The University of Vermont

The College Edifice,
now called the Old Mill

THE UNIVERSITY OF
VERMONT
THE FIRST
TWO HUNDRED YEARS

Robert V. Daniels, SENIOR EDITOR

UNIVERSITY OF VERMONT

Distributed by UNIVERSITY PRESS OF NEW ENGLAND

Hanover and London

UNIVERSITY OF VERMONT
Distributed by University Press of New England, Hanover, NH 03755
© 1991 by University of Vermont
All rights reserved
Printed in the United States of America   5   4   3   2   1
CIP data appear at the end of the book

The illustrations appearing in this book are from the
University of Vermont Archives and the Special Collections Department
of the University of Vermont Library.

Contents

Illustrations follow pages 120 and 218.

Preface

THE germ of this book goes back to the conversations among an ad hoc group of University of Vermont professors, including Edward Feidner of Theater, Connell Gallagher and Kevin Graffagnino of the Library, Samuel Hand and William Metcalfe of History, and Luther Martin of Religion, who felt that the bicentennial commemoration of the university's founding in 1791 ought to include a publication to illuminate the life and achievements of the institution's past and to make available the reflections of some of the people who were in a position to direct fresh inquiries into its historical record. The concept of a bicentennial anthology was embraced enthusiastically by President Lattie F. Coor, who made it an official part of the bicentennial program, committed the necessary university resources for its realization, and appointed an editorial board with the undersigned as senior editor. Members of the board are Professor T. D. Seymour Bassett (Library and History, retired), Professor George Bryan (Theater), Professor Jean Davison (UVM '44, Classics), Professor Feidner, Professor Lewis Feuer (formerly of the UVM Philosophy Department, now emeritus at the University of Virginia), Professor Gallagher, Professor Graffagnino, Professor Hand, Professor Martin, Professor Dolores Sandoval (Education), Professor Henry Steffens (History), Mr. Stephen Terry ('64), and Dr. Lester Wallman (Medicine, emeritus). (Mr. Ralph Nading Hill and Professor Thomas Sproston had agreed to serve on the editorial board, but tragically, died before the work got underway.) To the members of the board much appreciation is due for their efforts and advice in the execution of this project.

This work has been a collective undertaking in the best sense of the term. Contributors of the individual chapters were selected by the editorial board on the basis of competitive submissions of proposals, following criteria of inherent significance, feasibility, and suitability to the plan of the book. There were a number of excellent submissions that, unfortunately, could not be included in the project because of limitations of space. The final form of the anthology represents the cooperative efforts of authors and editors; all have striven to compose the most interesting and informative volume possible.

We have not attempted to produce an exhaustive or comprehensive history. Rather, it is a set of individual inquiries into interesting and important facets of the university's past, linked together by Professor Bassett's overviews of the main periods of this history. Taken as a whole, we hope the contributions to this book will offer an exciting and revealing account of UVM's growth, hopes, tribulations, and successes.

History always reflects the standpoints and judgments of its narrators. Each of the contributions to this work naturally expresses the views and conclusions of the individual author, intermixed with the suggestions of the editorial board and myself as senior editor. This is not an official history in the sense of conforming to any prior expectations on the part of university authorities; authors have been free to develop their topics and their judgments as they have seen fit, subject only to the editorial considerations of clarity in the narrative and of reasonable fit between related contributions.

Particular mention should be made of the help and advice offered by T. D. Seymour Bassett, beyond his signed contributions, in his inexhaustible knowledge of the history of the university and the state; by Robert Stanfield, Special Assistant to the President of the University; by Henry Steffens and Constance McGovern as UVM's representatives on the editorial board of the University Press of New England; by the State Archivist D. Gregory Sanford (M.A., UVM '74); by University Archivist Jeffrey D. Marshall and Assistant Archivist David J. Blow; by the staff of the Bailey-Howe Library and the Dana Medical Library; and by Sue Bronson of the UVM President's Office, and Jean Holt, Susan Kenny, and Kelly Thomas of the Bicentennial Office, in handling many logistical matters. A generous grant-in-aid was provided by the University Store at the University of Vermont, C. Hosmer Graham, manager.

The authors and editors involved in this effort all join me in the hope that the reader will find here an appropriate contribution to the celebration of UVM's bicentennial. We believe that we have put together a fascinating story of a unique institution of higher education in a unique state of the American Union.

R. V. D.

The University of Vermont

Introduction

ROBERT V. DANIELS

In our pragmatic, mobile, and present-oriented society, we tend to take most of the features of our life for granted, as givens, with no yesterday and no tomorrow. The communities, institutions, and assumptions that shape our individual lives are rarely appreciated as creatures of history that arose from obscure beginnings, grew, and changed into the forms we perceive in the present. Monuments and traditions of the past may be revived and revered for sentimental reasons, but they tend to be seen as disconnected from the real world of the moment. All too often we remain blind to the past reasons embedded in our present human environment that may continue to influence what we think and do.

It is easier to take the past more seriously when the focus is on a subject that is smaller in scale and more tangible in nature. The history of a familiar institution, explaining its present identity as the outcome of its past experience, is, like the history of one's hometown, a special kind of bridge between the personal and the cosmic. There are the old buildings still standing, the famous names whom one often knew as actual persons or whom one's parents or grandparents might have known, and the characters and happenings that live on in the oral traditions shared with one's contemporaries. But there are also the marks of the great national events, struggles, and transformations that have enveloped the institution and have linked it to history on the grand scale, which usually seems so remote from the ordinary individual.

Vermonters tend to think of themselves, their state, and their university as a world apart from the national mainstream. This is not ignorant provincialism but rather a long-standing, perhaps complacent sense that, by standing aside and holding back from metropolitan fashions of life and thought, Vermont and its university can retain the best of an earlier, simpler, better era. Meanwhile, the national mainstream reciprocates with the view of Vermont as a quaint irrelevancy, distinguished by skiing, maple syrup, and Old Vermonter jokes.

The two hundred years of the history of the University of Vermont reached in the year of this publication coincide exactly with the span of Vermont's existence as a state and nearly so with the history of the American republic. Naturally, the story of the University's creation and evolution into the multifarious institution it is today is closely interrelated with the history of those larger entities, more, perhaps, than members of the university family past and present have supposed.

One theme is common to all three levels, institutional, state, and national, of this experience. This theme is growth: in numbers, in complexity, in human powers over self and nature, and, one hopes, in the capacity to use those powers wisely. From its minuscule beginnings to today's megaversity of more than a thousand faculty, two thousand staff, and ten thousand students, the growth of UVM has mirrored the transformation of the American nation—and indeed of the entire world—that has taken place between the last years of the eighteenth century and the last years of the twentieth.

Less steady was the historical evolution of UVM's immediate constituency, the state of Vermont. Vermont grew apace with all of frontier America during UVM's earliest period, up to the middle of the nineteenth century. For the next hundred years, Vermont stood virtually still demographically, as the main currents of the country's industrial development and commercial sophistication passed it by. As a result, the University found itself beset by increasing tensions and contradictions, pressed by the nature of its educational mission to try to keep up with the worldwide explosion in knowledge and technology yet limited by the relative impoverishment of Vermont and the responsibility to the state that the institution has always borne. Then, in the past half-century, as Vermont was rapidly drawn into a metropolitan society, with all of its complications, UVM was able to respond with renewed growth in size, in scope of interests, and in sophistication. But these developments, in turn, made for a very different student experience; a new kind of faculty, recruited nationwide to offer specialized and professional instruction; and a far more complex structure of organization and governance, attempting to harness all of the centrifugal forces of college, departmental, and individual interests that drive the modern multiversity.

In its transformation during the past two centuries, UVM has been a microcosm of the American system of higher education and even of American society as a whole. We have been content with the appearance of stability while experiencing vast and usually unmanaged change. UVM's history has directly reflected the successive states of mind and philosophical outlooks that have marked our national life. Until the middle of the nineteenth century two intellectual currents dominated American university life that have since then been consigned to dim academic corners: the Classics and the Protestant religion. Until 1911 every UVM president but one was a Congregational clergyman or trained as such; until World War II every student who aspired to earn the B.A. degree had to have Latin and Greek. These traditions did not mean a uniformity of views or a suppression of original thought; within that framework fierce battles were fought between the orthodox and the liberal. In fact, considering its institutional frailty and inaccessible location, UVM in its first half-century held a remarkable place on the liberal side of these debates, both academically and theologically.

From the time of the Civil War, the basic tenor of American life changed fundamentally, thanks to rapid industrialization, urbanization, secularization, immigration, business empires, galloping technology, and the rise of science as the ultimate intellectual authority. But this was also the time when the mainstream of national development left Vermont aside, and when Vermonters began to take pride in being the contrary denizens of "a special world." UVM's special world was the Classical tradition in education, at which it had excelled in its early days but which became more and more difficult to reconcile with the demands of modern professionalism and specialization. Because of its own institutional culture and the state's penurious provincialism, UVM was always playing catch-up, usually too little and too late, until very recent times. Having pioneered in efforts to bridge the literary-philosophical realm and the scientific-professional realm (the "two cultures," long before C. P. Snow coined the term), UVM found it difficult to mobilize the resources and the expertise to excel in either one after they became hopelessly divorced.

After World War II, economics drew many old Vermonters away and permitted a growing number of more affluent and better-educated families to become new Vermonters. The political and cultural climate of the state was thereby transformed, as were expectations for the provision of higher education, professional training, and expert services. Like the country as a whole, UVM was shaken out of its old and comfortable assumptions.

If we look back a hundred or even fifty years ago, the contrast with the present that we see in the basic aims, values, and life-style of the university community is almost beyond belief. Not everything about those good old days will be missed. It is hard now to comprehend the snobbery, elitism, and prejudice that pervaded our national life. Until very recently—up to World War II or even later—American higher education, including UVM, reflected the distinctly hierarchical attitudes of a society that scarcely thought twice about contradicting the revolutionary principles expressed in John Dewey's democracy. Disparities of wealth were flaunted, as well as the dominion of whites over blacks and men over women. These polarities were overlaid by a scale of prestige or contumely expressed in the social pecking order of religious denominations, especially in the complacent Protestant exclusivity vis-à-vis Catholics and Jews. For its first half-century or more, UVM was a de facto instrumentality of the de facto established religion of New England, the Congregational Church, though of its more liberal branch. A college education, in this environment, was by and for a social and professional (and by the late nineteenth century, business) elite, for whom baptism by immersion in the Classics became the kind of special distinction that knowledge of so many thousands of characters conferred on the old Chinese mandarin class.

To be sure, if higher education was the badge of the elite, in America one could join the elite by acquiring that education, most particularly if it were at "the right schools." Thus, college became a key element in the powerful sweep of social mobility that ultimately undermined the old hierarchical, "prejudiced" mentality. The aim to "get ahead" helps to account for the tremendous surge in college aspiration among Americans in the twentieth century, which in turn contributed to the vast quantitative extension of higher education and the submergence of the old Classical, mandarin ideal. Elitism did survive in the order of prestige ascribed to different colleges and universities, and it fought a rear-guard action on the less prestigious campuses through the fraternity system. Racial and religious prejudices, at one time sustained like gender bias by the misguided rationale of Darwinian biology, were shaken by the horrors of the Nazi extreme in Europe; and the civil rights movement of the 1960s (reflected in the Kake Walk controversy at UVM) finally drove such thinking out of the domain of public discourse. Now the standard of equality in American society as regards race, sex, creed, and family connections is observed hardly anywhere as consistently as on college campuses.

The democratization of American higher education had its price. The old educational elitism was not indulgent but demanding; it stressed a standard of individual responsibility and achievement, and it aimed to create or sustain a cultivated upper and upper-middle class. The UVMer of a century and a half ago would be as shocked by today's collegiate culture with its materialism, self-indulgence, and intellectual lassitude, not to mention the sexual revolution in all of its aspects, as we today are repelled by the prejudices of the past. The UVMer of just fifty years ago would be—often still is— shocked just as much by the end-product of the "cultural revolution" of the past three decades.

One of the principal forces for change at UVM was sheer size. After its early years as a mere seedling, UVM roughly doubled its student body every twenty years; this added up to a twenty-fold increase in the first century and again twenty-fold in the second. From a clearing in the wilderness where one president-professor led a handful of students into the appreciation of Latin and Greek authors, the institution had become, a hundred years later, a recognizably modern college with a diverse faculty and the budding shoots of ramified professional training. After another hundred years UVM truly was a university, with all of its strengths and all of its problems, all of its triumphs and all of its frustrations.

Growth inexorably shaped the organizational character of the institution. Once a group of like-minded scholars who could hold a faculty meeting around the president's dinner table, the growing institution adopted in the first half of this century the national business model of board, chief executive officer, employees, and customers, probably not an organizational form best adapted to intellectual discovery. Then, as in all organizations overwhelmed by growth and specialization, the center effectively lost control and could only mediate among the various parts of the institution and between the institution and its public constituencies. As throughout American higher education, the expansion at UVM in numbers and purpose from elite to mass dissolved the old cohesiveness, first of the student body, then of the faculty, then even of the administrative apparatus. Simultaneously, the old humanistic intellectual unity of the institution was lost, and the disciplines of the humanities were progressively marginalized in the increasingly research-oriented institution. As the twentieth century approaches its close, UVM has achieved the ultimate form of the modern multiversity as defined by the late Clark Kerr, president of the University of California: a confederation of academic baronies held together by a common parking problem.

The contributions to this anthology are arranged, more or less chronologically, into four periods of the UVM experience. Professor Bassett introduces each of the four sections with an overview to provide continuity and help put the particular chapters that follow into a common context. Naturally, the divisions between the successive periods are by no means hard and fast, and individual authors have been free to extend their stories farther back or farther ahead, as their subject matter requires.

Kevin Graffagnino (B.A., '76; M.A., '78), curator of the Wilbur Collection in the UVM Library, opens part I with a biographical sketch of Ira Allen, the man credited with being the university's founder because he secured the Vermont Legislature's charter for a university in Burlington. Not to be neglected is the Reverend Daniel Sanders, UVM's president for its first fifteen years, who figures both in Graffagnino's account and in the following chapter, in which Professor Jeffrey Potash of Trinity College in Burlington (also a UVM alumnus, B.A., '76) traces UVM's early struggles for survival amid the swirls of religious controversy of that era and the rival ambitions of Middlebury College and Norwich University. Betty Bandel, UVM professor emeritus of English, endeavors to get inside the minds of UVM's early students, particularly as exemplified by the efforts in drama by the future national figure, Thaddeus Stevens. Then John Duffy, professor emeritus of English at Johnson State College, investigates the thought and career of the man who was arguably UVM's most illustrious intellectual figure, the Reverend James Marsh.

Part 2 of this history spans the long period of institutional development within a rapidly changing nation, from the middle of the nineteenth century to the early years of the twentieth. UVM Classics professor Philip Ambrose recounts the impact of these changes as evidenced in the University's instructional offerings and requirements; and Professor Bassett, in a chapter of his own, focuses on the man who personified UVM during most of this period, President Matthew Buckham. Bob Pepperman Taylor of the UVM political science department explores anew the background and career of UVM's most famous alumnus, the philosopher John Dewey. Three chapters, by Kevin Dann (M.A., '85), Dr. Wallman, and former dean of the College of Agriculture Robert Sinclair (B.S., '44; M.A., '55), then show UVM's evolution into modernity as exemplified in the fields of science, medicine, and agriculture, respectively.

In part 3, carrying UVM through World War II, we enter the age of living memory, permitting researchers to question directly those who participated in events or observed them. This was a time not so much of educational innovation as of consolidation, while the University tried to assimilate the changes and upheavals going on in the society around it and in the wider world. President for much of this time was Guy Bailey, whose era Professor Bassett recounts. Two succeeding chapters—about UVM's initiatives with respect to the role of women and about the development of the now-familiar collegiate life among students—are presented by Professor McGovern and by alumna Virginia Campbell Downs (B.A., '46). Jane Ambrose, professor and chair of the Department of Music, then describes UVM's growing involvement with the world of the arts.

Finally, part 4 brings the UVM story up to date, attempting to capture the multitudinous changes that the University has experienced since World War II. Two critical episodes in UVM's interaction with Vermont and with the nation are discussed in the chapter by Tom Slayton (B.A., '63, and *Vermont Life* editor) on changes in the University's links with the state and in the chapter by David Holmes, of the UVM education faculty, on the Novikoff affair. Alumnus Jules Older (B.A., '64) reports on the status of members of racial and religious minorities at the University. Patrick Hutton, professor of history at UVM, surveys the modern changes in knowledge and teaching reflected in the vastly ramifying curriculum. James Loewen of the UVM sociology department recounts the festival of Kake Walk and the movement that led to its abolition. Concluding the anthology as a whole is the study by Beal Hyde, professor emeritus of botany and former chair of the Faculty Senate, on the evolution of governance and the paradox of diminishing faculty participation within the growingly complex institution that UVM has become.

These contributions do not by any means exhaust the interesting and significant facets of the history of UVM. It would be impossible to compress within the covers of one book all that documents and memory recall of the past of this institution. This anthology aims only to offer a representative view of the main developments in UVM's first two centuries, touching on its presidents, its faculty and students, and its matrix in the state of Vermont and in the evolution of modern American life. We have omitted only the future. That we leave to another generation, to take stock of what we do now and what comes after us.

Part One

ORIGINS OF UVM, 1791–1833: OVERVIEW

T. D. SEYMOUR BASSETT

The early history of "Burlington College," as its first president and many Vermonters often referred to it, can be viewed as an aspect of the history of Protestantism in Vermont, as a story of village rivalry, as a footnote in the history of American drama and architecture, or in terms of its own subject, the history of higher education. The essays in this section address important aspects of UVM's first half-century. In chapter 1, Kevin Graffagnino describes the career of the founder, Ira Allen, who dreamed of locating a university in Burlington. Without his false promises—or rather, the pledge he could not redeem—there might have been a state university at Rutland, Middlebury, or Williamstown instead. In chapter 2 Jeffrey Potash focuses on religious controversy, economic adversity, and social constraints in the university's early struggle to survive and achieve preeminence (in the state's eyes) over Middlebury College and Norwich University. Betty Bandel (chapter 3) samples students' intellectual interests, and John Duffy (chapter 4) sketches the career and impact of one of UVM's greatest intellectual figures, James Marsh.

UVM's first fifty years were punctuated by a series of catastrophes that remind one of a serial soap opera, each installment ending in apparent disaster. Every decade after the charter of 1791 brought a blow: the competing Middlebury College charter of 1800, the closing of UVM when the army commandeered its building in March 1814, the fire of May 1824, and near starvation for want of students scared away by James Marsh's noble experiment and the temporary death of the medical department. Each crisis began or ended the term of one of the four principal presidents of this period, Daniel Clarke Sanders (1800–1814), Samuel Austin (1815–1821), James Marsh (1826–1833), and John Wheeler (1833–1848).

The Charter and Its Implementation, 1777–1799

The framers of the Vermont Constitution of 1777, looking over the state and seeing much woods and few people, called for one university as the crown of the state's future educational system of town common schools and county grammar schools. The General Assembly reserved land for that university in each town it chartered. Given the elite purposes of higher education in those days, the number of men in Vermont who would want what universities were supposed to offer (no women need apply), and the state's limited resources, one such institution was enough. But by 1834 there were three, with Dartmouth and Williams on Vermont's borders, and five other New England colleges, all competing for students and support. With that much competition, why did the state charter more than one college? Partly because local leaders knew that the presence of public institutions would increase the prosperity of their respective towns.

On October 25, 1791, Ira Allen marshaled 89 votes in the legislature for the bill that chartered the University of Vermont and located it in Burlington. Only 24 voted for Rutland; 11 for Montpelier, Berlin, or Williamstown; and 1 each for Danville and Castleton.

Having decided to have a university in Burlington, the Legislature the next day chose ten trustees, in addition to the governor and the speaker of the House of Representatives ex officio. Although UVM's charter emphatically stated that the University's "rules, regulations, & by-laws shall not tend to give preference to any religious sect or denomination whatsoever,"[1] the original corporation included ministers representing the state's four main religious groups. Caleb Blood of Shaftsbury, who served until 1808, was a leading Baptist pastor. Bethuel Chittenden, the governor's brother, tended his Shelburne farm and Episcopalians in northwestern Vermont. Asa Burton, Congregationalist of Thetford, had preached and taught theological students there since 1779. George Bowne was a New York City Quaker leader, merchant, and in 1789 part owner of Vergennes water power. Bowne and Charles Platt, presumably added to attract support from northeastern New York, never attended a corporation meeting.

The other trustees, like the vast majority of Vermonters then, had much less need for the religious hypothesis. Ira Allen was one, but he was out of the state most of the time until he resigned in 1804. Jonathan Arnold (1741–1793) of St. Johnsbury, revolutionary surgeon and landowner, congressman from Rhode Island and then a member of the Vermont Governor's Council, was replaced at his death by Joshua Stanton of Burlington, who had charge of constructing the president's house and the early work on the college building. Enoch Woodbridge (1750–1805), Vergennes mayor and Vermont Supreme Court judge, served until his death, though his attendance was irregular. Samuel Hitchcock (1755–1813) of Burlington, Harvard class of 1777,

Ethan Allen's son-in-law, Vermont attorney general (1790–1793), and U.S. District Court judge (1793–1801), was a weighty and active member until his death. Jonathan Hunt (1738–1823) was on the Governor's Council when chosen and later was lieutenant governor. This was a board representing major interests and regions of the state.

Why did it take nearly five years to build a frame house for the president and his first students and three more years to find a leader? The University's explanation of the delay was the appointment of a majority of trustees living too far away to attend corporation meetings. The Reverend Asa Burton saw a fatal defect in the fact that the University's orientation was not soundly orthodox Congregationalist. The evaporation of Ira Allen's £4,000 pledge required the Trustees to seek other funding at a time when the state had no resources. To be sure, there was no mindset against state aid to colleges; on the contrary, both the state and schools at all levels expected that government should foster education.[2] But Vermont's colleges continually had to compete with the public schools for funds.

Finally, with the aid of some $2,000 given by citizens of Burlington, the Trustees were able to build a president's house and to invite the Reverend Daniel Sanders of Vergennes to occupy it. Sanders moved into the house on November 16, 1799, and soon began to prepare a handful of students for college work.[3]

Sanders Tries Hard, 1799–1814

"Presidential history" is now out of style, but the old-time college president *was* the college, as modern promotional people say. When President Sanders opened UVM in 1800, this was literally true: he combined faculty, staff, and administration in his own person. For many years afterward, as in most American colleges of the time, the president personified the institution. He was spokesman to the constituencies: his town, the wider business community, the churches, alumni, and state legislators. He raised money and recruited students. As principal professor, who taught the keystone courses and hired the faculty, he could set the tone of instruction on which the institution's reputation in academic circles would be based. He was the chief disciplinarian. The handful of students who lived with President-Professor Sanders were apprentices to the master, as in any other craft. As time went on, the president had helpers, but he did not delegate much of the administrative work. This remained the style of leadership throughout the nineteenth century.

Daniel Clarke Sanders (1766–1850) was well fitted for his difficult task of bringing the college to life. A Sturbridge, Massachusetts, native, he was probably the first of his family to reach college. Helped by scholarships and loans, he worked his way through Harvard and graduated Phi Beta Kappa in

1788. That he was baptized only in 1789, when he decided to study for the ministry, suggests that his family had not belonged to a church. He "read theology" under a moderate Congregationalist, Thomas Prentiss of Medfield, Massachusetts, and made it his priority to help his parishioners work out their problems without splitting hairs about theology. He supported himself by teaching and, after he was licensed to preach in 1790, by supplying New England churches with sermons while he looked for a position as a pastor. In 1794, attracted by the potential of frontier Vergennes and Dr. Jabez G. Fitch's daughter, he accepted the call of the new church there and married Nancy Fitch. The couple had eight children, five of whom died in childhood before Sanders left Burlington.

Sanders was a strapping, stern young man, who once quelled an adolescent rebellion in his grammar school with physical force and, according to a former pupil, had no further trouble with discipline.[4] He had the usual rural skills and always farmed for some of his food. Those were the days when little cash circulated, and payments were usually made in kind. Burlington offered him a salary of $400 a year to serve as town preacher; his concurrent university salary was to be $600, but that was wishful thinking on the part of the Trustees, like Ira Allen's pledge. Picture Sanders, when not acting as town preacher or engaged in university business, felling pines at the edge of the ten-acre clearing around the president's house for more pasture, plowland, firewood, and view.

From the moment in November 1800 when the Legislature granted Middlebury College's charter, President Sanders was in trouble. He fought with all of his literary and lobbying might and, together with the other Burlington trustees, managed to keep the University's state lease lands from being shared with or transferred to Middlebury. He toured the state to collect rents, gifts, and students, but he had nothing like the Yale network supporting Middlebury. Sanders's most significant Harvard connection might have been the Reverend Samuel Williams (Harvard '61), his college science teacher and then publisher of the Rutland *Herald*. Williams had worked with Ira Allen to win the University's charter, but he was not chosen a trustee or president and does not reappear as a supporter of UVM until 1807. There were very few other Harvard men in the state.

The college building was finished in 1807, at a cost, together with the president's house, of $25,458. This outlay put UVM in a precarious financial position: barely half of the $5,000 lease-land rent had been collected, only a quarter of the $12 a year tuition had been collected, and debts totaled over $20,000. On the other hand, the University had a building, a few books, a magnet, and a few other pieces of "philosophical apparatus" for teaching physics. It gradually sold off its land to satisfy the most demanding creditors, until it owned scarcely more than the ground the building was on.[5]

But Sanders was finally in a position to expand enrollment, fill the new building, and recruit teachers. In his seven remaining years his college was gaining on Middlebury, though still behind. The faculty grew by 1813 to a total of four, counting Sanders. James Dean (Dartmouth '00) came in 1807 as a tutor and was promoted to professor of mathematics and science in 1809. Jason Chamberlain was added in Classics in 1811. Together Dean and Chamberlain represented two sides of UVM's curriculum coin: natural science based on mathematics and communication based on Classics.[6] Vermont Supreme Court judge Royall Tyler (Harvard '76) was a trustee while he was on the bench, 1802–1813, and seems to have given some lectures while holding the title of professor of jurisprudence, 1811–1814. From 1804 there was also a titular connection with Dr. John Pomeroy (trustee, 1807–1810, 1813–1822), but Pomeroy's medical instruction was an independent operation, as Lester J. Wallman shows in Chapter 9.

Just as the University's prospects were brightening, outside events clouded them. Burlington's Canadian trade suffered from the Embargo of 1807. At the same time the town's uneasy religious consensus broke down in a fight over the choice of preacher. In his first years Sanders had preached to the town, not to a particular church. Then, in 1805, he wrote a covenant and articles of faith for the "First Religious Society in the Town of Burlington." He tried in vain to attract a minister for this group who could satisfy all sorts and conditions of men. In 1807 Sanders gave up and resigned the town pulpit, partly because more students meant more work on the Hill and partly because the townspeople were no longer willing to be taxed for the support of religion. A Vermont law of the same year removed that obligation, completing the separation of church and state.

From 1807 to 1809, Samuel Williams did some preaching and lecturing in Burlington. Perhaps he was on hand in case there was a change in the administration of the University. He was mature, illustrious, and moderate, and a movement was forming to get rid of Sanders. The religious factions in Burlington gave up trying to agree on a minister and split into two churches. Sanders hesitated and then joined the smaller but more orthodox body, most likely out of political expediency.

In a last effort to enlist state support and to defeat the long-postponed consideration of Middlebury's 1805 petition for half of UVM's lease lands, the corporation asked the 1810 Legislature to take UVM "under their more immediate patronage." The Legislature accordingly granted a new charter requiring the governor, council, and General Assembly in joint session to elect fifteen trustees in staggered three-year terms. This corporation, including the governor, speaker of the General Assembly, and president of the University as ex officio members, would continue to control university property; make contracts, including those with the faculty and students; manage the lease lands; and report annually to the Legislature.[7] No one, not even Sanders, expected a state appropriation, which would have made UVM what we now think of as a state university. Vermont's original constitution assumed state support in terms of land endowment, but university shares were the poorest lands in each town, and most tenants, debt-ridden on the one hand and out of touch with their university landlord on the other, began to feel that they owned their farms.

Even more upsetting to UVM than these religious and economic problems was the War of 1812. As the collecting point for troops training to defend the Canadian frontier, Burlington suffered from "the demoralizing habits of an army," according to Governor Chittenden, and from war-induced inflation.[8] One thousand to five thousand recruits were piled into bare barracks and tents, and officers were billeted in every available dwelling in this lake port of some two thousand civilians.

In the summer of 1813 the army commandeered the forty-eight-room college building as an arsenal and posted a guard. Troops broke down Sanders's fences, invaded his grounds, trampled his grain, stole his corn, and smashed his pumpkins against the college steps. They rioted through the halls, breaking into rooms when the students were away and stealing their property. Studying almost stopped.[9]

Later on the army agreed to pay $5,000 a year rent plus damages, which seemed like a lifesaver to the now closed and debt-ridden college. For the conservative faction, moreover, the wartime situation provided a convenient excuse to get rid of Sanders. As students scattered to other colleges, enlisted, or found work, the Trustees "dismissed" Sanders and the faculty without making it clear whether they were to return later. James Dean returned to UVM in 1822 after teaching at Dartmouth in the interim. Sanders, who had just lost the last of five children to die in Vermont, collected what he could of his back salary and left Burlington. At forty-six he had spent twenty years of his prime in Vermont and seemed to have nothing to show for it.

Returning to his hometown of Medfield, Massachusetts, Sanders accepted the vacant ministry there and wrote his friend David Russell that wild horses could not drag him back to Burlington. His $700 salary was regularly paid by the town, and he tutored suspended Harvard students on the side. Though he chose to retire from the Medfield church when it was hit by the Unitarian-orthodox schism, he continued through a useful old age, gave patriotic addresses, and served several terms as selectman and in the Massachusetts legislature. He outlived his long-ailing wife and two of his three remaining children and died at eighty-two in October 1850. No prophet, he had honor in his own community.[10]

Austin and Haskel Imitate Middlebury, 1815–1824

The years after the War of 1812 were the most difficult period in all of UVM's history. The times were bad economically, fund drives failed, and few instructors could be retained for long. Proposals to unite with Middlebury College, under negotiation for two years, were a barometer of economic duress in both colleges. Hostile creditors revived their ancient claims when the University received $5,600 from the federal government for rent and damages to the college building during the war. Dr. Pomeroy, for example, sued for advances, suffered countersuits, resigned from the Board, and ended all connection with the University. Consequently, he took no part in the establishment of the medical department in 1822, the one bright spot in a decade of gloom.

The effects of the religious schism in Burlington continued to plague the University despite the trustees' decision to appear as loyal conservatives by appointing the Reverend Samuel Austin (Yale '83) to replace Sanders as president. The scholarly Austin found himself thwarted on every hand, and in March 1821 he resigned, broken in spirit. His health failed, both physically and mentally, and in 1830 he died.[11]

To replace Austin the trustees first took a bold step and invited Captain Alden Partridge to be the next president. Cashiered as commandant of the U.S. Military Academy at West Point because of his individualist character, Partridge founded the American Literary, Scientific and Military Academy at Norwich, Vermont. There he put a number of novel educational ideas into practice, marching the whole academy on field trips up Mount Washington or to Fort Ticonderoga to learn surveying the heights of mountains, military history, and the literary exercise of making reports. These exercises provided both physical and military training and publicized his philosophy of a citizen army. UVM would have been a different place if he had accepted its challenge. But why should he board a sinking ship? He chose to stay in Norwich.

In place of Austin and in default of Partridge's acceptance, the Trustees turned to Daniel Haskell, the man who had served the orthodox branch of Burlington's Congregationalists since the split of 1809. Haskell had little more success than Austin enjoyed. Perhaps with more years to season his administration he could have weathered the storms that universities are heir to. But on May 27, 1824, fire destroyed the college building and paralyzed, for the moment, his ability to act. Haskell, like Austin, left the presidency in a state of mental breakdown. Later he recovered enough to share in the compilation of a gazetteer of the United States.[12]

Professor James Dean was appointed acting president in the emergency but resigned when the Trustees overruled his dismissal of some students for scholastic failure. To fill the vacancy, the Trustees invited the Reverend John Wheeler (Dartmouth '16), pastor of the Congregational church in Windsor, who said he would come if his church approved; but they would not release him, and he would not go against their wishes. (He did serve on the Board of Trustees from 1825 until his ultimate election as president in 1833.) The

Reverend William Preston, who had replaced Daniel Haskel at the orthodox Congregational Church in Burlington, filled in for a year before going south to continue his ministerial career.

Raised Standards, Lowered Enrollments, 1825–1833

Fire, flood, and other accidents have never killed an institution that was not already moribund. The Burlington Establishment, which had for years let the college struggle along with its debts, seemed electrified by the crisis of 1824 and quickly subscribed enough to rebuild after the fire.

But whom could they entice to rebuild the student body and faculty? They turned to a Vermont-born Dartmouth alumnus (class of '17) who was teaching in Virginia, James Marsh. Marsh and his fellow students had taught themselves when Dartmouth was effectively shut down during the disturbances of 1816, and this experience had given him unorthodox notions of education, notably that students are capable of teaching themselves. It had exposed him to the German language and to German philosophy and theology, which had not yet won a hearing in the United States. So when Marsh came to Burlington in 1826, his head was full of reform ideas. A new team of young faculty came in with him, from the newer colleges (Dartmouth, Williams, Hamilton, and even UVM), with renewed emphasis on science and not-so-orthodox Congregationalism.

The overwhelmingly conservative trustees and faculty viewed the Jacksonian Revolution of those years with alarm. Marsh and his friends John Wheeler and Joseph Torrey had as students experienced the New Hampshire legislature's assertion of active control over Dartmouth College, and they did not want it to happen in Vermont. The first thing to do, they felt, was to end legislative election of trustees. On October 30, 1828, the governor and council concurred with the Legislature in a charter amendment allowing the Board to choose its own successors, with the proviso, like the one in Middlebury College's charter, "that this act may be repealed by any future legislature." [13]

The economic environment of Burlington was propitious in the mid-1820s, thanks to the new Champlain-Hudson Canal and the frontier market of northern Vermont. The town's population of 3,226 in 1830, up more than a third from 1820, made it the third largest in the state, just behind Middlebury and Bennington. By 1840, with 4,271 people, it was the "queen town" of Vermont, while Middlebury shrank. Verily, each town's college reflected the town's condition.

While President Marsh was working out a Christian transcendentalist philosophy and introducing German and Coleridgean idealism to this country, the University continued its original balance of Classics and science with an enthusiastic young group of science lovers. George W. Benedict (Williams

'13), who had trained under some of the leading scientists of the day, came in the spring of 1825 after seasoning as principal of the Newburg, New York, Academy. Zadock Thompson (UVM '23), was mathematics tutor during Benedict's first year and then took charge of the Burlington High School for Young Ladies at his home on the College Green; he equaled Benedict in his enthusiasm for the natural sciences. Joseph Torrey (Dartmouth '16) came in 1827 to teach Classics but had an abiding interest in botany as well as in art. George R. Huntington (UVM '26) took over mathematics from Benedict in 1829 and initiated instruction in civil engineering before he was replaced in 1832 by Benedict's cousin Farrand N. Benedict. The lecturers of the medical department completed the membership in the lively group of young Burlington scientists. In 1825 they incorporated the Medical Society of the University of Vermont, in 1826 they organized its College of Natural History, and in 1830 they formed the Burlington Lyceum to sponsor popular science lectures.[14]

Marsh and his faculty, after long discussion, proposed to break the traditional academic lockstep by letting students advance as soon as examinations proved they were ready, by admitting special students who did not intend to graduate, and by broadening the curriculum. One came to college, they thought, not just to take enough courses and spend enough time to get a degree but to learn how all knowledge is related, how to acquire this philosophical sense of its unity, and how to use it. One student wrote of UVM's "view of truth" as infinitely superior "over any other. . . . All science when rightly viewed constitutes a unity. . . . In the light of our Spiritual Philosophy, the insignificant [utilitarian] profit & loss systems commonly taught, dwindle into nothingness."[15]

With the president, three instructors, and a tutor, and a student body graduating at the rate of less than ten a year, the University offered a good education, but it was financially disastrous. Debts mounted again, and in 1833 President Marsh was persuaded to resign. Although a failure as a college president, Marsh did not follow the stereotype of the defeated, leaving town with tail between legs. Like many other Vermonters who fail to see how one office deserves more prestige than another, he stepped down to do what he did best—teach—with the strong approval of faculty and students.

A Hard Founding Father to Love: Ira Allen
and the University of Vermont

J. KEVIN GRAFFAGNINO

WHEN the University of Vermont's board of trustees assembled at Burlington on March 23, 1814, the school's future looked bleak. The U.S. Army, which had transformed Burlington into a major outpost in the northern theater of the War of 1812, had occupied the University's only building. The student body, some three dozen young men, had all gone home or transferred to other colleges. The entire faculty and administration—Professors James Dean and Jason Chamberlain, President Daniel C. Sanders—had been dismissed and were demanding payment of salaries that were sadly in arrears. Even with the rent from the army there was not nearly enough money in the treasury to settle UVM's debts. The Trustees passed various well-intentioned resolutions, appointed several committees, and adjourned to hope that things might somehow improve. Given their limited options, they had probably done all they could. There was only one thing missing: according to secretary Warren Loomis's detailed minutes, in two days of deliberations the Board apparently made no mention of and took no action on the recently received news of the death of the individual most responsible for the University's creation, Ira Allen.[1]

It is not surprising that UVM's trustees failed to mark Ira Allen's passing. Although he had been the driving force behind the move to obtain a charter for the University and to secure Burlington as its location in 1791, relations between UVM and its first patron had been strained ever since. Allen's failure to make good on his impressive 1789 pledge of £4,000, the deciding factor in the state legislature's selection of Burlington as the site for the new school, had left the Trustees scrambling for funds to get UVM started. Lawsuits, multiple deeds, and overlapping claims complicated the University's ownership of the Burlington lands Allen had offered for the campus. In addition to his troubles with the University itself, his checkered career as land speculator, state government official, and would-be Champlain Valley commercial titan had ended in poverty and disgrace. In 1814 and long after, Ira Allen was a hard founding father to love.

The establishment of UVM came in the middle of a busy lifetime for Ira Allen. Born in Cornwall, Connecticut, on May 1, 1751, he was the youngest of eight children of Joseph and Mary Baker Allen. The known details of his early life are quite sketchy, but he seems to have grown up in a family of moderate financial means by the standards of the western Connecticut frontier. Although his father died in 1755, the presence of five older brothers— Ethan, Heman, Heber, Levi, and Zimri—provided young Ira with a sufficiency of male role models. Judging by their later careers as authors, political theorists, and self-styled philosophers, someone must have instilled a powerful love of learning in all of the Allen brothers; however, we have no details on the youthful Ira's education. He appears to have had a more sedate youth than his siblings; at least there is no record of his participation in their occasional Litchfield County brawls and altercations in the 1760s. Perhaps as the youngest and smallest of a contentious clan, Allen simply learned early in life to rely on his wits to get what he wanted.[2]

By his late teens Ira Allen was ready to leave Cornwall and make his mark on the world. His brothers had become involved in the simmering dispute over whether New York or New Hampshire owned the territory between the upper Connecticut and Hudson rivers, and in 1770 Ira followed them to the area that had become known as the New Hampshire Grants. He invested his small inheritance from his father's estate in New Hampshire titles to Grants lands and then began exploring along the northern frontier on behalf of real estate speculators in southern New England. Following one quick week of study in Connecticut to learn the rudiments of land surveying, Ira spent much of the early 1770s running boundary lines and evaluating property in the unsettled townships east of Lake Champlain. Ethan Allen was leading the Green Mountain Boys in opposition to New York during the same period, and Ira occasionally joined in the guerrilla activities that effectively thwarted New York's attempts to govern the Grants. For the most part, however, he concentrated on learning all he could about the investment potential of land in what would become the state of Vermont.[3]

By 1773, Ira Allen had developed a plan to ensure the fortunes of his entire family. Convinced that the most valuable lands in the Grants lay in the Champlain Valley and along the Onion (Winooski) River, he persuaded his brothers to sell their lands in the southern half of the Grants and adopt a more northerly vision of the future. In January 1773, Ira, Ethan, Heman, and Zimri Allen and their cousin Remember Baker formed the Onion River Land Company to buy and develop New Hampshire–granted lands along Lake Champlain. The Crown had ruled that New York owned the Grants, and New York courts had invalidated New Hampshire's extensive land sales west of the Connecticut River, so the company was able to buy thousands of acres at bargain prices. Within a few months the Allens were offering 45,000 acres of northwestern Vermont real estate for sale through advertisements in Connecticut newspapers.[4] Ira built a blockhouse fort at the Colchester falls of the Winooski River in the summer of 1773 for use as company headquarters, then spent the next two years surveying, cutting roads, intimidating New York surveyors and would-be settlers, and buying more Champlain Valley property for himself and his partners. By the start of the American Revolution in 1775, the company claimed more than 65,000 disputed acres of northwestern Vermont lands, and Ira Allen's hopes for the future were firmly fixed in the valley he called "the country my soul delighted in."[5]

The outbreak of the Revolution drew the Allens, their land speculation activities, and the Yankee-versus-Yorker struggle for the Grants into the larger picture of America's fight against England. During the first years of the war the Allens were enthusiastic supporters of the American cause. Ira put his experience in the Champlain Valley to good use as an American scout in the months following brother Ethan's May 1775 capture of Fort Ticonderoga. That autumn Ethan was captured by the British in the first, abortive American attack on Montreal, but Ira marched north toward Quebec with Richard Montgomery's branch of the American army of invasion. On December 31, 1775, he helped lead the diversionary attack on Cape Diamond that preceded Montgomery's fatal assault on the main citadel at Quebec. Two months later, with the failure of the American campaign a certainty, Allen left Canada and headed back to the Grants.[6]

Allen found the Vermont area in turmoil on his return early in 1776. During his absence the leaders of the anti–New York contingent had begun a series of meetings at Dorset to discuss the political options the Revolution had created for the settlers in the Grants. By the time of the third Dorset Convention, which Ira attended in late July 1776, the Yankee faction west of the Green Mountains was ready to consider establishing a new and independent state between the Connecticut and Hudson rivers. With Ethan Allen still a prisoner of the British, Ira played a significant role in nurturing the new state movement. He participated in further conventions at Dorset and Westminster in the autumn of 1776, traveled extensively in the Connecticut River Valley to drum up eastside support for the statehood idea, and served as clerk of the January 1777 Westminster convention that declared the independence of the state of New Connecticut. The name would change to Vermont the following June, but for Ira the most important fact was that the Grants finally had an autonomous government pledged to defy New York and protect New Hampshire–granted land holdings.[7]

Despite his youth, Allen quickly became a major force in the political hierarchy of the fledgling state of Vermont. Elected the first state treasurer in 1778, he managed Vermont's finances for the next eight years in a fashion that ignored standard bookkeeping but kept the state solvent. As surveyor-general from 1778 to 1787 he directed the mapping of the northern wilderness and the profitable sale of new townships in the one-third of Vermont not covered by New Hampshire charters. His work as a member of the thirteen-man council (forerunner of the state senate), along with his duties as occasional secretary to Governor Thomas Chittenden, made him an important member of the small westside group known as the Arlington Junto, which exercised a precarious control over Vermont's wartime affairs. Allen's multiple offices and his frequent blending of personal and state objectives made him some influential enemies, but he managed to remain near the top of Vermont's pyramid of power throughout the Revolution.

Ira also performed a variety of important unofficial duties for Vermont during the war. In the summer of 1777, as a British army under General John Burgoyne swept south from Canada, he devised an ingenious plan to pay for raising two regiments of militia by confiscating and selling the estates of Tories. After Burgoyne's surrender at Saratoga that fall, Vermont continued to use the plan to produce revenues without levying unpopular taxes and as a convenient means of banishing and dispossessing troublesome Yorker settlers.[8] Allen frequently served as Vermont's ambassador to a hostile world, traveling to other states and to the Continental Congress to solicit support for Vermont's independence, to discuss the possibility of the state's admission into the federal Union, and to defuse the plans of New York, New Hampshire, Massachusetts, and others for dismembering Vermont. At home his negotiations with the many settlers in the Connecticut River Valley who opposed the Arlington Junto complemented the less diplomatic talents of his brother Ethan, whose return in May 1778 gave the Junto a much-needed sheriff-at-large for intimidating particularly stubborn dissenters. In addition, the two brothers became Vermont's most prolific authors, turning out fiery pamphlets, broadsides, newspaper articles, and other published propaganda that tied their cause to the Revolution, the natural rights of man, and the rhetoric of freedom and democracy. For a new state facing the pressure of numerous internal and external threats to its existence, Ira's efforts were significant contributions to the fight for survival.

Ira Allen's most hazardous service for Vermont during the Revolution came in what are known as the Haldimand negotiations. Beginning in 1780, a small group of Vermont leaders—Ira and Ethan Allen, Thomas Chittenden, Jonas and Josiah Fay, plus a few others—conducted clandestine negotiations with Frederick Haldimand, the British governor-general of Canada. The subject, a dangerous one for its Vermont participants with the Revolutionary War still going on, was the possibility of Vermont's rejecting the American cause and reasserting its allegiance to the Crown. From the start Ira was deeply involved in the negotiations, walking a tightrope between equally suspicious British and American observers. When he met with Haldimand's agents at Isle aux Noix for lengthy discussions, he assured them of Vermont's eagerness to rejoin the Empire; when he faced angry Vermont crowds amid swirling rumors and accusations of treason, he spoke eloquently of using the talks to save the state from another British invasion.[9] By the time news of Cornwallis's surrender at Yorktown reached the northern frontier in November 1781 and ended Haldimand's hopes of welcoming Vermont back into the royal domain, Allen had demonstrated a fair aptitude for espionage and intrigue.

Ira's political power in Vermont began to erode soon after the Revolution ended. With thousands of settlers pouring into the state from southern New England, much of the frontier character of Vermont society and government gradually gave way to more stable, mature communities and institutions. New issues replaced the concerns of wartime, and the ruling oligarchy of the pioneer generation soon faced serious challenges from younger, more sophisticated, and better-educated leaders. With his multiple state offices and his reputation for self-interest, Allen became a prime target in the struggle for power. Talented newcomers such as Isaac Tichenor and Nathaniel Chipman, on their way to heading the conservative faction then emerging in state politics, criticized Ira's handling of state funds, his management of the sale of new townships, and various reputed abuses of his official duties and privileges. Lacking a broad base of popular appeal and without the personal charisma to attract new supporters, Ira watched his political networks crumble under these attacks. He fought vigorously against his opponents but without success: by 1788 he had given up all of his state government positions and his place among the inner circle of Vermont's political elite.[10]

Ira's political eclipse did not signal the collapse of his dreams of riches and influence. With the removal of the military threat from Canada in 1783, the Champlain Valley once again became an area of vast potential for settlement and development. Settlers clamored for land along the eastern shore of Lake Champlain, raising the value of Allen's own holdings and those of the old Onion River Land Company. Revamping his plans for a vast commercial and industrial empire in the valley, Ira moved from Sunderland to the falls of the Winooski River at Colchester and set to work. He built sawmills, gristmills, and forges at Colchester and at other prime waterpower sites on rivers flowing into the lake; he bought, sold, and leased staggering amounts of area real estate; and he publicized the advantages and attractions of the Champlain Valley to every prospective settler and investor with whom he came in contact. His pace was remarkably hectic, but his vision of the future was strong enough to drive him onward.[11]

Ira did find time in the midst of his empire building for what seems to have been the only romantic attachment of his life. In September 1789, at the age of thirty-eight, he married twenty-five-year-old Jerusha Enos of Hartland, Vermont, gave her the wilderness township of Irasburg as a wedding present, and took her home to Colchester. The new Mrs. Allen presided over Ira's large household, developed an impressive garden and orchard beside the Winooski River, dealt with the confusion of Ira's financial affairs during his many absences, and bore three children—Ira Hayden (1790), Zimri Enos (1792), and Maria Julietta (1794)—to inherit the grand estate their father was determined to create. The marriage seems to have been an amicable one, even though Ira emulated his brothers Ethan and Levi in abandoning his family for long periods to chase the elusive goals of wealth and power. Allen apologized frequently for his absences, but he never did accede to Jerusha's requests that he place home and family ahead of business on his list of personal priorities.

Instead, Ira forged ahead with the development of his Champlain Valley properties. Working with his brother Levi, whose eventual choice of the Loyalist side and Canada during the Revolution had made him a more or less respectable British subject, Allen tried to establish a profitable trade between Vermont and Canada. The plan was relatively simple: Ira would ship the products of the Green Mountain frontier—potash, lumber, beef, grain, maple sugar—north from Colchester to the merchants of Quebec City; and Levi, who had established a trading post near the British fort at St. Johns, would acquire European manufactured goods to send south for sale to the waiting settlers of unindustrialized Vermont. If they were successful, Ira would become the dominant entrepreneur in the valley, and Burlington would become the thriving lake port he had envisioned when he first saw the wilderness township and its harbor in 1772.[12]

Certain that he could not fail, Allen made grand plans for Burlington's future. By 1789 he had included a college in his vision of what might become the intellectual center of the entire state. At the time there was no college in Vermont and only four—Harvard, Yale, Brown, and Dartmouth—in all of New England. Although Section 40 of Vermont's 1777 constitution had declared, "One grammar school in each county, and one University in this State ought to be established by direction of the General Assembly," nothing had come of that good intention.[13] Instead, the state legislature had unofficially adopted Dartmouth as Vermont's college, granting the 23,000-acre township of Wheelock to the Connecticut River school in 1785. But some Vermont leaders were beginning to feel that the state ought to have its own university. Four months after the Wheelock grant, Elijah Paine of Williamstown, Vermont, promised to donate £2,000 toward the creation of a college if the Legislature would order it to be built in his town. Although the Legislature appointed a committee to study Paine's proposal, eventually it was decided that Paine's offer alone was insufficient to support a new school. Nonetheless, the notion that Vermont might be ready for a college was now a subject for serious discussion, and Ira Allen decided to make certain that when the General Assembly did charter one it would be located in the town of Burlington.[14]

Ira launched his campaign for a Burlington university in September 1789. Drawing up a subscription form that declared education to be "Necessary for the promottion [sic] of virtue and for the happiness of civil society," he circulated it among his friends and associates in Chittenden County. Governor Thomas Chittenden of Williston was first on the list of subscribers, with a pledge of £300, but it was Allen's pledge of £4,000 that pushed the total to an impressive figure of £5,655. To accompany the list, Ira prepared a petition that praised Burlington's advantages over all other Vermont towns the legislature might consider for the school.[15] Burlington had excellent soil, good water, and ample raw materials to construct good roads; at one hundred miles from Dartmouth and close to college-less Quebec and upstate New York, it would draw many students from the northern frontier; and by virtue of its location on a major water trade route, it had the potential to grow into a commercial center. Not surprisingly, the arguments sounded remarkably similar to Allen's land-speculation spiels about Burlington; with a quarter-century of faith in Burlington's future behind him, it was not difficult to adapt his rhetoric for this new and worthy cause.

Ira was not working alone to seek a university for Burlington in 1789. Governor Chittenden helped prime the October session of the legislature to consider the question. The Reverend Samuel Williams of Rutland, a noted American scientist who had taught at Harvard before fleeing to Vermont ahead of a forgery charge in 1788 and who now hoped to use a connection with a new Vermont college to build a fresh career in the Green Mountains, was another principal ally. "My whole aim now," Williams wrote his wife, "is to influence and persuade the persons of note here to found a College."[16] Williams gave Ira much valuable advice on promoting the college plan. In September 1789, under the pseudonym "Respublica," he published "Observations on the Establishment of a University in the State of Vermont" in the Windsor Vermont Journal. Vermont would realize many benefits by cultivating the arts and sciences through a university, "Respublica" declared; as far as location went, a healthy competition among the interested communities would soon identify the best town.[17]

Ira Allen probably did not anticipate that it would take the General Assembly two full years to make a decision. Even though Allen was Colchester's representative in the House, his October 15, 1789, presentation before his fellow legislators resulted only in the appointment of two committees to study the issue and report back to the September 1790 session. Ira gathered more pledges from Chittenden County towns early in September of 1790 to bolster his case, but the Legislature took no action on his renewed petition.[18] The January 1791 General Assembly was too busy with the details of Vermont's admission into the American Union as the fourteenth state to pay much attention to Samuel Williams's impassioned call under the twin pseudonyms "Candidus" and "Impartiality" for a university for Burlington.[19] The best Allen could get was a promise that the autumn 1791 session might consider his proposal. As one of Vermont's revolutionary leaders, Ira must have deplored the snail's pace of Vermont's new generation of leaders in deciding on a state university.

Ira put the time between the January and October 1791 legislatures to good use on the college issue. Samuel Williams continued to feed him confidential advice on rounding up subscriptions and securing sufficient votes for a majority in the General Assembly,[20] and Allen worked hard to counter the promotional claims of various towns that had begun to challenge Burlington for the honor of becoming home to the state university. No doubt in large part because his £4,000 pledge remained by far the largest offer on the table, Ira's efforts were successful. The Legislature voted on October 24 to charter a college, a committee reported the following day that 89 of the 116 members polled favored Burlington for the school's location, and the act creating the University of Vermont for "the Education of Youth" and "the advancement of morality, virtue and happiness" became official on November 2, 1791. At last Ira Allen and Burlington had their college.[21]

Once chartered, UVM entered a long period of inactivity. The thirteen-man Board of Trustees appointed by the Legislature, including Ira, Governor Chittenden, and a mainly nondenominational mix of Vermont leaders, could not act without funds, and they soon found that money for UVM was exceptionally difficult to acquire. The Legislature had not made any appropriation and most of the individual pledges of 1789–1790, including Allen's, proved impossible to collect. Ira wrote to New York for a grant of land to benefit UVM on the grounds that residents of the northeastern portion of the Empire State would attend the school, but New York was unimpressed.[22] The only early progress came in June 1792, when the Trustees met in Burlington to select fifty acres of Allen's land at the top of the hill overlooking Lake Champlain as the site of the campus-to-be. This donation of land was considered equivalent to one quarter of Ira's original pledge.[23] The University now had a campus, but the only things on it were pine trees; there was no money in the treasury, there were no faculty or students in sight, and the prospects for addressing any of these shortcomings were less than bright. As the State of Vermont's hope for "the promotion of virtue and for the happiness of civil society," UVM was off to a slow start.

Ira's fellow trustees decided to get the University moving by forcing Allen to make good on the remaining £3,000 of his pledge. In addition to giving UVM the start-up funds needed to erect buildings, buy books and equipment, and hire faculty, a major gift would encourage other prospective donors to open their purses. Ira insisted that he meant to honor his promise but had not been successful in leasing any of his lands for the University's benefit.[24]

Nevertheless, in October 1793 he told the General Assembly that he would increase his original pledge by another £1,000 if the state would change the name of the school to Allen's University.[25] He had founded UVM "not only for the Benefit of the Present but for future ages," he explained in a separate memorial, and he was still working hard to promote the University's prosperity.

In Allen's vision of the future, UVM would be a shining beacon of American democracy and republican virtue:

It is not the Rich that I am Calculating so much to assist as the Poor[.] the Rich can send their sons to What College they Choose[.] But the poore have it not in their Power[.] yet they may have the most Promising Posterity[,] & if they can obtain Good Education may be in turn Rullers of the Land[.] . . . by Extending Knowledge & Sience to all Clases of People we may transmit to Posterity the Blessings of a free Government & on this Principle we must Principally Depend to Perpetuate those Liberties Obtained by the Loss of much Blood & Treasures[.][26]

The General Assembly considered Ira's proposal for two years before rejecting it. Although the legislators refrained from open criticism of his motives, they noted that he had proved better at making promises than at fulfilling them. He had paid part of his original pledge, an Assembly committee reported in 1795, "but the remainder we consider may be attended with uncertainty, and no way equal to what said Allen would have represented by this act for altering the name of said university." Adherence to the rhetoric of democracy and fine words about educating good Green Mountain republicans were not enough: the Legislature wanted to see cash or firm title to income-producing lands from Ira. Until then, there would be no Allen's University in the state of Vermont.[27]

By 1795 the General Assembly had good reason to be skeptical of Ira's financial prospects. The profitable trade he and brother Levi had hoped to establish with Canada had never materialized. The Quebec merchants had forced the Allens to sell low and buy high; the fluctuating water levels on the Richelieu River had made shipment of large timber rafts from the Champlain Valley a risky gamble; and the British authorities in Canada had vacillated between encouraging and discouraging imports from Vermont. Vermont's admission into the Union in 1791, which both brothers had opposed, had ended any chance of negotiating a separate free-trade treaty between the state and Canada. At home, Ira was facing challenges from other speculators and entrepreneurs who questioned the legitimacy of his title to tens of thousands of acres of Champlain Valley land. Deep in debt to merchants in Quebec, New York City, and Vermont itself but unwilling or unable to sell any of his property to raise cash, he lacked other reserves to protect his holdings, pay the taxes on his lands, or satisfy his creditors. His promises to UVM and the General Assembly notwithstanding, by 1795 Ira's financial empire was awash in red ink.

However, throughout his life, no matter how bad things looked, Allen always had a plan. In the autumn of 1795 he put his financial affairs in some semblance of order, renewed his bond to make good on the pledge to the University, and went to Boston.[28] Mortgaging his best lands for £4,000, he sailed to England, taking along an appointment from Governor Chittenden to solicit gifts for UVM, Chittenden's authorization to buy arms for the state militia (in which Ira held the rank of major-general), and an idea for revitalizing the Allen family's sagging fortunes.[29] That idea was to persuade the British government to connect Lake Champlain to the St. Lawrence River by means of a ship canal around the falls of the Richelieu River. Lake Champlain would become an inland sea and Burlington a major American port, sending Champlain Valley products across the Atlantic and receiving huge quantities of British manufactured goods in return. The benefits to Anglo-American relations, to the citizens of Vermont, Canada, and England, and (incidentally) to Ira Allen would be incalculable.[30]

Despite Allen's best rhetoric, the British were slow to respond to his scheme. When the wait stretched to several months, Ira moved on to Plan B. Crossing the Channel in May 1796, he went to Paris and suggested to the ruling Directory that the time was ripe for a rebellion in British Canada. If France would provide the guns, he would raise a force of ten thousand American volunteers and French-Canadian revolutionaries; together with a small French army of three thousand men they would overwhelm England's small Canadian garrisons and proclaim the new democratic republic of United Columbia. The spirit of the French Revolution would spread to a new land with an old French heritage, France's principal enemy would lose a substantial part of its colonial empire, and Vermont would have a new northern neighbor sure to be more open than its predecessor to a ship canal and free trade with the Champlain Valley. If everything went really well, Vermont might even secede from the United States and join United Columbia, especially if Burlington could become the capital of the proud new nation.[31]

The Directory took less than two weeks to endorse Allen's bold plan. By mid-July he had a portfolio of false documents to show that he was buying twenty thousand muskets and twenty-four cannon from France in his capacity as major-general of the Vermont state militia. On November 11, 1796, he slipped out of Ostend harbor with fifteen thousand muskets, aboard the small American ship *Olive Branch* and headed for America. Ira's prospects for finally realizing his Champlain Valley dreams looked bright; unfortunately, on November 19 the British warship *Audacious* caught up with the *Olive Branch* and confiscated its cargo as French military contraband. Allen protested vociferously and produced all of his fraudulent French documents but to no avail: back to England he and his gunrunning vessel went.

Allen spent the next eighteen months trying in vain to get a hostile British court system to let him and his muskets proceed to America. In May 1798 he went back to France in search of more fraudulent documents to bolster his case. He anticipated a warm reception from his fellow revolutionaries, but the membership of the Directory had changed since 1796, and Franco-American relations had deteriorated. Shortly after reaching Paris, Allen was arrested, and he spent most of the next year in jail, where his health deteriorated. He worried constantly about his Vermont properties while his chances of ever coming out on top in the *Olive Branch* affair grew steadily worse. By the time the French government set him free on September 14, 1799, Ira was nearly broken in both body and spirit.[32]

Allen lingered in France for more than a year after his release from prison, vainly trying to get the new government of Napoleon Bonaparte to revive the United Columbia idea. Delays in gathering documents for his *Olive Branch* case and the state of his health kept him from sailing for America until November 1800.[33] Ira spent the first months of 1801 in Philadelphia and Washington, trying to solicit support for the lawsuit he planned to file against England for damages in the *Olive Branch* debacle; then he headed north to Vermont. When he finally arrived in Colchester in May 1801, the European voyage he had expected to last seven or eight months had somehow stretched into an absence of 5½ years.

On his return Allen found his Champlain Valley empire in ruins. Ira's wife and his nephew, Heman Allen, were unable to maintain control of his holdings. Rival speculator Silas Hathaway of St. Albans had purchased Ira's 1795 mortgage and was now claiming possession of most of his best lands. Within his own family, Allen's nieces had obtained a court judgment that turned Ira's Colchester and Burlington mills over to them as compensation for their inheritance of his deceased brothers' shares of the Onion River Land Company. As soon as word of his return spread throughout Vermont, creditors and adversaries began to file lawsuits against him. The death of Thomas Chittenden in August 1797 had cost Ira his last powerful friend in state government; Matthew Lyon, another strong political supporter, had left Vermont for Kentucky; and Isaac Tichenor, Chittenden's successor as governor, had been Allen's enemy for twenty years. Ira worked feverishly to salvage something from the wreckage, but his problems continued to mount.[34]

UVM, on the other hand, had actually made some progress during Allen's long absence. Although Ira's occasional attempts to interest his contacts in Europe in UVM's welfare had produced nothing more than long-winded advice and offers to serve as president of the school if the salary and perquisites were right, the University's trustees had managed to raise enough money to erect one small house on the college "green" by the end of 1798.[35] That effort exhausted the Board's resources, and the house sat empty for a year while the Trustees grappled with the old problems of unredeemed pledges and nonexistent income. Finally, in November 1799, the Reverend

Daniel C. Sanders, a liberal Congregational minister from Vergennes, agreed to move to Burlington, occupy the local pulpit, and use the UVM building as a residence and school for young boys. Although this did not constitute a college, much less the thriving center of knowledge and education Allen had described to his friends in England and France, it was at least one small step in the right direction.

As the nineteenth century opened, the emergence of another college in Vermont forced the University's trustees to quicken their pace. When the state legislature granted a charter to Middlebury College in November 1800, UVM suddenly found itself with serious in-state competition for patronage and the support of the General Assembly. In the spring of 1801 the UVM board authorized construction of a large, three-story brick building on the east side of the College Green. The chronic shortage of funds delayed completion of the upper stories until 1806; in the meantime, the Reverend Mr. Sanders, who now bore the title of president, taught small classes of teenage boys in his nearby home and on the lower floor of the unfinished college structure. More than a decade after receiving its charter, UVM was in operation at last.[36]

Despite the severity of his own problems Ira Allen still took an interest in UVM's progress. He appears not to have held it against the Trustees that during his absence they had secured a court writ of attachment on his title to the town of Plainfield to try to extract payment of his original £4,000 pledge; perhaps he realized that the several challenges to his claim to ownership of the town would render the writ worthless to the University.[37] Less than two weeks after his return, he wrote a letter to the Burlington *Vermont Centinel* warning local speculators about to build near the College Green that he had set those lands aside for UVM's future expansion.[38] Two months later Ira informed the agent for the Trustees that he approved of the start of the college building and that he would donate £1,000 worth of English manufactured goods toward the costs of construction, but the shipment from England never reached Burlington.[39] For all of Allen's protestations of interest, his track record as a UVM benefactor was still weak on delivery.

Ira's inability to make good on any of his UVM pledges was evidence of the sorry state of his affairs after his return from Europe. The October 1801 session of the General Assembly granted him immunity from civil arrest for one year, but that was not nearly enough time to settle his massive debts. Levi Allen's death in December 1801 took away Ira's last brother, as well as one of his few surviving friends. None of the state legislatures he contacted would buy the *Olive Branch* arms he had left behind in Ostend, and the February 1803 bankruptcy of the New York firm he had authorized to sell the guns that had reached America killed all hope of a profit from that unfortunate transaction. The list of court cases against Allen continued to grow, his rivals began publishing newspaper advertisements to offer his property for sale, and early in 1803 a Canadian creditor had him jailed in Burlington for nonpayment of an old debt.[40] Allen managed to make bail, but he realized that he soon would be back in jail if he stayed within reach of his enemies. Aware that his creditors were watching him closely, he slipped away from home and family on a Sunday evening in April 1803, hurried to a boat waiting on Lake Champlain, and fled alone toward New York. Except for two brief visits the following year, Vermont had seen the last of Ira Allen.

UVM continued its slow progress after Allen's ignominious departure. The main college building, occupied in 1805 and completed in 1807, was an impressive home for the school. Financial concerns—low rents on UVM's lands, sporadic donations, the unsuccessful search for wealthy patrons—were still a problem, and President Sanders went unpaid for long stretches, but there were some signs of hope. Although Dartmouth and Middlebury were larger, UVM managed to turn out a steady stream of small graduating classes—four members in 1804; six in 1806; twelve in 1809—as proof of its contribution to education on the northern frontier. Unlike most of New England's other colleges, with their ties to specific religious denominations, UVM began to build a modest reputation for nonsectarian education and a student body not dominated by future ministers. Within a few years of Ira's flight, the residents of the Champlain Valley were pointing to his college's growth as proof of the development and prosperity of northwestern Vermont.

While UVM's star rose, Allen's descended. By the autumn of 1803 he was in Kentucky, where he took advantage of his old friend Matthew Lyon's local contacts and a lenient interpretation of the federal pauper law to declare bankruptcy.[41] Two months later he was in Washington, D.C., to ask the Jefferson administration for help in persuading England to reimburse him for his losses in the *Olive Branch* case.[42] In January 1804, confident that the Kentucky bankruptcy proceedings protected him against arrest for debt anywhere in the United States, Ira returned to Vermont to attend the state legislature's session at Windsor. He found the legislators cold to his petitions and lobbying efforts, and the fear that his Vermont creditors might persuade sheriffs and judges that bankruptcy in Kentucky meant nothing in Vermont soon drove him south again, this time to Philadelphia.

Once settled in the City of Brotherly Love, Allen received news that a British court had finally ruled in his favor on the *Olive Branch* appeal, but the accompanying bill from his London attorneys for £3,394 only added to his paper losses in the case. Securing damages from England or the United States, his last remaining hope, became an obsession. He returned to Vermont one last time in October 1804, but the trip went badly on all counts. The General Assembly's sole response to his *Olive Branch* petition was a facetious resolution authorizing him to hire the U.S. Navy's "Gunboat No. 1" to import arms for the state militia.[43] The courts rejected his appeals in the

Onion River Land Company and Silas Hathaway cases, and various enemies made plans to have him arrested again. Attending a UVM Trustees meeting just long enough to resign, he returned to Philadelphia, where at least he was safe from the troublesome writs, warrants, and summonses of the Green Mountain State.

Despite his failure in Vermont, Ira remained optimistic about his *Olive Branch* claims and turned out a series of pamphlets to inform the world of his position.[44] He renewed his petitions to the U.S. government, but none of his efforts—pamphlets, interviews with British officials in Washington and Philadelphia, meetings with high-ranking members of the Jefferson and Madison administrations, even a favorable ruling by the U.S. Attorney-General—had any effect.[45] The British government still insisted that it had dealt properly with the *Olive Branch* in 1797 and that any losses Ira had sustained then or since were his own problem.

Frustrated in the *Olive Branch* case, Allen also endured separation and alienation from his family after 1804. He had hoped to bring Jerusha and their three children to Philadelphia, but there was never enough money to make that possible. Ira apparently never saw Jerusha and his daughter Maria Julietta in the last decade of his life, and his sons Ira and Zimri visited him only a few times. Of his other relatives, nephew Heman Allen alone responded to his frequent letters and requests for help; everyone else distanced himself from Ira and his demands. Allen was bitter about this rejection; in his mind the family's future still lay in the realization of the dreams he had been pursuing since the 1770s.[46]

Allen's last years were unsuccessful and unhappy. He still wrote fruitlessly about the *Olive Branch* affair,[47] while dwindling financial resources forced him to move frequently, each time to cheaper Philadelphia lodgings. Despite Ira's distance from his family, the deaths of his seventeen-year-old daughter Maria Julietta in August 1811 and of his twenty-one-year-old son Zimri in August 1813 were painful blows. His own health, which had not been good since his imprisonment in France, grew worse as he entered his sixties.

Yet even as his prospects darkened near the end of his life, Ira found the strength for one last fling at empire building. In 1812 he met a group of Spanish-American adventurers who planned to invade the Texas region of northern Mexico and liberate it from Spanish rule. Ira convinced the group's leaders that his extensive experience in planning revolutions in Vermont and Canada would be valuable to their expedition. When the conspirators headed south to form a revolutionary army, Ira was sure that he would soon be the American ambassador of a new democratic republic in Texas.[48]

Despite Allen's high expectations the poorly organized invasion of Mexico collapsed early in 1814. By then, however, Ira was past caring. In January 1814 his health took a sudden turn for the worse, and on January 15, at the age of sixty-two, he died of "retrocedent gout." His estate, which had once included more than two hundred thousand acres of prime Vermont lands, was too small to pay the cost of burial, and his body went to a pauper's grave in Philadelphia's Free Quaker Cemetery. When the news reached Vermont early in February, the only public reaction was a two-line obituary in the Burlington *Northern Sentinel*: "In Philadelphia, on the evening of the 15th ult. General Ira Allen, late of Colchester, Vt. aged 64 [*sic*] years."[49]

After his death, Ira Allen quickly receded into the shadows of Vermont history, leaving the state's historical identity to revolve around Ethan Allen and the Green Mountain Boys, the stirring saga of brave Yankees battling avaricious Yorkers for control of the New Hampshire Grants, and the military excitement of the Revolution. Although he had clearly been one of Vermont's most important early leaders, Ira's commercial plans, his self-serving wheeling-and-dealing, and his political scheming fell outside the standards of the popular heroic tradition. Nineteenth-century Vermonters proudly compared Ethan Allen to Daniel Boone and Thomas Chittenden to George Washington, but Ira, whose closest national counterpart was probably Aaron Burr, attracted few admirers.

Allen's memory also faded at UVM, as the University developed a sense of its own history beginning with Daniel Clarke Sanders and the first students of 1801. In 1838 Ira's son, Ira Hayden Allen, had to write to Elijah Paine (whose attempt in the mid-1780s to establish a college at Williamstown had set the stage for Ira's more successful effort) to verify that his father had in fact played a prominent role in UVM's founding.[50] John Wheeler's historical oration at the 1854 ceremonies to mark the fiftieth anniversary of the first graduating class included a brief acknowledgment of Allen as the University's founder, but otherwise UVM continued to favor Sanders, James Marsh, and some of its distinguished early graduates as builders of the school's historical traditions.[51] As in Vermont state history, Allen's troubled career and scheming personal style made it difficult to work him into the pantheon of UVM's early heroes.

The University's first substantive attempt to rehabilitate Ira's reputation came in 1892 as part of the school's extended centennial celebration. At the 1892 commencement, librarian and Latin professor John E. Goodrich delivered a lengthy address on "The Founder of the University of Vermont." He detailed Allen's leadership in independent Vermont's government and his campaign to secure a charter for a college at Burlington, describing him in the terms Vermonters had reserved for their most beloved Founding Fathers and praising him at every opportunity for his selfless contributions to the state and college he had helped create. Vermont and UVM had both neglected Ira unfairly, Goodrich told the commencement audience, and the time had come to correct that oversight by establishing May 1, Ira's birthday, as Founder's Day, "a holiday forever, significant at once of her origin, and of the new life pulsing continually in her veins of perennial and ever bourgeoning [*sic*] prime."[52]

Goodrich's impassioned rhetoric proved effective. Beginning in 1894, Founder's Day became a tradition at UVM that lasted into the 1950s before evolving into today's Honors Day. The emphasis on Allen soon faded, however, until James B. Wilbur arrived to finish the job Goodrich had started. Wilbur, a wealthy businessman who had retired to an impressive country estate in Manchester in 1909, was an enthusiastic Vermont antiquarian and book collector. He developed a particular fascination for Allen and became convinced that it was "a sacred duty to undertake the writing of his life."[53] Although Wilbur's publication of a ponderous, adoring biography of Allen did little for his hero's reputation, his adoption of Ira's college as a favorite object of charitable largesse did a great deal for UVM. Under the skillful cultivation of UVM president Guy W. Bailey, Wilbur became the University's principal benefactor.[54] In 1921 he donated a statue of Allen; several years later he paid for the construction of Ira Allen Chapel at the northeast corner of the University green; and on his death in 1929 he left UVM nearly $3 million, still the largest bequest in the University's history. If having Ira Allen as a founder was not profitable for the University during Allen's time, it certainly was during Wilbur's.

The transformation of Allen's image has continued at UVM in the sixty years since Wilbur's death. The classical McKim, Mead and White chapel is an impressive monument to his memory; the University invokes his name frequently in its official literature; and membership in the Ira Allen Society is reserved for the school's most generous donors (who make good on their pledges). Posing for pictures under Ira's cap-and-gown-draped statue on the green has become a tradition for seniors at commencement time. True, UVM's modern sense of Ira has become hazy and one-dimensional, but that has allowed him to serve as an acceptable icon for a public institution's heritage. After nearly two centuries, he has become a respectable Founding Father.

Yet cardboard respectability is not what Ira Allen deserves from UVM. He was a complex and complicated man, one who demonstrated bravery, greed, determination, selflessness, vision, deceit, patriotism, and a variety of other good and bad human qualities. Any bland, uncontroversial representation of his character and career misses the fascination of this individual whose story is a colorful thread in the tapestry of northern New England's early history. The fact that he was no paragon of virtue in the Mason Weems tradition ought to be irrelevant today. What matters is that the early history of both the University and the state are incomplete without an honest picture of the life—virtues and faults, altruism and selfishness, deeds and misdeeds—of Ira Allen.

Years of Trial: Religion, Money, War, Fire, and the Competition with Middlebury

P. JEFFREY POTASH

THE simultaneous opening of the University of Vermont and of Middlebury College in the fall of 1800 was an unprecedented event in the history of New England, where only six colleges and universities had been chartered during the preceding century and a half. It reflected a frontier rivalry between "two growing and ambitious towns."[1] From the first settlement, town fathers both in Burlington and in Middlebury, strove to boost the fortunes of their respective towns. Each town had become its county shiretown, and each had organized an impressive assemblage of professionals, merchants, artisans, printers, and industrialists with which to bolster its claim to be the preeminent "central place" in its county.

The placement of the state's university was the ultimate prize in this competition. Although Ira Allen had claimed that distinction for Burlington in 1791, Middlebury seized on UVM's failure to commence operations as an opportunity to lobby visiting legislators on the "expediency" of their proposal to convert their "county grammar school" into a second institution of higher learning within Vermont. The Legislature granted the college a charter on November 1, 1800, albeit with the stipulation that it never be permitted to share the proceeds from state lands set aside for UVM.[2]

Although the UVM–Middlebury contest originated in the frontier spirit of entrepreneurial one-upsmanship, battle lines were quickly redrawn in the face of the cataclysmic religious event known as the "Second Great Awakening," the dramatic explosion of evangelical revivalism that by 1800 encompassed the entire nation. This "internal convulsion," to use Perry Miller's term, sought to contain the trend toward secularism that, in the minds of orthodox clergymen, had propagated "error, infidelity, and atheism," with consequent political factionalism and social disorder, during the two decades following the American Revolution.[3] The election of the non-Christian

Thomas Jefferson to the presidency lent urgency to the orthodox counter-revolution. Jeffersonians in New England were preparing to nullify the two-centuries-old "Standing Order" that supported the Congregational churches with public taxes in order to enforce moral behavior. In reply orthodox clerics warned of the impending collapse of the very foundations of American society. Insisting that immorality inevitably reigned where orthodox precepts of "innate depravity" were disregarded, Yale president Timothy Dwight concluded that "rational freedom cannot be preserved without the aid of Christianity."[4]

Frontier Vermont particularly aroused orthodox fears because of the scarcity of settled evangelical ministers. Congregational missionary Nathan Perkins, touring Vermont in 1789, found an abundance of "haters of religion" who lived "under no constraints in the indulgence and gratification of their inclinations, lusts, and passions."[5] Burlington in particular seemed a grim impediment to a Christian America. From its founding, Perkins observed, the town had been home to an "irreligious and immoral people," foremost of whom was Ethan Allen, author in 1785 of the first full-length treatise aimed directly at the destruction of Christianity, *Reason the Only Oracle of Man.* Though Perkins could take satisfaction in the recent death of Allen, "one of ye wickedest men yt ever walked this guilty globe," he found little solace in the fact that Burlington residents remained "all Deists and proper heathen." Nine years later, Timothy Dwight reported after visiting Burlington, "The morals of this town are uncommonly loose if we except a very moderate number of families." An attempt to form a Congregational church, he noted, failed when it was discovered that the town had fewer than ten religious inhabitants.[6]

In 1791 this bastion of secularism seemed a logical site on which to plant America's first public institution dedicated to the unfettered propagation of reason "without preference to any religious sect or denomination whatsoever."[7] Ten years later, as political and religious feeling polarized, this position was viewed by orthodox clerics like Timothy Dwight and orthodox communities like Middlebury as nothing short of sinister. Small wonder, then, that Dwight chose to ally himself with the fledgling Middlebury venture, releasing one of Yale's tutors, the Reverend Jeremiah Atwater, to guide the college as president. Atwater would ensure that Middlebury's roots were nurtured in the traditional soils of New England orthodoxy by copying Yale's Classical curriculum and its "Laws Regulating Student Behavior."[8]

Recurring religious revivals during the next three and a half decades imbued the contest between Middlebury College and UVM with a spirit of missionary zeal. Despite chronic financial problems plaguing both institutions throughout the period, the prospect of surrender was unthinkable both for UVM's advocates of a natural rights liberalism and for Middlebury's champions of the Calvinist belief in the elect and damned. But despite the steady progress of revivalism, culminating in the stunning climax of evangelical excitements during the "ultraistic" 1830s, UVM ultimately succeeded, in the 1840s, in claiming the title "Vermont's University."

Having been apprised of Middlebury's legislative request in October 1800, UVM's trustees rallied from almost a decade of quarreling and inactivity to appoint the Reverend Daniel Sanders as the first president. Although the selection seems to have aroused dissent among the few orthodox clergy on the Board, it certainly underscores the majority's firm commitment to sustain the liberal tenets of the charter. Sanders, nominally a Congregational minister like his Middlebury counterpart, displayed little attachment to Calvinist doctrines that stressed the eternal damnation of all humans save for those "elected" through a mystical infusion of God's "free grace." He publicly warned against "the dangers of self-delusion [through the use of] passions running to the extreme," and he privately admitted, "I lay very little stress upon what some divines call *conversion*." This was much closer to the Unitarianism evolving at Sanders's alma mater, Harvard, than to the orthodoxy of Timothy Dwight's Yale. Under Sanders's leadership the only religious requirement for admission to UVM was simple proof of "a good moral character"; and although laws "encouraged" students to attend to daily prayer, proof of Christian behavior was to be demonstrated through the cultivation of reason and a dedication to "good will" and "usefulness in society."[9]

The UVM trustees immediately followed up the appointment of Sanders with a yearlong fund-raising drive that produced a total of $2,300 in loans, pledged by Burlington's most distinguished professionals, merchants, and industrialists. Clearly, the generosity of Middlebury's local benefactors had not been lost on a Burlington elite that hitherto had relied on unfulfilled promises of funds from Ira Allen and from the Legislature.

During the University's first six years of operation Daniel Sanders performed as its sole instructor, principal fund raiser, solicitor of legislative funds, and overseer of the physical plant. The question arises, what measure of success did UVM record during this period, particularly when matched against its rival to the south? Figures for enrolled students appear to have been regularly exaggerated to impress legislators, but a comparison of total graduates and their occupational choices makes it possible to discern each college's contribution to society.

In simple numerical terms UVM was being rapidly outpaced by Middlebury. By the end of 1806, UVM had produced only thirteen graduates, compared with Middlebury's thirty-two. Middlebury was able to draw students (ten during this period) from traditional centers of conservatism in eastern Connecticut and Massachusetts. By 1806 it had graduated twelve orthodox ministers, whereas UVM had produced none.

This distinction notwithstanding, a majority of Middlebury (53%) and

UVM (77%) students who graduated prior to 1807 chose to enter careers in the law as either lawyers, judges, or public officials. This was part of a nationwide transformation in the legal profession, in Perry Miller's words, "from its chaotic condition of around 1790 to a position of political and intellectual domination" during the next two decades. In the law a generation nurtured on the vision of America as a revolutionary experiment aimed "to find a method, not for obstructing Utopia, but for making the historic wisdom of the law serve this uniquely American opportunity."[10]

Middlebury's financial situation, though better than that of UVM, remained precarious. Pointing to their superiority in producing graduates, in 1806 Middlebury's trustees lobbied the Vermont Legislature to nullify UVM's exclusive right to lease lands. For President Sanders this move violated the Middlebury trustees' promise "not to ask or to be considered as entitled to college funds." He told the UVM trustees that the request was an act of desperation: "If they [Middlebury] obtain no funds, I believe they cannot retain what scholars they now have." He sent to the Legislature a delegation led by trustee William C. Harrington. To sidetrack Middlebury's proposal they warned that the continued presence of two institutions of higher learning in Vermont was inefficient and counterproductive to the public good. The presence of "two colleges," Sanders observed, "can only be sores of painful rivalship, litigation, the hot-beds of intrigue and misrepresentation." The existence of Middlebury College "could only benefit a few individuals at Middlebury who wish to limit all public favors to that little spot of mire and clay."[11]

Although the legislators agreed to deny Middlebury public funds, Sanders had little time to savor the victory. President Jefferson proclaimed a total embargo on the lucrative Canada trade in March 1808 and commanded the Burlington collector of customs, Jabez Penniman, to join with military and civil authorities in using "all means in their power, by force of arms or otherwise" to disperse "insurgents . . . confederating on Lake Champlain." Burlington erupted in a frenzy of political protest; prominent citizens inveighed publicly against these "unconstitutional barbarous and tyrannical edicts" while privately flaunting their disregard for the law and reaping the profits gleaned from rampant smuggling.[12]

Despite Sanders's cautious efforts to steer a neutral course in both politics and religion, the whirlwind of unshackled rhetoric and uncontrollable emotionalism ensnared both him and UVM in its divisive trap. When Sanders resigned the ministry in the Burlington Congregational church, a newly formed orthodox faction steadfastly insisted that Daniel Haskell, a "respectable Hopkinsian" of strong Calvinistic convictions, be installed as minister. Unable to resolve the impasse, the church split into the First Congregational Society of Burlington (later Unitarian) and the First Calvinistic Congregational Society of Burlington.[13] Members of the newly invigorated orthodox church demanded that Sanders require students to attend their services. Sanders refused, publicly maintaining a policy of nonalignment while privately proposing to trustees that "we furnish our own preaching . . . in the chapel on the Sabbath," thereby notifying "the two clerical parties . . . [to] leave the college out of this foolish dispute." [14]

Amid heightening emotions, Sanders's position proved untenable. At the August 17, 1810, meeting of the UVM trustees, the three orthodox clergymen on the Board tendered their resignations, charging Sanders with being "so lax in sentiment as to favor one sect no more than another." Sanders, declared the Reverend Asa Burton, was "the most unfit person they [the Board] could well have appointed." With that the Congregational minister who had served on the UVM board for almost two decades promptly accepted a place on Middlebury's board. [15]

Burton's public repudiation immediately sparked fears among the remaining trustees that state legislators might exploit these resignations to reconsider UVM's special status and lease lands. It was to preempt such action that the Trustees secured a charter change from the Legislature providing for the election of the entire Board by that body. [16] But this amendment subjected Sanders and university operations to even greater pressures of partisan politics. In 1811 the newly installed Democrats on the Board tried to incriminate the former Federalist majority by charging Sanders with mismanagement. At the August 1, 1811, meeting of the Board, Cornelius Van Ness, a prominent Jeffersonian, collector of customs during the War of 1812, and later governor of Vermont, introduced a resolution asserting that "the interest and prosperity of Said University require that the Rev. Daniel Sanders, President of the University of Vermont, retire from said office." Sanders was a liability, a liberal Federalist who had incurred too many enemies. With the election of a more suitable president, Van Ness promised that "the college could not fail to flourish, scholars would come in crowds, and its treasury would be filled by the munificence of new patrons." [17]

Sanders weathered the attack, insisting that "the people of Vermont are not prepared to part with the rights of private judgment and conscience." Still, in the poisoned atmosphere of political and religious intolerance, he was not optimistic about his future chances. It was public knowledge, he wrote to a Harvard ally in September 1811, that the "whole weight of the Hopkinsian clergy and disciples are against us" and "do us what mischiefs they can." Moreover, partisan Democrats had gained control of the Board, leaving Sanders to feel that he was "almost the only Federalist who has not already been made a sacrifice." To a liberal Harvard friend he confessed, "I have long been ready to change my situation when a more eligible should offer." [18]

In 1812, Sanders published a remarkable monograph, titled *A History of the Indian Wars with the First Settlers of the United States, Particularly in New England*. This work opened the UVM president to another attack from his orthodox rivals at Middlebury College. In the recurring battles between Puritan founding fathers and Indians almost two centuries earlier, Sanders found a paradigm for his own persecution. His thesis argued that the rule of the "heart" over the "head" had led deluded Calvinists into slaughtering humans in the name of God. "Reason and conscience raise a voice which will be heard by all. . . . The Savage, who could not soon comprehend a metaphysical question, would be at no loss respecting what was right between man and man." The current import of this lesson was not to be overlooked, Sanders concluded. Only "when the useful arts shall have increased the means of subsistence, when something like science shall have thrown light into their darkened minds . . . then the mild religion of the Redeemer can be introduced with salutary effects."[19]

For Middlebury partisans, Sanders's philosophy invited an impassioned response. The Reverend John Hough, professor of divinity at Middlebury, made a scathing attack on Sanders's book in the November 1813 edition of the College's *Literary and Philosophical Repertory*. Sanders, Hough asserted, had "adopted the cant of every licentious advocate of infidelity and irreligion, and of every unprincipled and daring propagator of error and impiety and guilt." He accused Sanders of maligning the venerable fathers of New England in suggesting that "orthodox creeds do not always sanctify the heart and conduct" and in substituting reason and its "interested and mercenary motives" for "regeneration by the special agency of the Redeemer's righteousness." All of this made Sanders guilty of "the most barefaced and mischievous heresy."[20]

Hough's ferocious attack was a sign of the Second Great Awakening in Middlebury College. A revival took place at the college during the fall of 1811; it was followed by a second in the spring of 1812 and by a third, a "work of deep solemnity and power," in the late spring of 1814. The social and economic dislocations wrought by the embargo and by the War of 1812 were said to bear out the evangelicals' belief in the folly of reason and the propensity of the unconverted human toward self-gratification and "depravity." Middlebury faculty, exhorting "unconverted" students to release themselves from "the bondage of sin" and their "heavy hearts" and prostrate themselves before their lord," saw themselves creating a new community, purged of secular "wickedness."[21] For them, a mystical inner faith and "everlasting love" took the place of rational action to achieve economic and political betterment.[22]

While the unique combination of war and revivalism lifted Middlebury's fortunes to new heights, those of UVM plummeted. UVM graduated only twenty-two students during the first three years of war (1812–1814), compared to Middlebury's eighty-two. With Burlington subjected to British naval bombardments in March 1814, the Trustees were obliged to relinquish the university building to barrack U.S. Army soldiers and to suspend classes for the first and only time in UVM's history.

Middlebury's tight link with the Awakening was evidenced in a dramatic alteration in graduates' career choices. Whereas law and public service had predominated among graduates prior to 1807, more than half of those graduating between 1812 and 1815 (numbering 57, or 54 percent of those known) entered the orthodox ministry. By comparison, law attracted fewer than one quarter (24 percent of the graduating class).

Daniel Sanders's 1812–1814 graduates were a more diverse group. Although law remained most popular, the proportion had decreased from three quarters (1804–1911) to less than one half (45%). Five graduates became clergymen, and the remainder chose careers in medicine, business, farming, and education.

One can only speculate on Sanders's responsibility for UVM's inability to grow. In any case, he clearly had had enough. Two months after having been "dismissed" pending the outcome of the war, Sanders and his family "quitted that pleasant village never to return to it again."[23]

Sanders's departure and the army's subsequent vacating of the university edifice a year later presented the Trustees with a tabula rasa on which to start anew. Renouncing Sanders's philosophy, in July 1815 the Trustees appointed the University's second president, the Reverend Samuel Austin, an uncompromising advocate of "strict calvinism." Believing "that the providence of God indicated that he should accept the appointment," Austin pledged in his inaugural address to honor the Trustees' request that the "seminary . . . prepare its sons to guide the reins of civil government and to become skillful builders in the House of God." Transposing orthodoxy into university affairs, he observed that the "supreme value" of knowledge rested "in its subserviency to the extension of the kingdom of the messiah and the salvation of the souls of men." To guarantee that this overarching principle governed university affairs, Austin appointed a new academic faculty of three professors, Rev. James Murdock, Rev. Ebenezer Burgess, and Jairus Kennon, all men "of marked religious character." Finally, in a conscious reversal of his predecessor's policy, he struck a conciliatory note in relations with Middlebury College: "May it [UVM] act in liberal and friendly concert with all similar institutions, through this country and particularly with the sister institution in the state."[24]

Middlebury partisans doubtless watched with great interest to ascertain the degree to which Austin could promote change at UVM. In one area his influence seems to have effected a dramatic reversal: among students graduating from the University during his first four years (1816–1819), eight (57 percent) of those whose careers are known entered the ministry, a number equaling that of the preceding fifteen years. But Austin's progress did not meet his expectations. UVM managed to graduate only seventeen students during the period, compared with Middlebury's seventy-one. Furthermore, the postwar recession prompted several Burlington benefactors to revive long-standing debts against the University, which drained rent monies collected from the federal government for the wartime occupation of the college edifice and thwarted efforts to renovate the library and scientific facilities.[25]

As rumors flew of Austin's desire to resign UVM's presidency, departing president Henry Davis of Middlebury College proposed to his trustees in July 1817 that a plan of union with UVM be devised. If the Burlington campus were closed and Samuel Austin were appointed to head Middlebury, Davis contended, benefits would accrue "both to Middlebury College and the state . . . , and the institution would soon have the patronage of the Legislature, and of individuals in general throughout the commonwealth." However, Davis's proposal was rebuffed by Middlebury trustee and prominent benefactor Gamaliel Painter, who expressed "prejudice" toward a man who had tainted himself through association with UVM. Not to be outdone, the UVM Trustees forged an alternative proposal in the fall of 1819, suggesting that duplication could be eliminated if Middlebury defined itself as a theological seminary while UVM remained a collegiate institution. Committees from both institutions met several times over a period of two years with the hope of forging a mutually agreeable solution to the rivalry that had left both parties heavily indebted, but compromise eluded them.[26]

The demise of the union plan erased Samuel Austin's last hope for resolving UVM's pressing financial embarrassments. At the end of March 1821 he abandoned the effort and resigned. This step raised the fundamental question of whether the University could survive at all. With only $101.06 in the university treasury and outstanding debts exceeding $11,000, the outlook was dismal. Students warned the Trustees that unless "something decisive could be done . . . we shall think it to our advantage to dissolve our connection here immediately and remove to some other college." By the fall of 1822 only twenty-two students were left, and the faculty gave notice that instruction would cease at the end of the term.[27]

The appointment of orthodox Burlington cleric Daniel Haskell to serve as president and the receipt of a $2,500 loan enabled the crippled institution to stave off closure. On May 27, 1824, however, disaster struck when the college building was reduced to ashes by fire, started on the roof by sparks discharged from one of the building's tall chimneys.[28] The conflagration proved emotionally devastating for Haskell, and he suffered both physical and mental collapse.[29]

Fortunately, the destruction of the building rekindled a spirit of unity and commitment from Burlington's commercial elite. Subscriptions were solicited among town residents to erect a new facade. Twenty-nine men, including persons loyal to both the Unitarian and Congregational churches and comprising the elite of Burlington's mercantile and professional community, rallied together to contribute in excess of $8,000.

Still, university affairs continued to flounder, with Professor James Dean, Rev. Willard Preston, and Professor George Wyllys Benedict occupying the office of the presidency during the short span of two years. Only with the October 1826 appointment of the Reverend James Marsh was stability restored after a five-year hiatus. The construction of a new building not-withstanding, the sight that presented itself to Marsh when he arrived was forbidding. "The students," he later recalled, "were few in number, the funds not wholly free from embarrassment, the library and apparatus a mere name; and the impression seemed to prevail with many that an institution doomed to so many strange calamities was never to succeed and had better be given up by its friends."[30]

The Trustees' unanimous decision to offer the presidency to Marsh re-vealed an unprecedented regard for the youthful scholar. Though only thirty-two years of age, Marsh had already distinguished himself as a scholar of languages. In addition to his scholarship, Marsh provided UVM with a novel mix of orthodoxy and liberalism. His orthodox credentials were quite impeccable: an undergraduate degree earned at Dartmouth College and a degree in divinity from Andover Theological Seminary, a staunchly Calvin-ist institution organized in the wake of Harvard's 1805 defection to Unitari-anism.[31] Appearances were deceiving, however, for Marsh had exited from both institutions anything but a traditionalist.

In accepting the UVM trustees' monumental challenge "to re-establish the public confidence and favor an institution which seemed on the very verge of extinction," Marsh embraced the opportunity to experiment with broad curricular reforms. Echoing the sentiments voiced by Daniel Sanders more than two decades earlier, Marsh maintained that the sole objective of a collegiate education was to fully activate the rational senses and "to provide for the essential well-being of an individual and of a community." Notice-ably absent from his scheme was a reverence for religious observance. "We have had sufficient experience to be convinced," Marsh observed in his in-augural address, "notwithstanding all we may find to lament, that religion will best sustain itself, in its spirituality and efficiency, in the independent condition, in which we have placed it."[32]

Marsh's stark religious pronouncements rekindled the earlier antagonism between the university and Middlebury. For nine years prior to Marsh's installation at UVM, the Reverend Joshua Bates had guided Middlebury College along the unswerving path of orthodoxy. Following in the tradi-tion of his predecessor, Henry Davis, Bates was instrumental in nurturing two more major religious revivals at the college, one in 1819 and another in 1825–1826. Each yielded impressive numbers of converts and bolstered Middlebury's "distinguished character," in Bates's words, "for piety and holy enterprise."[33]

For Bates, Marsh's position was anathema. Education should be funda-mentally a religious enterprise. Reason, Bates insisted, "unaided by revela-tion . . . is altogether insufficient to lead us to a knowledge of the divine will, on which our duty, our destination, and our happiness depend." Religious instruction, with carefully monitored attendance at daily morning and evening services and the demand for irreproachable behavior, was viewed by Bates "as the most important part of education." Bible study was essential to "incorporate in the system of liberal education an explicit recognition of the truth and duties of Christianity" and thereby "correct the abuses of learning and purify the fountains of knowledge." Bates's Middlebury, in short, offered neither curricular experimentation and innovation nor sanctuary to the religiously ambivalent: only through the rigors of a traditional curriculum, illuminated by religious self-scrutiny and sustained by a rigid system of rules and punishments, did Bates believe the head and the heart would meld to produce "good learning."[34]

In the atmosphere of recurring revivalism Bates had extended Middlebury's preeminence over UVM. Between 1818 and 1826, Middlebury graduated a total of 184 students, almost three times the number produced at UVM. Fully one third had been drawn from the traditional bastions of orthodoxy in southern New England (as were only five graduates of UVM), indicating that Middlebury's bond with Timothy Dwight's "land of steady habits" remained intact. Further evidence of the college's orthodox commitment could be seen in the fact that 57 percent of all graduates during the period pursued careers as orthodox clergymen.

Nor would Bates and Middlebury relinquish their lead during the succeeding seven years that Marsh functioned as UVM president. Marsh's innovative programming did bolster the number of non-degree-seeking students at UVM, but between 1827 and 1833 only 46 were graduated, compared with 127 at Middlebury. Seemingly frustrated by "the various and distracting duties of his office" and anxious to return to his scholarly studies, Marsh resigned the presidency and took the chair of moral and intellectual philosophy at the University.[35]

Still, Marsh retained the support of the Trustees, who offered the presidency to the man he had personally recommended, Rev. John Wheeler of Windsor. In his inaugural address, Wheeler followed Marsh's lead in upholding a duty "to think as well as to act rationally, and to see that our connections of truth rest on the grounds of right reason."[36]

Prominent Burlingtonians shared the views espoused by Marsh and Wheeler, a fact confirmed in 1834 with the completion of a subscription totaling $30,000. In addition to repairing deteriorating buildings and paying pressing debts, Wheeler used the proceeds of the subscription to hire an additional professor and to buy $14,000 worth of "library and philosophical apparatus." "The influence of this subscription on the subsequent prosperity of the University," Wheeler later observed, could "scarcely be overrated."[37]

The rise in UVM's fortunes set the stage for one final contest with Middlebury College. Joshua Bates returned to the attack, inspired by the new vision of "ultraism," a new postmillennialism that anticipated imminent victory for evangelical religion through the intensification of revivalistic activity. He sought once and for all to quiet the forces of liberalism at UVM.

Revivalism in Vermont had been dramatically transformed in 1831 through the sudden appropriation of Charles Grandison Finney's celebrated "new measure" revival techniques. Refined by use in New York's "burned-over district," Finney's method employed "protracted meetings" and associated theological innovations; it permitted revivals to be generated seemingly at will, mitigating former fears that spontaneous enthusiasm exhibited in one locale might bypass neighboring congregations. These new measures appealed to many who formerly could not or would not submit to the orthodox creed. Their rapid diffusion across the Vermont countryside produced unprecedented yields; in a single year, 1831, more than half of the state's orthodox Congregational and Baptist churches (including Middlebury's Congregational church and Burlington's First Calvinistic Society) reported experiencing revivals totaling seventy-five hundred converts.[38]

In the same year, Bates held a four-day meeting for members of the senior class at Middlebury and secured the conversion of all but one of them. He explained his success by the carefully orchestrated use of "inquiry meetings" and "anxious benches," which constituted "a direct and exceedingly efficient means" to induce those "halting and doubting to take solid ground." This marked the beginning of a "new era in the ushering in of millennial glory."[39]

By 1833 revivals had slowed to a trickle, which forced Bates to temper his optimism. Anxious to rekindle the fire at any cost, he joined with several other clerics in issuing an invitation to the renowned, albeit highly controversial, itinerant evangelist Jedediah Burchard to undertake an extended tour of Vermont beginning in the fall of 1834.

Burchard had developed his tactics over a decade in western New York State; they included meetings of thirty days or more, during which he took his audiences on an emotional roller coaster. He depicted the horrors of hell in graphic terms and alternated tearful pleas for immediate repentance with threats of eternal damnation to any not acceding to his personal call. All of this was unlike anything ever before seen in Vermont. Nevertheless, Burchard's thirty-day stay in Middlebury, in November and December 1835, raised only a few quiet questions. More important was the "harvest of souls," alleged to be in excess of four hundred, or twice that of the 1831 revival.[40]

At the close of the Middlebury revival, Bates, Burchard, and Middlebury Congregational minister Thomas Merrill hatched a plan to attack UVM again. Given Burchard's unprecedented power to rout the forces of infidelity, they decided that he would go into the lion's den. An invitation issued earlier by Burlington's Calvinistic congregation was accepted. Then Merrill and Bates went to Burlington to join Burchard in his "labors and methods of proceeding," taking with them several Middlebury College students—"millennial laborers," Bates described them—who were to assist in the crusade.[41]

Although UVM president Wheeler and the Trustees had been careful not to publicly engage Burchard's followers in debate for fear of antagonizing clerics throughout the state, they left little doubt as to where their sympathies lay. In conferring an honorary degree upon Episcopal bishop John Henry Hopkins at the summer commencement ceremonies in 1835, UVM trustees publicly recognized one of the state's most fervent opponents of "new measure" revivals. Hopkins had just written a book, *The Primitive Church*, in which he charged the proponents of "ultraism" with a "lack of humility" for asserting that "new measures were revealed by God to accelerate Pentecost." Denying biblical sanction for any such connection, Hopkins sarcastically observed that "the apostles did not call upon the church to turn the entire stream of effort, collective and several, into a set of exciting, agitating, passion stirring movements which should suspend for an indefinite period the whole business of society."[42]

Former president Marsh, alarmed by methods he deemed "so palpably mischievous and absurd," felt "compelled to employ his pen and the whole force of his influence in opposition." He objected to Burchard's willingness to employ any measures, "revolting as they might be to the unbiased sensibilities of the pious heart," provided they yielded large numbers of supposed converts. Spirituality had been sacrificed for expediency. Thus, "a sensuous and accommodating utilitarianism had displaced or obscured truths, absolutes, universal and imperishable." In sum, Burchard's conversions were "spurious," based on an appeal to the superficial emotions that allowed his converts to backslide quickly into their old ways. "The great truths of religion," Marsh observed, "were not to be imparted from without, but awakened and developed from within."[43]

Marsh's devastating condemnation of Burchard's revivalism encouraged UVM president Wheeler and Professor George Benedict to voice their own misgivings. The University community remained wholly unreceptive to Burchard's efforts, and his adherents found him "not himself" in being able to prompt only four UVM students to seek conversions. Burchard's credibility suffered even more following a publicized run-in with two UVM undergraduates, B. J. Tenney and Charles Eastman. The two were hired by bookseller and publisher Chauncey Goodrich, Marsh's brother-in-law, to transcribe Burchard's sermons for publication. Having gotten wind of the plot, Burchard initially attempted to convert Tenney. Failing that, he tried to purchase the student's silence by "offering him a large sum." The fiasco intensified as Tenney pocketed the money yet refused to surrender his transcripts or absent himself from succeeding sessions. Frustrated in his efforts to eject Tenney and Eastman from the First Congregational Church, Burchard chose, as a last recourse, "to foil them . . . by holding his tongue." The lengthy silence that followed, according to an unsympathetic observer, provoked "the great vexation of his followers," who became "mad because they came to see the elephant and the elephant won't play for fear his tricks shall be noted down."[44]

News of Burchard's failure in Burlington emboldened formerly silent critics to join James Marsh in denouncing the colorful itinerant. By early 1836 a wave of antirevivalist sentiment swept through the state, with charges from various orthodox quarters that Burchard's motives originated in personal ambition. Middlebury College paid a heavy price for aligning its evangelical crusade so closely to Burchard and his "new measure" revivals. Enrollment plummeted from 168 in 1836 to 46 students in 1840; the number of graduates fell from a total of 250 students between 1830 and 1839 to 111 during the succeeding decade. The largest decline occurred in the southern New England contingent, which had furnished survival and prosperity from the outset. With the ignominious end to the revivals, the number of graduates choosing the ministry as a career also fell, from 108 during the ultraistic decade of the 1830s to 27 during the succeeding decade.

By comparison UVM's fortunes rose dramatically after 1837. Benjamin Labaree, Bates's successor as president of Middlebury, observed that UVM, having taken an open stand against Burchardism, came to be regarded as "the champion of order, of wisdom, and of religious prudence," whereas Middlebury College was held to be the sponsor of "irregularity, innovation, and radicalism."[45] UVM graduates more than trebled, increasing from 65 in the 1828–1837 decade to 209 between 1838 and 1847. Almost half pursued the perennially favorite careers of law and public service (43%), and one in eight chose either medicine, business or teaching (4.5% in each). The forty-four future clerics included twenty-seven intending to be orthodox Congregational ministers, equaling the total output of the preceding thirty-five years and underscoring the dramatic shift of Vermonters' allegiances from Middlebury to UVM.

In 1847, under circumstances completely reversed from a decade earlier, the Middlebury Trustees once again proposed legislation to consolidate UVM and Middlebury College "into one corporation to be called the University of Vermont."[46] This time it was UVM's board that rejected the proposal, calling it "wholly impractical." With, one suspects, no small degree of satisfaction UVM's Trustees recalled, "In its career, this institution has been subjected to scorn and faced calamities but it has always risen superior to them and now stands before the literary world as a powerful aid and contributor in the sublime work of educating a state and elevating the condition of its youth by the culminating and improvement of their intellectual and moral powers. Its origin, its career, its history, its character and evident condition forbid the idea that it should extinguish its light even in the hope of making ours more bright and glorious." [47]

With this cathartic rejection of union, UVM could finally savor victory in its rivalry with Middlebury, which, of course, would eventually recover but would never again seek to present itself as "Vermont's University." That distinction, earned by the efforts of Daniel Sanders, James Marsh, and John Wheeler, belonged permanently to UVM.

Student Debates . . . and Thaddeus Stevens

BETTY BANDEL

A T T I M E S poverty leads to good works.

The first decade of the nineteenth century was such a time, at least for the youths who entered the fledgling University of Vermont. Their purses were lean, and so were those of their pioneering fathers, some of whom only a few years earlier had been making clearings and building cabins on what was then the New England frontier. To go to college, at that time, was a privilege not to be taken lightly.

Speaking in 1854, at the semicentennial celebration of the University's first graduation, Charles Adams, who had been one quarter of the first graduating class (1804), said: "In 1800, the place where the college stands was a wilderness covered with primeval pines. . . . Burlington and this whole section was then poor. It requires some exertion, even on the part of those of us who were present and did Irish service in digging stumps, to recall to mind the state of things as then existing."[1]

The state of things as then existing prompted President Sanders to declare in 1807: "Tuition is 12 dollars a year. Room, books, etc., are gratis. . . . No college on the continent can be so cheap."[2]

Even in the 1830s, when both Burlington and the college had made some strides forward, UVM students stuck largely to business, as they had done from the entry of the first class. On many campuses in the turbulent years of the Jacksonian era, student riots were the fashion, but the young men who were working their way through UVM, most of them by teaching elementary school during the bitter winter months, had little time for such frivolity.

An enlightened administration, free from excessive paternalism, helped to minimize student grumblings; but in general their own natures and experiences led these serious, work-hardened, hopeful young men to believe that higher education was a privilege. There was no athletic program in this or any other American college of the day to occupy students' leisure hours. In many places they turned to carousing around town, but at UVM they preferred to attend meetings of their literary and debating societies. Such societies existed in most colleges, but it would seem that the paucity of other organizations or activities at UVM must have made the program of the debating societies loom especially large in the eyes of Vermont students.

Just two years after the University opened its doors, a literary and debating society, Phi Sigma Nu, was established at UVM. It was joined in 1810 by Phi Phi Adelphi, a purely literary society that stressed improvement in the writing and declaiming of Latin, Greek, and English compositions.[3] A few names of UVM students appear as members of both societies; and in the 1820s another debating society (the University Institute), the Society for Religious Inquiry, and the College of Natural History increased the choices that a student might make in selecting extracurricular activities to enrich his college experience.

As the leader among the student groups at UVM before the Civil War, Phi Sigma Nu played a prominent part in campus life, providing the students with a library that stressed literary and historic works, offering opportunities for debating contemporary problems, and presenting speakers, sometimes from among their own distinguished graduates. The society's meetings ended in 1862, when the call for soldiers in the Civil War was depleting college classes. After the war, with the rise of social fraternities, there was apparently no demand for the return of the debating societies. In 1868 Phi Sigma Nu donated its library to the University.

Fortunately, the reports of the society's meetings were preserved in large leather-bound notebooks. These records, now in UVM archives, open a wide window on student life and thought in the first half-century of the university's existence.

The first debate question to be recorded, that of March 27, 1805, was "Whether a person enjoys more happiness below a mediocrity of property than one above." In that halcyon day when boys brought their own firewood to college and when one boy provided "the use of a cow" for his boardinghouse, four gentlemen voted for "below mediocrity" and only two for "above."

Shortly there were more members than six to listen to and take part in debates. Membership was by invitation, but all students were invited to apply; and by 1810, when there were forty-three students in the University, Phi Sigma Nu had thirty-four members. Neither members nor honorary members took the society lightly. In Phi Sigma Nu's records are a number of letters from distinguished Americans who accepted honorary membership and regretted that the press of business made it impossible for them to accept in person. Among those accepting honorary membership, in addition to President Sanders, were such notables as Washington Irving, Henry Clay, Henry Wadsworth Longfellow, Oliver Wendell Holmes, and John Quincy Adams.

The society met weekly in its "hall" (one room in the one college building) and conducted its affairs with a formality suitable for a college that required its graduating students to wear lightly powdered hair and "small clothes" tied with velvet ribbons over silk stockings. From its beginning the society elected such customary officers as a president and treasurer but added to the usual list a librarian and a censor. It was the censor's duty to speak to members who failed to prepare their assignments for debates and declamations or who acted "out of character" (i.e., played cards within the University or committed other heinous sins; the rule against card playing lasted only from October 29, 1806, to March 8, 1807). If a member proved stubborn, the censor informed the society of the misdeed, and the society could admonish or even expel the erring member.

An important activity of the society was the building of a library, emphasizing belles-lettres that would complement the University's library of philosophy, theology, science, and the like. To this purpose was devoted a large part of the society's fund of dues and fines, running to about $1.75 per member per quarter. During the War of 1812, when the University suspended operations for a year while army troops occupied the college building, the society's library of 208 volumes (not counting 21 books found to be missing) was boxed and entrusted to J. Brownson, Esq., for safekeeping. When the college reopened after the war, the society continued to buy such works as an eight-volume Shakespeare, purchased from the Royalton Bookstore for $11, plus 25 cents "conveyance."

From the standpoint of history, surely the most significant of Phi Sigma Nu's activities was its choice of subjects for debate. America's interests and concerns, especially those that affected daily life in New England, are mirrored in the society's topics. Just as singing schools and writing schools provided a good part of children's education outside the towns' schoolrooms, so debating societies such as Phi Sigma Nu offered to college students much that courses such as political science were later to give as a part of the established curriculum.

In 1807, when America was edging uneasily toward war with Great Britain, debate questions included "Will it be politic for the USA to maintain a standing army?" (negative); "Whether, under present circumstances, war with Great Britain would be beneficial to America?" (negative); "Whether, in case of war with Great Britain, the conquest of Canada would be beneficial to the U.S.?" (negative).

The Embargo of 1807, restricting foreign trade in retaliation for English and French actions against American shipping and sailors, met with almost universal disapproval in New England. In 1808 Phi Sigma Nu, true to its New England heritage, voted for the negative on the question "Whether the

Embargo be beneficial to the USA." Surprisingly, however, the question "Is the Embargo a politic measure?" received an affirmative vote. For these voters on debate questions, *politic* still bore its broad meaning of *prudent* or *sagacious*.

Another question already agitating national opinion was considered by the society in 1808: "Would it be politic in the USA to emancipate her slaves?" The vote was 12 for, 7 against. Norman Williams, later a prominent Woodstock lawyer and Vermont's secretary of state, was among those voting in the affirmative. Voting in the negative was Jacob Collamer, later to be U.S. postmaster general and Vermont's representative and senator in Congress. Collamer's service to Vermont and the nation was such that he is one of two Vermonters, along with Ethan Allen, whose statues today stand in Statuary Hall in the U.S. Capitol. In March 1858, fifty years after casting his vote against emancipation in 1808, Senator Collamer rose on the floor of the U.S. Senate to make a powerful speech, titled "The Kansas Question," in which he opposed the plan to admit Kansas as a slave state.

Rounding off the year's debates in 1808 was the question "Has America sufficient reason to declare war against any nation on the Globe?" Jacob Collamer and Norman Williams, making up the negative team, won the vote.

Subsequent debate topics remained equally serious. In 1809 they were "Had the Spaniards who discovered America a right to drive off the natives and possess their territories?" (negative, 14 to 5); and "Should a man's religious tenets have any influence in excluding him from office?" (affirmative, 11 to 9). In 1810 the group debated the question "Can the people ever be justifiable in rebelling against a republican government?" The young men voted 12 to 2 for the negative.

Some of the questions debated indicate that, even in 1810, boys were boys. In that year the question "Is a state of celibacy productive of more happiness than a marrige [*sic*] state?" drew three votes for the affirmative, thirteen for the negative. Among the affirmative voters was Samuel Hunt Tupper, later a Methodist clergyman, who in fact was married twice, first to Miss Ann Wheeler, by whom he had four children, and then to Mrs. Sarah Hall. In 1811 the question "Is the use of tobacco profitable?" drew a tie vote (4–4) broken in favor of the negative by the president's vote.

By the beginning of 1812 the country, the state, Burlington, and UVM all felt the rising war fever. The dangerous business of smuggling, which had been going on between Vermont and Canada since the Embargo Act of 1807, was thriving in and near Burlington. In 1809 Congress had extended the embargo, which had previously barred international trade to and from ports of the United States, to cover all such trade using inland waterways or land routes. The situation reached a climax in April 1812; just two months before declaring war Congress laid an embargo on "all the shipping within the jurisdiction of the United States" for ninety days.[4] When the Vermont

Legislature met in October, the Federalists in that body asserted that the declaration of war had been "premature and impolitic." Throughout the state there was vocal opposition to the new state law forbidding dealings between any Vermonter and any Canadian without a special permit from the governor.[5] Equally loud was the grumbling against a new tax designed to equip the militia.

Early in 1812, Phi Sigma Nu had turned to the big question: "Would it be policy and justice for the United States to declare war against Great Britain?" (affirmative, 8; negative, 3). Then came the query "Whether it is right for any citizen of the United States to be neutral in his politicks?" (negative, 13 to 4). On a more timeless theme the young men turned from war questions to ask, "Ought foreigners be admitted to all the privileges of natural born citizens of the United States?" (negative).

The declaration of war made these issues even more insistent. On July 8 the society debated the question "Would it be policy for the United States under existing circumstances to declare war against France?" (negative). On September 12: "Is the present war a just one?" (affirmative, 11 to 2). Then followed "Would it be consistent to abridge the liberty of the press?" (negative, 9 to 4). And in 1813: "Would it be politic for the American government to conclude a peace with Great Britain on her acceptance of the proposals, heretofore made by the United States?" (affirmative, 10 to 6).

When the University suspended operations in 1814–1815, members of the class of 1815 were dismissed with recommendations to other colleges, and at least two of the twenty-four men in the class were graduated from other institutions—Wilbur Fisk from Brown and David Gould from Middlebury, both in 1815. (Fisk went on to become a Methodist clergyman and the first president of Wesleyan University.) The rest of the class apparently was content to abandon college education in 1814. As a result, when Phi Sigma Nu resumed operations in 1815, none but new names appear on the membership lists. Nevertheless, these new members continued to debate serious questions.

A number of men later distinguished in national and international affairs took part in the debates of this period. One discovers Jehudi Ashmun, later to be first governor of Liberia, acting as "compositor" of a debate of 1816 on the question "Would it be politick for the United States to emancipate their Negro slaves?" (negative, 5 to 4). But later the same year the society gave a resounding 9–2 defeat to the question "Is it policy for civilized nations to enslave the Africans?"

Ashmun, son of a New York farmer, transferred from Middlebury to UVM because of "an earnest desire of promoting the cause of religion in that institution." He received his B.A. in 1816 and an M.A. in 1817. After serving as principal of the Maine Charity School at Hampden (later Bangor Theological Seminary), Ashmun was licensed to preach and was made professòr of Classical literature. In 1819 he went to Baltimore and Washington to edit church journals, and in 1822 he was hired by the American Colonization Society to take charge of a group of free "colored emigrants" who were going to Africa. As the first governor of the new country of Liberia, Ashmun revealed administrative skills that helped his colony repel a sudden attack of some eight hundred far-from-friendly Africans. Because of poor health Ashmun returned to New Haven, Connecticut, where he died in 1828 at the age of thirty-four.[6]

A man whose life story stirred up a tempest in a teapot was Samuel Austin Worcester, class of 1819, who was for a time president of Phi Sigma Nu. Eighth in a Massachusetts father-to-son line of clergymen, Worcester heard the question debated in his student days, "Is it politick and has Congress the right to prohibit the introduction of slaves as a condition to the admission of new states into the union?" Apparently thinking deeply of man's inhumanity to man, he was ordained in 1825 as a missionary to the Cherokee Indians. His father, Rev. Leonard Worcester, pastor of the Congregational Church in Peacham, Vermont, preached the ordination sermon in Park Street Church in Boston.

Forthwith, Worcester went to New Echota, in the heart of the Cherokee country in Georgia. There gold had recently been discovered, and a frontiersman president, Andrew Jackson, was doing what he could to hand the land over to white frontiersmen. Worcester, championing the Indians' ancient treaty rights and refusing to swear allegiance to Georgia, landed in the Georgia state penitentiary to serve four years at hard labor. He actually served eighteen months, doing cabinet work by day and conducting prayer meetings at night. The American Board of Commissioners for Foreign Missions carried his struggle to the Supreme Court in the case of *Worcester vs. the State of Georgia* (1831–1832). In a historic decision written by Chief Justice John Marshall, the court upheld the inviolability of treaties made between Indian nations and the United States, thereby establishing the principle on which the country has tried to act ever since. Nevertheless, President Jackson would not send troops to enforce the order, and some fourteen thousand Cherokees were driven along the "trail of tears" to Indian Territory (Oklahoma). Worcester, fresh out of jail, joined his friends in Indian Territory and plunged into daily good works. Known as one of the "five great social pioneers" of the Congregational Church, Worcester is credited with providing the Indians with a printing press, helping to make them literate in their own language, teaching them something of public health, and waging war against drunkenness.[7]

Completing a trio of Phi Sigma Nu members who were champions of the underdog was Jonathan Peckham Miller, in his student days a member of the society's Prudential Committee, which apparently had oversight of the group's financial affairs. Born in Randolph, Vermont, in 1797, a great-nephew of Justin Morgan (the musical composer and owner of the first Morgan horse), Miller was orphaned at the age of two, and even with the help of those who brought him up he apparently had to make a determined fight for higher education. After serving briefly in the War of 1812, Miller enlisted in the regular army in 1817 and served for two years on the northern frontier. He returned to Randolph Academy and then went on to Dartmouth in 1821, but he transferred to UVM after a few weeks. Miller watched his hopes for the B.A. vanish in the fire that consumed "the College," with all of his books and possessions, in 1824. So he went off to Greece to help the Greeks in their fight for independence from the Turks.

Miller was twenty-seven when he arrived in Boston, en route to Greece. He had in his pocket a letter from Governor C. P. Van Ness of Vermont to the Honorable Edward Everett and other Bostonians prominent in aiding the Greeks. They outfitted Miller and sent him on his way. In Greece he was soon on the trail of the recently deceased Lord Byron and managed to acquire Byron's sword, which is today in the Vermont Historical Museum in Montpelier. While fighting in the twelve-month siege of Missolonghi, Colonel Miller earned the sobriquet "the American Daredevil."

Miller must have been among the first American soldiers to take it upon themselves to aid war orphans in theaters of operation. He adopted an orphaned Greek boy, Lucas Miltiades, and brought him back to Montpelier for his education. Miller himself established a successful law practice in Montpelier and received an honorary M.A. from UVM in 1829. He joined the antislavery movement vociferously and effectively. His adopted son went west to Wisconsin, to help build that state.[8]

Not all Phi Sigma Nu men lived the colorful lives that Ashmun, Worcester, and Miller knew, but many of them made substantial contributions to their towns and their country. It is not too much to assume that their student practice in debating both sides of important questions sharpened their grasp of the intricacies of problems they met in later life. The debates went on, year after year, until the Civil War disrupted all student life, as it did life in general.

No one would have enjoyed these debates more than a student who entered the University in May 1813 but who remained at UVM so short a time that in all probability no one thought to propose him for membership in Phi Sigma Nu. This student was Thaddeus Stevens, later to become the dominant figure in the U.S. House of Representatives during the Civil War and Reconstruction years—a figure described by one analyst as "the virtual prime minister of the United States."[9] Stevens had to wait until 1849 to be recognized by Phi Sigma Nu, when he was made an honorary member.[10]

Biographers of Stevens have ventured far afield in their search for the details of his education and for the nature of a play that he wrote during his school days. No account is more striking than Fawn M. Brodie's, in which she declares that Stevens spent two terms at "Burlington College" when "Dartmouth buildings were requisitioned by the government for troops during the War of 1812."[11] It was, of course, UVM's "Old Mill"—nearer the scene of action on Lake Champlain—that was requisitioned for U.S. troops during the war.

Stevens was born in Danville, Vermont, on April 4, 1792, and attended Caledonia County Grammar School in Peacham. Upon graduation in 1811 he entered Dartmouth College as a sophomore.[12] A tradition evidently came down in the Stevens family, and among other Danville and Peacham folk, that when he was a boy "Old Thad" wrote a play about Switzerland. The assumption, both by family members and by Stevens's biographer, Elsie Singmaster Lewars, was that the play was about William Tell.[13] Mrs. Lewars tells the story of how Stevens and other boys at Caledonia Grammar School got into trouble by defying school rules against the performance of plays and presenting a "tragedy" for which Stevens was "chief playwright." The part taken by Stevens, according to Mrs. Lewars, was "lengthy but not active, consisting of speeches delivered from the shadows."[14] In 1897, C. A. Bunker, principal of the academy in Peacham, told how Stevens, Wilbur Fisk, David Gould, Samuel Merrill, and nine other pupils were required to sign a statement saying that they recognized that their conduct in presenting a play had been "highly reprehensible."[15]

In the spring of 1813 Stevens transferred from Dartmouth to UVM, where he remained only until July of that year. He then returned to Dartmouth, from which he was graduated in August 1814. His reason for transferring is immediately apparent: at UVM Stevens could be reasonably confident, as he could not at Dartmouth, of being allowed to present his play. Dartmouth forbade plays and "all irreligious expressions."[16] At UVM plays written by students, only occasionally disguised as "dialogues," were presented from 1805 into the 1820s, usually at the graduation festivities. From about 1810 the afternoon before commencement at UVM was devoted to the "junior exhibition," which featured plays, original poems, and other products of the students' ingenuity and creativity. In time a sophomore exhibition was added to the festivities. When James Marsh became president of the university in 1826, this type of entertainment was given up.

When one learns that Stevens's play, *The Fall of Helvetic Liberty*, was presented at UVM during the Junior Exhibition of July 1813,[17] is Stevens's reason for moving from Dartmouth not clear? He was barred by lameness from competing with his fellows in many of the rough-and-tumble activities of New England frontier life. He had been reprimanded at school for presenting a play that probably grew out of his deepest convictions regarding manly conduct. Would he not have been disappointed when he discovered that Dartmouth, like Caledonia Grammar School, also barred plays?

Two of Stevens's school friends, who had appeared in his play in Peacham

—Wilbur Fisk and David Gould—had been students at UVM since the fall of 1812. Might they not have written to Stevens telling him of plays being presented at "Burlington College"? There was the drama "Duelling," written by Joseph Williamson of the class of 1812 and presented at the Junior Exhibition during the graduation ceremonies of August 1811. There was also the "dialogue" called "Quackery," written by Royall Tyler, Jr., and presented at the Sophomore Exhibition in November 1812. Royall Tyler, Jr., may have come by his playwriting skills naturally. His father, Royall Tyler, chief justice of Vermont, trustee of the University, and well-known writer, was the author of the renowned play *The Contrast*, the first comedy by an American to be presented by professional actors in this country. The younger Tyler unfortunately died in 1814, during his senior year at UVM.

Stevens arrived in Burlington, play manuscript firmly under his arm, in May 1813. In the UVM archives are the small, neat notebooks in which President Sanders carefully recorded the university's financial affairs. "T. Stevens" was entered for the first and only time during the spring–summer term of 1813, which began in mid-May and ended in late July. The fact that Stevens was a new student in May is clearly indicated by his being charged not only the $6 that covered tuition and room for the term but also 50 cents for a copy of the "printed laws of the University," always provided to entering students.

Stevens's play was indeed about freedom in Switzerland, but it was not about the medieval legend of William Tell. Titled *The Fall of Helvetic Liberty*, it dealt with Switzerland in the very recent years of the French Revolution. The play is convincing proof of the liberalism and far-reaching inquiry that characterized not only the young debaters of Phi Sigma Nu but also UVM as a whole in its formative years. That one of the great figures in the political history of the United States could begin his career as an advocate with the presentation of a play at UVM gives powerful support to the idea that the emerging university was a nursery for the training of men whose ideas were to prove significant in the history of the region and of the country.

Although the text of Stevens's play has been lost, an astonishing amount of information about both the play and its author can be gleaned from President Sanders carefully recorded the University's financial affairs. "T. Stevens" was entered for the first and only time during the spring–summer term of University's archives.

The surviving program indicates that Stevens's "tragedy" was given the place of honor in the Junior Exhibition. The program is headed: "University of Vermont, Burlington. Exercises of the Exhibition 27th July, 1813, the afternoon preceding commencement." Listed were music, orations in Latin and Greek, Stevens's and Gilman's English disputation, an English poem on Vermont read by Wilbur Fisk, the whole culminating in item 12: "The Fall of Helvetic Liberty, a tragedy in three acts, written by Thaddeus Stevens."

The cast was as follows:

French	Buonaparte	by Constantine Gilman
Generals	Brune	Isaac Holton
	Menard	Erastus Root
Swiss	Parvacina	Timothy Phelps
Generals	D'Erlach	Almon Warner
	Tiller	Wilbur Fisk
	La Harpe	Thaddeus Stevens
	Bay	Charles H. Perrigo
	Verres	Steven Cleaveland
	Stelguer	Steven Whittlesey
	Rhombleau	Nathan Whiting
Old Soldier		Royall Tyler
Boy		Calvin Pomeroy
Fop		Rodney S. Church
		Wilbur Fisk

Epilogue written by David Gould

To what extent is it possible to speculate about the actual contents of the play in the light of Stevens's known interests?[18] Did the play suggest the later development of Stevens as the "Great Commoner"? The events indicated by the characters in Stevens's play have to do with the impact of revolutionary France on the ancient federal republic of Switzerland in the 1790s. Swiss liberals, led by Frédéric César de la Harpe,[19] welcomed and even sought French support to force reforms upon the conservative oligarchs in the various semi-independent cantons. The French intervened militarily early in 1798, overwhelmed the conservative bastion of Berne in March, and imposed a new constitution for the "Helvetic Republic." The Swiss were left bitterly divided between those who collaborated with the French in the name of reform and those who tried to defend the historic independence of their unreformed cantons.

A comparison of Stevens's play with these events of the year 1798 in Switzerland will show how the young playwright worked. His cast of characters indicates that the play traced the lightning campaign of the French as they conquered Switzerland in the first five months of 1798. Since Buonaparte is in the cast, the play presumably began at some time and place at which that rising star could be present, probably Paris in December 1797, when we know that La Harpe sought the aid of the French leaders against the Swiss antirevolutionaries. A budding playwright of 1811–1813 who made La Harpe his protagonist would have had difficulty resisting a scene in which La Harpe met the man who by 1811 dominated Europe.

The cluster of Swiss generals whom Stevens picked out, some pro-French and some anti-French, makes it obvious that the tremendous fighting of March 1–6, 1798, occupied a central spot in the play. *Verres* is apparently a misspelling for *Verrer,* who died on March 1 defending Fribourg against the French. Tiller and Bay, twinned like Castor and Pollux, march through all of the accounts as principal leaders of the pro-French Popular Party in Berne. Berne's commander-in-chief, General D'Erlach, had to deal with them during those days in March when Berne was crumpling under the French attack and under the canton's own internal dissension and perplexity. D'Erlach, of course, would be essential in such a scene, as would the old mayor Steiguer (listed as *Stelguer* in the Stevens play). General Brune, the French commander, would also figure in this scene. General Menard had left Switzerland in early February; and if Stevens was careful in chronology, Menard might have been used either at the beginning of the scene dealing with the fall of Berne or in an earlier scene about the invasion of Vaud, La Harpe's homeland, in January.

The presence of Paravacina (listed as *Parvacina*) indicates that the play extended into the April and May attempt by the Forest Cantons to hold back the onrushing French under Schauenberg. It was Paravacina who led the men of Glarus in that last big battle of the campaign. There is no one in the cast to indicate that the play stretched on to the final battle at Stanz in September.

Since the play is in three acts, one is tempted to envision the following: Act 1—Paris in December 1797; act 2—Berne in March; act 3—Lucerne, Zurich, or the mountains to the east in May. It is possible, of course, that Stevens did not stick closely to actual scenes of the campaign and that he mixed his characters according to his dramatic needs. The tendency of people writing genuine chronicle plays, however—whether Shakespeare or Stevens—is to follow the major historical events rather closely, no matter what freedom the playwright allows himself in developing character. And Stevens's sources, both newspapers and books, give detailed, specific accounts of every move in the campaign.

It is a little difficult to see how Stevens fitted his stock characters from the old farces—the Old Soldier, the Boy, and the Fop—into so factual and so serious an account of contemporary history as his play must have been. The nature of the cast indicates that there were no battle scenes but, instead, the sharp debates that these perplexed leaders must actually have conducted— debates that would have been of special interest to a young man who was to develop into one of America's keenest lawyers and one of her greatest parliamentary debaters. Perhaps the stock characters were there to run on stage with messages from the battlefield. And perhaps the Fop was there because the tendency of some youths, newly resplendent in uniform, to give themselves airs as "macaronis" was known to every boy of Stevens's day who could whistle "Yankee Doodle."

It is, of course, impossible even to guess what the literary and dramatic merits of the play may have been. Stevens's later writings and speeches are packed with vivid and telling phrases and figures of speech. The command over language that he obviously possessed usually manifests itself early in life, so his youthful play may indeed have been powerful.

In 1866, Stevens's old schoolmaster, David Chassell, wrote to him, remarking that he remembered how Stevens and Wilbur Fisk "spoke and acted a dialogue, I think the last you both spoke and acted in Peacham Academy. I remember well I thought you both spoke and acted admirably." [20] If Chassell is referring to the "tragedy," here is praise for the play where plays reveal their virtues and defects most inescapably—on stage.

What sources of information and inspiration would a Vermont farm boy find to reconstruct these distant events? We do not know how Stevens first became aware of the revolutionary struggles in Switzerland, but there was plenty of printed material available in Vermont in newspaper and magazine accounts, pamphlets, and historical works, which Stevens could have read in Peacham or Danville or Hanover or Burlington anytime from around 1805 to the day of his play's presentation. Stevens would have found much drama in the weighty histories that he must have used as he prepared his plot. A principal source was evidently William Mavor's *Universal History, Ancient and Modern, from the Earliest Records of Time, to the General Peace of 1801* (New York, 1804). Mavor's twenty-five-volume history was in the Phi Sigma Nu library and probably in several other Vermont and New Hampshire libraries. Volume 18 contains the misspelling *Stelguer* that is picked up on Stevens's program. Since Mavor does not mention La Harpe, Stevens must have turned to such works as Alexander Stephens's *The History of the Wars Which Arose Out of the French Revolution* (London, 1803) for details of La Harpe's life and works.

It is from Vermont newspapers, however, that Stevens may have drawn the stirring bits of action, speech, and local color required in a history play. The *Green Mountain Patriot* reported on March 16, 1798, that the French Directory had forbidden Swiss officers to continue wearing prerevolutionary French decorations: "It might be expected," said the French, "that the eldest daughter of Liberty would not hesitate to discard that badge of slavery and servitude unworthy of the descendants of William Tell." Bennington's *Vermont Gazette* reported on April 20, 1798, that on January 22 in Basel, after the Tree of Liberty was planted, "young female citizens in white decorated with tricolored scarfs," attended by a military escort and by rural and patriotic music, laid garlands of flowers at the foot of the tree. The tricolor flag was hoisted to the top of the highest steeple, artillery was discharged, and there was a "superb ball." On May 31, reporting on the battle of early March, the *Gazette* related that the brave but poorly trained Swiss militia, "armed with scythes and clubs," in some cases placed themselves at the mouths of the French cannons—and were blown to bits. Among the six thousand French and Swiss dead on the battlefield after the engagement of March 5 were eight hundred women, the *Gazette* declared. These women soon lay dying on the pages of every newspaper in Vermont and neighboring New Hampshire—whether by a simple process of copying or by an early pooling of newspaper resources is not apparent from the record. Although the editorial sympathies of newspapers occasionally showed—as when the Federalist *Green Mountain Patriot* of September 19, 1799, was "happy to announce" the victory of the allies over French General McDonald—the news accounts were identical in most papers.

It is easy to see where Stevens could have gathered vivid details for his play. It is not so easy to see how much he knew about or precisely what attitude he took toward his leading character, La Harpe. As far as can be determined, none of La Harpe's writings had been published in the United States before Stevens wrote his play. When Frédéric César de La Harpe went to Russia as a young man to tutor the Empress Catherine's grandsons, he was awarded the rank of colonel under the Russian system of the time, which was to bestow military rank on civil servants fulfilling important functions.[21] He never served in the army, but when the Allies entered Paris in 1814, Czar Alexander I gave his old teacher the rank of a Russian general. This belated and tenuous generalship, bestowed when La Harpe was sixty years old, came too late for inclusion in Stevens's play; but apparently Stevens felt no hesitancy about awarding the rank of general to La Harpe, as his cast of characters indicates that he did. Perhaps in this respect Stevens confused La Harpe with his cousin, General Amadeus de La Harpe, an officer under Bonaparte who was killed in action in 1796.

La Harpe was a prime mover in the events that encouraged a foreign army to invade his native land. From the days of Aeschylus' *Seven against Thebes*, men who led foreign armies against their homelands had been the villains, not the heroes, of song and story, no matter how badly they thought their compatriots were being treated. La Harpe apparently did not dream that once the camel got his head inside the tent he would take over. Then too, Thaddeus Stevens was born in a state that, up to one year before his birth, had been sovereign, as the old Swiss cantons were sovereign. Ethan Allen, already a Vermont folk hero by the time Stevens was a youth, had openly considered which of several "foreign" powers it might be to Vermont's advantage to join. At the same time, Allen had indicated his undying allegiance to the principle of freedom. As Dorothy Canfield Fisher has said, Allen "was passionate about an idea—the ancient idea that men and women live best and most fruitfully in as much freedom and equality as is possible."[22]

In true idealist manner La Harpe gave every evidence of having believed that absolute freedom and equality are possible. In 1797 he published a work with the resounding title *To the Inhabitants of the Country of Vaud, Slaves of the Oligarchs of Fribourg and Berne*.[23] He helped to draw up and administer the constitution of the Helvetic Republic One and Indivisible, which, however badly its neat French national plan fitted the procrustean bed of Switzerland,

placed "sovereign power in the totality of the citizens" for the first time since
the Middle Ages.[24] On the other hand, although apparently considered loyal
by most Swiss, La Harpe seems to have approved the French government's
conduct toward conquered Switzerland, including its appropriation of the
wealth of those who had formerly been "oligarchs" in Berne and elsewhere
in the country.

Twenty-one-year-old Thaddeus Stevens must have seen in Switzerland
the prototype of the struggle for democracy and republican freedom. When
one examines his later career, certain similarities between his course and that
of La Harpe become immediately apparent. Like La Harpe, Stevens was an
uncompromising idealist; and like his Swiss model, the American fought for
the underdog. Nothing illustrates more clearly Stevens's adherence to the
principle of equality than the inscription he had placed on his grave in a small
cemetery in Lancaster, Pennsylvania:

> I repose in this quiet and secluded spot
> Not from any natural preference for solitude
> But, finding other Cemeteries limited as to Race
>   by Charter Rules,
> I have chosen this that I might illustrate in my death
> The Principles which I advocated through a long life:
> EQUALITY OF MAN BEFORE HIS CREATOR. [25]

Stevens refused to compromise on any point having to do with freeing
the slaves and granting them suffrage. Those who found this harsh and even
unrealistic in a world of political compromise would be obliged to admit
that, without his unremitting hammering at the foes of such ideas, the Fourteenth Amendment might not have follwed the Thirteenth. It was Stevens's
conviction that if a mild civil rights bill were passed instead of a constitutional amendment granting the Negro suffrage, it would be repealed as soon
as "the South with its copperhead allies obtain the command of Congress." [26]

Stevens's attitude toward Reconstruction in the South evoked bitter
hatred. Insisting that the South must be treated not as part of the Union but
as a conquered country with which a peace treaty could be made (since on
no other grounds could the North legally exact conditions from the South),
Stevens worked to ensure suffrage for the freedmen—as well as free schools
and forty acres for each family—and to have these provisions guaranteed
before the seceded states were readmitted to the Union. Stevens proposed
to confiscate the vast plantation holdings of the leading secessionists to get
the forty acres for each freedman, and it was only the power of President
Lincoln that stopped him and his fellow Radical Republicans from pushing
through Congress as early as 1862 a bill that would have stripped the Southern landowners of their property and ultimately of their political power.[27]
Thus, the course advocated by Lincoln prevented the United States from
following the road normally taken after a revolution, the road that leads to

the overturning of the previously favored ruling class by the expropriation of its property. It was not, however, Stevens's fault that this country did not go the way that the French Directory had gone in Switzerland.

There seems little doubt that playwright Stevens must have shaped La Harpe not only as the protagonist but also as the hero of his play. The play is called a "tragedy," but in all probability the term was used by Stevens, as it frequently was at the beginning of the nineteenth century, merely to designate a play dealing with a theme of high seriousness. Certainly, the play did not end in the death of La Harpe, Brune, or Bonaparte, all of whom were living in 1813. If tragedy in the narrower sense is implied, it must refer to that tragedy of narrow vision, selfishness, and internal dissension that made Switzerland ripe for revolution in 1798.

The newspaper and book accounts that Stevens could have read of the fall of the Helvetic Republic were largely antirevolutionary in tone. There was nothing revolutionary about Stevens's commencement address on the occasion of his graduation from Dartmouth. His speech was a defense of material possessions, even luxuries, as an incentive to work, invention, and progress.[28]

Yet when Stevens wrote his play, the future Great Commoner seems to have cast his vote with La Harpe, who did not oppose the French occupation of Switzerland as long as it subdued the Swiss oligarchs. Fifty years after he wrote the play, Stevens was advocating much the same measures in dealing with the conquered South that La Harpe had defended in his attack on the Old Regime.

Stevens's own weapon, like La Harpe's, was not the sword but rapier-sharp language. During Reconstruction days Stevens's enemies were addicted to calling him a Jacobin and likening him to Robespierre. When Stevens spoke out in Congress in March 1868 (just a few months before his death) to demand the impeachment of President Andrew Johnson, the *New York Herald* commented, "He has the boldness of Danton, the bitterness and hatred of Marat, and the unscrupulousness of Robespierre." The writer added that Stevens would make a fit leader for a Reign of Terror in the United States.[29] But his Republican constituents in Lancaster County, Pennsylvania, thought otherwise. Upon his death in office they resolved that "as a fitting tribute to the memory of our most able and distinguished champion of freedom and justice, the unanimous vote of the party be cast for the name of Thaddeus Stevens in the ensuing primary meetings and that arrangements be made later for filling the vacancy."[30]

Stevens was not Robespierre. He may, however, have been that other man, the one whose weapons were oratory and pamphleteering rather than bloodbaths, who focused unblinking eyes on an idea that drew him resistlessly forward. "La Harpe," says one biographer, "pursued his plan with the most unyielding inflexibility."[31] Thaddeus Stevens may have been not Robespierre but Frédéric César de La Harpe.

James Marsh

JOHN J. DUFFY

THE most important decision made by the University of Vermont Board of Trustees in the academic year 1826–1827 was the selection of a new president. Their choice, by unanimous election on October 17, 1826, at the autumn board meeting held in Cottrell's Inn, Montpelier, was James Marsh, originally of Hartford, Vermont, and at the time a professor of languages at Hampden-Sydney College in Virginia.[1]

In the late 1820s Jacksonian Democrats in Vermont were warmly vocal and sometimes an elected majority. The choice of James Marsh, the first Vermonter to serve as president of the University, might have been criticized on political grounds—as the grandson of Vermont's first lieutenant governor, Joseph Marsh, he was the scion of an elite founding family of Vermont, the Federalist-Whig Marshes of Hartford and Woodstock. (Ethan Allen called them "a Petulant, Pettifogging, Scribbling sort of Gentry."[2]) But James Marsh's preparation as a teacher and scholar was solid and extensive for a man only thirty-two years old. Certainly, his accomplishments as a student of languages distinguished him far above his predecessors. He had been reading German philosophy for ten years, and his Spanish, French, and Italian were regularly exercised on modern texts. He was grounded in Latin and Greek at William Nutting's Academy in Randolph, Vermont, preparatory to entering Dartmouth College in 1813.[3]

The background of James Marsh's service at UVM—first as president (1826–1833) and then, until his death in 1842, as professor of moral and intellectual philosophy—goes back to Hanover, New Hampshire, at Dartmouth College and particularly relates to three other Dartmouth men, two of whom also became presidents of UVM: John Wheeler, Joseph Torrey, and George Perkins Marsh, James's cousin. Torrey and Wheeler were in the class of 1816, James Marsh was graduated in 1817, and George was in the class of 1820. George Marsh, after reading law in Woodstock, moved to Burlington in 1825 to enter law practice; he ultimately gained national prominence as a congressman, diplomat, conservationist, and highly accomplished student of Scandinavian languages.

Dartmouth was still a small college during the first quarter of the nineteenth century;[4] from 1816 to 1820 only 157 degrees were awarded, and nearly half of those graduates entered the clergy. Like other early American colleges Dartmouth had deep religious roots, and like Middlebury it experienced an intense revivalist movement, led by divinity professor Roswell Shurtleff. In one month in 1815, 120 students and townsfolk, including James Marsh and his future wife, Lucia Wheelock (niece of the College's president), were formally accepted into the Church as a result of Shurtleff's sermons on such texts as "The harvest is past, the summer is ended."[5]

The Dartmouth faculty split on liberal–conservative lines, so violently that in 1817 the New Hampshire General Assembly proposed a rival university and closed Dartmouth College for a year. President Wheelock, ousted by conservative trustees, sued to get his job back, and Daniel Webster won this celebrated Dartmouth College case for him in the U.S. Supreme Court. Meanwhile, the Marshes, Torrey, Wheeler, and a few other friends resisted these distractions by regularly meeting in a literary discussion group, formed in 1813, to remedy the inadequacies of Dartmouth's formal curriculum and fill the void left by the disruption of academic life at the College.

James Marsh's intellectual life and literary interests grew in spite of Dartmouth. While teaching at Hampden-Sydney College in Virginia in 1826, he expressed his dissatisfaction with contemporary practice in collegiate education to his Dartmouth friend George Ticknor, who, after studying philosophy in Germany and traveling in Europe from 1815 to 1819, had assumed a professorship at Harvard. In 1826 he was in the midst of his vain attempts to reform the Harvard curriculum, when Marsh told him: "For several years now . . . I have been fully convinced that very essential changes were necessary in our whole course of early instruction. In many cases I have no doubt the present system is rather an injury than a benefit to the scholar since it confirms and flatters with the appearance of learning many who if left more to themselves would sooner become their own teachers."[6]

In the litigious atmosphere of Hanover, Marsh and his friends became their own teachers. They purchased books for the library of their club and met regularly to read and discuss papers written by individual members. Marsh took the lead intellectually. In 1821, Rufus Choate, an old friend from the Dartmouth group, who would soon distinguish himself as a lawyer, orator, and congressman, told Marsh that he had long since given up his German studies, for he felt like a cuttlefish following Marsh's wake through a German ocean of metaphysics, theology, and criticism.[7] Wherever Marsh went to study or teach—at Dartmouth, Andover, Hampden-Sydney, or Vermont—in his wake a school formed like the one at Dartmouth. In 1823 he wrote from Hampden-Sydney to Lucia Wheelock: "I was kept up last night till 12 o'clock, by a discussion in a society we have formed here, and which by the excitement and interest it is producing, reminds me of Hanover more strongly than anything of the kind I have enjoyed since the days of my tutorship."[8]

At Andover, Marsh had found the academic routine just as unsatisfactory as Dartmouth's, so he ignored regular classes at the seminary in order to study alone. He told Lucia Wheelock that he found nothing "more profit-less . . . than the constantly recurring routine of formal assemblies of any kind."[9] As a tutor at Dartmouth he had also objected to professors "who seem to know no way of managing young men, but by the terror of au-thority . . . , a method [that] tends to break down all the independent spirit and love of study for its own sake, which I thought it of so much importance to cherish."[10] His own independent habits of study were clearly fruitful. In February 1821 he recorded in his journal:

Of my progress in the German language, I have been more conscious than ever be-fore, and begin to feel as if I had conquered it. In Spanish, too, I have done something, and will conquer it within the year. My Hebrew I have some fears about, but I think I shall master it. . . . At the club on Friday, I was rather surprised to find that though I had devoted but half a day to the subject [the Apostolic Fathers], my knowledge of them was as good as anyone's. I do not make this record from vanity, but the fact is to me proof of the superiority of my system.[11]

Though perhaps not a system in a strict sense, Marsh's independent studies brought him to a level of learning that had seldom been seen in New England, certainly not in Vermont, in the first quarter of the nineteenth cen-tury. His accomplishments in languages by 1822 surprised Edward Everett, editor of Boston's *North American Review*, who told George Ticknor that Marsh's review essay "Ancient and Modern Poetry," published that sum-mer in Everett's journal, must have been written by someone with firsthand experience of Europe and its languages.[12] Actually, the longest trip Marsh ever made was in 1824, to Brownsville, Pennsylvania, to visit his brother Roswell, who had migrated west in 1813.

The time and the circumstances in 1826 were indeed propitious for a new presidency at UVM. In Burlington the newly completed college buildings, with the promise of a third to follow, as well as new equipment and books, evidenced clear improvement in the college's welfare. In his inaugural ad-dress in Burlington on November 28, 1826, Marsh told how his "system" of study would aim to reform and indeed revitalize education in line with the growing nationwide interest in this goal.

First, he affirmed a distinctively American principle: "the great object indeed of improving our condition, as a people, through the influence of education." Like almost every public speaker on American culture during the first half of the nineteenth century, Marsh acknowledged the shortcomings of American scholarship compared to that of Europe. But with improvements in the "practical skill and efficiency in our systems of elementary instruction . . . and time to accumulate at our Colleges and Universities the same means of giving and receiving instruction in the higher departments of knowledge . . . then . . . may we hope to rival our transatlantic brethren in the extent and variety of our individual attainments."

Some of James Marsh's contemporaries recalled that he was not a powerful public speaker or preacher, yet the peroration of his inaugural address reveals a vitality of mind as yet unknown to the small college he would lead.

We, too, like the nations of Europe in ancient and modern times, may hope to have our philosophers, and those worthy of the name—men of deep and mysterious thought . . . —the ventriloquists of human reason, uttering forth her untold mysteries, and
> 'truths that wake
> To perish never';
. . . men, who by the depth and justness of the principles which they announce, the living and productive energy of the ideas which they promulgate, shall impart wisdom to our teachers, and give laws to our legislators, thereby exerting a controlling power over the minds of their countrymen, and the future destinies of their country.[13]

Thus, Marsh proposed a role for the philosopher—for Man Thinking, as Ralph Waldo Emerson would describe the figure a few years later—through whom the power of ideas would prevail.

As John Wheeler recalled, President Marsh quickly went hard at the task of preparing the philosophers his address envisioned: "No sooner had Dr. Marsh entered upon the duties of his office than he brought before the Faculty for careful examination the course of study and habits of discipline in the University. . . . Discussion commenced at once in the Faculty on Education generally, and on the course of study, and discipline, best adapted to produce educated men."[14]

Early in 1827, President Marsh presented to the Board of Trustees the results of the faculty's examination of the system of education then in place at the University.[15] He opened his report by acknowledging that the topic of educational reform was a matter of concern throughout the country: "It seems to be very generally agreed among men of intelligence in the country that reform is necessary and our convictions fully coincide with the prevailing sentiment." The University's faculty of three—Marsh; George W. Benedict, professor of mathematics and natural philosophy; and tutor Solomon Foot—had concluded that there were five major problems needing correction: first, the present curriculum was too limited, preparing students only for the learned professions (i.e., law, medicine, and the clergy); second, instruction was too dependent on textbooks, discouraging original thinking; third, students did not achieve high levels of learning because they failed to challenge each other; fourth, degrees were earned simply by residing for four years at the college and seldom were refused for other reasons; and, finally, the brightest students quickly became bored by the curriculum and textbook-dependent teaching, although some, as Marsh knew from his own experience at Dartmouth, might develop habits of independent study.

The general purpose of collegiate instruction, Marsh reminded the Board, was to "call forth into conscious and active exercise the powers of the mind both intellectual and moral." Not only would instruction "communicate necessarily those departments of science and literature which are made use of as instruments for effecting that purpose, but we give him [the student] the most important knowledge of all, the knowledge of himself. We awaken the latent principles of his being into conscious existence." Marsh and his colleagues provided more freedom in the students' choice of courses. Moreover, they believed that opportunities to study at the University should be offered more widely in the community, even to young men who might not be able to complete a full degree because they were employed at other work as well. The discipline of student behavior ought to work through the moral influence of the faculty instead of by coercion and retribution; expulsion would be limited to the incorrigible.

Marsh then outlined the actual reform measures he and the faculty proposed to implement. They would define a set of entrance requirements and a course of study "considered best fitted for the purposes of mental discipline and at the same time of practical utility [comparable to that found] in our most respectable colleges." They would, for the first time, admit to the University young men who could pursue only a partial course of study and perhaps not complete a degree. Students would be grouped in classes according to the progress they made toward a degree, as determined by annual examination. Students willing and able would be "encouraged and assisted to pursue other additional studies which they should have the privilege of selecting subject to the advice and discretion of the faculty." Finally, annual examinations would determine actual accomplishments of learning, and such accomplishment would receive "appropriate marks" and publication "in the annual catalogue of the University." Those students who completed the partial course but did not receive a university degree "should on examination be entitled to receive a certificate to that effect with the College Seal."

The board accepted Marsh's proposal for reform. In 1828, after the reforms' first year in place, Marsh reported to the board on the initial results of the new curriculum. The college had been organized into four departments, including perhaps the first English department established as such, though it appears that activities in that department consisted mainly of readings in the Scottish rhetoricians Jamieson and Campbell and exercises in public speaking and debate. From the beginning Marsh had insisted that the new curriculum include the development of skills in oral communication—eloquence and oratory, in the educational nomenclature of his time—partly, perhaps, because of his own difficulty with public speaking but certainly also because of his belief, stated in his "Tract on Eloquence," that "oratory . . . is dependent on the same [powers of mind] as the dramatic or other forms of poetry."[16]

In the Department of Languages, instruction was provided in Greek, Latin, French, and Spanish by Joseph Torrey, who joined the faculty in 1827. Tutor George Allen of Milton replaced Solomon Foot as Torrey's assistant.

The Department of Mathematics and Physics offered instruction in geography, algebra, plane and solid geometry, differential and integral calculus, mechanics, optics, astronomy, chemistry, natural philosophy, and the philosophy of natural history, all taught by George Benedict.

The Department of Political and Moral Philosophy was the bailiwick of Marsh himself. He conducted lectures and recitations—something akin to modern discussion sections in which students were active participants—on economics, politics, "natural and revealed religion," logic, metaphysics, and ethics.

Marsh and the faculty felt that some of the problems of the old curriculum had been corrected in this first year of the new "system," yet others remained troublesome. The matter of textbooks remained problematic: the proper sort were not readily available. Marsh remained hopeful, however: "The results of examination will show that they have not been abused, but only used as subsidiary to a better understanding of the subject of which they treat."

One of the more radical reforms for its time, the admission of students to a partial course of study, seems to have had some promising success. "Some few students," Marsh told the Board, "have been received in the prosecution of a partial course of study and there is reason to suppose that many will avail themselves of the privileges thus offered."

Marsh and his colleagues at the University claimed that they had designed a curriculum with an organic form. Metaphoric organicism was a commonplace of thought in the late eighteenth and early nineteenth centuries, especially in the writings of some English poets and many German philosophers whom Marsh had studied carefully. A collection of ideas or activities characterized as "organic" was good, for it emulated the completeness of nature, the penultimate good. If the design of reading, study, discussion, and lectures in a curriculum took into account both the rational and emotional aspects of human experience, then such a design would lead to superior results in learning, in contrast with current practices. In his essay in *The North American Review* in 1822, Marsh had strongly criticized a modern sensibility that, in his view, found its "thoughts disciplined and guarded on every side by the fixed laws of philosophical inquiry": "We are taught to exclude the influence of feeling, and reduce the operations of the whole soul to the measured movements of a machine under the control of the will. We suffer no idea to take possession of us more fully, or to produce any greater effect upon our feeling, than prudence and cool reason dictate."[17]

Then, in a pointedly premonitory passage, Marsh struck directly at lifeless teaching:

The preacher does not converse with his church, he reads or declaims to them a written treatise. The instructor from his desk reads a written pamphlet. All is dead letter, with none of the spirit of living intercourse. We love and hate by letters. We wrangle and are reconciled by letters. . . . Our whole being depends upon our alphabet, and we can hardly conceive how it is possible for a child of this world to form and perfect his character without a book.[18]

A pamphlet of 1829, probably written by George Benedict, spelled out the organic scheme of education at UVM as Marsh and Joseph Torrey conceived it.[19] *An Exposition of the System of Instruction and Discipline Pursued in the University of Vermont* found its conceptual source in the writings of the English poet-philosopher Samuel Taylor Coleridge. Marsh had discovered Coleridge's ideas about organically formed schemes of knowledge and educational practices in the English writer's *Encyclopedia Metropolitana, or System of Universal Knowledge on a Methodical Plan* and his *Dissertation on the Science of Method, or the Laws and Regulative Principles of Education* (both published in 1818).

In Marsh's plan the four-year course of study at UVM was so designed that, after three years of studying languages, science, mathematics, and literature, the final year was devoted to philosophy under the instruction of Marsh himself. According to the "Exposition of the System of Instruction," philosophy was "the oscillating nerve, that should connect the various studies together." The senior year course "began with crystallography—the lowest form of organization" and discussed "the laws of all forms." Following Coleridge, the Vermont "system" imputed an ascending hierarchy of forms— "the geometry of all natural existence"—to all creation and so proceeded to display and examine the "laws" of biology, physiology, "psychology, and the connection of the senses with the intellect; the science of logic (the laws of the intellect); then Metaphysics—as the highest and last form of speculative reasoning, or of contemplation." As John Wheeler recalled the plan,

Within this pale [metaphysics] considered the spiritual characteristics of humanity as distinguished from all other existences. From this position Moral science was seen to issue; the ground of the Fine Arts was examined and made intelligible; the principles of Political science, as grounded in the truth of the reason but realized under the form of the understanding, was unfolded, and Natural and theoretical Religion was shown to open the path, when reason had reached her termination, to glory, honor, and immortality.[20]

An ancient but simple idea stood at the heart of both Coleridge's "method" of organizing knowledge and the "system" of instruction formulated by Marsh. The idea was first voiced in Greek philosophy and later given expression by the seventeenth-century Cambridge Platonists in England, then by the Germans Kant, Fichte, and Schelling, and most recently by Coleridge in England. Coleridge had said that knowledge was acquired either by the lower faculty of the Understanding, which responded to information provided by the senses, or by Reason, the superior faculty, which dealt with all that above and beyond simple sense experience. Reason, for Coleridge, was the source of principles; Understanding was the "faculty of Rules."[21]

By applying Coleridge's distinction between Reason and Understanding, in the final year's philosophy course President Marsh taught the young men of UVM to see, for example, "the principles of Political science, as grounded in the truth of the reason but realized under the form of the understanding."

The distinction between Reason and Understanding that Marsh found in both Coleridge and Kant satisfied a compelling need felt by Marsh, his colleagues at the University, and many of their contemporaries. John Wheeler, the only Vermonter actually to visit Coleridge in England (in 1829), later explained the aim of the Vermont system based on this distinction: "to give a *coherence* to the various studies in each department so that the several parts shall present, more or less, the *unity* not of an aggregation nor of a juxtaposition, nor of a merely logical arrangement *but of a development and a growth*, and therefore, the study in it, rightly pursued, should be a growing and enlarging process to the mind of the student."[22] Thus, the Vermont curriculum seemed to speak to the social and psychological dynamics of a young democratic society experiencing unprecedented stress.

Before the War of 1812, Vermont was a booming place; it had the nation's fastest rate of population growth between 1790 and 1810, and almost any commercial venture promised success, many doing handsomely. But by 1830 Vermonters had wantonly cut off most of their rich natural heritage of timber and, with the forest gone, had begun to experience the harmful effects of "dry spells." Then disastrous storms and floods washed out mills; carried away much of the rich alluvial soil of the intervales; destroyed bridges, barns, and crops; and drowned livestock. Grasshoppers, wheat rust, and general soil exhaustion caused declining harvests. The Champlain-Hudson Canal, Vermont's connection with the Hudson River and the Erie Canal, had promised a much-needed outlet for the state's produce in 1824, but instead it perversely carried away Vermont's sons and daughters, stricken with the "Western craze," while introducing competing products from the newly opened West.

The 1820s have been called the Era of Good Feeling in the United States, with special note given to the reconciliation of long-time opponents Thomas Jefferson and John Adams. But imputing national significance to the new friendship of the two Founding Fathers and their nearly simultaneous deaths on July 4, 1826, seems more a gesture of yearning for a mature national unity than a realistic characterization of the actual social and political conditions of the country. The rhetoric and ideology of rampant individualism could not provide both intellectual justification and emotional significance in a way that would tie together the experience of an individual in American society.

At the advent of the industrial revolution, Americans floundered between two worlds: the disappearing frontier and civilized progress. Their yearnings for a simple, transcendent unity were expressed in government by the Monroe Doctrine, in the arts by the repeated theme of a return to nature and antiquity, in religion by the revivalistic vision of a new heaven and new earth. Yet they lived in a society experiencing the strains of competing self-interests supported by the sanctity of contracts and private property.

At his inauguration Marsh had affirmed "the great object indeed of improving our condition, as a people, through the influence of education, and of attaining or approaching, at least, all those forms of ideal perfection in society, at which our religion teaches us to aim." Marsh was himself the product of an education, both institutional and independent, in which religion was intensely formative. Throughout his letters, the surviving fragments of his journal, his sermons, essays, and lectures, it is clear that he was heir to the tradition of New England piety. The religion of New England's Congregational Church, however, was just as disputatious and fractious as other aspects of American life in the first quarter of the nineteenth century. The Dartmouth College controversy, and the UVM–Middlebury rivalry were only battles in a war waged all over New England by disputatious clergy and college faculties.

In his thinking, writing, and teaching, and indeed in the Vermont "system of instruction," James Marsh attempted a synthesis of knowing, of intellect and emotion, of nature and spirit informed by traditional Christian faith. The lesson he sought to teach asked for intellectual rigor and promised revitalized Christianity, but the problem was how to reform the old orthodoxy without destroying certain features of it or denying the natural world it existed in. For Marsh, nearly all contemporary American thinking about religion had no meaning; Christianity had not been best expressed at Harvard, Andover, or Yale but by some "old" voices of seventeenth-century England and some ideas from a more contemporary Germany and England.[23] With their help he hoped to show that a thinking man "has and can have but one system in which his philosophy becomes religious and his religion philosophical."[24] Constructing such a demonstration posed two dangers, however. On the one hand, the Christianity he valued might be reduced to a speculative system in the manner of Unitarianism; on the other, through emphasizing personal and individual religious experience—"enthusiasm," in the eighteenth-century phrase—he might fall into the subjectivism of an individualistic faith lacking the power of Christianity to make over the world.

The late 1820s and early 1830s seemed to hold promise of success for James Marsh in his construction of a system in which religion was philosophical and philosophy was religious. In 1829 he prepared, with his own "Preliminary Essay" and notes, an edition of Coleridge's *Aids to Reflection* for publication by his brother-in-law, the Burlington printer Chauncey Goodrich.[25] By 1833 leading figures in the Transcendentalist Movement in Boston and Concord were reading and discussing Coleridge's book and Marsh's introduction to it. Frederic Henry Hedge, at whose house in Boston the first meetings of the Transcendental Club were held, recalled many years later how "the writings of Coleridge, recently edited by Marsh, and some of Carlyle's earlier essays . . . had created a ferment in the minds of some of the younger clergy of the day. There was a promise in the air of a new era of intellectual life."[26] When Ralph Waldo Emerson read Marsh's "Preliminary Essay" and notes, especially the sections dealing with Reason and Understanding, he told his brother that the distinction was "a philosophy itself."[27] Other Boston and Concord Transcendentalists later would credit Marsh's edition of Coleridge for "helping emancipate enthralled minds" and bringing benefits to American intellectual life that were, in Margaret Fuller's words, "as yet incalculable."[28]

In the world of practical affairs for which Marsh was responsible as president there were signs in the late 1820s that the University's fortunes might rise. Joseph Torrey had gone to Europe to visit intellectual centers, buy books for the University, and improve his German. Marsh wrote to him in February 1829 with news of promising developments for the University. The new medical building was almost complete, and lectures were being given by Dr. Benjamin Lincoln, "a very enterprising, promising, and agreeable young man," to a medical class of forty students; "and the prospects for the future greater still." The center part of the building, eventually to be known as the Old Mill, would be ready by the spring. George Huntington, a UVM gradu:.ce of 1826, was teaching mathematics and civil engineering, and George Allen of Milton, Vermont, was performing admirably as tutor in languages and literature. Undergraduate enrollments had not increased greatly since Marsh assumed the presidency, but the students were "taking higher ground in scholarship and several are preparing for examination on an extensive course of study" in Torrey's own language department.

The University's relations with the State of Vermont were changing. With assistance from Jacob Collamer, a Woodstock lawyer, a friend of the Marshes, and a member of the Board of Trustees, Marsh succeeded in getting the University's original charter "so altered [by the Legislature] that the Corporation hold their seats permanently and fill vacancies themselves when they please with power to increase the present number or suffer it to diminish." Marsh considered this "a great gain" in the governance of the University, even though the Legislature retained the right to change the charter to its original form at any time.[29]

Marsh continued to show concern for his students' learning skills and for the University's relations and service to the broader Vermont community.

He wrote to Torrey: "I gave, myself, several lectures in the fall of a practical character and in the Spring shall continue them on subjects calculated to be practically useful to all the students such as employment of time, use of books, modes of study etc."

In the meantime Marsh had been "engaged in various matters which I hope may indirectly benefit the University," addressing a larger audience:

We have kept up with some help from others a series of essays in the papers here on the subject of intemperance which I hope is doing some good and I have myself written more or less for the *[Vermont] Chronicle* about every week for eight or ten weeks. I am now engaged in a series of essays on Popular Education in which I am taking an extensive view of the subject in all its relations. Three numbers have appeared and I believe it is attracting some interest. . . .[30] Professor Benedict is giving lectures on Electricity to a crowded audience at Goulds Hotel and we are preparing the way for getting up a Lyceum among the people of the town. We think with pretty good prospects of success. . . . We are going to make [the people of Burlington] more cultivated and thereby better friends to the University.

While in Europe, Torrey purchased the first batch of European books, which would eventually put seven thousand volumes in the University's library before 1850. But money was difficult to obtain. Since the Panic of 1819, the credit policy of the Bank of the United States had been favorable to industrial development rather than mercantile interests, and Burlington in the 1820s was basically a village of merchants and shippers who had less access to cash than did men in commercial centers like New York City. Nonetheless, in July 1829, Marsh wrote optimistically to Torrey that he was "confident we shall be able to raise money for the College whenever it gets into the country again." There was additional good news: "In other respects our prospects are more encouraging and we have many reasons to believe that the College is gaining fast upon the confidence and good will of the public. Our prospect for a class this fall is good and among the rest we have two from Wheeling, Va., already here and shall probably have several more from that region drawn here by our peculiar system and the cheapness of living here."

Marsh had written a letter to Coleridge in March 1829 apprising the English poet-philosopher of the debt he felt for helping him understand the Reason–Understanding distinction.[31] In July of that year he told Torrey, "I was about republishing Coleridge's Aids to Reflection with a preliminary essay and illustration of his views from other works. . . . My object will be chiefly to point out the bearing of his metaphysical views on theology and the adaptation of the whole to the state of theology in this country."[32] Within four months of publishing *Aids to Reflection*, Marsh was able to write to England and tell Coleridge: "The edition of fifteen hundred published in November is so far sold and the work is engaging so much attention as to make it probable another edition may be called for in the course of the year."[33]

Interest and attention to Coleridge's *Aids* grew during the 1830s. In 1842 Emerson recorded in his journal: "Edward Washburn told me that at Andover they sell whole shelvesful of Coleridge's *Aids to Reflection* in a year."[34] In 1853, eleven years after Marsh died, W. G. T. Shedd, a former student of Marsh's and the first professor of English at UVM, published the first American edition of Coleridge's collected works, including Marsh's "Preliminary Essay." Shedd was simply finishing a job begun under Marsh's tutelage, a task that Coleridge's literary executor, Henry Nelson Coleridge, had originally planned for Marsh. Shedd's edition of Coleridge, never fully superseded, became the standard American text of Coleridge's prose and poetry for more than a century.[35]

As Shedd's work suggests, Marsh's students at UVM during his sixteen years as president and professor were deeply influenced by him. In 1854, at the semi-centennial celebration of the University's first graduating class, twelve years after Marsh's death, the Reverend Aaron G. Pease, class of 1837, set forth a "literary and philosophical creed of the Vermont alumnus." Pease expressed the debt that former students felt for their late professor and president as he read Article Four—"He believes in Colerige"—and Article Five: "He believes in Professor Marsh . . . for whenever one of these great names is pronounced, the other is not a great way off. He believes in Professor Marsh as the man to whom the University and the cause of education in this country, and his own mind, are more deeply indebted than to any other man."[36]

What seems to have attracted students to James Marsh was his encouraging attitude and supportive personal manner with them. These characteristics Marsh himself recognized when, as a tutor at Dartmouth in 1819, he objected to "the terror of authority." John Wheeler recalled that Marsh was "very instructive and not infrequently exhibited a playfulness of thought that made him quite entertaining. He was reverently loved by all who knew him, but none so much as by his pupils. To them he seemed as one always waiting to open thoughts of life and love."[37]

Marsh's teaching methods were also noted by students and colleagues. He assigned readings and questions on the readings, to be prepared before he would lecture on a topic in philosophy. At the following meeting of the class he would lecture on the topic first and then lead discussions—"oral explanations"—of the reading and questions. Henry Raymond, class of 1840 and founder of *The New York Times*, published an obituary of Marsh that recalled him as a teacher: "It was in the lecture room that his most patient labors were expended."[38] As total student enrollment did not reach one hundred until the last few years before his death in 1842, Marsh could also gather small groups of students in his home for discussions like those he organized and loved at Dartmouth, Andover, and Hampden-Sydney.

William H. A. Bissell, class of 1836, remembered an incident during his final year at the University that best displayed Marsh's encouraging way with students. President John Wheeler had arbitrarily assigned Bissell a commencement oration topic that failed to excite the young man's talents or interest:

After the rehearsal [of his speech, Bissell recalled,] Dr. Marsh took me aside. He said my oration was not worthy of me nor creditable to the University. I told him my grievance in [President Wheeler's] assignment of the subject. He admitted that it was not fair to me; "But," he said, "the subject you have can be made interesting if you will work at it." And he went on to ask it of me as a personal favor, that I would try and make it creditable. . . . I would have done anything for him, and I went to work on my political theme. . . .

On Commencement Day, as I came forward, I saw the audience getting into comfortable positions to endure a dull speech. But I soon had them in attitudes of close attention. . . . And my satisfaction was complete when I met Dr. Marsh at the Commencement Dinner; he shook my hand warmly and said, "Well, you did modify that as I wished."[39]

Bissell's experience with Marsh concerning the commencement oration illustrates the theory of education Marsh had outlined in 1830, speaking at the dedication of the chapel in the Old Mill: "The legitimate and immediate aim of education, in its true sense, is, not by the appliances of instruction and discipline to shape and fit the powers of the mind to this or that outward condition in the mechanism of civil society, but by means corresponding to their inherent nature, to excite, to encourage, and affectionately to aid *the free and perfect development of those powers themselves.*"[40] For Marsh, education was not a utilitarian drilling into conformity. Instead, he argued, if the sole purpose of education were to fit students for "success in the world, as merchants, for example or civil engineers, or as professional men, the results will be such a cultivation of their minds only as will . . . make their powers serviceable."

The point of the dedication sermon of 1830 suggests the actual end that Marsh's personal studies in Coleridge and German philosophy served. He drew a comparison between the ostensibly admirable powers of the understanding exhibited by great warriors and politicians like Napoleon and Talleyrand, on the one hand, and a simple Yankee, doubtless a Vermonter, whose "powers of understanding are . . . but imperfectly cultivated, but who, instead of rushing eagerly and unreflectingly into the pursuits of worldly interest and ambition had turned his thoughts to the knowledge of himself; who has communed with his own heart and cherished the powers of reason and self-consciousness. . . . He is the man in whom we recognize essential and inherent worth. In him we find unfolded the true and distinctive principles and character of our humanity."

The extent of the influence of UVM's "system," its curriculum, and the personality and manner of its deviser, James Marsh, is suggested by the eighty-one students from Marsh's era who went on from Burlington to become teachers throughout the country. With many other Vermonters during and after the 1830s, alumni of the University migrated west and south, carrying with them what they called "Marsh's philosophy." For example, Marsh's own sons, James, Sidney, and Joseph, all UVM alumni, migrated as far west as Oregon, where Sidney became president and Joseph professor at Pacific University; and even to Hawaii, where James became assistant minister of education, a member of the Hawaiian parliament, and publisher of the first Hawaiian-language newspaper.

For decades after his death Marsh's ideas continued to play a lively role in the education of Vermonters. As an undergraduate at UVM during the late 1870s, John Dewey had been a student and close friend of Professor H. A. P. Torrey, Joseph Torrey's nephew. Later, Dewey acknowledged that the general influence of Marsh's lectures on psychology and Coleridge's *Aids to Reflection*, which were used as texts in the younger Torrey's philosophy courses, was still sufficiently meaningful in the 1870s to shape irrevocably the thinking of many UVM undergraduates, including Dewey himself.[41]

But James Marsh's academic and intellectual life in Burlington was repeatedly distracted and weakened by the nineteenth century's "white plague," tuberculosis. His first wife, Lucia Wheelock, died in 1828, less than a year after he became president of the University. In 1830 he married her sister Laura, but she too died of tuberculosis, in 1838. From the early 1830s Marsh himself was seriously weakened by ill health. His control of the University's affairs waned soon after 1830, and the school again suffered financial troubles. His own salary was reduced from $1,000 to $600, and of that less than $100 was paid in cash. A committee of the Board of Trustees investigated the University's financial affairs and observed, "The treasurer seems to receive but little and of course he can pay out but little and embarrassments to all concerned are the immediate result." The fault for this grim state of affairs was laid at the doors of the faculty and the Board; they suffered from "a great want of energy."[42] Under this strain, Marsh resigned the presidency in 1833, and his old friend from Dartmouth, John Wheeler, took over. A member of the Board of Trustees since 1825, Wheeler traveled to Europe with Joseph Torrey in 1829 and on that trip became the only Vermont Transcendentalist to visit Highgate, England, and see Coleridge plain.

Marsh attempted to find a new position at some other college. Bowdoin and Dartmouth considered him, but his Vermont students having mounted a petition seeking his retention on the faculty, he was appointed professor of philosophy. After 1835 he seems to have considered moving to Ohio and founding a cooperative community with a former student, Zenas Bliss, and his sister and brother-in-law, Emily and David Read. His letters in the 1830s speak of waning strength and lack of time to complete any major work of scholarship. He died in 1842 of tuberculosis. *The New York Commercial Advertiser* prematurely announced his death on June 1 with an obituary notice titled "Another Light Extinguished." It was read to Marsh the day before he died.

On the one-hundredth anniversary of the publication of *Aids to Reflection*, John Dewey recalled Marsh's influence on generations of Vermont undergraduates in the middle years of the nineteenth century, long after his death. James Marsh, said Dewey, was "a pure personality . . . who wished to use scholarship and philosophy to awaken his fellowmen to a sense of the possibilities that were theirs by right as men, and to quicken them to realize these possibilities in themselves." Marsh's transcendentalism, derived from Coleridge and from German philosophy, was "the outer form congenial in his day to that purpose. The underlying substance is a wistful aspiration for full and ordered living." [43]

Part Two

THE CLASSICAL COLLEGE, 1833–1895: GROWTH AND STABILITY: OVERVIEW

T. D. SEYMOUR BASSETT

Institutions, like individuals, suffer a high rate of infant mortality. Many times during the founding and infancy of the University of Vermont, people thought either that it would not be born or that it could not survive. But at each crisis, supporters in Burlington, across the state, and beyond came to the rescue. In 1819, 1849, and 1864, UVM considered the possibility of sacrificing its identity and merging with Middlebury College and/or Norwich University. However, financial stringency was not severe enough and local pride was too strong to enforce surrender on the key questions: Whose campus shall we use? Which part of our program shall we give up?

Periodic financial panics between the War of 1812 and the gold rush of 1849, reflecting the worldwide shift from an agrarian to an urban-industrial society, threatened the very survival of the frail college. Moreover, in a country dotted with new denominational colleges, each fishing in the same pool for financial support, the competition was severe, and many a college town lost its college. At UVM, fortunately, the economic fluctuations of the 1850s and the still more severe reversals of 1873–1878 and 1893–1898 merely required slowdowns and retrenchment. In the 1850s Burlington and UVM marked time. From 1867 on, UVM had a steady income of more than $8,000 annually from its land grant fund, which exceeded its total receipts in 1866 and helped to blunt the force of the depression of the 1870s. By 1890 the land grant endowment provided less than a quarter of the growing institution's income,[1] but the larger tuition-paying enrollment cushioned the depression of the 1890s. The city of Burlington rode out those storms equally well, thanks to its industrial and commercial growth and the accompanying construction of factories, stores, institutions, and homes. Town and gown had a symbiotic relationship, with enough space between their centers to avoid the traditional tension.

The Whig–Congregational Pattern, 1833–1848

To replace James Marsh as president, the Trustees turned a second time to the Reverend John Wheeler (Dartmouth '16), who was a member of the board, and this time Wheeler was given leave to move by his Windsor, Vermont, congregation. Aided by Professor George Benedict, who served as his treasurer, Wheeler rebuilt the student body, increased the faculty to five, and raised some $30,000, thereby pulling the college back from the brink of disaster. Hard times after 1837 meant unpaid tuitions, unpaid rents on college lands, unpaid pledges. "The University was sued for a large debt; the . . . Library was attached, and advertised at a Sheriff's Sale," Wheeler reported.[2] Fortunately, he was able to borrow new money to cover old debts, and garnered UVM's first legacies. The faculty considered moving to a new site but decided instead to purchase the land connecting their three buildings. The team of president and faculty did not merely try to make ends meet; it aimed to move forward. From 1841 on, except for the abnormal war and postwar years 1860–1873, UVM graduated more students than did either Middlebury or Norwich.

The curriculum did not change; it included Classical languages, the physical and natural sciences, mathematics, philosophy, and weekly sessions at which some professor was assigned to hear prepared compositions declaimed. Z. Philip Ambrose expands on the early curriculum in chapter 5. A new course, labeled English Literature, appears in the catalogs with the coming of Professor William G. T. Shedd (1820–1894; UVM 1839) in 1845. The change in title from "Rhetoric" betokened a change in the nature and content of a study rooted in medieval Latin instruction, which eventually grew into speaking, writing, and reading the English vernacular. Shedd later moved on to the theological seminaries of Auburn (1852–1854), Andover (1854–1862), and Union (1862–1890), seeking to reconcile the new ideas of Kant and Darwin with the old orthodoxy based on Calvin and Locke.[3]

President Wheeler resigned in August 1848, after the longest service in UVM history until that time and the third longest ever. The reason he gave was the health of his wife, who died the next year, but his resignation, like that of George Benedict the year before, may also have been related to differences with the Trustees over the subscription campaign, which met its preliminary $50,000 goal early in 1847. Wheeler had conditional pledges for $17,000 more and may have wanted to continue the drive, but more cautious counsels prevailed.

Wheeler never wavered in his subsequent support for UVM. He served as trustee again, from 1849 until his death on April 13, 1862, and one of his last acts was a gift of land to the University. In 1856 the die-hard Whigs, those who refused to join the new Republican party and support John C. Frémont for president, nominated Wheeler for governor, but he declined to run. A well-traveled man of tact and diplomacy, much in demand for special occasions like UVM's semicentennial, Wheeler was one reason UVM and Burlington kept a cosmopolitan outlook.

The Classics and the Sciences, 1849–1861

To replace Wheeler the Trustees chose the Reverend Worthington Smith of St. Albans, who unfortunately was never well enough to give his full effort to the job, but the faculty was now strong enough to manage without him. He served chiefly to symbolize the survival of the Whig–Congregational alliance that Wheeler had exploited and to preserve the afterglow of James Marsh's charisma. His tenure saw the revival of the medical department, dormant since Benjamin Lincoln died amid the financial crisis left by Marsh when he stepped down.

Upon Smith's death in 1855 he was succeeded by the Reverend Calvin Pease, the first UVM alumnus ('38) and first UVM professor to become president. Pease also took pains to preserve the Whig–Congregational alliance and the James Marsh tradition. He was an experienced teacher of Classics, and although lacking seminary training, he was nevertheless licensed to preach and spent much of his time in nearby Congregational pulpits. As president he found that the cares of college business, clouded by the economic crisis from 1857 until war broke out, were a weight, not a challenge. So when the First Presbyterian Church of Rochester, New York, called him, he gladly resigned.[4]

Presidents Wheeler, Smith, and Pease, like their predecessors, were all Congregational ministers who maintained the traditional UVM connection between religious and political moderation. Presidents Sanders and Austin had both been Federalists, despite their theological differences. Their successors were National Republicans and Whigs, cool to any radical reforms whether against Masonry, slavery, or alcohol. Marsh, Wheeler, and Smith disapproved of the "new measures" of revivalist Jedediah Burchard. They also disapproved of the Canadian Rebellion of 1837–1838 and supported law, order, and neutrality against the rebels' movement for more self-rule in Canada.

The opinions of the presidents were well known from their public addresses, their chapel talks, and (up to Marsh's time) the traditional climax course for seniors, intellectual and moral philosophy. The course included some form of political economy in harmony with Whig or Republican party principles (no avowed Democrat has ever served as UVM president), a little general institutional history of ancient and modern Europe, morals, and an increasingly modernist Congregational theology. After the advent of John Wheeler the course was taught by another member of the faculty—by James Marsh until his death in 1842, by Joseph Torrey until his death in 1867, and by Torrey's nephew, Henry A. P. Torrey, until his death in 1902. Wheeler, who had no previous classroom teaching experience, set a new pattern: presidents continued to teach but did not carry a full teaching load along with their administrative duties. Each instructor of the senior course embellished his offerings according to his own experience and taste. Joseph Torrey conducted what amounted to tutorials with the remnant of students who did not go off to war. His emphasis on aesthetics resulted in his posthumously published lectures based on his visits to French, Italian, and German galleries.[5]

Teaching methods stayed the same: memorization of vocabulary and the rules of grammar and mathematics, recitations, and lectures. One form of memorization was copying the professor's lectures.[6] How much Socratic dialogue, or what we now call "discussion," was involved in recitation is not clear. President Wheeler wrote of James Marsh: "His method of teaching was by questions with oral explanation. The class being required to study the questions before appearing before him."[7] What student letters and diaries tell is whether they gave the "right" answer and whether one student who had not studied cribbed the "right" answer from another who knew it.

In the revived medical department, Dr. Samuel Thayer secured Swiss-trained Henri Erni, the first Ph.D. on the faculty, to teach medical and academic chemistry. Anatomical models and charts were scarce, though students dissected cadavers. When Erni moved on to federal government work, Edward Hungerford (Yale '51), who also had European training, took over chemistry and added geology. The clash of old and new teaching methods is illustrated in the folktale of President Pease's catching Hungerford (or it might have been Zadock Thompson) fishing for specimens with his students, and chiding, "Why aren't you in your classroom lecturing?"[8] Laboratory work in the physical sciences was nonexistent, as in almost all other antebellum colleges. Natural history had its collections of specimens of fauna and flora, classified according to Linnaeus, but again, no laboratory.

If the formal curriculum seemed arid, students could follow their own inclinations in the clubs. Saturday night meetings of the literary societies Phi Sigma Nu and the University Institute provided an opportunity for alternative education, where students learned to use their wits in political campaigning, parliamentary procedure, debating, literary composition, and satire. While the faculty bought books for the college library to meet their own needs, the societies maintained libraries focusing on student interests in literature, biography, travel, and current affairs. Pious students joined the Society for Religious Inquiry, which survived into the 1870s.

Students reacted against the rules by letting off steam in the taverns of the town, taking long walks in the country with a friend, or bathing, fishing, and sailing in Lake Champlain. The second quarter of the century saw student violence and protest all over the country, but it was mild at UVM. Blowing tin horns in the middle of the night, stealing grapes from nearby gardens, staying up all night drinking and singing (especially when visited by men from other colleges), outstaying lenient faculty permission to take a day off at the state fair, and tying the clapper of the chapel bell that called the students to morning devotions were normal pranks whose telling decorates many a college history. The faculty did not think it funny when President Wheeler, investigating a disturbance, was knocked down in the dark. Given the total lack of streetlights on Pearl Street until after the Civil War, no malice aforethought can be imputed.[9]

Assuming that the institution stood in the stead of parents, and believing in the patriarchal family (in spite of the phrase *alma mater*), the faculty dealt with student disorders by requiring public confessions and apologies, remanding malefactors to the care of their fathers for a period, or expulsion.[10] Rural parents, particularly, wanted a close guard to be kept.

The furor over some student behavior reflected the state of opinion on issues as important to students then as apartheid and the Vietnam War have been in the late twentieth century. They were steamed up on both sides of the issue of Jedediah Burchard's revivalistic methods in 1835–1836. Some sympathized with the democratic and republican aims of the Canadian Rebellion of 1837–1838. In 1843 the literary societies chose C. G. Eastman, editor of a Democratic weekly, who had been expelled from UVM six years earlier, to be their Commencement Poet, but the faculty successfully blocked his performance.

The first Greek letter "social fraternity" at UVM was also a kind of student protest. Lambda Iota (1836), known as the Owls from the owl on their pin, organized as a smoking club in rebellion against the college ban on tobacco. Its Greek initials stand for Lorillard Institute, because the New York tobacconist Pierre Lorillard, on being asked to become an honorary member, sent the boys a supply of smokes. Sigma Phi (1845), the first national fraternity at UVM, marked the diffusion of the social fraternity concept from campus to campus. The Alpha Chapter at Union College (1827) colonized Hamilton, Williams, Hobart, and then UVM. Two UVM seniors went to Schenectady in March 1845, were initiated, and brought back "the ideals and the secrets" to Burlington. All students belonged to one of the two literary societies, "the Blues evangelical" and "the Bloats riotous"; Sigma Phi recruited sixteen from each, against Owl opposition.[11] A third antebellum fraternity, Delta Psi (1850), was organized in the Antimasonic tradition as a protest against secret societies. Briefly bonded in an Anti-Secret Federation with similar societies at Williams, Amherst, Union, and a few other colleges, Delta Psi survived with the triple goals of scholarship, preparation for a career, and most important, social fellowship. For most of the nineteenth century, fraternities behaved like the literary societies. They met in the college building, then in downtown quarters until the beginning of the twentieth century.[12]

UVM stood out in the antebellum years for the place of natural science in its curriculum. George Benedict started this momentum before he resigned in 1847 to build telegraph lines. His patience may have been exhausted by the Classicists' lack of appreciation for his efforts to build a scientific museum, for which he demanded payment after twenty-one years. In any event he bought the Burlington *Free Press* in 1853 and continued to support the University and all other good Burlington institutions until his death in 1871. His son Grenville continued to run the *Free Press* until he died in 1907 and served as secretary of the university corporation.

The college replaced Benedict with the best and broadest scientists available—first, Zadock Thompson, the local amateur genius, followed, after his death in 1856, by James Marsh's younger brother Leonard (Dartmouth '27; M.D., '32), a man as capable in Classics as in "Vegetable and Animal Physiology," the name he gave to his biology course. Leonard Marsh's manuscript "The Practical Determination of Species," although primarily concerned with definition and classification, shows familiarity with the literature of the Darwinian controversy.[13] He published attacks on Democrats, spiritualists, and Unitarians, which few read; gave a series of lectures on work to the Burlington Mechanics Institute, which few attended; and exercised his brilliant mind all over the intellectual map.[14] Here was clearly a beloved old coot whom it was safe to ridicule, as in the *College Maul* early in the Civil War years:

FACULTY TUNK
Commencement Levee, Museum

Prof. Leonard was there, and, made bold by the sight
Of the animals stuffed, was exceeding polite,
And told—which delighted the guests not a few—
Of Radiates, Mollusks and Gastropods, too.

Chorus (Painfully suggestive of Animal Anatomy and the *reproductive* jokes of Leonard thereat):

Ri tu, ri nu
ri tu di ni na
Ri um ti nu di na.

(Tune: "Abe of the West")[15]

Young enthusiasts, well qualified for the times, taught the physical sciences. George Benedict's cousin, Farrand N. Benedict, handled mathematics and civil engineering through Wheeler's and Smith's presidencies. McKendree Petty (UVM '49), after an apprenticeship teaching in New Orleans—where he taught himself languages in his spare time and earned a University of Louisiana law degree—returned as tutor and then replaced Farrand Benedict in 1854. The first Methodist on the faculty, ordained in 1859, Petty frequently preached in churches around Chittenden County.

The State's University? 1861–1882

War is never good for colleges unless they try to educate soldiers. If they urge their students to keep on studying, they are unpatriotic; if they urge them to enlist, they go bankrupt. The Civil War was another in the series of setbacks UVM suffered during the nineteenth century.[16]

Following President Pease's departure, the Trustees turned to another professor and minister, Rev. Joseph Torrey, a thirty-five-year veteran teacher of Classics and philosophy, to keep the University going during the difficult war years. A major new source of support, as well as an impetus to change the University's sense of its mission, was the passage of the Morrill Act by Congress in 1862 on the initiative of Vermont's Senator Justin Morrill. It created a national network of land grant colleges and promoted higher education in agriculture, military science, and technology. My chapter 6 and Robert Sinclair's chapter 10 follow the tortuous path that agricultural education and relations in general between UVM and the State of Vermont took in the decades that followed.

In 1866 a young journalist from Rhode Island, James B. Angell, was picked to succeed Torrey in default of any available Congregational minister. UVM's first lay leader, Angell stumped the state during his five-year presidency to raise money and goodwill. He later commented that he found only three assets on arriving at UVM—the land grant fund for the new Agricultural College, the scholarly tradition, and Corporation Secretary Grenville Benedict. Among the poorly paid professors, "Dr. Torrey . . . was receiving a compensation less than the men then laying bricks in the construction of the Central Vermont Railway station." Wartime casualties, Angell sensed, had brought on a mood of discouragement in both the city and the state.[17]

Just as the original land grants included in Vermont town charters provided funds to support the University in its infancy, Morrill Act grants now sustained it. Vermont realized over $100,000 from the land scrip it received under the act, but Morrill expected each state to supplement this income. The Vermont Legislature's failure to appropriate such a supplement was the first sign of dissatisfaction with the UVM arrangement. Besides, UVM did not succeed in implementing the military training envisaged by the Morrill Act until the mid-1870s.[18]

Under Angell, the University did make an effort to provide instruction in the basic sciences related to agriculture, with Peter Collier (Yale '61; Ph.D., '69; Angell's brother-in-law) in chemistry and George Henry Perkins (Yale '67; Ph.D., '69) in natural history joining Leonard Marsh, who continued his Vegetable and Animal Physiology. In 1869 the first two B.S. degrees were awarded along with the traditional A.B., and the first C.E. (in civil engineering) was awarded in 1870. But very few farmers or their sons, in Vermont or elsewhere, were persuaded that they needed scientific instruction, and for years no one actually enrolled for a degree in agriculture. Along with his steps to expand the sciences, Angell's presidency was remembered for Angell Hall (also called the President's House) built in 1870 in a vain effort to keep him from moving to the University of Michigan, and for the Marsh professorship in philosophy, the University's first endowed chair.

To replace Angell, the trustees would have returned gladly to the clergyman-president model, but, probably with Angell's encouragement, they chose a man who acted like a minister but was not ordained and had never served a parish. Matthew Henry Buckham (UVM '51) had fifteen years' experience on the UVM faculty teaching English literature and Greek. The achievements of this longest-serving president (thirty-nine years) are detailed in chapter 6. They include the admission of women, the defeat of attempts to separate the agricultural program from UVM, and the steady growth of the medical department (achieved by keeping admission and graduation standards low), which Lester Wallman chronicles in chapter 9.

The Modern College Spirit, 1882–1895

A winning team brings the crowd behind it. From 1877 on, UVM graduated more students than did Norwich University and Middlebury combined (not counting the medical department, which awarded more degrees than all the rest of the University). Building after building began to give College Row its modern look—the remodeled Old Mill, the Billings Library, Williams Science Hall, and after the turn of the century, the gymnasium and Morrill Hall. Buckham boasted that UVM was in a class with Cornell and Yale, not with the small local schools. By 1895 continuing growth required two more dormitories, Converse Hall for men and Grassmount for women, and Commons Hall behind the Row, which students called "the Hash House."

Where antebellum students escaped college restrictions in Greek letter clubs and other off-campus activities, now those who had leisure from studying or working their way had additional extracurricular activities—publications and sports.[19] A good deal more "rah rah" worked its way into student mores in the Gay Nineties. Baseball came home with the veterans of the Civil War, but it was pickup or between classes until the late 1880s. The team took its first southern trip in 1891 and placed second to Yale for a quasi-national championship at the Chicago Columbian Exposition tournament of 1893. Along with the college games came college colors, green and gold. College yells and college songs enlivened the "smokers" or pep rallies before the games. Football, played with a variety of rules, was for a long time just a way of venting class rivalries, but in the early 1890s it became an intercollegiate sport.

Students imitated the Ivy League in founding *The University Cynic* in 1883, an all-purpose publication (weekly from 1908) with literary efforts and news—news for the alumni and other supporters as well as for the college community. Its title, the editors wrote in its first issue, "means that we shall honestly speak the convictions of our mind . . . ; that our objects are utilitarian; . . . that all things conflicting with the interests we represent we shall . . . combat." Their model was Diogenes, the most celebrated Cynic, who attacked hypocrites. Current literature, they continued, is afflicted with "affected aestheticism and prurient sentimentality."[20] A class yearbook, the *Ariel*, followed in February 1886, first published by the sophomores but eventually a junior enterprise. A separate photograph album of the graduating class, replacing the custom of exchanging *cartes de visite,* was published for several years and then incorporated into the *Ariel*. College humor had an outlet in the occasional issue of *The College Maul*.

Women were second-class citizens for their first twenty-five years on the campus. History professor Samuel F. Emerson, surveying the post–World War I secular trend from Christian humanism toward utilitarianism and specialization at UVM, acknowledged that Vermont had always recognized human equality and therefore women should share college opportunities. But he questioned, "Could the confessedly concrete feminine mind grasp abstract truth?" The answer of Professor H. A. P. Torrey about the women who took his courses in aesthetics, theory of morals, and psychology is not available.[21] Only ten women were enrolled in 1883, all but one of whom eventually graduated; of the ninety-nine men on campus that year, thirty failed to graduate. Of the 42 women enrolled in 1894–1895, 34 survived; again the men had a higher dropout rate: 41 leaving compared to 146 surviving. There were two sororities—Kappa Alpha Theta (1881) and Delta Delta Delta (1893); a third, Pi Beta Phi (1898), would soon join them.

Students still studied hard but had wider choices, both in the technical schools of medicine, engineering, and agriculture and in the humanities. Some of their senior theses have survived, indicating a new kind of study, undergraduate research by the German method. Professor Volney Barbour, almost alone in engineering since 1869, had three helpers by 1895, as well as the three professors in mathematics, chemistry, and physics. George Perkins alone occupied the chair of natural history when he came to UVM in 1869— actually a whole settee of the life sciences. The field now had four more instructors: W. W. Cooke in agriculture; Lewis R. Jones, later a leading plant pathologist, in botany; Joseph L. Hills, later dean, teaching agricultural chemistry; and Frank A. Waugh in horticulture, with a federally funded experiment station to work with. Professor Emerson came to teach Greek and modern languages in 1881, three years after graduating from Union Theological Seminary. By 1895 he was teaching history, and there were other specialists in German and French. A faculty of nine in 1883—twice as large as in President Wheeler's day—had doubled again by 1895. "By modern standards of scholarship they were not distinguished men. They were better than that. They were men of distinction," Thomas Reed Powell told a 1942 Founder's Day audience.[22]

Powell went on to say that he was glad UVM had finally abolished Greek as a requirement for the A.B. degree. He had studied it for five years, loved it, and remembered three or four phrases. Classics had originally been vocational training—Greek for divinity and Latin for law and medicine. The virtue of the Classics-based curriculum, Powell said, was that students, exceptional in talent and interest, "shared the same experience." Instead of "solos by the instructor," they learned in small classes by Socratic recitations, with "correction by the teacher and comment from fellow students." Controversy over college, church, or family sharpened their mental tools for their intellectual careers. A sense of consecration, of religious devotion, moved and bound the students in a fellowship.[23]

While the old ways of teaching humanistic principles gradually eroded, the Guardians of the Flame tried to keep the tradition alive by vaunting UVM history. After Grenville Benedict's 1891 oration celebrating the centennial of the charter, Professor John E. Goodrich was successful in instituting the observance of Founder's Day on Ira Allen's birthday. Goodrich also issued the first call from UVM to save the sources of the history of the state and its university. The books and papers of Lucius E. Chittenden and Rush C. Hawkins, given in response to this call, formed the nucleus of what became the Wilbur Collection of Vermontiana. Bibliophile Chittenden, President Lincoln's register of the treasury, was descended from Vermont's first governor. Hawkins, also a collector, focused on the Civil War.

In 1897 President Buckham reached sixty-five, the normal retirement age through most of the twentieth century. Whether a younger man could have done any better for his institution during the last thirteen years of his presidency is beyond knowing. It is clear, however, that the roots Buckham had sunk so deeply in the nineteenth-century classical-humanistic idea of a university made it hard for his successors to adjust UVM to the twentieth.

The Curriculum—I: From Traditional to Modern

Z. PHILIP AMBROSE

IN THE beginning there was no nineteenth century, no Victorian Age. No Matthew Arnold, John Ruskin, or Walter Pater had yet established the critical modes of the modern world by studying the past through the lens of the Renaissance. But in the beginning the faculty of the University of Vermont did create an innovative, unified curriculum in natural science and mathematics, Classics, literature, and philosophy. And even before President James Marsh's modifications that earliest curriculum had been grounded philosophically in belief in the utility of knowledge. Through the century this conviction underlay continuing debate about the UVM curriculum and its division into different programs. Is knowledge of one kind or of several? Is it to be pursued for its own sake or for practical application? Is it for the many or the few, for the preacher or the farmer? In reviewing the development of the UVM curriculum, we are really looking at the mentality that made the nineteenth century an epoch.

Erastus Root (1789–1829) of Guilford, Vermont, kept a "Journal of the Most Remarkable Proceedings, Studies and Observation" for the years 1815–1818.[1] Pursuing his "ambition for fame and literary glory" in preference to the family farm, in 1807 he put himself under the instruction of the Reverend Jason Chamberlain, then pastor of the Congregational church in Guilford, and in 1809 he passed the admission examination for Williams College. The next year Chamberlain was elected professor of learned languages at UVM, and Erastus Root left Williams to follow him, entering the sophomore class at UVM in July 1811. After graduating in 1813, just before the U.S. Army rented the "College edifice," Root read medicine in Guilford with Dr. Willard Arms of Brattleboro for seventeen months, sold his patrimony of $1,200, and returned to UVM to attend the medical lectures, under the private instruction of Professor John Pomeroy, M.D. In his daily journal, beginning with the ride back to Burlington, October 10, 1815, Root refers to his earlier years with Professor Chamberlain as the years of his "classickal studies."

The inaugural ceremonies of the Rev. Mr. Chamberlain as professor of the learned languages show how Latin was taken for granted in the world of the new university.[2] In addition to the Latin address by President Sanders, there were Latin replies by the inaugurand to the president, to Chief Justice Royall Tyler (who administered the oath), to the governor, and to the entire corporation (which included the professors and officers of the University). The inaugural address itself is evidence of the equation of the UVM bachelor of arts degree with Root's "classickal studies." But Chamberlain's opening sentence could have been pronounced by any anxious teacher of Greek and Latin during the next two centuries: "In the present age, some pretended philosophers have affected to undervalue the study of learned languages." Then as now, Vermont appeared to be extraordinary in these matters: "It is with the greatest pleasure, that I discover a disposition in the people of this State to encourage and patronize these studies."

In some respects Chamberlain's speech makes conventional, if valid, arguments for the study of Greek and Latin (e.g., in order to write and speak well). But some features of the argument suggest what the UVM curriculum aimed at in general: (1) that grammar is learned through learning one or more languages *by books*, none so "well calculated for this as the Greek and Roman"; (2) that our writers should possess that taste and refinement which distinguished the writers of the Augustan Age; (3) that the "Elysian fields of classick learning" covered a wide range of tastes and a wide range of knowledge;[3] (4) that these studies "excite youth to mental exertion, and lead them to form habits of industry and activity"; (5) that these studies are the source of "so much utility and pleasure, they ought to form a very considerable branch of polite education. They should be regarded as the first and fundamental studies, at every public seminary" (at the same time, Chamberlain welcomes the new interest in natural science: "The classicks, however, should not engross our attention so much as to exclude other useful studies. . . . Our Corporation, sensible of this, have recently established Professorships in the various departments of science, as well as in the learned professions; so that all the studies will be attended to in this University, which are necessary to complete a liberal, as well as professional education"); (6) that this classical education would prepare the student for the full spectrum of vocations. An exhortation to the students concludes Chamberlain's peroration: "Contend with that ardour and enthusiasm, which distinguished the combatants at the Olympick games . . . and you will be useful, respected, and happy in life."

Amidst the rhetoric of this oration one perceives not only the prominence given to the professorship in Classics but a conviction that the breadth of knowledge offered by the Classics was in harmony both with the vocations the students would enter and with the other subjects in the curriculum. This was not mere "politique inaugurale." The recurrent motif of utility in this twenty-one-page address suggests that the professor of learned languages intended to cooperate in a curriculum that would put the Classics to use as a guide and complement to practical knowledge. Chamberlain occupied the second regular professorship, joining James Dean, *Professor Matheseos et Philosophiae Naturalis* (of mathematics and natural philosophy, or science), for whom the "useful" was virtually his life's motto.[4] Chamberlain speaks not like a Latin and Greek teacher, a mere *grammaticus,* but as a Classicist who viewed the corpus of ancient authors as a thesaurus of knowledge for every sphere of life.

Although the study of Latin and, with the Renaissance, of Greek was traditional in the universities of Europe and America, that study had not been uniform through the centuries. In Harvard's first two centuries all instruction, though conducted in Latin, was much more concerned with philosophy than with literature. It concentrated on such learned languages as Greek, Hebrew, and Syriac and dealt not at all with Latin grammar and little with Latin literature.[5] By the end of the eighteenth century a revolution was occurring in the study of Classical antiquity. In Germany, *Altertums-wissenschaft*, a new concept of the study of antiquity, sought answers through the study of linguistics and literature to the anthropological questions that had arisen in the age of exploration and discovery. Classics was no longer content to be merely preparation for the professions. It had become the science of philology. That science would in turn spawn new children during the course of the nineteenth century: economics, anthropology, comparative linguistics, and critical theory in art and literature.

Burlington at the time of Jason Chamberlain's inauguration probably knew little yet of the revolution in Classics in Berlin. But from the vantage point of the New World, Burlington offered a fresh laboratory in which to study the Old World and to practise the modern science of philology. Here the Classics would be read for insights into the myriads of questions which had been raised by the discoveries of new peoples and places, questions about the nature of man, the origin of language and thought, the facts of natural history, survival in the new and often difficult world, and the purpose of life.

The development of the early curriculum at UVM fell generally into three phases: (1) instruction before James Marsh (1826); (2) the revisions made under Marsh, and (3) the subsequent addition of departments and divisions to the University.[6]

Even before the actual opening of UVM, the Reverend Samuel Peters, whom Ira Allen had importuned to edit his history of Vermont, wrote to the French scholar L'Abbé Vaire (who wanted a principal position in Ira's new college) concerning the laws and faculty of the college in Burlington for which the State of "Verdmont" had granted a charter.[7] His letter praised Vaire's plans for the college and further directed that the Trustees should appoint, in addition to a president and prefect, two professors for Latin and Greek, two for "the Mathematicks," one for history and geography, one for "Laws," one for "Drawing," and one for French. The curriculum was to be Classical and comprehensive, and the faculty was to be small, consisting of eight in addition to president and prefect. He added that the "Trustees [would] act wisely by appointing French gentlemen of literate abilities."

Peters hoped Ira Allen could secure Vaire's appointment as the president of the new university. Allen, languishing in a prison in Paris, could do little, but in a waywardly spelled and punctuated letter to Fulwar Skipwith, consul general for the United States, he gives some insight into his own educational views:

I had conserted measures to establish a most extensive Plan of Education not to be under the superstitions of the Clergy and in Place of Paying too much attention to the Hebrew, Greek, &c., &c. Institute the French and other Languages of the Present day, and such other studies as might be most useful and applicable to the ingenious [sic] and views of the students and to have s d University in connection with several Colleges, Academies, &c. to extend it's Influence &c. I mentioned these matters to Mr. Barlow [Joel Barlow, Yale, 1778] inviting him to the Presidency of said University and ment to have been more particular with him on the subject had oppertunity permitted.[8]

By this time Vaire clearly had been passed over, as had Peters's design for the University. For Ira Allen the promotion of French and other modern languages seemed to be allied with establishing a "useful and applicable" curriculum, a notion that in his view apparently was at odds with an emphasis on the ancient learned tongues. In default, however, of prompt support from Allen, the citizens of Burlington eventually brought the Reverend Daniel Clarke Sanders (Harvard 1788) to the post of president. With him the Classics were secure, but as the inaugural address of Jason Chamberlain suggests, the concept of the utility of education reflected in Ira Allen's letter was secure as well.

That education should be useful and that this utility inhered in Classical learning was in fact sealed by Sanders and trustees Samuel Hitchcock and William C. Harrington into the motto of the "Universitas Viridimontanae" adopted by the corporation in 1807.[9] They were apparently concerned not only with the motto but, as we shall see, with the seal itself. The words on this seal, *studiis et rebus honestis* are taken from Horace (Quintus Horatius Flaccus, 65–8 B.C.E.), *Epistles* I. 2. I offer a translation of the whole poem because it contains concepts essential to the UVM curricular philosophy:

While you were studying oratory at Rome, Lollius Maximus [a young student of law], I was at Praeneste rereading Homer, the author of the Trojan War. He states better and more clearly than the learned philosophers Crantor [of Soli, c. 335–c.

275 B.C.E., member of the Old Academy] and Chrysippus [c. 280–207 B.C.E., head of the Stoic school] what is beautiful, what is base, what is useful and what is not (*quid sit pulchrum, quid turpe, quid utile, quid non*). If you have time, let me tell you why I think so.

That story about the collision between Greek and barbarian in a stubborn war over Paris' love is a study in the passions of foolish kings and peoples. Antenor wanted to remove the cause of war, Paris did not, refusing to be forced to live in happiness and safety! Nestor tried valiantly to settle the quarrel between Achilles and Agamemnon. The latter was fired by love, and both by anger—and when kings go mad, the people pay for it! So it was with the Achaeans. Inside the walls of Ilium and out, behold: sedition, treachery, criminal lust and wrath.

Homer offers us Ulysses' might as a useful model of courage and wisdom. This vanquisher of Troy prudently observed the ways and cities of many people. Not to be drowned in the waves of adversity, he endured many a hardship to bring his men and himself home across the broad sea. You remember those Siren voices and Circe's cups. Had Ulysses been like his comrades who drank from them in lustful folly, he would have become a base and witless slave of a harlot and lived the life of an unwashed dog or a mud-loving sow.

In comparison with him we are mere ciphers, born to consume, like the suitors of Penelope or Alcinoüs' lazy troupe, wasting time tending their complexions, sleeping through the day or dulling their wits in the drone of the cithara.

Thieves rise in the night to strangle a man. Won't you at least wake up to save your life? After all, if you won't run for healthy exercise, you will when you have the dropsy. If you don't call for a book and a lamp before daybreak and apply your mind to virtuous studies and matters (*si non / intendes animum studiis et rebus honestis*), you'll twist in envy—or lust—and still not sleep! You are quick to remove anything which hurts your eye, so why do you put off until next year the cure of your mind? "Begun's half done!" "Dare to be wise!" Begin now! Postponing the good life is like the bumpkin who waits for an ever-flowing river to run dry before crossing.

Because men want money and a rich wife to bear children, the untilled woods yield to the plow. "Want only what you need, no more!" A house and estate, a heap of bronze and gold never cooled the rich man's fever or took away care from the mind. One should only ponder how to use possessions properly. House and property no more cure anxiety than painted murals aid a sore eye, or pillows the gout, or lyres an ear infection. "Whatever you put in a rotten pot spoils."

Spurn foolish pleasures bought with pain. "The greedy man is forever a pauper." Limit your desires. "A prosperous neighbor makes the envious man grow thin." Not even Sicilian tyrants could devise tortures greater than envy.

The man quick to anger will live to wish undone the works of his wrath as he forever rushes violently to gratify any hatred however small. "Anger is a passing madness." Control your mind or it will control you. Put it in reins, cast it in chains!

A trainer knows how to tame the tender neck and teach the horse to obey its rider. The great hound hunting in the wilds began his career as a pup yapping at stuffed stags in the farmyard. So, lad, drink in my words with a pure heart, give heed to your superiors. The pot will keep alive the same flavor with which it was first imbued. But whether you fall back or bravely push ahead—it's all the same to me. I don't wait for the sluggard or try to keep up with those who pass me by.

The appeal of this poem to the framers of the UVM motto is obvious. Admonitions to rise and shine, to burn the midnight oil over a book, to practise frugality and avoid envy, and especially to nurture the mind and character read like articles in the UVM Laws.[10] What is striking, however, is that although the third and final section of the poem is a scrapbook of traditional mottoes (intended by Horace as further proof of the utility of literature), the phrase *studiis et rebus honestis* is not among them. "Dedication to studies and honorable pursuits" (Lindsay's paraphrase[11]) and "Integrity in Theoretical and Practical Pursuits" (*The University of Vermont Officers' Handbook*, section 110.2) are attempts at turning the phrase into a motto. But in the very first years of the University, "studies and honorable pursuits" meant "literature," not only the Greek and Latin classics but any literature whose "rereading" was useful (in effect, Horace's definition of a classic at the beginning of the poem). Horace's argument for the utility of literature is made against the time-worn philosophic bias against poets, first expressed by Plato, on the grounds that poets, having no real knowledge, could not lead to virtue. Horace accepts the doctrine that knowledge leads to virtue but with equal confidence asserts that the literature of the great Classical poets brings that knowledge of the good necessary for virtuous action. With such convictions it is no wonder that UVM founded the first department of English literature in the country. It is interesting that the motto preserves Horace's dative case. A facile paraphrase to something like *Studia Honesta* would have obscured the source of the motto, a poem studied sometime in their second or third year by all students at UVM during its first half-century or so.[12]

If Ira Allen, in promoting the cause of "useful" education, may have wished to play down the ancient languages, Daniel Clarke Sanders grounded the curriculum on the Classics and in both motto and curriculum kept Horace as a champion of their *utility*. Although that curriculum would expand and develop in many ways, the concept of utility would continue as a major force in shaping it throughout the nineteenth century. The Horatian origin is even reasserted much later in the round seal incorporating the State Agricultural College. Just as Sanders's oval seal contained a globe between a drawing of the Pythagorean proposition and a quadrant, with a sun beginning to rise over the green mountains—all symbols of the early-rising students of practical and classical learning at UVM—so the later seal displays a shield (symbolic of a book) surmounted by a lamp. The lamp and book allude to the context of the UVM motto: "Rise before daybreak, call for a lamp and a book and turn your mind to *studiis et rebus honestis*."

The arrival in 1826 of James Marsh as president, with his interest in the philosophy of Kant and Coleridge and his role in the American Transcendentalist movement, marked a new turn in the UVM curriculum. Later, President John Wheeler looked back with enthusiasm on the revision of the curriculum undertaken by the faculty under Marsh's aegis.[13] The first result of the revision was the adoption and publication in 1827 of a system of bylaws and a modified course of "Collegiate Study," followed by an "Exposition of the System of Instruction and Discipline Pursued in the University of Vermont," which showed in a tabular synopsis what students had to cover. Wheeler claimed that the course of study was taken mainly from Harvard's and was "as extensive as in any of the New England Colleges"; he cited specifically the addition at UVM of chemistry and anatomy, "which were not usual in the other colleges."

Marsh set up four principal divisions, or "departments," of a "course of Collegiate Study" that was set forth in the Laws of the University: "first the department of English Literature, second, the department of Languages, third, that of the Mathematics and Physics; fourth, that of Political, Moral, and Intellectual Philosophy." Wheeler touted this Marsh curriculum as having "what no other course of collegiate study in the United States [had] so fully attempted. . . . It seeks to give a coherence to the various studies, in each department so that its several parts shall present, more or less, the unity, not of an aggregation, nor of a juxtaposition, nor of a merely logical arrangement, but of a natural development, and a growth; and therefore the study of it, rightly pursued, would be a growing and enlarging process, to the mind of the student." The four departments "should have a coherence, of greater or less practical use, with each other." Philosophy,

the highest department, . . . should be now the oscillating nerve, that should connect the various studies together, during the analytical instruction in each; . . . In Philosophy, the course began with crystallography—the lowest form of organization [the science of the forms, properties, and structure of crystals]—then the laws of vegetable life, as the next highest; to the laws of animal life, that is, to Physiology, as the next; thence to Psychology, and the connection of the senses with the intellect; thence to the science of logic . . . that is the laws of Universal thought as seen in language and grammar; and thence to metaphysics, as the highest and the last form of speculative reasoning, or of contemplation.[14]

Marsh found an able and cooperative faculty at UVM. George Wyllys Benedict had been appointed professor of mathematics and natural philosophy in 1825. The immediate addition of chemistry to his teaching duties increased his salary from $600 to $800. Writing to his brother Abner, Benedict offered a glimpse of his teaching: "I lectured 6 times a week on chemistry for 8 weeks and 12 times a week for 2 weeks more. Each lecture I had to prepare for in the Laboratory, besides making out the notes for the lectures. All this besides 2 recitations a day. I was completely *worn out*."[15] In another letter he advises Abner on lecturing: no more than forty minutes for the lecture except when it must be accompanied by an unusual number of experiments:

I made it my rule to exhibit before my class, as far as practicable, not only the experiment which was to prove a point, but the preparation for the expt. I endeavored also to illustrate the expt. with great plainness—recapitulating where there was the least chance of their misapprehending it. . . . On all subjects I pursued a strict *method,* and so far as I could according to the nature of the subject, I had a *similar* method through the whole.[16]

He mentions the few dollars he earned by eight lectures on a "popular subject," electricity, and two on "Galvanism" (study of electrical currents, named after Luigi Galvani, 1737–1798) before the "gentlemen & ladies" of the village, and he describes the "grand" electrical apparatus he had made during his vacation.[17] He had also had time, in 1826, to found a discussion society, the College of Natural History, with an initial membership of ninety people from the community and the University, which indicated the enthusiasm for science in the same period when Classics flourished at UVM.[18]

But Benedict's own interests were clearly not confined to science. He was chagrined by the resignation of William Augustus Porter as professor of languages. Soon afterward, as secretary of the corporation he wrote the letter of election to Rev. Joseph Torrey of Royalton as "Professor of Languages and Belletres" (sic) at a salary of $650. When James Marsh died in 1842, Torrey succeeded to the chair as professor of intellectual and moral philosophy. A scholar of Greek, Latin, German, fine arts, and English literature, Torrey had become a Classicist in the new interdisciplinary sense. Among some seven thousand volumes he purchased on his European trip in 1835 was Karl Ottfried Müller's 1833 edition of Aeschylus' *Eumenides*.[19] This work, treating the play as a phenomenon of ancient society, religion, music, and dance, can claim as much as any other single scholarly work to have transformed the study of Classics. Torrey's formation of the Phi Beta Kappa chapter at UVM in 1844 and his later service as president, 1862 to 1866, helped assure the Classical tradition in a period of pressure for the creation of "practical" courses of study, especially in agriculture.

Wheeler's description of the concept of intellectual growth in the Marsh curriculum is clear in its tabular form (see illustrations showing curricula and class schedules for 1835 and 1843). Note that in 1835, along with further work in Latin and Greek syntax and prosody, primarily historical authors are read in the first year, Homer and the orators in the second, and mostly lyric and dramatic authors in the third. In the fourth year, the culmination of the curriculum in philosophy, it is not surprising to find Plato, Aristotle, and Cicero. In the first year, mathematics courses taught the fundamentals of algebra and geometry, proceeding in the second year to calculus and such applied fields as surveying and navigation; in the third, to mechanical engineering, chemistry, and electricity; and in the fourth, to a review of algebra and calculus along with physics and astronomy. Lectures in history are first indicated in the second year and English literature in the third. There were special lectures on various topics as well as individual instruction in various modern languages and in Hebrew. A central part of every student's work was the preparation of declamations on topics of one's choice.

By 1840 a few minor changes had been introduced: mechanical philosophy, the course of the third-year fall afternoon class, was changed to two months of "statics" and two months of "dynamics." Two more months of Greek drama were added, displacing a month of Greek lyric and physiology. Another month of optics was added in the third-year summer term, and crystallography was put off until the beginning of the fourth year. The two months of "Plato, Aristotle, Lord Bacon" became simply one month of "Science and Logic." Among lectures and other exercises, "Latin and Greek twice a week through the year" is added in lieu of any regular class in the ancient languages in the last year.

An important innovation of 1843 was the division of the year into three terms: autumnal (ending on the first Wednesday of December), spring (ending on the second Wednesday of May), and summer (ending on the first Wednesday of August, Commencement Day). Another change was the addition of an eleven o'clock course, which may have made possible the temporary inclusion of French among the regular courses.

The 1851 catalog lists "private classes . . . in French, German, Italian, Spanish and Hebrew, under the general direction of the Professor of Languages," probably referring to the future president Calvin Pease, who knew Italian and German and in his diaries mentions teaching French. In 1854 French returns to its regular two-month slot in the second year, and the catalog states, "Instruction will be given during the second and third years, in the French and German Languages, by Prof. Erni" (the Swiss professor of chemistry, who must have been the first native speaker to teach modern languages at UVM).

When Calvin Pease became president in 1856, he offered a spirited defense of Classics (among which he included "comparative Philology"), mathematics, and philosophy (i.e., what he called the "old curriculum,") and confronted some of the issues that are still debated today. He distinguished between "popular science" and "an under-lying [*sic*] science" of which the former was a "fruit," and he disputed "the matter of doubt with some speculators on the subject, whether the *usefulness* [italics added] of the whole system of collegiate training has not had its day; and whether the wide diffusion of knowledge which now exists may not justify an essential modification of the system, and perhaps its entire abandonment."[20] In 1860 Pease noted in his diary,

The theory of collegiate study needs a strong and clear restatement [because of the] multifarious forms in which modern science, by which I mean natural science, are crowding their claims, and there is a very strong, but unthoughtful sentiment prevailing in admitting them into the places formerly, and in most colleges still, held by the classics. . . . They can never be a *useful* [italics added] substitute for the classics, mathematics, and philosophy, as these entered into the curriculum of Studies in New England Colleges at the beginning. The attempt to introduce mere Studies of that kind in the Curriculum of this University has impaired it materially. Nothing of much value is accomplished by the change, and much that's valuable has been neglected. I am glad to see a prospect of a return to the former ideas.[21]

In 1861, to cure the UVM deficit the corporation voted salary reductions of $200 each for professors and of $250 for President Pease and Professor Torrey. They abolished the chair of chemistry and geology and dispensed with Professor Edward Hungerford. The salary of the treasurer was also reduced. With these actions the Board stated its priorities: "If departments were to be eliminated, it was recommended that the last chairs to be vacated should be those of Moral and Intellectual Philosophy, Latin and English Literature, Greek Language and Literature, and Mathematics."[22]

Nevertheless, unhappy with the new curricular pressures, and convinced of the hostility of the Trustees,[23] Pease resigned in December 1861. What he had feared threatened to become a reality when Congress passed the Morrill Act in 1862 and the Vermont Legislature established the State Agricultural College in 1865, at a time when UVM already suffered low morale, fiscal weakness, and intellectual strife. President Angell, noting the demand for education for students with different preparation and interests, reaffirmed the traditional balance in the UVM curriculum, "thus meeting at once the classical and scientific wants of the age."[24] In 1866 Greek composition was dropped from the regular courses (it reappeared in 1871, melded with Cicero!), and four months of French were added in the second year and four months of German in the fourth year (changed in 1871 to eight months in the third year). The catalog's list of classics in French and German was expanded, though neither was as long as in those of the Greek and Latin authors.

As though an omen of the change that the College of Agriculture would bring to the University, a venerable tradition was broken in the year 1868: Juvenal displaced Horace from the pre-breakfast class in the first two months of the autumnal term of the third year. Horace was moved to the afternoon of the second year, sharing the spot with the *Odyssey*. In 1870 there was a further alteration: Horace, the very Horace so skeptical of the rhetoricians in *Epistles* I. 2, had to share class time for three months of the second year with that schoolmaster of rhetoric, Quintilian!

If Horace's new location was merely symbolic, the "Synopsis of the Course of Recitations and Lectures" of 1866–1867 showed a remarkable change. The curriculum whose evolution we have traced was said to belong to the "Academical Departments." The creation of the State Agricultural College as a part of UVM meant the establishment of parallel curricula with different admissions requirements. By the time Angell left in 1871, the catalog listed civil engineering, metallurgy and mining engineering, chemistry, and agriculture, leading to the bachelor of philosophy degree. Students might "pursue select courses without becoming candidates for a degree," a provision that allowed them to take courses with those seeking the bachelor of arts. All of the scientific programs included both French and German, a course in rhetoric, and exercises in rhetoric and English literature during the "whole of each course." Also described are the laboratory course and a "Course of Lectures for Farmers." The latter, open for a special fee, may have been an incipient agricultural extension service. The admission statement of the new agricultural and scientific "department" read: "Applicants for admission to this department must be at least fifteen years of age, and must bring satisfactory testimonials of good character, and be able to sustain an examination in all parts of a common school education, and particularly in English Grammar, Geography, Arithmetic, Algebra through Quadratic Equations, and in plane Geometry."

In 1872 there were three synopses of the curriculum, one each for the "Academical, Agricultural, and Engineering Department[s]." Agriculture and engineering still specified French and German, and the "academical" departments also included Greek and Latin. But what is most striking is the absence from the "academical" curriculum of the many courses formerly required in applied mathematics, geometry, and science. Algebra, geometry, botany, chemistry, calculus, physics, zoology, geology, and a bit of optics are crammed together with German into one month and still required of all, but gone are surveying, navigation, and civil engineering and the two months of optics.

In 1873 the "academical" course shown in the catalog is divided into five "sections": Rhetoric and English Literature; Language; Mathematics; Natural Sciences; Political, Moral and Intellectual Philosophy. The admission statement still required the fundamentals of arithmetic, algebra, geography, English, Greek and Latin grammar, and a wide reading in Greek and Latin authors.

Terminology again changes in the catalog of 1875, whose "General Statement" notes that instruction at UVM is in

three different Departments, viz:—The Department of Arts [the future College of Arts and Sciences]. The Department of Applied Science. The Department of Medicine. The first of these comprises the usual Academical Course in Languages, Mathematics, Physical Sciences, Philosophy, Rhetoric, Literature and History. The second is subdivided into Courses in Agriculture and related branches, Chemistry, Engineering, and Mining. . . . Students have full liberty to elect their course; but beyond this, options are not allowed to those who may be candidates for a degree, except that, to a limited extent, equivalent substitutions may be made by express permission of the Faculty. . . . All candidates for a Degree, except that of M.D., are alike required to pursue the regular Academic Course in Rhetoric and English Literature.

This important passage marks the entrance of the notion of optional courses at UVM. The statement seems not quite adequate to the problem because the separate admission requirements for the agricultural and engineering curricula would have left those students unprepared for the courses in ancient languages. But many of the courses in science, mathematics, rhetoric, and English literature were intended to be taken in common by students from all of the divisions. The decision to admit women in 1873 was not, for the time being, reflected in any curricular changes.

Admissions played a very important role in the reorganization of the University. The catalog of 1873 contains "Examination Papers" (entrance examinations) in geography, English grammar, arithmetic, algebra, Latin, and Greek. It is interesting that there are separate sets of questions in arithmetic and algebra for the "Classical Division" and the "Scientific Division," the questions in the latter being distinctly of a more practical nature.

By the last quarter of the nineteenth century the curriculum at UVM was basically set as it would remain through the next seventy-five years or so. If the "traditional" curriculum may look to some like a dream "core curriculum," this appearance was not by accident but by the design of a faculty still under the influence of the Transcendentalist James Marsh. The curriculum, for all of its particular changes, still strove to give the student a solid grounding in both cultural and natural history.

The "core" began to disintegrate with the addition of the College of Agriculture. That disintegration represented, in a way that can be appreciated only in hindsight, a severe challenge to the principle of the utility of the "academical" course implicit in the motto of the University. In the common view, utility had fled to the new departments of applied sciences; the Classics, of whose utility UVM and Horace had long boasted, acquired once again the aura of impracticality with which they had been wrapped by Ira Allen. In his inaugural address in 1871, President Matthew Buckham, a sometime professor of Greek, alluded to this pejorative connotation of the Classics and rephrased the Sanders–Marsh tradition of a comprehensive Classical and scientific curriculum: "We aim to inbreed in the scientific student the feeling and aspiration of scholarship, and to counteract the dreamy dilettante spirit of literary studies by the realistic spirit of science."[25] The negative attitude toward the utility of the Classics that Buckham sought to counter contrasts sharply with the spirit that led to the dedication of the window to George Wyllys Benedict in the former chapel, now the John Dewey Lounge. The inscription there alludes both to the more comprehensive view of utility of the earlier UVM years and to the spirit of the school motto: *Recti Pervicax Georgius Wyllys Benedict Prof:* MDCCCXXV–XLVII *constans adversus metus utilium sagax rerum* [G.W.B., Prof. 1825–47, firm in the right, constant against fear (Tacitus, *Histories*, 4.5), wise in the useful (Horace, *Art of Poetry* 218)].[26]

Concern about sufficient enrollments for the scientific curriculum led the University to try to counter the sense of division among its departments. The Trustees reported in 1876:

It has been asserted that farmers' sons, or young men studying agricultural science in a University, side by side with others pursuing classical or literary studies, will be under a sort of ban of inferiority. Nothing could be more absurd than such a notion, at least as regards this University, in which a large number of the students are and have always been Farmers' sons, and in which a democratic equality prevails to a degree unknown to the outside world. . . . It is to be noted, also that we have not here an independent Agricultural College by the side of another Institution, but one University of which all the students are alike members, those belonging to its different departments often reciting in the same classes, and all sharing its privileges and honors according to their merits without invidious distinctions.[27]

Despite such advertising, in fact there was no enrollment yet in the College of Agriculture! If the classicist Buckham appears to falter in his confidence in the traditional curriculum, it was because of an increasing sense that the University was not merely in but *of* Vermont. The crippling effect of the Civil War on the enrollment and the need for effectively trained people to labor in the booming, industrializing nation left the tiny and poorly tended institution feeling uncertain about its purpose. But as we have seen, it took more than two decades to stabilize the relationship between the University and the College of Agriculture.

As the partition widened in the structure of the curriculum, the catalog became increasingly explicit in describing the courses of study for the Department of Arts, in which five divisions of study were elaborated in 1878. In the first, rhetoric and English literature, one feature is the "general rhetorical exercise" held in the chapel every Wednesday afternoon (in 1886 every Saturday morning), "at which the members of the Junior and Senior Classes are required to present original declamations. One oration for presentation in public is also required each year after the first." In the second area, languages, there were two sections: Greek and Latin, and modern languages. In the study of the ancient languages, "effort is made to consider each author read in his relations both to the history of his own time and to general literature. Along with the customary oral recitation of passages specially prepared, written translations and translations at sight are frequently required. Some attention is given to the comparison of these languages with each other and with the modern languages studied in the University. . . . Recitations are had also in Greek and Roman history." Whereas the catalog of 1878 speaks of both oral and written work in modern languages, that of 1880 suggests a return to the model of instruction in the ancient languages, with primary focus on reading.

In 1885 a remarkable innovation appeared: the announcement of The Sauveur School of Languages, a summer session attended by more than four hundred students from all parts of the United States and from Canada. "Instruction was given by what is known as the 'Sauveur' or 'Natural' method in the French, German, Italian, Spanish, Latin, Greek, Hebrew and Sanskrit Languages, and by Lectures, in the literatures of the same." In 1886 this summer school became the Stäger School of Languages, intended to be located permanently in Burlington for "teachers and others" to put a summer vacation "to good account" by gaining instruction in modern languages from "accomplished native teachers."

The following year the catalog again revised the method of instruction in modern languages for the regular term: there would be "literal translations and constant exercises, oral and written. . . . Constant attention is paid to conversation; and for this purpose the 'Meisterschaft' system is recommended, though the 'natural method' is not pursued at the expense of a completer knowledge of the language." It is clear that there were differences of opinion abroad about the best approach to the study of foreign languages. UVM's philological and literary approach to the Classics, which had clearly impressed itself on the teaching of modern languages, was working out an accommodation with the so-called oral approach. There must have been considerable enthusiasm for modern languages in this period. Three women of the class of 1889 studied languages abroad in their senior year: Ella Evarts Atwater, A.B.; Emma Mary Chandler, Ph.B.; and Isabella Midler Chandler, Ph.B. The list of authors read in German and French had grown considerably by that time.

In contrast with the developments in languages, there were few in mathematics or in natural science during the 1870s and 1880s. In the pinnacle division, Political, Moral, and Intellectual Philosophy (in two parts: 1. Political and Social Philosophy; 2. Mental and Moral Philosophy), there are also few changes. One entrenched textbook was the published lectures *The Theory of Fine Art* by the "late" Professor Joseph Torrey, UVM's answer to Matthew Arnold, John Ruskin, and Walter Pater. The very title anticipates John Dewey's *Art as Experience*. As an evangelist of independent thought, Dewey was well served by his teachers, Goodrich in Classics, Buckham with his Socratic method, and H. A. P. Torrey in philosophy. The catalog of 1879, Dewey's class year, concludes the description of this division with words altogether characteristic of Dewey's own philosophy of education: "The student is encouraged to raise questions and to present difficulties, and the aim of instruction is not so much to impart a system, as to stimulate and guide philosophical inquiry."

In the 1885 catalog the "Literary-Scientific Course" was presented in tabular form for the first time. Those who did not pursue Greek were provided additional exercises in Latin and English, and certain students in the sciences might follow this literary-scientific course. In 1889 such students were also provided French and German.

By 1889 the Department of Arts had been increased to six divisions by splitting philosophy into "Political Science and History" and "Moral and Intellectual Philosophy." The general description of courses in that year's catalog was much more elaborate, and a precise list of authors and works was added for each course (e.g., for the third term: "Latin: Horace, Satires and Epistles, 4 times a week, Professor Goodrich"). The following year there was a complete revision of the curriculum in the "Course in Liberal Arts." The seven divisions no longer reflected the culmination of study in philosophy, the heart and soul of the Marsh curriculum; they were listed in the following order: (1) social and political science, (2) moral and intellectual philosophy, (3) languages, (4) mathematics, (5) history, (6) natural science, (7) rhetoric and English literature. Social and political science met three hours weekly in the second half of the junior year and two hours weekly during the whole senior year. The course was required of all students in the "Classical Department," optional in civil engineering and chemistry. In the last half of the senior year it was devoted to the study of the Constitution of the United States. Philosophy also was required in the junior and senior years and dealt with the history of philosophy as well as psychology, "theism," ethics, metaphysics, and fine art (the last two being elective). Greek and Latin were required in the freshman year but were elective in the sophomore year for those who passed the freshman examinations. In the sophomore year, Horace's *Epistles* were still read! French I or German I was required of sophomores. Freshmen were required to take mathematics and, in the division of natural science, physiology (a series of talks on personal hygiene). Classical, medieval, and modern history were required in the sophomore year and an elective course, "Reformation and Revolution" in junior and senior years. English rhetoric and composition were required in the first year and a half, English literature in the remaining years.

By this time UVM had entered the era of the elective college course. The catalog of 1890 reflects some discomfort with the concept under a discussion of "Elective and Required Studies": "The abuse to which a system of perfectly free optionals is liable is avoided by the requirement of a course which secures a certain degree of completeness and symmetry of discipline, while the number of electives permitted gives room for the development of special talents and the following out of individual predilections." That catalog was the first to state that students omitting Greek and taking additional work in Latin, English, French, German, and "certain of the sciences" would earn the degree of "Bachelor of Philosophy," earlier designed for students in engineering. The evolution of the originally innovative curriculum from "traditional" to "modern" had taken place.

A dramatic illustration of the ties between the University and the state during these years is the life of Roswell Farnham, an elective trustee of UVM and member of the State Board of Education, who in 1880 was elected governor of Vermont by 25,012 votes, the second-largest majority to that time in the history of the state. Farnham was born in Boston in 1827 and raised in Bradford, Vermont. Lacking funds to enter college, he remained at Bradford Academy to complete the first two years of the UVM course of study and did not enter the college until 1847, as a junior. He graduated in 1848, the last year of the presidency of John Wheeler, and was clearly a sterling product of Calvin Pease's "old curriculum." In his senior year Farnham kept a personal journal,[28] showing a man of serious scholarship; a member of Lambda Iota, a literary society devoted to Minerva (hence, the "Owls"); a man whose religious sincerity did not prevent him from appreciating the fair young women to be observed in church on Sundays; and a student not untouched by a tendency to rowdyism (consisting of late-night dancing to the fiddle). Farnham's journal also helps flesh out the meaning of the courses listed in the catalog.

This typical entry gives the schedule of a student's day:

Today [October, 20, 1848] has been one of a great many rainy, cold, disagreeable days of which we have had any quantity this fall. As a matter of course, the bell roused me before sun-rise this morning to go into prayers, though I failed of getting up until it began to toll. Immediately after prayers we have a lesson in Psychology which lasts until breakfast. Our next lesson is not until an hour before sunset. Today we finished Astronomy, in which we have been writing to [i.e., taught by] Proff. F. N. [Farrand N.] Benedict otherwise Little Ben. Our next study is to be "central forces," which I have had the pleasure of copying. From morning until afternoon recitation we study, read, write, or anything we choose. In the evening we do the same. . . . Every day is the same. One is so like another that I cannot tell them apart when I look back and endeavour to remember some particular circumstance . . . so I hope a description of one will suffice for the whole.

There is no doubt about the substance of Farnham's learning. His polished translation of Aristophanes' *Clouds* exists in manuscript, allegedly translated by a certain "Heliogarbalus" and, as a note on the back of the final page indicates with humor, read as a "tragedy" to Professor Calvin Pease in the spring term of 1848 by the entire junior class (whose members are then listed).

Like Erastus Root and many other undergraduates, Farnham made ends meet by teaching in a common school in Burlington.[29] In this activity began an important relationship of UVM with the community and state, even before the problems posed to the University by the Morrill Act, for these young teachers were disseminating the UVM philosophy of education throughout Vermont. Both Root and Farnham leave in their diaries frequent and often poignant notes on their work in the common schools. After graduation, Farnham continued to teach, for a while in Dunham in Lower Canada (now Quebec) and then as head of the Franklin Academical Institution in Franklin, Vermont. Later he taught at the Bradford Academy before turning to law and politics.

Farnham's unpublished inaugural address as head of the Franklin Academical Institution is interesting testimony both to the philosophical unity of the Marsh curriculum at UVM and to the evangelical spirit with which it was promoted in the primarily privately funded academies (as distinct from the district schools) of Vermont.[30] With a prose whose purple could only be described as "viridimontane," Farnham explains the "practical utility" of every discipline in the academies: algebra, geometry, surveying, grammar, declamation and public speaking, botany, astronomy, fine arts, mental philosophy. The academy in the abstract—whether the privately funded high schools or the colleges and universities—becomes the primary inspiration of not just a very few but of everyman:

The farmer at home, the mechanic in our cities, the gold-digger in California, the Green Mountain Boy everywhere is acting under the influence of principles and habits instilled into his mind at home and modified by his teachers at school. The dying Hero, upon the battle field of Mexico, lying on the bank of a stream polluted by his own and the blood of his countrymen, as he lifts the reddened flood to his lips, thinks of the cool streams that flow down the shady glens in Vermont, thinks of the precepts of his mother, and, as dizzy and faint from the flow of life's purple current he lies down to die in a distant land, the death ring in his ears mocks him for the moment, and he listens to catch the distant tolling of the Academy Bell: Alas: that he shall hear nevermore—it is the knell that is calling him fast to Eternity.

The "school spirit" and even the sense of pathos in the rhetorical crescendo of this peroration are foreshadowed in Farnham's first day's entry in his student journal at UVM:

We are fifteen only, for there have been proscriptions, and sickness and various other causalities that have cut us down to our present pitiful remnant of a class. We have been proscribed on various slanderous accusations, such as drunkeness [sic], laziness, horn-blowing, "magna pars fui," etc. etc.: yet the spirit of the class is not the whit the less. Hence as a matter of course the individual spirit of each one is increased in a direct ratio as the class is diminished.

If there is yet one unbroken tradition at UVM, it is the energy with which the faculty of many departments, including Classics, have attempted to serve collegially with teachers in the secondary schools of Vermont. Though the University was tiny in Farnham's college days, the philosophy of education it represented was widespread in the state. It was thus that he was able to complete the first two years of the UVM curriculum under the sole tutelage of a teacher at Bradford Academy and thus that Erastus Root could complete the first year's work under Jason Chamberlain before the latter's call to UVM. So today, at both the institutional and individual levels, there is an effort to coordinate the curricula of the secondary schools with that of the University. Because the University has actually grown much more than the state's population has in the last one hundred years (a factor of about 80 for the University, against less than 2 for the state), this policy of cooperation is both sound and possible.

All things change. A curriculum changes. But change is not death. The nineteenth-century UVM curriculum survives in some respects even today. Few universities have such strong entrance and graduation requirements in foreign languages, and UVM is still widely known for its Classical studies. The division of opinion that underlay the development of the nineteenth-century curriculum also has survived. Although UVM continued to require Latin and Greek for the B.A. degree until the early 1940s, the establishment of other colleges within the University has perpetuated some of the division between humanistic and scientific or between theoretical and practical courses of study which characterized the last quarter of the nineteenth century at UVM. In the ongoing debate on the nature of the curriculum, "innovative," "interdisciplinary," and "relevant" are terms used frequently to justify change. It gives one pause to consider how the term "useful" seems to have preempted "relevant" in the construction of the very innovative and interdisciplinary curriculum of UVM in the nineteenth century. And it inspires respect that the truly useful was sought not in the passing and topical but in the very fundamentals of knowledge, *studiis et rebus honestis*.

President Matthew Buckham and the
University of Vermont

T. D. SEYMOUR BASSETT

MATT walked to the bow of the Cunarder that late summer day in 1854 and scanned Liverpool harbor. A cold, misty rain mixed with the smoke of the tugboats softened the starkness of the docks in the early morning light. To the average American recently graduated from college, the seaport would have presented an unfriendly face, but not to Matthew Henry Buckham. A native of Leicestershire, son of a Scottish dissenting minister who named him after one of his favorite Puritan divines,[1] he was glowing with anticipation at the chance to taste imperial Britain, rise a notch above his competitors by acquiring more European culture through study and travel, and discover his own roots.

Born on the Fourth of July, 1832, Matthew Buckham had come to America as an infant and moved with his family as his father, the Reverend James Buckham, served Congregational churches and ran private schools in Chelsea, Vermont; Ellington, Connecticut; and nearby parts of Quebec.[2] When Matthew was ready for college at fifteen, his father moved to the Congregational mission in Winooski so that his sons could live at home and attend the University of Vermont. As a frugal parson's boy, Matt walked between his father's house and classes and so did not participate in dormitory life. During vacations he taught school. His aloof bearing concealed warmth within once you got to know him, as his brothers in Sigma Phi did. His senior year, they helped him to the post of delivering the address at the "burial of June training," an annual spoof of the militia. Those who recalled him as student, tutor, or professor and had negative reactions did not specify; perhaps they thought of him only as a strict grammarian in Classics and English literature.[3]

By 1854, when he returned to England, Buckham had already discovered his vocation, to be a college professor, and was looking forward to completing his preparation for it at University College, London. Though second youngest in a class of nineteen at UVM, he was graduated as valedictorian in 1851 and then taught for two years at Lenox Academy in the Berkshires. He knew, after another year as tutor at his alma mater, that he liked teaching, even as drillmaster on the lowest rung of the academic ladder. He had saved enough as a bachelor schoolmaster and tutor to afford a year or two abroad, with the family safety net under him. This put him in the vanguard of a growing stream of Americans who chose to prepare themselves in the sciences and letters by study abroad.

Buckham carried a letter of introduction to Dr. John Hoppus, his father's classmate at Rotherham, an Independent (Congregationalist) college. Hoppus, he wrote to his father, supported "the same doctrines . . . which we were taught" at UVM.[4] Oxford and Cambridge universities were virtually closed to Dissenters and Roman Catholics, because of their religious tests, until the Tests Act of 1871. On the other hand, the University of London, founded through the influence of Lord Brougham and James Mill, was a haven for Dissenters. Hoppus was appointed its first professor of philosophy of mind and logic in 1829.

At UVM, Buckham had a patron in the person of Calvin Pease, who had taught Greek and Latin there since 1842 and had functioned as president de facto when illness kept President Worthington Smith at his home in St. Albans. Probably Buckham had an oral understanding that if he studied Classics in London, he would be the leading candidate for the Classics post at UVM if Pease officially became president. The practice of sending a man to study in Europe after assuring him of an appointment had been well established ever since Yale's president, Timothy Dwight, appointed Benjamin Silliman professor of chemistry in 1802 and then sent him to Edinburgh to acquire the requisite competence. Buckham's future was not yet so firm when he embarked because the UVM trustees had demurred at President Smith's request to resign in June 1854 and left him nominally in charge until November 1855, when they elected Pease as his successor. Whatever happened at UVM, Buckham knew that when he finished his "graduate work" he would be a superior candidate to teach Latin and Greek almost anywhere in the United States.

Buckham's professional career unfolded according to his hopes, although his family life had its difficulties. He returned to a classics professorship at UVM, and after his probationary year his father married him to Elizabeth Wright of Shoreham, a relative of Vermont Congressman Charles Rich and of John Dewey. By the 1860s his father was living in the next house east of the Allen House on Main Street, with a garden connected to Matthew's house on Tuttle (now South Prospect) Street. In 1862, along with the rest of the faculty, Buckham accepted a $200 cut and agreed to stay and carry the University "through to a permanent success," although he probably had better immediate opportunities elsewhere.[5] He had to dismiss their servant, which left his wife with a household of little children—she had five in a decade. As president's wife from 1871, Elizabeth Wright Buckham was an invalid much of the time; she died August 24, 1886.[6] The children remembered their father's thoughtful care. He read to the whole family on Sunday afternoons from John Bunyan's *Pilgrim's Progress* in the sitting room on the sunny second floor, hid nuts and candies behind the sofa of his large library-study, and took them on annual excursions to Malletts Bay.[7] Family reticence and the state of nineteenth-century health science conceal the nature of Mrs. Buckham's illness. President Buckham bore his burden privately and alone.

Did Buckham conceive of the possibility of a college presidency, which turned out to be his life work, much more so than teaching? His two-year cosmopolitan interlude, including travel on the Continent, contributed to his eligibility, but the choice was mainly circumstantial. When President Angell left in 1871, Buckham was there, able and willing. He was a loyal alumnus and a loyal member of the faculty with fifteen years' experience; he was already active in city and state educational affairs, well connected throughout the Congregational Conference, and willing to deal with difficult problems. He had served as Burlington superintendent of schools (1866–1867) and as a member of the State Board of Education (1867–1874). The scientific and technical goals of the State Agricultural College would have to be melded with the Classical goals of the original university. The admission of women, determined at the same commencement at which Buckham was inaugurated, had to be effected. Angell's enthusiasm had put the college back on its feet, after he found it lying wounded by the loss of students who enlisted in the Civil War and by the dropouts who preferred moneymaking to college studies. The University's shaky condition, however, would not attract a large flock of candidates for the presidency.

No one could foresee that nearly forty years after Buckham's inauguration in August 1871 he would still be president, virtually identified with the institution. So the eulogists at President Buckham's funeral in December 1910 echoed Emerson in saying, "He *was* UVM." But he was not the personification of the institution as hundreds of alumni had earlier thought James Marsh to be. He was the person who spoke for the University when he raised money among the alumni, when he marshaled the team that kept enemies from seducing the State College of Agriculture from its marriage to the old Classical college, and when he assured his alumni supporters that the curriculum was what James Marsh taught in the 1830s while increasing the emphasis on science, modern languages, the history of civilization, English literature, political economy, and other modern departures. He was, as his fraternity magazine said, "a man of today and ready for tomorrow, without having forgotten yesterday."[8]

The Discouraging Seventies

The alumni were amazed that little Matt, whom they had known too well as fellow student or teacher, had been chosen to succeed Angell. They considered President Angell an exception as a layman. Surely, the Trustees could have found some minister on the model of the first four successors of James Marsh, one with moneyed connections, willing to give up an urban parish to maintain the Marshian tradition against the modernizing trend of science and technology.

But the Trustees, who had been through a long selection process only a few years before and knew the slim field of availables, did not give any opposition to Buckham time to rally. Although there is no direct evidence that Angell chose his successor, the retiring president had watched Professor Buckham for six years and must have concluded that he had executive ability. Evidently, Buckham had already decided, for he took only five days after receipt of the Trustees' offer to accept. When the students and the Queen City Band serenaded him that evening and he just happened to have refreshments ready, he told them that their support, communicated to the corporation, had helped him toward his difficult decision. Angell, introducing Buckham at his inauguration in August 1871, asserted, "The students, the alumni, and the public have heartily expressed their approval," and the trustees were unanimous. Buckham's "friendship and counsels have been of . . . inestimable value to me," he added.[9]

Because Angell and Buckham lived on the same campus and could consult on university matters without leaving a paper trail, we cannot analyze Angell's assertion. Professor Buckham put the argument against Angell's moving to Michigan in providential terms: "Your course would be plain enough but for the state of things here, and this seems to me to present a *providential obstacle to your going anywhere.* . . . The most you can say is this: 'If God had not put me here, I should have thought He wanted me to go there—but now that he has sent me here, I cannot see any evidence that he releases me from the task he gave me to perform, now when it is not half done'."[10] Here spoke a man theologically and biblically educated by his reverend father but too modernist to risk being examined for ordination by neighboring clergy of more conservative beliefs.

In his letters to Angell during the year after his predecessor left UVM, President Buckham seemed to be seeking approval from a valued colleague for the changes they both favored: the terms of the admission of women, ways to deal with rowdyism, heating the president's house, shifting to gas lighting to keep the same recitation hours throughout the year, the terms of Angell's contract to landscape the front and back campuses, whether or not to dispense with the marking system, what could replace shallow Guizot as the basis for the president's history of civilization course. There seems to have been little contact after 1872, except when Buckham congratulated Angell on his 1880 appointment as ambassador to China. Did the controversy with Angell's brother-in-law, Peter Collier, cool the connection? [11]

At the end of his first year Buckham had already made two innovations. Two women had been admitted, and the long vacation had been shifted from winter to summer. When Professor Henry W. Haynes examined Ellen Eliza Hamilton in Greek for admission, Buckham wrote Angell, he found her "as good as the best we have." [12] Buckham explained the advantages of the new calendar to the trustees in 1872:

A long vacation in the summer months enables young men to earn more money and with greater advantage to their health than by teaching school in the long winter vacation, while the winter months are more valuable for . . . study. The wisdom of the changes has already become apparent. Every young man in College who needs to do so, has already found opportunity to labor at much better advantage than he could by teaching. This arrangement is especially favorable to members of the scientific classes, who readily find employment which is both remunerative and improving, in the practical departments of their chosen profession.

Women had been gradually taking over the profession of teaching, and pay had declined. [13]

There were other consequences of the change in calendar: higher fuel bills from longer winter sessions, professors traveling or "camping" by the lakes and in the mountains in the summer. "I can't say that I enjoy, personally, this long summer vacation," Buckham wrote to Angell after the first summer. "It is too long for rest & recreation; next summer I think I shall lay out some work." [14] Among the "most pressing wants" he listed for the Trustees in 1875 were "better facilities for exercise in winter, especially a bowling alley." [15] In the 1880s Buckham put the idle campus to summer use by renting buildings to private language schools.

Modern student activities gradually bloomed under Buckham after the establishment of the fourth fraternity (Phi Delta Theta, 1879), the first sorority (Kappa Alpha Theta, 1881), *The University Cynic* (1883), and *The Ariel* in 1886. By the 1890s athletics and Greek life dominated student interests, with the vaudeville-like Kake Walk moving toward stage center to raise money for sports.

The images an institution presents to its alumni and to the world where the alumni live, to its community and its state, and the icons that symbolize those images are perhaps the most important "facts" about that institution. In his inaugural address Buckham promised to carry on the educational philosophy of James Marsh. Perhaps this cliché—I'm carrying on the tradition—is what they all say at the changing of the guard. But the president's close contemporary, Professor John E. Goodrich, affirmed this in his funeral eulogy. Buckham, he said, was "the last man active in college affairs who received and transmitted that earlier discipline . . . , an independent, vigorous, fruitful method." [16] Whatever it meant to the philosophers in terms of German and Coleridgean idealism, to generations of alumni it meant confidence that the new could be combined with the old. It meant modernist Protestantism, incorporating the findings of archaeology and the Higher Criticism into what Congregationalist Buckham felt was evangelical Christianity. It meant not worrying about the deterministic implications of Darwinian theory, leaving it to the professors of philosophy and natural history to claim that evolution and religion were compatible. It meant that there is a unity in life, and you discover its ramifications and connections at the university. The image of UVM as the place where James Marsh had been philosopher was not only the one that satisfied the alumni but the one that identified the University in the world of higher education.

Near the end, when Buckham came back from a summer's R & R abroad in 1910, unrefreshed but still facing forward, he tried to clarify this image for the returning students. UVM was always the state university, he claimed, never "Burlington College." Where colleges concentrate on liberal arts, universities (on the English rather than the German model, he said) combine liberal arts with professional schools. Our responsibilities are to the whole state and the whole broad span of learning. [17]

UVM had in fact been called Burlington College since its beginning, and in one real sense it was the city's college. The executive committee of the corporation was made up of local businessmen who in any emergency were ready to raise money among their colleagues or render an opinion for the hard-pressed president as to what the Board would probably favor when it met for its annual meeting at commencement. Local donors provided quick money for the dining hall (Wells, Richardson Company, manufacturers of patent medicines and aniline dyes) and for the first gymnasium or baseball cage on the back campus (Frank R. Wells, '93, of the same company). Town-gown tension, presumed to be a given in college towns, was virtually nonexistent except among the Democratic minority of Burlingtonians.

In 1871 the country was heading for a depression, putting the new president in a difficult position for solving the interlocking problems of public relations, finance, agriculture, and enrollment. Most immediate and hardest to solve was the question of the State Agricultural College. UVM had accepted the challenge of the Morrill Act when Middlebury and Norwich would neither take it nor share it, and the State Agricultural College was wedded to the old UVM in a unique dual corporation that was intended to reflect the philosophy that "the Aggies" were not attending a mere trade school. What Morrill wanted—and he was very vocal in saying what he wanted throughout his long and illustrious terms in the federal House and Senate—was to provide not only technical courses on farm machinery or plants and soils but also some appreciation of Vergil's *Eclogues* and *Georgics*, glorifying the pastoral life, and some understanding of the society and culture farmers live in.

The land grant colleges were expected to teach "mechanic arts" (i.e., technology) and military science as well as agriculture. Angell recruited Volney G. Barbour (Yale Ph.B., '67) to teach civil engineering, and UVM granted its first B.S. and C.E. degrees before Buckham took office. From Angell's time on, UVM sought West Point–trained officers or regulars with Civil War experience to drill the students. President Angell had difficulty persuading any of the eighteen eligible retired U.S. Army officers or a civil engineer with Civil War experience to take a UVM assignment. The executive committee even offered the salary of a professor of physics and civil engineering in addition to army pay. In 1867–1868, Captain Charles Ormsby French was secured to teach military tactics "nearly the whole year" as an experiment, according to Angell's 1868 report, "and doubtless contributed somewhat to insure us exemption from illness." In other words, Angell considered military drill a form of physical education and intended to alternate it with gymnastic drill. Charles Denison (Williams '67) is listed as gymnastics instructor for 1868–1869, but there were no others in either field until 1874. From 1874 on there was always a PMST (professor of military science and tactics) on campus, as called for in the Morrill Act.[18]

Some $8,000 in income from the Agricultural College fund helped to shield university finances against the depression of the 1870s, so by 1879 Buckham could report to the Trustees that the "outside debt" had been paid off, leaving "only" the borrowing from the scholarship fund. How had he done it? His Scotch thrift, doing without, accounted for most of the savings, as the depression dried up the sources that had provided $100,000 in Angell's fund drive of the prosperous 1860s. Salaries had not been raised. Buildings had not been repaired. Practically *no* books had been added since the library building was completed, during the early years of the Civil War, except free federal documents. However, Buckham did not cancel subscriptions to the expensive British quarterlies that John Dewey, for one, found so significant in his undergraduate years.

Continuing his quest for financial resources and sensing the approach of a fight over the State Agricultural College, Buckham reopened the old question of a merger with Middlebury College and/or Norwich University. In 1874 he wrote to one of the Middlebury trustees, ex-Governor John W. Stewart:

Can anything be done at this juncture to bring our two Institutions together? . . . [It is] my duty . . . to watch every opportunity for putting these two Institutions into such relations with each other, and with the common cause of education, as shall be for the greatest general good. If . . . any feasible plan either for uniting or differentiating the Colleges has occurred to you, . . . no advantage would be claimed on our side on account of the temporary depression of your circumstances.[19]

Nothing came of the Middlebury gambit, but Buckham meanwhile turned his sights on Norwich University, a financially struggling institution that had just relocated in Northfield, Vermont, after a disastrous fire in 1866.

He stated confidently in his 1876 report to the trustees that Norwich seemed about to close and that the board should therefore be ready to negotiate a merger of the residual property. Again, Buckham's expansionist ambition came to naught.

The first attempt to separate the new State Agricultural College from UVM was a compound of various resentments. Burlington's fight to be the state capital, after the State House fire in 1857, had created enemies. Burlington's size and steady growth outdistanced and antagonized other towns in the state, which were fearful of their life blood draining out through emigration. Rutland alone kept pace with Burlington, but it was not ready to make the large investment of capital necessary to maintain an agricultural college and receive a few thousand dollars a year from the federal endowment. UVM needed a demonstration farm to show Vermonters how scientific agriculture meant a better income, but for many years, in spite of Senator Morrill's urging, the University did nothing. Buckham thought he had two spokesmen to defend his stewardship of the State Agricultural College fund: George Perkins in natural history and Peter Collier in chemistry. Collier, supposed to be Buckham's spokesman on the State Board of Agriculture, became the Board's spokesman for the separation. However, after seven years the Patrons of Husbandry (the state Grange), the State Board of Agriculture, and Peter Collier lost the fight, and Collier was dismissed from the faculty.[20] The town–gown conflict of most colleges was a university–state tension in Vermont.

UVM's gain in enrollment over its in-state rivals reflected a new, utilitarian attitude toward higher education. When good jobs were scarce after 1873, many students chose college to prepare themselves for better jobs when times improved. Nationwide, young men (and a few women) were beginning to think of college not just as preparation for "the learned professions" but as a boost for a business career. Other women went to college either for a superior preparation for teaching or other occupations then open to women or to marry a college man; possibly some went because, like some men, they enjoyed study. Women had no other college to attend in Vermont and only Mount Holyoke, Elmira, Vassar, Smith, Wellesley, and Radcliffe in the northeast; still only nine graduated from UVM in the 1870s, and eight dropped out. There was a slight increase in the total number of graduates during the decade, from twelve in 1871 to eighteen in John Dewey's class (1879) and twenty in the class of 1880. Total enrollment, not counting the medical department, did not reach one hundred until 1884.

Expansion and Innovation, 1881–1895

Every historian of UVM, looking at Buckham's administration, has featured his monument in brick and stone. The bulk of the buildings were raised and paid for in a fifteen-year period, completely transforming the campus to serve the growing enrollment and more diverse activities. However, one looks in vain for a campus plan harmonizing the whole, like the one Frederic Law Olmsted prepared for the University of California at Berkeley. To those who preferred the early-nineteenth-century styles of Grassmount and the Wheeler House, College Row deserved Professor Frederick Tupper's quip about "the Seven Lumps of Architecture," which his generation would understand as a pun on the title of John Ruskin's 1849 book, *The Seven Lamps of Architecture.* Of the six buildings along University Place only the President's House, built in 1870 as a vain inducement to keep Angell from going to Michigan, had survived unchanged from Angell's time. Its stylish mansard roof was matched when Trenor W. Park, whose money came from a New York City department store and was multiplied in railroad management, gave UVM $10,000 to put a mansarded third floor on the library to create an art museum. Park (1823–1882), a legislative trustee in Angell's time (1865–1867), remained a potential donor but drew away into benefactions to other institutions.[21]

Then came John Purple Howard, who learned innkeeping from his father on the north side of City Hall Park in Burlington and then made a fortune with a hotel in New York City. In the early 1870s he gave UVM money for landscaping, including a flagpole that students chopped down; a fountain, still gracing the green; and a statue of General Lafayette by the popular sculptor John Quincy Adams Ward, on the College Street axis. Howard's major contribution came later—the modernization of the main college building, called "the Old Mill" by students since the 1840s. The old tin-roofed dome with a small cupola, probably designed by John Johnson in the Jeffersonian style of the early nineteenth century, had been a shining landmark for more than fifty years, identifying UVM to thousands. Now, breaking with the classical past, J. J. Randall of Rutland supplied plans to replace the dome with a high belfry (a "birdcage," students called it), peaked much like the lesser towers adorning the Hill residences of Burlington's affluent. More substantial improvements than this symbol of modernity were sixty furnished dormitory rooms on the upper two floors, with several water closets, and improved recitation and lecture rooms.[22] As with the Waterman Building later, bachelor professors (notably Nathan F. Merrill, who taught chemistry for some thirty years) were provided quarters to keep the lid on students and be accessible to them. The Old Mill thus became the original living/learning center.

The other four buildings on the Row were new in Buckham's era. On the site of Professor Petty's home, between the "old" library and the President's House, Frederick Billings of Woodstock, who made his money as a lawyer in the California gold rush and later in railroads, spent well over $100,000 for a Richardson-designed library "worthy of Oxford University," as Buckham said. It housed—first in the apse and then in a new wing to the east—more than twelve thousand volumes of the library of George Perkins Marsh, which Billings bought for UVM after direct negotiations with Marsh to acquire his library broke down. The main collection, with the remnants of the libraries of the defunct literary and religious societies, was spread out along the present North Lounge. On its completion, President Buckham reported to the Trustees that UVM was now in a class with Cornell, Yale, and Harvard. "Weaker" colleges like Middlebury and Norwich were no longer rivals. Just before he died in 1891, Billings gave another $50,000 to fill the shelves, and his widow gave more. Landscape architect Frederic Law Olmsted was paid $100 to mark the paths around the building—a pity he was not commissioned to design the whole campus.

The old library building was moved northward, back of the President's House, to serve as the museum and art gallery, with exhibits in natural history, Indian anthropology, and geology, plaster teaching models of great sculpture, and paintings. The president's son Charles, fresh from the architecture department of Columbia University, superintended the move and designed the mansard-roofed third story for the art gallery. The building, now known as Torrey Hall, houses the Pringle Herbarium. On the site of the old library, Wilson Brothers, a leading Philadelphia firm, designed a state-of-the-art science building with its own power plant and motifs echoing those on the Billings Library and the Old Mill on either side of it. The donor was Edward H. Williams of the Baldwin Locomotive Company of Philadelphia, who, although he was not a UVM alumnus, developed a loyalty to Vermont through his connection with the Williams family of Woodstock. In the 1960s Williams Science Hall was still deemed too sturdy and solid to tear down.

John Purple Howard had hinted that he would give a gymnasium and an observatory, but he died in 1883 with nothing in his will for UVM. Several other wealthy Burlington trustees, Buckham pointed out to the Board at the time, had died within a few years, and none had remembered their university.

In 1888, Buckham asked the Legislature for $20,000 to build the Justin Morrill Drill Hall (i.e., gymnasium), to be matched by private gifts, plus a dozen years' annual appropriations of $2,400 for senatorial scholarships and $3,600 for salaries of professors in the "industrial arts." He put the question, shall UVM be only nominally "a State institution" or should the State put its money where UVM's name was? The answer from the State was "Only nominally."[23] More than twenty classes had clamored for a gym before the early Christian basilica (now Royall Tyler Theater) rose just southeast of the Old Mill in 1900–1901, with a baseball cage attached to its eastern side a few years after. A contemporary committee asked the trustees for playing fields southeast of the Old Mill.

From early in the century the Johnson family, descended from the designer of the original college building, had lived in a house on the south end of the Row; the family sold the site for Morrill Hall, the first state-funded building. The president's son, Charles Wyman Buckham of New York City, designed it. (The original frame house was relocated and is now just above the tunnel on Williston Road.) The seventh campus "lump" was Converse Hall, in bluish gray marble, the first of a series of donations by John Heman Converse (UVM '61), president of Baldwin Locomotive.

Buckham's thrifty soul favored the recycling of buildings, not only in the case of the old library and the Old Mill but also of the old medical building (Pomeroy) and the Harry Bradley–Levi Underwood mansion, where the Dewey Building now stands, made over into a medical building. Grassmount, the private mansion of lumber tycoon and trustee Lawrence Barnes, became the first "girls'" dormitory in 1895. The president's want list that year included art and engineering buildings.

What Buckham built showed his practical priorities. Though he personally would have preferred a chapel, the first need was for an all-purpose, up-to-date Old Mill that would house more students and give them more classrooms and laboratories. Second priority was the very best library that money could buy. Then a temple of science, followed by a museum, with a balance of exhibits in science and art. Then a marble dormitory for the students attracted by a good library, a teaching museum, good laboratories, and good classrooms. Last, what the students wanted first, a gymnasium, and what the state wanted first, a center for agriculture. John Purple Howard would have given the money for a chapel, but Buckham never reached the chapel on his priority list, so he did the best he could by enlarging and beautifying the chapel in Old Mill.

The very eclecticism of the whole building program, the emphasis on decoration rather than on the plain Puritan simplicity of the age before 1840, and the opportunist placing of each individual building piece by piece rather than according to plan—all reflected the individualistic Gilded Age, the age of the robber barons. The principal donors—Howard, Billings, Converse, and Williams—represented the key industry of the age, railroads, together with their locomotives and hotels. Buckham was careful to procure icons, in portrait and bust, for each donor, whereas earlier heroes of the intellectual life, such as James Marsh, George Benedict, and Joseph Torrey, were memorialized in the chapel. Angell raised money for an endowed Marsh professorship in philosophy; Buckham found endowments for natural history, chemistry, and commerce and economics.

Buckham generally chose faculty in the humanities who were, if not trained theologians, at least pious believers and who taught "hard and tight thinking on the basis of premises not too skeptically questioned," according to Thomas Reed Powell. Whereas many under this discipline became rigid pedants, opposed to innovation, some long-term teachers, particularly H. A. P. Torrey, John Goodrich, and Samuel Emerson, "had the liberal temper that can face new views with calmness and can choose between the old and the new as reason and judgment dictate." Their acceptance of Darwinism probably kept them from full-time preaching, although they were always available to supply nearby pulpits and took their turns, of course, at college chapel. They did not present mere compiled information; they presented their point of view, to be discussed.[24] Each professor was married to his teaching, till death parted him from it. When President Benton asked his heads of departments in 1916 to share the responsibility for appointments and removals, Professor Tupper replied, "During President Buckham's administration a man was retained on the faculty long after his colleagues were convinced that he should be asked to resign because no member of the staff, through considerations of esprit de corps towards colleagues, felt free to suggest the removal." That was tenure!

Deep down inside Matthew Buckham was the hard core of the Classics. "The Dead Languages, Forsooth!" he titled one address. He had started out as a professor of Greek with a sideline of English literature. "A pity that the charm and culture and philosophic insight of President Buckham . . . were drafted from the work for which he was superbly qualified and turned to tasks which he did less well"—teaching political science and economics— wrote Thomas Reed Powell.[25] Buckham's enthusiastic, perspicacious review of *Oedipus Tyrannus*, when it was performed in the original Greek at Harvard, shows his admiration for the Classical tradition in Cambridge and was reflected in his preference for Harvard graduates to teach Greek at UVM.[26] Greece was Buckham's Holy Land as much as Palestine.

Drifting into the Twentieth Century

Buckham rode his horse and buggy into the twentieth century. He accepted the "merriment" of students in their extracurricular life, provided they had worked hard at their studies to "deserve" it. The student leaders, at least, accepted this bargain, but more and more of the rank and file came to college to get a favorable start on their careers, to be "gone out with," to understand science and the modern world.

President Buckham exploited the Old Home Week movement in a 1904 centennial of the first graduating class. It was vastly celebrated with pomp, speeches, parades, and banquets, much as his successor celebrated his inaugural in 1912. He took occasion to launch a Centennial Fund drive for $1 million. Otherwise, beyond his functions as host and master of ceremonies, he confined his role at the centennial to the traditional baccalaureate sermon at his College Street Church.

Buckham could have gone out in that blaze of glory and let others bring the University into the twentieth century. He was seventy-two and healthy (he had just had a baby daughter by a second marriage), with wide acquaintance among the respectably rich; he would have been valuable as director of development for the forthcoming drive. But directors of development appeared only after World War II, and Vermonters never really retire. George Perkins Marsh died in office at eighty-one as minister to Italy. Justin Morrill, in Congress forty-four years, died in office at eighty-eight. George H. Perkins, only sixty in 1904, continued teaching until he died at eighty-nine in 1933. Buckham likewise died in harness, at seventy-eight, on November 29, 1910.

A new opportunity, which a younger man with more political savvy might have exploited more effectively, was the national trend for the professional education of teachers. In 1905, UVM offered a new professorship of education to Walter E. Ranger, state superintendent of education, but he declined in order to become Rhode Island's commissioner of education. Then a federal act of March 1907 appropriated money for teacher training, and within a year UVM had a College of Education almost ready to go, expecting the Legislature to match the federal money and fund the college. But the young new president of Middlebury College, John M. Thomas, outlobbied UVM and won an annual grant of $6,000 "to establish and maintain a department of pedagogy" for high school teachers. Thomas cleverly argued that the state's normal schools prepared teachers for the grade schools, but secondary education was the weak link. Besides, he pointed out that since 1888 the Legislature had funded the three Vermont colleges equally. Buckham went ahead anyway with a teacher training curriculum, hiring James Franklin Messenger, an energetic, breezy midwesterner, to start an education department and a summer school. Both flourished.

Buckham was also hospitable to home economics and defended its introduction, along with other new departures, in the alumni magazine in 1909: "The very essence of liberalism," he argued, was "to give every new idea a chance to show its merit, and . . . to appropriate whatever merit it can show. . . . The new branches of study which the university has introduced within the past few years, studies in Agriculture, Engineering, Mechanics, Forestry, Home Economics, Teaching, are . . . disciplines in knowledge and virtue and good living" if taught in the right spirit.[27]

In 1907, Buckham delivered the presidential address to the Association of American Agricultural Colleges and Experiment Stations. He reiterated his holistic educational philosophy: literature from the Hebrews and Greeks on down, history, social science, and nondogmatic religion, to balance the modern obsession with engineering and natural science.[28] Sure of his style after long years of practice, Buckham called attention to UVM by widely distributing his speeches to his colleagues elsewhere. And he pressed on with the fund drive until UVM reached its million-dollar goal in 1910. Burlington citizens, including the president himself, had given $50,000. But Buckham had spent himself for the cause, and after a summer abroad that failed to restore his health, he said his "Nunc dimittis" and died after Thanksgiving, leaving his widow and children only $5,000 worth of property.[29] The trustees summed up his character: "President Buckham combined that conservatism which tests all things, with an open-minded and prophetic comprehension of the necessity and conditions of progress."[30]

Buckham was a holdover from an earlier age, as Professor Goodrich, also a holdover but retired, said in his funeral eulogy. Buckham preferred to use a quill pen and wrote an essay on why it was better than a steel one. His style changed little from his first addresses of the 1860s, except for ease and polish, and his message remained the same; though he perhaps came to realize more clearly the publicity value of printing and distributing his speeches (which was facilitated as more funds became available and a friendly printer was found in the jobbing department of the *Burlington Free Press*). He believed that people who valued experience, including his predecessor, James Angell, would give a sympathetic hearing to a man long in office as he discussed the properly balanced course for a university.

Goodrich and the president's son, the Reverend John Wright Buckham, had access to Buckham's papers and prepared an edition of his speeches, taking its title from Buckham's 1907 convocation address, *The Very Elect*.[31] Buckham spoke on public platforms early and often, but the writings that survive, including the manuscripts his literary executors chose to publish, are mainly products of his last years. Most likely, the editors chose the pieces they had heard themselves and most readily remembered. Still, the speeches in *The Very Elect* demonstrate the Buckham blend of Classics and Christianity, as if to say, "These principles are still valid." Copies of this literary monument graced many an old-guard professor's shelf in subsequent years, and the faculty referred repeatedly to its principles as they refought the fight against Buckham's modernizing successor, Guy Potter Benton. The old guard of Buckhamites prevailed, and UVM had to wait until after World War II to come fully abreast of the twentieth century.

Ira Allen

President Daniel Sanders

Plan of original "College Edifice"

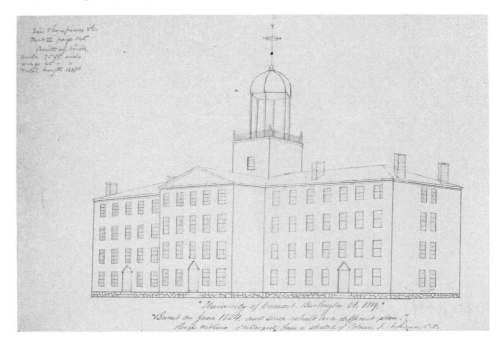

Burlington, ca. 1812

President Daniel Haskell

President Willard Preston

President John Wheeler

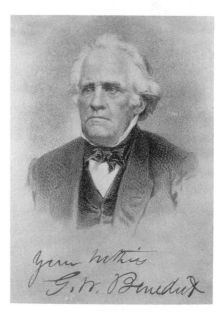

Professor George Wyllys Benedict

President James Marsh

Synopsis of the Course of Study.

AUTUMNAL TERM.

Years.		September.	October.	November.	December.
I.	A. M.	ALGEBRA.	ALGEBRA.	ALGEBRA.	ALGEBRA.
	P. M.	HERODOTUS. GREEK FORMS.	HERODOTUS. GREEK FORMS.	LIVY. LATIN FORMS & QUANTITY.	LIVY. LATIN FORMS & QUANTITY.
	Lectures and other exercises.	English Grammar. Translations or English Composition once in two weeks.			
II.	A. M.	TACITUS.	TACITUS.	ODYSSEY.	ODYSSEY.
	P. M.	CONIC SECTIONS.	PLANE & SPHERICAL TRIGONOMETRY.	TRIGONOMETRY.	TRIGONOMETRY.
	Lectures and other exercises.	History and Chronology. Exercises in Composition and Elocution.			
III.	A. M.	HORACE.	HORACE.	THUCYDIDES.	THUCYDIDES.
	P. M.	MECHANICAL PHILOSOPHY.	MECHANICAL PHILOSOPHY.	MECHANICAL PHILOSOPHY.	MECHANICAL PHILOSOPHY.
	Lectures and other exercises.	Greek & Roman Literature. Mathematics & Nat. Philosophy. Practical Levelling and Surveying. Elocution and French as in the second year.			
IV.	A. M.	PSYCHOLOGY.	PSYCHOLOGY.	SCIENCE OF LOGIC.	SCIENCE OF LOGIC.
	P. M.	ALGEBRA AND CALCULUS.	ALGEBRA AND CALCULUS.	PLATO, ARISTOTLE, LORD BACON.	PLATO, ARISTOTLE, LORD BACON.
	Lectures and other exercises.	Greek & Roman Literature. Mathematics & Nat. Philosophy. Original Exercises in Declamation or Forensic.			

BIBLICAL INSTRUCTION on the Sabbath, through the whole course. GERMAN, ITALIAN, or SPANISH Languages. Instruction in NATURAL

SUMMER TERM.

		March.	April.	May.	June.	July.
I.	A. M.	HERODOTUS.	HERODOTUS.	LIVY. ROMAN ANTIQUITIES.	LIVY. TACITUS. ROMAN ANTIQUITIES.	TACITUS.
	P. M.	ALGEBRA.	GEOMETRY.	GEOMETRY. (PLANES AND SOLIDS.)	GEOMETRY. (SPHERICAL, &c.)	GEOMETRY.
		Greek Syntax and Antiquities. Practical Logic and Rhetoric. Elocution by Classes weekly through the year.				
II.	A. M.	SURVEYING, NAVIGATION, PROJECTIONS.	PROJECTIONS. DIF. CALCULUS.	DIF. & INT. CALCULUS.	CALCULUS.	CIVIL ENGINEERING.
	P. M.	ODYSSEY.	QUINTILIAN.	QUINTILIAN.	GREEK ORATORS.	GREEK ORATORS.
		History and Chronology. Practical Levelling and Surveying. French, twice a week. ... as in the first year.				
III.	A. M.	LATIN DRAMA.	GREEK LYRIC POETRY.	GREEK DRAMA.	GREEK DRAMA.	PHYSIOLOGY.
	P. M.	CHEMISTRY, GALVANISM & ELECTRICITY.	CHEMISTRY, MAGNETISM & ELEC. MAG.	OPTICS WITH EXPERIMENTS.	OPTICS WITH EXPERIMENTS.	CRYSTALLOGRAPHY.
		English Literature. Electricity, Galvanism, Chemistry, Magnetism, etc. Composition by Classes once in two weeks through the year.				
IV.	A. M.	CENTRAL FORCES. ASTRONOMY.	ASTRONOMY.	MORAL PHILOSOPHY.	PRINCIPLES OF GOVERNMENT.	EVIDENCES OF NAT. & REV'D RELIGION.
	P. M.	METAPHYSICS.	METAPHYSICS.	CICERO DE OFFICIIS.	PRINCIPLES OF RHET. AND FINE ARTS.	EVIDENCES OF NAT. & REV'D RELIGION.
		Political Economy. Chemistry, Anatomy, Physiology. Hist. of Philosophy. Disputation weekly, by divisions through the year.				

Private classes may be formed, during the two last years, in the Hebrew. HISTORY will be given in connection with the College of Natural History.

University of Vermont, Nov. 1835.

Curriculum and class schedule, 1835

Years.	Times of Recitations and Lectures.	AUTUMNAL TERM. Ending on the first Wednesday of December.			SPRING TERM. Ending on February.	SPRING TERM, the second Wednesday of May.			SUMMER TERM, Ending on the first Wednesday of August.		
		September.	October.	November.	February.	March.	April.	May.	June.	July.
I.	Morning.	ALGEBRA.	ALGEBRA.	ALGEBRA.	LIVY.	LIVY.	LIVY. TACITUS.	TACITUS.	TACITUS.	TACITUS.
	11 o'clock, A. M.	GREEK FORMS.	GREEK SYNTAX.	GREEK SYNTAX.	ROMAN ANTIQUITIES.	ALGEBRA. ENGLISH GRAMMAR.	PRINCIPLES OF GENERAL GRAMMAR.	PRACTICAL LOGIC AND RHETORIC.	PRACTICAL LOGIC AND RHETORIC.	PRACTICAL LOGIC AND RHETORIC.
	Afternoon.	HERODOTUS.	HERODOTUS.	HERODOTUS.	ALGEBRA.	GEOMETRY.	GEOMETRY.	GEOMETRY.	GEOMETRY.	GEOMETRY.
II.	Morning.	TRIGONOMETRY.	TRIGONOMETRY.	CONIC SECTIONS.	QUINTILIAN.	SURVEYING. NAVIGATION.	NAVIGATION. PROJECTION.	NAUTICAL ASTRONOMY. CALCULUS.	CALCULUS.	CALCULUS.
	11 o'clock, A. M.	CHRONOLOGY. HISTORY.	HISTORY.	HISTORY. HEAT.	FRENCH.	FRENCH.	FRENCH.	MINERALOGY. BOTANY.	BOTANY. PRACTICAL SURVEYING.	PRACTICAL SURVEYING AND LEVELING.
	Afternoon.	ODYSSEY.	ODYSSEY.	ODYSSEY.	ANALYTICAL GEOMETRY.	QUINTILIAN.	GREEK ORATORS.	GREEK ORATORS.	GREEK ORATORS.	HORACE.
III.	Morning.	HORACE.	HORACE.	THUCYDIDES.	DYNAMICS.	THUCYDIDES. LATIN DRAMA.	GREEK DRAMA.	GREEK DRAMA.	GREEK DRAMA.	GREEK DRAMA.
	11 o'clock, A. M.	CHEMISTRY.	CHEMISTRY.	ENGLISH LITERATURE.	EXPERIMENTAL ELECTRICITY.	ZOOLOGY. NATURAL PHILOSOPHY.	NATURAL PHILOSOPHY.	BOTANY. GALVANISM.	GALVANISM. ELECTRO MAGNETISM.	LATIN OR GREEK LITERATURE.
	Afternoon.	STATICS.	STATICS.	STATICS. DYNAMICS.	THUCYDIDES.	HYDROSTATICS. HYDRO-DYNAMICS.	ELECTRICITY. HYDRO-DYNAMICS.	ELECTRICITY. MAGNETISM.	OPTICS.	OPTICS.
IV.	Morning.	PHYSIOLOGY.	PSYCHOLOGY.	PSYCHOLOGY.	SCIENCE OF LOGIC.	METAPHYSICS.	METAPHYSICS.	MORAL PHILOSOPHY.	PRINCIPLES OF GOVERNMENT.	EVIDENCES OF NAT'L & REVEALED RELIGION.
	11 o'clock, A. M.	ANATOMY. PHYSIOLOGY.	CENTRAL FORCES.	CHEMISTRY.	NATURAL HISTORY.	ASTRONOMY.	ASTRONOMY.	CICERO DE OFFICIIS.	PRINCIPLES OF RHETORIC AND FINE ARTS.	PRINCIPLES OF RHETORIC AND FINE ARTS.
	Afternoon.	CRYSTALLOGRAPHY.	MATHEMATICS. ASTRONOMY.	MATHEMATICS. ASTRONOMY.	SCIENCE OF LOGIC.	PLATO.	PLATO.	METAPHYSICS.	POLITICAL ECONOMY.	EVIDENCES OF NAT'L & REVEALED RELIGION.

English Compositions or Translations once in two weeks, and Declamation, by divisions, weekly, through the first two years.

English Compositions, and Original Declamations weekly, through the last two years.

University of Vermont, October 1, 1843.

Curriculum and class schedule, 1843

Roswell Farnham's diary

President Joseph Torrey

President Calvin Pease

President Matthew Buckham

President James B. Angell

Angell Hall, formerly the president's house

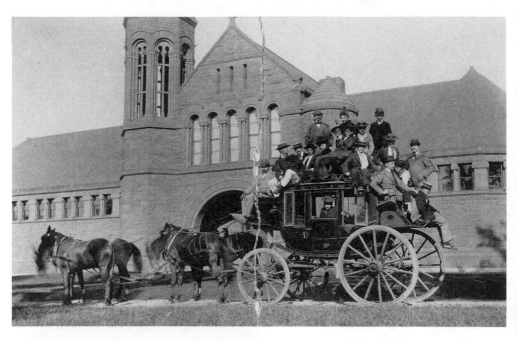

Billings Library, ca. 1890

George Washington Henderson,
Class of 1876

Frederick Billings, Class of 1844

UVM medallion (1804)

John Dewey, Class of 1879

Dean George H. Perkins

UVM seal (1865)

Cyrus Pringle

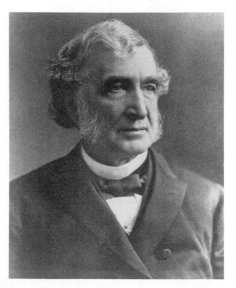

Senator Justin Morrill

Dean Joseph Hills

Dean J. E. Carrigan

John Dewey's Vermont Inheritance

BOB PEPPERMAN TAYLOR

I T I S the University of Vermont's special claim on posterity to have educated John Dewey, the man whom Alfred North Whitehead would herald
during his lifetime as "the typical effective American thinker; . . . the chief
intellectual force providing that [American] environment with coherent purpose."[1] The honors that were bestowed on Dewey, the influence that he
exerted, not only on other professional philosophers and educators but on
men and women throughout American society and in all walks of life, and
the prestige he enjoyed as a man of ideas are unparalleled in American history.

Nonetheless, among Dewey scholars there is no single view of the role of
Dewey's Burlington and UVM background in the subsequent development
of his democratic political theory. Some view Dewey's political philosophy
as a reflection of small-town New England culture. Others think Dewey
rebelled against his background and developed a perspective greatly at odds
with the values and philosophy of his childhood and youth. My view in
this essay is that the intellectual influences on Dewey at college and church
were much greater than is usually appreciated. On the other hand, the influence of the political culture (that is, the political institutional and ideological
context) of Burlington on Dewey's democratic sensibilities has been greatly
exaggerated, or at least not properly understood.

Dewey returned to his alma mater for five official visits during the course
of his long professional career. During these visits (1890, 1904, 1929, 1939,
and 1949) he always exhibited a respectful attitude toward the University.
In fact, during his 1929 visit he delivered an address commemorating the
one-hundredth anniversary of the publication of James Marsh's "Introduction" to Samuel Taylor Coleridge's *Aids to Reflection*, a work of profound
significance to the whole UVM community in the nineteenth century and
one that Dewey, as a member of the class of 1879, had read as an under-

graduate. Toward the end of this talk Dewey reflected on his own Vermont background and education at UVM in an often-quoted passage:

If I may be allowed a personal word, I would say that I shall never cease to be grateful that I was born at a time and a place where the earlier ideal of liberty and the self-governing community of citizens still sufficiently prevailed, so that I unconsciously imbibed a sense of its meaning. In Vermont, perhaps more than elsewhere, there was embodied into the spirit of the people the conviction that governments were like the houses we live in, made to contribute to human welfare, and that those who lived in them were as free to change and extend the one as they were the other, when developing needs of the human family called for such alterations and modifications. So deeply bred in Vermonters was this conviction that I still think that one is more loyally patriotic to the ideal of America when one maintains this view than when one conceives of patriotism as rigid attachment to a form of the state alleged to be fixed forever . . . [so that one should heed] the claims of a common human society as superior to those of any particular political form.[2]

Thus commemorating the greatest of UVM's presidents, Dewey paid tribute to what he understood to be the best of his Vermont inheritance and suggested that the independence, flexibility, and common sense contained in this heritage had greatly influenced the development of his mature political thinking—and continued to do so even fifty years after his graduation from UVM. Nor were these public comments the only kind words he had for Marsh and the tradition Marsh represented. He once said to his friend and colleague, Herbert W. Schneider, that Marsh's edition of Coleridge's book "was our spiritual emancipation in Vermont. Coleridge's idea of the spirit came to us as a real relief, because we could be both liberal and pious; and this *Aids to Reflection* book, especially Marsh's edition, was my first Bible."[3]

Dewey, however, was not entirely uncritical of his Vermont background. To be sure, in his only published autobiographical statement, an essay titled "From Absolutism to Experimentalism," he maintained a respectful attitude toward his experience at UVM. For example, he commented on the importance for him of his "senior year course" in social and political ethics, taught by President Buckham, and of a number of books that he read, especially Thomas Huxley's textbook in physiology.[4] He also had kind words for his teacher of philosophy, H. A. P. Torrey: "I owe him a double debt, that of turning my thoughts definitely to the study of philosophy as a life-pursuit, and of a generous gift of time to me during a year devoted privately under his direction to a reading of classics in the history of philosophy and learning to read philosophic German."[5] Nonetheless, there was a strong ambivalence in these reflections. Although Torrey was a fine teacher, Dewey commented, "In a more congenial atmosphere than that of northern New England in those days, [he] would have achieved something significant."[6] The implication is clearly that there was much in this "northern New England" environment that really was uncongenial, presumably because it in some way prevented complete intellectual freedom and self-expression.

Dewey explained that his attraction to Hegel in graduate school and during the early part of his professional career served an almost therapeutic function for him, necessitated by his "uncongenial" Vermont background:

It [Hegelianism] supplied a demand for unification that was doubtless an intense emotional craving, and yet was a hunger that only an intellectualized subject-matter could satisfy. It is more than difficult, it is impossible, to recover that early mood. But the sense of divisions and separations that were, I suppose, borne in upon me as a consequence of a heritage of New England culture, divisions by way of isolation of self from the world, of soul from body, of nature from God, brought a painful oppression—or, rather, they were an inward laceration. . . . Hegel's synthesis of subject and object, matter and spirit, the divine and the human, was, however, no mere intellectual formula; it operated as an immense release, a liberation.[7]

As the very title "From Absolutism to Experimentalism" suggests, Dewey viewed his own intellectual development as a movement away from the "absolutism" of his youth. His later instrumentalism represented a break from the philosophical and religious dogmatism of his youthful environment.

Organized religion played a profound role in Dewey's early life and in the life of the communities to which he had belonged in Burlington and at UVM. Later on, he reacted quite explicitly against this background. In *The Quest for Certainty*, for example, he argued that the exclusivity of religious communities was one of the most divisive of human practices. "Men will never love their enemies until they cease to have enmities. The antagonism between the actual and the ideal, the spiritual and the natural, is the source of the deepest and most injurious of all enmities."[8] In *A Common Faith*, Dewey writes in a similar vein: "The opposition between religious values as I conceive them and religions is not to be bridged. Just because the release of these values is so important, their identification with the creeds and cults of religions must be dissolved."[9] By 1934, when this book was originally published, he had come a long way from his early Congregationalist piety. He could now view organized religions as no more than cults subscribing to unjustifiable dogmas.

Dewey's biography is very much the story of a man who left his hometown far behind him. He was born to a solidly middle-class family: his father was a modestly prosperous, humorous, and well-loved but not overly ambitious storekeeper in Burlington, and his mother was a deeply pious evangelical Christian who was actively involved in philanthropic work among the local poor. Dewey grew up mixing with the economic and political elite that dominated social and cultural life in Burlington.[10] His family always assumed that he would attend the local university,[11] and he graduated from UVM in 1879. He then spent a brief period teaching school in Oil City, Pennsylvania, after which he returned to Vermont to teach school in Charlotte. During this time he resumed private studies with Torrey and then decided to attend graduate school in philosophy. In 1882 he left to study at Johns Hopkins University in Baltimore (where, it is worth noting, he was singularly uninterested in the course he took with Charles Peirce, the founder of pragmatism [12]). For all intents and purposes the move to Johns Hopkins signifies Dewey's permanent break with Vermont. After graduate school he would hold faculty positions at the Universities of Michigan, Minnesota, and Chicago, as well as Columbia University. From 1904, when he moved to Columbia, until his death in 1952, Dewey would be a central figure in the intellectual life of New York City. He enjoyed life in the big city, once commenting that he could not understand why so many of his colleagues vacationed in Vermont: "I don't see why you fellows want to go back to summer places in Vermont. I got out of there as soon as I could." Vermont was, he confided to another friend, "that God-forsaken country." [13]

Dewey's discomfort about his Vermont background is nicely illustrated by his appearance at a celebration held for him at UVM in honor of his ninetieth birthday in 1949. Arriving in Burlington, he and his wife were greeted by marching bands and cheerleaders, much as though he were an athletic hero.[14] Dewey took a tour of Burlington and met with a few people he had known during his childhood. But like a man who had been away from the city long enough, he boarded the return train to New York well before the dinners and speeches were held in his honor that evening. John Dewey had had enough of his hometown and wanted to go back to his adopted home in the city.

John Dewey was not unusual in his diffidence about his Burlington and UVM background. It is not surprising for people to feel negative or confused about their origins, upbringing, and early life. Nevertheless, the literature on Dewey commonly emphasizes how his mature thinking reflected values "imbibed" or inherited from the democratic political culture of Burlington and Vermont. Thus, Jane Dewey, John's daughter and biographer, writes, "His boyhood surroundings, although not marked by genuine industrial and financial democracy, created in him an unconscious but vital faith in democracy." Again, "In spite of the especial prestige of the first few families, life was democratic [in Burlington]—not consciously, but in that deeper sense in which equality and absence of class distinctions are taken for granted." [15] Sidney Hook, too, argues that Dewey's egalitarianism can be explained by the democratic Burlington of his childhood: "It was a community in which no great disparities of wealth or standards of living were to be found, and in which a man was judged, as the saying went, not by what he had but by what he did." [16]

These are but two well-known interpretations that explain Dewey's democratic sensibilities by reference to his Burlington background. Dewey is thus frequently thought of as giving the ideals and sensibilities of small-town democratic America their highest philosophical expression. In a more critical vein, Dewey is sometimes thought of as bound by his background, unable to break out of his provincialism. For example, Neil Coughlan writes: "If Dewey's provinciality left him enabled and emboldened to propose comparatively simple answers to great problems, it also imposed some of his limitations too. In his pursuit of a model of all human behavior, he was oddly blind to behavior that was not earnest, methodical, and goal-oriented." [17] Whether admiring or critical, however, all of these authors think of Dewey's philosophy as reflective in some way of his small-town New England heritage.

Some Dewey scholars, by contrast, have emphasized the distance between the intellectual background of Burlington and Dewey's mature democratic theory (produced, significantly enough, in the great cities of Chicago and New York). Neil Coughlan and Lewis Feuer, for example, both agree that we must look to Dewey's experiences after he left Vermont to discover the origins of his political beliefs and social theory.[18] They see a great gulf between Dewey's Republican background and his mature democratic socialism, his Congregationalist background and his mature view of religion, the presumed Protestant dogmatism of his teachers at UVM and the pragmatism of his mature instrumentalism. For Feuer, "Dewey resented his Puritan upbringing because of the repressions it had imposed." [19] Dewey's mature ideas have to be understood as expressions of his rebellion against Vermont.

We find, then, in the secondary Dewey literature a tendency to make connections, however vague and weak, between the tone and sensibilities of Dewey's philosophy and his Vermont background. Other scholars emphasize the substantive distance between Dewey's professional work and the intellectual environment of Burlington and UVM.

My general claim is that the views described above are as misleading as they are helpful in understanding the development of Dewey's ideas. On the one hand, the view of Dewey as a reflection of small-town New England culture points in a useful direction, but it does so in a most misleading way. As I will argue below, Dewey has much more in common with his teachers and peers in Burlington than is usually recognized or than is reflected in vague comments about Dewey's Vermont sensibilities. On the other hand, the view of Dewey as a rebel against his Vermont origins is in many ways more satisfying—the intellectual distance between Dewey and his Vermont background is generally more carefully drawn than the contrary claims. Yet my contention is that this literature has not paid enough attention to the ideas of those who influenced Dewey. When we look more carefully at these ideas, we find that Dewey had much more in common with the folks back home than even he understood or appreciated.

Consider first those who understand Dewey's intellectual development as an extension of his Vermont inheritance. There is a common tendency in this literature to assume that the Burlington of Dewey's childhood was a sleepy, homogeneous little New England town with little or no class conflict or the political strife found in larger urban settings. Although it is true that Dewey's ideas and values owed much to his experiences in Burlington and his education at UVM, it is simply untenable to contend that he was deeply impressed by a sleepy little New England town and its "town meeting" political culture.

Burlington was much more of a city during Dewey's childhood than this stereotype would allow. The growth of the lumber trade had made it the nation's third largest lumber center as of 1850.[20] Town meetings were abolished when Burlington was incorporated as a city in 1865, when Dewey was only six years old (although they survive to this day in surrounding towns). Dewey's childhood actually coincided with the dramatic growth in Burlington that prompted municipal incorporation. This was accompanied by sharpening class, ethnic, and political cleavages. In the five years following the end of the Civil War and the establishment of city government, the population of Burlington doubled, causing serious public health problems, overcrowding, and social and political friction between the old Protestant Yankees and the immigrants who were primarily French Canadian and Irish Catholic working people. It was the growth of these working-class and Catholic groups that led old Yankee business leaders to fear that they would lose control of town meetings and thus political power. This, along with concerns over public health and public works in the face of population growth, led to the adoption of the city charter in 1865. In short, the sociology of Burlington during Dewey's childhood and adolescence belies the mythology of Dewey as a product of small-town America.

The real lesson Dewey seems to have learned from the political culture of Burlington had less to do with town meeting democracy than with America's leap into modern urban industrial society. The world of his childhood was a rapidly changing and expanding one, in which the personal, informal, and small-scale institutions of the earlier American experience were quickly becoming inadequate. This was the lesson that Dewey was sensitive to even as a college student at UVM. It was to inform the central message of his lifelong philosophical project.

Consider, on the other hand, the views of those who have emphasized the great distance between Dewey's mature political thinking and activism and the conservative Republicanism of his Vermont heritage.[21] What is most unsatisfying about this version of Dewey's development is that it leaves so little room for any substantive influence from his early life. It is true that Dewey did rebel against his Vermont background; when he left for graduate school in 1882, he left pretty much for good. Nonetheless, even in this rebellion, in this break with his childhood and youth, there was much more continuity than is conventionally recognized, even by Dewey himself.

John Dewey's academic career at UVM was respectable but not striking or outstanding. Max Eastman wrote, "He slid through his first three college years . . . without throwing off any sparks, or giving grounds to predict anything about his future."[22] The story is often told, however, about his reading during his junior year a physiology text by the Darwinian T. H. Huxley that had a deep impact on him. Dewey himself dated his interest in philosophy from this event.[23] He then went on to perform very well in his senior year, particularly in his course with President Buckham. In this final year of study he improved his rather average academic standing enough to graduate second in his class of eighteen.[24]

There is evidence, however, primarily in the form of library records of his reading habits, that Dewey was interested in philosophical and political affairs quite early in his career at UVM. During his first year of study, for example, Dewey read Walter Bagehot's *Physics and Politics*, Alexis de Tocqueville's *Democracy in America*, and a more obscure but, for our purposes, very interesting volume by Richard Josiah Hinton, *English Radical Leaders*.[25] Bagehot's book is a discussion of the importance of Darwinism for political thinking and institutions. Tocqueville's monumental work is, of course, one of the most insightful studies of the nature of America's democratic political culture. Hinton's book is a series of profiles of liberal and progressive English politicians, "a class of men who seem destined to lead their nation through the peaceful ways of ameliorative reforms, into the larger liberties and ordered equities of a practically democratic future."[26] These three books indicate that even in his first year of college Dewey was sensitive to major intellectual changes (most notably the development of Darwinist scientific and social theory), social changes (the growth of the labor movement, the increasing concentration of capital, the woman's movement), and the importance of these developments for democratic politics and society.

This first-year interest was not short-lived. Dewey's sophomore essay was a discussion of municipal reform, a topic of some significance in Burlington, which had incorporated as a city a little more than a decade earlier.[27] His commencement speech, titled "Limits of Political Economy," was also obviously of political interest.[28] Throughout his four years at UVM Dewey read extensively in the most advanced literary, philosophical, and political periodicals of the time, including the *Edinburgh Review*, *Westminster Review*, *North American Review*, *Atlantic*, and *Journal of Speculative Philosophy*. In addition to his course work he read Herbert Spencer, J. S. Mill, and Auguste Comte, among others.[29] In all of this reading, Dewey was confronting the most advanced English-language philosophical and political discussions of the period.

Dewey comments in "From Absolutism to Experimentalism" that at this time what interested him the most in Comte's writings was "his idea of the disorganized character of Western modern culture, due to a disintegrative 'individualism,' and his idea of a synthesis of science that should be a regulative method of an organized social life."[30] In general, Dewey learned from all of these readings about a tremendous flux in traditional ideas and social practices, a sense of openness and change in the future, the importance of new developments in science, and the excitement and apprehension accompanying these profound intellectual and social developments. His college reading makes it clear that his early sensitivity to the changes going on in American society led him to seek out literature that would help to explain these developments and project their future. Jane Dewey comments, "English periodicals which reflected the new ferment were the chief intellectual stimulus to John Dewey at this time and affected him more deeply than his regular courses in philosophy."[31] At the very least, UVM provided Dewey with the environment and resources necessary to pursue this interest.

But there were more direct influences at UVM. Dewey was grateful to H. A. P. Torrey, both for the educational attention he provided and for the encouragement he gave to pursue philosophy as a vocation.[32] Torrey was primarily a teacher and never wrote very much. Looking back over the written materials he did leave, one is at first struck by the great differences in tone and perspective between Torrey's and Dewey's writings. For example, after Abraham Lincoln's assassination, Torrey wrote an essay (unpublished) in remembrance of the dead President.[33] The morality and stern piety of this discussion of the Civil War reminds one that Torrey was only the latest descendant of a long line of Puritan thinkers in New England. To Torrey, the war had been a conflict between the just and righteous Union and the evil and ungodly Confederacy; and God, working through Lincoln, had assured the Union victory: "For if ever the Hand of Providence is visible in human history, it is visible in the history of this war, and in the career of him whom God chose to guide the nation through it."[34] Two things in this document are in striking contrast to Dewey's later political writings. First is its extreme moral certainty. There is no attempt to understand the complexity of the Civil War nor the possibility of moral guilt on the part of the North as well as the South. Torrey views the conflict in much simpler terms, as a conflict between good and evil, with the former triumphing. Dewey would never be guilty, in his mature work, of exhibiting such a lack of sensitivity for moral complexity. Although he would never lose the capacity for moral indignation, he would spend much of his adult life attacking precisely the "quest for certainty" so clearly illustrated in Torrey's essay.[35]

Second, Torrey's understanding of the political world is still one informed by Puritan orthodoxy on this subject: the basic reason for political organization is original sin. Because of human sin, war is and always will be a necessary institution in human life, for "persuasion comes more of suffering than of conscience."[36] In fact, "the strength of government is still in the sword."[37] Dewey would become very critical of the conception of original sin, which he considered to be indicative of philosophical laziness (for assuming that which needs to be explained). He once commented to Sidney Hook, referring to Reinhold Niebuhr's insistence on the importance of original sin, "A man doesn't have to be an S.O.B. S.O.B.'s are made, not born." [38]

A series of articles that Torrey wrote in 1885 suggest that Dewey and his old teacher had more in common than the above comments would imply. In "The 'Theodicy of Leibnitz,' " Torrey criticized Leibnitz for practicing philosophy on a level too highly abstracted from the realities of life as experienced by everyday men and women. Referring, for example, to Leibnitz's definition of suffering as metaphysical evil, Torrey sarcastically observed, "The philosopher may define suffering as metaphysical evil, but the victim is not eased by the definition." [39] His point, of course, was that Leibnitz's proposed definition is a pure abstraction, removed from the facts and realities of life as it is lived. In terms of pure, metaphysical knowledge, Torrey suggested, the problem of theodicy—God's tolerance of evil—may be intractable (at least until the "end of history"). Yet this was not the only kind of knowledge, nor even the most important knowledge available to Christians in daily life. Torrey suggested that "light comes more from living than from thinking. Moreover, this practical way of dealing with a problem too hard for the intellect is like that which God himself has offered to our consideration and acceptance." It is possible, through Christian faith, to live and to feel the solution to theodicy, if not to strictly "understand" it in philosophical terms. [40] There is a hardheaded practicality to Torrey's discussion here. It is this type of appeal to lived reality and the distrust of purely "philosopher's problems" that suggest a strong similarity with Dewey's later pragmatism. Torrey wrote, "Pessimism is artificial, non-natural. Every man is at heart an optimist." [41] Dewey, too, was an optimist, although by no means an uncritical or complacent one.

Much in Dewey's mature writings appears almost diametrically opposed to Torrey's thought, but there are also elements of similarity between the two. When we look at some of the other figures of intellectual importance to Dewey at UVM and in the Congregational Church during these years, we find the same mix of elements. President Buckham was viewed by the UVM community "as the very embodiment of tradition, a kind of fortress of conservatism," [42] hardly what we would recognize in Dewey. On the "college ideal of life" Buckham writes: "It would not have human life dominated by the philosophy of the average man. It says to that philosophy, there are more things in heaven and earth than you have dreamed of." [43] This elitism and idealism is a far cry from the thought of the "philosopher of the common man," as Dewey was not infrequently called. [44] Buckham's Horatio Algerism, a belief that through hard work and determination individuals are able to overcome all obstacles and adverse circumstances in their lives, is incongruous with both Dewey's mature communitarianism and his analysis of the organizational and structural constraints in complex urban industrial society. [45]

Yet despite these differences with Dewey, some of the other elements in

Buckham's writings are strikingly paralleled by the sensibilities of Dewey's later work. Like Dewey, Buckham was committed to an understanding of the moral life as an activist life: "The life nurtured by Christianity is a life of action."[46] Although he warned his students against the temptations of radicalism, Buckham was very sensitive to the changes taking place in American society and the need to rethink many moral and political ideals and categories.[47] Most interesting, however, is his attack on what he understood as too great an emphasis on individualism and individual rights:

We in this country . . . have been living too long in the primitive stage of human society. We have built our social fabric too much out of a mere assertion of rights. At times we have been lifted into a glorious forgetfulness of our selfishness, but have soon dropped back again into our old ways. Save as religion modifies the temper of our people, the spirit of American life is too much that of individualism. Every man is for himself. Politically we are democratic: socially we are intensely aristocratic. The strongest are the best.[48]

In fact, a society built merely on the assertion of individual rights would be a chaotic one. In Buckham's mind America had been saved from this chaos only by its all too infrequently recognized Christian morality and fellowship:

To found society on the rights of man, his rights only, is simply to incorporate the principle of multiple self-assertion. The experiment has been tried, and its various phases have been hate, cruelty, bloodshed, anarchy, insurrections, massacres, the reign of terror, military despotism. History furnishes no single instance of a community beneficently organized upon a mere assertion of rights. The French anarchists were fond of justifying themselves by appealing to the American Declaration of Independence. But that document represented the spirit of American liberty only when taken in connection with the profound respect for law and the deep sense of religion which formed the substance of the American character.[49]

Clearly, Buckham, like Dewey, believed that unbridled individualism was both morally wrong and empirically incorrect.

During his college years and directly afterward, while still living in Burlington, Dewey was active in the First Congregational Church; he was elected president of the church's newly founded youth group in 1881.[50] From the minister at this time, Lewis Orsmond Brastow (subsequently a professor at the Yale Divinity school), Dewey certainly heard much Congregational orthodoxy. In a discussion of religion and government, for example, Brastow torturously attempts to prove that ours is a Christian state and can therefore favor Christian activity and morals even if there is a formal separation between these two spheres. He concludes his case by observing, "It is God, not man, who creates government."[51] Nonetheless, at the state convention of the Congregational Church in 1879, the year Dewey was a senior at UVM; Brastow bravely defended toleration of diverse opinions within the Church from an attempt by conservatives to impose tighter doctrinal standards.[52] After his death, one of his colleagues at Yale eulogized him as a man whose theology "arms one against all movements in the direction of intolerance and dogmatism."[53] Like Dewey, Brastow firmly believed that "doctrines that fear liberty confess weakness."[54] From Brastow also, Dewey probably heard criticisms of the individualism in contemporary life.[55] Most striking are comments Brastow made in a special sermon during Dewey's senior year in college, "The True Estimate of Life," emphasizing the importance of personal growth and development: "Every man is a man of whom more might have been made. No one attains his full measure. We all die half-grown. . . . It belittles a man not to grow."[56] Life as a moral opportunity for personal growth would, of course, become an idea of central importance for Dewey's moral and political theory.

Probably the most significant intellectual presence at UVM when Dewey attended was the ghost of the late president of the University, James Marsh. Marsh expounded a philosophy highly critical of the Lockeanism that he (like Coleridge) believed dominated contemporary philosophy and moral theory. He felt that Lockean epistemology was subversive to religious orthodoxy because it radically split the worlds of faith and reason.[57] To the contrary, Marsh argued, "Christian faith is the perfection of human reason."[58] The worlds of reason and of faith are complementary when properly understood, rather than antagonistic or simply unrelated. Philosophy and religion are mutually compatible and, in fact, interdependent. True religion must be philosophical, just as true philosophy must become religiously informed.[59]

With this perspective Marsh was very critical of philosophical systems that had purely intellectual integrity but seemed far removed from the concerns of Christian life and activity. Joseph Torrey commented in his "Memoir" that Marsh "felt altogether dissatisfied with the old method of the Scotch and English philosophers, which he thought too formal, cold and barren. They did not, he said, keep alive the heart in the head."[60] Philosophical thinking must grow out of the actual experiences that individuals have in the course of their daily lives. In turn, for philosophy to be significant, it must influence the living of these lives: "No living and actual knowledge can be arrived at simply by speculation. The man must become what he knows; he must make his knowledge one with his own being; and in his power to do this, joined with the infinite capacity of his spirit, lies the possibility of his endless progress."[61] Marsh was thus impatient with philosophical systems that held purely academic or speculative interest. Philosophy must be activist and directly concerned with the moral problems raised by the facts of everyday life.[62]

Marsh believed that this moral perspective was in direct conflict with what he understood to be the emphasis on individualism and self-interest found in currently fashionable Lockeanism.[63] Philosophy must be intimately associated with, if indeed not subordinated to, the claims of religious and moral duty. Marsh and those who followed him at UVM held that we are obliged to think seriously not because it is fun or interesting or exciting or creative but because without doing so we would simply not know how to live appropriately. Any philosophical system that does not inform such concerns and is not proved in the living is false, vain, or merely irrelevant.

Even though Dewey would eventually retain few if any of Marsh's religious beliefs, there is a great deal of common ground between himself and his Congregationalist forebear. Marsh, Dewey points out in his centennial address, condemned all attempts to separate knowledge from action. "Marsh constantly condemns what he calls speculation and the speculative tendency, by which he means a separation of knowledge and the intellect from action and will."[64] Dewey also makes a great deal out of a passage from Marsh's speech dedicating the UVM chapel in 1830, on the democratic nature of American government:

We can hardly, indeed, be said to be the subjects of any state, considered in its ordinary sense, as body politic with a fixed constitution and a determinate organization of its several powers. . . . With us there is nothing so fixed by the forms of political and civil organizations as to obstruct our efforts for promoting the full and free development of all our powers, both individual and social. Indeed, where the principle of self-government is admitted to such an extent as it is in this state [i.e., the United States], there is, in fact, nothing fixed or permanent, but as it is made so by that which is permanent and abiding in the intelligence and fixed rational principles of action in the self-governed. The self-preserving principle of our government is to be found only in the continuing determination and unchanging aims of its subjects.[65]

Dewey finds that his own pragmatic perspective and understanding of democratic values is not greatly different from the view that Marsh set forth here.

When we look at these intellectual influences of a few key individuals on Dewey as a young man and student, we find many more similarities between Dewey's own developed democratic philosophy and the ideas of his teachers and clergy back home in Burlington than the secondary literature or even Dewey's own personal reflections would lead us to expect. It was common for him to hear criticisms of philosophical individualism and conventional Lockean theory. It was equally common for him to hear criticisms of all philosophy and intellectual life that was not intimately involved with human activity and life as it is lived. Individual growth and development was held by others in Burlington and at UVM to be of ultimate moral concern for personal moral life and social life in general. Democracy, at least as it was understood by Marsh, is less a fixed form of government than an open opportunity for development and growth by citizens. And finally, all of those in a position to have influenced Dewey strongly opposed any radical separation between the world of facts and the world of values, between intelligence and morality, between means and ends. On all of these counts, which are so important to Dewey's mature democratic thought, there are important precedents in the thought of those who taught and influenced him while he was growing up in Burlington and studying at UVM.

Dewey's democratic political theory is distinctive in a number of ways. He distrusted the individualism of much conventional liberal theory, both in its natural rights (Locke) and utilitarian (Mill) incarnations. His criticisms were twofold: on the one hand, the theory is empirically inaccurate (especially in the twentieth century); on the other, it has become a mere rationalization for institutions and social behavior that are actually contrary to the spirit of the liberalism from which it developed. On the first count, liberal individualism simply fails to understand the objective interdependency of individuals in the modern world. Because of this the theory is not terribly useful in guiding moral action in the world that individuals actually live in. Thus, in *The Public and Its Problems* Dewey refers to "the enormous ineptitude of the individualistic philosophy to meet the needs and direct the factors of the new age."[66] In an equally characteristic passage in *Liberalism and Social Action*, Dewey argues that the "beliefs and methods of earlier liberalism were ineffective when faced with the problems of social organization and integration."[67]

On the second count, Dewey argues that it is largely because of this theoretical limitation that liberalism has so easily been corrupted and vulgarized as an ideology serving narrow, selfish interests. Thus, for example, liberal individualism has come to be associated with the rights of capitalists to engage in unrestricted economic activity, regardless of the consequences for the community as a whole.[68] The individualism of earlier liberal democratic theory, which had been formulated as a theory of freedom for all members of the political community, has easily been co-opted and put to work for particular class interests.

The political implications of Dewey's democratic theory are strongly participatory: against the thrust of much twentieth-century political theory he warns us to be wary of the power of political experts and elites. As social and political life have become increasingly complex, centralized, and national (or international) in scope, the temptation for democratic theorists is to give up on the possibilities for direct citizen participation and to view democratic politics as primarily a method whereby the mass of citizens have electoral mechanisms through which they may periodically control the behavior and policies of elites. In fact, the tendency has frequently been for theorists to attempt to protect and isolate political elites as much as possible from the influences of mass opinion so that they will be able to develop the expertise necessary for political activity and have the power to practice their skills.[69] Dewey, by contrast, argued that the challenge for democratic politics in the twentieth century was to find new ways for citizens to participate meaningfully in political affairs despite the increasing complexity and impersonality of those affairs. To hand over political life to a class of political experts would be a disaster because their expertise is illusory. "A class of experts is invariably so removed from common interests as to become a class with private interests and private knowledge, which in social matters is not knowledge at all."[70] If politics is concerned with common affairs, then it is the individuals who hold those affairs in common—that is, the citizenry—who must, to the greatest degree possible, participate in the direction and determination of public life.

This characteristic of Dewey's democratic theory is very much related to a third, and perhaps most important, characteristic of his thinking: democracy is viewed not simply as a political form or a set of institutions but as a way of life. From Dewey's perspective the ultimate moral value, as far as we can define such a thing, is found in what he refers to as individual growth: "Growth itself is the only moral 'end.' "[71] Because this is the highest of all social goals, democracy is to be valued as the greatest of social values because it maximizes the opportunities for personal growth for all individuals in a society. "Democracy has many meanings, but if it has a moral meaning, it is found in resolving that the supreme thrust of all political institutions and industrial arrangements shall be the contribution they make to the all-around growth of every member of society."[72] The way democracy promotes this value is through its insistence on free and open communication, which allows every member of a community the opportunity to contribute to the development of social life and shared interests. Thus, "regarded as an idea, democracy is not an alternative to other principles of associated life. It is the idea of community life itself."[73] To the degree that community life is truly achieved, the opportunity for individual growth and communication with others is maximized. Dewey's theory is, obviously, a highly moralized theory of democracy, rather than simply descriptive or empirical (like much contemporary democratic theory). For Dewey, democracy places a premium on communication, and "Of all affairs, communication is the most wonderful."[74]

Dewey emphasized that democracy as a way of life was more than a particular set of institutions or political practices. Although elections and constitutional protections of the individual are essential to a democratic political society, according to Dewey they are not enough to form a community where communication is nurtured, protected, and stimulated. The institutions necessary for real democracy depend on the needs and particularities of each community. In small communities, for example, the town meeting may be a very appropriate and effective vehicle for democratic participation. In a large urban area different institutional arrangements (for example, neighborhood organizations) become necessary. The final form of a democratic state, therefore, cannot be defined, nor should a fetish be made of current or past institutional arrangements: "The formation of states must be an experimental process."[75] Dewey emphasized democratic process, change, and development and was hostile to overly formalistic, static, or ahistorical theories of democracy. He saw nothing sacred in particular political forms in and of themselves. Only to the degree that they continued to cultivate democratic life were they to be valued.

Dewey's theory is a response to the tendency in much contemporary political thought and political practice to separate political means from political ends. In a 1937 essay, Dewey wrote:

The fundamental principle of democracy is that the ends of freedom and individuality for all can be attained only by means that accord with those ends. . . . The value of upholding the banner of liberalism in this country . . . is its insistence upon freedom of belief, of inquiry, of discussion, of assembly, of education: upon the method of public intelligence in opposition to even a coercion that claims to be exercised in behalf of the ultimate freedom of all individuals. . . . But democratic means and the attainment of democratic ends are one and inseparable.[76]

The maintenance and protection of democratic society requires not only that we use democratic methods but that we reject the split between facts and values found in much contemporary philosophy.[77]

What we find in Dewey's mature political thinking is a theory based on strong communitarian and participatory principles, which views democracy as much more important than political institutions alone and, in fact, as a way of "associated life." His theory is pragmatic and antiformalistic, conceptualizing democracy as an experimental process of development rather than something achieved once and for all. Finally, Dewey emphasizes the importance of understanding the intimate relationship between means and ends, and he argues that to sacrifice democratic means is also to sacrifice democratic ends.

Given Dewey's personal ambivalence about his background, as well as the emphasis in much of the secondary literature on the gulf between Dewey and his Vermont origins, it is at first a little surprising to find that those with whom he came in contact when he was a young man studying at UVM prefigured so many of the ideas in his later philosophical work. Perhaps the most striking similarity is in what we might call the pragmatic perspective of all of their writings. Dewey agreed with his teachers that thought divorced from the problems of action is at best vanity and at worst dangerous and irresponsible. There was a profound sense of earthly vocation in the writings of Dewey's teachers, alive and dead, and their strong religious sensibilities served less to divorce their thoughts from this world than to moralize the entirety of their worldly activities. Although the theological component of this moralism would disappear from Dewey's profoundly secular, nonreligious philosophy, the moral perspective of instrumentalism is very much in the tradition of his Puritan forebears. Paul Conklin was one of the few to recognize this relationship; he writes: "He [Dewey] never repudiated most of the values of his childhood. Instead, he correlated them with a new knowledge of man and his environment, a knowledge never possessed by his less sophisticated forebears."[78] In his pragmatic perspective Dewey "was the best of the Puritans."[79] He had no tolerance for philosophy apart from the real problems faced by common men and women in everyday life, any more than his forebears had tolerance for those who professed religious belief but did not allow this belief to guide them in the mundane details of living.

This characteristic of Dewey's Vermont inheritance may have led him to overemphasize the significance of philosophical activity. It is the Puritan in him that made him believe that wrong thinking leads necessarily to wrong acting, in ways, I think, that simply cannot be sustained empirically. This view, for example, led him to overemphasize the importance of the tradition of Kantian idealism for the growth of German political absolutism before both world wars.[80]

On the other hand, it is this same characteristic that made Dewey so important to his own generation and potentially to ours. He always had, even in his choice of reading at college, a strong sense of the movement and change in his society. This was not unusual for men and women of his generation—in fact, the Progressive movement as a whole, of which he was a central figure, was very much a movement struggling to come to terms with the new American society emerging from the post–Civil War era. What made Dewey so important and attractive to his peers was not the uniqueness of his concerns so much as the strength of his vision and his supreme sensitivity to the problems of social change. If it is true, he argued, that the world has changed so that our old ideas are no longer guides to us in facing the moral challenges in everyday life, then it is our intensely moral task to try to develop new ways of thinking so as not to be cut adrift in this new world (which, he was afraid, was becoming more and more the case). All the while he insisted, in the good tradition of James Marsh, that it was unacceptable to separate our moral from our intellectual concerns and that to do so was not only an intellectual error but a grave danger to our integrity as moral actors. The philosopher must maintain an engagement in the world in order to give his or her work moral significance and philosophical integrity.

Cushing Strout has rightly observed of Dewey: "He was a man of notable common sense and decency, and if he seems remote now it is partly because we find it difficult to conceive of a philosopher so effective in the world."[81] This effectiveness was a result, at least in part, of his early moral and intellectual training in Burlington and at UVM. Although Dewey rejected its particular religious form, he accepted and developed the moral perspective from which his forebears worked. It was not simply intellectual curiosity that drew the young Dewey to the debates about Darwin and Comte, Spencer and Hegel, in the intellectual journals found in the UVM library. It was the same moral concern that would later lead him to attempt a "reconstruction in philosophy," to make philosophy a more effective tool for action.

Dewey's objection to the theological perspective was not that it was overly moralistic but that the moralism it brought to bear on life would not do the job required of it. In fact, he argues that if we are to maintain the moral concern and responsibility of such great importance to his Puritan elders, the content of their theology and philosophy must change. This position is nicely illustrated by an article written in 1935 by Dewey's childhood friend, John Wright Buckham, the son of President Buckham, discussing Dewey's book *A Common Faith*. A professor at the Pacific School of Religion in California, Buckham had stayed much closer to the Congregational orthodoxy of his youth and was quite unsympathetic to Dewey's pragmatism (which he understood only very imperfectly). He sensed, nonetheless, that he and Dewey had maintained a much closer similarity in moral perspective than he had previously appreciated—in fact, he believed that in *A Common Faith* Dewey had transcended his pragmatism and returned, as it were, to the fold.[82] Buckham was both right and wrong in his evaluation. Dewey had not renounced pragmatism, nor had he really returned to the fold. Yet he was not as far away from the traditional moral commitment as Buckham had previously believed.

This connection is crucial in understanding the complex relationship between American secular democratic theory and the theistic philosophies out of which it grew. Dewey's democratic theory was neither a total rebellion against Congregationalist society nor the simple reflection of the values of the supposed political culture of his youth. His preoccupation with the democratization of American life grew quite naturally out of his moral and intellectual education at church and the university. In this sense, as the observations of John Wright Buckham suggest, he had more in common with the folks back home in Burlington than most commentators have realized.

The Natural Sciences and George Henry Perkins

KEVIN T. DANN

The Rise of Science at UVM

WHEN George Henry Perkins arrived in Burlington on January 3, 1870, it had been twenty-two years since any single instructor had taught all of the natural sciences at the University of Vermont. For an equal span of years, George Wyllys Benedict had performed that role, before leaving the University in 1847 in frustration over its lack of support for his efforts on behalf of scientific research and education. Since then a number of men had taught at various times some of the subjects that Benedict had encompassed: Zadock Thompson took over natural history for a few years in the 1850s, Edward Hungerford lectured intermittently on geology, and Leonard Marsh taught "vegetable and animal physiology" from 1857 until Perkins arrived.[1]

Perkins was brought to UVM by President James Angell to strengthen the link between the University and the new commitment to agricultural education that he had addressed in his inaugural speech. In those days the need for science was defined as much by the surrounding community as by universities themselves. Just a year after Angell's inaugural address, Burlington hosted the Annual Meeting of the American Association for the Advancement of Science (AAAS). Thirty-eight Burlingtonians, only a few of whom were scientists, were elected as new members at the meeting. However, a harbinger of the coming shift from community-oriented to professional science in a national scientific institution was a proposal at the same meeting to adopt new and more stringent membership rules that reflected professionalization. In American colleges before the Civil War, science had been almost universally community-oriented, but by the end of the nineteenth century, according to Charles Rosenberg, the "scientist's basic unit of orientation" was his discipline. It was his discipline that "define[d] his aspirations, sanction[ed] ambitions, reward[ed] ultimate achievement." Though some historians feel that the professional and community-oriented patterns of science coexisted only until the 1870s, at UVM this coexistence continued for at least another fifty years.[2]

Over the next half-century, UVM made considerable strides toward achieving the sort of balance Angell called for. The curriculum and the physical plant necessary for adequate scientific instruction were strengthened, largely through the efforts of Angell's successor, Matthew Buckham. But if it had "opened its ears" to science education, there was a limit to how fully UVM might heed the call. This was largely because of the same constraint that had frustrated Benedict during the first half of the nineteenth century— money. Another problem was the lack of men with the ambition and vision of Benedict and Angell; such men usually opted for institutions with greater opportunities for professional growth. The sciences at UVM were left in the capable but cautious hands of men who were content to practice a largely local science, endearing them to generations of UVM students who did not necessarily pursue scientific careers but leaving those with higher scientific aspirations unsatisfied.

Perkins, the seminal figure of science education at UVM throughout this period, illustrates this limitation. Universally loved and admired, he gave generations of UVM students an appreciation of the natural world, yet he never produced any graduates who made significant contributions to natural science. Perkins came to UVM with a newly earned Ph.D. from the Sheffield Scientific School at Yale, where he had pursued his research under A. E. Verrill, a student of Louis Agassiz. His dissertation, "The Molluscan Fauna of New Haven," was in the tradition of descriptive natural history and would have made fine reading for Benedict and Thompson. It lacked, however, the theoretical foundation and inductive reasoning that would make it *science*. In this respect it foreshadowed the pure description of the natural world that Perkins would publish over the next six decades while mainstream American science moved toward a more experimentalist mode.[3]

The establishment of Harvard's Lawrence Scientific School in 1847 and Yale's Sheffield Scientific School in 1854 led a trend of developing science education within the Classical curriculum. Until the time Perkins arrived, UVM still required no scientific competence for admission except elementary algebra. The Morrill Act of 1862, however, added to the momentum of practical education. By 1869–1870, almost a quarter of the students (fourteen of fifty-nine) were enrolled in the "Agricultural and Scientific Department," whose courses were taught by chemistry professor Peter Collier, engineering professor Volney Barbour, and Perkins. Morning and afternoon recitations for all entering students in this department, whether hopeful engineers, chemists, or "scientific" farmers, consisted of algebra, geometry, and chemistry while their peers in the Classical curriculum digested Xenophon, Herodotus, and Cicero. Second-year science students would choose between three courses of study while juniors and seniors enjoyed a fledgling elective system. Civil engineers studied railroad surveying, bridge construction, and steam engines, and prospective mining engineers and metallurgists could study ore assaying, hydraulics, and tunnel design—though none elected this last course of study. Chemists could make use of the newly furnished and supplied rooms on the ground floor of the North College for their experiments. For the agricultural course, Professor Perkins was prepared to give lectures in February and March, when young Vermont agriculturalists were at liberty to leave their farms to come and hear about agricultural chemistry, physical geography, and other subjects that were likely of little interest to the average farmer.[4] This scientific training was largely utilitarian in approach, paralleling the entire nation's approach to science. When motivated by a practical need, Americans produced innovations ranging from the telegraph to anesthesia, but they fell short in the fields of pure science.

The Darwinian Revolution

Science arrived at UVM at a time when "pure" research was being revolutionized by Charles Darwin's theory of evolution by natural selection. The notion of evolution had been developing well before the publication of *Origin of Species* in 1859; at UVM it was often touched on in discussions in the College of Natural History. The local specimen-collecting efforts of this society, like others of its era, brought it face-to-face with large scientific questions, particularly that of the variation of species.

Professor Joseph Torrey, who had started an herbarium of local flora in the early 1840s, was intrigued by the question of evolution. Dissatisfied with both the old Linnaean system and the more theoretical "natural method" of classification that was beginning to replace it, Torrey stressed how important systematics were to the eventual discovery of a "law of vegetable life"— that is, evolution. He thought the doctrine of special creation was a fallacy, and he called the idea that nature creates all species independently "unphilosophical and unsatisfactory." His own ideal systematics anticipated Darwin: "It is upon [the] idea of the vegetable world as an organic whole, interpenetrated and connected by the energy of one and the same law, and passing into gradual development through the various individuals . . . that the only truly scientific and natural method of classification can be constructed."[5]

Torrey's prescience seems not to have been shared by Leonard Marsh; Lucius Bigelow ('61), a capable amateur botanist, said that Marsh "did not teach us botany in the field nor anywhere else; he gave us nothing but repulsive dry bones of drudgery and a mere boy of sixteen I *shunned* his classroom."[6] In geology, Marsh limited his lectures to elementary mineralogy, bedrock geology, and geomorphology, with little attention to contemporary scientific issues, particularly those raised by the publication of *Origin of Species*.[7] In 1869, however, Marsh's poor health prompted his temporary replacement by someone with a tremendous interest in evolutionary theory—John Bulkley Perry.

Perry had grown up in Burlington and had been a student of Torrey and Benedict. Early on he had expressed a desire to devote his life to his age's most pressing intellectual task—reconciling science and religion. After his graduation from UVM in 1847 he studied at Andover Theological Seminary, and became pastor of the Swanton Congregational Church in 1855. There he continued his own fieldwork in geology and actively entered into the nineteenth century's great geological controversies. Perry's brief UVM appointment gave him a forum to test his ideas on science and religion; he closed the course with a lecture on the "Relation of Geology to Scripture."[8] Much later, in 1868, he was hired as a paleontologist by Louis Agassiz at Harvard's Museum of Comparative Zoology.

More prepared than his mentor, Agassiz, to accept Darwin, Perry still adhered to the pre-Darwinian concept of a divinely ordained Great Chain of Being. After surveying the whole of the animal kingdom, he concluded: "All the comprehensive systems of life which have passed in review before us are the work of Creative Wisdom. Their several places have been exhibited upon the face of the globe from age to age during the long and unmeasured past. Each in due order was called into existence, then entered upon its appointed work." When Perry said that each system of life was "called into existence," he seemed to be standing on the side of special creation, yet most of his writings suggest that he did not hold Agassiz's view to this effect. Many scientists were either "for" or "against" evolutionary theory, but Perry was one of those committed to both science *and* Christianity who seemed at home between the two conflicting outlooks: "Some take the ground that God acted before all time. Others that he acts through all time. There is trouble in both positions. The error is in assuming one and excluding the other. Properly we must hold to both alike and exactly."[9]

Perry returned to Cambridge in 1870, and George Perkins took up the geology lectures. Though he had been trained more recently and was thus in a better position to interpret the scientific side of evolutionary theory, Perkins's own work seemed to sidestep evolutionary conclusions. This was not because of any ecclesiastical qualms but rather because of his parochial scientific tendencies. The son of a Congregationalist minister, he had had some aspirations of his own toward the ministry. Like Perry, Perkins represented the typical Congregationalist effort to reconcile evolution with faith and to propagate evolutionary theory for the lay public. Predisposed as they were to demonstrating God's mastery through the grandeur of the natural world, the American Protestant theological intelligentsia actually allied themselves more solidly with Darwin than did the scientific community.[10] Perkins's father—Frederick Trenck Perkins, a well-respected pastor in Galesburg, Illinois—upon learning of his son's decision to answer his calling to natural science, expressed an easy acceptance: "The field of scientific study is a glorious one. God's thoughts in his works are to be studied, expounded, and made use of for the salvation of mankind." [11]

It seems likely that Perkins presented evolutionary theory to his students in the 1870s from the perspective of some form of "Christian Darwinism." Christian Darwinists understood Darwin's theory and in their effort to reconcile it with their faith left it substantially intact. While scientists at other universities were actively challenging Darwinian doctrine, "Perk" was not a man for controversy. The only example preserved in print of an "attack" of any sort by him against intellectual antagonists was in a paper titled "The Antiquity of Man": "There are here, as elsewhere, wild and extravagant views which have been eagerly adopted by those who would overthrow all faith, and hotly snatch at anything that seems to be likely to further their own ends; but because error has tried to force truth into service, we are not on that account to quietly let it be so, and refuse truth in its rightful place when it seeks it." Just who at UVM held what "wild and extravagant" views is unclear; Perkins may have been referring to the use of evolutionary theory to deny the existence of God. [12]

UVM students participated in the evolutionary debate more vociferously than Perkins did, and the students' views largely mirrored those of society. Author Wilford Hall's attacks on evolution (as well as on gravitational theory, the wave theory of sound, etc.) in his book *Wilford's Microcosm* were ridiculed by William Stiles, science editor of the *Cynic*, who in 1883 labeled Hall "one more of the uneducated or half-educated men" who considered science and religion contradictory. The following year Stiles reported on University of Minnesota president W. W. Folwell's address to the meeting of the AAAS in Minneapolis, which Perkins and A. H. Sabin (professor of chemistry and physics since 1880) were attending. Stiles quoted Folwell as affirming that "we are all, in some sense, evolutionists." In another issue, the *Cynic* considered the question, "What position shall the college student take on the question of evolution?" The response, after a balanced discussion, was a firm vote for Christian Darwinism. [13]

Perkins's publications reveal no particular viewpoint regarding the specifics of evolutionary theory. Between 1870 and 1911 he published eleven articles on a variety of subjects in the *American Naturalist*, which espoused the "American" (i.e., neo-Lamarckian) theory of evolution based on the inheritance of acquired characteristics. The *American Naturalist* was waging an ideological battle with its rival, the *American Journal of Science*, and rarely published articles by those who disagreed with its stance. A clearer picture of Perkins's position is provided by an address he gave in Burlington, "The Relation of Theories of Evolution to Religious Belief," in December 1895. Avoiding the ultimate question, "Is it true?" Perkins stated, "It is possible none of the existing theories will be finally accepted." But he fully embraced the evolutionary model: "The growth of a globe of vapor to an inhabitable earth, and the growth of a nation from the family to a tribe and through savagery to barbarism and from this to civilization are each an evolution. . . . To the evolutionist the present is not the final condition of everything. That is in the future and toward that future in which he believes he continually turns his eyes, and with blessed optimism sees there the undoing of evil and the enthronement of good."[14]

By the time Perkins delivered this talk, evolutionary theory had thoroughly infiltrated American thought and culture, and the lecture drew a large and sympathetic crowd. The response might have been different a quarter of a century earlier, when the *Burlington Free Press*, in a review of Darwin's *Descent of Man*, pointed out how the book traced "the origin of the race back beyond the monkey, to the oyster, which perhaps explains the 'affinity' of mankind for that affectionate bivalve."[15] Though Perkins did not recommend *The Descent of Man* in his 1895 lecture, he did suggest more palatable fare: Henry Drummond's *Ascent of Man*, Joseph LeConte's *Religion and Science*, G. F. Wright's *Studies in Science and Religion* (all three among the principal texts for the Christian Darwinists), and Darwin's less controversial work, *Origin of Species*.[16] Records show that President Buckham himself read *The Descent of Man* in 1895, perhaps on the recommendation of Perkins.[17]

The Practical Sciences

The relationship of mollusks to man was just what Perkins wanted to explore with his students in the practical, laboratory-oriented manner of his Ph.D. training. In 1875 he instituted a comparative anatomy course, where each student dissected animals of four different classes. Just what creatures were being sacrificed is not certain, but a *Cynic* article some years later notes Perkins's use of Burlington's stray cats in a lab demonstration. Laboratory study, begun under George Benedict in the early years of scientific education at UVM, had progressed primarily in chemistry, albeit slowly. In 1866, $450 was given to Eli Blake, professor of chemistry and physics, to purchase apparatus and chemicals, and to contract for lab tables to be built. A few months later President Angell submitted a plan for a chemical laboratory to be built on the ground floor of the North College. Otherwise, for years the University did little financially to advance laboratory training; the combined equipment expenses of the chemical, civil engineering, and natural history departments was about $300 per year all through the 1870s. In 1878 the Trustees splurged and bought almost $500 worth of chemicals.[18]

Despite these hindrances William Stiles could report in 1883: "UVM has now the best College laboratory in New England, outside of Yale and Harvard." UVM graduated at least one chemist before the Civil War, Frederick V. Hopkins ('59), who became professor of chemistry and geology at

Louisiana State University, but there was very little employment for chemists outside academe. Andrew Carnegie recalled that even in the early 1870s chemistry was "almost an unknown agent in connection with the manufacture of pig iron." Before Stiles's declaration of a new era UVM's few graduates in chemistry usually found jobs either in teaching at other universities or at state agricultural experiment stations. The same was initially true of the single physicist, C. K. Weed ('71), who taught high school physics before becoming professor of physics at the University of Michigan. However, by the late 1880s he had left academic life for the private sector and then joined the U.S. Patent Office.

The Patent Office's work in this field was mushrooming as a result of the increasing employment of chemists by private industry, and UVM's graduates demonstrate this trend. Between 1889 and 1893 UVM graduated seven chemists, all but one of whom went to work for a variety of manufacturing companies. The seventh, H. A. Torrey ('93), son of Professor H. A. P. Torrey, delivered a commencement address, "The Extension of the Laboratory Method," that was the first given by a future scientist. He went on to get a master's degree and a doctorate at Harvard before returning to teach at UVM in 1899. Earlier graduates in chemistry had pursued advanced degrees in Europe. Horatio Loomis ('76) studied at Wiesbaden and Leipzig. W. O. Atwater went on to receive a Ph.D. from Yale in 1869, but continued his schooling in Berlin and Leipzig. Nathan E. Merrill, who presided over chemistry at UVM from 1885 to 1914, had spent three years at Heidelberg, Leipzig, and Zurich. President Buckham aided aspiring scientists considerably by moving the traditional winter recess to summer, thereby freeing students for better-paying and skill-improving work in their prospective fields.[19]

William Stiles was representative of the postbellum UVM student in his belief that science was more useful than the Classical curriculum and that it paid better; he went into manufacturing after college. In the debut issue of the *Cynic* his editorial "More Room for the Sciences" argued that the average college student would use his knowledge of science ten times "while he reads one line of Greek." He wrote another piece that compared the graduate who taught in a country academy for $400 to $800 per year and the chemist who could expect $1,200 to $1,500. After graduation he worked as a color chemist in Montreal for eight years before becoming the superintendent of a paint works in Flushing, New York.

Underclassmen following Stiles reflected the growing attraction of utilitarian science. Even as an undergraduate, Charles Whiting Baker ('86) wrote about developments in underwater armaments. He later became an engineer and editor-in-chief of *Engineering News*. Baker's classmate Frederick J. Mills wrote a *Cynic* piece announcing the death of pure science and holding that only practical applications were worthwhile: "Our condition depends, not so much upon what we know, as upon what we use, and such being the case, it requires no prophet to foretell the final victory of utilitarianism." It comes as no surprise that Mills's career epitomized the triumph of utilitarianism. After working for the Union Pacific Railroad for five years he served in the Idaho legislature, became lieutenant governor, and then did irrigation engineering for the state and the U.S. Army.[20]

A more complex example of the "new" UVM graduate can be found in a Burlington native who graduated just before Stiles, Baker, and Mills entered the University—John Dewey. In an earlier age Dewey might easily have become a minister, but along with this option modern society presented a variety of secular careers. Reading Thomas Huxley and Herbert Spencer, as well as Matthew Arnold's critique of religious orthodoxy, Dewey began to see the world as his science professor, George Perkins, saw it—evolutionary and progressive. For Dewey and his peers science was the new religion.[21] Huxley seems to have introduced Dewey to the idea of the interdependence of the parts of biological organisms and to have suggested the possibility of a similarly organic philosophy. Perkins, like Dewey's other UVM professors, showed him how to balance contemplation and action, and this contributed to his pragmatic philosophy.[22]

Perkins's Legacy

Though Burlington was far from the centers of American scientific activity, UVM students kept up to date via publications and the work and contacts of their professors. Perkins's scientific circle was fairly large; he exchanged geological and paleontological specimens with A. E. Verrill, L. J. Smith, and O. C. Marsh of Yale University, Joseph Henry at the Smithsonian, Elliot Coues of Columbia University, and Nathaniel Shaler of Harvard. He read widely in all of the sciences, from zoology (Cuvier's *Regne Animal*, Agassiz's *Contributions to Natural History*, Wilson's *Ornithology*, Holbrook's *Herpetology*, and Say's *Entomology*) and geology (*Geology of Canada, Geology of Illinois, Geology of Iowa*) to botany (Darwin's *Variations of Animals and Plants under Domestication*). Though his Ph.D. was in zoology, his first professional publication was in geology: an 1870 description of a landslide on a New Hampshire mountain. He had a budding interest in anthropology when he came to UVM and made ample use of the few works relating to local natural history (Hitchcock's *Geology of Vermont*, Thompson's *Natural History of Vermont*). By 1890 his reading suggests that anthropology was his most particular interest. In sum, Perkins practiced an applied science that alternately drew him in and out of various scientific fields following society's fluctuating interest in them. He served as state entomologist from 1880 to 1895, a time when the federal government was battling insects on American farms, and his tenure as state geologist (1898–1933) spanned the period of the rise of the slate, granite, marble, and other extractive industries in Vermont. In 1898 he became dean of the Department of Natural Sciences. Though he published articles in a variety of scientific journals and in annual government publications, his work was equally visible in lay publications. Between 1871 and 1895 the *Burlington Free Press* published twenty-six articles that Perkins had extracted from his lectures and scientific publications. In addition, the *Green Mountain Freeman* published his popular writings throughout the late 1870s and early 1880s. His style in these articles was plain and simple, whether the topic was prehistoric man or local plant life.[23]

Perkins's real gift was for teaching, and he often shared this gift outside university classrooms. His honest, unadorned manner made him a great popularizer of science throughout the state of Vermont. He demystified natural history, acting as the voice of authority on subjects as diverse as geodes, ancient pottery, tent caterpillars, and the "hygiene of house plants." In suggesting to the lay public what the appropriate human emotions should be toward weasels and cutworms, leaf rollers and liver flukes, Perkins served as an important public relations liaison for the University for more than half a century.[24]

For all of Perkins's scientific erudition in the eyes of laymen, he did not want for critics of his work among his peers. Ezra Brainerd, president of Middlebury and second only to Cyrus Pringle in his knowledge of Vermont flora, had this to say about Perkins's *General Catalogue of the Flowering Plants of Vermont* (1882): "Perkins' catalogue filled me with intense disgust. He corrected a few misprints in the copy he sent me but overlooked the ten times worse [nomenclatural] errors. . . . His work is useless—is a disgrace to the state."[25] When Perkins's *Flora of Vermont* was issued in 1888, he tried to explain away the faults of the earlier edition by attributing them to the printer, but the real failing lay in his lack of botanical expertise. His heart was in the right place in wishing to see a Vermont flora published, but it could not be rushed. Brainerd and Pringle could have produced a much superior work but ended up consenting to act as editors for Perkins's 1888 work.[26]

In 1901 Perkins the botanist became Perkins the ornithologist with the publication of "A Preliminary List of the Birds Found in Vermont." Scientific reaction was swift and sharp. R. H. Howe, a Longmeadow, Massachusetts, ornithologist, who had been planning a similar publication, faulted both errors in Perkins's list and his failure to include a preface on the relationship of bird distribution to topography, plant communities, and "faunal areas." Howe, a younger man in touch with the blossoming science of ecology, did, of course, include such a discussion.[27] Perkins was in a position to author such comprehensive lists because botanists and ornithologists from around the state sent him their observations. Though appreciative of his efforts on behalf of natural history study, these devoted amateurs could be critical as well. Frances Horton wrote from Brattleboro to protest mildly that the scarlet tanager, warbling vireo, pine warbler, and hermit, wood, and Wilson's thrushes were all common in southern Vermont—not rare, as Perkins's list suggested.[28] Even Perkins's skills as an entomologist were called into question. Though he had served since 1888 as the Experiment Station entomologist, the station's Board of Control dismissed him in 1905.[29]

It was only natural for the good dean's capabilities to be questioned because he remained a generalist while specialization in science moved forward. A review of Perkins's "fieldwork" gives some idea of how thinly spread his efforts at science were. Back in his hometown, Galesburg, Illinois, for his wedding in August 1870, he collected geodes along the Illinois River. Throughout the decade of the 1870s he made local collecting expeditions to the "Frink Farm," or "hemp yard," archaeological site in Swanton (now known as the Swanton Cemetery, an early Woodland Indian burial ground) and along Lake Champlain. In 1878 Henry Loomis and the University provided funds for Perkins's summer collecting efforts, and the Lake Champlain Transportation Company provided free passage.[30] In 1883 one of Perkins's former students, J. W. Griffin ('73), donated money for summer research and travel expenses that allowed him to collect fossils in the Dakota Badlands after attending the AAAS meeting in Minneapolis.[31] This was the last time Perkins would receive even minor research assistance. Paid sabbatical leave, though instituted as early as the 1870s at some of the research universities, was not widespread at UVM until the 1960s.

Perkins's expedition budget never afforded him an assistant. His wife, Mary, sometimes served as field companion, though she seems not to have shared his collecting enthusiasm. In the summer of 1899 the Perkinses traveled to British Columbia, where Mary recorded these sentiments in a letter to her son Harry:

We . . . have roamed through the Indian village, watched the silver-smiths and basket-makers at work in their unspeakably filthy houses, seen (*smelled*) their salmon on poles in the outside huts drying. . . . People are "stocking up" in baskets and halibut hooks, etc. for gifts and cabinets, while your father selects the dirtiest and lowliest specimens he can find, as having been actually used and as more characteristic, for his two Museums. He is out now and will come back with leprosy and small-pox combined, I haven't a doubt.[32]

Perkins was determined to extend their northwestern foray to include the Muir Glacier in Sitka, Alaska, and Mary explained to her sister the reason for the long journey:

It is becoming more and more evident that if George is to hold a College position now, at his increasing age, and in this day of specializing, he must add to his equipment in the ways which are open to him, by all possible means. I see quite a difference between his enthusiasm for these things now, and when we first began to see mountains together. Not that he is less appreciative, but more cautious and deliberate. He has kept up wonderfully in his departments of study, considering the pressure which his *work* keeps on him all the time. And so long as he is to hold a place in College he *must* keep up. . . . These investments of a part of his salary in tours for field work and study are keeping him equipped for further work.[33]

Generally, Perkins failed to turn his summer trips into profitable scientific publishing ventures. His Alaska travels added a totem pole and grave chest and other exotic items to the museum, but they yielded no contributions to the scientific literature. A review of his 1904–1906 research in paleobotany in the Brandon lignite deposits concluded: "From a botanical viewpoint the venture was virtually valueless. Almost every minor variation in size, shape, and preservation was named as a new species."[34] His 1907 trip around the world took him to a wide variety of places where he might conduct research; he spent a number of days at the British Museum in London with both the ethnology/archaeology collections and the paleontology collection, but the closest he came to doing research was to look over the museum's collection of fossil fruits for comparison with his Brandon specimens.[35]

The Growth of Scientific Education

Substantial financial support for the natural sciences at UVM began in 1880, when John Purple Howard gave $50,000 to endow a chair in natural history and provide Perkins with a salary of at least $1,500 per year, plus not less than $300 per year for specimens and for the repair or purchase of apparatus needed for natural science instruction. In 1882 John N. Pomeroy, a longtime UVM trustee who had been active in the College of Natural History, gave $20,000 to endow a professorship of chemistry and natural philosophy, and in 1893 Edwin Flint ('36) gave $50,000 to set up the Flint Professorship of Mathematics.[36] As generous as these patrons were, their conception of science was out of date. Though Perkins was indeed a "natural historian," at other universities such chairs were being replaced by professorships for the various specializations—botany, zoology, geology. Frederick Billings's gift of the George Perkins Marsh library was a boon for the historian, but it did not contain the modern scientific periodicals and texts needed by chemists and geologists. Science at UVM paled in comparison to the strides that were being made elsewhere. Harvard's Museum of Comparative Zoology, begun by Louis Agassiz in 1858 with a $5,000 gift, was worth $700,000 in 1885 and backed by $600,000 in invested funds. The University of Pennsylvania received a $60,000 bequest the same year simply to promote the scientific investigation of spiritualism. It was only in 1885 that Perkins got his first assistant, a student who received 15 cents an hour. Four decades later, reminiscing about the conditions of the zoology lab, Perkins related how microscopic demonstrations were carried on at that time. There was only one microscope for lab demonstrations (a Crouch binocular bought slightly used in Philadelphia at one quarter of the original price), and students lined up one after the other to see the specimen, approaching on tiptoe because the floor was so shaky.[37]

Thanks to the Hatch Act of 1887, appropriating funds for research at state agriculture experiment stations, Perkins gained a colleague, Lewis Ralph Jones, who was appointed assistant professor of natural history in 1888 and professor of botany in 1892. Jones made an enormous contribution to UVM during his twenty-year tenure, as both a research scientist and an inspiring teacher, as well as in public relations as the Experiment Station reached out across the state. He laid the foundation for an excellent research program in phytopathology, the first research specialty to become associated with the University and one that continues today. He also cultivated an early interest in forestry at the University, both by his teaching and through his public efforts to promote scientific forestry throughout the state. He promoted the use of effective teaching methods in "nature study" in the public schools, by guidelines he developed at UVM and by his statewide lecturing before educators and administrators. He prompted university officials to acquire land locally for research and teaching opportunities. He followed the earlier Perkins pattern in service activities (the Vermont Botanical Club, the UVM Botanical Club, the Vermont Forestry Association, and the Burlington Board of Park Commissioners). His pioneering studies in plant pathology attracted significant recognition, which eventually led to his being wooed away from UVM to the University of Wisconsin.

Though Jones's leadership in American plant pathology is associated with his later years at the University of Wisconsin, he had a significant impact on at least one cohort of students before leaving UVM. Before his arrival UVM had turned out no botanists. Beginning in 1890, UVM was producing one or more students annually who went on in botanical work.

UVM conferred its first master's degree in 1874, an M.S. in engineering awarded to Charles Simeon Denison, who later became professor of mechanical drawing at the University of Michigan. Then there was nearly a quarter-century hiatus before the University began regularly granting the M.S. In 1890, Jones had begun collecting parasitic fungi, assisted by two students: Abel J. Grout ('90) and Herbert Isaac Collins ('93). William Allen Orton continued their work and in 1898 received a master's degree for his thesis, "A Preliminary List of the Parasitic Fungi of Vermont, with Notes on the Species of Economic Importance." Orton was one of many students who assisted Jones in his work while an undergraduate and then created his own research agenda. He had shown promise early on, winning sophomore honors in botany, the "junior prize for progress," and an honorable mention for "thesis of conspicuous merit" at graduation. Along with field and lab work, Orton spent much time putting the University's herbarium of fungi in order, remounting specimens and arranging them taxonomically. Professor Jones once reminisced that Orton, who was partially deaf, even as a freshman always sat in the front row "eyes open, lips parted, eagerly 'drinking in' every idea." Jones hailed Orton as a representative of the "heroic" in science, attributing this (as a fellow Congregationalist might) to his ancestry and upbringing—he was related to Ethan and Ira Allen.[38]

Orton's master's thesis was a simple list, supplemented by observations on the life cycles of the species of fungi that had economically important plants as hosts—grapes, gooseberries, vegetables, and cereals. For UVM botany students like Orton, the master's degree, funded as it usually was by experiment station money, was a direct entrée to a position with either another state experimental station or the Bureau of Plant Industry at the U.S. Department of Agriculture. That, in fact, is where Orton went after finishing his degree, and a number of other UVM experiment station alumni followed him there. Phytopathology provided crucial assistance to the increasingly monocultural American agricultural industry and was perhaps the most important agricultural science of that era.

UVM awarded its first Ph.D. degree to Alfred Hills Campbell in 1888, but it was granted "upon examination"; he never wrote a dissertation or enrolled in any courses. The only other Ph.D.'s awarded before World War II were in botany: Arne Peitersen was awarded the degree in 1916 for his study of *Rubus*; and E. J. Dole and L. H. Flint both received Ph.D.'s in 1923, Dole working on transpiration in *Pinus strobus* and Flint on the metabolic effects of fertilizers on various crop plants. All three men were affiliated with the Experiment Station while working toward their doctoral degrees.

Along with progress in plant pathology the major international development in botany in the closing years of the nineteenth century was the growth of plant ecology. Clifton D. Howe's 1901 master's thesis—"Flora of Burlington and Vicinity"—though primarily a catalog of plants from the Burlington area, is also a preliminary attempt at applying the principles of plant ecology and geography to those flora. His model was H. C. Cowles's paper "The Physiographic Ecology of Chicago," published in the *Botanical Gazette* that same year. Howe's twin brother Carleton wrote a thesis on Cowles's successional theory of plant communities developing in a well-ordered chronological sequence. However, despite the promise in the Howe brothers' work in plant ecology, they ended up in other fields. Carleton became a school administrator, though he always maintained a vital interest in nature study. Clifton went on to get a Ph.D. in botany at the University of Chicago and then joined the faculty of the University of Toronto, becoming head of the forestry department in 1920.

All of Jones's students took courses with Perkins as well; but because Perkins had no systematic research program of his own, the only two master's theses pursued under his aegis were done so more by default than design. In 1910, A. R. Atwood, who had graduated in 1899 with honors in geology and had gone on to Harvard Divinity School (1900) and Andover Theologi-

cal Seminary (1904), applied to work for a master's degree. His proposal was
to study geology and evolution, reading the major theorists and interpreters
(Darwin, Lamarck, Huxley, Mivart, Spencer, Cope, etc.) and then producing a thesis on the glacial geology of Quincy, Massachusetts. Unfortunately,
his thesis turned out to be only a poor copy of Perkins's own scientific
work, a rambling discussion of economic geology and paleoenvironments.[39]
In 1913 master's student Roy F. Leighton did an excellent study of sixty-
five trephined (surgically perforated) prehistoric skulls from the American
Museum of Natural History, but though he acknowledged Perkins's guidance toward an interest in anthropology, he received his practical assistance
from others.

Meanwhile, more needed to be done to upgrade science facilities. President Buckham, noting that UVM was now competing with the best colleges,
warned in 1886, "Our weak point is the lack of endowments."[40] Alumnus
Edward H. Williams proposed donating money to build an art museum at
the University. Buckham and trustee John H. Converse (Williams's business
partner) persuaded him to designate the money for a new science building
instead. Williams Science Hall, a copy of the Oxford Museum in London designed by John Ruskin, was completed in 1896. The building symbolized the
dual aspirations of the University: to improve both scientific *and* humanistic
education. Ruskin's aim, like that of the Philadelphia architects who copied
him, had been to humanize science by housing it in Gothic architecture.
Dissection, distillation, and electrical demonstration might go on inside,
but the building's elaborate terra-cotta trimmings, high-pitched roof, and
plethora of arches and gables invoked the devotion to God that had been the
foundation of the institution. The cathedral-like exterior reminded students
that their laboratory studies were conducted within a framework of a religious, moral, and aesthetic tradition that superseded science's novelty. The
three medallions on the facade were of men dedicated equally to science *and*
God. Facing the green were Louis Agassiz and Joseph Henry, the leaders of
the American scientific elite at midcentury, and Samuel F. B. Morse, whose
practical science had helped to transform modern life.

As impressive as the Williams building itself was the state-of-the-art
apparatus that filled it. The Department of Electrical Engineering had a
dynamo room equipped with $6,500 worth of motors, alternators, arc-light
machines, and power scales; a photometer room; and an electrometallurgy
room. Though the wish list drawn up by Professors Perkins and Jones for the
Department of Biology contained "nothing which is not of immediate use,"
it was an enormous improvement over the scarcity of the past. It had taken
Perkins a dozen years to acquire ten microscopes for his physiology lab; now
he was to get twenty at once, plus micrometers, Bunsen burners, scales, and
dissecting equipment. The mineralogy lab was updated with a ganiometer, a
spectroscope, and a cutting machine for making thin sections of rocks. There

were also to be twenty-six rock hammers, assuring the ability of each student in Perkins's geology class to take samples on their excursions to Rock Point and Willard's Ledge.[41]

The other institution that experienced significant growth in the late nineteenth century was the University Museum. Since its creation along with the College of Natural History in 1826, this variegated collection of objects from the natural world had been a joint venture of the University and the surrounding community. It was the one institution that was psychologically "owned" by farmers and merchants (and doctors, lawyers, and other professionals) as tenaciously as by University faculty and students. Its maintenance and growth, however, were largely due to one man—Perkins. When the Trustees passed a resolution mourning Perkins's death in 1933, the first quality they recognized after his "progressive spirit" was his role as a "museum builder."[42] After Perkins became curator in 1873, he increased the collections by nearly half with the deposit of more than 10,000 zoological and 5,000 geological specimens. He continued for nearly sixty years, through his own collecting and solicitations from others, to build a respectable natural history museum. Just as George Benedict before him had aspired to create a miniature version of the great musuems of Europe, Perkins often used the large, well-established museums of the Northeast as a yardstick for his own progress. He was both proud of his museum and frustrated by it; to Peabody Museum director F. W. Putnam he reported, "Our Vermont collections are in a newly fitted up room and are many times larger than when you saw them and are better arranged for exhibition. . . . I wish that the Peabody Museum were where I could have more frequent access to it for study. In my anthropological reading I am all the time coming to points which study of collections would greatly elucidate."[43] Lack of space was always a problem; Torrey Hall, housing the museum since 1863, became more cramped when a third story was added in 1874 to house the Park Art Gallery and again in 1898 when the Cannon Room was added. The extra space from these additions was simultaneously offset by the bric-a-brac (and expectations for more of the same) that came along with them.

The fundamental problem with the natural history museum was the paucity of benefactors and the lack of any systematic scientific investigation for which the collections might provide support. The expansion of natural history museums at other universities was largely the result of participation by associated faculty in sustained field investigations. Such activity was rare at UVM. The lament expressed by Perkins to Putnam was somewhat misplaced, for Perkins's own archaeological research efforts tended to be unfocused and antiquarian. Aside from their limited use in classroom demonstrations and their entertainment value for the general public, there was no real focus for the collections, and it was inevitable that they would eventually seem superfluous.

The same could not be said for one particular branch of the museum—its botanical collections. The herbarium begun by Joseph Torrey had been augmented over the years by both UVM and outside botanists, but in Perkins's hands it had remained a modest collection because botany was not his particular passion. However, in 1902 Professor Jones persuaded the Trustees to bring Cyrus Pringle and his herbarium to the University. Pringle, a native of Charlotte, Vermont, had matriculated at the University in 1859 but never attended because of family obligations. By the time of his move to UVM he had become the most prolific plant collector in history. The initial endowment for what would come to be known as the Pringle Herbarium was a sum of $10,000 contributed by UVM trustee Dr. W. Seward Webb; Pringle, as "Herbarium Keeper and Collector," was to be paid a lifetime annuity of $600, with an additional $350 annually for maintenance and acquisition expenses. With the arrival of Pringle's collections, UVM's herbarium became the largest in New England except for Harvard's Gray Herbarium. Supplying specimens to more than fifty museums throughout the world and corresponding regularly with an almost equal number of botanists, Pringle was essentially a one-person research institution of international reputation.[44]

The "Progressive" Sciences: Anthropology and Eugenics

Like that of many of his contemporaries, George Perkins's interest in natural history encompassed the study of man; and for Perkins, anthropology was "anything pertaining to man; the study of the past to understand the present, the present to understand the future." He began presenting this evolutionary view of the study of man to UVM students in 1885 in the second anthropology course ever taught for credit in an American university (one was begun in 1879 at the University of Rochester). His interest in anthropology likely stemmed from his role as curator of the University Museum after 1873. A number of local collectors—D. S. Kellogg of Plattsburgh, New York, A. D. Halbert of Essex, Vermont; H. B. Williams of Monkton, Vermont; and many others—donated hundreds of artifacts, mostly from the Champlain Valley. By the mid-1880s Perkins was making a special effort to solicit Vermont archaeological material for the museum.[45]

All of Perkins's seventeen publications in anthropology were of an archaeological nature, largely descriptions of objects collected by others. Though he pursued some fieldwork and corresponded with more experienced men, he never developed a feeling for archaeological methods, and contemporary archaeologists continue to be confounded by the paucity of provenance data for the collections. Little or no site information such as the stratigraphic record accompanied the artifacts, rendering them largely useless to archaeologists seeking to reconstruct possible activity at their prehistoric sites.

Perkins's anthropology course was always extremely popular, partly because of its light work load; students referred to the course as "My Trip
around the World." Meeting in the sunny atrium on the top floor of Williams Hall or later at Perkins's house on South Prospect Street, students were
treated to "Perk's" view of world civilizations, derived from his readings
of authors such as Edward Tylor and Lewis Henry Morgan, who believed
that social evolution universally followed a pattern of progress from savagery through barbarism to civilization. In his teaching of anthropology,
as in his instruction in other disciplines, he conveyed this underlying belief in progress. He embraced the theory of evolution as a metaphor for all
of life, telling students, "Things are what they are because of growth. Anthropology is a study of growth, of action, of the law of development in
mankind." [46]

Perkins held onto his anthropology course until three months before his
death at age eighty-nine. There was no incentive at UVM for more up-
to-date instruction in the discipline. Franz Boas and other cultural anthro-
pologists had long since begun to disprove the assumptions that cultural
differences had a racial basis and that racial and linguistic groupings were
equivalent, which Perkins and his peers held from their nineteenth-century
training. In his first lecture each year Perkins painted a picture of Paleo-
lithic brutes enduring much suffering, with little intelligence to advance
themselves technologically. He went on to elaborate about racial differences,
equating small stature (he did not include himself though he was only a little
over five feet tall) with racial inferiority and flat noses with "degraded races."
The Celts were "impetuous, narrow in their religions . . . , not given to profound investigation"; Slavs were "the least civilized of any people, fond of
barbaric shows . . . , warlike" but "great linguists"; the Finns and Lapps were
"simple-minded," their idea of religion being that "when in danger they are
very devoted to the Scriptures and Hymns"; the Chinese had "no ability to
invent." Teutonic people, however, "lead the races and in a sense control the
earth." Communicated with his characteristic genteel good humor and illustrated by maps, lantern slides, and an array of curiosities, many of which
he had collected himself, his propositions were impressed on students in a
memorable manner. [47]

One of the students in those early anthropology lectures was the professor's son, Henry Farnham ("Harry") Perkins. Harry had a passing interest
in natural history but hardly possessed his father's zeal for the natural world.
Indeed, many of his classmates were much more intrigued by the affairs of
science. At his 1898 commencement four addresses spoke to the realms of science and nature: Anna May Clark, "The Struggle for Existence,"; Clifton D.
Howe, "Enjoyment of Nature," Marian Rustedt, "The Attitude of Modern
Poetry to Science"; and J. C. Torrey, "The Element of Design in Evolution."
Harry Perkins's topic was "Education and the Labor Problem." Although

his father was progressive in the sense of having a general belief in progress, Harry was a Progressive who took the idea of progress as a mandate for social reform.

Despite his reformist inclination and minimal interest in biology, Harry followed his father's path by enrolling for graduate study at Johns Hopkins, arguably the leading center of biological research and education in the United States, where he came under the tutelage of William Keith Brooks. Brooks, though a descriptive morphologist himself, was producing graduate students who were pioneering the experimentalist tradition in American biology. Brooks's own work focused on the life history of jellyfish, and Perkins's Ph.D. study followed his mentor's lead.[48]

Even though he accepted a position at his inland alma mater, Harry Perkins seemed destined for a career in experimental biological research like his contemporaries at Johns Hopkins and other leading coastal research universities. After becoming instructor in zoology at UVM in 1902, he continued his scientific work along this line. In 1905, funded by the Carnegie Institution of Washington, he studied coelenterates from the moat at Fort Jefferson in the Dry Tortugas.[49] After research work for the U.S. Bureau of Fisheries on Lake Champlain mollusks,[50] he was back at Johns Hopkins in 1917 as a "Fellow by Courtesy," doing work on jellyfish physiology. Though he continued to teach comparative anatomy and embryology, his research in the field ended by 1920. Burlington was no place to make great strides in experimental biology or even descriptive morphology of marine animals; the best Perkins could to to offer students opportunities for such research was to lobby the administration to subscribe to the Marine Biological Laboratory at Woods Hole. UVM was a member institution for twelve of the years between 1919 and 1938, but only a few students—J. Allen Scott in 1924, Lyman Rowell and Flavia Richardson in 1928—ever did research there.[51] The incentive to produce scientific research at UVM came almost exclusively from outside the University, there being no institutional demands or support for it. Perkins's scientific community centered on the Vermont Bird and Botanical Club of which he was vice-president in 1915 and president in 1922. He did some banding of gulls on the Four Brothers Islands but seems to have had far greater enthusiasm for photography than for ornithology. He taught a course in photography and was familiar to students via the lantern slide show of the campus he gave annually to incoming freshmen.[52]

Perkins's zoology teaching load, consisting of courses in "Elements of Animal Biology," comparative anatomy and embryology, and an occasional seminar in bird biology, had remained relatively light over the years. Though he taught no course in genetics or evolution, he did touch on the "principles of heredity" in his embryology class. In 1922 he wrote to C. B. Davenport, director of the Department of Genetics of the Carnegie Institution of Washington at Cold Spring Harbor, New York, to ask for ideas for student research projects on heredity. Davenport sent an enthusiastic reply, suggesting work on eye color, height and weight, and color blindness and added that "family histories of local orphanages will reveal very interesting data of great social, if not biological, moment." He also invited Perkins to send his students to Cold Spring Harbor to continue their work.[53]

In 1924 Perkins began to teach a course devoted to human heredity and channeled students to just the sort of projects that Davenport had suggested. In procuring the data he had help from a UVM colleague, sociology professor A. R. Gifford, who was president of the Vermont Children's Aid Society in Burlington and gave him access to the society's records. The following year, with the assistance of President Guy Bailey, Perkins found a patron for the eugenics program he was building at UVM. Vermont native Mrs. Emily Proctor Eggleston of Berkeley, California, gave UVM $5,000 for a "eugenical survey of Vermont." (Mrs. Eggleston was a native Vermonter, daughter of former governor Fletcher D. Proctor and a benefactor of the Children's Aid Society of which Bailey was treasurer.) The funds were distributed to Perkins, who established an office on Main Street for his Eugenics Survey of Vermont.[54] "Eugenics" was the term coined by Charles Darwin's cousin, Francis Galton, to denote the science of improving the genetic condition of the human race. Less a natural science than a crude social science effort, its proponents believed in the reality of racial stereotypes, accepted the myth that certain races (particularly those of northern Europe) possessed a monopoly of desired characteristics, and thought that human differences were invariably caused by heredity and thus were resistant to modification.

All but the genetic elements of the eugenics equation had been imparted to UVM students since 1885 by George Perkins in his anthropology course; he added genetics in 1900 when Gregor Mendel's classic 1866 paper on crossing peas was rediscovered. The elder Perkins read up on the field, and at Johns Hopkins, Harry Perkins actively absorbed the infant science from teachers who were tentatively applying Mendelian techniques to their research. During the rise of the eugenics movement (roughly 1905 to 1930) there were few people in Vermont with any substantial training in genetics, leaving Harry Perkins as the sole "expert" in hereditarian theories of human behavior. Perkins often invoked his natural science training when presenting eugenics to the public. Commenting on the work of the eugenics survey, he remarked, "This investigation happens to be under the direction of a laboratory-trained biologist. He looks upon the rural community as a biological organism, its heredity and its environment show numerous parallels to the kindred processes in plant or animal." Such expert status was also claimed by Henry Taylor, director of the Vermont Commission on Country Life, founded in 1928 as an extension of the eugenics survey's work. At his own request Taylor was designated "Research Professor of Agricultural Economics" for the three-year tenure of the commission and thus became UVM's first officially appointed research associate.[55]

Eugenics at UVM died hard. Harry Perkins continued to teach his course on eugenics until his retirement in 1945, and to honor him the University invited one of America's most strident eugenicists, Henry Pratt Fairchild, professor of sociology at New York University, to give a lecture at Ira Allen Chapel on "Population and Peace." Hovey Jordan, who had been a student of Perkins's at both the undergraduate and graduate levels, joined the UVM faculty in 1919 and taught the same doctrine in the zoology department and in the medical school. He served for a number of years on the advisory council of the American Eugenics Society. Paul Moody continued to teach eugenic principles in his zoology courses into the 1960s.[56]

Perkins's eugenics survey was not the only manifestation at UVM of a "scientific" endeavor to transform American life. Beginning shortly after his arrival in 1921, psychology professor John T. Metcalf administered intelligence tests to each incoming freshman class. Metcalf was particularly qualified to initiate such a program; he had served as one of eighteen commissioned officers who helped conduct the U.S. Army's massive intelligence testing program for recruits during World War I. Metcalf's testing at UVM preceded widespread use of psychological testing in American universities. It was not until 1925 that the College Entrance Examination Board offered tests developed by Princeton's Carl Brigham to assist colleges with admissions. At UVM, intelligence tests were being actively used by 1926 to "track" students into particular courses of study and also to assist in decisions of academic dismissal. Outside UVM, Metcalf's expertise was often called upon by a number of organizations, including the Vermont Children's Aid Society, the Vermont Department of Public Welfare, and the Eugenics Survey of Vermont.[57]

Twentieth-Century Adjustments

In 1930, George Perkins retired from the curatorship of the University Museum, passing it on to Harry, with the prospect of a new era for the collections created by the soon-to-be-completed Fleming Museum. However, despite the new director's background as a natural scientist, the natural history collections were displaced by fine arts, the new darling of the upper class. Besides occasional requests for money for teaching specimens, Harry Perkins did little to augment the collections or to maintain what he had inherited from his father. Ironically, he oversaw the dismantling of the natural history collections that his father had worked so long to build. Remnants of the various collections were moved to the anthropology department, to Torrey Hall, and to the geology museum in Perkins Hall. Still, the museum continued to be linked to the community through a series of regular radio broadcasts given by Perkins and his assistant, Horace Eldred, and a museum-centered nature study program.[58]

Meanwhile, the utility of the Pringle Herbarium was questioned by university officials, though it was actively used by a variety of students, faculty, and community members, as well as by scientific correspondents from all over the world. The stature of old-fashioned taxonomy was eclipsed by newer plant sciences such as ecology and plant physiology, and these increasingly preferred the exotic over the local. For example, in the 1940s, G. P. Burns, chairman of the botany department, recommended to President Millis that the salary of one of his staff be frozen to persuade him to leave, because his botanical knowledge was limited to Vermont and thus his scientific authority was reduced.[59] This case highlighted a tension that had not previously been felt at UVM—that of professional competency. No one would have dreamed of leveling a charge of parochialism against George Perkins, and it displeased no one that his replacement in geology, E. C. Jacobs, was equally parochial. Jacobs assumed Perkins's old mantle of state geologist, under which, despite a limited budget, he churned out annual reports on Vermont copper mines, clay deposits, and talc prospects and a popular piece on the state's physical features. The largest grant he ever brought to the University was the $3,000 he obtained from the National Research Council for a seismograph in 1933. As departmental head he was not pressed to publish scholarly pieces more innovative than the State Report fillers (mainly to appease the Legislature).[60]

In 1944 Professors Jacobs and Burns retired, and a year later Harry Perkins retired from the curatorship of the Fleming Museum. The natural sciences were now in the hands of younger men, whose training and research experience were much more narrowly focused than that of their predecessors. After World War II, the sciences at UVM would grow to resemble the highly specialized, self-examining disciplines that they had already become at America's larger research universities. The return of veterans from World War II, coupled with the popularity of Vermont as a vacation resort for people from southern New England, New Jersey, and New York began to expand the geographical constituency that had always limited UVM's growth. Research programs in the natural sciences, often stymied during the late nineteenth and early twentieth centuries by lack of financial support, had remained largely ad hoc even after the post–World War I rise in enrollment. UVM was not alone in this regard. In 1920 fewer than twenty-five American universities were seriously committed to research as an institutional goal. Beginning in the 1940s, however, geologists, zoologists, botanists, and other scientists at UVM were almost without exception involved in research work and enjoying sustained outside sources of financial support. Some of these scientists became involved in research efforts sparked by the war. Professor Jacobs, for example, assisted in the reopening of the Vershire/South Strafford copper mines, and the Experiment Station grew a species of dandelion that it was hoped could be used to produce rubber.[61]

The new research programs drawing UVM scientists into ever-widening professional and intellectual circles during and after World War II have many roots in the previous century of scientific investigation and teaching. The work of the Maple Research Laboratory can be traced back to the pioneering efforts of experiment station chemist C. H. Jones in the 1890s, and the forestry department continues a tradition begun by George Perkins and Lewis Jones. Since the late 1960s renewed interest in the archaeology of the Champlain Valley among members of the anthropology department has answered many of the questions first asked by Perkins and his contemporaries. Specimens from the Pringle Herbarium still circle the globe to assist botanists interested in Vermont flora. UVM geologists, with plate tectonic theory as well as rock hammers in hand, visit many of the same outcrops that Perkins and Jacobs and their students did. All of these sciences have changed in their methods and materials, but they still remain part of a tradition of inquiry that has been sustained by the University for nearly two centuries.

Medicine at UVM: From Skilled Craft
to Learned Profession

LESTER J. WALLMAN

LYMAN ALLEN, University of Vermont professor of surgery, wrote "In Vermont, doctors were born and not made."[1] In eighteenth-century America and well into the nineteenth century there was no external control over qualifications for care of the sick and injured. Nor was there even agreement about the education or experience physicians should have. Whoever chose to could adopt the title of "doctor." In the spirit of the "common man," citizens of Vermont opposed any regulation of the practice of medicine by the Legislature.[2] Having attained the freedom to manage their own business and family affairs, they brooked no interference with their choice of anyone to help with their health problems, and they rejected the idea of a monopoly by any group of healers.

However, they did recognize and respect competence. So UVM, from its very beginning, was able to market training programs for young men who wished to be physicians. There was public acceptance, and at times in the early history of UVM, medical students outnumbered all others combined. But medicine everywhere was slow to grow from an empiric art to a learned profession based on science, and the medical department at UVM followed a correspondingly gradual path from a trade school outside the mainstream of the University to its present position as a national but distinctive academic resource.

Background

Faculties of medicine began in Paris, Naples, and Cambridge in the thirteenth century, followed by others in the next hundred years. Although medicine early became a recognized university discipline in Europe, university-trained physicians, interested primarily in theory, became philosophers, priests, teachers, and elite physicians for the nobility. Care of the masses was left to craftsmen—apothecaries and barber-surgeons.

In colonial America the M.D. degree was not in great demand. A few young men studied in Europe, but most became apprenticed to established physicians. Harvard College had functioned for 146 years before its medical faculty was organized in 1782.

By the time the Republic of Vermont was established in 1777 there were schools in Philadelphia, New Haven, Boston, and New York that awarded the M.D. degree and were staffed in part by European-trained professors. Few Vermont boys had either the opportunity or desire to attend those schools. Their families were too poor to employ physicians except in extreme cases, nor could they spare their sons from farm work for the study of medicine. Sawyers, blacksmiths, and coopers were in great demand, and established artisans took apprentices usually for about seven years of supervised work.

Physicians were also being trained by apprenticeship, but it took them only three years with an established practitioner before they could take up medicine as an occupation. Such pupils may have had a little more preliminary schooling than the artisans, and the quality of the training varied greatly from doctor to doctor. It was easier to identify shoddy workmanship in a joiner or smith than in a physician. Community acceptance of the young physician depended partly on the reputation of his preceptor. Practitioners of all sorts offered their services, and many who made no claim to any form of training flourished on the basis of self-professed native ability to cure. As late as 1833 Benjamin Lincoln, medical professor at UVM, lamented, "Of all the methods of getting a livelihood invented by Yankee ingenuity no one secures its object so effectually and with so little expense of Mental Labour as 'turning doctor.' "[3]

County medical societies, formed in Vermont in the late eighteenth and early nineteenth centuries, examined candidates recommended by their preceptors for membership.[4] Acceptance into the society indicated that the new doctor had been properly trained and could be distinguished from the "irregulars," the quacks, and the unorthodox healers.

Early in the nineteenth century, in order to gain additional credentials for practice, young men began to supplement the skills they had learned from their preceptors by going to school for the M.D. degree. Addressing this opportunity, physicians set up medical academies offering courses of lectures. Some were purely business ventures, usually short-lived when their proprietors were unable to secure legislative authority to grant degrees. Others developed into respected institutions. Following a two- or three-month course of lectures, the student would go to his preceptor for three or more years of practical training. He would then return to the academy to attend the same lecture series, presumably understanding the presentations better than he had the first time. After examination he would then be awarded the M.D. degree. The system was not very rigid. As long as the student paid his fees, he might drop out and return at any time, and many attended the first course in one school and the second in another.

The UVM Medical Department: 1804–1836

The story of medicine at UVM begins with Dr. John Pomeroy, who had had the customary apprenticeship with Dr. James Bradish in Cummington, Massachusetts.[5] In 1787 Pomeroy went to Cambridge, Vermont, to set up practice, but he moved his young family to Burlington in 1792 after deciding that the outlook was better there. The city did grow, and Pomeroy's reputation as physician and surgeon attracted patients. By 1800 he also was known as a teacher. He found a number of young men interested in sampling "physic" before making long-term commitments, and he began to take pupils in his home. Recognizing his ability, the university corporation appointed him lecturer in "chirurgy" and anatomy in 1804, just three years after President Sanders began instruction in the college building on the hill. However, the University provided neither lecture space nor financial commitment, so Pomeroy's classroom was his office and home on Battery Street, and he made whatever financial arrangement he could with his students. In 1809 the university bestowed an honorary M.D. on Dr. Pomeroy and awarded its first and only bachelor of medicine degree to one of his pupils, Truman Powell. No further medical degrees were awarded until after 1823 when, with the beginning of regular classes, the degree was the M.D.

During the War of 1812 the University was forced to suspend teaching (its one building having been taken over by the army), but Pomeroy's course on Battery Street was not affected; he even expanded to a rented building next door. When the University reclaimed its building in 1815 and repaired some of the damage done by the military occupation, Pomeroy and other professors he had recruited were permitted to use the upper floor for medical instruction. This concession was easily arrived at because few nonmedical students had presented themselves for enrollment.

After a shaky start Pomeroy's enterprise prospered. Although he himself had been trained by a preceptor, men with more prestigious qualifications joined him. Nathan Ryno Smith, B.A. and M.D. Yale, set up practice in Burlington and became professor of anatomy and physiology. He persuaded his famous father, Nathan Smith (of Dartmouth, Bowdoin, and Yale), to move to Burlington and teach theory and practice of medicine.

Nathan Smith, the founder of Dartmouth's medical college, was born in Massachusetts in 1762[6] and subsequently moved with his family to Chester, Vermont. Doctor Josiah Goodhue of Putney, Vermont, went to Chester and performed a leg amputation out in a field. When he asked for a volunteer to help hold the leg, Nathan, age twenty-one, stepped forward and maintained enough composure to help tie off the arteries in the stump. Following the operation he asked Dr. Goodhue to accept him as an apprentice, but he was told first to secure enough general education to satisfy the requirements for admission to Harvard College. After a year of study he was back with Dr. Goodhue for a preceptorship of three years, and at twenty-five he started practice in Cornish, New Hampshire.

In 1825 Harvard graduates William Sweetser and John Bell, who had M.D. degrees from Bowdoin and Dartmouth, became professors at UVM. In 1828 Benjamin Lincoln, a Bowdoin graduate who had studied with the well-known Boston physician George C. Shattuck, came to lecture, and the following year he was appointed professor of anatomy and surgery. These young men had already distinguished themselves as teachers and medical authors. Lincoln, a particularly popular professor, attracted students from as far away as Boston. One of them, Edward Jarvis (Harvard '26), had difficulty deciding on a profession. Medicine appealed to him, but he found the society of physicians "not very congenial to a cultivated mind"; most had little interest in literature, philosophy, or even medical science, and there were many uneducated quacks. When he did decide to attend Harvard's medical department, he spent some time in Burlington first with Professor Lincoln.[7]

Throughout most of the nineteenth century the University and the medical department operated in parallel, with separate budgets and sources of income. Each had its ups and downs, though not always concurrently. As a proprietary institution, like most schools of its time, the UVM medical department was owned by the professors and depended on student fees. There was little profit for the teachers, who supported themselves by the private practice of medicine. The medical department needed the University for the prestige of its academic appointments and the authority to grant degrees. Unless it could offer the M.D. degree, it would suffer in competition with other schools. In turn, the University gained credibility as a stable institution thanks to the reputations of the medical professors, many of whom were well known beyond Burlington. And by including the names of the medical students it could double its roster.

Between 1815 and 1822 the college on the hill graduated thirty-four students. Records of medical students during those years have been lost, but from 1823 to 1834 the university awarded the M.D. degree to 115 candidates, whereas the academic graduates numbered but ninety-two.[8] However, the college was in session all year except for three vacations totaling twelve weeks, whereas the medical department lectures lasted only twelve to fourteen weeks.

It was possible to have a functional medical college with just a few teachers to give lectures, a few anatomical preparations, and a minimum of chemical apparatus. Interested Vermonters were assured that they could do as well and much more cheaply in Burlington, where the climate was healthier than in Boston. The course of instruction was similar to that of the more prestigious colleges in the big cities. In any case it was preceptorship, just as available in Vermont as anywhere else, that provided the practical experience considered more useful than the lectures on theory. In 1834 Charles Caldwell of Transylvania medical school in Kentucky worried that more medical schools were being started than were needed, and he advised young people who wanted to study medicine to go to country schools because "the incentives to vice of all sorts are more numerous and powerful in large cities than in small ones."[9]

By 1830 there was a glut of physicians in New England. Some young men, after trying their luck in several communities, were forced to give up medicine entirely. In Vermont there were medical colleges in Burlington, Castleton, and Woodstock, and competition for the shrinking pool of potential students became severe.

When Castleton tried in 1831 to lure prospective Burlington students with reduced tuition, Dr. Lincoln, the leading light of the UVM medical department, published "An Exposition of Certain Abuses Practiced by Some of the Medical Schools in New England."[10] The drastic reforms he proposed for medical colleges would prohibit advertising and soliciting for students; professors would be paid salaries and would not be dependent on fees from students, and only students who had passed examinations in English, Latin, Greek, mathematics, and natural science would be admitted. Every course of study would begin with anatomy and physiology and progress to the application of these basic disciplines (an early attempt at a graded curriculum).

Lincoln was far ahead of his time. The relationship between medical practice and a Classical education or even exposure to the medical theories of the time was not generally accepted. In the climate of intense competition among schools any attempt to increase academic requirements for admission or graduation was bound to be resisted. Students found it easier to study at Castleton with its more relaxed standards, and Burlington's share diminished along with the income from the sale of lecture tickets. Dr. Pomeroy, outclassed by better-educated professors, had long since left teaching to concentrate on his practice and other civic ventures, and by 1834 Drs. Bell and Sweetser had moved on to other institutions. Benjamin Lincoln remained as the only faculty member, assisted by George Benedict, who acted as dean and taught chemistry. But Lincoln was already ill and soon went home to Maine, where he died in 1835. Benedict appointed a small faculty, at least in name, and one degree was awarded in 1836; after that no students were enrolled until the school was reactivated in 1854.[11]

Medicine in Early-Nineteenth-Century Vermont

The Vermont physicians of the early 1800s were a mixed lot with varying levels of education (often very little), but in the society of the time they performed a useful function, and most were able to hold their own against the "irregulars." Abby Maria Hemenway records that Dr. Benjamin Chandler of St. Albans, a well-respected practitioner who had been trained only by a country doctor, became "a fair classical scholar," "studying Latin by the kitchen fire."[12] She wrote that Dr. Stephen Peabody of Cambridge, Vermont, had "not much education." His brother warned him, "You have not the learning for a great doctor and you must not give harsh medicine, but the mildest you can."[13] Dr. Peabody had the reputation of being intemperate, but he always waited until he was sober before attending a patient.

With no common agreement on the efficacy of various systems Vermonters had to choose between various unorthodox practitioners and the regulars. They often made do with home remedies and many in rural areas did without any medical attention at all. In Boston and New York care was distributed according to social class, the well-to-do patronizing their social equals, the educated physicians, leaving the increasing numbers of poor without much attention. In Vermont there was less social stratification, and the one or two physicians in a community tended all citizens. Most of those who availed themselves of medical services could afford to pay something. It was not rare for a physician to operate a farm or other business along with medical practice, and some became quite prosperous.

It is interesting to note the relative financial rewards of physicians and artisans. In 1827, when a pair of shoes cost 67 cents, one Rufus Chaffee charged 20 to 37 cents to mend them and would make a pair of boots for $1.25. In 1824 Dr. Joel Fairchild of Shelburne charged 20 and 25 cents for medicine he dispensed, "visit and cathartic 50 cents," obstetric care $2 or $3. Payment was often accepted in kind. The account book shows that Fairchild allowed a patient 75 cents for two bushels of oats and peas, $2 for two quarters of beef and a calf skin. The overseer of the poor in Panton, Vermont, paid a Dr. Bradford 88 cents for "doctoring a stranger." Families who "took in" indigent persons were paid 75 cents or $1 a week. Dr. Joel Holton billed $357.23 in his first year of practice and $601.80 in his eighth year, but this included his wife's earnings (making a bonnet, 34 cents; a frock, 50 cents; a cloak, 83 cents).[14] In the 1830s few New England physicians earned more than $500 a year in money and kind. Twenty-six of thirty-four doctors in Worcester, Massachusetts, left unsettled debts at death.[15]

Doctors' offices were in their homes, and their expenses included only the cost of a horse and perhaps a wagon, a few instruments, and books. They stocked medicines that they sold to their patients.

The Vermont physician of the first half of the nineteenth century was more craftsman than professional. The theoretical basis of his treatment was shaky at best and far from being generally accepted even by his peers. Medical science in the present sense was unknown. Most patients had little interest in the reasons for any course of action; they wanted results, and they exercised their right of choice between the regulars, the herbalists, and the local lay people who claimed curative powers. Of course, today's patients also want, above all, to be relieved of their troubles, but modern physicians have behind them the tremendous popular acceptance of "medical science" over which they claim a monopoly. The graduates of UVM's medical department between 1804 and 1836 had no such advantage, and it was practical experience, gained from their preceptors, that helped them compete with the numerous other purveyors of care. Only gradually and incompletely did the stamp of competency provided by the M.D. degree and the approval of the medical society impress consumers.

The Reconstituted Medical Department: 1854

One wonders why Dr. Samuel White Thayer of Northfield, Vermont, a country practitioner, persevered in the difficult task of restarting a medical college in Burlington. It took thirteen years for him and Dr. Walter Carpenter of Randolph to persuade the university Trustees and to elicit support from Burlington doctors. The medical school in Woodstock was faltering, and Burlington was growing. Thayer may have seen an opportunity for personal advancement just as Dr. Pomeroy had sixty years before. Certainly, Drs. Thayer and Carpenter later were among the most prominent members of the Burlington medical community. There was already a building, as well as some books and laboratory apparatus that the Trustees would let them use, provided the enterprise, including faculty salaries, "shall have no power to charge the corporation with any pecuniary liability whatever." [16]

When the medical department of UVM was reconstituted in 1854, the world outlook had changed. In the first half of the century well-to-do young men from Boston, New York, and Philadelphia went to France to supplement their education from American medical schools. Brilliant and popular teachers such as Pierre Louis in Paris had stopped theorizing about vital principles and whole-body reactions of irritability and sluggishness. Instead, taking advantage of the large number of patients in the city hospitals, they applied statistical methods to the outcomes of disease, did autopsies, and studied tissues under the microscope to define changes in body organs.

After 1840 Germany was the place to go.[17] Laboratory science was rapidly expanding there, not in the hospitals but in the universities, where the experimental method was used. The great professors' laboratories were well supported by the state, and discoveries in physiology, pathology, and later, bacteriology were revolutionary. Bacteria were shown to cause many infectious diseases, and the potential relevance of science to the practice of medicine became obvious. Young men from America and from all over Europe flocked to Berlin and Leipzig and returned home full of excitement and enthusiasm. But the application of these advances was slow all over

America, especially in Vermont. Not until 1886, after six years of repeated attempts, did the Vermont State Medical Society succeed in getting the Legislature to establish a board of health;[18] the state laboratory was not built until 1899. Only then could Vermont doctors submit specimens for bacteriological diagnosis of diphtheria, typhoid fever, and other contagious diseases.[19] Midcentury American medical schools, dependent as they were on student fees, were not ready to subsidize investigators. They were teaching the art of medicine, and they wanted professors who were successful practitioners. Textbooks written in England and France were imported and translated when necessary so that medical education could be offered in a rural setting.

The UVM medical department of 1854 was again set up as a proprietary enterprise. It was owned and operated not by the university Trustees but by the professors, who were, in effect, partners in the business. Like other American medical schools it was not a graduate school. The only admission requirement was the payment of a fee, and although some students had had some Classical education, the majority had not.

Student recruitment was small at first. The Dean's Book (kept in the UVM registrar's office)[20] records nine students in 1854, six of whom had had previous lectures in other institutions. Six were graduated. In 1855 there were fourteen students and three graduates. Optimistic projections were justified as enrollments for 1856, 1857, and 1858 were thirty-four, forty-seven, and sixty-five, respectively; the corresponding numbers in the academic department averaged around one hundred.

Though enrollment on the academic side was disrupted by the Civil War, the number of medical students continued to increase. By the 1863–1864 session medical students outnumbered all of the others, sixty-four to forty. The growth in medical enrollment continued after the war, reaching 230 in 1884. In that year there were 101 graduates, only 11 of whom had already earned bachelor's degrees. In 1875 there was a total of 859 UVM alumni, of whom 578 had been awarded the M.D. degree. By 1890 there had been 1,101 graduates in arts and 1,368 in medicine.[21]

It has been said that changes in the structure of medical education are a function of who pays the bill. Although philanthropic support of education did not reach a flood until after 1900, vast sums of money were being made in business and industry by that time, and most medical colleges were starting to get their share of gifts. But the medical department at UVM, proprietary until 1899, remained almost entirely dependent on tuition. There was some help from private citizens to construct the medical college building of 1829. The more spacious one, renovated and made available in 1884, was donated by Burlington philanthropist John Purple Howard.[22] In 1908 the State of Vermont made its first appropriation to support medical education, perhaps recognizing that UVM had provided a substantial number of physicians for its citizens. More than one thousand M.D. degrees had been awarded since 1854. Probably a third of the students were from Vermont, and about the same proportion of the total stayed to practice in the state.

The Curriculum: 1854–1900

During the second half of the nineteenth century the UVM medical college strove to improve academic standards while at the same time maintaining a competitive position against other schools. Woodstock and Castleton succumbed in 1856 and 1859, but there were still Bowdoin, Albany, and Dartmouth, and with increased affluence and mobility Vermonters could consider more choices. UVM not only survived; it managed to increase its student roster.

The catalogs of the medical department during the 1850s and 1860s read like advertisements, as indeed they were: their purpose was to attract students. In part they represented only pious hopes for each coming year, and the announced regulations were often bent to serve individual circumstances.[23]

In 1855 the requirement for admission was payment of a $3 matriculation fee and $50 for tickets to all of the lectures. The catalog lists six professors, whose lectures covered the major branches of medicine. The regular course lasted sixteen weeks, beginning in March. To qualify for the M.D. degree the candidate had to be twenty-one years of age, "intelligent and of good moral character, must have studied medicine with a respectable physician for three years and have attended two full courses of public lectures, one of which must have been in this University." Submission of a written thesis on some medical subject also was required. At the conclusion of his second course of regular lectures, the student was examined by the medical professors, representatives of the university corporation, and a committee of the state medical society.

At the annual meeting of the state medical society in 1865 the "delegates to examine students of the Burlington Medical College" reported: "Teaching has been thorough and practical and it was clearly apparent that the students had been taught to use their reason and judgement and not rely on their memory alone."[24]

By holding its lecture term in the spring, Vermont attracted well-known professors from New York and other cities, who could teach at country medical schools when the term (usually winter) was over in their home colleges. It was not unusual for a professor to teach in three institutions in one year. The catalogs from 1859 on indicate the addition of professors who went to Burlington—sometimes for an entire term, more often for six weeks—to teach special subjects that reflected advances in medical practice.

The first and for a time the only medical teacher at UVM who could be called a scientist was Swiss-born Henri Erni, who joined the faculty in 1854.[25] He had studied chemistry in Zurich, and in the academic college at UVM he taught chemistry, physics, natural science, and for good measure, French and German. At the same time, he taught chemistry by lecture and demonstration in the medical department. For an extra fee in the winter, medical students could get instruction in "practical chemistry." It is doubtful that Erni could have had time for original research, and his list of publications, twenty-four in all, is not spectacular. Most were completed before his arrival in Burlington or after he left in 1857.

In his introductory lecture to the medical class of 1857 Erni predicted, "The era of a truly rational system of medicine will come, and it is near at hand, requiring a medical student [to acquire] a thorough acquaintance with Natural Science as the only sure and true basis to build upon." Physicians of the "old school," these "practical men" who considered chemistry or the revelations of the microscope unnecessary, Erni warned, had either closed their eyes or were "vexed at having first to learn the elements of science in order to appreciate advances in medicine."[26] Like Benjamin Lincoln twenty-five years earlier, Erni was ahead of his time. Although his medical colleagues might agree that practice should be based on science, medical education still remained practical and would reflect the "This is how I do it" approach for years to come.

In the mid-nineteenth century, American physicians saw ambulatory patients in their offices and made home visits to treat the sicker ones. Hospitals were charitable institutions, providing a refuge for the poor who were unable to afford home care. It was not until the 1870s that hospital trustees permitted the use of some of the patients for teaching students. Thus, clinical instruction became more available in Burlington with the opening of the Mary Fletcher Hospital in January 1879. Dr. D. B. St. John Roosa, Special Professor of Eye and Ear since 1875, traveled up from New York to speak at the ceremony, saying it was worth the trip north even in January because of the importance of the new facility to the citizens of the town and its value to medical education. "It is essential to proper training of doctors. . . . A hospital is a medical school." But it was not a place for private patients. "It is a place for the poor. It is inconvenient for a mother or a father to be sick at home. Their care requires much self-sacrifice. But the idea of a home will soon be lost if the well-to-do people resort to hospitals and we will be on the road to communism, to the breaking up of the home and family."[27]

During the post–Civil War decades, along with its counterparts in the big cities the UVM medical department gradually incorporated science into the curriculum and tried to raise the general educational level of its students. In 1865 a course in jurisprudence was added, taught by the well-known New York physician, lawyer, and Classical scholar John Ordronaux. In 1875 President Buckham joined some of the other academic faculty in offering a short course in English literature, "to promote the spirit of culture" among the medical students. The course is not mentioned in subsequent catalogs.

In 1871 Harvard became one of the first medical schools to insist on some academic preparation for admission. Nevertheless, as President Charles W. Eliot tried to raise standards to a university level, he found resistance from the faculty, who feared losing students to the competition. At UVM it was not until 1890 that an entrance examination was required, and it was waived if the applicant had had one year of college or three years of high school.

In the 1880s the medical college adopted a graded curriculum, in which basic disciplines came first and more advanced courses later, with at least a fifteen-month interval of practical experience between the two. In 1898 the faculty adopted a four-year curriculum, and the course of lectures was lengthened to six months, January through June. Faculty names in the catalog of 1900 show big-city addresses for the professors of special subjects, whose courses ran about six weeks. Almost all were distinguished specialist practitioners from New York and other centers, with teaching appointments in their home cities as well.

The UVM medical graduate of the reconstituted school was prepared by lectures and demonstrations to recognize, diagnose, and treat most of the injuries and diseases he would be likely to see in practice. The medical education of these men did not greatly differ from that of most other schools. Their books were the same, and many shared the same professors. However, unless they were lucky enough to have had especially good preceptors, few had much chance to examine personally or treat live patients.

The Graduates: 1854–1900

When the UVM medical department general catalog was compiled in 1904, 335 graduates of the department were living in Vermont, most presumably practicing there;[28] 148 towns or well over half, were represented. In addition, many graduates assumed local government and other civic responsibilities, became officers in medical societies, and wrote articles for medical journals.

Dudley B. Smith of the class of 1856 wrote a history of the town of Plainfield, Vermont. Charles F. Taylor of New York became a prominent orthopedic surgeon, innovator, and author. Philo J. Farnsworth ('58) became professor of materia medica in the State University of Iowa. Alfred F. Holt ('60) was president of the American Public Health Association. William McNutt became professor of medicine in the University of California. Irving A. Watson ('71) was secretary of the American Public Health Association and of the First Pan-American Medical Congress. George Packard ('74) was a prominent orthopedist, author, and teacher in Denver. Homer Crowell ('75) was professor of gynecology at the University of Kansas. Charles S. Benedict

('82) was chief of the infectious disease department of the New York City Department of Health. Charles P. Thayer ('85) was professor at Tufts Medical College. Charles Dennison ('89) was professor of medicine at the University of Denver, and Albert Nott, of the same class, became dean at Tufts.

The minutes of the Chittenden County Medical Society tell something about the professional lives of those graduates who settled in the Burlington area.[29] Despite busy practices they attended the meetings to share professional experiences and to promote contact with developments in the outside world. Papers were read on everything from the microscopic study of urine to the artificial feeding of infants. In 1875 there was an epidemic of smallpox in Burlington, and thirteen people died, nine of whom had been vaccinated. A committee was appointed to evaluate the usefulness of vaccination.

In 1894 the role of bacteria in infectious disease was discussed. One doctor said that the specific germ of scarlatina was not known and that there might be some other agent. He cited a case in which the disease was carried by a pair of stockings worn by a sick person a year previously and another in which a dog was the carrier. In 1895 the society considered whether it should offer financial help to a member who wanted to spend time on scientific research. There was an opinion that it was not fair to have patient fees subsidize research. No action was taken. In 1909 a course of postgraduate study for members was proposed: two meetings a month, one on anatomy and the other on diseases of the organs studied. There was a call for a place on the program for original research—again, no action.

In 1908 a society member reported discovery of the spirochete of syphilis by the German Fritz Schaudinn three years earlier. Pointing out that microscopic diagnosis of syphilis was now possible, he offered the hope that serum treatment would soon be available. In 1910 the society was informed that serological tests for the disease had been developed, that treatment with a compound of arsenic (Salvarsan) was being tried in Austria and in Germany that same year.

The members of the society had not made great contributions to scientific literature, and perhaps none had the surgical skills of some of their Boston colleagues, but one gets the impression that their medical college professors would have been satisfied with the products of their efforts. They had come a long way since the days of the medical craftsman.

The Twentieth Century

In 1899 the University took over control of the medical department. As a proprietary institution up to that time, owned by the faculty, it seemed to be doing well. Under Dr. Ashbel P. Grinnell, dean from 1874 to 1877 and again from 1886 to 1898, student enrollment had greatly increased. But Grinnell, popular with the students and a good lecturer, had kept the benches full by relaxed academic policies and by accepting promissory notes in place of cash for tuition. In 1898, 15 percent of the students were in arrears for a total of $2,234.16.[30] The professors were faced with a reduction in salary, and when the dean also resisted raising the academic standards, they voted to replace him. The students and a minority of the faculty rushed to Grinnell's defense, and dissension threatened the future of the school. The University Trustees, having secured a legal opinion that they could do so, assumed control, asked all of the professors to resign, and then reemployed most of them for one year while tempers cooled. Grinnell was out, and the Trustees reassured the community of the stability of what was now the Medical College.

It has been said that not until the twentieth century did a patient have an even chance of benefiting from a visit to a doctor. The statement reflects a modern bias; it ignores the fact that nineteenth-century physicians knew a lot about the course of disease and had much to offer in counseling, symptomatic and emotional support, and prognosis. But there were few definitive cures.

By 1900 the great surge in experimental medical science was influencing the day-to-day practice of medicine, making it possible for the doctor not only to understand the internal workings of the body but to apply this knowledge to treatment. Medical educators promoted the value of research to produce new information and to give the student facility in the scientific method. To this end they adopted the progressive education teachings of John Dewey: learning by doing. The leading schools, with large budgets, were able to recruit instructors who had studied with famous scientists in Germany and to expand laboratory courses. In 1904 students at Washington University in St. Louis were spending half of their medical school hours in autopsy rooms, laboratories, clinics, and hospital wards.[31]

UVM could not afford such luxuries. Expanded curricula put an end to the era of itinerant medical professors, so UVM could no longer share the faculty of the big city schools. When the medical building burned in 1903, it was promptly rebuilt with minimum disruption of classes. But the fire interfered with student recruitment, and the faculty felt obliged to assume responsibility for interest on $40,000 borrowed for the new building.[32] Furthermore, with decreasing enrollment, the already modest stipends paid to the faculty were lowered to the point where many were contributing their services almost gratis, which caused some of them to look elsewhere. The drastic cash flow problem forced Dean Henry Crain Tinkham to cut corners at a time when the expectation of rising standards was already closing some medical schools and costs were rapidly outrunning tuition fees. Now UVM also had to face the process of accreditation from outside the University.

The Association of American Medical Colleges (AAMC), reestablished in 1896 after an earlier poor start, set standards of performance and admitted schools to membership as they met the standards. From its beginning in 1848 the American Medical Association (AMA) also had been interested in improving medical education, though it had little influence until 1904, when its Council on Medical Education was formed. This body began to inspect medical colleges and to rate them A, B, and C, the last designation signifying "hopeless."

Market forces were already at work eliminating the poorest of schools, but the Council felt the need of some outside authority to back up its attempts at raising standards. It persuaded the well-financed Carnegie Foundation for the Advancement of Teaching, which already was involved in studying general education, to investigate the state of American medical education. The foundation engaged Abraham Flexner, a nonphysician, to do the job.[33]

Flexner, brother of the famous Simon (director of the Rockefeller Institute for Medical Research), had attended Johns Hopkins University, whose medical school, founded in 1891, was a radical experiment for the time and far outclassed all other American schools. Richly endowed and with a major commitment to medical research, it attracted an outstanding faculty. Its carefully selected students, all college graduates, were taught to be scientific investigators as well as physicians, and a large proportion of them became leaders of American medicine. Excited by the scientific developments he had seen in Baltimore, Flexner expected that a relatively small number of good schools could supply enough physicians who, properly trained in science, could provide a high quality of medical care to all. He impatiently concluded that a system approximating the one at Johns Hopkins was an attainable and urgently necessary goal. Flexner visited 155 medical schools, spending just a few days at each. He found conditions "deplorable." Schools of poor quality were producing a glut of inadequately trained physicians who were a menace to society, a society that, he wrote, deserved to benefit from the increasing wonders of medical science.

With regard to New England, Flexner found it badly overcrowded with poorly educated physicians. It "will need no more—for years to come; it can of course begin none too soon the process of substituting a higher grade of physician for what it now has. . . . The clinical departments of Dartmouth, Bowdoin, and the University of Vermont [should] certainly be lopped off; there is no good reason why these institutions . . . should be concerned with medicine at all."[34]

The Flexner Report, published in 1910, received wide attention and accelerated changes in medical education already in progress; the inadequate schools were slowly being eliminated anyway. But in his rapid tour of the United States Flexner had had little opportunity to evaluate the quality of medical care. In New England, particularly, he presented scant evidence to substantiate his low opinion of physicians. Dean Tinkham, in speeches and in private argument before the councils of the AMA and AAMC, tried to show how Flexner had been unfair to small schools and to UVM in particular. Vermont graduates were doing well on state board examinations and had become successful practitioners in the community. At home, with the help of President Buckham and some members of the faculty, Tinkham was able to extract $2,000 from the Trustees and $10,000 from the Legislature, allowing an increase in the full-time basic science faculty from one to four. As a result, the college was admitted to membership in the AAMC in 1912.

The reprieve was incomplete and of short duration. The medical college had difficulty maintaining admission standards acceptable to licensing boards in other states, blaming the quality of Vermont secondary education for the paucity of qualified applicants. In 1936 both the AMA and the AAMC put UVM on probation and threatened to withdraw accreditation because the clinical teaching, all by part-time faculty, was poorly controlled and because there was practically no scientific research. Dr. A. Bradley Soule, representing the faculty, went to a meeting of the education committee of the AMA to plead Vermont's case. The chairman walked in, said that discussion was useless and that there was no need for a medical college in Vermont, and then walked out. The other members of the committee were willing to listen, but Dr. Soule went home discouraged, though not ready to give up.[35] UVM again pulled itself together. Harold Pierce, Ph.D., was recruited to develop biochemistry, assured by President Bailey that he would be provided enough resources to meet the national standards. Ray Daggs and Ferdinand Sichel, also scientists from "away," were appointed in physiology. It was said that the clinical faculty gave up some of their small part-time stipends to help fund the research men.

The medical college survived the vicissitudes of the Flexner era and the accreditation problems of the 1930s by producing doctors for rural Vermont. The citizens were appreciative of access to medical education for their children, many of whom returned to their hometowns to practice. Well into the 1950s—when medicine was still a separate item in the university budget— the legislators, grateful for the physicians trained by the medical college, supported it with taxes at the rate of $2 per capita (the national average was 50 cents).[36]

By World War II it was clear to everyone that a first-class medical school could not get by only on research in the preclinical sciences; the medical and surgical faculties needed to become involved as well. At first there was resistance on the part of some physicians. When Wilhelm Raab, a well-known European clinical investigator, came to UVM in 1940, he did not get an appointment in medicine but was offered laboratory facilities as professor of "Experimental Medicine," becoming, as he was heard to complain, a "rat doctor."

With the appointment of William E. Brown as dean in 1945 the fortunes of the College of Medicine began to change. No longer struggling to maintain its accreditation, it moved toward a secure first-class position. Brown, formerly professor of preventive medicine at the University of Cincinnati, had served with the army and in the U.S. Public Health Service; posted as consultant to the Greek government, he had helped restore the hospital services in Athens shattered by the war.[37] He gained the confidence of the Vermont medical and legislative communities, helped patch up some of the rivalries between the two Burlington hospitals, and secured better support from the Legislature. More important, he built up the faculty. During World War II a large number of recent medical graduates, many from well-known university programs, joined the armed forces. When the war was over, this pool of well-trained young doctors was eager to reenter academic life, and Dean Brown grasped the opportunity to fill out his faculty with promising young people. With a reasonable prospect of earning a livelihood from practice in Burlington, these physicians were glad to accept clinical appointments at little expense to the University. They would also enjoy the stimulation and perks of a university position, the opportunity to teach, and the possibility of some subsidy for research.

During the postwar years medical school research, previously supported by private philanthropy, expanded greatly with federal support. Large amounts of money became available for laboratories, salaries for investigators, and enhancement of the faculty with established scientists. George Wolf, dean of the College of Medicine since 1952, was ready to compete for grants. He also raised funds from alumni, friends, and private foundations so that the college could move from the inadequate 1904 building on Pearl Street to new quarters adjacent to the Mary Fletcher Hospital.

The golden age of American medicine had arrived. The profession was held in high esteem, spectacular new discoveries and techniques were quickly applied to the treatment of the sick and injured, and there seemed to be plenty of treatment to go around. UVM graduates were welcomed in academic and scientific circles. The College of Medicine now qualified as a first-class institution.

A Learned Profession

Webster lists medicine, law, and theology as the three learned professions. The *Oxford English Dictionary* defines "learned" as "having profound knowledge gained by study, especially in language or some department of literary or historical science." From early in the nineteenth century there were indeed people of "profound knowledge gained by study" in the UVM medical department. Benjamin Lincoln, for example, taught anatomy from the standpoint of a philosopher. Perhaps it is the implication of the Oxford phrase "especially in language or some department of literary or historical science" that until recently caused the rest of the University to consider the medical degree a class below the Ph.D. As late as the 1950s and 1960s, in the faculty committee that recommended promotion and tenure, this writer encountered resistance in justifying tenure for a physician compared with a history or philosophy scholar.

In the nineteenth century, American medical students were often illiterate and considered a rough lot. The requirement for some preliminary education improved the image of the profession and raised its social status. And as medical practice became more sophisticated, it seemed inappropriate for a young person a few years out of high school to care for the sick; adding some years to his education would make him more mature. Furthermore, with the rising importance of medical science, students needed some physics and chemistry before medical school. With so much to cover, the professors refused to spend time teaching fundamentals.

Medical science has been worshiped by consumers and politicians, and the best and brightest of college students have competed for places in medical schools. But there is now concern that medical practice, overwhelmed by technology, is losing the human touch. Health care has become enormously expensive. Hospital budgets rise exponentially, and we have life-support systems and organ transplants that appear to extend life but lower its quality. Contrary to our expectations of forty years ago, we find limits to what the providers can supply; some form of rationing is inevitable. Cost becomes the operative word for politicians, journalists, sociologists, and company executives. The golden age may be tarnishing. Medical schools are accused of being insensitive to the needs of the poor. Concerned about genetic engineering and animal rights, activists try to block the erection of a university biology laboratory.

American medical educators react to these challenges in part by cutting back on laboratory science and increasing students' exposure to societal issues. We may be sliding toward a less intellectual environment in which the "practical" is again gaining prominence in medical education.

No human endeavor, least of all medicine, can be out of context with the society of which it is a part. For almost two hundred years UVM has offered preparation for the practice of medicine, conforming to what the public it serves has believed to be true, good, and useful. But it has never had to give up completely the two-thousand-year tradition of the profession. The craftsman who deals with wood, iron, or leather has simpler material to work with than the physician who tries to understand the functions and dysfunctions of the human body and mind. While modern medical schools teach the skills necessary for the practice of medicine, they must also bring to bear all available scientific and humanistic resources. Learning, as society understands it and when it can afford it, remains a valued commodity; and medicine, as taught at UVM, still qualifies for a place among the learned professions.

Agricultural Education and Extension in Vermont

ROBERT O. SINCLAIR

It was not easy to launch agricultural education in Vermont, even though in the mid-nineteenth century half of the state's population lived on farms. The crucial step was enactment in 1862 of the Morrill Act, sponsored by Vermont representative Justin Morrill. But decades of effort, distinguished by the leadership of Dean Joseph Hills and Dean Joseph Carrigan, were still required to bridge the gap between rural Vermonters' suspicions of "book-farming" and the University of Vermont's tradition of classical learning. Ultimately, in the early years of the twentieth century UVM did achieve the coordinated program of teaching, research, and extension that has proved so successful in modernizing the agricultural base of the American standard of living.

Beginnings

Agricultural schools had existed in Europe since the early nineteenth century, and societies for the improvement of agriculture were active in the United States by that time, but the first state-supported agricultural college came only in 1855, the Agricultural College of the State of Michigan (now Michigan State University).[1] In Vermont the concept figured in the plan for the forerunner of Norwich University envisaged by its founder, Alden Partridge. As early as 1841, Partridge proposed to Congress a national system of colleges combining the arts, sciences, and practical studies, including agriculture, to be supported by the sale of public land—the basic idea of the Morrill Act. In 1849 a resolution of the Vermont House of Representatives endorsed Partridge's proposal, though it took no further action.[2]

Justin Morrill, the man who made national agricultural education a reality, began his career as a storekeeper in Strafford, Vermont, where he had been born in 1810. Largely self-educated, Morrill presumably learned about Partridge's ideas through his partner, Judge Jedidiah Harris, who was one of the incorporators of Norwich University. According to Charles Plumley, a more recent president of Norwich and later congressman from Vermont, "There are many people now living who believe that the land grant colleges have Alden Partridge to thank for having inspired Justin Morrill," though Morrill obviously became aware of other efforts of this nature in both Europe and the United States.[3]

In 1854, Morrill was elected to the U.S. House of Representatives, moving up in 1866 to the Senate, where he served until his death in 1898. He was known as an independent but popular legislator, responsible for much of the government building program in Washington, including the Library of Congress, in addition to the land grant college program that bears his name.[4] Senator George Hoar of Massachusetts declared at Morrill's funeral, "He was contented to be responsible for one man; to cast his share of the vote of one State; to do his duty as he conceived it, and let other men do theirs as they saw it. . . . He never grew impassioned or angry. He had in high degree what Jeremy Taylor calls 'The endearment of prudent and temperate speech.' "[5]

Morrill's first land grant bill was vetoed by President Buchanan, but he persevered, and President Lincoln signed the Morrill Act into law in July 1862. The goal was to place science and its technological applications in the hands of the many, rather than the privileged few, so that America's natural resources could be developed most rapidly and efficiently. Land grant colleges in each state should make science, not literature, the center of the educational process. At the same time, anticipating John Dewey's educational philosophy, Morrill stressed that the colleges should keep cultural and practical education in the proper proportion to make men both "thinkers and doers" because a liberally educated and intellectually disciplined citizenry alone could guarantee the perpetuation of democracy.[6]

Morrill was unhappy over the term *agricultural schools,* inserted by a clerk in the title of his bill. In the fifty years or more following the passage of the act there was great controversy over the nature of the education to be offered in these new institutions, but there was never any doubt in Morrill's mind. Speaking at the Massachusetts Agricultural College in 1887, he explained:

The land grant colleges were founded on the idea that a higher and broader education should be placed in every State within the reach of those whose destiny assigned them to, or may have the courage to choose industrial vocations where the wealth of the nations is produced; where advanced civilization unfolds its comforts and where a much larger number of its people need wider educational advantages and impatiently await their possession. The design was to open the door to a liberal education for this large class at a cheaper cost from being close at hand and to tempt them by offering not only sound literary instruction but something more applicable to the productive employments of life. It would be a mistake to suppose it was intended that every student should become either a farmer or a mechanic.[7]

Unfortunately, Morrill was never able to convert farmers and their organizations to his goals. Some of the states followed the model of Vermont and established their land grant college as a part of a classical state university. For example, New Hampshire originally established its land grant school at Dartmouth, and in New York it became a part of Cornell University. Other states established independent colleges of agriculture and mechanical arts (the A and M's). More vocational in nature, often requiring students to work on the college farm for part of their academic credit, the A and M's were often criticized as deficient in academic standards and intellectual rigor. In return, fears were expressed that if the "aggies" were placed in the same university as the classical scholars, they would be looked down on and discriminated against or would benefit from a double standard of entrance requirements and scholarship expectations.[8] The dilemma over whether a college of agriculture should teach basic science applied to agriculture or agricultural practices and skills was to be argued in the Vermont farm community, in the Legislature, and even in the curriculum committees of the college for years to come.

The College is Born

The Legislature of the state of Vermont responded to the Morrill Act with an alacrity seldom seen before or since. On October 29, 1882, it authorized acceptance of the land scrip available to Vermont and instructed the governor to receive donations of land, buildings, and funds to help establish the new college. But around the state there was not much enthusiasm for it.[9]

In September 1863, John Adams, secretary of the Vermont Board of Education, an alumnus of UVM, and a classmate of Governor John Gregory Smith, revived the idea of a union of UVM, Middlebury College, and Norwich University. This consolidated institution would receive the land grant fund and establish a land grant college. Governor Smith endorsed the proposal and included it in his report to the Legislature. A bill to incorporate the "Vermont State University and Associated Colleges" was introduced into the Legislature with the vigorous support of three UVM alumni members, and it passed despite vigorous opposition from the town of Middlebury and Middlebury College. The UVM trustees and the Norwich University trustees voted to accept the proposal; Middlebury College declined.[10]

Before the Legislature met in 1864, several Vermonters, led by sheep farmer Edwin Hammond of Middlebury, issued a broadside addressed to "Farmers and Mechanics of Vermont," demanding that a separate agricultural college be created. Accordingly, on November 22, 1864, the Legislature passed a bill creating the Vermont Agricultural College, with Justin Morrill and Edwin Hammond as two of the incorporators. The land grant monies were to be awarded to this college, provided that its trustees were able to raise at least $100,000 through public subscription in the ensuing twelve months. Several large subscriptions were pledged, including $1,000 from Justin Morrill, to be raised to $5,000 if the college were located in his home town of Strafford. When it became evident that the public subscription was a failure, the trustees again approached Middlebury and Norwich to see if either would accept responsibility for the college. Middlebury immediately rejected the offer, and the trustees of Norwich equivocated. Because Norwich did not have the money to meet the subscription, the trustees of the agricultural college turned once more to UVM. In spite of vocal opposition from the alumni, the UVM trustees agreed to "adopt" the Vermont Agricultural College if they could be assured that the University's property would be protected and that it would share in any increases in land grant funds. On November 9, 1865, the Legislature passed and the governor signed the bill creating the University of Vermont and State Agricultural College (UVM & SAC).

The act of 1865 provided that the University of Vermont and State Agricultural College would be governed by a board of eighteen trustees, with the governor of the state and the president of the University serving ex officio. Nine of the trustees would be appointed from the original board of the University of Vermont and would be self-perpetuating. The remaining nine would be elected by (not necessarily from) the Legislature for six-year terms. All property of the University of Vermont would go to the new institution, as would the land grant funds. The Trustees were directed to provide a four-year course of Classical studies that was not inferior to that previously taught at the University of Vermont, and to develop new courses in military tactics, agriculture, and the mechanical arts, in conformity with the intent of Congress. At their discretion the Trustees could acquire land to be used as an experimental farm, provided that students were not required to perform agricultural labor. The permanent location of the institution was to be at Burlington, although the door was left open for Middlebury or Norwich to unite with UVM &SAC. The Trustees were required to make annual reports to the Legislature. Finally, in the event that the new corporation failed substantially to carry out the provisions of the act, the Vermont Supreme Court was empowered to dissolve the corporation and equitably divide the assets of the institution.

The Struggle to Exist, 1865–1900

Thus, the land grant college of agriculture in Vermont came into being. Justin Morrill was elected as a legislative trustee and was reelected every six years until his death in 1898. Edwin Hammond, the farm leader who had initiated the agitation for a separate agricultural college, was also elected to the board but declined to serve, which portended a lack of support from prominent farmers in the state.

Almost simultaneously with the legislation setting up the College of Agriculture, the new president, James B. Angell, stressed in his inaugural address the Morrill Act and the drive for agricultural education. The University would "train and equip men for every department of scholarly research and for every useful position in life."[11] Presidents recognized the value of public relations even then.

Under Angell the University responded quickly to its broader mission. The expanded Board of Trustees voted in 1866 to establish professorships in modern languages, "Chemistry and Its Application to Agriculture and the Mechanic Arts," geology, mineralogy, and mining; and a Department of Military Tactics. It is noteworthy that the first professor to teach anything of a specifically agricultural nature was a doctor of medicine, Leonard Marsh, in his course "Vegetable and Animal Physiology."[12]

Notwithstanding the new name of the University of Vermont and State Agricultural College, agricultural instruction was initially organized only as a part of the Agricultural and Scientific Department (becoming a separate department in 1888 and a college only in 1911). The initial curriculum of the Agricultural and Scientific Department provided a three-year course leading to the bachelor of science degree in analytical and agricultural chemistry, in civil engineering, or in mining and metallurgy. By taking an additional year, a student could acquire the degree of bachelor of philosophy. Students who did not wish to matriculate for a full three years selected certain portions of the course. Finally, a series of lectures especially adapted to the needs of agriculturists would be offered in February and March each year.

Students in all three options of the Agriculture and Scientific Department took the same course of study except for one course each year. In the freshman year students took three terms of chemistry, two terms of geometry, two terms of French, three terms of English composition and declamations, and one term each of algebra, free drawing, and bookkeeping. The second year included English composition, drawing, mathematics, trigonometry, analytical geometry, geology, mineralogy, general chemistry, analytical and agricultural chemistry, laboratory practice, applications of chemistry to agriculture, analysis of soils, relations of soils to vegetable and crop production, vegetable anatomy and physiology, habits of domestic animals, and insects injurious to vegetation. French was an elective.

In the third year students took English composition and German throughout the year, chemistry, laboratory practice, mineral analysis, metallurgy, mechanics, optics, astronomy, and physical geography. Obviously, this was an ambitious course of instruction for a faculty of about a dozen all told, of whom only three were specific to the scientific fields.

For its first three decades, agricultural education at UVM was pulled two ways. The University and its trustees approached it as a mere extension of the prevailing classical and scientific curriculum while the farm community, unreconciled to the merger with UVM, wanted practical vocational training. They saw little relationship between the Classics and pure sciences and the needs of farmers, and even though most students at the University had come from farms, they feared that the students in an agricultural course would be derided by the others. The trustees reported reassuringly in 1867, "It has been made evident by the experience of the past year that there is no ground for fear, which was cherished by some, that there would be a lack of harmony and kindly feeling between the students of the Academic and those of the Scientific Department."[13] But this was beside the point because there were no students enrolled in the agricultural curriculum as such. The curriculum existed on paper only, and the few students enrolled in the agricultural courses came from the classical program.

The following year, acknowledging mounting criticism of the University and its commitment to the agricultural program, the trustees tried to explain how the basic sciences course, suitably shaped, could provide practical information for farmers: "We propose only to examine and teach those laws by which God has ordained that crops shall grow and animals be propagated. Is the study of these laws not worth the attention of every young farmer, nay, of every man?"[14]

When Matthew Buckham replaced Angell as president in 1871, the University's mood swung from the new pragmatic notions of education back toward the Classical. Buckham commented that he was content to discharge the new agricultural responsibilities of the institution with one course within the already established scientific curriculum. A perceptive alumnus wrote, "Is not the new Agricultural College Corporation . . . a bundle of whimsies?"[15]

There was still no distinct school of agriculture in 1873–1874, when the Trustees protested that it would be most expensive, that it was something "novel and full of peril to the whole enterprise," and that there was no demand for it. They might consider appointing a full-time professor of agriculture, but they still felt that the University could avoid the expense of its own farm because the professor could use farms around the state. Arguing that they were "honestly and faithfully carrying out the agreement to give instruction in *branches of learning related to agriculture* [italics added]," the Trustees maintained that "a young man intending to be a farmer—let us say, intending to be a man, an educated man, and a farmer—could hardly qualify himself better for his work and place in life, than by taking a course in the sciences, in literature, in history and philosophy, as this institution can give him."[16]

This direction of policy defied the rumblings of criticism that had already begun in the farm community. In 1870, Zuar Jameson, secretary of the Orleans Agricultural Society, told a meeting of farmers in Glover, "The studies taught are not acceptable to sons of toil and have no direct application to agriculture."[17] Jameson was appointed to the Vermont Board of Agriculture in 1871, and in 1874 he and two other members of the board again attacked the University, alleging that the institution was not spending its land grant funds in accordance with the intent of Congress.[18] Accordingly, in the session of 1874 the General Assembly created a Joint Special Committee on the University "To Inquire into the Expenditure of the Fund Paid by the State of Vermont to The University of Vermont and State Agricultural College."

The Joint Special Committee could find no great difference between the University's two options, the Classical and the industrial (i.e., scientific). Because no student had requested instruction in practical and experimental agriculture, no money had been spent to purchase a farm. The land grant money went into a "pooled fund," from which more was spent on the industrial program than on the agricultural course as such. A contrast was drawn with other states that were supporting their land grant colleges with substantial appropriations.[19] The committee appeared to have given the University a reprieve, but much more serious accusations were to follow.

In 1875, led by Zuar Jameson and E. P. Colton, the farm community stepped up their vocationalist campaign by urging establishment of a new school, where "the sons of the poorest farmers may secure a practical education and pay (in part) in labor . . . and work on a farm."[20] The University responded by offering lectures around the state, with some success after the first year or two, and experiments to demonstrate the benefit of commercial fertilizers drew a number of farmers to cooperate. The Trustees asserted optimistically, "Intelligent farmers are coming, though slowly, to appreciate the practical utility of scientific knowledge."[21] Two trustees even established a contest with two scholarships as prizes for boys under eighteen who raised the largest crops of corn and potatoes on one eighth acre of land. In 1881 there were 102 entries in the corn production contest, with a top yield of 122 bushels per acre equivalent, and 105 entries in potato production, with a top yield of 492 bushels per acre—yields that would be respectable even today.[22]

Meanwhile, when Justin Morrill came up for reelection to the Senate by the state Legislature in 1878, his opponent, legislator and former state supreme court chief justice Luke P. "Brass Buttons" Poland, introduced a bill calling for a new investigation of UVM. He repeated the claim that the University had misused land grant funds and accused Morrill and his fellow trustees of breach of trust. Poland's bill provided that any ten citizens could petition the Vermont Supreme Court to investigate the University, pending which the state treasurer could not make payments of land grant funds to the University. Morrill mounted a spirited campaign for the first time in his political career and eventually caused Poland to withdraw from the Senate contest.[23]

Though Poland's investigation was dropped, the University finally responded to the political heat. In 1884, *seventeen years after the establishment of the so-called Agricultural Department,* the Trustees announced that they had decided to appoint a professor of agriculture. They invited Vermont farmers to nominate a man "who shall give his whole time to scientific and practical agriculture as a speciality, and who, as Professor of Agriculture, shall give instruction both in the institution and throughout the State," even if UVM had somehow to "take a young man of the right character and *train him for the place*" (italics added).

In 1886 the first permanent professor of agriculture, W. W. Cooke, was hired. He was also appointed state chemist, with responsibility for the analysis of fertilizers as required by law. In announcing the appointment, the Trustees affirmed:

We trust that Professor Cooke's labors among the farmers of the State will tend to promote good will and confidence between the College and the farming community. If Professor Cooke succeeds in convincing the farmers, or the more intelligent among them, that such work as a college can do, through laboratories and experiment stations and the like, is of real value to practical husbandry, it will be a very simple matter also to convince them that for the proper development of this work, greatly increased reserves are needed, and that Vermont must follow the example of almost all the other states and make some adequate appropriations for carrying forward such an enterprise.[24]

Accordingly, the Trustees approached the Legislature in 1887–1888 with a request to add $100,000 to the land grant endowment, arguing that "Vermont, whose representative in Congress and now honored Senator was the father of the act creating these colleges, is almost alone in allowing her University to struggle unaided with the immense task of meeting these demands of the new learning."[25] Senator Morrill also addressed the Legislature to plead for state support of the University but to no avail.

When the University was reorganized in 1888–1889, agriculture finally gained separate departmental status with seven professors (of whom Professor Cooke was the only one actually trained in agriculture). To encourage enrollment a new two-year course in agriculture was instituted, along with a winter short course that ran for eleven weeks. No tuition or laboratory fees were charged to agricultural students, and they could eat at Commons for $2.50 per week, a subsidy being paid by the university general fund.

In 1888, Professor Joseph L. Hills appears for the first time on the roster; his name was to be synonymous with the College of Agriculture for the next half century. Long afterward Dean Hills recounted the shortcomings of agricultural education in those early years:

During the first period (1866–1890) there were no agricultural students save at its very end when a few were in residence. There was but one agricultural instructor who arrived 21 years after the college had been launched. Little attempt was made either to plan for their training, had students come, or to get them to attend. . . .

A farcical agricultural curriculum was outlined in the catalogs. No one took it. . . . Much emphasis was laid in the early days on the fact that underlying sciences rather than agriculture itself were to be taught. . . . The trustees of 1867 plumed themselves on the fact that the agricultural course was "in operation" whereas in many states it was "not organized." As a matter of fact, it was not in operation. There were no instructors and no students either then or for 20 years succeeding this baseless statement, which was doubtless made for legislative consumption.[26]

One problem for all of the new land grant colleges was that there were precious few scientific agricultural principles to teach, as sophisticated farmers recognized. Thirteen states, including Vermont, had responded by establishing experiment stations prior to the passage of the Hatch Act in 1887, providing federal support.[27]

The Vermont Board of Agriculture (dating from 1870) first voted in 1876 to establish an experiment station under its control, with Professor Henry Seely of Middlebury College as its superintendent, "to give without remuneration, a portion of his time to . . . such investigations and experiments as shall seem to him likely to simplify and explain the relations of science to agriculture, make additions to our knowledge and skill in the cultivation of the soil, and raising and care of stock, and protect us from fraud and imposition, *such investigations to be without expense to the Board or State*" (italics added).[28] Lack of financial support and Seely's poor health doomed this effort.

The Vermont State Grange entered the fray in 1885, complaining in a resolution, "The farmers of Vermont have received no adequate returns or benefits from the government fund for the establishment of agricultural colleges"[29] and calling for the establishment of an experiment station. Meanwhile, the University asked Professor Cooke to prepare arguments for the establishment of an agricultural experiment station similar to the one at New Haven, Connecticut, and in several other eastern states. The Legislature responded favorably and passed the bill drafted by Cooke to provide an annual appropriation of $3,500. This was soon supplemented by the Hatch Act, signed by President Grover Cleveland on March 2, 1887, which initially provided $15,000 annually to each state to establish an agricultural experiment station *under the direction of the land grant college in that state* to conduct research related to agriculture and rural life. Thus, the second leg of the so-called three-legged stool of agricultural education—teaching, research, and extension—was firmly in place. With funding assured, UVM's trustees in 1891 finally purchased a farm on upper Main Street in Burlington, which was to serve the college and the experiment station for the next seventy-five years.

Even these steps did little to silence the University's critics. A bill in the 1888 Legislature to establish a separate Vermont School of Agriculture died in committee, but the Legislature called on the governor to appoint a committee to study the idea. At the same time the Grange appointed its own committee to do the same thing, and there is some evidence that the two committees functioned as one. The House and Senate Agriculture Committees also made a cursory visit to the UVM campus, and raised the old issue of integrating agriculture into the traditional college: "If, as claimed, the Agricultural Department of the institution has proved to be a failure, it is through no fault of the management, but rather for the reason that our young men decline to take an agricultural course *in connection with those who are pursuing a classical one*" (italics added).[30]

While controversy simmered in Vermont over agricultural education, the federal government had been considering further aid to the land grant colleges. Senator Morrill first introduced a bill for this purpose in 1872; it took him eighteen years to secure passage. The bill provided for an initial $15,000, increasing in annual increments of $1,000 to an eventual $25,000 per year, to each of the land grant colleges of agriculture. No distinction as to race or color was to be made in the admission of students, although if separate institutions for white and black students were maintained, the funds must be divided among them in a just and equitable, but not necessarily equal, manner.

The new Morrill Act money—nearly $40,000 per year—heartened the proponents of an agricultural college separate from the University. As the battle lines were drawn in the 1890 Legislature, those against the University and for a separate agricultural college included the Vermont State Grange, the *New England Homestead*, the *Rutland Herald*, the *Montpelier Argus*, the Vermont Dairymen's Association, the Farmers' League, and many individual farmers and state politicians. Arguing for the University were President Buckham and the Trustees, *The Burlington Free Press*, many legislators who were alumni of the University, and fifteen "agricultural students" who went to Montpelier to testify.

A separation bill passed the state house of representatives, but the main battle occurred in the senate. In spite of a petition favoring separation signed by more than five thousand farmers, the senate eventually voted 18 to 12 against it, much to the dismay of its advocates. There were the usual cries of fraud, favoritism, bribery, and "wait until next year." To blunt this criticism, the University initiated a major drive throughout the state to recruit agricultural students, using the new federal money to offer them free textbooks, exemption from laboratory fees, free room rent, and a promise that work would be available to pay for board, all in addition to the free tuition offered two years earlier. One might think that students would be beating down the doors to take advantage of the opportunity; actually, only twelve were admitted to the agricultural curriculum in 1891.

There were no further serious attempts to separate the agricultural school from the University. The battle had been won, but the price was very high. The suspicion and hostility toward UVM & SAC on the part of many key legislators, farmers and their organizations, and the farm press would have an adverse impact on the institution for years to come. Indeed, during the ensuing twenty years of President Buckham's incumbency, he made no approach to the Legislature for funding.

The Dean Hills Era: 1900–1941

In 1893, Professor Cooke left the University, and Joseph Lawrence Hills, five years after coming in as agricultural chemist, was named professor of agriculture and director of the Vermont Agricultural Experiment Station. He was to serve the University faithfully and honorably for the next forty-nine years. The first agricultural student had received his degree in 1892, and two more were graduated in 1893. All later graduates, until 1942, received their degrees from Dean Hills. There were twenty-three agricultural students in 1893, and the agricultural faculty consisted of Dean Hills, Dr. Lewis R. Jones, botany; Dr. Frank A. Rich, veterinary science; Professor T. R. Gulley, horticulture; and H. B. Chittenden, farm manager.[31]

By 1900, when Hills received the title of dean, thirty-five years after the formation of the University of Vermont and State Agricultural College, the state had a school of agriculture in substance as well as in name, but it had taken a major threat from the Legislature to separate the college from the University before the institution was willing to honor its commitment. According to the 1900 university catalog, 9 of the 62 faculty members and 23 of the 283 students were in agriculture, with eleven courses available. Other than the farm, the only building for the department and the Agricultural Experiment Station was the old medical college building on Main Street.

In his unpublished memoirs Hills wrote about the early years of his incumbency. "The 1891–1915 period [was] characterized by earnest endeavor by the University administration to mend its ways and to forestall criticism by means of greater agricultural student attendance in 4-year and short courses; by liberal financial concessions . . . ; by increased instructional facilities; by improved but far from ideal situations in respect to student relationships; by the inception of extension work; by increased cordiality and receptiveness on the part of farmers; and at its close, by a most unfavorable report made by the Educational Commission."[32]

One of Hills's major accomplishments was to gain funding from the State for the construction of Morrill Hall. The University had always relied on private benefactors for its buildings, but the chances of getting private funding for agriculture were practically nonexistent. Ironically, there was no building named after Senator Morrill on the campus of his own university. Arguing first on the basis of need and second on state pride, Hills drafted a bill and approached the Legislature for funding. Fortunately, the chair of the Agriculture Committee was a personal friend of Hills's, Representative George Aitken of Woodstock, a muscular, two-hundred-pound Scotsman who corralled his committee into a room to consider the $60,000 appropriation. He locked the door, put the key in his pocket, and refused to let them out until they unanimously agreed to support the measure. The bill met with some opposition in both the house and the senate, but it passed in the 1904 session.[33]

Morrill Hall was erected in 1906 and dedicated in 1907. The appropriation specified that the building should be used exclusively by the agriculture department and the Experiment Station, and it was of more than sufficient size to meet the needs of the sixty students and faculty of eight to ten when it was opened and for the next twenty years.[34]

In 1905 the question of the instruction of young women in "household economics" arose. After a committee of three alumnae made a fruitless report, Dean Hills and Professor Jones met successfully with President Buckham to "put the bee on him about home economics." In the fall of 1909, Professor Bertha Terrill, the first woman faculty member, appeared on campus to head the program in home economics in the Department of Arts and Sciences. The first courses were offered in 1909–1910. A second professor was added in 1912, as enrollments grew, and in 1917 the program was transferred to the College of Agriculture, where it received a much more sympathetic welcome and where it thrived for the next fifty-seven years. Professor Terrill headed the department until her retirement in 1940.

When Guy Benton succeeded Buckham as president of the UVM & SAC in 1911, he made a sweeping new offer: "If the Legislature of Vermont will extend to the Agricultural College the financial help necessary to release it from the limits of Burlington and Chittenden County, we shall be glad to cover the State with extension courses so that by cooperation between the trained specialists in the Agricultural College and the earnest farmers of the State we may make the barren and waste places to blossom as the rose. This is no time for niggardliness."[35] The State had already shown its responsiveness: in 1908 its appropriation to the University was increased from $6,000 annually to $16,000 and in 1910, to $26,000 of which $10,000 was earmarked for the medical college, $2,400 for student tuition, and $13,600 for education, arts, and the industrial sciences. In 1912, thanks to Benton's challenge, the subsidy was nearly doubled, with $4,800 designated to subsidize agricultural students' tuition and $8,000 to develop agricultural extension work in the state.

In 1911 the University was reorganized again, and the former departments were renamed colleges, so for the first time there really was a College of Agriculture. A whole new generation of farm-raised and college-trained instructors was entering the teaching field; adequate texts were being supplied; the laboratory, the farm, the field, the orchard, the dairy, and the livestock judging ring were coming into use. The number of "ag" students was slowly increasing, though Hills admits that many of them were poor farm boys taking advantage of the free tuition to attend the scientific curriculum in agriculture and hoping to get into the College of Medicine.

Despite these gains the old question of an antiagricultural bias within the University was raised again in a 1912–1913 study by the Carnegie Foundation for the Advancement of Teaching, which had been brought in by a special state commission to investigate the entire educational system in Vermont. The commission's findings were, to say the least, rather uncomplimentary to the College of Agriculture:

1. The University farm is used by the Experiment Station but is of no use to the college.
2. Professors cannot use the farm as an aid in teaching, students are never seen on its premises, and the barns probably should be condemned as unsanitary.
3. There is poor coordination between the scientific and empirical parts of the college.
4. There is a striking absence of the more familiar agricultural courses.
5. Poultry husbandry is taught by a nonresident lecturer at a cost of $150 per year.
6. Agricultural equipment is meager or nonexistent.
7. There are few agricultural books, almost no collection of scientific literature.

To sum up the situation with respect to the College of Agriculture, it may be said that the courses are not based upon a consistent educational policy, the equipment for teaching is meager, that on their practical side the courses seriously lack equipment, and that by reasons of these conditions, the College of Agriculture is not adapted to serve well either the needs of the boy who desires to be a practical farmer or those of the youth who looks toward a scientific training in agriculture; and finally, that this whole situation has lent itself to a regime under which the college has a very slender connection to the agricultural industries of the State. It does not help or guide these industries in any such way as should be expected of an efficient agricultural college.[36]

While the study characterized the faculty and administration of the college as "excellent men" who had "done admirably" with the means they had at their command, it faulted the policies of the Trustees toward the college, finding that only $5,481 of the $50,000 received from the federal government had been spent for agricultural education.

The agricultural college and the students in it have lived for many years in an atmosphere in which the prejudices of the trustees, of faculty, and most of all of students, were directed against them. It is not surprising that in this situation the trustees should lend themselves to a policy that enabled them to build up the parts of the University in which they really believed and to devote to agriculture a meager remainder. . . . In a word, the appropriation of the general government for agricultural education has been used . . . for the benefit of the general educational development of the University, and in the process *the agricultural college has been milked dry*. [italics added.]

The Carnegie Commission did not believe that the function of an agricultural college was merely to train farm boys in their vocation. Whereas the advocates of a separate college in 1890 favored a "trade school," the commission seemed to feel that the real function of a college of agriculture was the "promotion of scientific agriculture and the maintenance at the same time of right relations to elementary agricultural training schools." Yet the report concluded: "Our experience of fifty years in agricultural education goes to show that a trade school will not grow in a university atmosphere," and it recommended that, in the interest of providing more state support to primary and secondary education, "subsidies to higher education should cease." [37]

Some of the criticisms in the report were valid. Hills admitted that throughout the early 1900s it was not uncommon in most states to "milk the Agricultural Experiment Station," that is, to use federal funds appropriated for research for nonapproved purposes. According to Hills, President Buckham honestly believed that he was doing God's service when he diverted federal funds from their proper usage to university coffers. Part of Arts and Sciences dean Perkins's salary was paid from experiment station funds for years even though he made no contribution to it. Such practices were eventually ended by tighter federal auditing, although it must be admitted that teaching salaries of agricultural faculty on joint station appointments were often subsidized from the research funds.

One of the recommendations of the Carnegie report called for a more sympathetic attitude toward vocational training in agriculture. The Vermont Dairymen's Association had called for state support of a secondary school of agriculture in 1908. In 1910, Theodore Vail, president of American Telephone and Telegraph, endowed a school of agriculture in conjunction with Lyndon Institute, with the stated objective of providing practical instruction in agriculture to Vermont boys who had neither the money nor the inclination to attend a four-year college. This was followed by legislative action in 1910 to establish a school of agriculture in Randolph Center. In 1915, Vail turned the Lyndon school over to the State, and in 1921 its agricultural program was dropped. The school eventually became Lyndon Teachers' College. [38]

The forerunner of the Extension Service was the farmers' institutes. Started in 1871 and continued sporadically, they were cosponsored by the state board of agriculture, later by the commissioner of agriculture. After the 1890 legislative battle, short courses were offered during the winter, especially in dairy processing, and for several years these were well attended. During the first decade of the twentieth century the program expanded rapidly.

One experiment, started in 1909, was particularly successful—the Better Farming Special Trains, intended to take the college to the farmer. With the cooperation of the state's railroads, several baggage cars were adapted so that about three fourths of the car was devoted to exhibits, with the remaining one fourth containing seats. Subject matter of the exhibits and the faculty lectures included soils, fertilizers and fertilization, crop varieties, orcharding and propagation, forestry, dairy management and milk testing, dairy cattle selection, and home economics. The usual procedure was to have a one-hour program at each station: a half-hour lecture followed by a half hour to see the exhibits. In one four-day period in 1911 more than seven thousand people visited the train.[39]

Educational exhibits also were prepared for the county and state fairs. Hills reports that at the White River Junction State Fair in 1911 he met Theodore Vail and James B. Wilbur, the benefactor whose endowment created the Wilbur scholarship fund at the University. As a result of these discussions Hills received private funding to employ three county agents, one year in advance of the passage of the first state appropriation to support extension work.

That support came in 1912, when the Vermont Legislature granted $8,000 annually for two years "for the exclusive use of the College of Agriculture. . . . , which shall be expended solely for work in agricultural extension, including the establishment of extension schools, correspondence courses, lecture and reading courses, of demonstration plots, the issuance of educational leaflets and bulletins dealing with agriculture, the support of district field agents in cooperation with the office of farm management of the United States Department of Agriculture, and kindred enterprises bearing direct relationship to the agricultural advancement of the State."[40] Pursuant to these terms, the University appointed its first director of extension, Thomas Bradlee, and seven county agricultural agents.

Two years later, the federal government gave its backing to extension services through the Smith-Lever Act, authorizing funds to the land grant colleges "to aid in diffusing among the people of the United States useful and practical information on subjects relating to agriculture and home economics, and to encourage the application of the same."

The Smith-Lever Act used the term "Cooperative Extension Service," and it was clear from the beginning that this was to be a joint venture of the U.S. Department of Agriculture, the land grant college, and the local people, not only in program development but also in program management and funding. To guarantee local participation county committees, which came to be called farm bureaus, were established.

Hills actively encouraged the establishment of county farm bureaus and worked closely with E. B. Cornwall, the first president of the Vermont Farm Bureau, organized in 1918. For his cooperation and support Hills received the Distinguished Service to Agriculture Award from the American Farm Bureau Federation in 1941, one of only two Vermonters ever to be so honored.

The Vermont Farm Bureau undertook to support the annual appropriation of the Legislature for the Extension Service. Although in 1922 the executive committee of the Vermont Farm Bureau declared its "independence" of the Extension Service, county farm bureaus continued to share offices with that agency for more than thirty years and served as the supervising committees for county extension work. County extension agents organized farm bureau membership drives, and I remember Lamoille County agent Frank Jones coming to my parents' farm each fall during the 1930s to sign them up as farm bureau members. I myself organized farm bureau membership drives in Washington County, where I served as county agricultural agent in the 1940s. But the tie created a problem, as Deacy Leonard, a past executive director of the Vermont Farm Bureau, explained: "Farm Bureaus . . . soon began to outgrow the [county] agent. The agent was forbidden to engage in economic or legislative work (because of federal funding) and the leaders of the Farm Bureaus came to realize that they could not become a strong pressure group until they could escape the ties of the Extension Service." [41] As the farm bureau at both state and national levels became more politically active and started to engage in commercial activities, the tie became less defensible and suffered criticism by other farm organizations, by legislators, and by other agricultural agencies. The connection was officially dissolved by the Vermont Legislature in 1952.

With the establishment of the Extension Service the land grant college was complete. This coordinated system of research, on-campus instruction, and off-campus education and service carried out by the same faculty under the aegis of the college is followed not only in this country but throughout the world, and its achievements in agriculture are widely acclaimed. [42]

Significant changes occurred in Vermont agriculture during the next twenty-five years, many of which were in part the result of the land grant system. Farm-to-market roads were improved so that farmers could get produce to market year-round. Campaigns were initiated to eradicate bovine tuberculosis and brucellosis in cattle. Extension agents started pushing farmers to keep records and to use good farm management practices. The improvement of railroads and the introduction of refrigerated rail cars made it possible to ship fresh fluid milk and cream to the Boston area, and these developments started the decline of butter and cheese making. Dairy herd improvement (milk testing) associations were promoted by the Extension Service, and with the availability of accurate production records, sire selection and herd improvement programs became possible. During the Depression programs created by the Roosevelt administration were of great benefit to farmers. Rural electrification, subsidized lime and fertilizers, subsidized credit, and the development of milk market orders and the classified milk-pricing system were essential to the development and survival of Vermont agriculture. The comparative economic advantage of milk production led to a highly specialized dairy industry and the decline of general farming.

The period 1920–1942 might be characterized as one of relative stability for the College of Agriculture. Enrollments were stable, and financial support to the Experiment Station from state and federal sources increased slowly, with emphasis on applied rather than basic research. In the Extension Service, home demonstration clubs for women and 4-H clubs for rural youth were increasing in number and membership, and the farm programs were becoming more readily accepted by farmers.

The university farm had been forced to operate from its own resources after federal auditors ruled that federal experiment station funds could not be used to subsidize it. Deterioration of the farm was not reversed until the Legislature made appropriations for it in 1927 and 1928. By 1937 the Legislature was providing state funding to match federal research funds, and by 1940, the land grant units of the University were receiving nearly $300,000 in federal funds in addition to the original land grant funds; the Extension Service was receiving about $65,000 per year from the State to support its work. As a result, when the University discovered its fiscal crisis in 1940, the College of Agriculture was the only unit that had not run a deficit. According to figures published just before Hills's retirement, the faculty of the college had grown to 20 (out of 264 in the entire university), and the undergraduate enrollment totaled 208 (out of 1,266). The 1940 entering freshman class in agriculture was the largest on record.[43]

Joseph Hills retired as dean at the end of June 1942 after serving in that position for forty-one years. He had skillfully guided the college, the Experiment Station, and the Extension Service through their formative years, often with lukewarm support from the Vermont agricultural community and perennially with modest financial support from the university and the state. The honors and accolades he received, both within and outside of Vermont, were glowing in their praise of his leadership. Perhaps a Burlington *Free Press* editorial says it best: "There is a forward looking and optimistic spirit among the farmers of Vermont which, we believe, is due in large measure to the guiding genius, the cheerful and lovable personality, the unfaltering courage of Joseph Lawrence Hills."[44]

The Carrigan Years and After

Joseph Carrigan, named by the Trustees in 1942 as the replacement for Dean Hills, was a graduate of the UVM College of Agriculture and began his career as Addison County agricultural agent, later becoming assistant county agent leader for the state. Following the death of Director Bradlee in 1932, he was named director of extension and retained this position when he became dean; he also served as director of the Experiment Station.

Dean Carrigan was appalled at the inadequacy of the buildings and equipment of the college, and following the war he mounted a major campaign to get state support for new buildings. The college administration shared Morrill Hall (the only state-financed building on campus) with the Extension Service, Experiment Station, Department of Home Economics, creamery, and seed-, feed-, and fertilizer-testing laboratory. Other college departments were scattered among five other buildings. There were few adequate laboratories, and equipment was obsolete. Realizing that without new facilities the college would be unable to accommodate the influx of returning students and World War II veterans, Carrigan created an Agricultural College Advisory Committee, including prominent rural leaders, representatives of all of the major farm organizations in the state, leaders in farm-oriented businesses, and legislators, to educate the state about the inadequate conditions at the college. He carefully spelled out the major needs: state aid to lower the $350-per-year tuition, additional faculty for teaching and extension, and a series of new buildings.

Thanks to the state funding thus generated, the next six years saw the completion of the Carrigan Dairy Science Building, the Hills Agricultural Science Building with associated greenhouses, the Bertha M. Terrill Home Economics Building, a poultry plant, and an agricultural engineering building, as well as the purchase of the Hoag farm on Spear Street, which was subsequently to be the site of a modern college farm. Additional funds were appropriated to provide $200 scholarships for every Vermont student admitted to the College of Agriculture. A new administrative unit, the Division of Related Services, was created to supervise all income-producing units of the college, such as the farms, dairy plant, and testing service. The college also took over the Morgan Horse Farm in Weybridge from the federal government and purchased a farm off Shelburne Road for horticultural research.

The Extension Service entered the realm of mass communication in 1922, when a license was obtained to operate a radio station, the first in Vermont. WCAX ("College of Agriculture Xtension") began regular broadcasting in 1924 with Professor Leon Dean as announcer. The college continued to operate the station until 1932, when it was sold to private owners. In 1956 the Extension Service put on its first television program, with Dean Carrigan as guest. Carrigan was so enthusiastic about the merits of television that he persuaded WCAX-TV to sponsor a daily program, "Across the Fence," the longest continually running farm program on the air in the United States.

Dean Joe Carrigan retired on January 1, 1957, after thirty-nine years of service to agriculture and fifteen years as dean during the period of the greatest development and growth of the college. He had inherited a weak, poorly funded unit with limited enrollment and inadequate facilities. He turned over a strong, growing land grant college, well positioned to meet the needs of the second half of the twentieth century.

Carrigan was succeeded in the deanship by his associate dean and director, Paul Miller, and Robert P. Davison was named extension director. This administrative organization was to continue until 1988, when the Extension Service was again placed under the dean of agriculture.

Miller's tenure was a time of consolidating the gains made during the

Carrigan years. Student numbers continued to increase, and new faculty were employed to teach them. A significant improvement in facilities was the construction of the Spear Street dairy complex, at the time a modern dairy farm well adapted to research activities. At state appropriation of about $600,000 financed this construction in 1966.

Miller retired in 1965, and Thomas W. Dowe, who had been director of the Experiment Station, was named dean. During the next several years enrollment in the college grew rapidly. Major revisions were being made in the curriculum, with opportunities for students to major in agricultural business, foreign agriculture, rural land use planning, biological science, recreation resources management, general agriculture, and environmental studies, as well as the traditional options. The 1973 university catalog listed fifteen options in seven departments in the college, and enrollment totaled over 1,200 students.

Early in 1972, President Edward Andrews appointed the Task Force on Collegiate Reorganization under the chairmanship of Professor Wallace Christensen of the forestry department. The task force met for nearly a year before submitting a bombshell to the president. Their recommendations would have combined the College of Agriculture and Home Economics with the College of Technology to form a College of Applied Sciences. Most agricultural programs, including the Experiment Station and the Extension Service, were to be combined into a Department of Agriculture, and botany and agricultural biochemistry were to be transferred to a new Department of Biological Sciences in the College of Arts and Sciences.[45]

Regardless of the merits of some of its proposals, the task force report stirred up a hornet's nest within both the University and the state. The administration and faculty of the College of Agriculture and Home Economics saw it as a threat to their survival, and they went to their constituency within the state to assist in the struggle. A Burlington *Free Press* editorial was headlined "UVM Reorganization Silly,"[46] and the Rutland *Herald* called for retaining the identity of agriculture.

Most of the recommendations of the task force were disregarded, but in 1973 the Department of Home Economics became a separate School of Home Economics, until 1988; forestry, wildlife management, recreation resource management, and resource economics became the nucleus of a new School of Natural Resources; and a separate interdisciplinary environmental studies program was established. Although the College of Agriculture retained its basic science programs, enrollment in the college was reduced to about seven hundred students.

Thomas Dowe left the deanship in 1979, and this writer was selected to replace him. When I retired in 1987, Donald MacLean was named dean and continued until 1991. But these years are too close to us to include in an objective historical narrative.

In Conclusion

Justin Morrill wanted an institution in Vermont that would make science, not literature, the central idea and discipline of the educational process. He wanted an institution where theory would lead to practice, science to technology; an institution that would provide greater access to a college education by the "industrial classes." And he wanted a college that would maintain in proper proportion the cultural and practical in education to make men both thinkers and doers. The leadership and faculty in the College of Agriculture have tried to hold fast to these goals, as has every land grant college in the nation. In no small part the activities of the land grant colleges have transformed American agriculture from the man with the hoe to its present high-technology, science-based characteristics. That the land grant system has been successful in this endeavor is largely the result of three fortunate circumstances: first, the combination of on-campus undergraduate and graduate instruction and off-campus programs under the aegis of the land grant university; second, the federal–state partnership in research and extension with joint funding from federal, state, and (for extension) local funding, which has assured a stable, continuing financial base with a large measure of local control; finally, the strong institutional mission of the land grant colleges to address the problems of society and to apply the tools of science and technology to the solution of these problems.

The system today, both in Vermont and nationally, is under stress. State and federal funding have not kept pace with inflation, and university policies have precluded using tuition income to support nonteaching programs. The great decline in the number of farms since 1950, both in Vermont and nationwide, has reduced the pool of students interested in an education in production agriculture. The 1980s have seen a rapid growth in basic science programs, especially in biotechnology and business management. Resources must be reallocated to help these expanding areas address the needs of modern agriculture and agriculture students if UVM's land grant college is to retain its twentieth-century role as a leader in agricultural and rural affairs in the twenty-first century.

Part Three

A SMALL UNIVERSITY
WITH IVY ASPIRATIONS,
1895–1940: OVERVIEW

T. D. SEYMOUR BASSETT

An impartial outsider could conclude that in the years after World War II the University of Vermont finally caught up with the twentieth century before it departed. In the first half of the century the basic nineteenth-century character of the institution seemed frozen, though changes occurred beneath the ice cap. Numbers multiplied, first in enrollment, especially of women, and then in faculty and staff; facilities, funding, and curriculum expanded accordingly. Change went on during the quiet compromises of Matthew Buckham's last fifteen years, during the turbulence of Guy Benton's wartime efforts, during the prosperous 1920s while Guy Bailey was testing the chances for increased state aid and the opportunities for private donations, and in the hard times of the 1930s.

The Centennial College, 1895–1910

President Buckham made the concessions he had to make in defense of what his senior professor, Samuel F. Emerson, called "the mediate university."[1] This "noble self-deception," as Professor Emerson put it, tried to mediate between humanistic ideas and culture on a Christian-Classical base and the new criteria of utility, industry, and facts. The mediate university protested "while silently surrendering to hard realities," contemplating absolute truth while glancing sideways at the "immediate values" of the new courses teaching how to make a living. The utilitarians lauded the humanities but only as a veneer; UVM "faced the stars but moved relentlessly earthward."

This pragmatic trend was symbolized by the relocation of the University's formal occasions. As a growing institution, UVM had become too large and too secular by 1880 to hold its major ceremonies in Congregational houses of worship. Commencement moved to the new Howard Opera House that year and to the new Strong Theatre in 1905.

A formal occasion that started feebly in 1893 but grew into the major student-centered winter carnival event during Guy Bailey's presidency was Kake Walk, the minstrel-show derivative dissected by James Loewen in chapter 19. In the days when Blacks were "darkies," few lived in Vermont, almost none since George Washington Henderson ('77) had attended UVM. Kake Walk brought together on the campus all kinds of white townsfolk and alumni.

Besides athletic and Kake Walk competitions, students had prize speaking and debating. Old-fashioned "rhetoric" or oral English was only a small part of the English professor's duties after Frederick Tupper assumed that chair in 1894. Thomas Reed Powell ('00) recalled Tupper as adviser to Histrionic Devilings, the student dramatic group. On one of their trips to the hinterland, Tupper surveyed the hall crowded with empty seats and told the troupe, "It's time to begin; the audience are both here." It could have happened to the Banjo and Mandolin Club. Small clubs formed around many special interests, from sailing to religion, or gathered alumni of particular secondary schools. However, there were no organized winter sports or outing clubs before World War I.

With the centennial of the university charter in 1891, the establishment of Founder's Day in 1892, and the 1904 anniversary of the first graduating class, UVM put increased emphasis on inviting its alumni to come back to the campus. But finances were again precarious. The medical building burned down in December 1903, and medical enrollment fell. A major fund drive was slow in starting. Nevertheless, there were signs of hope. The University announced the acquisition of the Ainsworth farm off East Avenue for athletic fields and laid the cornerstone of the new medical building, built on borrowed funds. And the College of Agriculture, subsisting for over forty years in leftover space, finally got its state-funded Morrill Hall in 1907.

For his last six years Buckham continued to preside, to proclaim his humanistic philosophy, and to see that the new vocational developments—in teacher training, summer study, and home economics—were liberally inspired. A younger man more skilled in lobbying might have prevented Middlebury College from winning public money for its pedagogy program. A more rigid Classicist might have refused a home economics program. A feebler president could not have completed the million-dollar fund drive in six years or earned so much publicity through his finely crafted addresses. He believed he had mediated successfully between the old and the new. Nevertheless, after he died in 1910, his successors found much work to do to adjust UVM to modern times.

Benton's Bible Classes, 1911–1918

Guy Potter Benton was expected to be a fresh breeze from the Middle West to blow away the cobwebs of the classical college and make "Vermont," as the press called the University more often than "UVM," the truly state institution that Justin Morrill had hoped for in his land grant colleges. Benton had been president of Miami University of Ohio since 1902 and before that a professor of history and administrator in Kansas and Iowa colleges and in the Kansas school system. But the UVM Old Guard, thoroughly entrenched in faculty and alumni brigades, resisted Benton's efforts. Seven years later they maneuvered him out by questioning his patriotism (specifically for supporting a suspected spy, the professor of German).

Benton presumably had a mandate to clean house, though there is no record to show how he was briefed about UVM's situation. His inauguration imitated the centennial splurge of 1904, in contrast to Angell's inauguration in 1866 and Buckham's in 1871, held before modern-style publicity and in a period of dire distress. Benton's big splash seemed an unusual beginning, although he was merely following the current national practice. It was therefore wise of Guy Bailey when he took over officially in 1919 to omit the whole ceremony and make his traditional statement of goals in the first fall convocation.

In his first speeches Benton gave the usual assurances that he would honor and continue the great tradition of his predecessors and try to help the University be of even greater service to the state. He moved into the President's House at the north end of College Row and also took over a quarter of the main floor of the 1904 medical building for administrative offices. No longer would the University be run personally by the president, as it had been by Buckham, informally consulting his constituents and recording with his quill pen his own decisions or those of the Trustees, faculty, or committees. Buckham had led the University from his home next door to the humanistic library; Benton administered from his office next door to practical scientists.

The appointment of Laurence Wardell Swan, Benton's private secretary at Miami, to be "Secretary of the University" alienated the Old Guard at the outset. Buckham's nephew, James Dewey Benedict ('93) had been eager for the job. A New Yorker, descended from Professor George Benedict, he could have linked Benton to the Burlington elite, but Benton persisted in the selection of a man familiar with his own style and ideas.[2] Nowadays it is considered normal for the coach to bring some loyal players with him to his new job.

Benton's style was that of the owner of a business. After five years' experience on the campus he called thirty "full professors" together in April 1916 and presented a set of bylaws dealing comprehensively with governance. These departmental "chairmen," or head professors, as they were called for the first time, would have none of it. Thereupon Benton issued the bylaws without faculty approval.[3]

Although Benton meant in his inaugural to soothe the humanists by guaranteeing the humanistic curriculum, he clearly intended its guardian, the College of Arts and Sciences, to be a diminishing proportion of an expanding whole, as the state of Vermont was in the nation. Few, however, disagreed with his goal of wooing the state into funding broader services in education, agriculture, engineering, medicine, and social welfare. The Trustees rejected the advice of the Flexner Report and the Carnegie Foundation study to close the medical college and told Benton to go for a state appropriation for medicine instead. Benton noted that the Carnegie report "had failed to find that the University was a State institution,"[4] but the Board preferred not to deal with this issue.

Methodist Benton was the first UVM president who was not a Congregationalist, and he suffered for it. He was like the leading character in Sinclair Lewis's *Babbitt*, perhaps not sufficiently low-keyed about religion. To be sure, Buckham's administration had required and checked daily chapel attendance, although students were getting restive. In 1907, Buckham wrote to Levi P. Smith, editor of the *Cynic*, "You would not wish in rallying students to a more decorous behavior in chapel to tell our other constituents that chapel is disorderly. But the last issue of the Cynic gives that impression."[5] The Reverend Isaac C. Smart, pastor of Buckham's and Bailey's College Street Church, had the title of university chaplain and taught Bible. After daily chapel was abolished under Benton, Smart continued to perform as chaplain at university religious functions through the 1920s, and the Reverend Raymond A. Hall of the Charlotte Congregational Church succeeded Smart. For over half a century the main-line Protestant churches—Methodist, Baptist, Presbyterian, Congregational, Disciples of Christ—had felt a common "evangelical" bond and had had common enemies in Roman Catholicism and secular materialism; yet Benton's evangelical fervor, perhaps derived from his circuit-rider grandfather, alienated key UVM personnel.

Benton believed that UVM was a Christian institution in a Christian state. To a Methodist of that day a good Christian was a teetotaler with a puritanical approach to sex. In a welcoming speech to the Vermont Medical Society in 1913, Benton took occasion to disparage "the prurient advocates of sex hygiene."[6] At his first faculty meeting he demanded total abstinence: "A beer-sipping, wine-bibbing . . . professor . . . will not be tolerated beyond the meeting of the Board of Trustees [after] . . . his discovery. . . . I will not serve on a teaching body with any man who uses intoxicating liquors." Professor Tupper, already a distinguished and popular English teacher with considerable seniority, promptly went to him and declared that he sometimes had wine with his dinner. He was not dismissed. A faction developed, including Tupper, Samuel Bassett, and Judge Henry B. Shaw ('96), dedicated to Benton's own proposition that he should not serve on that faculty.[7] It called itself "the Benton Bible Class," after the adult Sunday school class Benton taught in the First Methodist Church downtown, and exercised wit in private at Benton's expense.[8]

Benton's faculty and alumni enemies used war-borne anti-German super-patriotism to pull him down. Anton Hermann Appelmann (1884–1929), professor of German at UVM from 1913, with a Ph.D. from study at five European universities, was rumored to be a German spy. An alumni investigating committee exonerated him, and the Trustees concurred. However, Appelmann, an enemy alien after the United States declared war, tendered his resignation. The Board first accepted it, only to back down when Benton threatened to resign himself. Appelmann nevertheless left and went back to Germany.

At the same time, Benton reaffirmed his own patriotism by taking a year's leave of absence to serve as a YMCA administrator with the American troops in France (later extended to two years).[9] In fact, his term as president was over. On his return from Europe he became president of the University of the Philippines, resigning in 1923 after contracting a tropical sleeping sickness, of which he died in 1927. Dean J. L. Hills commented, "He may not have fitted into the Vermont picture as well as might be wished," but "he fitted right well into the world wide picture."[10]

The Failure of a Dream: Guy Bailey, 1917–1940

Guy W. Bailey (1876–1940), a trustee of the University since 1914 and comptroller since 1917, was well positioned to succeed Benton. He was a native Vermonter, an alumnus (Phi Beta Kappa, '00, with honors in Greek), and a politician who knew the ropes. During his nine years as Vermont's secretary of state Bailey had formed a wide acquaintance over the whole state and knew the Vermont economy. Although, like Calvin Coolidge, he was capable on appropriate occasions of extended discourse and flowing conversation, Bailey built an image of dignified taciturnity. He was middle-aged and vigorous, a solid Congregationalist Republican, already being spoken of for governor. He was a man all UVM constituencies could trust.

During Benton's years in Europe the venerable dean George Perkins, in his seventies and with a half-century's experience on the UVM campus, carried the title of acting president. But Bailey, who was more in touch with the overall operation of UVM than anyone else, really did the work of the president, even before the Trustees voted him the title in August 1919.

Bailey's role as president between the world wars and his preparation for it are elaborated in chapter 11. His long tenure (1919–1940) was divided in half by outside forces: a period of expansion, when prosperity brought more students, buildings and endowment; and the Depression years, when the

University had little to cheer about, except that elsewhere things were worse and UVM was still alive.

In his first decade, ended by the October 1929 crash, Bailey lived up to his implied promises for the professional schools. They expanded with the prosperous times but basically reflected the limited needs of their local constituents. And although the teacher-training program continued to expand both through regular courses and through summer school, Bailey was unable to persuade the State to establish a single college of education in Burlington.

The postwar feminist movement contributed to the most notable change in UVM's profile, recounted by Constance McGovern in chapter 12. During the first period of the presence of women at UVM, 1872–1895, the problem was to accept them in classes. When classes were over, the girls disappeared into private homes off campus. The period 1895–1919 started with Grassmount as the new women's dormitory and ended with six more. Home economics, entirely a women's program initiated by alumnae in 1909 and fostered under Benton by the persistent Professor Bertha Terrill, made a substantial contribution to the women's side, as Professor Sinclair observes in chapter 10. Summer school and teacher training brought many more women to the campus. As Professor McGovern shows, the postwar flapper generation developed its independent UVM institutions, governance, rules, and festivities and edged steadily into the coeducational scene.

College "boys" in their sweaters, jackets, and slacks (not jeans) and "girls" in their pleated skirts and sweaters still shared "college spirit," although the scale of student life had expanded with the much larger and more heterogeneous enrollment. In chapter 13, Virginia Campbell Downs ('46) recounts the evolution of the collegiate atmosphere during the first half of this century. This was the heyday of the Greek letter fraternities, their social season climaxing in Kake Walk. Fraternities began to meet on Monday evenings instead of Saturday nights, as in the 1890s, because so many dances were scheduled after the games. After Saturday classes almost everyone, by unwritten rule, went to the football or baseball game and yelled the college cheers. Few blushed to sing, "We'll trim Harvard, we'll trim Yale, and there ain't no team that we can't whale; Rah rah for *Ver*mont," and so on.

Off in his medical college office, President Bailey made many minor decisions about individuals as well as the major policy decisions: dismissing an instructor, finding a donor, buying an estate, and negotiating its price. He consulted his senior staff members individually; usually accepted their recommendations for books, equipment, and instructors; and generally won Board approval at the annual meetings. He entered into the national effort to persuade wealthy businessmen to support the expansion of educational institutions but landed his biggest catch right in Vermont in the person of James B. Wilbur, donor of the Wilbur Fund and the Wilbur Collection. Wilbur shared with Bailey the Ivy League ideal of the university as a training ground for leadership, the premise of every president and professor from Daniel Sanders to George Perkins, though not the premise of Guy Benton.

Could Bailey carry out this Ivy League policy during the Depression decade? Probably no one could have to the extent required for the full flowering of the idea. But UVM was already on this track, and Bailey added significant increments. The faculty continued to come from the Ivies or by slow promotion from within—slow because senior professors did not retire; they taught until they were incapacitated or died. Unlike many Depression-hit presidents, Bailey did not cut salaries. They were simply not raised at the normal prosperity rate. As a larger proportion of UVM's income came from tuition, Bailey increasingly turned to his network of donors to pay the tuition of deserving poor students and maintain enrollment.[11] This meant, as the income of most donors was also constricted, that Bailey could find little money for new initiatives, not enough even for ongoing commitments. An exception was buildings, which attract the easiest money even in the worst of times. Bailey combined gifts, federal funds, and money from the sale of building lots to professors to build Slade Hall and the Southwick Women's Center on the Redstone campus; and he acquired a number of former Hill residences for offices or student housing as loyal alumni or professors died.

The great legacy that built the Waterman Building in 1940–1941 concealed the University's precarious financial situation. With $1,250,000 made from mining, railroads, and banking, the University put into one building the facilities to meet needs that had been accumulating for decades. Into the center of the Waterman Building went stacks for a large part of the overcrowded library, staff offices, and a rare-book room (the present Memorial Lounge). In the subbasement were installed new machinery for the College of Engineering and two bowling alleys. The space released to the medical college when the administrative offices moved to Waterman helped ward off a renewed threat of the loss of accreditation.[12] In addition, Waterman provided much-needed classroom and office space, along with the University Store (moved from the Old Mill). After the "Hash House" behind Williams Science Hall—more formally known as Commons Hall (1885)—closed in 1931, there was nowhere to eat closer to the main campus than Grassmount, boardinghouses near campus, or fraternity houses. A dining hall in Waterman, opposite the University Store, met that need. When UVM could not compete for the instructors it wanted by offering higher salaries, it could offer a few low-rent bachelor apartments on the top floor of Waterman.

The Waterman Building went a long way toward raising those standards that could be improved by adding space, but it could not balance a budget. In fact, so sour were UVM finances when Waterman was completed, there was no money to run the elevators, no money for full maintenance of the new building. No one since the audit of 1941 has yet had the heart to examine the financial history of UVM during the Depression. We therefore do not know whether it was in trouble from 1929 on, when western mortgages and other securities went bad, or whether, as the auditors said, Bailey's borrowing from earmarked funds began in the late 1930s. Vermonters trusted Bailey, but unlike President Buckham, for instance, he did not tell the Trustees what the real troubles were. Professor Paul D. Evans, chair of history for a decade under Bailey, called him "a one-man show and a 'silent operator.' "[13] Guy Bailey heard the parties in a conflict, consulted the experts if he felt it necessary, assured himself what the rules and the policy called for, decided, delegated, and usually told the Trustees.

No wonder the public was amazed to read in the papers after Bailey's death that UVM owed some half-million dollars to the banks. Once again, as with President Worthington Smith (from 1849 to 1855), a president had failed to resign when he became too sick to manage. The gathering gloom seemed no time to celebrate the charter sesquicentennial or to publish the university history that English professor Julian Lindsay had been preparing since 1938. Institutional histories, like sundials, like to record only sunny hours.

When the state, the city, and the alumni prepared to rally behind their university, they came bearing all kinds of advice as well as gifts. George W. Alger ('92), a successful New York lawyer born on Texas Hill in Hinesburg, Vermont, and long a consistently large donor, recalled the good old heyday of Buckham's peak years. "We had . . . the education of a gentleman, with the classics . . . , philosophy, modern languages, and a relatively small amount of science." Narrow as this curriculum was, it produced articulate, well-mannered, poised, well-dressed, cultured, attractive personalities—"the most successful graduates the University ever has had," he believed. The younger crop he saw at New York Alumni Association meetings were awkward, tongue-tied, mannerless. "There is more difficulty in placing these Vermont youngsters because of their cultural backwardness than for any other reason." Alger continued, "For a long while the cultural aspect of education has been neglected" at UVM, he wrote. "I went a few days ago to the KAKE WALK. . . . It simply made me sick. . . . The stunts were silly and pointless. . . . The gawkiest, rawest, and most uncouth student in the University in my time got it started. He subsequently went insane." No student body with any cultural standards "could find this form of entertainment continuously alluring," yet it was the most important expression of student culture. Alger hoped that aptitude tests could help freshmen know their weaknesses in time to remedy them and that after UVM got over its financial worries it would choose an educator-president with "vision which is still practical."[14]

A door opened and a door shut in November 1941, as the new administration of President John S. Millis moved its offices from the Medical Building to the new Waterman Building. On November 15 the bell in the Old Mill tower, which had rung so many students to chapel and classes and in latter days for athletic victories, was taken down. A month later the United States entered World War II, and long-range planning had to be shelved while the University scratched for survival. Coasting into the twentieth century and then aspiring both to fuller state university and Ivy League status, UVM left many wondering in the 1940s whether a near-bankrupt institution could have any status at all.

Guy Bailey and the University of Vermont

T . D . S E Y M O U R   B A S S E T T

Each person has various gifts. Some cultivate them, and some by a confluence of events use their gifts and growth to advantage, or make do with what little they are given. My purpose in this essay is to sort out what gifts Guy Winfred Bailey was given when and after he was born in Hardwick, Vermont, May 7, 1876; how he developed those talents; and what opportunities at the University of Vermont he found to use the abilities he developed until his death on October 22, 1940. How did the combination of gifts, cultivation, and opportunities in Guy Bailey make him different from all other UVM presidents, and how did he reflect or change UVM?

Bailey was blessed with enterprising parents. His father, John Winthrop Bailey, was born in Greensboro on October 11, 1849, of parents born in Greensboro when it was scarcely a generation out of the wilderness. With a $1,000 note endorsed by his half-brother Charles, John Bailey took over an old-fashioned woolen mill in Mackville, a mile and a half south of Hardwick post office. He could not compete with the higher-tech, larger-scale mills of modern times and went into bankruptcy. Moving to Essex Junction in 1882, he found work in the monument business.[1] He certainly had observed the Hardwick granite sheds if he had not worked in them. In 1888 his wife (born Laura Cahill in Greensboro) and others of the Essex Junction Marble and Granite Company leased a lot south of Maple Street on the railroad for an expanded monument works. By 1907 the Bailey Granite Company had moved to the east side of Railroad Avenue, opposite the station, occupying the main floor of the village auditorium. After Guy Bailey's mother died in 1915, his father moved to the Lincoln Inn, continuing in the monument business to within a year of his death in 1922.[2]

Guy worked in the shop as a high school boy of fifteen and as a college student living at home. He learned a bit of carving, as well as lettering and tracing. In later life the biographical material he supplied the press did not emphasize his Puritan background; only one sketch mentioned that his ancestor James Bailey came to Rowley, Massachusetts, in 1640 and that another, John Bailey, served in colonial wars. Guy Bailey's forefathers came to Greensboro via Newburyport, Massachusetts; Portland (then Falmouth), Maine; Peacham and Troy, Vermont.[3] His mother was descended from the Scots-Irish settlers of the Craftsbury–Glover area. There were no other children surviving to adulthood. The membership register of the Essex Junction Congregational Church includes neither Guy nor his parents; nor did he or his wife ever join the College Street Congregational Church in Burlington, although they attended regularly.

The Baileys were ambitious for their lad, and paid tuition at Burlington High School to give him the best education they could afford. He commuted the six miles by the Central Vermont Railroad (which ran five shuttle trips a day) or by the trolley (extended to Essex Junction in the late 1890s) and continued to commute throughout college and even when he was comptroller of UVM from 1917 to 1919. His law partner recalled, "Many times while he was a student at the University he walked from the campus to Essex Junction because he did not have sufficient pennies to pay his fare on the electric car."[4] Memory being what it is, that means at least twice. Guy was a village boy, not a country boy. When he filled out the military manpower survey of faculty and staff in 1918, he confessed that he could not ride a horse, although he could handle a team; and he could not drive an automobile, nor swim, nor cook.

Entering UVM at twenty, older than the average, Guy proved his manhood on the freshman class football team (the sophs won the annual contest 60–0) and pledged Alpha Tau Omega. Records do not show whether he was in the underclassmen's fight at Athletic Park (then located down the hill from Riverside Drive off Intervale Road) the first Saturday of his first term, nor whether he went downtown to "the vicinity of" the Howard Opera House (on the southwest corner of Bank and Church Streets) on October 5, 1897, to take part in "the fiercest cane rush in the history of the University," stopped by Police Chief Dumas when the sophomores were ahead.[5] He was a "townie" who attended classes, went home, worked in his father's shop on Saturdays, and studied, yet withal a popular young man.

Bailey's other extracurricular activities were what his fraternity called on him to do and the offices his peers recognized his ability to perform. In his sophomore year he was class poet and on the class banquet committee. As a junior he joined the chess club, was one of four sergeants of the university battalion, and was president of his class. Many of his associates recalled his playing chess for relaxation all through life. In his senior year he was first lieutenant of the battalion and on the class book committee that prepared the *Portfolio*. (He was not on the *Ariel* board.) He also chaired the general committee arranging commencement events for the graduating seniors. He was *not* among the nine senior orators (including Thomas Reed Powell, son of the treasurer of the University), nor one of the ten Class Day officers. He made Phi Beta Kappa, and although not a member of the Classical Society, graduated A.B. in 1900, one of four with special honors in Greek. It may be significant that besides specializing in Classics, he studied German with Lewis J. Huff, an ordained minister who lost his Southern Baptist faith after exposure to Darwinism.[6]

Even before he graduated from college, Bailey pointed himself toward politics by registering his intention to study law with Brown and Taft of Burlington. He struck up a friendship with Allen Martin, the long-time Essex, Vermont, town clerk, soon after Martin opened his Essex Junction law office in the fall of 1898 and clerked with him from graduation until he was admitted to the Vermont bar in October 1904. Joining the Mount Mansfield Lodge, Knights of Pythias, in Essex Junction in 1900, he had become Grand Chancellor in the Grand Lodge by 1906. Later he would join Rotary, the Elks, Odd Fellows, Masons (awarded thirty-third degree), Sons of the Revolution, and Loyal Legion, and he became governor general of the Society of Colonial Wars. The spring after he graduated he was elected town moderator in Essex, and he kept being elected to that office (except when he was sick in 1915) through 1922, a year or more after he moved to Burlington. And he was president of the Village of Essex Junction, 1902–1904 and 1914–1915.

A signal that he had settled his career direction was Bailey's marriage December 22, 1905, to Mabel Gertrude Brigham, a New York native then living in Essex Junction. Until they moved to Burlington, they lived in a white frame house on the corner of Main and Pleasant Streets in Essex Junction, within walking distance of Guy's law office of Martin & Bailey on the Five Corners between Maple and Main. He began to deal in real estate. Winthrop, their first and only child, was born at home August 12, 1905, but died four months later of "congenital malformation of heart."[7] Henceforth Bailey's parental love was diffused among all of his constituents and students. He served as president of Kurn Hattin Homes, the orphanages in Westminster and Saxtons River, Vermont, from 1920 to 1940, and as treasurer of the Vermont Children's Aid Society. "Few men in Vermont had a wider circle of friends," wrote Edward F. Crane, Burlington *Free Press* editor, after Bailey's death.[8]

By 1904 Bailey was prepared to enter state politics. Elected to the Vermont House that year, and the only Essex representative reelected to more than two years' service between 1825 and World War II, Bailey served from the start on important committees such as Judiciary and Ways and Means. He was also clerk of the commission to edit the *Public Statutes*, 1904–1907, and then a member of the commission.

In 1908 the Republican state convention nominated Guy Bailey for secretary of state over Walter K. Farnsworth of Rutland, secretary of the state senate. Bailey won 59 percent of the votes. Election over his Democratic opponent the following November was a foregone conclusion. The Montpelier *Journal* called him "one of the best known young men in the State, combining excellent executive ability with an engaging personality," who "has always played a prominent part in municipal and state affairs."[9] In his first statewide public office, Bailey "spoiled that job for sitters," the Northfield *News* declared. He observed the legislative turmoil over aid to UVM, Middlebury, and Norwich, and so when he became president, he was able to end the strife and diplomatically shift the debate, according to one press comment, to the question of what Vermont higher education really needed.[10]

Progressive Republicans in Vermont adopted much social welfare legislation during Bailey's tenure as secretary of state. As a member of the Commission to Formulate an Employer's Liability and Workmen's Compensation Law and of the Commission to Formulate a Uniform System of Accounts,[11] he helped codify the new programs. He was not only a workhorse bureaucrat; he kept his hand in politics, attending the national Republican convention in 1916 as a Hughes delegate. He expanded the state's role in promoting tourism and the sale of summer homes and inaugurated the State Bureau of Motor Vehicles. Samuel R. Saiger (UVM '22) recalled Bailey's royal administrative style, which never changed after he came to UVM. Saiger tells how when he was seventeen he went with his father to Guy Bailey's in Essex Junction to get an operator's license. (Not until World War I did the secretary of state have an office in Montpelier when the legislature was not in session.) Bailey knew the law, which allowed him to issue a permit to anyone over sixteen if he was satisfied that the applicant could drive. He decided on the spot: "I think Sam had better wait until he is eighteen before he starts driving."[12]

In 1914 Bailey was elected a UVM trustee. Then in 1917 President Benton appointed him comptroller, combining the functions of treasurer, registrar, superintendent of buildings and grounds, and president's administrative secretary, in other words, his number-two administrator. In his statement to the press on accepting the appointment, Bailey said in praise of his president, "During the last few years, the University of Vermont has been more and more fulfilling its mission to the people of the State. . . . I am assured [by the Trustees] that I may have a part in . . . the work of making the University more serviceable."[13] The functional division of responsibilities between Benton and Bailey was just what troubleshooter Packer recommended in 1941, after Bailey's twenty years of exercising the presidency without divesting himself of the comptrollership. Bailey had been considered a leading candidate for governor; the press generally assumed that as UVM's business manager he was only temporarily out of contention and that he would be in touch with the Legislature and with politics. In fact, he was permanently out of contention, because he did not want to be governor, but he was never out of politics.

In April 1917, Bailey had voted with the majority of trustees and against President Benton to accept German professor Anton Appelmann's resignation, now that his country was at war with the United States, but also voted to let him teach the rest of the term. When the Trustees unanimously accepted the report of the committee of the Associate Alumni exonerating Appelmann of anti-American activities, "Mr. Bailey . . . explained that he could not approve the [4–1] majority report unqualifiedly because he thought the record disclosed that Dr. Appelmann had been guilty of indiscretions which the majority report should have noted with censure."[14] Against the resistance of several trustees, Bailey did vote with President Benton in June, when Benton threatened to resign unless the Board reappointed the controversial Professor Appelmann. But events moved rapidly, thrusting Bailey into the driver's seat. On September 1, 1917, President Benton started his year's leave of absence to serve with the YMCA in France, and Bailey wound up his work as secretary of state.

For two years mayor of the palace under titular Acting President George H. Perkins, then in his seventies, Bailey managed the difficult times when male students went off to war and soldiers drilled on the back campus. In August 1919 the Trustees appointed him Perkins's successor as acting president, and he took charge of what was nearly the smallest of northeastern colleges (only 301 students in 1921).[15] He gave what amounted to an inaugural address on "opening day," the fall convocation exercises. He would not "resume the argument as to whether the University is or is not a State institution," he began. Then in fact he did resume the argument. He believed the founders thought "they were establishing a State University."[16] He quoted Governor Jonas Galusha in 1811, referring to the charter amendment of 1810, reversed in 1828: "This University has now become a State institution."

But the right to be the state university, Bailey continued, is based on "service as well as law." He pointed out that graduates of Vermont high schools approved by the state Board of Education were admitted without examination—an arrangement President Buckham had resisted during his last years—and suggested that Vermont might need a junior college for those less prepared for university work. The alternative was better preparation in high school. The University would merit state support, Bailey went on, by the quality of its instruction, research, and "extension and extramural activities" in *all four colleges*. He promised a caring advisory system and job opportunities for students working their way, with scholarship financing so that "every possible student should be saved . . . without sacrificing standards."

At the same time, Bailey emphasized medical and agricultural achievements in research and extension—Experiment Station reports, research on poliomyelitis, the work of the state laboratory of hygiene associated with the medical college, the work of seniors in the fall and winter of 1918 at the Waterbury State Hospital. He concluded: "The University should be the clearing house for information respecting the State's needs and its problems." An annual nonpartisan conference of politicians, bureaucrats, and other citizens should deal with issues "in a good old fashioned way," including "women's duties and her legal rights."

Against this background Bailey showed where his main push toward the public sector would come—in teacher training. First he pointed out that UVM was already preparing two thirds of the high school teachers of agriculture, and many high school home economics teachers. Foreseeing the "discontinuance" of the normal schools, he suggested that the University might have to provide training for teachers in the elementary grades, at any rate for grades 5–8. With four fifths of UVM students residents of Vermont, and therefore likely to teach there, the University, with good practice schools nearby, was well equipped to be the state's college of education. Bailey did not mention preparing high school teachers; Middlebury College had state subsidies for that program.

The test came in the early 1920s with the apparent opportunity to concentrate teacher training in Burlington. This field had grown mightily at UVM for a dozen years under Professor James F. Messenger's administration. President Benton had helped persuade the 1912 Legislature to establish an education commission, which in turn initiated the Carnegie Foundation study and accepted its findings. Vermont Supreme Court judge John H. Watson, speaking for the commission, deplored wasteful duplication of efforts and preferred no appropriations to any private college, including UVM. He pointed out that Vermont spent much more on education in proportion to its total property valuation than did New York or any other New England state. He recommended that secondary schools train elementary school teachers, that Middlebury College train secondary school teachers, that the State Agricultural College prepare teachers of agriculture, and that both the Johnson and Castleton normal schools be closed.[17] Both Johnson and Castleton had temporarily closed in 1920, and a special 1921 report to the Legislature recommended a single teachers' college. The Carnegie Foundation offered $100,000 and UVM earmarked $200,000, but the senate-approved bill to accomplish this consolidation was killed in the House.

Once more opportunity knocked when Castleton's main building burned down in 1924. Caroline Woodruff, who as principal had raised Castleton from the dead in 1921 and knew how eager UVM was, rushed to rouse Castleton's alumni. They raised the money to rebuild while Woodruff rallied political support, presumably including alliances with Johnson, the new Vail agricultural institute at Lyndon, and Randolph Agricultural School. If Castleton closed for good, would Johnson be far behind? Bennett Douglas, the new UVM professor of education and director of the summer session, may have had other goals, requiring good relations with every part of the state's educational system. Likewise President Bailey had to balance UVM's needs for other state aid. At all events, the votes were not there for a single state teachers' college, and they never have been. Bailey continued to build UVM's education program as primus inter pares, first among equals.

Women were entering UVM in unprecedented numbers for many other reasons besides teacher training. Their war experiences had widened their awareness of new career possibilities. New dormitories had to be found, first by buying private homes. The president had been active in Essex real estate, and he was at home in the field when it came to acquiring residence halls. In 1921, Bailey gave the Kappa Alpha Thetas permission to establish the first sorority house on campus by acquiring the Carroll house, 215 South Prospect Street (where Catholic bishop Rice had lived until 1919). Other sorority houses were bought or built during the Bailey administration—on Main Street (Delta Delta Delta and Alpha Chi Omega) and next to Redstone (Pi Beta Phi).

In the long run, women had to be assigned a place in the campus plan in a kinder, gentler environment, sheltered from the brutal rough-and-tumble of the men's campus. Soon after Bailey took office, UVM bought the Redstone estate, occupied by the family of the professor of ophthalmology, Dr. M. C. Twitchell. It provided contiguous open space beyond the Experiment Station, with three stone buildings, solidly built in the late 1880s and needing little renovation to make elegant dormitories, a dining hall, and a professor's house.[18]

Although Guy Bailey loved students, he could be stern with them. He imposed a prohibition on coed smoking, although Dean Patterson would have relaxed it. He fired an instructor because his baby came too soon after his marriage. Irene Allen ('25) recalled that the Baileys' home in Essex Junction "was quiet and immaculate . . . but it wasn't a place a child felt really at home in." She endured her first semester with her mother and the Baileys at Wheeler House but escaped for the spring term to Grassmount. Bailey made no exceptions for alumni and friends of the University whose sons had flunked out of Ivy League colleges and applied for admission to UVM. On the other hand, he had the politician's real interest in individuals when he shook hands with freshmen in the receiving line.[19] When Dorothy Barrows ('25) reminded the president that girls being evacuated from Angell Hall (when it was ready to be torn down) had been promised their choice of rooms, he became very indignant and denied her request. That evening he phoned, apologized, and reversed his decision. He did not hesitate over decisions. When Professor Harry Perkins saw the excellent laboratory work of math major Lyman Rowell, he sounded him out for an instructorship in zoology upon graduation. *The very next day* Perkins told Rowell, "The

President says it's all right to hire you." No contract, no procedure, no advertising in the national (including minority) media. Just a word from Guy Bailey.[20]

Bailey kept in touch with students individually, as he called them in to discuss their problems. For example, Elmer L. Nicholson ('39) had an argument with his basketball coach and quit the team in midseason. The president, who had found him the money to stay in college, pointed out that he played for UVM and not for a coach and persuaded him to finish the season.[21] Bailey also used Boulder, the men's senior honorary society, as an arm of his administration when he felt he needed help from the student body. But no senior committee was appointed to canvass the class as to whom they would like to address them at their graduation. Students, faculty, staff, and alumni might suggest, but Bailey decided.

Whether Bailey's goal was to persuade Vermonters to support their state university by sending students and voting appropriations or to attract potential private donors, he needed a modern public relations staff. He mobilized the alumni, appointed John O. Baxendale ('12) alumni secretary, and started the *Vermont Alumni Weekly*.

There was a network of UVM faculty and staff working with Vermont citizens and schools through many channels. Walter Hill Crockett, editor of university publications, who had worked with Guy Bailey when he was secretary of state, and Leon W. Dean, English instructor who also helped with extension publicity, teamed with Baxendale. Crockett and Dean created a high school publications network, with conferences and prizes. Max W. Andrews ('99) and his successors in the "elocution" field coached strong debating teams, which they recruited through their connections with high school debate. The state YMCA and YWCA were other connections through Older Girls' and Older Boys' conferences. The home demonstration staff and Elwyn L. Ingalls, who directed state 4-H Club work, reached other groups of potential students and supporters.

All through the staff and faculty, there were people with such personal connections. Thus, small-scale fund raising was the ultimate result of a series of interlocking networks persuading Vermonters that UVM was *their* college. It was helped indirectly by the establishment of the University's radio station in 1924.[22] But as L. F. Killick, director of alumni relations, wrote for the 1962 self-study, "until ten years ago," fund raising was a "one-man band," barely self-supporting out of the money it raised.[23]

After failing to win state aid for an expanded UVM teacher training program, Bailey turned to soliciting a share of the private fortunes made in World War I and before, that continued to grow in the booming 1920s. Most of these prospects were out of state, but one wealthy businessman, James Benjamin Wilbur (1856–1929), had moved to Manchester shortly before the war. About 1915 he bought the nearby Eagle Square Company of South

Shaftsbury for his son to manage and first interested himself in the Bennington County Improvement Association.[24] Then Wilbur discovered Ira Allen. He convinced himself that Ira, not his brother Ethan, was the true Hero and Founder of Vermont and of UVM. Naturally, he showered his blessings on Ira's university, first with a small icon in the form of a statue on the campus displacing that of Lafayette, looking down College Street. Then he gave a chapel, designed by UVM's architects, McKim, Mead and White, displacing the President's House at the north end of College Row. President Buckham would have been pleased. President Bailey was not displaced by the new construction. He had moved from Essex Junction into President Wheeler's old house, 133 South Prospect Street, late in 1920, leaving Angell Hall available as a women's dormitory. By 1924 he had moved to the Albert C. Whiting mansion, 203 South Willard Street, recently given to the University, a short walk from campus, surrounded by quiet citizens, not students.

In 1928, Wilbur published his laudatory documentary biography of Ira Allen.[25] The next year he died, but his benefactions continued. By major expenditure of staff energy for a decade, and by letting him have his way when he became a trustee, Bailey was able to persuade Wilbur to provide in his will a $3-million endowment for scholarships to Vermonters. This was the climactic gift, but it was not all. Wilbur also donated the library that he had assembled to write the biography of Ira Allen, with a $150,000 endowment to develop it further, and contributed to the building fund for the Fleming Museum (1931) for an addition to house that library.

Residuary legatees contested Wilbur's will on the ground that UVM had failed to meet his requirement that enrollment at UVM never exceed one thousand. However, after long litigation, in 1932 the court accepted the argument of Warren R. Austin, UVM counsel, that Wilbur intended to restrict only the College of Arts and Sciences, the heir of the original University of Vermont, to which various professional schools had been added since the Civil War.

What do Wilbur's gifts show about the direction of Bailey's policy for UVM? Beyond the statue and the biography, traditional ways to memorialize a great man, the larger gifts were what Bailey wanted, although it was incongruous to give deist Ira Allen a chapel for a gravestone. The scholarships, on the other hand, continued the dual purpose of Ira Allen's original concept of UVM, started with a state endowment of land and his own private endowment. In 1930 the state was giving only a few thousand for medical and agricultural training. But Wilbur's bequest helped some of Vermont's best high school graduates go to UVM—something that states farther west and south provided by subsidizing a lower in-state tuition.

Implicit in all of this was Wilbur's and Bailey's Jeffersonian idea of a state university as the place to prepare its natural aristocracy for leadership. The Ivy League, northeastern institutions mostly of colonial origin that enjoyed large endowments, shared this ideal. There was no contradiction between this elitist goal and providing more scholarships for the best scholars in each graduating class. With liberal funding UVM could divert a larger share of the most gifted Vermont youth from out-of-state Ivies to Burlington and at the same time attract nonresident children of successful alumni and other leaders in the nation's centers.

In this way excellent graduates would be prepared by the confluence of leisure, space, wealth, and contact with instructors trained in the Ivy League. Wealth would provide a favorable faculty–student ratio and rich resources in buildings, grounds, and equipment; in libraries and laboratories; and in living, learning, and recreational arrangements. Space would be guaranteed by limiting the numbers using these resources. Instead of chance acquaintance with those most likely to succeed (all that was possible in institutions with large numbers of undergraduates), students could be sure of exclusive contacts with other potential leaders. The fraternity system, an elitist palliative in large universities, carried exclusiveness a step farther in the Ivies. Leisure, prerequisite for the creativity that enables leaders to keep ahead in their fields, would be the result of having wealth and space. With enough scholarship aid, students' time would not be cut by the need to earn their expenses. This approach meant channeling students upon graduation from high school, rather than letting upward mobility depend on one's college record. With enough microscopes, a student's laboratory time would not be shortened by the need to share equipment. With enough dormitory space, including common, dining, and recreation rooms, or enough money to afford apartments in town, a student's energy would not be misdirected toward defending turf. Leisure is an intangible, dependent also on ideals fostered by recognition in art shows, performances, and other forms of attention to achievement. Seminars, independent study, and foreign travel, while reducing class time, needed funding to promote students' independent development.

Although there was no requirement during Bailey's administration that professors have Ph.D.'s or that they publish their research, in 1919 more than half of the faculty in the College of Arts and Sciences had doctorates and, thanks to their training, naturally published the results of their studies. Other instructors in the larger departments often did not complete their graduate work until long after they began to teach at UVM but were allowed to continue even if they never completed their dissertations. Tenure was an informal assumption that if an instructor survived his first year on probation he would be continued indefinitely. Although President Benton proposed bylaws for the faculty in 1916, only in 1945 did the faculty draft them, including an AAUP statement on tenure and dismissal that President Millis and the Trustees approved.

Those professors who published were not funded by grants, except in fields touching agriculture, such as George P. Burns on white pine and Marshall B. Cummings on apples, whose research was federally supported. When the medical college examiners in the late 1930s found weakness in faculty research, appointments of such people as Harold B. Pierce and Wilhelm Raab were made to meet this criticism. As director of the Fleming Museum, Harry Perkins launched the Old Buildings Project and hired architect and photographer Herbert Wheaton Congdon. Its products were an exhibit, a book, and the deposit of the film and prints in the Museum.[26] With defense industry prospering toward the end of the 1930s and the price of copper rising, the Vermont Copper Mining Company gave the University the largest research grant to date, to explore the Orange County copper belt. A research team directed by State Geologist Elbridge C. Jacobs analyzed the findings and concluded that Vermont Copper could remine their mine tailings.

The first privately funded research project at UVM was the Eugenics Survey of Vermont, directed by Harry Perkins for a decade beginning in 1925. Biased in its assumptions and crude in its methodology, the project nevertheless served to justify the eugenic sterilization of two hundred or more "feebleminded" and other "unfit" in Vermont institutions, under a Vermont law urged by Perkins's organization and passed in 1931. However, it is a far cry from President Bailey's accepting $5,000 a year from Mrs. Emily Proctor Eggleston for the Eugenics Survey, at one end of the spectrum, to Nazi racism at the other.

George W. Alger, the alumnus of 1892 who posed the educational standard of "a gentleman," was a trustee from 1935 to 1941. He shared the president's Vermont background and his social philosophy, but he did not respect Bailey's cultural leadership of the campus. Alger criticized Bailey for choosing "a long succession of uninspired and generally dull speakers" to visit the campus.[27] A trustee's steady diet of commencement addresses probably developed an allergy, evinced in Professor Francis Colburn's famous parody.[28] The speakers, from the Japanese Christian pacifist Toyohiko Kagawa to Canon Allen Pearson Shatford of Montreal, were people whom UVM could afford and who were willing to swerve a day's journey off the main line of the speakers' circuit.

Alger particularly faulted Bailey for his lack of broadening travel. He wrote after Bailey's death, "President Bailey, with all his good qualities, came from a very narrow background. He scarcely left the state in his life."[29] Alger, whose career was a Horatio Alger success story like Bailey's, was showing his metropolitan prejudice. Bailey's trips away from his desk were to inspect the University's farm mortgages in the northern Great Plains, to "visit with" (his habitual way of making an appointment) alumni and other donors in Atlantic seaboard cities, and to go fishing for a week or so on the Averill Ponds in the Essex County woods near the Canadian border.

On two different occasions the Trustees urged Bailey, at whatever university expense, to take vacations and trips whenever he chose and for as long as he chose, but he never did.[30]

This expression of complete confidence betrayed the Trustees' failure to supervise their chief executive as his health declined or to persuade him to retire when he should have. There was insufficient communication between the Board and the president and also a gap between the president and his subordinates. A chief executive leads a lonely life unless he delegates important matters to his assistants and keeps in close touch with them. One way to develop their responsibility is to go away and leave them in temporary charge. Since the president "never took a vacation," he lost another opportunity to develop those who could carry the ball as his own strength ebbed.

About 1937 the Alumni Council commissioned Martha Greta Kempton to paint the president's portrait. It now hangs near the Bailey/Howe Library circulation desk. Ms. Kempton had a practice of letting her subject converse with a friend during sittings. Chester B. Eaton ('34), active in alumni affairs and then with the Boy Scouts of America in New York City, took time off to "sit" with Guy Bailey at Kempton's New York studio. Eaton remembered clearly the president's exhortation: "Mr. Eaton, don't make the mistakes I did. Don't fail to work very closely with persons younger than yourself. There are times I don't have anybody to turn to except persons my own age," or former Boulder men, like you, he added. Bailey was already sick and knew that he could not transfer his adeptness at persuading the affluent to give to UVM, even if he took a younger man with him to present UVM's case. During the Depression the president was accustomed to visiting his prospect list toward the end of each year, armed with specific knowledge about each loyal supporter, what individual students' needs were, and what UVM's deficit would be. In the late 1930s he no longer had the strength, and perhaps his benefactors, surmising that the president's life was ebbing, no longer had the confidence to give.[31]

As comptroller, Guy Bailey resorted to various devices to make ends meet, including persuading people to give now and receive annuities. This is a common practice, but it requires investing the proceeds and not touching them until the annuities end. Bailey used the funds because UVM needed them for current operations. Nationally, gifts to higher education were down, returns on investments were down, and student needs were up. In order not to show how large the annual deficit was (from 1936 to 1940 it accumulated to $716,000, with another $200,000 shortfall predicted for fiscal 1941), Bailey raised the valuation of university properties, notably the Wilbur Timber Company tract on Vancouver Island and the Billings Library. The annual accountings showed a deficit of only $6,000 in 1937 and just above an even balance otherwise. The 1939 audit of Jurgs, Murray & Densmore, reviewing the annuity contracts and the table of deficits, showed nothing different. As his admirers who compiled *Thank You, Guy Bailey*, wrote, he "had spent money he had no legal right to spend" but for good purposes.[32]

From the spring of 1939, Bailey was confined to his bed by tuberculosis of the spine and shoulder, and his bedroom became his office.[33] The Trustees came to his house for their annual meeting that June and again in 1940 and for the special meetings concerned with the Waterman legacy and the building, up to their last meeting with him October 12, 1940, ten days before his death of a heart attack.[34] Guy Bailey's will involved an estate of not quite $15,000, after payment of some $36,000 in debts—a $14,000 note to the Burlington Trust Company and loans on his life insurance. One wonders whether he had dipped into his own pocket to meet the most pressing demands on UVM in his last months. He had suggested that the Howard Bank, trustee, pay Mabel Brigham Bailey an annuity of $350 or more a month.[35] She lived in Beverly, Massachusetts, until her death in the 1950s. "He freely gave instead of creating an estate," wrote his close friend Allen Martin.[36]

Many of the president's loyal supporters believed, as Edwin B. Abbott, Bailey's bookkeeper, wrote, "If he had lived, there was a good chance he would have succeeded in making up the deficit."[37] He clearly intended to. Preparation for war had turned the economy around so that surpluses were again there for the winning. But could Bailey's style have coped with the upheavals of 1941–1945? As temporary president Paul Packer warned in 1941, the day of the Lone Ranger in the president's chair was over. No individual could deal single-handedly with businessmen and bankers, students and alumni, faculty and staff, townspeople at Rotary, and visitors from the Outer Isles.

Bailey was benevolent first selectman and town representative of a university village. Although no ballots were cast to elect him except for the unanimous approval of the Trustees in 1919, he continued to rule by common consent. Let later generations not assign to him tasks that were not his. Let us leave praise and blame behind and look straight at a mountain of a man, "too large to see around and too deep to see into," as Irene Allen recalled.[38] His reign spanned two decades; he left tangible and intangible monuments; he was first in boom, first in bust, and first in the hearts of his alumni.

Professor Frederick Tupper

President Guy Benton

Professor Samuel Emerson

Professor Samuel E. Bassett

President Guy Bailey

James B. Wilbur

Laying the cornerstone of Ira Allen Chapel, 1925

Women students, ca. 1885

Lida Mason (l.) and Ellen Hamilton (r.), first women to graduate from UVM and first anywhere to be elected to Phi Betta Kappa

Professor Bertha Terrill

Dean Pearl Wasson

Dean Mary Jean Simpson

uvm baseball team, 1893

ATO fraternity brothers, ca. 1912

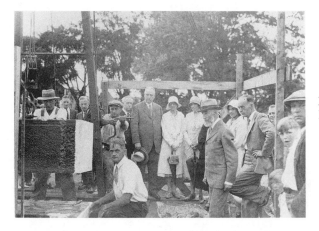

Laying the cornerstone of Fleming Museum, 1932

Cast of *The Covenant* (written by Jan Goldstein and David Lash, Class of 1973), Arena Theater, 1973

President John Millis

College Green, ca. 1950

Presidents Carl Borgmann and William Carlson

Dedication of Aschen-
bach sculpture, Bailey
Library (l. to r., Pro-
fessor Edward Feidner,
Paul Aschenbach, and
President John T. Frey)

Dr. Alex Novikoff receiving honorary degree from President Lattie Coor, 1983

Kake Walk

Kake Walk king and queen, 1950s

Freshmen, Class of 1961

Ira Allen statue

Lieutenant Governor Thomas
Hayes addressing Vietnam
protest rally, 1970

Women at UVM

CONSTANCE M. MCGOVERN

Lᴵᵀᵀᴸᴇ did the Trustees of the University of Vermont realize, when they voted in 1871 to admit women students, the extent to which their decision would alter the character of the University and the lives of its students. Immediately, the University had to heat the library; but more fundamentally, the Trustees would be faced with a whole array of issues—expanding the curriculum, investing in dormitories, hiring women as professors, addressing issues of gender inequities, and contending with differential giving from graduates. For the women themselves the decision of UVM's trustees offered new opportunities for careers or a chance to bring a sense of social responsibility to their marriages. It changed their expectations for their daughters as well, however little this was anticipated in 1871.

As the governing board of the first East Coast university to admit women, UVM's trustees, like those of the few western coeducational state universities of that era, had mixed motives. Most of those eighteen trustees were thoughtful, generally liberal-minded, middle-class men, but by no stretch of the imagination were they, or their wives, the shakers and movers of the nineteenth-century feminist world. George Grenville Benedict, for instance, was adamantly opposed to woman's suffrage, but as editor of the *Burlington Free Press* he reprinted articles lauding UVM's decision to admit women students. He, like others who had taken note of the arguments for the higher education of women, thought it only just to offer the opportunity to women like his own sisters or daughters. Another Vermonter and trustee, Justin Morrill, had long argued for the democratization of higher education, and for him it seemed a matter of course that the daughters of Vermonters, as well as their sons, should benefit from a university education. For the other trustees who were willing to tackle the "much agitated question of the collegiate education of women" it made more sense, as they reported to the

Legislature in 1871, for young women to pursue their studies "under the accumulated advantages which colleges have been elaborating for centuries" rather than create "separate colleges for women."[1]

The receptive environment at UVM had been enhanced by James Burrill Angell's term as president between 1866 and 1871. Angell believed that a state university should be committed to the higher education of women. After he left UVM to become president of the University of Michigan, he was even more outspoken on the issue. With his wife, Sarah Caswell Angell, he missed no opportunity to discuss the advantages a university education gave teachers and delighted in pointing out that collegiate studies had not harmed the good health of women students.[2]

At UVM, however, Angell's public expression of his commitment to the higher education of women often took second place to his campaign to set the University on a sound financial footing. Only three young men had graduated from the University in 1866, eight in 1867, five in 1868. And as the entering classes showed no signs of recovering numbers, speculation abounded about the reasons for declining enrollments and the consequent impoverishment of the University. Some thought that the University had "suffered from the patriotism of its students" when a disproportionate number of young Vermont men had enlisted, and had died, in the Civil War, diminishing the student pool. The Trustees also lamented the "declining interest of the youth of Vermont in higher education," blaming the decline on the "growth of the mercantile spirit." Others thought that the affiliation of the newly created agricultural college "frightened away students who wanted a liberal education."[3]

Whatever the reasons, Angell remembered that UVM was "prostrate" when he arrived in 1866, and he thought "in fact the case looked hopeless": the campus fence was dilapidated, the green had run to hay, funds were low, the city had little faith in the institution, and the five poorly paid professors were dispirited. Despite overtures from Michigan, Angell stayed on to prevent a "terrible disaster" and to reestablish the University on a sound financial basis.[4]

Moreover, early in 1871 the faculty of Middlebury College, equally concerned about their low enrollments, had entertained the idea of admitting women. The faculty of UVM also considered the idea, but in May of that year voted to postpone any further action until the fall term. They wanted to "ascertain so far as possible the state of public opinion" and to obtain the reactions of the "leading academy and High School Teachers" of the state about the wisdom of offering higher education to women. For the UVM Trustees, however, the risk of competing for what seemed an ever-shrinking pool of male students, the prospect of additional tuition payments, and their commitment to the idea of higher education for women, proved compelling. On the first of August 1871 they voted to admit women for the spring term; only two of the eighteen trustees cast dissenting votes.[5]

Those who dissented wondered if the admission of women students would raise questions about the rigor of the University's reputation, perhaps making it in some people's eyes a mere "bundle of whimsies"; or they worried that women were reaching beyond their proper sphere. Education might only "addict" them to professional life, some thought, while others warned that "college life, manners, discipline, and surroundings" were inconsistent with the nature of women, that such a life would bring "ruin to the women." C. Carroll Parker, a UVM trustee, did not believe that "Academic and Scientific courses" were "adapted to the womanly mind and womanly physique" and warned that the "attempt" to educate women at UVM would "be perilous in the extreme." In the same tone an 1857 alumnus complained that the idea of admitting women to UVM "seems to me monstrous." But the Trustees prevailed, and the St. Albans *Messenger* commented that since Burlington had "fewer things than most cities where colleges are located" to "lead the young astray," the women would be relatively safe at UVM.[6]

At his inaugural in August 1871, President Matthew Buckham welcomed all young women to "those studies that are congenial and helpful to all minds alike." Lida Mason, a young Burlington woman, was the first to enroll in the spring of 1872, and Ellen Hamilton of Brunswick, Maine, soon followed her in the fall term. They "addressed themselves to their work with great zeal," Buckham noted, and showed "themselves quite capable of meeting the demands of severe studies as successfully as their classmates of the other sex." They "receive[d] no favors and desire[d] none," according to the Trustees. At their graduation in 1875, Buckham reflected that Mason and Hamilton had "carried" themselves with "good sense and modesty." They had done much more; they had pursued the traditional Classical course, had graduated in the top third of their class, and had been elected as the first women members anywhere of Phi Beta Kappa.[7]

Mason and Hamilton were but two of the first generation of 118 women who had graduated from the University by 1900. These young women were largely middle-class Vermonters, most of whom had relatives (often a brother or sister) who had attended UVM. They already had considerable education: for admission, the University in the late nineteenth century required a knowledge of common arithmetic, algebra, ancient and modern geography, and English, Greek, and Latin grammar. Additionally, applicants had to demonstrate before a group of UVM faculty an ability to read at least five books of Xenophon's *Anabasis*, three books of Homer's *Iliad*, and large sections of Sallust, Caesar, Cicero, and Virgil.[8]

Once on campus, this new generation of young women pursued the traditional Classical courses. It was not long, however, before they were requesting instruction in new areas, such as Italian and food chemistry. They saw no reason why they should not have courses in physical education on Saturday mornings while the young male students were engaged in military drills. In 1902 UVM became one of the first to offer these courses, which were conducted by male faculty but chaperoned by a "lady of the faculty" (presumably the wife of the instructor).[9]

Women students earned as many honors prizes as the men, often taking the top award in Greek, biology, or mathematics. And like other college-educated women of their generation, many remained single or at least postponed marriage and childbearing. For those who remained single and pursued careers in teaching, their university education broadened the cultural background they brought to their students. It benefited their careers as well; nearly twenty percent of them became school administrators. Those who married brought the same cultural advantages to their families and became the backbone of community services or women's clubs and charity organizations. The more adventurous, like Jessie Elvira Wright (1884), practiced law with their husbands or, like Jean Alice Christie (1886), joined their spouses as medical missionaries.[10]

Despite the presence of women at UVM it was clear until the turn of the century that ideas about traditional gender roles remained intact: the men of the Young Men's Christian Association, for instance, discussed topics such as "The Winning Side," while the members of the Young Women's Christian Association considered "The Supreme Gift" and "Perfect through Suffering." And in keeping with Victorian ideas about proper behavior for women, it was considered a matter of course that the female students would be excused from the semipublic chapel recitations. They also were less prone than the male students to escapades of stealing cadavers from the medical school or playing billiards in the city saloons.[11]

In general, during the first three decades of coeducation, the women at UVM lived in a male culture. The *Cynic* pages were filled with photos and accounts of the young men's activities, with only an occasional mention of a happening at one of the sororities or the YWCA. Only men appeared in group pictures in the *Ariel* and in the class books. There were no women professors, and the first woman in the library, Ella Evarts Atwater, was hired only as a secretary to the librarian in 1890 and promoted to assistant librarian in 1892. And not until the mid-1890s did the University open a women's dormitory, at Grassmount, and list in the catalog scholarship support for "students of limited means" rather than just "young men of limited means." Proportionately few in number, women students exercised little manifest influence on the institution or its rituals.[12]

Change was brewing, though. When in 1885 the editor of the *Cynic* poked fun at the entering class for creating a second vice-president and bestowing the office on "one of their fair candidates for M.A. (Maid of Arts)," he had to admit that the move was taken to "keep 'peace in camp'" among the first-year students. As the twentieth century dawned, no one at UVM or across the nation suggested any longer that women should not go to college, but some worried that they would pursue careers and not marry. Many parents sought a course of study more suited to the domestic role of women and thought of college as a "convenient parking place" for their middle-class daughters and a "waystation to a proper marriage." Ellen Richards, a chemist at the Massachusetts Institute of Technology, and Marion Talbot, dean of women and professor of sanitary science at the University of Chicago, were among the educators who responded to these conservative concerns by combining their commitment to women's higher education with their interest in the application of science to the home. Both women became charter members of the American Association of University Women and founders of the American Home Economics Association (AHEA). In 1909, one year after the founding of the AHEA, UVM organized its own Department of Home Economics to meet the needs of a new generation of college women, and, under some pressure from UVM alumnae, hired its first woman faculty member, Bertha Terrill.[13]

A Vermonter by birth, Terrill had been an 1895 graduate of Mount Holyoke, where she had majored in Greek. Soon, however, she became fascinated by the new discipline of home economics. She studied for a year with Ellen Richards in Boston, spent a summer at Harvard, then studied with Marion Talbot in Chicago and became a charter member of the AHEA. When a 1905 state appropriation for the building of Morrill Hall provoked the alumnae of the University to put pressure on the Board of Trustees for a course in home economics, she emerged as the likely candidate. Unabashedly, she admitted that her status as a Vermonter, her experience as a college roommate of President Buckham's second wife, and her training as a Classicist worked to her advantage. She remembered that there was "little enthusiasm for such a practical science" among the faculty. Nevertheless, she "cleaned out a basement storeroom at Morrill Hall to make a classroom" and, over the course of the next thirty-one years, built her department, expanded women's roles in the Extension Service, established home economics courses in over seventy Vermont high schools, and generally gained the respect and devotion of faculty and students alike. Moreover, the "intrepid Miss Terrill" had "worked the back roads of northern Vermont, urging farm girls to come to college" and, as Mary Jean Simpson later remarked, "no one ever knew how many girls Bertha helped finance out of her own pocket."[14]

As the national trend in women's higher education turned to producing skilled housewives rather than moral leaders, the Department of Home Economics became the focus of the collegiate training of many UVM women. Jennie Rowell was hired as an instructor of chemistry in the Department of Home Economics in 1911, Josephine Marshall was named an assistant professor of home economics in 1914, and numerous regular faculty appointments for women followed. By the time Terrill retired in 1940, the department boasted six full-time teaching professors and three research professors.[15]

Apart from home economics, teaching drew the bulk of women students in the first third of the twentieth century. The Department of Education was established in 1911, a formal teacher-training program in 1921, and a four-year elementary education training course of study in 1927. As a response to the influx of students in the 1920s and to the changing social mores about the purposes of women's college education, a secretarial course was begun in 1921. Faculty appointments of women followed the student enrollments.[16]

It was not until 1943 that Mary Jean Simpson and Hovey Jordan of the medical school recruited Faye Crabbe, then at Teachers' College at Columbia, to establish a department of nursing at UVM. Crabbe designed a baccalaureate program, created affiliations with the major hospitals in Vermont as well as with many in major cities in the Northeast, and operated the Wasson Infirmary. A woman of indefatigable energy, Crabbe also traveled throughout the state to teach evening classes for graduate nurses. By the time she retired in 1960, the Department of Nursing boasted three separate programs. Crabbe brought federal grants to UVM to create programs for public health training in rural Vermont and for special programs in psychiatric nursing. In 1956 this woman who had begun the Department of Nursing with one faculty member (herself) and two students saw her department become one of the first in the nation to receive accreditation from the National League for Nursing. By then the program had grown to 14 faculty and 140 students.[17]

A few women among the early-twentieth-century students chose different paths. Alma Carpenter of Foxboro, Massachusetts, became the first woman graduate of the College of Agriculture in 1909; she had studied botany and later worked for the U.S. Department of Agriculture. Marie McMahon of Burlington received her degree in civil engineering in 1915; she taught mathematics and science at high schools in Vermont and New York for five years until she married a UVM alumnus. In 1920, when two thirds of the Class A medical schools already admitted women, the College of Medicine at UVM capitulated by admitting its first female student, Dorothy Mary Lang of Cambridge, Vermont; she received her medical degree in 1924. A handful of women continued to study in those schools, but most female students were concentrated in what had become the feminized areas of study—home economics and teacher education. The constrictions of gender socialization and the limited professional opportunities available to women graduates dictated their choices, as did the relative conservatism of this second generation of college women. In general, they were less apt to prepare themselves for lifelong careers, and although they were admiring of the pioneers in women's higher education, they had no desire to emulate their spinsterhood nor take up their political causes. Instead, they pursued teaching as a means of earning a livelihood before marriage or home economics as a way to prepare for their married lives.[18]

For all of its activity in the early decades of the twentieth century, the University practiced a relatively casual policy concerning issues important to women students and faculty. The much hailed step of appointing Bertha Terrill as the first woman faculty member, for instance, was a response to pressure from the alumnae rather than a deliberate step to address the needs of female students. Even when the Trustees had finally approved the measure in 1909, it was the alumnae who raised $1,000 for equipment for the department.[19]

Other steps were responses to pressure from the women students and faculty. The female students had petitioned the president and faculty for physical training in 1894; eight years later they finally prevailed. Once again, in 1916, women students pressured the Trustees to hire an additional instructor in "physical culture" by proposing to raise the women's athletic fee from $2 to $5 a year to defray the salary of just such a new female faculty member. It was the women students who raised funds to start repair work on the floors of Grassmount. And in 1917, Bertha Terrill requested that she be freed to do "war work" but only after she already had arranged for her departmental colleagues to cover her classes and other duties. Her male colleagues had been given leaves of absence with pay from the start; not until 1918 did Terrill request and the Trustees grant the same privilege to her.[20]

However casual the University may have been toward the presence of women and however conservative Americans' attitudes toward the higher education of women had become, the many activities of the female students in the first decades of the twentieth century gradually altered the climate on campus. The *Cynic* began regularly to cover women's academic achievements, as well as sorority entertainments, fund-raising events, and picnics. Not an issue went by in the 1910s and 1920s without articles about baseball games between the young women of the various classes or the tennis matches with Middlebury. In 1921 a multipage section on women became a regular feature of the *Cynic*, and every spring the *Cynic* published a special women's issue.

This strong emerging female subculture flourished on campus in the 1920s and 1930s. For the first time women moved into positions of decision making on the *Cynic* staff, and women's organizations such as the literary Blue Stockings and other clubs became more active than the men's clubs. In many co-educational activities, such as debating, drama, and honor societies, women students took the lead. Indeed, when the *Ariel* rules were changed in 1936 to allow a woman to be editor, the male editor of the *Cynic* wondered: "Are the men going to stand by and let the co-eds invade another field once held without any effort?"[21]

The Women's Athletic Association (WAA) flourished in the 1920s as well. It had been founded in 1913, but the tenure of Eleanor C. Cummings as the women's athletic director (1920–1951) gave the association new life. Cummings expanded the program of activities and arranged for UVM women athletes to participate in national competitions in advanced apparatus work, dance, hockey, track, basketball, and rifle shooting. On campus the WAA sponsored track meets at Grassmount and basketball and hockey intramural tournaments, as well as volleyball, baseball, rifle, and gymnasium teams. The *WAA Handbook*, written and published by the female students, governed their activities and the young women strove to "bring about a healthier, happier womanhood in Vermont." The WAA Health Council proffered advice on nutrition, mental health, personal appearance, skin care, posture, and other issues of interest to the young coeds. Field days, Winter Carnival, and women's athletic activities of all kinds came under their aegis. And the weekly Women's Mass Meetings, although sometimes devoted to lighthearted sings, more often addressed topics like career opportunities for women.[22]

The Women's Student Government Association (WSGA), founded in 1920, was the most powerful women's organization. The WSGA was the first self-governing student body at the University. It was an autonomous body, not a subcommittee of any other student organization. Every female student was a member, and WSGA leaders planned and supervised all of the extracurricular activities of women on campus. They governed the women's dormitories, regulating and enforcing norms of conduct for all female students. They ran programs such as Freshman Camp for incoming women students, the only orientation program for any new students. Maintaining collegiate social traditions like the Big/Little Sister pairing of new students with older, wiser juniors and operating fire safety programs, courses in group living, and leadership training workshops were just a few of the other activities of the women of the WSGA.[23]

The decades of the 1920s and 1930s were a time of tremendous influx of faculty women. Between 1920 and 1930 seventy women taught at UVM. Some of them served for only a few years, but the overall effect was to raise the proportion of women on the faculty from a mere nine percent, representing five women faculty members in 1920, to twenty-one percent, representing thirty women on a faculty of 144 by 1930. Proportionately, that high mark of women on the faculty would not be reached again until the mid-1980s.[24]

For Bertha Terrill in her early years at UVM, female companionship on campus had been scarce, although "The Ladies of the Faculty" began meeting in the very year Terrill arrived on campus. The organization consisted of the wives of faculty, trustees, and medical students—and "unmarried members of the faculty" (presumably Terrill). "The Ladies" struggled to sponsor teas and entertainments for students, to uplift themselves through attendance at lectures, and occasionally to reprimand student clubs that permitted "improper postures in dancing." There was little on their agenda in the way of intellectual stimulation, however, and Terrill and the later women faculty members never played a major role in the organization. The Faculty Research Club, founded in 1905, refused to accept women professors until 1942. This and like instances contributed to the sense of isolation of the early women professors.[25]

Gradually, the number of women professors increased. As the years passed and more women came on board, they shared interests and friendships often based on earlier connections. For instance, Sara Holbrook, a professor of education, who joined the faculty in 1924 and became the close companion of Terrill, had studied at the same school in Hartford, Connecticut, where Terrill had taught. Terrill and Sarah Potter Fletcher (physical education, 1916–1918) had both taught at the Abbott Academy, also in Connecticut. Nellie K. Doud, an instructor in Terrill's department, also had studied at the University of Chicago, and Eleanor Stenson Cummings (physical education) had studied at Harvard summer school, where Terrill had brushed up on her chemistry. Julia Louise Hurd (home economics, 1917–1920) and Alice Emma Blundell (home economics, 1919–1937) were classmates at Iowa State, and Doud, Hurd, Cummings, Sarah Elsie Potter (home economics, 1916–1919), and Josephine Atlee Marshall (home economics, 1913–1917) all had a Columbia connection. These women shared a sense of mission, and the support they provided one another went a long way toward alleviating their sense of professional isolation.[26]

In 1918 women students had gained the University's official recognition of their particular needs when President Guy Benton had asked Pearl Randall Wasson to become the first fulltime dean of women. Others, starting with Bertha Terrill, had filled the role unofficially among their other duties, but Wasson was the first woman hired specifically for the purpose. She spent a year studying college administration at her alma mater, Wellesley College, and began her duties at UVM in the fall of 1919. She had been prominent in women's circles in Vermont, serving in important positions in the Vermont Federation of Women's Clubs, the American Red Cross, and the Vermont Council of the YWCA, and on the Waterbury Board of Education. In her short tenure as dean of women, Wasson promoted the founding of the WSGA, gained UVM the recognition of the American Association of University Women, and inspired the women students of UVM to recognize what historians call the "bonds of womanhood." Remembering her impressions of the Tree Day ceremonies at Wellesley and the May Day tradition at Bryn Mawr, Wasson initiated Lilac Day at UVM. She hoped that the day "might become one of the beautiful memories for the women of the University." Alumnae have remembered those ceremonies that took place annually for the next twenty-five years; Lilac Day became a "genuine Women's Day on campus" for them, "complete with *Parade* and *Pageant* and *Planting*." They remembered, too, Wasson's inspirational "Vermont Creed" in which she importuned them to have vision and enthusiasm, work hard, practice good judgment, and follow tradition—a creed they lovingly hand-copied for each new member of the Mortar Board Society.[27]

Wasson's good friend and successor in 1922, Marian Patterson, was quite different in personality and in accomplishment. Patterson had done advanced library work after graduating from Wellesley and volunteer work for the blind. In a time of family crisis, like many other single women she experienced what Jane Addams called the "family claim," temporarily gave up her own career, and returned home. During World War I she worked for the U.S. Employment Service and later went to Burlington to help out her friend Wasson. She stayed on to become a bedrock of common sense to the thousands of women students who came under her guidance in the next fifteen years. To them she was an "intelligent, dedicated and resourceful" woman, one who "seemed to breathe life and energy." She looked out for their welfare, and as one alumna recalled, "there was no waiting for an 'appointment,' you were welcome and she listened." She was quick to admonish them for their late night trips up the fire escapes but never asked a roommate to reveal more than she thought she could. She arranged for individual study cubicles in the Redstone library rooms, wrote articles of advice for young women graduates in the *Vermont Alumni Weekly*, and was known affectionately as "Dean Pat."[28]

Upon Patterson's retirement in 1937, President Guy Bailey offered the position to Mary Jean Simpson. At that time Simpson was director for the state of Vermont in the Works Progress Administration in Washington, D.C., and her supervisor promised a salary of $4,000 if she would continue. The University offered her only $2,100, plus a $400 living allowance, but she took the job anyway. Both the students and the women faculty would benefit during the 1930s, 1940s, and early 1950s from Simpson's professionalism. She remained traditional, as illustrated by her hard and fast rules about women wearing skirts unless the temperature plunged below ten degrees; but her standards for herself were high, and she expected no less of her students nor of UVM in preparing them for their lives and careers. Recognizing her students' need for "self-development and self expression," she argued indefatigably not only for the recognition of the volunteer work of women but especially for the necessity of increased technical training in the teaching, nursing, and social work courses.[29]

Simpson's seventeen years at UVM were years that would have challenged anyone. In the late 1930s women students continued to feel the tensions of the Depression in the advice they received; Dean Patterson, for example, had urged them to seek avocations rather than careers. Yet Simpson's office and the WSGA regularly sponsored workshops to help them prepare for their careers, although those opportunities were limited to social work, health and recreation activities, secretarial and store work, food and textile preparation, interior decoration, or journalism, advertising, and book retailing. In 1934 women were allowed for the first time to take part in the management and production of Kake Walk. Ironically, as women moved into these responsible positions, some groups on campus were reflecting American society's growing emphasis on women as public sex objects: in 1935 ROTC chose a "beauty queen" and the *Ariel* sponsored a beauty contest, both for the first time.[30]

Not all of the young women acquiesced readily to the idea of limited opportunities and the status of mere sex objects. The coeds on the *Cynic* staff replied in a humorous vein to such suggestions by printing an anecdote about a questionnaire circulated at the University of Pennsylvania asking if the average male preferred pretty girls or smart ones. The Penn coeds, they reported, simply had sponsored their own questionnaire asking if the respondents liked intelligent men or typical college men. Others examined the strengths of women students, especially in less traditional fields like medicine. For instance, Elizabeth Mandigo, the only woman in the 1936 class of the College of Medicine, proclaimed that women did not have "any special qualifications" for medicine, but they had "no characteristics as a sex which should handicap them" either.[31]

Such issues were quickly pushed into the background with the outbreak of World War II. During the war years women students outnumbered civilian men on campus by a ratio of 5 or 6 to 1. Yet despite their numbers, women were expected to play a rather traditional, passive role. While Mary Jean Simpson supported the possible wartime draft of women and expected that senior girls would sign up for the Women's Army Air Corps or the Marine Corps Women's Reserve as the campus recruiters advocated, she advised the underclass women to "carry on the full tradition of Vermont" so that the University would be financially and academically healthy "when the boys come back." She told the "girls" that they "must prepare for the companionship their men will be demanding when this war is over"—they must be ready for marriage and motherhood.[32]

For all of her patriotic zeal and traditional approach to the roles of women, Simpson fought for her students. She knew it was the enrollment of women students that kept the University open during the early 1940s, and she admonished the faculty and Trustees to recruit even more women. Nor did she hesitate to report the "discontent" of the women students. The female students' complaint "has not been due simply to the absence of men," she said in 1944, "but to the fact that some students feel that they have not been getting what they came here to get because too much attention has been given to the air cadets." Indeed, a glaring example of this neglect was the directive that women students were not allowed to enroll in regular physics classes because those were reserved for the cadets; women could take only classes in household physics. And although UVM women students might have been complimented by the parting sentiments of some of those air cadets, who thought of them as "friendly and unsophisticated" and were grateful that they were not a "Vassar edition of Veronica Lake or a Bryn Mawron with ropey hair and dungarees," they took pride as well in the way they managed the campus organizations during the war years. They held offices in formerly male-dominated organizations, sponsored international conferences, and generally enjoyed their new opportunities.[33]

The postwar years, however, brought changes that would catch up with Mary Jean Simpson's "girls." UVM ordinarily had received six hundred to seven hundred applications per year; in 1946 thirteen thousand young people applied. Like other women across the nation, UVM female students experienced pressure to make room for the returning soldiers. Simpson talked to them about their "sacred duty as women," and for all intents and purposes, coeds disappeared from the public eye. No longer were there special columns in the *Cynic* devoted to women's activities. Rather, women students were berated for the "fad of wearing sneakers" because the habit made them appear unfeminine and sloppy, put them at risk for sweaty feet and fallen arches, but most of all, created unglamorous enlarged ankles. Later writers in the *Cynic* complained that "calfy coeds" were the "result of walking from Redstone."[34]

On the few occasions in the 1950s when women's sports made the newspaper, their teams were referred to as the "UVM Kittens." Photographs in the medical alumni magazine featured a typical graduate student's family: father busily poring over his books, mother and baby playing contentedly on the floor. And even in the face of the shortage of engineers in the mid-1950s and a more welcoming atmosphere for women in that field of study, the *Cynic* writers still found it necessary to ask of the women engineering students, "But how about dating? How do the guys react to slide rules and surveying?"[35]

Ironically, increasing numbers of women would enter the work force in the 1940s and 1950s, yet their education would continue to be geared toward their roles as wives and mothers, and young college women would continue to be treated as children. When Anna Rankin Harris replaced Simpson as dean of women in 1954, she was asked for her thoughts about dress codes (no slacks; "girls should not be ashamed to be feminine"), smoking (no moral behavior connected with this habit), and drinking ("many people do it because they're afraid not to") but not her ideas about academics.[36]

Curfews for women students were enforced until 1968, and a dress code for class and dining halls did not fall by the wayside until that year. By then, of course, many students had what seemed to be more global concerns. Stories about the war in Vietnam filled the pages of the *Cynic*, as did articles about draft evasion. News about drug probes and arguments about legalizing marijuana competed with items about the student evaluation of faculty and the production of Henrik Ibsen's *Hedda Gabler*. Nevertheless, the women of the WSGA, perhaps taking their cue from Ibsen, persisted in their quest for greater autonomy by calling for a referendum on ending curfews for women and by organizing a protest on the lawn of President Lyman Rowell's house.[37]

This successful protest was one of the last acts of WSGA. The organization had not found significant areas of activity to replace those, like Freshman Camp, that had been taken over by the larger campus administration and other administrative arms of the University. According to the various memos of Mary Jean Simpson, the women of WSGA for years had been placed in a position where they had "to beg each year" from the male-governed Student Association "for a reasonable sum with which to do their work." In 1969 there was so little interest in WSGA that candidates for some of the offices were not to be found. By the end of that year, because the "added problems which have evolved from coed housing" could "no longer be solved within the existing governing structures," WSGA cooperated in its own demise by agreeing to disband in favor of the Inter-Residence Association.[38]

By 1971, when the editors of the *Cynic* celebrated the admission of women to the University with a centennial edition, the women of UVM had shed a separatist approach and were well on their way to integrating themselves and their ideas into the whole spectrum of student and faculty affairs. Pockets of resistance persisted as captured in a special *Cynic* column entitled "I Remember When Women . . . ." A male chemistry professor who previously had thought women students were just nice to look at, for instance, now stated that he was "beginning to realize that women are people," that they were "getting better as students," and that they had "a great deal more to offer than [just] their gender." But a former male dean thought that "for the most part women . . . valued their privileged status as being apart and superior, and accepted with grace and charm their position on a pedestal."[39]

The image of a woman on a pedestal had long ceased to satisfy UVM women, who, in the 1970s, were mobilizing on behalf of themselves. Like women on the national scene, they responded to Betty Friedan's challenge to the "feminine mystique" and Kate Millet's theory of "sexual politics." Consciousness-raising groups, the organizational techniques and political strategems of the civil rights movement, and a quest for justice and equity informed their activities. UVM women challenged traditional attitudes about the limits of women's abilities, organized workshops to address the new careers opening to women, and planned "mini-crash survival courses on 'how to make it in a man's world.'" Women faculty and students alike took every opportunity to suggest what "educators [could] do for the cause of women's liberation." Since "only a minuscule 7%" of college women "think that the activities of the adult woman in American society should be generally confined to the home and family," they suggested that the University address admission policies, challenge the cultural stereotypes that relegated women students to traditional fields of study, and hire more women professors. They pressured President Edward Andrews to establish plans for affirmative action hiring and to appoint an equal opportunity officer, and they urged the Student Association president, the chairman of the Board of

Trustees, and the chairman of the Faculty Senate to address issues of equal opportunity and gender discrimination as well.[40]

By the late 1970s the proportion of women faculty was on the rise (climbing toward 20 percent after having declined to 15 percent in the 1950s). Relatively few women were available for professorships as universities expanded in the 1960s because of the national failure in earlier decades to encourage young women to pursue professional careers. Women who had persisted in their intellectual pursuits had been clustered in a few limited disciplines like nursing and home economics, often those marked as feminine and underpaid. As a 1979 report of the UVM chapter of the American Association of University Women pointed out, women faculty at UVM were disproportionately represented in the ranks of lecturer, instructor, and assistant professor. And like other universities, UVM exploited the available labor pool of faculty wives, especially in the areas of language instruction and first-year writing courses. Tenured women faculty, however, gradually moved more visibly into university politics and administration. Judith Anderson, Virginia Clark, and Dolores Sandoval chaired the Faculty Senate in successive terms from 1976 to 1982, and Jeannette Folta, appointed as the first woman academic administrator in 1972, opened the way for women in administration. Finally, the more favorable climate of the late 1960s for women to pursue academic careers cast its mark on the character of the 1980s university.[41]

At the same time, the number of women students multiplied until, in the 1980s, women constituted half of the student body (in the 1910s there had been a quota of 20 percent). They lived in coed dormitories, majored in non-traditional disciplines, and participated in campus politics. Together with faculty women they called for curricular changes. Where there were women faculty available to teach the emerging feminist perspective in the 1970s, classes on women and society, women and culture, women in literature, and women's history entered the course of study. In the 1980s the women of the College of Arts and Sciences designed a minor in women's studies, including additional courses on women in psychology, economics, religion, nursing, and education. Outside the classroom UVM students organized a campus chapter of the Society of Women Engineers, and others formed the Women's Organization and Resource Center (WORC). The women of WORC sponsored feminist speakers, put on film festivals, participated in "Take Back the Night" demonstrations, and organized marches on Montpelier and Washington, D.C. In an era that many feminists nationally bemoaned as a period of doldrums for the women's movement, UVM faculty, students, and staff climaxed their decade of activities with a successful call for a President's Commission on the Status of Women.[42]

In 1871 the Trustees of UVM could not have anticipated the changed world of the 1990s, but their decision to admit women started the forces of change in motion. Seldom on the cutting edge of innovation after that time,

UVM nevertheless responded to the changing images and roles of women. For UVM women that sometimes meant the retrenchment that accompanied the domestic and consumer images of the 1920s and the return-to-home movement of the 1950s. But UVM quickly offered opportunities for young women to gain a quality education. Bertha Terrill's courageous work in building a new department in an environment less than welcoming inspired the dozens of faculty women who followed her. They, in turn, laid the groundwork for the accomplishments and activities of the spiritual daughters and granddaughters of Terrill. Those faculty and students of the 1970s and 1980s created an educational environment that more closely reflected the world students would enter as UVM alumnae than at any other time in the history of the University.

UVM Goes Modern: Student Life in
the Collegiate Era

VIRGINIA CAMPBELL DOWNS

THE times were intoxicating for students of the University of Vermont that first year of the twentieth century. Change was in the air. The Spanish-American War, just ended, had opened the nation to an international frame of mind. UVM had begun to loosen itself from the bonds of Classical education, joining other major schools around the country in assuming the shape of a modern university.

Traveling to Burlington by train and horse-drawn carriage that fall, the 235 men and 44 women who made up the student body found a campus astir with newness.[1] There were now dormitories for both men and women, a winter carnival called "Kake Walk," and football and baseball teams carving their niche in intercollegiate sports. These were to be seeds for the growth of a strong college spirit among the students.

Student life at UVM changed profoundly during the first half of the twentieth century, as the institution evolved from the elitist atmosphere of the nineteenth century, offering a Classical education for the few, to a university sensitive to the socializing needs of its students as well as their varied academic interests. This transformation becomes clear when we follow the tenor of campus life from the last ten years of President Matthew Buckham's administration through two world wars, the Great Depression, fraternity antidiscrimination reforms, and the first real attempt at student government.

The stirrings of college spirit were in evidence by 1904 when former president James B. Angell spoke at the University's centennial celebration. He mentioned "the college yell which has been invented, and also the athletic craze in reasonable proportions."[2] Student extracurricular activities were moving into high gear. The *Cynic* began publication in 1883 and the yearbook *Ariel* three years later, just in time to document the beginnings of the sports era at the University. Changes in the curriculum reflected the growing emphasis at UVM on preparing students for careers and for life, which brought an enthusiastic response from practical-minded parents. More of their sons and daughters began to arrive on campus, substantially increasing enrollment.

Campus Social Life

Until after World War I, cars were a rarity on campus, and drinking was not customary. Many students were forced to work after classes in times of pinched family finances. Saturday football and baseball games were high points of the week.

UVM had been in the forefront of colleges in the East to recognize the need for dormitories. When the four-story Converse Hall was constructed in 1895, with a ninety-man capacity, and Grassmount, a private residence, was purchased the same year to house twenty women, Columbia University had yet to begin building dormitories. Still, the two dormitories at UVM in 1900 could house only half of the students; the others had to find lodging in private homes around Burlington. Eventually, a growing number of fraternities and sororities bought or built houses where some members could live. Sigma Phi was first in 1902.

Dormitory life would provide the atmosphere of a home away from home. For women students for many decades to come, a live-in woman supervisor enforced strict observance of rules. In 1911, when Mabel Watts Mayforth ('15), a native of Waterbury, arrived on campus, a small new dormitory facility had opened in the house built by Civil War General O. O. Howard on Summit Street, across from Grassmount, where the girls took their meals. Mrs. Mayforth remembers with warmth the feeling of safety and belonging that Howard Hall provided for new students who suffered from homesickness, knowing that during the whole school year they would see their families only at Christmas. After World War I the house became the first cooperative dormitory for financially needy girls, who cooked and cleaned to pay much of their board and room.

"We walked to all our functions . . . . Nobody had a car," Mrs. Mayforth recalls.

If it rained at the time of the Junior Prom, it might be important enough to have a cab. There were horse-drawn cabs. . . . A man kept a livery stable and supplied conveyance for people in town and for students. The dances in the gym were mostly waltzes and two steps at first, then by my senior year some of the new dances, like the Turkey Trot.

A couple of us girls could have our young men come in, and have a chafing dish with crackers and fondue in the kitchen. Miss Marshall [Josephine Marshall, the matron] was in residence and she acted as chaperone.

This close-knit, informal climate on campus, with professors and their families taking a personal interest in their students, encouraged students to work hard at their studies, George Kidder ('22) firmly believes: "Professors knew us individually." Like most Burlington students, he commuted to school from home. He remembers that one final exam in Greek consisted of reading a play in Professor Samuel Bassett's home. Mrs. Bassett often served oyster stew to groups of students after football games.

In the first decade of the century clubs began to flourish. They were the twentieth-century version of the speaking and literary clubs on campus that had begun with the Phi Sigma Nu Society, founded in 1803, but had waned in the second half of the nineteenth century as the fraternity system grew. The men's old mandolin and banjo clubs would soon give way to glee clubs. As a sign of change, the Green and Gold Debate Club sometimes included women members. A dramatics club with both men and women members put on lively performances. Mabel Mayforth recalls an annual June highlight as women students of Greek put on an outdoor play. "Grassmount had a great deal of privacy with a cedar hedge and a picket fence and so it was a natural amphitheater for a Greek play. We made our own costumes . . . and students and faculty people attended."

As a convenient railway stopover between New York or Boston and Montreal, Burlington was already a mecca for world-class entertainers, who appeared in the Strong Theater or UVM's gymnasium. Opera and theater companies and renowned musicians thrilled audiences in those years when the radio and movie industries were barely underway and recreation was limited. In the 1920s and 1930s the concert tradition continued in a series promoted by Arthur Dow, class of 1910. The University believed that its students, so remote from urban areas, should be exposed to the best of cultural and intellectual stimulation.

Dan Dyer ('24), a farm boy from Albany, Vermont, who was an agriculture major, recalls being inspired by his first real exposure to classical music. With no pocket money to spend, he climbed up the gymnasium fire escape to peer in at the great Czech violinist Jan Kubelik during his recital. Afterward he shook his hand, "the softest hand you can imagine."

Athletics and College Unity

Not all students were drawn to such cultural events. Intercollegiate sports, along with Kake Walk, are credited by alumni as being the extracurricular events most responsible for building college spirit. The first baseball team suited up in 1886, and a year later a football squad was organized. By the time UVM became officially the school of the green and gold in 1892, serious competition in intercollegiate athletics had arrived in Burlington, and a sense of college unity was in the making.[3]

Baseball and track reigned supreme among university athletic programs by 1910, attracting large turnouts for home events. Larry Gardner and Ray Collins, 1909 classmates, gave the college a glorious baseball record, leading their team in victories over such Ivy "greats" as Harvard, Brown, and Dartmouth. Clarence DeMar ('11) and captain Al Gutterson ('12) set the pace for a spirited track team and went on to win fame as world-class athletes. DeMar won the prestigious Boston marathon seven times, and Gutterson took the Olympic gold medal in the broad jump the July after his graduation. The gym (now the Royall Tyler Theater) was used in cold months for practice and meets.

Freshman rules early in the century mandated male attendance at all home games as well as at "smokers" in the gym to learn the college yells and songs so that they could root loudly for the teams at game time. Dan Dyer remarked, "They didn't have to tell me that! There was a lot of spirit for baseball—they filled the stands."

Enthusiasm for track and baseball in those glory days was shared by the coeds, for attendance became a major social event. Mrs. Mayforth recalls, "I became very enthusiastic about baseball. . . . Hal [classmate Hal Mayforth was to become her husband after World War I] was catcher." She describes football's fascination in those years. "At my time in high school there was no football, so it was a new game for most of us. . . . Hal was quarterback. We girls usually went in a group and there were faculty women who were very considerate who would sit with us. Then we were invited to the home of one of them for hot chocolate and sandwiches afterwards."

The football team, however, fell on hard times. *Cynic* editor Ed Crane ('16) reflected in a 1915 editorial the campus concern that the sport might be dropped.[4] He wrote that the team had been daunted by frequent changes of coaches and policies and was the victim in a David versus Goliath role, meeting teams with more weight and experience from larger colleges with bigger budgets. Intercollegiate basketball in those years suffered a worse fate; it was dropped in 1913 for financial reasons despite a campus-wide petition to the Athletic Council for renewal of the sport. For years basketball would be confined to intramural contests.

Sophomore–freshman "scraps" were a tradition for men at the University, a legacy handed down from the nineteenth century when they were referred to as "horse-shedding." Interclass rivalry got the college year off to a spirited start with fountain fights, tugs-of-war, kidnapping and tieing up of freshmen, and cane rushes during the halves at football games. Seth Johnson wrote in his diary on September 29, 1911, "The Sophs had the Freshies out tonight. . . . We went over to the dorm and got 29 freshmen and ducked them all in the fountain along with some other cute stunts." George Kidder speaks of the scraps as "vicious" at times. "Class identity was much stronger then than it is now." The freshman–sophomore cane rush was dangerous, as Dan Dyer relates: "A lot of canes got broken and the splinters on the ends caused injuries." When hose fights became popular, the fire department provided the two-inch-wide hoses that the two classes aimed at each other, progressively increasing the water pressure to stinging streams.

Dan Dyer recalls that as a freshman he crawled on all fours up the Converse Hall stairs, spurred on by the well-placed whacks of paddles wielded by sophomores. He recalls, too, an unplanned junket: "There were six of us freshmen and along came a truck. They took us down on Church Street and said, 'All right, you get up on that mailbox and tell everyone that you're a senator. . . . Now get down from there.' Then we got into the truck and they took us down on Shelburne Road. Another fellow and I got out and I said I don't know about getting back into Burlington but I think I'll go into this house and by God out comes a dog. I think if I'd been timed for that I'd've made 100 yards in 10 seconds."

Dyer was on campus the year one freshman-sophomore skirmish resulted in a tragic accident. It was the annual "Proc Nite" when the custom was for sophomores to paste proclamations of freshman rules on telephone poles throughout the city, pursued by freshmen tearing them down. During the Proc Nite boxing match in the gym on November 20, 1920, a freshman was knocked onto the hard-packed dirt floor by a sophomore and never regained consciousness. Dyer recalls hearing the sad news of the death the next morning at breakfast in Commons Hall. George Kidder remembers the grief on campus after the accident, the tragedy of it from the point of view of the sophomore involved in the match, who was "the gentlest fellow you could imagine."[5]

Proc Nite was canceled for the next year and a half while campus leaders grappled with the issue of whether to keep the tradition, with modifications, or to abolish it. Urged by UVM's oldest honorary society, the Boulder Society for men of the senior class, and by senior class president Richard Holdstock, abolition was voted on May 6, 1922. Interclass scraps waned thereafter as a rapidly increasing college enrollment turned the student focus toward campus-wide activities and away from emphasis on class identity.

Fraternities Come to UVM

UVM was not far behind an important new trend in American college life in the mid-nineteenth century, the development of the social fraternity system. The first American fraternity, Kappa Alpha, was founded in 1825. UVM's Lambda Iota, a local fraternity, was organized in 1836, setting off an enthusiastic movement to create more of these secret societies. The first issue of the *Ariel* in 1886 lists six fraternities, including Kappa Alpha Theta, the first women's secret society on campus, founded in 1881. Two years later the second sorority, Delta Delta Delta, was founded. Fraternities answered a felt need for companionship, were a focus for planning dances and parties with members of the opposite sex, and provided a more informal style of extracurricular life. Typical of the new collegiate zest for fun was the hazing of fraternity pledges. George Kidder recalls the frenzy of fraternity hazing in post–World War I years: "I remember one case in which they put them [pledges] in a silo. . . . [They] had to break their way out of it and get back to town. They were completely disoriented. . . . The reason for it all was for a feeling of being together and cooperating to do something. You take a half dozen boys out in the countryside and dump them and there is going to emerge a leader and also they are going to have some feeling of cohesiveness which is a good thing in a way."

Dan Dyer, a Phi Mu Delta, saw his fraternity experience as a positive one. He entered so enthusiastically into the brotherly spirit that he became president. His fraternity brothers taught him to dance so that he could enjoy campus social life. "We had a lot of fraternity dances and had a great time at the Junior Prom," Dyer explains. "You had a dance program and you'd dance with this one and that one." He recalls that fraternity brothers built up group spirit through interfraternity sports and would also find help for those having trouble with course work. In contrast, girls' fraternities (as they were often called in those years) sponsored genteel social occasions. Mary Jean Simpson ('13) wrote to her family in Craftsbury about an evening thimble party her Kappa Alpha Theta sisters had enjoyed.[6]

Miss Simpson was a campus leader in her day, devoted to her sorority but also intent on broadening her horizons by working for the *Cynic*, doing YWCA service, and enjoying such community offerings as Verdi's *Il Trovatore* at the Strong Theater. The sewing classes offered by Bertha Terrill, who became head of the new home economics program while Miss Simpson was a student, failed to impress this free spirit. "Had to take out the tucks on my ruffles three times because they were not straight," she wrote her parents. "I simply cannot get things *straight*. . . . Tra la, what matter will that make a hundred years from now." Nevertheless, Miss Simpson epitomized the young woman of the day for whom, as Professor Terrill put it in high school recruitment talks, "there are opportunities in the future." Graduating Phi Beta Kappa, Mary Jean Simpson returned to her alma mater as its third dean of women in 1937.

Some students felt frozen out in those years by the nine fraternities and three sororities. Fortis Abbott ('13) was one of the agriculture students who felt slighted. He described himself as one of "a bunch of farm boys from Brookfield. . . . We were ostracized as far as the University was concerned. We cowhide boot boys were never invited to join Greek letter societies [Abbott, however, was named to Alpha Zeta, an honorary agricultural society.] . . . You didn't feel right playing tennis with these boys whose education and financial backgrounds were so much better than ours."[7] Dan Dyer, also an agriculture major ten years later, believes the disdain for agriculture students had lessened by then, perhaps because of the boost the football team received from "Aggies" who played a strong game. "The feeling was there to some degree, though. I remember one incident. When a girl found out someone she was going to date was an Aggie she lost interest."

Mrs. Mayforth described the sensitivity of English professor Frederick Tupper and his wife toward these country boys who were not invited to join fraternities. "He invited them to his home quite frequently because he realized that these boys had never had the exposure to city living and dinner parties."

Abbott lived in the university creamery's milking plant, bringing his own bedding and food staples from home. He milked the cows twice a day and worked in the mail room, earning 15 cents an hour to pay his rent. During vacations he stayed on campus and tended furnaces, substituting for students who could afford to go home.

A new informal local fraternity called the Commons Club (later reorganized as a chapter of the national Phi Mu Delta in 1918) answered the social needs of boys like Fortis Abbott. They held meetings in the basement of Converse Hall. A *Cynic* article in 1915 described the Commons Club as "absolutely democratic and inexpensive." In spirit it was the forerunner of the Independent movement that appeared in the late 1920s, offering membership to all men on campus who cared to join. Phi Mu Delta attracted many agriculture and engineering students. Long afterward, in 1959, a new fraternity, Alpha Gamma Rho, was formed, designed for students majoring in agriculture.

Mrs. Mayforth tells what attracted her to membership in Kappa Alpha Theta. "They were good students, quite serious, conspicuous for their talents on campus, but a very friendly group. We didn't have a sorority house. We had meetings Saturday nights on the second floor of a house on North Prospect Street that belonged to one of the older alumnae." She estimates that no more than 25 percent of students were fraternity members. "The girls who weren't asked to join sororities were a little more downcast than the girls today because now there are so many social organizations or other outlets which there weren't in my day." In the *Ariels* during her years five organizations besides sororities were listed: Home Economics Club, YWCA, Young Women's Instrumental Club, Cercle Française, and Classical Club. "But those girls adjusted and some of them were very good friends of sorority members, but I think they felt a little left out."

A college man arriving as a freshman on campus in those years took a casual attitude toward housing, since the one dormitory, Converse Hall, might be filled. Dascomb Rowe ('21) came from Peacham with the UVM tuition scholarship for highest academic standing in his class, knowing that he would have to work for his room and board. "I got on the train and when I hit Burlington I didn't have the slightest idea where I was going to stay. I met a couple of upperclassmen on the sidewalk and they told me about a third floor room in a private house down on North Winooski Avenue so that's where I stayed my freshman year. I ate in a boarding house for three dollars a week, three meals a day." He washed dishes and cleaned out the chicken coop at the boardinghouse and harvested crops at the university farm for room and board money.

World War I and Its Aftermath

The conflict in Europe would drastically change the educational plans of Rowe and other UVM men. Soon after Congress declared a state of war with Germany and President Wilson made his famous "make the world safe for democracy" speech, throughout the country the now-familiar posters appeared with the message "Uncle Sam Wants You." A *Cynic* editorial (May 27) urged undergraduates to remain in college because only twenty-one- to thirty-one-year-olds were being conscripted. But patriotism inspired Rowe and many classmates to enlist. That fall the college newspaper bore the headline: "Intercollegiate Sports at University Discontinued." Interclass games were to take their place.

Women came into their own in student activities for the first time, as men left for service in increasing numbers and campus organizations lost their leaders. In March 1918, Catherine Casey ('19) became the first woman editor of the *Cynic*, a role she would keep until May 1919, when the men began to return and Perley Hill took her place. Hill paid tribute to the women who had kept the newspaper going during that year in an editorial that applauded Business Manager Margaret Patten Gilbert ('19) for leaving the *Cynic* "in the best financial condition it's ever been."

Mrs. Gilbert explained the dynamics of pioneering as a woman in a leadership role. "Many men were opposed to our taking over, so we took it quite seriously. . . . Our name was at stake and we wanted to make good. Where those before hadn't worked at it very much, we went around town and got lots of ads."[8]

Sorority functions became more important as UVM took on the appearance of a woman's college and the popular campus dances and Saturday games were suspended. A member of Pi Beta Phi, Mrs. Gilbert recalls the makeshift circumstances back then when her sorority rented two rooms and a bath for their meetings in the Klifa Club (the women's social club on Pearl Street), washing their dishes in the bathtub.

Patriotism rallied the students to turn over their 1918 Kake Walk proceeds of $908.77 to the Red Cross. They joined Burlington citizens in selling Liberty Bonds, creating an atmosphere of goodwill where rowdyism during Freshman Week and hazing activities in the past had caused periodic grumbling. Instead of publishing the traditional yearbook in 1919, a special edition of the *Cynic* included a forty-five-page *Ariel* insert dedicated to UVM servicemen. President Benton had brought acclaim to the University during his leave of absence to take charge of YMCA work in Paris, looking after American soldiers. Twenty-two UVM men lost their lives in the war.

Influenza, the war's accompaniment, had its impact on campus in 1918. As the deadly disease swept the country, it was decided to delay the opening of the fall semester at UVM until October 23. Nevertheless, an epidemic then broke out, and the Sigma Nu and Sigma Phi houses became hospitals for flu patients. The signing of the Armistice on November 11 brought about further interruptions in the college routine as the University prepared to welcome back its returning veterans and discontinued special classes on campus for the Student Army Training Corps. A recess was granted from December 13 to January 2 to make postwar arrangements. The returning students were told that there would be a quarantine because of the flu epidemic; all college extracurricular activities were suspended for the winter semester. However, class and fraternity meetings were allowed to resume.[9]

Mrs. Gilbert recalls serving as a volunteer nurse's aide. "There was a shortage of nurses and during the flu epidemic some of the sick were housed in the Ethan Allen Club [a men's social club in Burlington] where I worked. They were desperate times—all you could give them was aspirin to try to make them comfortable. Most of the pregnant women didn't survive the black flu."

In February 1919 the University returned to more normal circumstances, as intercollegiate athletics resumed. The baseball team, coached by A. C. Engle (a former Red Sox teammate of UVM graduates Larry Gardner and Ray Collins), rallied the campus to a renewed college spirit with a stunning season's record. *Cynic* editor Perley Hill must have expressed the enthusiasm of a student body elated at a return from crisis to normal college pursuits when he described the baseball squad as "the best everyday team in the United States." At the end of the school year, he reported in his last *Cynic*, "The end of a successful baseball season. Coach Engle won every home game and 71 percent of the whole season."[10] In the meantime work on a new Centennial Field resumed after having been disrupted by the war.

These were building years for the football and basketball teams under Coach Tom Keady. Alumni would claim that the 1922 Green and Gold gridiron was the best Vermont had ever seen: the team whipped unbeatable Dartmouth 6–3.[11] Keady's basketball hoopsters also finished a dazzling 1921–1922 season, winning fourteen of eighteen games. Students thronged to Centennial Field for every home game and thrilled to the traditional tolling of the bell in the Old Mill belfry at victory time.

With the war behind them students were glad to get back to normal, gearing up for the high point of every year, the frenetic preparations for Kake Walk. A large part of Dan Dyer's decision to go to UVM dates from the "sub-freshman" weekend when he and other high school seniors in the state were invited to visit the campus and attend Kake Walk. He was struck by the magic of the occasion with the hushed gymnasium in darkness and the spotlight on the walkers in splendid satin costumes, kicking their legs in rigorous dance steps. "There was something about 'Cotton Babes' and Joe Lechnyr's trumpet that set you up. That sort of settled it—I was going to the University!"

Fraternity politics appeared to bother some thoughtful students in those postwar years. Then as later the *Cynic* editor was the gadfly, urging the student body to practice fairness in student elections. Perley Hill took fraternity men to task for "a tendency to make a practice of nominating for office their own men for Student Union or class meetings." He urged students to consider "college first, fraternity second," and counseled "democratic and friendly ways, smiling at others on campus."[12]

Echoes of Rebellion

The "roaring twenties" brought to the campus echoes of the rebellion of America's "flaming youth." Coeds switched from long skirts and hair demurely pinned up to short skirts and bobbed hair.

Joseph C. Carter ('32) described the "flapper era" in letters to his parents back in Calais: "I cannot endure that boyish bob." He remarked that there was a collegiate fad where "many students don't buckle their overshoes—they just let them flop," and men wore hair pomade called "slikkum."[13]

Though they were mostly the affluent out-of-state students, some men showed up at games in raccoon coats, sometimes with secret hip flasks. Prohibition, reinforcing the college drinking rules, was a challenge to this type. It was a short trip to the Canadian border from Burlington, and the few students with access to a car found themselves popular. Kitty Bassett Hagar ('29), daughter of Professor Bassett, heard about some who thought "the most dashing and daring possible thing you could do would be to go to 'Gallagher's' just over the border, a beer place, and people would go up there for dinner."

By this time dance music had begun to reflect the popularity of American jazz and swing. Lyman Rowell ('25), a Lunenburg native who would become head of the UVM zoology department and later UVM president, from 1966 to 1970, sometimes practiced his dance steps at the Campus House (a girls' rooming house where Waterman Building is now located, acquired by the University after World War I as enrollment climbed to more than 1,000). "They would have the rugs rolled up and the victrola going and I'd stop off for a few dances before I went back to study at the Owl house [his fraternity, Lambda Iota]," he recalled.[14]

Although the University was expanding rapidly, Rowell described a bucolic campus when he enrolled on a mid-August day in 1921. Angell Hall, the President's House, was still standing. (It would later be torn down to make way for the Ira Allen Chapel, completed in 1926.) "A little stream ran across the campus at the point where Wills Residence Hall is—pine trees came down at the edge and . . . the cattle which grazed over the hill towards East Avenue were fenced away from us. We had a nice picnic under the pines."

The campus must have buzzed with anticipation when the *Cynic* headline announced, "Former Stars to Coach 1923 Baseball Team." Red Sox pitcher Ray Collins and third baseman Larry Gardner were returning to their alma mater from Big League ball careers to lead the college nine on a triumphal course. The 1924 team proved to be in good form, with its record of sixteen wins, nine losses, and two ties. Tom Keady's basketball team was also drawing cheering crowds to their games in those years with a record from 1921 to 1925 of fifty-six won and fifteen lost.

Women's athletics picked up more life and significance in 1921 when Eleanor Cummings was hired as athletic director. The program had begun in Mrs. Mayforth's day with weekly classes in swinging Indian clubs and dumbbells in the "gym," a former horse barn on the Howard Hall property. Miss Cummings arranged track meets, softball, volleyball, and intercollegiate tennis matches. The year after her arrival a rifle team was organized. It showed great promise from the beginning, winning its two matches in the first year of the sport. Two years later four UVM girls shot a perfect score.

Dorothy Nash Davis ('31) of Lyndonville was one of the crack shots on that team during her years at UVM. But she recalls, "Tennis was my big love in college. I liked Professor Pooley [James Pooley, Classics professor] because we had tennis in common. We had tennis tournaments between faculty and students and the day I was supposed to play with him I got a stitch in my back and couldn't play."

Ten years later the first woman's ski team would be organized. Dorothea Smith Hanna ('41) was captain of the first squad. The small varsity team practiced four days a week on Mt. Mansfield's Lord Trail. "There was no tow," team member Elaine Burns Little explained, "You just climbed up." It was sport for the truly dedicated skier because meets during Kake Walk weekend meant that the women missed a lot of the carnival fun.

Streetcars were still municipal transportation when Pauline Sullivan Bosworth ('27) was a student. She rode from her home on Shelburne Road, wearing a long coat to hide her baggy gym bloomers. "It was a pleasant time on campus and we were unworried about the state of the world."

Rules continued to curb the girls' activities, with a strict set of nighttime curfews and behavior regulations. Mrs. Bosworth speaks of Dean Marion Patterson's dress code for coeds: "She insisted that we wear hats west of Willard Street. That would be going downtown. And she didn't mean scarves tied around our heads, either. She said, 'There are downtrodden women in Europe who have to wear babushkas and they would give anything to be here where they could wear a regular hat!' The message was ladylike behavior and dressing properly. West of Willard Street was getting downtown where the public was. You had to look good in public. Of course, blue jeans and slacks hadn't been thought of."

Dealing with rules infractions was one of the tasks of the Student Union's Judiciary Committee. Although the organization's main function was to promote college spirit, its constitution contained rules governing women's life on campus. Kitty Bassett Hagar reflects that her position in the Student Union—she became president in her senior year—was unusual because she lived at home without campus restrictions. She recalls, "The men could smoke but Mary Spargo [class of '30] smoked a cigarette in the Old Mill one time and she was campused for two weeks."

By the 1920s increasing numbers of Catholic students, primarily from Burlington, had begun to enroll, and fraternity discrimination became more evident. Margaret Mahoney Farmer ('29) joined Alpha Xi Delta her sophomore year. "It was known as one of the sororities which would take Catholics without any limit at all. That wasn't the reason I finally joined—it was because of the girls." Then in her senior year she remembers that at pledging time "there was one girl in that class who was Catholic and we were rushing her. One particular girl made the remark, 'We have enough of her type.' She didn't say religion, but we knew and it hurt us terribly, and they didn't pledge her."

That same year national Alpha Xi Delta headquarters had issued new rules and regulations limiting the numbers of Catholics who could hold sorority offices, Mrs. Farmer relates. She and some sorority sisters planned to turn in their pins, but "we decided first to discuss it with Father Joyce [the future Bishop Robert Joyce who was principal of Cathedral High School at the time] before we did anything rash." With Father Joyce's advice the decision was to retain their membership in deference to Sister Martha O'Neil, a nun at Mt. St. Mary's School, who had been a founding member of the sorority in 1915.

Mrs. Hagar, who was a Kappa Alpha Theta member, remembers sorority rules when she was a student as generally fair in the rushing process. "They tried to keep it simple and have everybody have the same budget and guidelines. You were allowed to have an open house and then the final rushing party where they pulled out all the stops, perhaps a progressive dinner. And they all did it the same." During her UVM years the first Jewish sorority, K.E.L., a local, was formed in 1926.

Freshman male students reading the 1935–1936 student handbook received some thoughtful hints. "Choose the group you wish to join as the group with which you would prefer to be cast upon a desert island. A jail with the right companions, it is said, can be paradise."

When the Wall Street Crash hit in 1929 and kicked off the Depression years, many students suffered additional hardships in finding money for education. They had a sympathetic friend in tall, affable President Guy Bailey, whose door seemed always open to students looking for scholarships and loans. From the time he was installed in 1919 until his death twenty-one years later, he seemed to have the gift of alchemy when a student or an athletic team faced the hazard of being terminated for lack of funds.

Joseph Carter wrote to his parents in Corinth that he had talked to President Bailey about his younger brother, Stan. "He never lets a freshman stay out a year because of difficulties," he wrote. President Bailey granted Stan a loan. Carter also spoke to the president on his own behalf, receiving the promise of $350 for the next semester and "altogether $1000 for the next three years."

Carter was among a small number of students who began to have their eyes opened to world issues of the day. Encouraging their interest were the International Relations Club, founded in 1926, and the John Dewey Club, formed a year later. Under their auspices a lecture series began to attract national figures. Carter wrote of meeting Calvin Coolidge, the famous UVM alumnus and philosopher John Dewey, Bertrand Russell, Lowell Thomas, and athlete-alumnus Clarence DeMar. "We have discussed all the important problems and are trying to make a new world," he reported in one of his letters.

A campus issue reflected in Carter's letters was the opposition by some students and faculty to compulsory ROTC. A vigorous leader of that cause was Louis Lisman ('31), who was an activist editor of the *Cynic* and campaigned against compulsory military training in the paper. Student reaction, however, was "antagonistic," he reflected. "They wanted to leave everything the way it was. Of course, you have to understand the student body in those days was very small and they were there to get degrees and nothing was going to interfere with that."

In those Depression years Lisman was able to work for spending money to supplement the tuition scholarships he received from UVM as top scholar at Burlington High School and as recipient for three years of university-sponsored debating awards. He earned money playing piano for the silent movies Saturday afternoons at the Majestic Theater and tutoring students in math.

The year Lisman entered UVM had brought crisis to the state and to the University. The devastating flood of November 1927 swelled Vermont rivers, wrecked bridges and houses, and swept cattle downstream. Students were organized under the guidance of the ROTC and sent out in trucks to help in stricken areas. Freshman Louis Lisman went to the devastated town of Waterbury, where the students were sent to various places in the town. "I was one of a small group that went to the store in Waterbury and we shoveled dirt from the cellar. We began getting blisters on our hands, so we went upstairs to get some gloves and as we were leaving he [the proprietor] asked us to pay for the gloves, which we did."

A Battle with Campus Politics

As editor of the *Cynic*, Lisman's first goal was to fight the prevailing fraternity politics, a recurring issue since the beginning of the fraternity system. He assumed the editorship in February 1930 after a mass meeting had denounced the habit of *Cynic* editorial boards to promote their fellow fraternity members for positions on the paper. Lisman printed a page-one article calling for the election of editors on a purely competitive basis. Promotion on the paper was to be based on the amount of work produced for the *Cynic*.

"Fraternities had become the political parties," Lisman explained. "It was not a case of every fraternity being its own political party but in every election on every issue fraternities banded together, one group against another. In order to be elected [to the *Cynic*] you had to get into the successful group. It was so in everything, even in sports when they elected the captains of the teams."

An exception was Lisman's own election to the newspaper, based on campaigning for himself among editorial board members and winning their interest in his cause to stop fraternity control of campus politics. His own fraternity, the newly organized Jewish fraternity Phi Sigma Delta, had yet to gain status on campus. It had just begun in 1928, formed by pledges from Tau Epsilon Phi (UVM's first Jewish fraternity, established in 1919), who bolted en masse from TEP in rebellion against what they viewed as too restrictive rules.

Lisman's years were weak ones for UVM's football team. "Our problem was that there wasn't enough money to support sports," he recollects. "The football team had to support itself by playing two major teams at the beginning of the season. They would play us for practice and in return they would give us large guarantees. With the money we were able to carry the entire season. The trouble was that by the time they got through with us, we weren't good for anything. Half the team was out crippled."

Henry Farmer ('33) came to UVM from Sherman, Maine, having worked on the family farm for five years after high school to help with college expenses. He made the football team, but, he explains, "We didn't have any great teams in those days because of the Depression years. The University wasn't promoting football. Coach Dunn stayed a couple of years and then he left and then John Burke came in and he stayed a couple of years. . . . If you don't have a winning team, they don't keep you around very long."

A member of the baseball squad, Farmer got his first chance to take the pitcher's mound in his junior year on the southern trip, where he was credited with winning the Lehigh game. Coach Gardner brought out the best in his players, he remembers. "As far as he was concerned he wanted to win but it was supposed to be a fun sport. He didn't want you to break your neck to win. He had a great sense of humor and always told you jokes."

The year Henry Farmer entered UVM an alumnus of the class of 1927, Archie Post, took on the formidable task of coaching the shaky track team. Post described the sorry state of track when he was a student in the 1924–1925 season: there was no coach and no team. When it was discovered that Jack Latty, professor of French and Spanish, had been a track man, he was chosen to fill the void.[15] The following season, Post's junior year, Latty's team won the state championship. In 1937, Archie Post's Catamounts won both the eastern intercollegiate and state championships.

By 1932 sexual equality had begun to appear in campus organizations. For the first time women were invited to join the men in the International Relations and John Dewey clubs. When Bernard Lisman ('39) of Burlington was president of the John Dewey Club, lively programs were sponsored. He recalls the thrill of corresponding with John Dewey to arrange his appearance to deliver the traditional Founder's Day address in the spring of 1939. The august gentleman surprised his audience when he said, "College students now have far better manners than in my day, when there was much horseplay, much boisterous joking, which necessitated correction by the teacher. . . . 'Boys will be boys' is applicable but in a different manner than it was in the 1800s. Steam now escapes on the diamond field or track."

A member of the class of 1941, who preferred to remain anonymous, could have enlightened Mr. Dewey about new male antics on campus. He recalls some of his Phi Delta Theta brothers conducting panty raids in sorority houses. "And at that time there was the goldfish craze. I remember a Phi Delt party one weekend. They had bowls of goldfish all along the table. It was a dinner but instead of flowers they had goldfish. You reached in and pulled out a goldfish and down it goes! It would shake up the girls and that was the reason we did it."

Hazing was under control by then, the Phi Delt member claims. "We tried to scare them a little." A popular trick was leading pledges through the fraternity basement where some engineering students had rigged up devices to simulate hell. As the pledge walked through the dark room a transformer transmitted mild electrical shocks along the wet floor while the fraternity brothers chanted "sands are hot."

The Phi Delt house had "house mothers" in those years, and according to this source, "It never occurred to us not to have one. It made us feel good because it made the girls more comfortable." The presence of live-in directors of fraternity houses was somewhat haphazard, encouraged by the administration but not enforced, according to George Kidder. He remembers that the cook in residence in the Kappa Sigma house during his college years was "a fine influence on our lives." By 1946, as the campus returned to normal after World War II, seven of the nine functioning fraternities had house directors.[16]

Independents Back "Vermont First"

The Independents began to grow in the late 1930s, with a constitution, intramural teams, and the announced aim of serving college interests above their own. "Vermont First" was their motto; their purpose, to provide social outlets for unaffiliated men. Nonsorority girls attended their dances at Southwick on Redstone Campus.

The time seemed right for a similar organization for the women on campus who had not joined a sorority out of choice, for financial reasons, or because they were not invited. With advice from Independent president Frank Livak, Ruth Hopkins McCarty ('41) got a committee together, and the Independent Women's organization was formed in 1940, similar to the men's, with membership open to anyone interested. "A large number of girls did not belong to a sorority, had no voice on campus and complained that there was no place to meet anybody," Mrs. McCarty explains. "It was really just a start, a medium through which women could have a little bit of social life, because most of those activities on campus were controlled by fraternities and sororities."

One new tradition created at that time built enthusiasm as spring arrived and the campus inevitably experienced a post–Kake Walk anticlimax. This was the Dean Hills Sugar Party, initiated in 1937 to celebrate Dean of Agriculture Joseph L. Hills's fifty years of service with the university. Sponsored by the Home Economics and Aggie clubs, the celebration featured sugar on snow, sour pickles, doughnuts, and coffee, as well as singing of school songs and dancing, at a charge of 25 cents a head.

However, school spirit seemed to have dipped in those years. In the spring of 1938 a *Cynic* survey lamented the lack of supporters at games, small attendance at chapel and class meetings, and students' apathy toward learning school songs. The record of constant team losses was a major culprit, some felt; others blamed fraternities for handicapping school spirit; and some pinpointed the scattered male population away from campus, with Converse Hall still the only dorm.[17]

A change in the University's athletic destiny was about to take place at the time of that survey. It could largely be traced to UVM's first concerted attempt to recruit promising high school seniors with top marks and shining sports records as football and baseball rookies. Alumni eager to see a reversal of intercollegiate fortunes spearheaded the effort. Joseph Corbett ('43) remembers the arrival at his school in North Tonawanda, New York, of UVM's new freshman football coach, John "Fuzzy" Evans, scouting schools with successful teams. Joe's older brother, Jim ('41), was tapped as one of a group of talented players to arrive on campus in 1937. In October 1937 the *Vermont Alumnus* crowed to its readers, "An unprecedented number of first year men galloped over the greensward in freshman uniforms . . . , giving promise of fat years to come."

Joe Corbett remarks, "One reason those young people could come up was the alumni got them jobs and they lived in the third floor of the Rock of Ages building (located on Bank Street where a parking garage is presently situated) of which the Patricks were executives." (Roy L. Patrick [UVM '98] was president of Rock of Ages and Eastern Magnesia Talc Company.) Corbett, who was to join his brother and other recruits two years later, recalls that "by cleaning up the offices in the evening we were able to get our room for nothing. They let us use the board room to study in and found some of us jobs to earn our board."

The recruiting effort paid off. The following year the new athletic stars helped put UVM back in the headlines. Their varsity teams won state championships in football, baseball, basketball, and track.

This surge in athletic victories was a tonic for the beginning of a new decade that would sorely test students' mettle. Arriving on campus in the fall of 1941, they found themselves in the center of a financial crisis that threatened to close down the school as a result of the Depression's incursions and the late President Bailey's injudicious financial maneuverings. Then the news came that the Vermont Legislature had come to the rescue by appropriating a two-year loan. However, it would still be necessary to mount a vigorous campaign by alumni, students, and university friends to raise $150,000.

Students hailed the legislative action and paraded down Main Street eight hundred strong, carrying "Vermont Saved" banners, then returned to build bonfires on campus and sing college songs by torchlight.[18] Mary Thornton ('46), an "army brat" from Camp Lee, Virginia, who had just started her freshman year, remembers the relief students felt. "It meant we didn't have to pack our bags and go back to the railroad station and head south. After that we went back to try to be average, normal students."

Wartime Again

Circumstances would not permit that return to normalcy. On the Sunday afternoon of December 7 the campus felt the reverberations of a nation pushed into world conflict once again. "As the mood struck the campus, a lot of men wanted to leave immediately," Miss Thornton recalls. The women too responded to the patriotic urge, some leaving to join the WACs or WAVEs. Mary Thornton returned to her home in Virginia to work for a year at Camp Lee.

War and financial troubles would cast their shadows on the UVM campus for the rest of the 1940s, causing constant disruptions through the wartime years and forcing adjustments afterward. George Kidder, Classics professor at the time, likened the World War II situation to the years when these students' parents were in college: "World War One had its Student Army Training Corps and in World War Two we went through that again." As UVM men exited from the campus, U.S. Army Air Corps cadets arrived to take a full roster of courses, as servicemen had in World War I. "We were in a desperate financial situation at the time," Kidder explained. "We had just acquired the Waterman Building, President Bailey had died and Jack Millis came facing this problem. . . . Close to half of the enrollment had disappeared." The army took up the financial slack in payment for billeting and education of the cadets.

The strong focus on sacrifice in the interest of the University was expressed in many ways during the war years. George Little ('43), a Burlington native, recalls the fundraisers put on by his fraternity, Delta Psi, and others to help the University pay back the state of Vermont for its emergency funding. "I can remember they had gatherings on campus, 'Buy Bonds for UVM' fundraisers, and there was a barbershop quartet that went around the state promoting the sale of these bonds."

Cynic editors took up their cudgels again as the disruptions of the war years threatened to dampen morale. Wrote editor John Corliss, "Show some old UVM American fight. . . . Get busy on the War Council, do your bit for the USO, get out those knitting needles for the Red Cross."[19] Before the paper was published, he and a large group of enlistees were on the train bound for Camp Devens. For seniors like George Little it would be the end of their college years. Their diplomas were awarded in February because a new quarter system had allowed them to accelerate their class standing by taking summer courses.

It was a bittersweet time for campus sports. After winning state championships in baseball, basketball, and football, UVM had to suspend intercollegiate sports for "the duration" in the spring of 1943.

Again women were thrust into leadership roles as they had been in World War I. This time, during a longer war, they made greater gains toward equality. Twins Margaret Donahue Davis and Frances Donahue Leach ('45) led a movement to make the ROTC band coed. Opposition was overcome when servicemen who had been band members and called themselves "Joe's Boys" wrote their approval to band leader Joe Lechnyr. The coed band made its first appearance in the fall of 1943. Meanwhile, Frances Donahue Leach became the first woman *Cynic* editor since World War I and brought more recognition to the Independent Women. Julia Fletcher Averett ('44) became president of the new student government body, U.V.M. Students. Gradually, the International Relations Club, once solely a men's organization, became exclusively one of women.

Mary Thornton describes the early history of UVM student government which began in 1942, as "a very polite encounter. The administration would invite us in. . . . It would be a conversation on both sides, not a confrontation. . . . The administration gave us a voice but we had no policy function." A formal constitution was drafted, and all students automatically became voting members upon payment of an activity fee. As part of the organization's attempts at self-government, a student court was formed, with representatives elected from each undergraduate college, to hear infractions of rules as reported by the students' executive committee.

Finding candidates for student government positions became a problem in the war years. When Mary Thornton became *Cynic* editor in 1945, she zeroed in on the apathy about new ways of doing things, such as an honor system. Under the banner headline "About Face, UVM," she challenged students to come to grips with lack of interest in campus elections, dishonesty at student election polls, and lack of support for student government. She wrote, "We hope this exposé makes you mad—if you are aware that something is lacking in the spirit of UVM."[20]

A kind of revolutionary spirit began to stir on the campus as news from the battlefronts came back. In late 1944, Frances Donahue Leach's boyfriend sent a letter describing what he saw as one of the infantrymen who liberated a concentration camp. She read the letter at an open meeting on campus. Students were incensed at what they heard about atrocities in Europe, and there was a mood to take a look at racial and religious discrimination at home.

In the fall of 1945 the University had its opportunity to respond to these issues. Jules Older recounts in chapter 17 what happened in the fall of 1945 when Alpha Xi Delta sorority pledged one of the few black girls on campus. Suspended by the national sorority headquarters, the Vermont chapter refused to yield, even though it meant its disbandment. The upshot of the affair was an agreement by the eight sororities on campus to do away with racial and religious restrictions. Representatives met at the home of philosophy professor George Dykhuizen. "We said it's about time we eradicate discrimination on our campus," Miss Thornton explains. "We were just saying that, for the unusual individual who finds greater friends among someone not of their race or religion, that individual, in a democracy, should be accommodated." All sororities on campus adopted the Greek Letter Reform proposals, agreeing to "discard all discriminatory acts written or traditional." As the campus became fully coeducational again with veterans returning, fraternities also complied with the reform movement, revising their chapter bylaws.

Their education paid for under the new G.I. Bill, the veterans eased back into the college routine, eager to put war memories behind them. Torrey Carpenter ('48), a Burlington native, relates what it was like to return to academic life after he had left school as an enlistee in 1943. "Most of us were happy to forget [the war]. I think when I came back most of us were more serious." Carpenter married Dorothy Fraser ('47), a Long Island native, before his senior year. "I got all A's that year, the first time. We associated with the other married students. . . . We weren't carousing downtown as we had previously."

Entering as a freshman in 1947, Lawrence Kimball ('51) of St. Johnsbury saw the older men as a positive influence. "The vets were quite serious in terms of careers, more practical," he recollects. "One of my distinct impressions is of a frat brother [Kappa Sigma] who was actually 32 at the time. He was extremely young looking and he used to get infuriated when we'd go to a bar and they'd ask him if he was 21."

The traditional Junior Week Peerade, first sponsored by the men's Wig and Buskin Club in 1921, was reactivitated in May 1946 after a four-year suspension. Kimball recalls the intense concentration on constructing a float for the springtime event during his years at UVM. He remembers the 1949 Peerade and the Kappa Sigs' float, which evoked the displeasure of the judges. "It was the time when Ingrid Bergman went off to Italy—Stromboli." [The popular actress scandalized the American public when she left her husband and child to live with film director Roberto Rossellini.] "Our slogan was 'If I'd known you were coming I'd have baked a cake!'" The judges found the allusion distasteful and the execution even more upsetting. The crepe paper creation of a Mount Vesuvius volcano on the float caught fire, requiring the attention of the fire department. The upshot was social probation for the following fall semester.

The in loco parentis regime still had a firm grip in the late 1940s. Larry Kimball recalls, "Life was controlled on campus by controlling the women. Week nights they had to be in by ten and weekends by midnight, and though there were no rules for men, you had to get your date back to the sorority or dorm, and that sort of ended the evening."

Dress continued conservative, men wearing neat trousers and jackets; the women, skirts, sweaters, and saddle shoes. Jeans had just made their appearance but were seen only on weekends. When the coldest winter winds howled on campus, allowances were made for girls to wear slacks to class. Jerome Agel ('52), who commuted to campus from his Burlington home, recalls, "There was a temperature chart and if it fell below zero Fahrenheit, the girls could wear slacks."

Agel, who was UVM's sports publicity director in his sophomore through senior years, remembers that athletics picked up strength in 1946 as if the war had never happened. Leading an enthusiastic vanguard of veterans returning to campus life, Burlingtonian Larry Killick ('47) brought luster back to the basketball court as top scorer with 309 points in the 1946–1947 season, when the team scored nineteen victories out of twenty-two games. The next season the team won its seventh straight state championship. Football equaled its 1923 high. Coach Archie Post shaped a track squad that won the state crown in 1947 and 1948. His 1950 cross-country team won all four dual meets and the state championship and tied the University of Maine for the Yankee Conference title.

By his junior year Agel sensed the lack of a strong cultural program on campus, which had been curtailed by the war. "I decided that my contribution to the University was going to be working out a concert series," he explains. During his summer vacation in 1951 he concentrated his efforts on contacting national figures for engagements. The result was the UVM Program Series, bringing a rich palette of nine productions, including author Carl Sandburg, poet Dylan Thomas, artist Norman Rockwell, and a troupe of African dancers. The *Cynic* called it "a giant step towards improving the tone of the University as a whole."[21] The Program Series evolved into the Lane Series. The top ticket price for all nine programs was only $4.50, and the 1,143 subscriptions were sold out within three hours.

As the 1940s drew to a close, the University seemed to be back on a normal peacetime course. The women's housing problem had long since been resolved with the construction of several small dormitories and the facilities on Redstone Campus. The construction in 1950 of three new men's dormitories, Chittenden, Buckham, and Wills, marked UVM's continuing growth. As the 1950s opened, however, history repeated itself with the eruption of the Korean conflict. For the third time in as many decades UVM students prepared to adjust to the demands of a nation at war.

The View from Midcentury

Students played an important part in this critical half-century at UVM as the University struggled to achieve a firm footing as a broader-based institution. Those fifty years had been painfully harsh, with two wars and a major depression draining the University's resources and curtailing student life, particularly in the field of athletics. However, students proved resilient through those years, perhaps because of financial hardship. Many were forced to focus on surviving academically to keep scholarships and on beating the competition for jobs after class.

Student protest would not be forthcoming for another decade and a half; meanwhile, dorm rules in 1950 still forbade dancing and card playing on Sundays and mandated that radios and Victrolas be kept at low volume. Cars were just appearing in small numbers on campus.

At the midcentury mark, the University had accomplished an impressive transformation, its enrollment of three thousand in 1950 totaling ten times what it had been in 1900, with eleven fraternities and eight sororities to choose from.[22] The seeds had long since been planted for racial and religious tolerance in the fraternity reform movement. Although geographically insulated from the urban turmoil that lay ahead as Vietnam War protests touched off a rash of student rebellions, UVM students showed their sensitivity in the characteristically quiet Vermont way. Much later they were to speak up against apartheid in South Africa, where the University had stock holdings, and voice outrage that ethnic diversity was not adequately represented on the UVM faculty, for the University had begun to mirror the rich complexity of America's ethnic makeup.

In the 1950s students could not possibly have foreseen the coming demise of Kake Walk and of football, which was to be replaced by ice hockey as UVM's stellar sport. Interest in forming a hockey team in those earlier years had started and failed regularly, discouraged by weather uncertainties that made practice games on the flooded rink behind College Row (where Lafayette Hall is now located) undependable.

By the middle 1960s the baby boom had produced another upsurge in the student population, to more than four thousand. Dormitory facilities had been outgrown, and Dean of Women Anna Rankin Harris responded to the housing crisis by permitting women at least twenty-one years of age to live off campus.

This was a gentle beginning for a social revolution sparked by the Vietnam War, with its flood of students' rights issues. Feminism arrived, and unisex dorms appeared on the campus in the 1970s, with liberal room visitation rights. Dress codes vanished. Fraternities faced a roller coaster course in popularity ratings, and they are still perceived as shaky at UVM.

As the last decade of the twentieth century approached, the campus seemed to be bursting at the seams. In the fall of 1989, more than eight thousand full-time students enrolled, making UVM a bustling community larger than most Vermont towns. The little school of the horse-and-buggy era had grown to a highly respected state university.

The Arts at UVM: A Retrospective

JANE P. AMBROSE

RALPH WALDO EMERSON, in his 1841 essay on self-reliance, writing of the individual's need to seek an original means of expression, rejected fashion, tradition, "foolish consistency," and cant in his injunction "Do not imitate." This was a key to New England originality. The history of the arts at the University of Vermont is a history of originality, innovation, and imagination, sometimes indeed in a cultural wilderness but always demonstrating the will of the individual to persist in spite of the odds.

Although academic departments in music (1925), art (1947), and drama (1946) did not exist until well into the twentieth century, the arts have always been an integral part of life in the state and at the University. The independence and vigor of Vermont's citizens have characterized their various and diverse artistic contributions, often inspired by Vermont's "wilderness." The grandmother of Royall Tyler, chief justice of the Vermont Supreme Court, trustee of the University, our only professor of law, and author of the first American comedy, wrote, "He [Royall] professed to me that he was going to Vermont, then considered the outskirts of creation by many, and where all the rogues and runaways congregated, and for that reason considered a good place for lawyers."[1] And undoubtedly for writers, artists, and musicians as well. Another UVM playwright, Thaddeus Stevens, was said to be "as sincere a fanatic and as dangerous a one as Robespierre."[2]

Museums

It would be hard to exaggerate the value of "the museum" in its various permutations in the overall education of students at UVM. Both ethnographic and fine arts collections have been seminal parts of several departments' endeavors from the early nineteenth century to the present, when disciplines as diverse as art history and anthropology teach from museum materials.

In 1826 a voluntary society of members and friends formed the College of Natural History as a "society" for "the acquisition and diffusion of knowledge in every department of natural history, and the accumulation of books, instruments and all materials which can advance these ends."[3] Members paid $3 to join. Professors George W. Benedict and Joseph Torrey, among others, contributed to the "cabinet" of historical curiosities. "Organick remains from this town" also became part of the collection. In 1827 the Colchester jar, perhaps the finest example of early New England Indian pottery, was given to the College by Luther Loomis, who had bought it from Captain John Johnson, a Burlington surveyor. Archaeologists believe that it was left in Vermont by Iroquois Indians from New York on a hunting trip.

In 1849, when the collection of the College of Natural History was incorporated into the University's holdings, it was valued at $1,200. Although the college membership was more than one hundred by then, display space was inadequate, and university support was both desirable and necessary. Apparently, the mounting of "specimens" in the "cabinet" was particularly difficult: "We have ascertained that the space underneath one of the cases is sufficient to receive the swan, and that by removing four or five of the shelves from the case and bringing the feet of the heron as near together as possible he may be deposited within it. We are not certain, however, but in order to do this it will be necessary to abridge somewhat the length of one of his toes, but his foot would be completely hidden from view."[4] The College of Natural History was disbanded in 1851 because of financial difficulties.[5] In 1862 Torrey Hall was built to house the university library and the collection of minerals, costumes, birds, insects, orientalia and other objects that had been accumulating in the Old Mill since the College of Natural History was founded. In 1894, when Torrey Hall was moved to the northern edge of campus to make room for Williams Science Hall, a room for the ethnographic collection was added. The building still stands, housing botany department classrooms and the Pringle Herbarium.

The museum as teaching facility had long been a concern of the University. Professor Torrey had begun instruction in fundamentals of art theory as early as 1834, along with his primary fields of ancient languages and intellectual and moral philosophy. In 1874 his lectures, "Principles of Rhetoric and the Fine Arts," were published posthumously as *A Theory of Fine Art* by his daughter Mary, herself a figure of local renown as a composer and pianist.

Reading those lectures today gives one a sense of Torrey's dedication to clear explanations of the principles of aesthetic theory, never an easy task. He states in the introduction that the course is designed for the senior year "after the plan pursued in some of the European universities." The language of his age gives him scope to expound on the ideals of creative expression: "[The orator] must avail himself of the rhetoric of a great number of well-arranged thoughts welded together by the two fire streams of logic and passion."

H. A. P. Torrey succeeded Joseph Torrey as professor of intellectual and moral philosophy in 1868. Using his uncle's published lectures, the younger Torrey taught from the paintings and plaster casts in the museum collection. Together, uncle and nephew taught the principles of art to UVM students for seventy-five years.

"There are so-called art-galleries containing hundreds of pictures whose total value for purposes of art-culture is not equal to that of one first-rate picture. Our enterprise will not, therefore, be a failure, if we succeed in contributing to the University's resources for culture only two or three masterpieces of native or foreign art, provided there be no second or third-rate pieces admitted to degrade the standard and confuse the effect." So read the announcement of the founding of UVM's Park Gallery of Art in September 1873.[6] In that year Trenor W. Park, Esq., of Bennington donated $5,000 for the construction of a third-floor addition to Torrey Hall. Park, a railroad magnate, had made a fortune on the sale of Panama Railroad Company stock; his estate was worth $7 million when he died. Galleries were still a rarity on university campuses when the Park Gallery was completed in 1874. Glenn Markoe writes, "During the previous decade, some two dozen university museums were founded, mostly as cabinets of natural history. In the field of art, however, there was very little precedent. Yale University's Trumbull Gallery, opened in 1832, was the first of its kind. By the 1850s prominent institutions such as Harvard and the University of Michigan were beginning to collect art."[7] Perhaps unknowingly, Park was building a bridge of imagination as well as of reality to link the University's significant "cabinet of curios" and its first real "fine arts" collection.

The Park Gallery remained the University's fine arts museum for the next fifty years. During that time it acquired the famous Egyptian mummy, surely the best known of the Fleming's thousands of artifacts; the "East India curios and bric-a-brac" exhibited for many years in the room named for their donor, LeGrand B. Cannon; and the Mary Fletcher collection of American landscapes, donated in 1885. In the same year the art program gained a substantial amount of space when the library was moved from the second floor of Torrey Hall to its splendid new home in the building designed by leading American architect H. H. Richardson and erected with funds provided by UVM alumnus Frederick Billings.

Exhibition catalogs in the Wilbur Collection[8] indicate that the Park also served as a sales gallery and in some cases as a showcase for substantial artists. The 1877 exhibition included the Alfred Bierstadt *View of the Sierras* for $750 and Joseph Francis Cropsey's *Greenwood Lake* for $200. The 1878 exhibit included George Inness's *Autumn near Hastings-on-Hudson* for $450 and his "Twilight" for $125! By 1882 the ninth annual catalog looked, finally, like an exhibit catalog rather than a sales catalog.

Museum acquisitions lists can send our sense of time reeling. Although we tend to think of drugs on campus as a recent phenomenon, the 1891–1892 acquisitions list shows the gift of an "opium smoking outfit, pipe, cleaning tools, etc." from Miss A. O. Taft.

When George H. Perkins became museum curator in 1873, he used the newly acquired space to increase the holdings in the ethnographic collection. Additions included alumnus John Converse's gift of a carved Assyrian stone slab from the palace of Assurnasirpal at Nineveh, oceanica purchased by Perkins at the Chicago Exposition, a carved shield from the Trobriand Islands, and three gifts of native American material from the Southwest. The town of Williston presented the museum with a giant mounted bear. Perkins made collecting trips in 1899, 1905, and 1910, each time adding substantially to the ethnographic collections from such diverse locations as the Pacific Northwest, Hawaii, India, and the Mediterranean. He purchased the Twenty-fifth Dynasty mummy during his trip around the world in 1910. Although it is far from the most valuable article in the museum's collections, the mummy is certainly the best known and was unquestionably one of the least expensive acquisitions. Harry Perkins recalled his father saying, "I never thought I would see the day when my son would pay $350 for a case to hold the mummy that I bought for $35."[9] In 1927 Perkins senior retired as curator and was succeeded by his son, already professor of zoology. Between them the Perkins father and son, like the Torrey uncle and nephew, served the University for seventy-five years. At the inauguration of the Fleming Museum in 1931, the eighty-six-year-old Perkins senior reminisced about the old quarters: "The new building was very plain, just a brick box. I saw, as we entered, a small but good collection of birds, a few mammals, shells and Indian relics, more minerals and a very few geological specimens. . . . As a museum it was not very important or attractive, but it was to be *my* museum."[10] Indeed, the name Perkins and museums were synonymous on the UVM campus for many years.

The Robert Hull Fleming Museum was in major part the gift of Katherine Wolcott, who contributed $150,000 of the total cost of $300,000 in honor of her alumnus uncle. In July 1930 construction began on the McKim, Mead and White building. Additional funds were provided by James Wilbur, who was interested in housing his Vermontiana collection. Miss Wolcott was also actively involved in the design and furnishing of the building, and helped keep the museum alive with a further contribution of $150,000. Modest, sensible, firm, but not demanding, she provided excellent guidance to the new undertaking.

Director's reports issued by Harry Perkins starting in 1935–36 document activity in the new building.[11] In that year Perkins recorded some of the problems of the building: " 'No' . . . has to be said frequently, or the store rooms will become swamped with 'junk.' " Unconditional gifts ranged from maps to arrow points to a gift from Professor Paul Moody of a "popular log about 1 ft long cut by beavers" to "two old wooden planes" from Professor Lyman Rowell, horned toads from California and Texas, and a smallmouth black bass. A project was established to collect examples of all existing Vermont mammals. The facility was open from two to five daily, and it was "not rare" for five hundred to seven hundred people to visit in a day; one Saturday saw the attendance of one thousand persons. The next year more Vermont materials, twenty-five dolls in the costumes of their countries, and a "beautiful gift" of antique watches from Mrs. W. S. Webb of Shelburne were added. The name of Henry Schnakenberg, a Vermont artist and collector who donated works by such outstanding fellow artists as Peggy Bacon, Isabel Bishop, and Reginald Marsh over a period of thirty-five years, appears on the advisory committee. In 1937 an "After-School Club" offered fifty students 1½ hours each of instruction in drawing, painting, modeling, and nature study under the supervision of two interns. This formally began the instructional programs of the museum. Soon after the museum was opened, interest began to shift from its original emphasis on zoology and ethnography toward its present focus on the fine arts. The new building sparked local interest in the latter area, and Perkins noted in his report for 1938–39 that he had been "persuaded" to subordinate his enthusiasm for zoology.

Although one could wish that Perkins had pursued the art collections of Electra Havemeyer Webb and Joseph Winterbotham, which went elsewhere, he was nevertheless responsible for many acquisitions. Henry Schnakenberg's gift of fifty prints and drawings in 1933 was the first major gift of this nature since the Fletcher bequest of 1885. Other major gifts in the early Fleming years, such as the Grout and Catlin Zulu beadwork materials and the carved ritual masks from Sri Lanka, given by Mrs. Chester Griswold (daughter of LeGrand Cannon), increased the value of the ethnographic materials. The photographs and drawings documenting 140 notable architectural monuments constructed before 1850, collected as part of Herbert Wheaton Congdon's "Old Vermont Houses" project around 1940, were deposited in the Wilbur Room archives.[12] Perkins's leadership skills were tested when the university deficit of $500,000 was discovered shortly after the death of President Guy Bailey in 1940. Perkins held the museum program together and continued to mount exhibits and accumulate gifts and donations until his retirement and replacement in 1945 by his assistant of fifteen years, Horace Eldred, who served until 1954.

Since the opening of the Fleming, donors have contributed continually to the costume collection. Several items date to the early twentieth century, and a few date as far back as the late eighteenth century. Included are wedding dresses, day and evening dresses, undergarments, nightwear, hats, shoes, jewelry, parasols, a large collection of fans, and a group of Kashmir, Paisley, and Chinese silk shawls. The Fleming also has some men's clothing and military uniforms of those periods, as well as a selection of children's clothing and infant gowns. The ethnic collection has clothing from most countries, notably including robes, vests, shoes, skirts, and wall hangings from China.

Although suggested in 1948, it was not until 1954 that an art historian, Alan Gowans, was named museum director. It was at this time that the focus of the museum changed from a "general" museum to "fine arts" and anthropology. Gowans and his successor, Thomas McCormack (1956–1958), stressed the educational relationship between the museum and the academic departments. During this time important paintings such as Thomas Hudson's *Ann Isted* and George Romney's *Anna Seward* were added to the collections of paintings. Important acquisitions were added to the ethnographic collection as well. Collections were relocated and remounted, and important additions were made. The museum was used for cultural events such as concerts and symposia—again, an anticipation of future times.

Richard Janson, director from 1958 to 1977, and Margit Holzinger, curator from 1957 to 1974, added American and European prints and drawings, early American ivory miniature paintings, and further valuable ethnographic works to the collections. Important exhibitions of contemporary art were held during this period. An exhibit of Montreal Op Art was mounted to honor the founding of Canadian studies in 1965, and exhibits of the 1970s included works of American artists James Franklin Gilman and Louis Lozowick and a retrospective of Clair van Vliet's work at the Janus Press. William Lipke (1977–1980) reinstated the Cannon Room and sponsored two major publications in conjunction with special exhibits—one focusing on tools and technology, the other on educational toys in America since 1800. For the 1976 United States bicentennial celebration, Lipke mounted a major exhibit, "Vermont Landscape Images." Special exhibits, symposia, and a major renovation reorienting the entrance toward campus and remodeling several interior spaces marked the directorship of Ildiko Heffernan (1980–1990). The work was a collaborative effort of Glenn E. Markoe, curator of collections from 1984 to 1988, and Fleming Museum designer Merlin Acomb, who has provided stability, common sense, and professional standards to museum operations. The museum was reopened to the public in the fall of 1984.

Grants, especially from the National Endowment for the Arts and the National Endowment for the Humanities and their state affiliates, from the Institute of Museum Services, and from friends and volunteers, have made the last decade of the museum particularly fruitful. There has been a recent inventory of the entire holdings, an on-line catalog of the museum's seventeen thousand objects is underway, and the costume collection has been rehoused. The ethnographic collection has yielded fruit in the exemplary publication of the Read Collection of the Northern Plains Indians by Markoe following an NEA-funded assessment of the ethnographic items in the permanent collection.[13]

Art Instruction

Art instruction has a long history at UVM. Joseph Torrey's "Principles" course, begun in 1834, was one of the country's earliest college courses on the fine arts. Emphasis continued to be placed on theory until 1906, when the first real art history course was initiated by Samuel Eliot Bassett, professor of Greek. He introduced Greek sculpture and architecture, lectured on Mycenaean art, and discussed painting, ceramics, terra cottas, bronzes, gems, and coins. In 1920 a historical survey taught jointly by Bassett, George Perkins, Arthur Myrick (professor of Romance language and literature), and Samuel Emerson (professor of history and sociology) was first listed in the UVM catalog. Other distinguished faculty members lecturing on art in the early years of this course were Lester March Prindle and George V. Kidder, both from the Latin department. In 1939 Greek art and European painting became separate courses, and in 1954 the faculty began to expand the departmental offerings further. At present the department covers the full spectrum of historical and ethnographic possibilities of both the Western and non-Western worlds. The latest new course, "History of Optical Media as Art," demonstrates the commitment of the art history faculty to cover the entire chronology of their discipline.

Studio art courses were initiated by Elizabeth Colburn (1921–1942), who, as an art educator, believed that liberal arts students needed their own art curriculum. She and Isabel Clark Mills (1945–1964) carried the practical curriculum until the arrival of artist-in-residence Francis Colburn (1909–1984, no relation to Elizabeth) in 1943. After graduating from UVM in 1934, Colburn had studied in New York at the Art Students' League and at Bennington College. He became the first faculty member not involved in either art education or "arts and crafts." Colburn's presence on campus remains in the legacy of his Vermont humor and in his many paintings hanging in distinguished places on campus. In some ways his ideas are a modern reflection of Torrey's ideas. Tom Slayton quotes Colburn's educational philosophy in his introduction to the exhibition of Colburn's work at the Fleming in 1984: "To just what kind of star have you hitched your wagon? You are old enough to consider some of the stars. You are old enough to realize that a life dedicated to no truly big idea is in danger of going around in awfully small, awfully boring circles." Recalling Colburn's humor, Slayton wrote, "Colburn was born in Fairfax and used to say that being a native Vermonter on the UVM faculty made him something of a curiosity, like being 'the last surviving member of President Garfield's cabinet.' "[14]

For those who know the subject, autobiographical paintings always capture the essence of the character of the sitter in spite of surrealistic settings among artifacts of the sitter's life. A good example is Colburn's self-portrait in Heffernan's catalog, *Picnic ca. 1955*. The Vermont Council on the Arts presented him their Distinguished Service to the Arts award in 1968. In 1974 the University conferred an honorary degree on him and named a gallery for him. Other prizes were awarded by the Springfield Museum of Fine Arts, the Boston Institute of Contemporary Art, the San Francisco Palace of the Legion of Honor, and the Fleming Museum.

At present fifteen full-time faculty and eleven part-timers teach the full range of courses in studio art and art history. Faculty members Richard Janson, William Lipke, Christie Fengler-Stephany, Edward Owre, Francis Hewitt, Paul Aschenbach, and William Davison have all given the department the kind of stability that comes from longtime service and commitment. The department thrives and offers an exemplary curriculum in spite of pressing space requirements for both faculty and students.

Music

That music was alive and well at UVM long before there was a music department is evident in the listing of musical organizations in the first *Ariel* (1888). There was a chapel choir of ten men; Phi Delta Theta had a double quartet; Sigma Phi, a quartet; ATO, a sextet; and Delta Psi, a double quartet. Phi Delta Theta had an orchestra with the somewhat bizarre combination of two violins, two cornets, a piccolo, and a cello, and Sigma Phi had a banjo club consisting of two banjos and two guitars.

UVM got its official school song in 1882: "Champlain," composed by D. David Fischer. But the real school song for many years was Percy Weinrich's "Cotton Babes," played first by the Burlington Military Band, then by the ROTC band, and finally by the university band at Kake Walk, the focus of Winter Weekend activities from 1893 until its replacement in 1969 by a more ordinary winter carnival.

The University and the Burlington community enjoyed active performance life long before the George Bishop Lane Series was established in 1955. Performers stopped en route between Boston and New York and Montreal to perform at Fleming Museum, Southwick Ballroom, and Ira Allen Chapel. Announcements from New York managers sent directly to Howard Bennett suggest that these programs were run from the music department almost from its inception in 1925. World-famous soloists and orchestras frequently performed at UVM before they had established their reputations, a tradition that has continued with the Lane Series.

The idea for a memorial to George Bishop Lane, UVM class of 1883 and founder of the *Cynic*, came from his widow, Nellie Lane, and Florence Barbour, wife of Lewis Barbour, the adopted son of Nellie and George. They approached President John Millis in January of 1947 with a proposal "to make a suitable memorial to a fine man and, at the same time give the University of Vermont something which will increase its ability to serve." Mrs. Lane suggested an organ for the chapel because "Mr. Lane was very fond of music." Alternative suggestions were a hospital room or a leisure reading room. In a letter to Mrs. Lane, Millis suggested other possibilities, including "an endowment fund to support an annual concert or concert series which would be of great help in satisfying the desires of students who greatly appreciate the opportunity of hearing great artists." In April, Millis and Mrs. Lane agreed that a concert endowment was the most suitable memorial and that any extra monies could be used "within the Music Department or to create other memorials to George Lane."

At first Mrs. Lane provided for the endowment in her will, bequeathing a sum of approximately $300,000 in stocks for this purpose. Then, in April 1954, President Borgmann received a letter from Mrs. Lane's lawyer stating that she had decided to make the gift during her lifetime. Borgmann welcomed the news, and on April 30 he announced the gift as part of the festivities celebrating the 150th anniversary of the University's first commencement.

From 1948 to 1951, Professor Ippocrates Pappoutsakis served as a "concert committee." He joined the Lane Working Committee in 1954. In the meantime (1951–1952) the Student Association undertook to support the "University of Vermont Program Series," that Jerome Agel ('52) had proposed and organized because "there was no cultural activity on campus to speak of." The Student Council ran the series in Southwick Gymnasium and Ira Allen Chapel; however, it was more for lectures than for music. The year's only controversy occurred over the performance of a jazz group in Ira Allen Chapel on a Sunday evening. Ticket prices that year were $2.50, $3.50, and $4.50. The student-run series had three successful seasons before the Lane endowment took effect.

In the fall of 1954 a working committee of six students and five faculty members was appointed, with Dr. Jack Trevithick, professor of English, as executive secretary. Mrs. Lane knew and approved of the faculty–student involvement in the series, although she died in April 1955, before the first season actually opened the following fall with a performance of Shaw's *St. Joan* by the Canadian Players. Mr. and Mrs. Barbour attended the performance of the London Philharmonic on November 17, and after their visit Mrs. Barbour wrote to Trevithick, "We are especially pleased with the Concert Series. It is splendid in every way and we know that Mother would be happy too. We like the student–faculty control and we like the selection of offerings this first year. We certainly congratulate the committee."

Trevithick remained director of the Lane Series for twenty-one years. "Dr. T." worked well with students and faculty, and his responsibilities over the years eventually increased to the point where he was employed full-time. During his years the Lane Series established an enviable reputation for the bringing "the best" to Burlington in all areas of entertainment. Upon his retirement in 1976, Trevithick was succeeded by Terrance

Demas, who had been manager of the Student Association Concert Bureau. By this time, however, the musical scene in Burlington, as elsewhere, had changed markedly: artist fees had escalated, audiences were complaining about Memorial Auditorium's strange acoustics and unacceptable concert ambience, and there was competition from newer presenters. In his twelve years with Lane, Demas continued to bring only "the best," sometimes under extremely difficult circumstances and in facilities always less than ideal.

The present writer was appointed director of the Lane Series in June 1988 by President Lattie Coor. The endowment is now worth some \$2.4 million dollars through growth as part of the University's portfolio, individual contributions, and local capital campaign efforts in conjunction with an NEA matching grant. Four percent of the total of the endowment is returned to the series each year as part of the base budget. The 1988–1989 program, for example, had thirteen events, ranging from classical chamber music to theater, dance, and family entertainment. We have, as well, revived the old Lane film series, "The Best of the Art Cinema," with financial support from several programs and departments. Lane remains a vital force in community life.[15]

Music Instruction

The music department opened its doors at 85 South Prospect Street in September 1925. Formerly the residence of General W. W. Henry, the house had been occupied by Delta Psi fraternity and then used as a women's dormitory. Under the leadership of Howard Gordon Bennett, recipient of a master's degree from Harvard and recently returned from a year of study in Vienna and Paris, the department flourished. In that first year Bennett taught music appreciation (earliest times to Beethoven), history of choral music, elementary harmony, and a teacher training course. He also conducted the glee club. Two new instructors were added the next year—Miriam Marston in piano and public school music and Elizabeth Bradish in voice. Bennett added advanced harmony and a second semester of the appreciation course to the curriculum. By May 1927 the glee club and choir were able to perform Purcell's *Dido and Aneas*. Already the department reflected the three concerns that shape its present curriculum—performance, history and theory, and music education. Equipment in 1926 consisted of two grand pianos, two upright rebuilt Steinways, a Duo-Art reproducing piano, a large Brunswick "Panatrope" and more than three hundred rolls and records. A large modern organ "will be installed . . . in the new University chapel."[16]

In 1927 a large, modern Welte-Mignon organ with "reproducing player attachment" was installed in the new Ira Allen Chapel. For UVM students paying \$275 tuition that year plus a student activity fee of \$27.50, music lessons were \$35 a semester for one a week, \$60 for two. Practice room "rent" was \$5, and organ practice was \$25 per semester. During Bennett's chairmanship the department grew almost to its present strength of ten full-time and another dozen part-time faculty. Making way for the construction of the Waterman Building in 1939, the department moved to 70 South Williams Street and later expanded next door to Booth House and then to the old carriage house behind it. Frank Lidral became department head on Bennett's retirement in 1960 and remained chair until 1973, when his dream of seeing the music department in a new facility was realized. In that year construction was begun on the current building attached to Southwick on the Redstone Campus, designed by Burlington Associates.

The new building was dedicated on Sunday, February 22, 1976, with a concert and remarks by William Metcalfe, Lidral's successor as chair; Lieutenant-Governor Brian Burns for the State of Vermont; Edward Feidner, director of drama, for the arts at UVM; and Lyman Rowell, former president of UVM, for the community. Since that time the department has presented hundreds of concerts for the University and for Vermont communities.

Meanwhile, James Chapman became chair upon Metcalfe's return to the history department, and in June 1988 the present writer assumed that position. The department offers several hundred students a complete range of courses, lessons, and ensembles leading to the degrees of bachelor of arts, bachelor of music in performance or theory, and bachelor of science in music education. Current departmental priorities include the addition of an electronic music laboratory, an upgrading of facilities and equipment, and the reinstatement of the graduate program.

Remarkable longevity of faculty has marked the sixty-three-year history of the music department. Recent retirees were all hired during Bennett's time at UVM, and most of the current senior faculty have been at UVM for more than twenty years. The record is held by Professor Pappoutsakis, who taught at UVM thirty-five years before he "retired" in 1975. During that time he conducted the orchestra for twenty-five years, taught dozens of courses, and directed the first high school summer session and the Elizabethan Institute. He continued to teach music literature in the evening division until his death in 1990.

Theater and Drama Instruction

At the time of the dedication of the new Royall Tyler Theater in 1974, UVM theater historian George B. Bryan wrote:

The twin muses of drama are not alien to the University of Vermont, for the theatrical arts have been fostered at UVM since the days of its first president, Daniel Clarke Sanders (1800–14). To placate delicate sensibilities, dramatic presentations were called "odes and dialogues" or "colloquies," and as such formed a basic part of the commencement ceremonies from the institution's first in 1804. The courthouse, situated where the City Hall Auditorium now stands, was the scene of the earliest commencement at UVM, which included a "Dialogue on the Languages" as well as two other similar presentations. . . . Disguised theatrical presentations continued to be a part of each commencement through the 1820s.[17]

Although Greek drama and English literature courses assured that classics of the theater were read on campus, dramatic activity itself was not extensive outside the presentations at forensic events. In 1892, "Histrionic Develings" were begun as a means of underwriting athletic activities. On April 17, 1896, for instance, the group presented "The U.V.M. Minstrels and Histrionic Develings" Baseball Benefit at the Howard Opera House.[18] Tickets were 50 cents and 75 cents, and $102.65 was raised for the UVM Athletic Association. In part 1, the UVM Minstrels, complete with interlocutor, tambos, and bones, presented their part of the show. One of the actors was a Mr. Harry Stedman ("Watch out for him all de time"). There followed a potpourri entitled "Old Black Joe," including a choral version of the "Colored Four Hundred." Part 2, vaudeville, was an "Imitation of Bones with Accessories." The show concluded with Thomas J. Williams's one-act farce "Turn Him Out." Cultural diversity was already a fact of campus life although in a form that contemporary society might find unacceptable.

Titles of nineteenth-century dramatic productions show us some student predilections: class of 1810, Norman Williams, "The British in Philadelphia or The Battle of the Kegs"; class of 1812, Joseph Williamson, "Duelling," and Royall Tyler, Jr., "Quackery, or the Dumb Gent"; class of 1813, Ira Bellows, "Physiognomy"; class of 1818, A. A. Parker, "Pedantry". There was also Thaddeus Stevens (who would have been class of 1815). By the turn of the century, dramatics organizations flourished; and men's and women's dramatics clubs performed on and off campus.

There followed a century of achievement, marked by the dramatic productions of Professor Wilnetta Sproul Taggart from 1922 to 1942, the founding of the Department of Speech under the direction of Robert B. Huber in 1946, the founding of the University Players in 1952, and the creation of the Arena Theatre, a 1957 transformation of the Fleming Museum's basement into a 250-seat auditorium. Long-time faculty members Edward J. Feidner (1958), William Schenk (1965), and George B. Bryan (1971) have shaped the direction of the department over many years.

The Champlain Shakespeare Festival and Royall Tyler Theater

Founded in 1958, the Champlain Shakespeare Festival has presented the highest-quality productions of the plays in accord with historical performance research. From 1965 to 1970 the festival was supplemented by the Institute of Elizabethan Arts and Letters. This interdisciplinary institute offered high school teachers of English literature the opportunity to study the

Elizabethan arts and to observe the preparation and performance of Shakespearean plays. Festival performances were held in the Arena Theater, which provided an intimate four-tiered arrangement with a raised stage and the audience on three sides. The festival offered more than forty performances each summer to a cumulative audience of twelve thousand patrons. For years Edward Feidner was producer of the festival, and William Schenk was the scene designer and technical director.

Dramatic performances now take place in the Royall Tyler Theater, a facility that was envisioned by Feidner after grandiose plans for a magnificent arts center to house art, music, and theater fell through in the early 1970s. It utilized the old gymnasium, the elegant if simple structure designed by Boston architectural students of the famous H. H. Richardson, creator of the present Billings student center.

Historical precedent for artistic productions in the old gym is documented by Bryan in the Royall Tyler Theater dedication program:

The first public exhibition of the new Gymnasium, held on 14–16 October 1901, was a gala one, as it housed the Vermont Musical Festival, featuring the Boston Symphony Orchestra and a choir of four hundred. A spacious hall, the Gymnasium seated 1200 at each of the five concerts and at many others afterward. The structure proved a suitable location for physical activities, military drill, dances, Kake Walk, baccalaureate and commencement exercises, but especially for musical entertainments. Over the years the roster of artists whose talents inspirited the building is most noteworthy and includes John McCormack, Jascha Heifetz, Fritz Kreisler, Geraldine Farrar, Mischa Elman, Alma Gluck, Amelita Galli-Curci, Jan Kubelik, John Philip Sousa, Sergei Rachmaninoff, Ruth St. Denis and Ted Shawn, Carolina Lazzari, Efrem Zimbalist, Ernestine Schumann-Heink, Anna Pavlova, and Paul Whiteman, who presented Gershwin's "Rhapsody in Blue" soon after its original performance in New York.[19]

Artifacts at the theater, such as the lamp carried by Helena Modrzejewska in her farewell tour and given to Feidner by Emma Frederick, as well as the Thomas Gould bust of the great Shakespearean actor Edwin Booth, synthesize theater history.[20]

The new theater was dedicated on March 14, 1974, with the UVM Brass Ensemble and Choral Union joining their theatrical colleagues in celebration. Since then the theater has welcomed the UVM Baroque Ensemble, music department recitalists, Lane Series artists, Gilbert and Sullivan entertainments, art exhibits, seminars, and other activities, in addition to presenting dozens of plays on its boards. There is a long history of cooperation between the music and theater departments. Together they have presented offerings as diverse as Carmen, The Three-Penny Opera, and Gilbert and Sullivan operettas.

The Shakespeare Festival and the theater department are the more recent manifestations of dramatic activity on campus. The festival has given young professionals a chance to perform at a level that might have been impossible elsewhere; and the department itself, in its forty-two years, has combined course work and practicum effectively to prepare each student generation for the theatrical work that most of them undertake after graduation.

The arts have had a long and prosperous life at UVM. At present we offer all of the standard historical and practical courses, an extraordinary number of exhibits, dramatic productions, concerts and symposia, and dozens of activities ancillary to our major programs. We have, however, suffered from budget insufficiencies, so our departments are presently in need of substantial upgrading and modernization of spaces and equipment. One victim of budgetary constraints is the Champlain Shakespeare Festival itself, which had to suspend operations during the summers of 1989 and 1990. Nevertheless, as we enter the University's third century, the faculty remain committed to the continued excellence of preparation of our students and the presentation of the widest variety of artistic activity at the highest possible level.

Part Four

THE MANY-SIDED UNIVERSITY, 1941–1991: OVERVIEW

T. D. SEYMOUR BASSETT

Within days after President Bailey's death on October 22, 1940, the Trustees became aware of the University's huge debt, nearly $1 million. They resolved it the following year under the leadership of Newman K. Chaffee, Rutland banker, UVM trustee, and acting president between November 9, 1940, and August 16, 1941, who commuted to Burlington to oversee the headless administration. State aid, private gifts, and bonding were combined to solve the problem. However, the state demanded a complete audit, together with strict new accounting procedures and an acting president as troubleshooter, as well as a long-range plan to restore financial solvency and public confidence and a new president who could implement it.

On the recommendation of the Carnegie Foundation, Paul C. Packer, dean of the College of Education at the University of Iowa, who had reorganized the University of the Philippines and made other site evaluations, was appointed to take first steps. Packer worked on campus from April 1941 to the end of June to prepare a report. In August the Trustees elected him temporary president, along with Major General Brice Disque as temporary business manager, to restore confidence as an outsider. They retired seven professors aged sixty-seven and over on half pay, including Joseph Hills, Elbridge Jacobs, and Frederick Tupper, apologized for the lack of a pension system, and froze hiring.[1]

In September 1941, Governor William Wills called a special session of the Legislature, which voted to appropriate $500,000 provided UVM raised the rest to cover the total debt. Twelve eminent and faithful trustees resigned because they had not been able to blow the whistle on their president, who, from his sickbed, was privately carrying an impossible burden as both business and educational leader—or as they put it, they resigned "to clear the decks and permit the rehabilitation groups to work."[2] Bailey's assistant comptroller and registrar, Forrest W. Kehoe, carried on, also covering purchasing and buildings and grounds. J. Howard Moore, president of the Alumni Council, resigned from the Board as of November 1, 1941, to run the alumni side of the drive to match the legislature's appropriation. "Operation rescue" collected $383,000 by June 1942, university affairs taking center stage in Vermont in spite of the war.

During the interregnum, temporary president Packer and the Trustees addressed the debt problem and moved to prevent more deficits by cutting expenses and expanding income. Packer envisaged a radical consolidation of instruction, by reducing the twenty-six "top-heavy" departments in arts and sciences to six or eight fields, such as life sciences, physical sciences, social sciences, and foreign languages, that should cover everything and lead to just two degrees, A.B. or B.S. Arts and Sciences would provide the basic general education as well as preprofessional studies. The College of Engineering should be closed, but since this was more drastic surgery than Packer could expect, he urged that the college concentrate on one branch of engineering. He called emphatically for a larger state medical subsidy and provision by the state for a new agricultural plant and equipment. He warned that unless the debt could be refinanced, a competent president could not be attracted. The Trustees must delegate financial management, contracts, conveyances, and auditing to their executive committee, and meet, not once a year as hitherto, but several times. He would remove both the president and the governor from the Board and let the governor appoint half the members representing the state, with two thirds of the state senate approving. Above all, he declared, "It is no longer possible for the president personally to handle both the educational and business affairs of the University." The treasurer should manage banking and endowments, while the comptroller or business manager handled financial reports, property records, buildings and grounds, and central purchasing. Packer accepted Bailey's idea of two residential campuses and recommended that women's dormitories be added near Redstone and men's dormitories near Converse Hall, avoiding further encroachment on the Hill residential district around the Waterman Building. Except for the streamlining of courses and colleges and the reorganization of the Board itself, most of Packer's recommendations had been addressed if not achieved by 1950.

Who would stop the drift and tackle the task of stabilization? After several candidates for president had been considered, a committee consisting of Packer, Asa S. Bloomer (UVM '13, a trustee and a power in the legislature), Howard Moore for the alumni, and George A. Ellis, banker and businessman of New York and Bennington, accepted the recommendation of the Carnegie Foundation to appoint John Schoff Millis, dean of administration at Lawrence College in Wisconsin, currently on leave from Lawrence to work with the foundation. Millis's career had gone from high school coaching and mathematics teaching to professor of physics and then dean at Lawrence.

Millis recalled the whirlwind of events. Two days after he met the trustee committee in New York he was elected president, on November 1, 1941. He called his wife: "We're moving to Burlington." "Where's that?" she asked. Millis's father, chair of the National Labor Relations Board in Washington, read the news in the paper, phoned him in his Hotel Vermont room at 6 A.M. the next day. "You damn fool, what have you done *now*? Get out of bed and get to work!"[3] He did, that day, without the luxury of any inauguration then or later.

Up to 1941 every UVM president except Angell and Benton had close Vermont connections. Millis was not only an outsider but the first of five natural scientists to serve as president of UVM in the next thirty-five years and the first Episcopalian. However, he was "a brilliant and hard-textured administrator" who took the necessary drastic measures regardless of where the chips fell, according to Lyman Rowell, then one of the Young Turks of the faculty. Millis was "challenged by the faculty," who kept up the pressure for a pension plan and won trustee acceptance of their statement on academic freedom.[4]

President Millis had scarcely settled into his new Waterman office when war broke out. For the next five years his administration had continually to juggle the housing and instructional needs of transient military trainees. War had always brought heavy enrollment losses, and twice before—in 1814–1815 and 1917–1918—the army had disrupted UVM life when it came on campus. Intercollegiate sports were suspended in 1943; playing fields became parade grounds. Employees entering the armed services were not replaced and were not guaranteed employment after the war. Faculty not drawn off to war "taught . . . often in new and unfamiliar fields," Lyman Rowell recalled. Francis Colburn, who came as artist in residence in 1942, was drafted to teach English; Howard Bennett, head of the music department, taught mathematics. Students leaving for war had the choice of getting cash back for the part of the semester they missed or tuition credit for their enrollment when they returned. Of the 2,454 UVM alumni in the armed services, 78 were killed in action.[5]

The army presence offset the wartime decline in civilian enrollment, from nearly 1,400 in 1940–1941 to less than 900 in 1944–1945. Premedical and preengineering programs were conducted for the Army Specialized Training Program, as well as basic education for U.S. Air Force cadets and a program for high school students not yet of draft age. Military substitutes for full-time civilian students were not satisfactory, but they were better than nothing. Arrivals were irregular and could not be well planned for, despite a complete revision of the university calendar. The military took over the Redstone campus and used the Waterman cafeteria as their mess hall. Instead of the soprano chatter of coeds on their way down South Prospect Street to classes, residents heard the marching songs of uniformed men. In fourteen months some 2,500 men were processed, with twenty full-time and sixty-five part-time instructors as of November 1943. Some of these students, assigned to UVM involuntarily, chose to come back on the GI Bill after the war.

Meanwhile, new gifts helped improve the University's position in cash and in real estate. One last attempt by the Grange to detach the agriculture college from UVM was beaten back; instead, the state was persuaded to pay for the new university farm and to commence regular appropriations for agriculture. Some three hundred friends of UVM gave over $32,000 to buy the house built by President Wheeler in 1842, to serve now as the Student Health Service and infirmary (named in memory of Pearl Randall Wasson, first dean of women). In 1945, Governor Mortimer R. Proctor gave the Maple Research Farm in Underhill, and Joseph Winterbotham gave the large property on the corner of Main and South Willard Streets, later sold to the Burlington School Board, then to Champlain College. Many other Hill homes, willed by friends of UVM, were used for a while as dormitories and then sold.

UVM bounced back after the war, reaching an enrollment of 2,006 students in 1946–1947, and observers noted a career-oriented seriousness, especially among the married veterans in the trailer village near Centennial Field. Nevertheless, the dominant mood was first cousin to the postwar 1920s, with "a lot more hard drinking and related activity," as one former air force pilot put it.[6] Kake Walk remained the greatest campus event, followed by other fraternity affairs and sports.

In the immediate postwar period, people assumed that the state's intervention on behalf of the University had been temporary. Yet the experience prepared the state for later long-term commitments. Emphasis on UVM's public character led to increased biennial appropriations, not only for the Colleges of Medicine and Agriculture but temporarily for the College of Education. Total state support rose from $219,000 in 1941 to $430,000 in 1942, dropped to $234,000 in 1945, and then rose steadily to nearly half a million by 1949, practically all for medicine and agriculture, as the teacher-training component dwindled. In addition, the Hills Building, the first expansion of the plant of the College of Agriculture since Morrill Hall, was built with state money; likewise the Terrill Home Economics Building and the Carrigan Dairy Science Building, all in 1949. Responding to questions about the University's public service to the state, Millis asked the Trustees in December 1947 what constituted fulfilling Morrill Act obligations, suggesting that Buckham had discharged the bare minimum. A year later Governor Ernest Gibson told him that "he felt the University was working in the direction of becoming a State University."[7]

When President Millis resigned in 1949, the Trustees picked Burlington coal-and-oil dealer Elias Lyman to be acting president and chairman of the search committee (consisting of six trustees, alumni representatives, and a faculty representative from the new Policy Committee). To continue the effort to make UVM more like a midwestern state university, the choice fell on William Samuel Carlson, a geologist and president of the University of Delaware, who took up his duties in Burlington in April 1950.[8]

Carlson knew that he was expected to set many initiatives in motion, and he did so. He appointed committees on general education and on long-range planning, and he advised academic acceleration when the Korean War caused a 10 percent drop in enrollment. He launched the School of Dental Hygiene, proposed a Department of Community Service, and instituted the Government Clearing House and a foreign study program. Centennial Field was rented to a semiprofessional baseball team. Faculty apartments went up at University Heights. UVM acquired the Morgan Horse Farm in Weybridge, Vermont, from the U.S. government. Finally, Carlson removed the last prop from Classical studies when he persuaded the Trustees to abolish the ten scholarships requiring the holders to win a grade of B or better in at least one Classics course each year.

Up to World War II, UVM presidents did not think of themselves as career administrators who would move on from one university to another that could best use their talents and pay accordingly. Carlson could not resist the chance to head the New York State University system and resigned in 1952. Many senior faculty polled by the Policy Committee for suggestions of a successor reacted resentfully. They wanted "some one who will *stay,*" "who will be loyal to the University," not one of those "fair-haired boys" using UVM as a stepping-stone. "Deliver us," wrote one, "from another Mid-western apostate from scholarship." Lyman Rowell, among a substantial minority preferring an insider, pointed out that they knew only the plus side of outsiders but both sides of locals. He recommended someone who would grow in the job and mentioned history professor Paul D. Evans (in the memory of the writer and others, much too gentle for the job), then chemistry professor C. Ernest Braun.[9]

On the other hand, younger professors called for someone like Carlson, who would continue his policies, willing to give five or six energetic years before he went on. This has been the UVM pattern of presidents from Millis on. Their median tenure at UVM has been only six years. The only recent deviation from this norm was President Lattie Coor, who went through several unsuccessful candidacies with other institutions before he found the right fit with Arizona State University.

Responding to the new transient character of the presidency, UVM gradually adopted the procedures common to institutions all over the country in searches for chief executives. Each program would first contribute to a profile describing UVM, its goals, and the kind of leader it needed. Then the Trustees appointed a search committee assisted by an advisory committee intended to represent all constituencies—alumni, state, city, staff, faculty, students. The search committee advertised nationally, including the minority media in response to federal affirmative action law, and screened a large number of candidates according to the criteria established in the self-study. More recently, UVM has assigned the advertising and screening to agencies specializing in filling university presidencies. Finalists (but no longer their wives) come to the campus to inspect and be inspected, followed by debate within the search committee, its recommendation, and the full board's choice. Spouses of candidates increasingly tend to have careers of their own. In any case, the character of the spouse has become irrelevant to the selection process, except that the president's family has lived since 1958 in Englesby House, the facility staffed by the University for official entertaining. As in other nomination processes, a political deadlock between frontrunners sometimes has led to the appointment of a third candidate.

One consequence of UVM's effort to be more like a state university was the conscious elimination of the Protestant image. Although UVM had not had a Congregational minister for a president since the Civil War, the laymen chosen between 1866 and 1940 were churchgoing, religious Protestants who believed that religion was important to the life of UVM. Presidents after 1940 were in varying degrees religious men, but their outlook on their jobs was secular, judging by their public speeches and their limited attention to religious affairs on the secular campus. Although there had been a few Catholics in the student body in the nineteenth century and after and both Jews and Catholics on the faculty beginning early in the twentieth century, recruitment became truly religion-blind only after World War II. Protestants, Catholics, and Jews united in building a small chapel in the basement of the Ira Allen Chapel for their joint use. Catholics used the auditorium upstairs for Sunday mass, and the B'nai B'rith Hillel Foundation maintained a rabbi for several years, with Professor Harry H. Kahn (German and Hebrew) as adviser. By the late 1950s convocation had replaced Wednesday chapel, and a coordinator of religious activities had replaced the chaplain, leaving formal religious activities to the Protestant Cooperative Ministry, the Newman Center, and Hillel. However, as Jules Older ('62) shows in chapter 17, prejudices continued.

President Carlson's ultimate replacement turned out to be Carl Borgmann, from the University of Nebraska. Like Carlson, Borgmann announced that he would be happy to stay in Burlington until he retired, though ultimately he could not resist the repeated offers of the Ford Foundation. Chapters 15 and 16 in this volume focus on major events during his administration. David Holmes recounts how Alexander Novikoff, a brilliant biochemistry professor in the medical college, was fired by the Trustees—

against the recommendations of the faculty, his dean, and a special investigating committee—because he had refused to testify before a U.S. Senate committee about his putative Communist associations before and during World War II. Thomas Slayton retells the story of how, two years later, the General Assembly revised the university charter to make UVM "an instrumentality of the State"—a phrase picked up from earlier documents by university counsel Louis Lisman in 1948.[10] Were these events connected? If Borgmann had supported Novikoff, instead of just trying to see that Novikoff had a fair trial and then voting to fire him, could he have achieved his goal of persuading the state to assume more financial responsibility for educating Vermont students at UVM? Some feel sure that the idea of changing the charter had not occurred to Borgmann until after the Novikoff trial ended on August 31, 1953.[11]

When Borgmann left in 1957, he was succeeded, as acting president for a year, by Lyman Rowell, who had moved from his professorship in zoology to the directorship of the summer session. Going through the new and complex selection procedure, the Trustees chose John T. Fey, a former law professor, Maryland legislator, and clerk of the U.S. Supreme Court, with the aim of giving body to the initiatives of Borgmann's administration. Instead of the persuasive, personable, warmly human Borgmann, Fey was a driving, demanding administrator who was able to get difficult decisions accepted.[12] As total enrollment climbed rapidly, infrastructure needed to be built to support it. Fey built dormitories, dining halls, and a new library; recycled Billings into a student center; added a new gymnasium; converted the old one into the Royall Tyler Theatre; and did much more.

Fey was an expansionist, adding costly Ph.D. programs as well as buildings, though he encountered faculty resistance in fields that prided themselves on undergraduate teaching. In order to teach graduate students and conduct one's own research, the postwar requirement of a Ph.D. for any rank but instructor extended the standard that had applied to almost all heads of departments since World War I. Fey fostered the development of interdisciplinary foreign area studies; whereas Vermont studies, taught by Walter H. Crockett and Leon W. Dean since the 1920s, was favored with more space in the new Bailey Library and by my appointment as local history specialist. Faculty efforts in this area were given a focus with creation of the Center for Research on Vermont in 1974. Vermont's growing ecological sensitivities were addressed by the administration of President Edward Andrews when it established the interdisciplinary Environmental Program under Carl H. Reidel in 1972. Special Collections was established in the library in 1962 under John L. Buechler, who built up the rare book collection. To try to restore some cohesion among the diverse parts of the University, Fey created the post of dean of faculty, filled by former chemistry chairman Clinton D. Cook.

As enrollment swelled after World War II, there was a problem with the Wilbur Fund because of its restriction limiting enrollment in the College of Arts and Sciences to one thousand students (plus an allowance for population growth in Vermont) on pain of losing the fund to the Library of Congress. (President Carlson had reported to the Alumni Council in June 1951 that current enrollment was 999.) To maintain compliance, those programs thought most nearly vocational were transferred to other colleges of the University. Home economics had been part of the College of Agriculture since 1916, but teacher training was not moved out of Arts and Sciences until the College of Education and Nursing was established in 1946, following the wartime stimulus for a nursing school. Likewise in 1946, mathematics, chemistry, and commerce and economics were made part of the College of Technology, along with engineering, and still, through the 1950s, arts college enrollment pressed on the Wilbur Fund ceiling. With his previous legal and governmental experience, President Fey was able to get legislation through Congress in 1960 waiving federal rights under the Wilbur bequest. Wilbur's heirs went to court to win back the family fortune, contending that the donor had intended to help a small college, but the University successfully argued that Wilbur could not have foreseen in 1929 the postwar expansion of higher education, or he would not have added the afterthought of an enrollment restriction. Five thousand students had been helped by Wilbur scholarships.[13]

Fey left UVM in 1964 to become president of the University of Wyoming (eventually returning to Vermont as head of the National Life Insurance Company). Lyman Rowell, who had assumed the post of dean of administration newly created by Fey, once again took over as acting president for a year.

Another full-dress search was undertaken to replace Fey with the kind of president many of the faculty had pined for in 1952: someone who would *stay,* appreciate teaching and research, and be approachable by students, someone like Bailey. The search settled on Shannon McCune, a competent geographer, experienced as assistant to the presidents of the Universities of Massachusetts and Illinois, who seemed to fill the bill. McCune immediately created the "troika" of three vice-presidents—Melvin Dyson, finance; Clinton Cook, academic affairs; and Lyman Rowell, administration. But the business executives among the trustees, the deans and vice presidents, and especially the medical college with its many grants and a hospital merger about to take place, were frustrated by what they saw as McCune's administrative incompetence. They told him so in April 1966, but McCune felt he had a mandate to do it his way; therefore, in August they forced his resignation and elected Rowell president, recognizing his competence as acting president in 1964–1965.[14] One has to go back a century to the choice of Pease, Torrey, and Buckham to find a board that bypassed the usual canvass of prospects.

President Rowell responded to numerous faculty suggestions. The Experimental Program, for example, was launched in Coolidge Hall in 1969 (making it the University's first coed dorm); it demonstrated in its five years' life both the values and the drawbacks of the satellite college concept and unstructured programs (see Patrick Hutton's chapter 18). However, the objectives of student self-motivation, interdisciplinary study, faculty residence with students, and small satellite living/learning groups remained and informed the Living/Learning Center established under President Edward Andrews in 1973.

Students in the past quarter-century have peacefully protested, demonstrated, occupied buildings, and otherwise shown that they are concerned and want to participate in university governance, but students, faculty, and administration have succeeded in communicating with each other during crises without police interference. The student presence in governance has slowly opened up: in 1972, for the first time, a student (Cajsa Nordstrom (a medical student and member of the class of 1970) was chosen to serve on the Board of Trustees, and in 1976 the Legislature added two specifically student seats to the Board. Since then, students have regularly been represented on all manner of advisory committees and search committees.

In 1969 student activists persuaded the University to abolish Kake Walk as racist (see James Loewen's chapter 19). President Rowell and the Trustees supported the move in spite of protests from alumni and townspeople that no offense was intended. Faced with a severe budgetary crisis, the Andrews administration that followed Rowell in 1970 abolished baseball as an intercollegiate sport after the 1971 season and football after the 1974 season, with minimal student complaint. (Baseball was reinstated in 1978.) Superior ski, soccer, and hockey teams made up for the loss of football and attracted their share of students. Athletic scholarship aid increased from $397,000 for fiscal year 1981 to $985,000 a decade later.

Neighboring Middlebury College and Dartmouth have at times threatened to close all Greek letter societies. At UVM they live a precarious, minority life in the twilight zone between campus and town. By 1990 they provided only about four hundred beds or 10 percent of those available on campus and attracted only about twelve hundred affluent members, or 15 percent of the undergraduate body. On the dark side, they epitomized partying to disorderly and dangerous excess. On the plus side, they developed leadership, polished the rough diamonds entering as freshmen by interaction within a small group detached from the thousands on campus, and performed community service projects.

By the time President Andrews left in 1975, his administration had decided to confront all of the problems created by the University's accelerating expansion—parking, housing, buildings, and campus crowding in general—by putting a cap on total enrollment. In 1980 the Trustees decided not to build any more dormitories, although the City of Burlington was already complaining about the impact of off-campus students, seeking independence or privacy, on the Burlington housing market. Students' cars cluttered parking for blocks beyond the campus. By the fall of 1989, 55 percent of the eight thousand undergraduates were living off campus, together with all of the fifteen hundred graduate and medical students and thousands of non-degree students, and this crush brought the city residential situation, in both economic and behavioral terms, to the point of crisis.

By the late twentieth century, as Patrick Hutton shows in chapter 18, the old intellectual unity of the University had been lost, despite efforts under Carlson, Rowell, and Coor to restore an imagined unity to the curriculum. The College of Arts and Sciences was "no longer the academic center around which the professional colleges revolved."[15] James Marsh's synthesis had gradually fragmented. When President Buckham attempted to fit the study of agriculture into that unity, his detractors saw only the devious siphoning of income from the land grant funds to the Classical curriculum. Each vocational addition, except medicine, was supposed to fit in the same way, and even the medical students were reminded by Professor Peter Collier in the annual convocation address in 1876 of their mission to care for the health of human beings.[16] Bertha Terrill, the founder of the Department of Home Economics, had a Classical education and had taught Classics. James Franklin Messenger and his successors Bennett Douglas and Thomas King continued the humanistic tradition in education. President Benton, for all his concern for the A. and M. side of the University, had taught history in Kansas. But as UVM's second century closed, eight thousand undergraduates and a thousand enrolled in the Graduate College, each with a personal agenda, stretched dedicated teachers thin to satisfy such diverse needs.

In considering the most recent events, it is easier to be journalistic or autobiographical than truly historical. During the Coor administration from 1976 to 1989, rigidities inevitably crept into every aspect of the institution as a result of its size, its fear of litigation, the requirements of federal grants, the polarized procedures in faculty–administration relations, and the restricted conditions under which personnel could be fired, to name the more obvious. The Coor years left UVM facing a series of crucial questions.

With a population not much over half a million and a comparatively limited tax base, could Vermont maintain quality education in the four state colleges and the University? With the resources available, could UVM both maintain its national reputation as a "public ivy" university[17] and persuade Vermonters, particularly the General Assembly, to support the state's university generously? Not without the out-of-state contingent and a fourfold increase in the public relations budget to nearly $1 million. Facing all of the uncertainties in the national and world economy, could Coor's successor, George H. Davis, avert the buzz saw of restricted income, faculty demands for salary raises, and ever-escalating costs by restoring the goodwill that a smaller, different university once had in the city and across the state? Or would he, like President Bailey before him, have to rely on the private sector? In any case, there remains great strength in the institution. The early twentieth century College on the Hill will move into the twenty-first century as the University of the Valley, making a tremendous, often intangible contribution to the quality of life in Vermont.

UVM, Carl Borgmann, and the State of Vermont

TOM SLAYTON

WHEN Carl Borgmann accepted the presidency of the University of Vermont in 1952, he assumed he was taking over a public university, pure and simple. "Believe it or not," he said in 1989, "when I arrived, I thought it *was* a state university."[1] Borgmann quickly discovered that his assumption was wrong. UVM wasn't what he thought of as a public university. But it wasn't exactly a private college either. In fact, in the 1950s, as in the 1980s, there was considerable uncertainty and debate on campus about whether the school was actually public or private. What Borgmann had won was the leadership of a very complicated legal entity.

To begin with, the school had not one charter, but three.[2] A long and complex legal history had created three corporations: the University of Vermont (1791), the Vermont Agricultural College (1864), and the merger of the two—the University of Vermont and State Agricultural College (UVM and SAC, 1865). Further, although authorities agreed that the State Agricultural College was clearly a public school, elements peculiar to private colleges had crept into the other two charters, raising questions in the minds of many as to just how public UVM actually was.

When Borgmann asked his staff shortly after he arrived on campus if it wasn't about time to start preparing the University's appropriation request for the state legislature, he was told that the state didn't give UVM an appropriation per se, only scattered grants for specific programs. He was surprised to find out that a good many people considered UVM to be essentially a private school. Even Governor Lee Emerson felt that way. "He seemed to have quite a different impression of what the status of the university was, other than what I had imagined," Borgmann said in a 1972 interview. "He took the old line, that it was strictly a private institution, whereas I had the myth of a state university strongly imbedded in me."[3]

Borgmann's "myth" stemmed from his midwestern origins. A forty-seven-year-old engineer and administrator from the high plains, Borgmann came out of an educational tradition that was considerably different from Vermont's. Born June 3, 1905, in Missouri, he had grown up in Nebraska and was steeped in the educational populism of the midwestern United States. Young, smart, and ambitious, he had paid his $25 tuition to attend the University of Colorado at Boulder and had earned his bachelor's degree in chemical engineering before going into teaching and later administration.

The assumptions out West about college were simple and straightforward. First, it was assumed that if you had the brains and wanted to go to college, you could; money would not be a problem. And second, all public and private resources were channeled to make sure the state university was the best place to go. Those were the assumptions that Borgmann brought east with him in 1952.

But eastern higher education, the new UVM president learned on arriving in Vermont, was different. In the East the high-status schools were private, exclusive, and expensive. Public schools, especially in New England, were relegated to the second rank. To get the best education for your child meant getting him or her into Harvard or Dartmouth or Middlebury or some other Ivy-League sort of college. Failing that, you could always get into a state university, although it wouldn't be as good or as prestigious.

UVM, despite its name and the facts of its founding, had not been clearly defined as a public school in more than one hundred years. How had this come about? The University had only public trustees elected by the Legislature until 1828, when the Legislature amended the charter to have new trustees chosen by the remaining members of the Board, with the proviso "This act may be repealed by any future legislature." In the view of former trustee Chester R. Eaton of Rutland, this change was one of the key elements, along with the lack of systematic state funding, giving UVM the appearance of a private school. He explained: "Sincere and dedicated leaders of the University, in the absence of needed financial support from the State, utilized the myth of the private/public dichotomy to attract substantial gifts for many worthy and necessary purposes from private benefactors."[4]

The self-perpetuating Board of Trustees of the original University of Vermont corporation was carried forward into the board of the University of Vermont and State Agricultural College corporation in 1865, while the provisions of the Morrill Act gave the agriculture college a clearly public character. This duality accentuated the private/public concept on which subsequent university administrators relied for securing financial support. President Buckham tried unsuccessfully to push the balance in the public direction; a *Cynic* editorial in November 1888 reported:

An appeal has been made to the present Legislature for that material support which was pledged many years ago; and humble as the petition is, if granted, the University may look forward to a renewed and more energetic existence. . . . For nearly a hundred years the "University of Vermont" has been a State institution, but in name only. Now it is proposed to make the college something more than a nominal State institution. Other States have persevered in the plan initiated in Vermont. . . . Why should Vermont bring up the rear in these great living issues?[5]

The first state-funded building on the UVM campus was Morrill Hall, built in 1907 for the agriculture college. In many other ways, UVM by this time behaved much like any other public university. It admitted all qualified Vermont residents before considering out-of-state applications, and it received state funds to allow some—notably prospective teachers and medical students—to pay lower tuition fees. It offered a variety of short courses for business and industry and maintained a high level of instructional quality, as required by the Morrill Act.

When Guy Bailey became president of the University in 1919, he tried first to address the problem of state financial support that had frustrated his predecessors. Then, in Chester Eaton's words, "President Bailey chose to utilize the private/public myth and thereby secure substantial contributions payable to the original University of Vermont corporation that enabled many worthy students in all branches of the University to complete their educations and provided the University with needed physical plant as well."[6]

Many associated with the school during the Borgmann years recall the fervor with which the question of UVM's legal status was debated on campus and in the community at large. Richard Hopwood, head of public relations for the University at the time and a former professor of English, recalled, "There were as many legal opinions as there were lawyers in town."[7] Emeritus professor of English Betty Bandel still feels strongly that UVM could have called itself a public school any time it wanted to: "In my opinion, when UVM was founded by the State of Vermont, it fulfilled two of the three legal requirements of any public university. It was open to any resident of the state who was eligible, and it was chartered by the state, as the state university."[8] The third requirement she referred to, that the state actually run the university in question, has often been bypassed by other schools in the interest of educational autonomy and academic freedom.

Nevertheless, in many minds the legal status of the UVM and SAC remained unclear on the day that Dr. Borgmann arrived in Vermont. UVM's governing board still had equal numbers of self-perpetuating and legislature-elected trustees, and the school received only scattered and largely inconsequential state funding. Vermont resident students studying in the Colleges of Arts and Sciences and Engineering paid the same tuition rate ($625) as out-of-state students, the highest in-state tuition then charged by any state university in the United States (as Borgmann noted repeatedly).

A chart, possibly prepared by Dr. Borgmann himself as part of his campaign for UVM charter revisions, shows that in 1950 UVM received a total of $486,519 in state funds, of which the largest single sum ($175,000) went to the medical college. An even larger total, approximately $257,000, went to various programs within the agriculture college, including the Extension Service ($100,000) and the agricultural experiment station ($52,815). By contrast, teacher training scholarships totaled only $33,000.[9] Although the scholarships and grants for medicine, agriculture, and teacher training were renewed from year to year, they were unpredictable. There was no such thing as a state appropriation for the university as a whole. Even more surprising for the new president was the fact that most UVM administrators seemed quite satisfied with the situation.

But Borgmann didn't get discouraged, and he didn't accept the status quo. Immediately and instinctively, he felt that UVM should be the state university, that it should be the best school in Vermont—or at least the best school it could be made to be—and that it should provide top-quality higher education for all Vermont young people at a reasonable, affordable price. That meant, in effect, that the state legislature would have to be persuaded to support the University on a much broader basis than it had ever done before. And that undoubtedly meant that UVM would have to give up some of its governing autonomy, and state-named trustees would have to have a clear majority on the board. Nevertheless, Borgmann took his vision whole. He was willing to reshape UVM, if necessary, to make it a truly public state university. "I thought from the beginning that the State ought to support it," he said. "I told the Trustees, 'We've got to get on the ball and be one or the other [public or private]. We can't play both ends against the middle.' "

For many years, of course, UVM had received some public and some private financing. That was what Borgmann was referring to with his "both ends against the middle" comment. The University had stressed its public nature when seeking state money from the Vermont Legislature for the medical college and the College of Agriculture and had stressed its quasi-private nature (and the extra dollop of perceived status that conferred) when approaching potential private-sector benefactors. "Inevitably," recalled Professor Hopwood, "there were times when, if we were seeking public money, the public institution would emerge. And if the institution were interested in money from Rockefeller (or some other private source), we would become *very* private."[10] It was that tradition Borgmann sought straightforwardly to replace by making UVM a bona fide state university.

By the time Borgmann arrived, UVM's finances had largely recovered from the crisis left at his death by President Bailey, thanks in part to an emergency state appropriation. Still, there was never an ongoing, overarching state appropriation, and the University's fiscal health was not robust. Faculty salaries were still relatively low, and student tuition fees were still relatively high. Broad state funding could alleviate both problems and secure forever what Borgmann saw as UVM's proper relationship with the State of Vermont—its role as a fully public state university.

What was predominant in his thinking, Borgmann was asked in 1989—

was his primary aim to get the additional money he needed from the State of Vermont to help lower tuition and pay higher faculty salaries, or was he mainly seeking to make UVM legally and clearly a state university? "They went together," he replied, as twin aspects of his single goal. Underlying the money question was the larger issue of what sort of school UVM was to be. Borgmann, as an educational populist from the Midwest, did not want it to slip further into the private school mode that was (and is) fashionable in New England, becoming another Middlebury or Dartmouth, another exclusive school for the wealthy with an enrollment of perhaps 10 or 12 percent Vermonters.

Borgmann wanted something quite different. In one of the dozens of speeches he made in his remarkable campaign for that something different, he described his vision clearly: "Should the youth of Vermont have the same chance for a college education as any other young person in America? There can be only one answer," he declared. "Yes, of course, young Vermonters deserve the same opportunity. The people of every other state provide at least one university of high academic standing which their children can attend at low tuition rates. The people of Vermont can and should do the same." [11]

Fueling Borgmann's concern was the fact that whereas in the nation as a whole, 33 of every 100 high school students went on to college, only 22 of every 100 Vermont graduates did so, and a dismaying 60 percent of the top quarter of Vermont high school students ended their education forever after leaving high school. He felt that the reason for the low aspiration rate of Vermont students was a lack of educational opportunity, and he repeatedly said that UVM's high tuition was keeping Vermont students away. "All major courses of study should be equally available at the university to all qualified boys and girls," Borgmann wrote in a memo. "Appropriations for this cause can truly be regarded as investments in the future of the people of Vermont." [12]

Borgmann launched his campaign for state support in earnest in the summer of 1954 (after the storm over the ex-Communist biochemistry professor Alex Novikoff had ended with Borgmann acceding to Novikoff's dismissal). With the biennial election coming up in November, Borgmann set himself the task of meeting and talking over his plans with as many prospective members of the 1955 Legislature as he could contact. He met with them in their kitchens, over coffee, and at public meetings. He later met with them at the State House in Montpelier. "I worked like hell," he recalled thirty years after that summer and fall. "I drank an awful lot of coffee." At the same time, and right up until the opening of the 1955 Legislature in January, he made the rounds of the rubber-chicken circuit, speaking to Rotary clubs, service clubs, local groups of educators, and just plain citizens. Any group that would listen got a visit from the UVM president and a heartfelt introduction to the virtues of having a bona fide state university that would provide good, low-cost college education for all Vermont students.

By that time Borgmann was backing a specific proposal, one that had been drafted by attorney Fred Smith, a young Burlington lawyer and former House member retained by the University. Although it was complex, at its heart the bill offered a simple trade-off: more state-appointed trustees on the UVM board in exchange for an appropriation. However, nothing about the University's governing structure was, or is, simple. As noted earlier, UVM at that time comprised three chartered corporations: the University of Vermont, the Vermont Agricultural College and the University of Vermont and State Agricultural College. The bill drafted by Smith did not change the legal status of any of them, but by adding three governor-appointed trustees to the board that ran the show—the Board of UVM and SAC—it changed the way the University was governed, giving control to the Board's state-selected members by a 12–9 majority.

Smith said that the corporate structure of UVM had to remain essentially unchanged, in legal terms, for the school to protect several of its endowments and scholarship funds, especially the Wilbur Fund, for years the major source of UVM scholarships for Vermont students. Along with his legislative supporters he argued that by leaving the University's corporate status unchanged, yet giving the governmentally named trustees majority control of its affairs, the bill in fact made UVM an instrumentality of the state and therefore a bona fide state institution. "We are adapting what we already have to our present needs," Smith explained.[13]

This solution was a compromise between a completely public school, run by the state, and the organizationally scrambled institution UVM had long been. The bill was long and involved, but it was presented and understood in the Legislature as the reasonable trade-off described above—three governor-appointed trustees, confirming public domination of the UVM Board in exchange for the right to a continuing appropriation from the state. And that was the way the UVM president presented it to legislators. He visited every senator and about half of the 246 members of the prereapportionment House of Representatives. "You can't accuse me of lobbying," he said in 1989. "I didn't ask for a single vote. I just said that I wanted to supply them with some facts and let them make up their minds on this business. That was my line from the beginning, and it was an honest line."

The Burlington *Free Press* praised Borgmann's arduous campaign in behalf of the bill: "President Carl W. Borgmann of the University of Vermont is giving a tremendous amount of time and energy to the job of telling Vermonters about the requirements of the university, if it is to do the job in this state that he and the members of the Board of Trustees feel it should do."[14] The paper stressed a couple of Borgmann's arguing points: that UVM was at the time the only state university that didn't give all resident students a tuition break, with the results that fewer Vermont high school graduates went on to college than in most other states and that the percentage of Vermont students at UVM was declining. "Vermonters should thank President Borgmann for making these facts and others clear in his pilgrimage to various parts of the state."

Borgmann's campaign not only won over the *Free Press* editorial writer; as events were later to prove, he had made similar progress with the Legislature itself. Borgmann was not a brilliant orator, according to those who remember him from the mid-1950s, but most agree that he was a convincing person, one whose intelligence, friendliness, and integrity made him very believable. Professor Bandel remembers him as the most outstanding president of UVM that she has known. Above all, it was Borgmann's straightforward approach that won people over. They felt they could trust him, Professor Hopwood recalls.

However, Borgmann's direct manner did result in one face-off before the Legislature opened. At a social gathering at a UVM trustee's house, Borgmann had been outlining his plans for the upcoming 1955 session when George Ellis of Old Bennington confronted him on the issue. As Borgmann tells it, Ellis was a wealthy man (he was a former New York City stockbroker, instrumental in the 1941 bailout of the University) who felt that UVM should never become a public school, and he told Borgmann so. "He came up to me and said, 'If you go ahead on this, I'll fight you in the Legislature, and I'll knock you down,'" Borgmann recalled. "He sure was determined it wasn't going to happen."

Borgmann believes that Ellis went on to organize and possibly finance the only serious opposition to the UVM bill in the 1955 Legislature. No one in 1989 remembered for certain what the Bennington man's motivation might have been, but Borgmann felt it was based on snobbery—the fact that New England's public schools were held in lower public esteem than private ones. In his own way, Ellis may have been trying to protect UVM's reputation from the changes brought to it by an upstart midwestern populist. Whatever the reasoning behind it, a counteroffensive against Borgmann's campaign was mounted in mid-January, after the Legislature had convened, by an organization calling itself Research and TV Education Inc. A former attorney general, F. Elliott Barber, Jr., was the spokesman and lobbyist for the group.[15]

Barber announced his group's opposition with a formal statement to the press on January 25, when the bill was being studied by the House Education Committee. He fought the measure unrelentingly for the rest of the session. And although he and his group eventually lost, they made the going rough for Borgmann and the University. The final lopsided votes in favor of the charter change do not indicate the difficulty of the fight, according to those who were there at the time. "It wasn't an easy victory, by any means," Hopwood remembered. "We had to stay right on top of things all the way through."

The arguments of Borgmann, Smith, Leon Latham, and others representing the University centered on two basic points: first, that to end the historic confusion over its legal nature, the University should be clearly defined as a state school and should get a state appropriation; and second, that the University had a responsibility to provide good, affordable education to all eligible Vermonters. Just as he had made those two points to individual legislators the previous autumn, Borgmann made them again to the committees and public hearings of the sitting legislature. And he backed them up with disturbing facts about the low aspiration rate of Vermont students.

Barber, in opposition, argued that the UVM bill was not aimed at "clarification" but would bring about substantive change in UVM's legal status, jeopardizing its present endowments and crippling its ability to find private endowments in the future. Further, the opponents argued, the change would make UVM a favored institution and put private colleges such as Middlebury, Norwich, and St. Michael's at a significant disadvantage. And, Barber went on, the State of Vermont did not have enough funds to increase its support of UVM substantially and also continue to offer financial assistance to public elementary and secondary schools.

There was a few days' sparring in the halls of the State House and in the House Education Committee, prior to a public hearing in the House of Representatives the evening of January 27, 1955. That hearing marked the crucial moment in the legislative history of the charter change, Borgmann recalled. He confronted Barber at the hearing, attacking his arguments and pointing up inconsistencies and inaccuracies. "It was important in knocking Barber out of any possible influence he might have had with the legislature."

The clerk's notes of that 2½-hour hearing and contemporary newspaper accounts suggest how dramatic the confrontation between Borgmann and Barber was.[16] More than two hundred people were in attendance, listening as Barber charged that the charter changes were designed to make UVM a "favored institution" in Vermont, one that would attract students away from the state's private colleges. But Borgmann countered: "We are not going after boys who go to Middlebury, Norwich, or St. Michael's—we are going after the boys who go nowhere at the present time."[17] Spectators cheered that. Barber had outlined a plan the day before to make UVM a private school by shearing away those colleges that were then getting public money—the agriculture college and the medical school—and setting up an impartial state board to grant scholarships to deserving Vermonters.

Borgmann challenged the idea: "In separating the colleges of Agriculture and Medicine from the University of Vermont, what would you do with elementary and junior high education?" (Young people studying at UVM to teach in Vermont public schools already got state assistance.) Barber's response—that he would make education training part of the College of Medicine—must have sounded as lame in 1955 as it does today.

Borgmann followed up his opening quickly, asking Barber what he would do about endowment funds, which were, at the time, being prorated equally to all colleges. Would they be allotted only to the private university that Barber had proposed, thus requiring greater state support for medicine and agriculture? And what about UVM's real estate and buildings? Which school would assume ownership of them? "Barber had no answer for these questions," the committee record notes laconically. Borgmann's cross-examination of Barber was the high point of that decisive hearing. Even with the backlog of support and goodwill that his autumn visits with the legislators had built up, the issue could have gone down to defeat had he allowed Barber to muddy the waters with an alternative proposal. His counterattack at the hearing made it obvious that he, not Barber, was in control of the facts and the issue. Shortly afterward the House Education Committee voted 12–1 to recommend passage of the bill, and less than two weeks after the hearing, on February 9, the full House, after two hours of debate, voted 200 to 24 to approve the measure.

Although the question of money—a state appropriation and tuition fees for Vermonters—had not been directly addressed as the charter bill passed the House, newspapers of the day make it clear that it was understood that once UVM was under state control, state dollars to help reduce Vermonters' tuition would not be far behind. An editorial in the Bennington *Banner* just after the House vote noted that the margin of victory was more than 10 to 1, and said that Senate passage of the bill appeared virtually assured because of the large majority gained by the bill in the House. "Vermonters, however, should now brace themselves and adopt the proper attitude as far as taxes and financial support of the university is concerned. If we are willing to accept control of the institution, we must be as fully prepared to assume its finances." [18]

On March 8, three days shy of a month after it had been passed by the House, the charter bill won strong preliminary approval in the Senate, 28–0, after five proposals of amendment were defeated. Final passage came on March 9, and the bill was then signed into law by the newly elected governor, Joseph Johnson. [19] As far as everyone at the time was concerned, passage of the bill established UVM as the state university. There remained the question of precisely how much state support UVM would receive in return for becoming an instrumentality of the state. Dr. Borgmann and his supporters proposed an appropriation of $478,000 to reduce in-state tuition in all colleges to $225 per year. But Governor Johnson recommended that the state appropriate only $220,000, which would have resulted in a tuition of $425 per year in the College of Arts and Sciences and $225 in the College of Agriculture (which got federal money under the Morrill Act) and for Vermont students enrolled in a preteaching curriculum. [20] Finally, late in the session, the Legislature split the difference by appropriating enough to set College of Arts and Sciences tuition at $345 per year (a familiar way of compromise).

All in all, Borgmann had won a major victory. He had won a university-wide appropriation for UVM, he had cut tuition for most Vermont students nearly in half, and he had also established the principle de facto that the rate of in-state tuition was directly related to the size of the appropriation provided by the State of Vermont.

More important to Borgmann and his supporters, however, was their feeling that passage of the bill established once and for all that UVM is a public school. Despite their many differences, that was the one point that Borgmann and his rival Barber agreed on. Barber, in arguing against passage of the legislation, said the bill would make UVM forever "a public charge"; and although Dr. Borgmann phrased the matter quite differently, he repeatedly declared during his legislative campaign and afterward that his intent was to make the legal status of UVM as a state university clear for all time. As he told legislators during the debate on the bill, his proposals "represent a bona fide offer by the trustees to define—once and for all—the University of Vermont and State Agricultural College as the university of the State of Vermont."[21] And forty years later, asked about his intent in promoting the bill that made UVM a state instrumentality, Borgmann said emphatically, "I wanted to be perfectly clear [with legislators] that if they took that action, that this was it—that the University of Vermont was a state university, once and for all."

However, things have not remained that clear. Despite Borgmann's hopes for UVM, the ambiguity has arisen again. In fact, since Borgmann's presidency UVM's status as a public institution has been clouded by the actions of the University itself, which in more recent years, for a variety of reasons, has not wanted to be defined clearly and unequivocally as a public institution. The University's long-standing tendency (detested by Borgmann) to be public in some instances and quasi-private in others has resurfaced and appears likely to continue in the future.

The first legal ruling on UVM's status came in 1959. A lending company had raised this question because of a state law that said no private corporation organized for educational, literary, scientific, charitable, or religious purposes could hold more than $10 million worth of property. Attorney General Fred Reed ruled that the law applied to private corporations only and that he was "satisfied beyond any doubt" that UVM was a public corporation. Therefore, the law didn't apply, and UVM, which held more than the maximum allowable $10 million worth of property, did not need to be bound by it. Referring to the 1955 charter changes, Reed said that the Legislature had done much more than simply adopt the words "instrumentality of the state." "The state has assumed some financial responsibility for the maintenance of the corporation," he wrote in his opinion. "Even more important, in our view, is the element of control." He pointed out that the 1955 act gave the State of Vermont "a clear majority on the board of trustees," as well as transferring all property of the University to the corporation known as the University of Vermont and State Agricultural College. The legislature had asserted its control of the University in 1955 by setting maximum tuition rates for Vermont students (40% of the out-of-state rate) and by other actions, Reed argued.[22]

But in the years since then, the public/private issue has seemed far from settled. The University itself and its faculty have on more than one occasion argued both sides of that question. The clear-cut answer—and the educational mission—that Borgmann sought have become obscured in more complicated times. Among the first to reject a call to a more public mission for the University were some members of UVM's faculty. In 1962, Philip H. Hoff, an articulate Burlington lawyer with a strong interest in public education, was elected Vermont's first Democratic governor in modern times. He quickly let the University know that he wanted to establish much closer links between the State of Vermont and UVM. "I wanted to reorganize the University–state relationship along the lines of the midwestern model," Hoff said in an interview in 1990.[23] "Under that system there's much more cooperation between state government and the state university. There's a free flow back and forth of information and personnel."

Hoff wanted UVM to become a research institution for state government. He was convinced that Vermont's leaders were making many decisions without enough accurate information, and he wanted the University to help supply more of that information. He talked with Lyman Rowell, who was then president, and he recalls that Rowell liked the idea. "But it was an idea that died in the process of being born," Hoff said, "because the faculty, led by Lyman Gould, fought it. They never did buy into it."

History professor emeritus Robert V. Daniels, who saw both sides of the UVM–state relationship as a university faculty member and as a state senator from Chittenden County, said that intrafaculty politics may have led Professor Gould into opposing the Hoff idea because Hoff had worked closely with Professor Rolf Haugen, with whom Gould had clashed. Also, Daniels said much of the UVM faculty opposition to the Hoff idea then and since may have come from professors who feared that their research on state projects wouldn't make national scholarly journals and therefore would not help them secure tenure or promotions.[24]

Hoff's conversations in later years with President Lattie Coor persuaded him that his idea would never be accepted by the University, so he dropped it. Like others, Hoff is clearly irritated by the University's propensity to call itself public at some times and private at others, depending on what suits its purposes of the moment. "That's the dilemma of UVM," he said. "It's a state university when it wants money from the Legislature and a private institution when it comes to undertaking activities for the State of Vermont." He said that under Coor the University used private fund raising to expand into many new program areas, then expected the state to pick up the tab for continuing those programs. "We'd just get handed the bill," said Hoff, who spent several years as a state senator some years after he was governor. "It was like a kid buying a new car on time, and expecting his father to pick up the payments. The State had no voice in it [UVM's program expansion] at all."

Professor Daniels believes that the university administration began playing serious games with the state appropriation in the early 1960s when then-president John T. Fey merged the medical college appropriation with the total UVM appropriation, leaving no specific line item that showed precisely how much state money the medical college was receiving. "There's a lot of talk about the inadequacy of the [state] appropriation," Daniels said in an interview in early 1990. "But it's the cost of the medical school that makes the appropriation inadequate." His view is that by masking how much state money goes to the medical school, UVM is able to keep its prestigious medical college well-heeled and then "teaches all the arts and sciences on the cheap."

Several UVM and state officials disagree with that assessment. Former medical college dean George Wolf, who for years was the person making the UVM medical school's pitch in Montpelier, said that President Fey made the change because it was "better administrative practice." "None of the other colleges made a separate presentation to the legislature," he explained. It was felt that it wasn't needed for the medical college either.[25]

Former governor Hoff said that even with a separate line item in the budget for the medical college, no significant change would occur in the relationship between UVM and the State of Vermont. He noted that UVM's direction and goals—its mission, for want of a more precise term—tend to change as its presidents change. Borgmann and Coor were very different men with different ideals. "Their visions were quite different, and they led to quite different results." Rather than changing under different leaders, Hoff said the University should achieve a clear definition of its purpose and stick by it. What needs to be done, according to the former governor, is for state officials to determine the proper role of UVM and to ensure that UVM then fulfills that role. "No one has ever asked what kind of university does the State of Vermont want," Hoff said. "We ought to have an overall cohesive plan for higher education in this state, and the University ought to act within the scope of that plan."

Needless to say, neither Reed's 1959 opinion nor Hoff's failed attempt to give UVM a role in state government was the last word on the volatile public–private question. As recently as a 1987 discrimination case, to avoid having to open sensitive records, UVM's lawyers claimed that the state open-meeting law did not apply to the University, on the ground that "UVM is not a public agency subject to [the law in question]." "UVM is neither a branch or authority nor a political subdivision of the state," they argued in court documents. Nevertheless, U.S. District Judge Franklin S. Billings ruled that both the provisions of the open meetings law and the public nature of the University required that it abide by the statute.[26]

Even so, the University has continued to insist regularly that it really isn't as public as its regular state appropriations and the membership of the Board of Trustees would indicate. In 1988, when a bill to extend the State Labor Relations Act to UVM threatened to abet a faculty union organizing drive under way at the time, the university administration argued vigorously though unsuccessfully against the public status for which Borgmann had struggled so hard. Failing in the Legislature, the administration turned to the National Labor Relations Board (NLRB) to argue again that UVM should be judged private, in hopes that the NLRB would apply the 1980 "Yeshiva Decision" of the Supreme Court, holding faculty members at private colleges to be managerial personnel ineligible to organize a union. However, the NLRB agreed with the arguments of the state and faculty members who wanted to be able to form a union and ruled that UVM is an instrumentality of the State of Vermont: "We find the university was created directly by the state, so as to constitute a department or administrative arm of government, and that the university is administered by individuals who are responsible to public officials or the general electorate."[27] The decision was hailed by faculty union organizers, who questioned the state university's growing reluctance to describe itself as public. When the U.S. District Court subsequently upheld the NLRB decision as well as the 1988 legislative action, philosophy professor Will Miller said, "It's a major victory for the employees of the University and it's a major victory for Vermonters because this holds back the drift toward privatization at UVM."[28]

As UVM's political battles continued through 1989 and 1990, the public/private issue was debated several times in newspaper articles as well as in court hearings. There were rumors on campus that UVM's administration was planning to seek a charter amendment that would place the school clearly in the private sector, and one member of the school's administration, reminded that Dr. Borgmann had amended the charter to make the school a public institution in 1955, responded: "Yes, but they're sorry now that he did it."[29] In a January 1989 editorial entitled "UVM—Fish or Fowl?", the Rutland Herald took note of the continuing uncertainty over the school's legal status: "The answer to the basic question is that UVM is neither a private nor a state institution, but at different times, it may be represented as both. When the university's convenience has been studied, it has been represented as private, while at other times for different reasons it has been called a state university."[30] Should the University's legal status, then, be clearly defined once and for all? The Herald editorial writer thought not because legal flexibility on that point might make it easier for the University to survive and prosper: "As for the question of whether UVM is an arm of the state or a private institution, it's better for it to continue as quasi-state and quasi-private, or half fish and half fowl."

Nevertheless, in gaining legal flexibility, the University has had to sacrifice the clear-cut sense of educational mission that was central to Carl Borgmann's 1955 campaign for public school status. That vision is blurred today. Rather than arguing, as Borgmann did, for a lower tuition to attract more Vermont students, the administration in the 1989 session of the Legislature blamed its budget deficit on an unexpectedly large influx of Vermont students in the face of a set appropriation. More Vermont students mean less tuition income, said then-president Lattie Coor and others. Thus, Borgmann's logic was reversed. Vermont students were not seen as an educational opportunity but as the cause of a budget deficit.

Necessity is partly to blame for this apparent shift in vision. The state has consistently underfunded the school because Vermont is a small and relatively poor state without bottomless coffers of tax revenue. The creation in 1965 of the Vermont Student Assistance Corporation (VSAC) also helped obscure Borgmann's vision. The scholarship funds provided by the State of Vermont through VSAC can go to virtually any accredited school, public or private, that Vermont students choose to apply to. In fact, VSAC exactly fulfills one of the proposals made by Elliot Barber and opposed by Borgmann during the 1955 session: a state agency providing scholarships to many colleges, not just UVM.

Meanwhile, the Vermont State Colleges, small normal schools when Borgmann was in charge at UVM, have developed into full-campus colleges with widely ranging interests. Like VSAC, they annually demand millions of dollars of state funds to operate. Former governor Hoff and others believe that the state colleges are more warmly viewed than UVM in the Vermont Legislature because they have taken over the mission that Borgmann wanted UVM to have: basic responsibility for entry-level higher education for Vermont youngsters. In the early 1960s, Hoff recalls, UVM "could do no wrong" in the Legislature. But by the late 1980s UVM was engaged in a running battle with leading legislators over many of its policies. "Meanwhile, the state colleges have become the vehicle that has served what I call the common Vermonter," Hoff went on. "They do a good job of it, and the Legislature has a deep attachment to those schools because they can see what they're doing for our kids."[31]

In the late 1980s and into 1990, the Legislature's sparring with UVM grew increasingly intense. House Appropriations Committee chairman Michael Obuchowski, a Rockingham Democrat, precipitated a face-off in 1989 by demanding answers to a series of aggressively phrased questions showing clear distrust of the University. For example, Obuchowski wrote, "Excessive Administrative Salaries: . . . It is clear that the salaries of administrative personnel are excessively high. There is no acceptable rationale or excuse for this circumstance." A later "question" continued: "Low faculty salaries: Lack of competitive salaries paid to UVM faculty threatens to undermine the quality of education at the university. Please develop a blueprint for the re-distribution of existing resources such that faculty salaries may be more closely aligned with salaries in our sister New England states."[32] A legislative commission that studied UVM later that year announced findings that, not surprisingly, seemed to confirm Representative Obuchowski's charges, but the Board of Trustees, led by Chairman Jack Candon, a former House member, vigorously denied the allegations, and public sentiment seemed to shift slightly back in favor of the University.[33]

Regardless of who "won" that particular round, that dispute and other battles between UVM and the Legislature were a clear indication that times had changed drastically from the days when Carl Borgmann and his trustees convinced legislators to radically increase state support of the University. Vermont is a state with strong egalitarian traditions, and the University's effort in the 1980s to seek national academic status as one of the "Public Ivies" may have contributed to the increasingly difficult relations between the school and the state. As UVM promoted itself as a quasi–Ivy League college and attracted larger numbers of higher-paying out-of-state students because of that image, and as the state colleges took on more of the role of purveying higher education to the Vermont masses, did legislative distrust of the University increase? It appeared so, especially in the wake of the public uproar that followed the disclosure in 1989 that UVM admissions policy made special allowance in recruiting wealthy out-of-state students.

A column in the Burlington *Free Press* in 1989, by a university professor disgusted with his school's policies, gives some of the flavor of the public discourse at that time. "Now we discover that the university had a policy [in admissions] not only favorable to out-of-staters but to rich ones," wrote political scientist Garrison Nelson. "I am afraid that our elected state Legislature, which contributed to the problem [by underfunding UVM] will use this latest revelation to deprive the university once again of needed money. . . . A plague on both your houses," he concluded. "Justin Morrill's heirs may want his good name back from the UVM building it graces. And I, for one, would not blame them."[34]

Given Vermont's complex higher educational structure and the increasingly complicated battles, legal and otherwise, that UVM has had to fight, it is not surprising that UVM's share of the state's total budget has shrunk since 1955, even though the absolute amount of the University's appropriation has risen substantially with inflation. The $1.6 million that UVM received from the state in fiscal 1956 amounted to 7.7 percent of the state budget that year. The figure grew until, in 1964, some 10.9 percent of the total state budget went to UVM. But by fiscal year 1989 UVM's percentage (measured against a greatly expanded base of state responsibilities) had dropped to only 4.7 percent of the total.

How much of UVM's total budget does the State of Vermont now appropriate? That contribution is also falling as a percentage of the total university budget. In fiscal 1956 the state gave UVM 28.3 percent of its budget. In fiscal 1958 almost exactly one third of UVM's budget came from the state, the largest that share ever got; it has steadily declined since then. With the broadening of the University's base, including grant-funded research and a larger proportion of out-of-state students paying full tuition, the state's 1989–1990 appropriation of $28.6 million represented only 12.8 percent of the total UVM budget of $224 million that year.[35]

What all of these figures mean is stated in the *Chronicle of Higher Education*: Out of all fifty states in 1990, Vermont was forty-ninth in its per capita support for all higher education (including VSAC scholarships). When the figures are adjusted by measuring the state's contribution to higher education against per capita personal income, Vermont still comes out only forty-fifth in the United States.[36] Those figures tell why UVM is losing the promise that Borgmann saw for it. According to Dean Wolf, "Borgmann wanted to apply midwestern ideas to the University. The only thing that went wrong was that they [the Legislature] didn't fund it adequately." As UVM turned to emphasize its private school aspects, Carl Borgmann's attractive vision of a single, top-quality state university, open to all qualified Vermonters at a reasonable price was obscured, if not lost. Chester Eaton sees recent events as "an unfortunate replay of factors, including inadequate state funding, that had created the financial and philosophical confusion concerning UVM facing President Borgmann when he arrived in Vermont."[36]

What, then, is Borgmann's legacy to the State of Vermont and its university? The increased state funding Borgmann won for UVM and the later proceeds of state building bonds helped the school with its remarkable academic and physical plant expansion in the 1960s and 1970s. There are thousands of Vermont students, graduates of UVM today, who would not have been able to attend the school had tuition not been halved for them in 1956. Borgmann himself believes that if he had not won his case in the 1955 Legislature UVM could have remained solvent only by taking the private road, with a largely non-Vermont clientele and the higher tuition rates these students paid.

So the State of Vermont has Carl Borgmann to thank that UVM is as public as it is. Even though his vision of a true state university, open at reasonable rates of tuition to all Vermonters, has been receding, UVM is a more open school today because at a critical point in its history Carl Borgmann was its president. "We thought we had a damn good school," he said in 1989. "We felt with a state appropriation and public status, it could only become better. That gave me the determination to make the fight."

Academic Freedom and the Novikoff Affair

DAVID R. HOLMES

From the time of the visionary Ira Allen, who helped bring the state of Vermont and its university into being, Vermont has been known as a land of political independence and as a sanctuary for those who march to a different drummer. An unwritten theme in Vermont tradition, according to Dorothy Canfield Fisher, is "the unquestioned right of anyone to practice variations—harmless to others—from the way of life generally accepted by the majority of his neighbors."[1] What Vermonters have believed about personal freedom has shaped the ethos of the state and of the University of Vermont as well.

Vermont's self-perpetuated reputation for tolerance has not always been matched by practice. Three episodes at UVM in this century, involving controversial political activities by members of the faculty, raise troubling questions about how Vermonters respond when political emotions are heated and individuals have staked out unpopular ground. The Appelmann case of 1917, the Novikoff case of 1953, and the Parenti case of 1971 all raised delicate questions about the meaning of academic freedom and the uncertain line between acceptable political expression and behavior deemed incompatible with appointment as a university faculty member. This chapter will focus on the Novikoff affair. It is instructive, however, to set the scene for this story by reviewing the concept of academic freedom and the circumstances that brought Professors Appelmann and Parenti their troubles with the UVM board of trustees.

Political Dissent and Academic Freedom

Since the birth of the first American college at Harvard in 1636, there have been arguments and controversies about the appropriate place of higher learning in American society. The American habit of balancing powers among contending parties was captured in the design of our colleges, where external lay boards of trustees assumed broad policymaking authority (especially, in hiring the president and in establishing overall budget parameters), while on-campus administrators and faculty were granted primary responsibility for curriculum, academic policy, campus life, and faculty personnel decisions. This division of responsibility has sometimes lapsed, however, when outside pressures have prompted trustees to assert their legally established authority over internal college matters.

Reacting to such intrusions by trustees into academic matters, faculty have argued for preserving the concept of academic freedom and the idea that the college or university must be protected from passing political pressures or willful administrative fiat. To support these principles, the American Association of University Professors (AAUP) came into being in 1915 at the urging of John Dewey and other leading professors at America's elite universities.[2] The concept of academic freedom, an inheritance from the German university, was shaped and codified by the AAUP over the next quarter-century in response to cases of professors under fire from university administrations. The AAUP expanded on the German conceptions of *Lernfreiheit* and *Lehrfreiheit* (the absence of administrative coercion in the classroom; the freedom to inquire and teach) by identifying two professional expectations of college faculty: in their teaching, faculty should remain neutral on controversial issues, and in the public arena they should not speak out as professionals on issues outside their areas of professional competence. It was understood, however, that faculty in their *civic* roles held the same constitutional privileges of free speech as any other citizen.

Interpretation of these principles has produced disagreement and heated controversy. The thorniest problems have arisen when faculty have acted in the political arena in ways that offend segments of the population, especially newspaper editorial writers, politicians, and trustees of universities. Although the AAUP principles of "acceptable academic practice" (codified in the AAUP statement of 1940 on academic freedom and tenure) have been recognized by almost every institution of solid reputation, faculty have been pressured to drop political activities, and many have been fired. Safeguards such as carefully defined procedures of due process and tenured appointments are commonplace in American colleges and universities, yet willful presidents and trustees have acted, often successfully, to override these standards.

The intersection of political activity and academic rules presents difficult decisions about the meaning and limits of academic freedom. To what extent will a university tolerate dissent aimed at the prevailing political regime or against the university itself? Should offenses against the body politic (e.g., a conviction for civil disobedience, refusal to answer the questions of a congressional committee) be deemed offenses punishable by the university? Specifically, what kinds of off-campus activities are inconsistent with reasonable expectations of faculty behavior? UVM has not been immune to situations and dilemmas of this kind.

The Appelmann and Parenti Cases

In 1916, as the United States plunged toward a declaration of war against Germany, UVM took up the case of A. H. Appelmann, a professor of Germanic languages and literature, who was known to be sympathetic to the cause of Germany and rumored to be a spy. As T. D. Seymour Bassett notes in his discussion of President Guy Benton, the Trustees exonerated Appelmann and, under Benton's pressure, retracted their initial acceptance of his resignation. Nevertheless, UVM alumni and segments of the Burlington community kept up a stream of criticism about Appelmann's German sympathies, and in the fall of 1917 he resigned again to return to Germany, leaving UVM for good.[3]

Following a stint as a visiting associate professor at the University of Illinois, Michael J. Parenti joined the UVM Department of Political Science in September 1970. To the surprise and consternation of many Vermonters, Parenti brought from Illinois a history of political and legal controversy. After the killing of four students at Kent State University in May 1970, he participated in sit-ins, made speeches to campus dissidents, and was arrested during a bloody confrontation with Illinois state troopers.[4] He was indicted by a grand jury in June 1970 on a variety of charges, including aggravated battery of a state trooper. During his first months in Vermont, Parenti's troubles with the law in Illinois came to the attention of Vermont newspapers, Vermonters who penned letters of distress to editors, and the UVM Board of Trustees. After he was found guilty by the Illinois courts in October, several members of the Board moved to suspend him from the faculty. When the full Board refused to act against him at its December 1970 meeting, Trustee John Beckley resigned in protest.

In accordance with university bylaws, the Board had the statutory responsibility to approve personnel actions, including the renewal of faculty contracts. Growing public criticism of the hiring of Parenti, exacerbated when he engaged in an angry argument in the Billings Center with an undergraduate, an ex-Marine, prompted the Trustees to reject (by a 15–4 vote) the renewal of his appointment even though it had been endorsed by the dean of Arts and Sciences and by President Andrews.[5] At the conclusion of his duties in May 1972, Parenti left the University.

Coming at times of overseas military conflict and heightened patriotic consciousness, the actions of both Appelmann and Parenti were deemed unacceptable behavior on the part of a faculty member. Although Parenti had the additional problem of his conviction for violating the law, suspicion of providing aid and comfort to the enemy was a trigger in both cases.

Alex Novikoff's confrontation with the UVM Board of Trustees in 1953 was more complicated, with roots going back to his political record in the 1930s. The common factor in all three cases, however, was an intolerance, fueled by patriotism and war, of "un-American" actions. In each instance the AAUP definition of academic freedom, especially the idea that citizenship responsibilities are separate from academic duties, succumbed to the popular will.

A Former Communist Settles in Vermont

Under the leadership of Dean William Brown, the UVM medical college strove in the late 1940s to enter the front rank of schools nationally. There was increased emphasis on medical research and a willingness to search widely for promising academic talent. When a cancer research laboratory was formed under the direction of Bjarne Pearson, UVM sought someone to join Pearson in the enterprise. In the spring of 1948, Pearson received a recommendation from a prominent cancer researcher, Van R. Potter at the University of Wisconsin. Potter suggested Alex Novikoff, a biology professor on leave from Brooklyn College, who was working with Potter on a fellowship funded by the American Cancer Society. Novikoff's collaboration with Potter had been highly productive, leading to five papers in scientific journals.[6]

Novikoff visited Vermont, where he was interviewed by Pearson, Dean Brown, and members of the school's small faculty. Novikoff, then thirty-five, was a man of boundless energy and evident enthusiasm and capability for scientific research. He impressed the UVM staff, including biochemistry professor Arnold Schein, who had known Novikoff in New York City in the early 1940s when both had been officers of the American Association of Scientific Workers. He testified that Novikoff was "famous as a fabulous biology teacher at Brooklyn College."[7] Based on Novikoff's résumé, the recommendation from Wisconsin, and the favorable interview, an offer was made: a position as professor of experimental pathology and associate in the cancer laboratory. No inquiries about Novikoff were made at Brooklyn College.[8]

What Novikoff's new employers did not know in 1948 was that he had been a political activist at Brooklyn College during the late 1930s and early 1940s. The precocious Novikoff joined the Brooklyn faculty in 1931 at age eighteen after receiving his undergraduate degree from Columbia University and then being rejected by medical schools. He enrolled in the doctoral program in biology at Columbia and did part-time laboratory work at the new city college near his home in Brooklyn. By 1935 he had established himself as an excellent scholar and a vigorous advocate of faculty rights.

This was a time of lingering economic crisis and political tumult in America, and the campus of Brooklyn College was beset by controversy.

Bitter conflict between senior professors and administrators and the younger, leftist faculty politicized the campus and exposed activists such as Novikoff to backlash. A few months after a branch of the Communist Party was started on campus, Novikoff joined the party and quickly assumed a leading role. He helped edit an anonymous party paper, participated in party meetings and training, and joined the campus local of the Teachers Union, an affiliate of the American Federation of Teachers (under Communist control in New York City).

Novikoff survived an attempt in 1938 to deny him a promotion in a case publicized and won by the Teachers Union. The political tide, however, turned against the Communists in 1939 and 1940. When Stalin abandoned his anti-fascist line and signed the nonaggression pact with Hitler, the American Communists were exposed to ridicule from the left as well as from the right. The party lost many members as well as useful alliances with other left-wing organizations. As German forces pushed across Europe, national security assumed a more prominent position in American politics. Eventually, various government entities decided to investigate the Communist "menace," including the FBI, the House Committee on Un-American Activities (known as the Dies Committee from its chairman, Martin Dies of Texas), and a New York State legislative committee, the Rapp-Coudert Committee.

The Rapp-Courdert Committee achieved a major breakthrough in November 1940 when Bernard Grebanier, a colleague of Novikoff's at Brooklyn College and a former Communist, named thirty Brooklyn faculty members as Communists, including Novikoff. Novikoff was subpoenaed in February 1941 but refused to discuss his activities. Called to testify again in July, he denied—falsely—that he had ever been a Communist.[9] Because none of the Brooklyn Communists was named by a second informer (the event that would have triggered the full sanctions of the authorities), they were not fired by the Board of Higher Education.

Novikoff, like many of his colleagues, lived in professional limbo for the next several years. Although his research and writing grew in stature and significance, he was widely suspected of being a Communist. He left the party in 1945, but he did not know whether a second informer would come forward to destroy his budding career as a scientist.[10] Novikoff took the Wisconsin fellowship in 1947 with the idea that this move might lead him permanently away from his troubles in New York.

When UVM decided to hire Novikoff in 1948, they knew nothing of this past. Dean Brown and Professor Pearson did not approach his superiors at Brooklyn College, and Novikoff volunteered only that he had been an active union member during the 1930s and 1940s.[11] Despite his notoriety (he was mentioned in the New York newspapers during the committee's proceedings and was well known as an activist on the Brooklyn campus), the Rapp-Coudert episode went unnoticed at UVM. Five years later Novikoff's political history would burst on the scene in Vermont.

McCarthyism Reaches into Vermont

After Novikoff's arrival in Vermont the cancer laboratory earned several grants and regular publicity in the Vermont papers. This was a time of personal happiness for Novikoff—his professional reputation advanced in the cancer research field, and his wife and two small children found Burlington a comfortable place to live. On the national scene, however, politics became increasingly embittered and rough as Senator Joseph McCarthy carried his anti-Communist message to the American people.

By 1952, enhanced by the consolidation of Soviet control in Eastern Europe, the end of the American monopoly of atomic weapons, the "loss" of China, and the war in Korea, the Communist threat was the dominant issue in national politics. Beginning in the congressional elections of 1946, the anti-Communist rhetoric and actions of politicians such as McCarthy and Richard Nixon planted the idea in the minds of many Americans that the "international Communist conspiracy" was making headway. Now, prodded by McCarthy and his allies, congressional committees were committed to finding and exposing allegedly disloyal employees in government, the entertainment industry, and education.

In September 1952 the Senate Internal Security Subcommittee traveled to New York City to investigate unresolved allegations of Communist activity among faculty members at New York City colleges, allegations that went back to the Rapp-Coudert investigation in 1941. Novikoff's luck ran out when a former Brooklyn College colleague and friend, Harry Albaum, told the committee in a private session that Novikoff had been a Communist.[12] In the spring of 1953 the committee, chaired by newly appointed Senator William Jenner of Indiana, resumed its investigation, and on March 19 it subpoenaed Novikoff to testify. With this action, anticommunism invaded Vermont politics, and Novikoff's life was forever changed.

On the afternoon that Novikoff received his subpoena, UVM's new president, Carl Borgmann, and the University's attorney, Louis Lisman, visited Novikoff at home to discuss what should be done. Lisman, a graduate of UVM and Harvard Law School, was a member of a prominent family in Burlington's small Jewish community. It was agreed that he would contact the Jenner committee and try to delay or cancel the subpoena.[13] In the meantime, on the chance that Novikoff might actually be called to testify, Borgmann and Lisman moved quickly to set the University's rules in order. After consultations with members of the Board of Trustees and the Policy Committee of the Faculty Senate, Borgmann announced on March 26 a new policy concerning individuals called to testify before congressional committees:

1. No known Communist will be permitted on the staff of the University.
2. Any faculty member claiming privilege under the Fifth Amendment will be immediately suspended. A faculty–trustee committee will be set up to investigate

the circumstances of the case, and upon its recommendation appropriate action will be taken.

3. A faculty member who admits previous membership in the Communist party, but who now claims that he is no longer a member, will be investigated by a faculty–trustee committee who will make recommendations on his fitness to continue on the staff of the University.[14]

When this policy was promulgated, Borgmann knew from his discussions with Novikoff that, if required to testify, he would take the Fifth Amendment. On the other hand, he had heard Novikoff say that he had been free of any political activities or affiliations since his arrival at UVM in 1948.[15] The new policy, therefore, was nicely tailored to the particulars of Novikoff's situation.

In their rush to protect the University from an embarrassing incident, however, Borgmann, Lisman, and members of the board committed an unfortunate error. The procedures set forth in the policy, primarily the creation of a special faculty–trustee committee, violated provisions of the UVM *Officers' Handbook*. Borgmann, still in his first year as president and not yet officially inaugurated, failed to notice that existing university bylaws already provided a special procedure for "a termination for cause of a continuous appointment," namely, a board of review made up of the Board of Trustees, the Policy Committee, and four additional faculty members from the accused's college. Three months later, in the midst of its proceeding against Novikoff, the University would be forced to start over in accordance with the existing bylaws.

Novikoff's troubles in Washington became known in Vermont on April 23 when, despite his efforts to avoid public testimony, he went before the microphones and cameras in Senator Jenner's committee in the Old Supreme Court Room in the Capitol. Novikoff denied that he was a Communist but refused to talk about his activities prior to going to Vermont. He invoked the Fifth Amendment several times in his testimony.[16] The afternoon Burlington *Daily News*, a William Loeb newspaper with a conservative editorial slant, hit the streets with a banner headline, "UVM Prof Not a Red Now."[17] This revelation, especially Novikoff's turning to the Fifth Amendment, set in motion events that would consume Vermont politics and university attention for the next five months.

Testing Vermont's Reputation for Tolerance

Although Vermont was distant from the political tumult experienced by Novikoff in New York City and from the tempest created by Joe McCarthy in Washington, the state was not unaffected by the country's anti-Communist fever. The Wallace presidential campaign in 1948 caused problems for Vermonters who identified with Wallace, including a dean at Lyndon State

Teachers College, Luther K. McNair, who was forced out because of his role in the statewide Wallace organization.[18] In 1950 the nationally syndicated columnist Westbrook Pegler charged that Vermont's tolerance of a left-wing summer population indicated that Vermonters were "suckers" for Communist infiltration.[19] Despite Vermonters' instinctive ambivalence about the many "flatlanders" who poured into Vermont in the summer, Pegler's assertions had little impact on a state that benefited considerably from the dollars brought to Vermont by summer visitors. Representative Charles Plumley began a four-year effort to convince Vermonters that the state had been selected as a testing ground for Communist ideas and infiltration. His campaign came to a feeble end, however, when his proposal to create a state board of censorship for school textbooks was rejected by a 202–11 vote of the Vermont House of Representatives.[20]

The governor of Vermont in 1953 was Lee Emerson, a conservative Republican. He had come into office by the traditional "stepladder" pattern of serving in the Vermont House, in the Vermont Senate, and as lieutenant governor before winning the governorship in his second try in 1950. Emerson showed his concern about the international Communist threat in his 1951 inaugural address, when he actually called for a declaration of war by Congress so that chapter 306 of the Vermont Sabotage Prevention Act could be brought into force.[21]

Although these rumblings of concern about Communism had very little effect on Vermont life, Vermonters were inclined to accept the messages from Washington about the Soviet threat and the dangers of internal subversion. Vermont editorial writers reinforced this view. In early 1954 a Columbia University political scientist (formerly of Bennington College) carried out a study in Bennington that suggested that almost half of Vermont's adult population approved of the methods of Senator McCarthy.[22] To the extent that this study was indicative of thinking across the state, Vermont was in step with public opinion nationally.

UVM's response to the Novikoff problem reflected the thinking of the national higher education community about the Communist threat. In early 1953 the AAUP joined distinguished legal scholars Zechariah Chafee and Arthur Sunderland, Rutgers president (and former Bennington College president) Lewis Webster Jones, and the prestigious Association of American Universities in asserting that invocation of the Fifth Amendment would raise questions about an individual's fitness to serve as a faculty member. Chafee and Sunderland stated that a faculty member would be "neither wise nor legally justified in attempting political protest by standing silent when obligated to speak. . . . The Fifth Amendment grants no privilege to protect one's friends."[23] Jones stated that "negative attitudes of non-cooperation (with congressional committees and university panel(s) constituted unacceptable professional behavior."[24] Borgmann and UVM attorney Lisman fell in step with this thinking when they formulated special procedures for handling a faculty member under investigation, assuming that (1) the congressional investigations were justified, (2) past or present Communist affiliation was a relevant consideration in judging the fitness of a faculty member, and (3) invoking the Fifth Amendment was a misguided action. On the matter of a suspected Communist, Vermont and its state university definitely were *not* marching on an independent path.

Governor Emerson and President Borgmann responded in predictable ways to Novikoff's testimony before the Jenner committee. Emerson, as an ex-officio member of the UVM Board of Trustees, told reporters that he wanted a "thorough investigation" of Novikoff and emphasized to Borgmann that "we do not want to intimate in any way that the University of Vermont has Communist professors, but we do want to be assured that everything is being done by the University authorities to see that the faculty is 100 percent pro-American and anti-Communist."[25] Taking his cues from other campuses and from the governor, Borgmann moved immediately to carry out the provisions of the policy approved on March 26, a step that overlooked the procedure called for in the bylaws of the University.

Borgmann appointed a six-person faculty–trustee committee chaired by Father Robert Joyce, a Rutland priest and later bishop of the Burlington diocese. A UVM graduate and World War II veteran with duty in Europe as an army chaplain, Joyce was a natural leader with the bearing of an athlete. Novikoff and Joyce had not met previously, but the events of 1953 would lead to personal affinity and friendship.

Just seven days after his testimony in Washington, Novikoff met with the committee in a 5½-hour session. The committee also interviewed several of Novikoff's professional colleagues, two students, and a Burlington rabbi, Max Wall.[26] After deliberations that carried through May, the committee concluded that Novikoff had not been a Communist since coming to UVM, was respected as a person and a scientist, and "even though he did invoke the Fifth Amendment, he should be retained." Although the committee members guessed that Novikoff "might have been" a Communist while at Brooklyn College, they did not seek information from sources in New York and therefore were still unaware of the Rapp-Coudert investigation or of the extent of Novikoff's Communist activities in the 1930s and 1940s.[27]

On June 12 the committee reported its findings to the Board of Trustees, with a 5–1 vote in Novikoff's favor. At this point Vermont politics entered the scene, with profound consequences for Novikoff. Governor Emerson had declined all previous invitations to attend a trustees meeting. However, he came to the June 12 meeting on the Novikoff matter and argued strenuously against accepting the recommendation of the Joyce committee. Split by Emerson's argument and wishing that the problem would go away, the Board decided instead to go to Novikoff and ask him to return to Washington and testify openly about his past activities. At a meeting with a delegation from the Board led by Borgmann, Novikoff explained that "in all conscience" he could not change his course.[28]

A week later Governor Emerson, joined by President Borgmann and nine other trustees, took a step that established clearly the position of the Board on the Novikoff matter. Emerson gained endorsement by a 11–5 vote (with Father Joyce in the minority) of the following motion:

That Dr. Novikoff be indefinitely suspended without pay from any further duties at this institution as of July 15, 1953, unless on or before that date he advises the president in writing of his willingness to go down and appear before the Jenner Committee and answer fully and freely any questions that the Committee may see fit to put to him and that before that date he offers to the Jenner Committee to do so.[29]

Although the motion had a tone of reasonableness to it ("We will let you, Dr. Novikoff, determine the board's action in your case"), the action was a repudiation of the Joyce committee and a harsh outcome for Novikoff. Novikoff knew immediately that, since he would not go to Washington to testify, "indefinite suspension" was tantamount to his firing.

Borgmann told the press, "A member of an institution of higher education has special responsibilities with respect to his willingness to answer frankly the questions of a properly authorized investigating committee."[30] With Borgmann's vote in favor of Emerson's motion (and his willingness to communicate the logic of the action on behalf of the board), university policy and Vermont politics had converged. The Board of Trustees, the governor of Vermont, and Vermont public opinion were now on the same channel. The idea that elimination of suspicion comes only through "confession"— the essence of McCarthyism—was now university policy.

The Dissenters Step Forward

The first public reaction to the Board's action, soon referred to as the "talk or walk ultimatum," was decidedly favorable. Governor Emerson announced proudly, "In fact, I made the motion."[31] The Burlington *Free Press* stated that the University had acted "logically."[32] The Burlington *Daily News* offered its "heartiest congratulations" and pointed out that "this forthright and American type of action is in contrast to the disgusting vacillations and chicken-heartedness of the administration of Harvard University which allowed various members of its faculty to remain at Harvard University after they had refused to answer reasonable questions propounded to them by various Congressional committees."[33]

In the face of official enthusiasm for the Board's action, a few people in Vermont began to raise serious questions about the proceedings. William Van Robertson, a UVM biochemist and a friend of Novikoff's, anguished over the University's failure to protect a faculty member and submitted his own resignation. Although Robertson withdrew his resignation after intense discussions with his dean, he became a vocal defender of Novikoff as the summer went along.[34] Bernard O'Shea, editor of the weekly *Swanton Courier*, asserted, "Senator Jenner has no right to inquire into your beliefs or ours; into anyone's politics."[35] This argument brought the suggestion from another newspaper that the *Courier* was "communist minded."[36] A storm broke over Burlington when eighteen local clergymen, led by Rabbi Wall, Episcopal bishop Vedder Van Dyck, and The Reverend Harold Bucklin, released a letter they had sent to the Board of Trustees. The letter revealed for the first time publicly that the Trustees had overturned the 5–1 vote of the Joyce committee and warned: "The action taken by your board in the case of Alex Benjamin Novikoff seems to us to be a dangerous blow to academic freedom."[37] Although the letter elicited sarcastic reactions from the editorial writers at the *Free Press* and the *Daily News* and from the governor, it seemed for a few days in early July that public opinion might turn in Novikoff's favor.

A sad part of the story began to unfold when a few concerned UVM faculty turned to the national AAUP in Washington to seek help. UVM had a small AAUP chapter on campus headed by Andrew Nuquist, a political scientist. Arnold Schein, Novikoff's close friend, consulted with him and Nuquist and then wrote the executive secretary of the AAUP, Ralph Himstead. Schein had noticed that the policy under which the Board of Trustees had acted was in violation of dismissal procedures established previously by the University. He asked that the national AAUP intervene in the Vermont case and press the University to delay a final decision. Although the July 15 deadline for Novikoff's "indefinite suspension" loomed close, the AAUP took several days to respond to Schein's fevered requests. Their first act was to require Novikoff's written permission before taking up the matter. Before AAUP action on the local or national front could be formulated, the July 15 deadline passed, without Novikoff's stepping forward to testify. Emerson's motion automatically took effect, and Novikoff was removed from his duties.[38]

What Schein did not know was that the national office of the AAUP was paralyzed by rigid, ineffectual leadership and by ambivalence about how to respond to the McCarthy era. Though it had acquired wide prestige by censuring institutions for violations of academic freedom, the AAUP produced no reports during this time of crisis for hundreds of faculty members and had censured no one.[39] Time and again during the summer of 1953, Schein and his colleagues called on the Washington office, with profoundly disappointing results.[40] The national AAUP was a weakened organization, and when it got drawn into the Novikoff battle in August, it was no match for the political consensus already built in Vermont.

The combined effects of a letter from Novikoff, pressure from the local AAUP, and two petitions signed by UVM faculty members finally persuaded President Borgmann that he had committed an error in ignoring the UVM bylaws. He called a faculty senate meeting for July 30. Before a crowded auditorium (closed to the press and other outsiders), he retreated:

At this point, I want to say that I have assumed that the "indefinite suspension" of the Board was to be interpreted as dismissal. I have been informed recently by the University's attorney that such an interpretation is an improper one. It seems clear to me that the procedure outlined in Article X, Section 14 . . . ought to be followed in arriving at a final determination of Dr. Novikoff's future status.

In response, Nuquist, the AAUP chapter president, presented a motion recommending a "complete rehearing" of the case. The motion passed with only two dissenting votes.[41]

To the frustration of the editorial writers and the governor, the actions of the Board of Trustees were now without force. Borgmann wrote the Trustees that a board of review should be formed so that "the rules on tenure be completely followed."[42] This was an intermediate but important victory for the supporters of academic freedom in Vermont. The Novikoff case would be tried anew; there was still hope. The most politically astute observers knew, however, that this victory only delayed the inevitable.

The Political Tide Rolls over Novikoff

The board of review for Novikoff's August 31 hearing included the University's twenty trustees, five faculty members from the Policy Committee, and four faculty members from the College of Medicine. Paul Evans, a history professor who had argued for Novikoff's right to due process at the June 30 faculty senate meeting, was elected chairman. Novikoff hired a lawyer, Francis Peisch of Burlington, and asked Ralph Himstead of the national AAUP to support his case. After weeks of supplications from Vermont, Himstead finally agreed to present the AAUP point of view at Novikoff's hearing. On the surface this was an important breakthrough because Himstead had not made a personal appearance at any other faculty hearings during the McCarthy era. As events developed, however, he played a nearly invisible role. Novikoff and Peisch realized belatedly that local resentment of "outside" interference was damaging to Novikoff's position.[43]

Under the glare of publicity and recognizing that their credibility was at stake, the Trustees were committed to prosecuting their case against Novikoff to a successful conclusion. Borgmann, university attorney Lisman, and Governor Emerson sought information from the FBI about Novikoff's past. Emerson received in his office an oral summary of the Novikoff FBI file from a special agent of the Albany office. If there had been any doubt previously, the FBI information made clear that Novikoff had been an active

Communist during his years at Brooklyn College. Lisman went to Washington and, with an introduction by Vermont senator George Aiken, contacted Robert Morris, counsel to the Jenner committee. Morris provided the names of former Communist Party members at Brooklyn College who might be willing to testify in Vermont. Lisman traveled to Wilmington, Delaware, and to Boston to contact possible witnesses.

At a planning session prior to the final hearing, Lisman told Novikoff's lawyer that he had recruited witnesses to testify about Novikoff's Communist past and that the FBI had provided secret information about Novikoff's involvement in "germ warfare" for the Soviets.[44] Available evidence suggests that Lisman's statements were intended as intimidation: no witnesses had agreed to come to Burlington to testify, and the charge of germ warfare does not appear in the FBI files on Novikoff. After Novikoff chose not to testify openly before the Jenner committee in April (as Lisman apparently expected), Lisman's feelings toward Novikoff grew bitter.[45] At the final hearing he accused Novikoff of "moral turpitude" for invoking the Fifth Amendment.

The temperature approached ninety degrees as the board of review convened on August 31 in Memorial Lounge in the Waterman Building. This was the climactic moment of one of Vermont's most celebrated political controversies. Novikoff's task was to convince the board that his refusal to talk about his political past and his invoking of the Fifth Amendment did not warrant his dismissal from the University. He knew, of course, that his actions fed the suspicions of those who feared the Communist threat. He knew also that, by the rules of this inquisition, the route to exoneration was to talk about the past. Remembering his successful testimony before the Joyce committee in May, Novikoff made an unexpected offer. He agreed to testify *off the record* about all of his past political activities.[46] He wanted to demonstrate that his past activities were not in any way threatening to national security and that they were almost completely focused on local campus issues. His offer was a retreat from his "moral position" against testifying under duress before a committee of investigation, but it was his last resort.

The board of review decided that off-the-record testimony was unacceptable. They feared that, hearing Novikoff's testimony, *they* might be vulnerable to a subpoena from Washington to testify. The contemplation of such a possibility raised great anxiety within the group. Moreover, many trustees believed that the central issue was the invocation of the Fifth Amendment and therefore that details about Novikoff's past were irrelevant. Thus, whether an act of personal cowardice or of courtroom pragmatism, the board voted, 11–8, not to hear Novikoff.[47] Novikoff's only chance of changing the political dynamics of the hearing evaporated.

After a day of testimony from Novikoff supporters and periodic haggling over procedural points, the board of review convened in executive session at 4:45 P.M. to determine Novikoff's fate. To the surprise of several trustees, Father Joyce revealed that he was not the lone negative vote against Novikoff (in the 5–1 ballot) in the earlier subcommittee proceeding. He went on to express continued support for retaining Novikoff on the faculty.[48] Joyce's comments had little effect. Three hours into the executive session, the board of review voted, 14–8, to dismiss Novikoff from the University. This recommendation was transmitted the following week to the full Board of Trustees. They first voted 13–2 against Novikoff, with one trustee abstaining. After hearing additional testimony from Lisman about Novikoff's Communist past, the Board voted again, with a 15–1 tally. In the end the only trustee to vote to retain Novikoff on the UVM faculty was Father Joyce.[49]

In a statement prepared for release to the press, the Board emphasized that Novikoff was fired because "he has failed to display to a sufficient degree in his actions and statements during the past five months, both before the committee of Congress and before University bodies, the qualities of responsibility, integrity, and frankness that are fundamental requirements of a faculty member. The actions referred to include, but are not limited to, his invoking of the Fifth Amendment."[50] Thus, after five months of proceedings, the Board of Trustees fell into step with the anti-Communist campaign that had swept the nation.

Reconsidering the Past

Novikoff was a brilliant scientist and a respected faculty member. The evidence is persuasive that he was inactive in the Communist Party after 1945. Only by the most extreme interpretation was he ever a threat to national security. He refused, however, to clear himself of suspicion by naming other Communists before the Jenner committee. Even under threat of dismissal he refused to retreat from his position, except to offer off-the-record testimony about his past to the UVM board of review. The logic of McCarthyism prevailed in Vermont, and President Borgmann, Governor Emerson, and other Vermonters joined in an action that stands as a permanent blemish on the history of the University and the state.

In the years that followed the downfall of Senator McCarthy and the curtailment of the anti-Communist inquisition, there emerged a sharper, more profound understanding of political rights and the precepts of academic freedom. First, many professional authorities concluded that the prevailing interpretation of the Fifth Amendment during the early 1950s was much too narrow. These constitutional scholars argued that invoking the Fifth Amendment in the manner of Novikoff and many others was appropriate and protected by the Constitution. Second, many university administrators and faculty came to believe that political activity and affiliations of the kind engaged in by Novikoff, ought to be tolerated by higher education. His activities, even his membership in the Communist Party, although distasteful, were not illegal or prohibited to other Americans. Moreover, it was argued that as long as professors did not impose their political views in the classroom, the right to hold these views should be protected. Of course, this revision of thinking came too late for Novikoff and approximately one hundred other faculty members around the country who were fired during the height of the McCarthy period.[51] The damage was already done.

A considerable period of time elapsed before UVM reexamined its action against Novikoff. It was not until 1983 that UVM came to terms with what had happened thirty years earlier. Prodded by a petition started by Merton Lamden, a colleague of Novikoff's at the time of his firing, the University chose to give Novikoff an honorary degree. Novikoff, who had gone on to a distinguished career in cancer research at the Albert Einstein School of Medicine in New York City, returned to campus for the commencement ceremonies.

President Lattie F. Coor welcomed Novikoff back to the University and saluted his "integrity and courage."[52] It was a moment of institutional atonement and personal restoration. Later in the day Novikoff visited Robert Joyce, who had retired as bishop but was, in his eighties, still active in civic affairs. Novikoff and his sole defender on the Board of Trustees permitted themselves a brief expression of triumph. At last, the University had emerged from one of the darkest episodes in its history.

Jews, Blacks, and Catholics: UVM's
Anomalous Minorities

JULES OLDER

"What Are You Lookin' At, Ugly?"

SHORTLY before midnight, on a warm spring evening in 1961, I was walking home from Redstone campus after a date. Passing Waterman, I glanced at someone dumping beer bottles into the corner mailbox. He yelled, "What are you lookin' at, ugly?"

Then, without further conversational gambit, he bounded across Prospect Street and proceded to beat the living daylights out of me. Drunk though he was, there was enough Jew-hating in the words he was hurling along with his fists that I realized two things: he knew me, and he was probably another student.

I didn't recognize him. But from the ground where I lay bruised and bloodied, I got the make of his car and the first two letters of his license plate as he sped away with the lights off.

Two weeks later, driving with a friend along South Prospect, I spotted the car heading away from Redstone campus. We did a fast U-turn and followed him to Kappa Sigma fraternity—the Animal House.

My unsought encounter with anti-Semitism helps answer the question, What constitutes a minority? The dictionary first defines it as "a group numbering less than half of a total." By that definition, just beneath the surface everyone is a minority. Democrats, Episcopalians, Baltimoreans—all were minorities when I was a student at UVM.

The second definition is more specific: "A racial, religious, political, national, or other group regarded as being different from the larger group of which it is a part."

That clarifies things. My Baltimore-ness never had the slightest effect on my life at UVM; my Jewishness colored the experience for the full four years, from 1958 to 1962.

That's not what I was looking for when I came this far north. I came in part to broaden my life beyond the safe but bland familiarity of the Jewish ghetto of northwest Baltimore where I grew up. I also came because UVM accepted me, shaky high school record and all.

Most of the friends I first made on campus weren't Jews. I was thrilled that college, whose function was to Broaden Your Experience, was actually doing just that for me. It wasn't until the beginning of second semester that I realized experience broadening could be painful.

At the end of the 1950s, male social life was almost completely dominated by fraternities, and I joined the gaggle of freshmen eager to pledge one. The rules for rushing stated that you had to visit every fraternity, presumably to keep a single house from locking promising candidates in the basement until they agreed to pledge. As we trooped from house to house, I came to see how the world was divided.

There were three Jewish fraternities on campus. Two were not exclusively Jewish—the few black students and an occasional white Christian usually ended up in Phi Sigma Delta and less frequently in Tau Epsilon Pi. But I felt mixed about Phi Sig, didn't like TEP, and had no interest in the strictly Jewish house, Alpha Epsilon Pi. Instead, I wanted more of this broadening that I was so enjoying. But as we freshmen made our way among the houses, it became clear that some fraternities were intent on narrowing.

Alpha Tau Omega, for example, kept emphasizing that it was "a Christian fraternity," an emphasis that 1950s Jews instantly recognized as the equivalent of real estate ads that proclaimed "Churches Nearby" or "Restricted." Kappa Sigma—the Animal House—was less subtle. They simply hung a large Nazi flag in one of the bedrooms and made sure we all got a good look at it on our way through. Maybe my attacker had spent too much time living under the flag.

Other fraternities were polite, but most were distinctly uninterested in minority students of any kind. At least one, Sigma Nu, did take in an occasional Jew, but, despite my longing to join that Gentlemen's House, I was not chosen as the Jew from '62.

I was crushed. After a day of hurt and sorrow, I gathered what was left of my pride and joined the University Players, about to put on *The Three Sisters* under the direction of a new faculty member, Ed Feidner. The Players proved uninterested in actors' ethnicity, I landed a small part, and I was, at least for the moment, fraternally unattached.

In the course of the next several months I had time to consider fraternities outside the frenetic hustle of rushing. Phi Sig had taken in what they considered a disappointing group of pledges, whom they disparagingly referred to as "the radicals." Perhaps because of their slim pickings the brothers made it known that it wasn't too late for me to join.

I was also made welcome at a considerably less likely house, Acacia. Known as a "farmer's frat" with Masonic connections, Acacia had neither the sophistication of Sigma Nu nor the drive of Phi Sig. I'm sure they'd never had a Jewish member. I'm not sure what the basis of our mutual attraction was, but we liked each other. I had dinner there several times, and they too invited me to join.

I also considered staying independent, as had a few of my friends who had either not rushed or had been turned down by the fraternity of their choice. But after surveying the relatively meager social and civic options open to non-Greeks (fraternities controlled Kake Walk, had a lock on some of the honor societies, and dominated most other aspects of campus life), I joined the radical pledges of Phi Sigma Delta.

Over the next three years the broadening I had come to university for yielded to a shrinking back to the safe, bland homogeneity of Jewish northwest Baltimore, now transported to North Prospect Street in Burlington. A saving grace was that the radicals (whom I quickly came to see as kindred spirits) dated with little regard to religion or ethnicity. My own two big college loves were a middle-class WASP from Rochester, New York, and a farmer's daughter from Brownington, Vermont. I married the farmer's daughter.

I tell you all this—the unprovoked attack by a student bigot, the ethnic mix of friends, the demarcation of Jewish and non-Jewish fraternities, the warm welcome at Acacia, our college dating patterns—to give you a picture of UVM at the end of the 1950s from the perspective of a male Jewish student.

"And Episcopals with Episcopals"

At the same time there were rumors that female Jewish students were being segregated, not by sororities—which, after all, were private clubs and therefore sacrosanct in their right to discriminate—but by the University itself. In 1989, thirty years later, I remembered the rumors and thought I knew whom to see to check their veracity.

Professor Raul Hilberg is, at the end of the 1980s just as at the end of the 1950s, a somewhat frightening figure. Now, as then, he is not known for suffering fools gladly, and now, as then, I always feel particularly fool-like in his presence. I asked him about the rumors.

Professor Hilberg sits very still; he speaks slowly and deliberately, weighing every word for accuracy and delivering each one with maximum impact. "Yes," he said, "the rumors were true. The dean of women, Anna Rankin Harris, and her assistant, Margaret Wing—for whom two dormitories are now named—maintained a policy of strict segregation of freshman girls by religion.

"In 1959, Professor Harry Kahn, the head of Hillel, made a list of Jewish freshman girls at UVM. I systematically went through the directory and found all the Jewish girls were assigned rooms with other Jewish girls."

Hilberg paused for effect. "Then I found that Catholic girls were assigned rooms with other Catholic girls."

Pause. "And Episcopals with Episcopals."

By now I was starting to laugh. He continued his slow-paced delivery. "And rich girls with other rich girls."

Now even Hilberg was laughing, subvocally. "There were three criteria— religion, money, and . . ."

"Yes? Yes?"

"And *height*! This was social engineering! If you were short and Protestant and poor, chances are you would be living with someone else short and Protestant and poor."

I suddenly remembered how remarkable we all thought it was that my girlfriend (now my wife) was paired with a near twin—another poor, rural, Protestant Vermonter . . . of identical height.

In 1959 Hilberg wrote to Lyman Rowell, then dean of administration, demanding an end to "the segregation of Jewish freshmen girls in the University dormitories." In his letter he quoted from a statement by one of them. She said, in part: "One comes to college to broaden one's ideas, philosophies, and human relations as well as to pursue higher academic studies. By stating religious preference, one automatically receives a roommate of similar background. This confines a student to association with the type of person he already knows about and leaves no room for expansion."[1]

Hilberg pointed out that segregation "collided head on with the Constitution of the United States" and quoted cases, including *Brown v. Board of Education of Topeka,* to back it up. He demanded that application blanks delete questions of race and religion and that room assignments be made independent of these factors. Hilberg's letter concluded, "You have my assurance that the results will be checked in the fall."[2]

The practice ended soon after. "But," he pointed out with feeling, "we still have two dormitories named after those bigots."

"Dartmouth Is a Christian College"

Jewish students faced discrimination in the 1950s and 1960s, but those years marked the end of a long era in which it was difficult, perhaps all but impossible, for a Jew to become a member of the faculty. This was not just the case at UVM; rather, anti-Semitism was routine at American (as well as Canadian and European) colleges and universities.

In 1930, New York University, which had the biggest Jewish student body in the world, had not one Jewish professor.[3] In 1942 sociologist Talcott Parsons wrote, "Jewish representation in the academic field . . . is entirely negligible."[4] In 1945 the education secretary of the American Dental Association stated that too many dental students seemed to come from "one racial strain."[5] The president of Dartmouth College said, "Dartmouth is a Christian college founded for the Christianization of its students."[6]

Former UVM professor Lewis Feuer (now emeritus professor of sociology and government at the University of Virginia at Charlottesville) told me a story told to him by the late professor of history Paul Evans: "Evans said that Harvard had recommended a new Ph.D., Frank Manual, for a teaching position at UVM. The President, Guy Bailey, refused to consider the recommendation because Manual was a Jew. Manual went on to become one of the country's leading scholars in European history. He had a named professorship at NYU, and he lectured at Stanford."

This is but one of many stories of scholars being turned away from American universities because of their religion. Where race was involved, discrimination—against professors and students alike—was even more blatant.

"Going to the Mixer"

I was talking about the subject with UVM's dean of allied health, Lawrence McCrorey. When I told him Hilberg's story of segregating students by ethnicity, he immediately stood up and began pacing the floor of his office. "I believe it," he said, "I believe it." He shook his head. "When I went to the University of Michigan in 1944, there were about five thousand freshmen on campus, and maybe fifty of us black. The school put on a weeklong orientation for all the incoming students. After the fact, I found that somebody in the administration had taken the trouble to go through the orientation packages of the whole damned five thousand and pull all of the social invitations from the black kids' packs. People around me kept talking about 'going to the mixer,' and I couldn't figure out why I didn't know about it."

Still pacing, he laughed without humor. "They still send me letters asking for my alumni donation . . . , and this year I finally told them why I send my money to the United Negro College Fund instead."

McCrorey's Michigan experience typified American university attitudes toward minority, especially black, students until well into the second half of the twentieth century. The worst—and this included most state universities throughout the south—practiced unfettered segregation, banning black students by law or decree. The main campus of UVM was not among this number, but at times in its history the College of Medicine was, as we shall see.

"It Is Not Barely *Toleration,* but *Equality* Which the People Aim At"

Excluding medicine, UVM has for most of its history been one of the more liberal American academic institutions. This openness goes back to the

University's beginnings and to the ideals of one of its original supporters, the Reverend Doctor Samuel Williams. Williams was a descendant of Puritan educators, ministers, and free-spirited Eunice Williams, who had been captured by Indians, married an Indian chief, converted to Catholicism, and refused to reconvert "despite theological fulmination, family entreaty, and a bribe of a grant of land."[7]

Samuel Williams described Vermont as a place of great religious openness. He wrote:

Some of the people are Episcopalians, others are Congregationalists, others of the Presbyterian and others of the Baptist persuasion and some are Quakers. All of them find their need of the assistance of each other. . . . It is not barely *toleration,* but *equality* which the people aim at. Toleration implies either a power or a right in one party to bear with the other, and seems to suppose that the governing party are in possession of the truth, and that the others are full of errors. . . . The body of the people in this community carry their ideas of religious liberty much farther than this."[8]

Dr. Williams's ideals, and those of his student (and UVM's first president) Daniel Sanders, set the University on the liberal and unorthodox course described by P. Jeffrey Potash in chapter 2. UVM was the twenty-fifth college founded in the United States but the first to encode in its charter the requirement that its "rules, regulations, and by-laws shall not tend to give preference to any religious sect or denomination whatsoever." UVM historian Julian Lindsay credits Williams for this early stance against discrimination, enthusiastically concluding, "This is evidence of enlightenment for which most of the world waited long."[9]

After his experiences at Michigan and at the University of Illinois where he took his Ph.D. degree, Lawrence McCrorey came to Vermont to test this enlightenment for himself.

"We've Been Silent Too Long"

McCrorey came to UVM in 1966, intending to stay five years. Instead, he's stayed the distance, largely because of his continuing impression that "in terms of racial progress, UVM is one of the better universities. Not because it's not steeped in racism—hell, all of them are. I've stayed because this school has the potential to make things better. You can make inroads here. Lattie Coor's agreement with the minority students is a prime example."

The agreement McCrorey referred to was signed on April 22, 1988, climaxing a campus confrontation that had begun four days earlier. At noon on April 18 a group of students from a variety of racial and ethnic minorities took over the executive offices in Waterman Building, demanding "an end to overt and institutional racism on campus." The takeover was supported by large numbers of other students who sat, sang, and slept outside the locked doors of the corridor until the demonstration ended. More than two thousand students signed a petition backing the minority students, and the Burlington city council passed its own resolution of support.

The takeover had its beginnings nearly twenty years earlier, when, in response to student pressure, the University agreed to take steps toward making itself a more pluralistic institution by recruiting minority students and faculty.[10] For a while, that's what happened. From six black students in 1970, UVM went to seventy-two six years later. But the numbers began to fall in 1976, and were down to forty by 1988. At the same time, black members of the faculty increased from two in 1966 to a high of eleven in the mid-1970s. But over the next decade there was no further increase, perhaps because other universities mounted more effective affirmative action programs. After the takeover, President Coor acknowledged, "Try as many have on this campus, our record in recent years has not been impressive."[11]

Some blame Coor for that record. Professor Dolores Sandoval put it bluntly; she told me, "People give Coor credit for his handling of the takeover, but for fifteen years he has been a roadblock to minority progress on campus. All the positive figures stop in 1976 when President Andrews left and Coor arrived. Now we're picking up from there."

Her views were echoed by another black faculty member, Harry Thompson. Both he and Sandoval credit what progress UVM has made in minority hiring to President Andrews and to the former dean of the education college, Dean Corrigan.

Other faculty faulted the minority students for their takeover tactics. In a *Free Press* article Professor Robert Daniels wrote, "Neither the students' right to protest nor the virtue of their goals are at issue here, but rather the coercive tactics and inflamatory ignorance."[12] A similar view was expressed by a staff member when the student occupation began. Told to quickly vacate the premises, she responded, "There's no sense in alienating the staff. We might agree with your cause." A student answered, "We've been silent too long."[13]

Takeovers are confrontational by nature, yet it says something about the quality of campus life at UVM that when President Coor suggested each side choose a mediator, the students chose a white, Jewish faculty member, sociology professor Stephen Berkowitz, and the administration chose a Black one, Dean Lawrence McCrorey. Berkowitz and McCrorey then chose a third mediator, sociology professor S. Frank Sampson.

At the end of four days Coor announced an agreement. The key points included:

1. Beginning in 1989, each incoming out-of-state class should roughly reflect the proportion of minority high school graduates in the country.

2. No less than four minority faculty would be hired each year for the next four years.

3. The University would significantly increase its courses in ethnic studies.

4. A three-week program on race relations and ethnic diversity would be offered to all incoming students beginning in 1988.

5. A racial awareness and sensitivity program would be developed for faculty and staff.

6. Faculty and staff evaluations would include performance on affirmative actions matters. Punitive sanctions would be taken "for any member of the University community who blatantly engages in or insinuates racist remarks or actions."

7. Specific steps would be taken to provide a minority presence on the UVM Board of Trustees.[14]

"Life Is Selective . . ."

The 1988 takeover was not the first example of student involvement in what Dean McCrorey calls "making inroads." There had been a silent procession and another sit-in three years before to protest the University's continuing investment in companies doing business with apartheid-ridden South Africa. Following the action, a divided board of trustees voted to divest the university portfolio of South African–related shares within eighteen months.[15]

James Loewen describes another example of student involvement in his chapter on Kake Walk. And before that, in 1946, 1957, and 1960, UVM students involved themselves in antidiscrimination fights that helped change the school, the state, and the nation.

In 1946, a year after the end of World War II, Alpha Xi Delta sorority pledged Crystal Malone, a black student from Washington, D.C. Ms. Malone (now Crystal M. Brown) describes the campus then:

The university students, mostly girls, were young, impressionable with dreams of a better world. This was a fun time for me. My dreams and aspirations were the same as all others, my educational preparations as strong; I lived as an American coed and loved every minute.

When I arrived on the campus in 1943 as a freshman, there was one other Black student, a junior from Washington, D.C. . . . When you have so few Blacks on campus, there seems to be no need to show open antagonism. I never felt unwelcomed or unwanted. I may have been an oddity to some, but I was always comfortable in this setting. . . .

I never expected to be asked to join a national sorority. I had grown up in a segregated world. However, I participated in all the open activities of the school along with other students, joining in the pleasures of being a UVM student. When I was asked to join Alpha Xi Delta, I remember being pleased—the spoken emotions and feelings after the war made me think it was possible.[16]

The pledging of Crystal Malone by a hitherto all-white sorority was probably sparked by a UVM conference on religion. In November 1945 four clergymen, including a rabbi and Reverend Ben Richardson, a black minister, spoke on campus. Anti-Semitism and "anti-Negroism" were among the themes of the conference.

Whatever the speakers said, they must have said it effectively. The *Cynic* reported that when the meeting ended, one hundred students "thronged the lounge to elect a committee to investigate the quota system and abolish it on this campus." The committee "is contacting the national organizations in an effort to do away with the Quota." [17]

The "Quota" or "quota system" was a means of keeping down numbers of Jews at universities and medical schools by maintaining a quota—a percentage of acceptances—that would not be exceeded. The Quota came to be applied to other minorities by other institutions, including fraternities and sororities. The *Cynic* editorialized:

Finding the time ripe for a definite plan of action to wipe out organized intolerance on this campus, Rev. Richardson led student discussion and inspired the abolition of the Quota. We owe him a profound thanks for waking us up to the utter incompatibility of democracy and Quota. To the student leaders who inaugurated the student committee we offer congratulations. Here is a movement *of* students, *by* them, and *for* them and it is significant that outstanding students have taken on a serious responsibility to which their talents are suited.[18]

The following January the *Cynic* announced that the "Pan-Hellenic Society had adopted in its new rushing system the objectives of the Greek Letter Reform movement. . . . Henceforth, all sorority rushing will be on a basis of no racial or religious discrimination towards any girl." It added, "All fraternities will adopt these objectives." [19]

Alpha Xi Delta took the issue seriously and pledged Crystal Malone. The national sorority took *that* seriously—the president, Mrs. Beverly Robinson, traveled to Burlington to try and dissuade eighteen-year-old Crystal from joining. She did not succeed. As a direct result, the UVM chapter was suspended by the national organization. Mrs. Robinson told *Life* magazine when it reported the affair, "Life is selective, and maybe it's just as well to learn it while we are young." [20]

The Vermonters countered, "[We] are proud to be sorority sisters of Miss Malone." [21] They backed their words with a momentous deed—they burned their charter. Doing so meant that no group, including themselves, could use the name Alpha Xi Delta for five years. Knowing this, the chapter decided to close its doors if Miss Malone could not be a member. It was a dramatic stand—if we can't be Alpha Xi Delta with Crystal, there will be no Alpha Xi Delta.

But before taking this drastic step, Alpha Xi made it clear to the UVM administration that "prolonged censuring of the sorority would mean its end at the University of Vermont." According to the *Cynic*, President J. S. Millis responded, "This is a matter between the local sorority and the national."

Dean of Women Mary Jean Simpson "declared it was not a matter of University of Vermont policy."[22] (Dean Simpson, too, has a dormitory named after her.)

The administrative bow-out did not go unnoticed. In a letter to the *Cynic*, veteran and student Peter Mallett wrote, "The sickening part of the whole affair is the pathetic indifference of the administration. . . . Not taking a stand assures the maintenance of the *status quo,* the continuance of racial discrimination at the University of Vermont."[23] In less than a year the suspended Vermont chapter, severed from its national body and unsupported by the university, acknowledged defeat. It did not take part in rushing and soon disbanded.[24]

"A Small-Minded Inn-Keeper Didn't Like His Color"

Ten years later, in 1957, another black student was the leading campus hero, the captain of the UVM football team. But hero or not, when Leroy Williams, Jr., brought his Kake Walk date to a Burlington motel where he had reserved a room for her, she was refused accommodation. As the *Cynic*'s editorial stated:

The Captain of our team was not allowed to put his girl up at the motel because the color of his skin was not the same as ours. The man who led our team on to so many victories, the fellow who gave the spirit and leadership to our team, the guy who symbolized the entire University as he struggled with our foes on the gridiron was "not allowed" because a small-minded inn-keeper didn't like his color.

It is obvious that an injustice has been committed, an injustice which involves not only the people of Burlington but every member of this University and every member of this state. . . . There is a need of a Civil Rights bill in this state, so that a public licensed institution such as a motel shall not be able to legally bar anyone from use of their facilities because of race, creed or religion."[25]

The editorial's sentiments were echoed by political science professor Albert Churchill Ettinger, who also pointed out that the Burlington *Free Press* had buried the story between two ads on the comic page.[26]

By the end of the week, in the raw winds of early March, some four hundred students joined a rally directed by the captain-elect of the football team, Richard W. White, to protest the discrimination. The rally featured speeches by a number of Burlington clergy. Among them was a young minister new to the city, the Reverend William H. Hollister. Perhaps in response to the *Free Press* comic-page burial, he said, "The problem is that many people in Burlington and at UVM do not believe there is a problem."[27]

The rally spawned the UVM Council on Human Relations, headed by Herzl Spiro, Mary Macey, Joseph Siegel, Robert Wolfe, and Richard Fiske. The council drafted and circulated a petition urging the passage of an antidiscrimination bill and began investigating discrimination at UVM and around the state.[28]

Two months later, on April 23, 1957, the Vermont General Assembly enacted legislation prohibiting discrimination in places of public accommodation.[29] At the same time, William Pickens, a black student, was elected president of the UVM Student Association by a 2-to-1 margin over his nearest rival.[30]

The Pickens landslide occurred when the campus was overwhelmingly white. No one I've interviewed from the 1940s through the 1960s can remember more than a handful of black students on campus at any one time.

"It Is Only Harming Innocent People"

In 1960 a protest against another form of racial discrimination took UVM students to the streets. Specifically, it took them to Church Street, in front of the Woolworth store.

On Saturday, March 25, at least twenty undergraduate students and one faculty member took part in a nationwide student movement protesting the chain store's refusal to integrate the lunch counters of its southern branches. According to the front-page article in the next week's *Cynic*, "Some [passersby] laughed, some sneered, some entered the store, and more than three hundred signed the boycott petition that members of the group held."[31]

The day before the picketing, in response to a delegation of fifteen students, the Student Association "passed a resolution whereby qualified students who have been expelled from their universities and colleges in the South, because of their participation in the non-violent demonstrations against discrimination, should be invited by President Fey and the administration to attend the University of Vermont with a possible reduction in tuition."[32]

Cynic columnist Roger Zimmerman, one of the Woolworth pickets, took to task Governor Stafford and ex-President Truman, who "told the NAACP that the Negroes should 'behave themselves.'"[33]

Editor-in-chief David H. Steele supported the pickets, arguing in an editorial, "Segregation is morally wrong. . . . Pressure such as that applied here in Burlington can result in change in the South."[34]

But in a letter to the editor, student Sheila Whitney countered:

I think that the UVM students' action of picketing Woolworth's store here in Burlington is a disgrace to UVM. Not only was this action a disgrace, but it is embarrassing for the students who did not participate and who did not want to participate. . . . I truly feel that this picketing did not represent even one-third of the student body at UVM. In taking a poll of one of my classes one student out of fifteen said that they definitely approved of the demonstration. I think that you will discover that this is true throughout the campus.[35]

She was probably right. A month later the Student Association "condemned the actions of students who have picketed Burlington business enterprises," declaring it "unjust to picket Burlington business establishments which have no control over the present crisis in the South."[36] The *Cynic* disagreed. A rare front-page editorial described the Student Association resolution as "one of the most shocking things to come out of SA in recent years. . . . It has, in effect, put its seal of approval on the 'status quo' in the South."[37]

In the same editorial the *Cynic* reiterated its lack of faith in the effectiveness of the earlier SA resolution on admitting dismissed southern students to UVM. And now there was evidence to support its stand: the board of trustees had decided that "favored admissions policy for any special group could be offered only at the cost of prejudice to individuals who have applied in good faith." The paper concluded: "Need the CYNIC reiterate that the SA's resolution is ineffective?"

Either the editorial or the resolve of the pickets (who had returned for a second Saturday on the line) turned the tide. In early May, SA rewrote its antipicketing resolution to read: "Student Association Council respects the rights of students to protest in any lawful manner acts of discrimination against people for reasons of race, creed, or national origin," cautiously adding, "Such protests are not to be construed as necessarily representing the views of Student Association."[38]

A week later, on May 19, 1960, in an editorial headlined "Victory in Nashville," the *Cynic* triumphantly reported:

A recent news item from Nashville, Tenn., announced the ending of lunch counter segregation in that city. White *and* Negro citizens, it continued, met TOGETHER and decided that lunch counters would henceforth be integrated in Nashville.

The students who picketed the local Woolworth's branch recently have been told again and again that their picketing has had no beneficial result, and that it is only harming "innocent people." . . . Now at last it can be proved that the pickets, by showing their active support of the Negroe's [*sic*] cause, have had a positive effect toward desegregation. . . . The CYNIC feels that picketing should proceed until every lunch counter is desegregated, and that then pickets should turn their efforts to other facets of the problem of Civil Rights.[39]

"How Can There Be an Intellectual Catholic?"

Whereas discrimination against Jews and blacks has been nearly ubiquitous throughout the United States, widespread discrimination against Catholics largely died out well before the middle of the twentieth century. But Vermont had long been a hot spot for anti-Catholicism, in part because Catholicism in Vermont has been associated with a foreign nationality and language.[40] A significant proportion of Catholics in northern Vermont are of French Canadian descent, and they have more often served as the objects of local prejudice than Jews or blacks.

Here is how Vermont historian Rowland Robinson described Vermonters of French-Canadian descent in 1892:

For years the State was infested with an inferior class of these people, who plied the vocation of professional beggars. . . . They were an abominable crew of vagabonds, robust, lazy men and boys, slatternly women with litters of filthy brats, and all as detestable as they were uninteresting. . . . The character of these people is not such as to inspire the highest hope for the future of Vermont, if they should become the most numerous of its population. The affiliation with Anglo-Americans of a race so different in traits, in traditions, and in religion must necessarily be slow, and may never be complete.[41]

Robinson's prediction of incomplete affiliation was supported by a scholarly study of ethnic relations in Burlington during the 1930s. Sociologist Elin Anderson not only found a city divided by ethnicity but a university at least perceived to be a fortress for one of the sides:

. . . Division of the community [of Burlington] is enhanced by the presence, on the one hand, of many Catholic institutions, especially the headquarters of the Catholic See of Vermont, and on the other hand, of the University of Vermont. The University is a public institution, but in contradistinction to the Catholic colleges near at hand it is Protestant in tone. As the Old American Protestant group retreats from commercial power in the city, the last stronghold of its traditions will be on the campus.[42]

This "tradition" may have lasted considerably later than the 1930s. Raul Hilberg told me that his department chairman in the late 1950s would not hire a Catholic as a member of the political science department. Hilberg added that he considered anti-Catholicism a more serious problem at UVM thana prejudice toward blacks or Jews.

Former professor of philosophy Lewis Feuer disagreed on both counts. He remembered the political science chairman as a liberal man and added that not once during his years at UVM (from 1951 through 1957) or in his capacity as president of the local chapter of the American Association of University Professors did a case of anti-Catholic discrimination come to his attention.

Thomas Geno, an associate professor of Romance languages and a practicing Catholic, wasn't sure about discrimination but had no doubts about prejudiced attitudes. He said, "I hear it being talked about in the faculty lounge—'How can there be an intellectual Catholic?' and 'How can a Catholic be educated?' I haven't experienced prejudice practiced against my own being, but I think attitudes like this belie one's own underpinnings and own formations of prejudices. It's the same as attitudes toward Jews and Blacks."

Geno wasn't the first to observe this similarity. Anti-Catholicism has been called the anti-Semitism of intellectuals. Especially prior to the election of John F. Kennedy as president, American Catholics were often regarded as authoritarian, dogmatic, and anti-intellectual. And in Vermont, anti-Catholicism was heightened by xenophobia. UVM historian Robert Daniels told me, "If you go back before the late 60s, you will find . . . the anti-French effect was a mood in Vermont society at large (and self-limitation of the French regarding college aspirations.)"

I asked Professor Geno if Vermont Catholics regarded the University as a Protestant institution. He thought for a moment before answering: "It was always bandied around in Catholic circles that UVM was the layman's school, not the Catholic one—in French, *école sans Dieu,* the school without God. Having been here twenty-five years, I think a study would show that deans and chairmen and presidents at UVM are overwhelmingly WASP."

Former Vermont governor Philip Hoff acknowledged the attitudes that Robinson evinced, Anderson recorded, and Geno observed. He wrote for a 1983 report of the U.S. Commission on Civil Rights, "Franco-Americans have been the victims of anti-Catholic, anti-foreign sentiment in the past, and of negative stereotyping in much of the 20th century."[43] Without implying discriminatory practice, the report noted that in 1975, only 7 percent of UVM students had an identifiable French surname. By 1979 the figure had risen to 9.4 percent. The report concluded: "The figure still suggests underrepresentation. . . . Nevertheless, it appears to be the case that more Franco-American students are entering Vermont's largest university."[44]

"I Don't Like It, but I Do It"

I asked one of these students about his experience at UVM. Christopher Bilodeau is a history major in the class of 1991. He grew up in a bilingual family in a region of Maine where French is the language of commerce and social life:

Before UVM I went to Hebron Academy, a small, private, nondenominational high school in Maine. At Hebron my background had absolutely no effect on anything— it simply never came up. If a person was Jewish, I wouldn't know about it. You dealt with people as individuals, not as stereotypes.

When I got to UVM, I realized that ethnicity definitely was an issue; whether you're Catholic or Jewish or Filipino or Black became a trait that people judged you by—"Oh, he's Jewish," and that told you something about his personality.

As far as being French here, I quickly learned that they weren't really the most loved people. French Canadians have a different style and culture. It tends to be a bit flashy and gaudy sometimes, and that style creates some tension between Americans and French Canadians. They're looked upon as shallow in intellect and moral behavior—which isn't very nice.

UVM has definitely heightened my awareness of ethnicity. Now, when I meet a new person, I say, Oh he's Black or a Jew or Filipino, and I start from there. I don't like it, but I do it.

"Well, There Went All My Dreams and Aspirations"

Samuel Williams may have set the university on a liberal path, but the College of Medicine was long a largely separate institution. As such, it developed its own mores and traditions, one of which was maintaining a student body that was overwhelmingly white and male.

The medical school's historian, Martin Kaufman, wrote, "Although in 1871 the [UVM] trustees had decided to admit young women and 'colored students,' they tabled and in effect defeated a motion allowing females to attend lectures on midwifery, but they voted to admit Negro students to the medical lectures."[45]

But medical lectures are only a part of medical training. Although lectures from the core of the preclinical years, experience with patients is the next— and crucial—step toward graduation. And the medical school was far from ready for black doctors to touch white patients. According to Kaufman:

Until well into the twentieth century the students at the Medical School were almost exclusively white males. . . . over the years a small number of blacks had been enrolled. Black students, however, had a difficult time being accepted by the local citizenry. [Although this is possible, I have found no evidence for it. Alternatively, medical deans may have justified their own prejudices by attributing them to local citizens.] There was a general feeling that they should minister to black patients, and there were so few blacks in Vermont that black medical students were often sent south for their hospital training. In 1922 Dean Tinkham noted in a letter that "what few colored students" there were at the University had been referred "to the South for hospital service," since "it is not logical to have a colored man acting as an intern at a hospital where the patients are practically all white."[46]

The consequences of that policy are best illustrated by the case of James Kingsland.

Among the four alumni receiving Alumni Achievement Awards at the 1989 UVM reunion was Dr. James Kingsland, class of 1935. The program said the award was for his distinguished medical and military careers and for his enormous community service.[47] What it didn't say was that Dr. Kingsland was pushed out of the College of Medicine because he was black.

As a UVM undergraduate, Kingsland was a member of Gold Key Honor Society, sports editor of *Ariel*, and member of the football and basketball teams. He applied for entry to the medical school, but when successful candidates were announced, his name was not among them. Instead, he got a note directing him to report to the medical dean, James N. Jenne.

According to Kingsland, "Dr. Jenne told me that even though they had accepted candidates whose record was lower than mine that I was being denied entrance to medical school because my not being white was not acceptable. He stated that in the later years it was custom to have students go about the state and serve short periods with various practitioners in private practice, and that I would not be acceptable to them. Well, there went all my dreams and aspirations which I had harbored through the years!" Kingsland went to President Guy Bailey, who "listened to my story. He said he would look into the matter." But Kingsland heard nothing from Bailey over the summer and with trepidation returned in the fall to register. Jenne "was indignant that I would open up the subject" but after consultation with Bailey "told me that I could enter but that I had to agree to leave the school at the end of my second year."[48] Kingsland applied to a number of other schools and was turned down by all except the black-run Howard University. He graduated from Howard with an M.D. and launched a long and distinguished career.

This wasn't the last time a qualified black candidate was denied entry. When Elizabeth Gourdin applied for admission in 1944, Medical Dean C. H. Beecher informed her that the college did not "have the clinical facilities for teaching negro students." She was advised to apply somewhere else. When concerned Vermonters—among them, utopian author and environmentalist Scott Nearing—wrote on her behalf, Dean Beecher prevaricated, saying, "The student in question was not refused admission." Rather, "she was advised to go to a school that had adequate clinical facilities for teaching negro students."[49]

"Protecting the Serenity of the Campus"

In 1968 the Student Council expressed concern about "the all-white nature of the medical student body" and recommended the creation of a five-year program for students from black colleges who had not received adequate premedical training. The next year and the next, other voices echoed the need to recruit black students, and "after a long discussion, the [medical school] chairmen agreed that it would be justifiable to reduce admission requirements for blacks by using the same standards for them as those applied to Vermont residents."[50]

But it was not to be. Kaufman wrote: "For a number of reasons the chairmen were hesitant to take this action. The majority seemed to feel that minority representation was not nearly 'as important as protecting the serenity' of the campus. 'Many were worried about black students as potential rioters.' Others feared the development of a program 'which might graduate second class physicians.' Finally, it was argued that the clinical facilities in Burlington were inadequate."[51]

Perhaps because of this lukewarm support, nothing much came of the good intentions. Although other minorities have cracked the whiteness of recent medical classes, blacks are still notable for their absence. The medical school has failed to graduate even one black student since 1976.

The school has been a little more successful in hiring black staff. In 1959 Moses Alfred Haynes joined the preventive medicine department as the first black faculty member. In 1962 Jackson J. W. Clemmons was recruited by the Department of Pathology, and in 1966 Lawrence McCrorey was hired by the Department of Physiology and Biophysics. Both proved to be outstanding lecturers; in 1970 McCrorey was named the medical school's Teacher of the Year.[52] Dolores Sandoval told me she credits McCrorey and Clemens with bringing more minorities to campus: McCrorey for keeping the pressure up on behalf of students, Clemens for prodding the university administration to hire black faculty and for welcoming the candidates and urging them to accept the offered positions.

"The Jewish Student Does Not Fit into Our Scheme Here"

Jews have encountered both discrimination and acceptance at the College of Medicine. At least one of the discriminators was Dean James N. Jenne, the same Dean Jenne who ensured that James Kingsland did not graduate. In a 1934 reply to an inquiry from Rabbi Morris Lazaron, leader of the National Council of Christians and Jews, he wrote, "I would say that our Jewish students have achieved scholastically as well as Gentiles; but the Jewish student does not fit into our scheme here."

Why didn't Jews fit into "our scheme"? For the same alleged reason James Kingsland didn't fit: "We are making every effort to provide the rural towns of New England, and Vermont more particularly, with doctors. There are very few Jews in these rural communities." Jenne added, "This is a state-supported institution, and we feel it necessary to take care of the sons and daughters [*sic*] of the tax-payers and the men and women [*sic*] from our own University before considering non-resident applicants. This accounts for our small number [*sic*] of out-of-state residents."[53]

This was more false than true. I've found no evidence that rural Vermont communities rejected Jewish doctors. The daughters of taxpayers were hardly "taken care of" by a school that had accepted so few of them. And the College of Medicine drew heavily from other states for students.

But by the late 1930s, at a time when many, perhaps most American medical schools still discriminated overtly or covertly against prospective Jewish students,[54] UVM reversed course and accepted them despite pressure-verging-on-blackmail not to. The pressure came from a respected national body, the Association of American Medical Colleges.

When A. Bradley Soule became acting dean in 1937, the medical school was in deep trouble. It had been put on probation by the Council on Medical Education because its teaching standards were not up to those required of a medical faculty. This was not the first time the school had been disciplined by a national body, and the pressure to clean its slate was considerable.

In November 1937, Dean Soule met with Fred Zapffe, secretary of the Association of American Medical Colleges. Zapffe, who had been one of the Council's inspectors, seemed to have extraordinary power over UVM's College of Medicine. He okayed the retirement of certain department chairmen, deemed two prospective chairmen acceptable, advised that "a local man" should become the new dean and, according to Dean Soule, "declared that he was opposed to the admission of Jewish students, especially those from New York City."[55]

Either from idealism, economic necessity or a mixture of the two, the medical school did not kowtow to Zappfe's demand. Historian Sam Hand and medical historian Lester Wallman both told me the College of Medicine continued to admit Jews, some of whom went on to become outstanding Vermont doctors. And despite its refusal to discriminate, the medical school came off probation at the end of 1940.[56]

"Throw All Protestants off the Staff"

The College of Medicine's uneasy relationship with the Catholic diocese has a long history. Underlying tensions surfaced in the 1920s with the construction of a Catholic hospital in Burlington. Sociologist Elin Anderson described its effects:

The growth of the two large hospitals in the community affords another interesting indication of the way in which a community enterprise is split on a religious basis. One of the hospitals, the Mary Fletcher, established in 1879, is a private, non-profit institution serving all people of all classes and creeds from all parts of the State. Until 1924 there was in addition a small Roman Catholic hospital on the outskirts of the city, but in that year a large one, the Bishop DeGoesbriand [named after the first bishop of Burlington, Louis DeGoesbriand], was built in the center of the city. The erection of this hospital, following as it did close upon the building of the parochial high school, seemed to many people to mark one more step in the tightening of the lines in the community according to affiliation with the Protestant or the Catholic faith.

No Catholic [in the mid-1930s] is a member of the Board of Directors of the Mary Fletcher, no Protestant a member of the Board of Directors of the Bishop DeGoesbriand."[57]

Tension between the two institutions rose and fell over the next several decades but was always a palpable presence. The University and the medical school were frequently dragged into the melee. Two medical school deans, Hardy A. Kemp and William Eustace Brown, worked hard at bringing the DeGoesbriand into the medical college program in the 1940s. Martin Kaufman reports that Bishop Edward Ryan met with Brown and asked "why Catholic hospitals were second- and third-rate institutions. Brown responded that Catholic hospitals traditionally selected their staff on the basis of religious affiliation rather than professional competence. As a result of the discussion, an agreement was drawn up giving the College the right to approve staff appointments at the Hospital." But this move threatened the status of some of the DeGoesbriand physicians, heightening animosity rather than abating it. The president of the DeGoesbriand medical staff observed, "Catholic DeGoesbriand staff . . . seemed to have a real hatred of the Medical School and for the doctors associated with it."[58]

In 1949 it was the Protestants' turn to hit the roof. Bishop Ryan, wanting to prevent abortions at the diocese hospital, appointed a devout Catholic doctor to head the Department of Obstetrics and Gynecology, and he did so without consulting the dean. According to Kaufman, "rumors spread that the Bishop was going to 'throw all Protestants off the staff' of the DeGoesbriand, that members of the Obstetrics Department of the Hospital 'were going to be subject to a new czar' . . . and that 'a grand plot was under way to embarrass the University.' "[59]

A Jewish surgeon, Arthur Gladstone, helped bring the warring Catholic and Protestant camps together. In 1954, Gladstone offered his services as a liaison officer for the two institutions and thus became a one-person communication conduit between them. Kaufman says that by 1957 Gladstone's presence had so improved morale at DeGoesbriand that the new dean (George Wolf) and the new bishop (Robert Joyce) began the process of exploring "what steps can be taken to formalize and integrate the DeGoesbriand program with the College of Medicine."[60]

The dean and the bishop set up a "tri-institution committee" to bring peace between the medical school and the DeGoesbriand and Mary Fletcher hospitals. After a number of fits, starts, and skirmishes, the two hospitals became one on January 17, 1967, now known as the Medical Center Hospital of Vermont. Finally, the great divide between Protestant and Catholic was bridged.

Conclusions

The recent history of minorities at UVM is a story of indifference and idealism, head-banging frustration and triumphant success. It is a story inextricably linked to social change, for the opening of American universities to religious and racial minorities has had to be fought for time after time. As I read and listened to the words of those involved in the struggle, certain patterns emerged:

* Universities are usually ahead of the general populace with regard to minority rights.

* From its beginnings and at many points in its history, UVM has been ahead of most universities.

* Faculty used to be ahead of administration, both at UVM and elsewhere, but in the last two decades that relationship has often been reversed.

* Students have consistently been ahead of faculty and administration, both now and in the past.

* The main campus was and is well ahead of the medical school.

* And everybody is ahead of the trustees.

* Within each group, a relatively small number has levered a sometimes unwilling majority either into action or at least acceptance of action toward the improvement of minority status. The tactics of this minority have always been criticized as too pushy/strident/impolite . . . too something.

* Resolution often precedes action by many years. Fraternities and sorori-

ties discriminated against minorities for decades after both Pan-Hellenic and Inter-Fraternity councils outlawed discrimination. Cultural pluralism existed on paper for twenty years before a student takeover pushed for renewed implementation.

* At UVM the editorials of the student newspaper have consistently set the tone for change. The University—first students, then faculty or adminis-tration, finally trustees—has sometimes grudgingly, sometimes willingly, gone along.

* Finally, UVM has at times risen to the challenge of minority involvement and at times utterly failed to do so. The Crystal Malone affair, the keeping of blacks and Jews out of the medical school, the naming of dormitories after bigoted administrators were low points in our history. The resolute sisters of Alpha Xi Delta, the medical school's refusal to go along with the Association of American Medical Colleges' anti-Semitism, and the student fight against racial segregation are among the high points.

Epilogue

This chapter opened in 1961 when Kappa Sigma was the Animal House, complete with Nazi flag, and Alpha Epsilon Pi was an exclusively Jewish fraternity. In 1989 I went back and visited both. I began with Alpha Epsi-lon Pi.

Along with the two predominantly Jewish fraternities, AEPi disbanded a decade or so ago, but in 1986 it was revived by a small group of Jewish stu-dents. Today about a third of its small membership is not Jewish. When last year's prospective pledges appeared to be overwhelmingly non-Jews, some of the Jewish members suddenly felt overwhelmed. To keep AEPi's Jewish identity, they made a conscious effort to target Jews as prospective pledges. The small, impoverished-looking fraternity is still struggling with its mixed identity—a Jewish organization that does not discriminate against non-Jews.

Kappa Sigma is no longer the Animal House—ironically, Sigma Nu now seems to hold that title. It's no longer anti-Semitic; probably a third of its members are Jews, and the others were surprised to hear me refer to Jews as "minority students." (Neither Jews nor Catholics now fall within the national criteria for "minorities.")

I had expected to conclude this chapter by saying, "And of course, Kappa Sig no longer has a Nazi flag hanging in one of its bedrooms." It doesn't, and the brothers were shocked when I told them it once did. But Kappa Sig does have two large Confederate flags hanging in one of its bedrooms. I asked my hosts if they didn't think this might look the same to a prospective black pledge as that swastika did to me. Although they denied the intent was in any way racist, they did agree that it might be taken that way.

The Curriculum—II: The Comprehensive University of the Twentieth Century

PATRICK H. HUTTON

SHORTLY before the turn of the century, John Converse, a graduate of the class of 1861, made a gift to the University of Vermont for the purpose of inaugurating a new program in commerce and economics, one of the first in the country. At a ceremony honoring him for his generosity, Converse remarked on the challenge of integrating a general education in the humanities with a practical one in the professions in the curricular offerings of the University as it entered the twentieth century.[1] It was a speech that might still be given today in that it expresses the problem of curricular diversity with which educators at UVM continue to wrestle. UVM has from its earliest days been a pluralistic institution of higher education. The present system of colleges, inaugurated in 1911, was already prefigured in the departments established in 1889.[2] Each of these, in turn, had emerged autonomously during the nineteenth century, and each had fostered its own intellectual traditions.

But UVM was not without a unifying tradition as it entered the twentieth century. Implicit in all of the individual courses of study was an underlying vision of the way in which they related to the larger curriculum of the University. Each college may have designed its own courses of study, but each did so on the basis of a larger consensus about an education as a formation in a particular tradition of learning. In all fields of intellectual inquiry, whether they were as practical as engineering or as imaginative as the humanities, the curricula were prescribed in clear and coherent patterns. From the late nineteenth century, these were delineated in an annual bulletin, course by course, sometimes even noting individual readings that a course was to include. Until the eve of World War II, the bulletin provided an extensive reading list of books considered essential as a preparation for the entrance examination, and nearly all courses of study were presented in graphic form so that entering students might see at a glance what was to be expected of them in the programs they were about to pursue. For the faculty, the curriculum of the University was the formalized expression of a common intellectual tradition into which students were to be initiated. They might choose any of a variety of courses of study in which they would learn quite different things, but the terms of each were well understood, and they fitted in a complementary way into a larger conception of the framework of knowledge.

Nowhere else was this sense of the grounding of the curriculum in an intellectual tradition more deeply acknowledged than in the College of Arts and Sciences, whose courses of study well into the twentieth century continued to display the hallmarks of its heritage in Classical languages. Until 1942 the A.B. (*Artium Baccalaureus*) degree was awarded only to students completing the Classical curriculum, which demanded proficiency in both Greek and Latin. The consolation prize was the Ph.B. (Bachelor of Philosophy), conferred on students in the literary-scientific and the general science curricula. But even these students were expected to satisfy a requirement in Latin. In 1934 a social science curriculum was added to these offerings. Students in this immediately popular program were permitted to substitute a modern foreign language for an ancient one, but like the others, this program emphasized the importance of foundational learning.[3] In all of these "group elective" curricula, course work in mathematics, English composition, English literature, and philosophy was also required, together with a cluster of elective courses drawn from three broad areas of learning (languages, social science, and natural science) and sequences of courses in more specific major-field and minor-field concentrations.

In 1942 these curricula were consolidated into a single "liberal arts" program, for which a B.A. (Bachelor of Arts) degree was awarded. As the translation of the degree title from Latin into English suggests, intellectual attainment in Classics was discarded as the distinguishing trait of the well-educated graduate. Courses in ancient languages, together with those in mathematics, were dropped from the required list. At the same time, the college reaffirmed its commitment to the principle of a common curriculum by requiring courses in subjects judged essential for all students pursuing the B.A. degree. The announcement in the bulletin for 1947 spoke of the need for rigorous training in languages, "particularly in English, as the mother tongue and chief tool of thought and expression."[4] The college therefore continued to prescribe introductory courses in English composition, literature, foreign language (ancient or modern), and a laboratory science. For advanced work, three tracks of "group electives" were prescribed: language, literature, and music; social science; and science and mathematics. Basic courses in literature, history, and mathematics respectively were designated as prerequisites for entry into these fields. These subjects, then, acquired a special prominence in the curriculum as the keystones of a liberal arts education.

For the faculty, these new requirements underscored an ongoing commitment to the principle of a common intellectual formation. But a subtle shift in thinking about the curriculum was in the making, away from required courses (a core curriculum) toward elective fields of study (a distribution requirement). Not since the turn of the century had particular courses been required; the 1942 reforms, in carrying forward the prewar scheme of required courses at the introductory level and required disciplines at the advanced level (group electives), reflected a lingering sympathy for a core-type curriculum. But the long-range trend was away from content-oriented requirements, which implied a universally accepted intellectual tradition, toward procedure-oriented ones, based on a search for a more practical principle of curricular organization in an era in which the consensus about that tradition was breaking down.

The curricular reform of 1969 crystallized this trend. In that year a distribution requirement was substituted for the modest remnants of core offerings. Students were thenceforth permitted to choose any three courses from three of four broadly defined areas of learning (languages and literature, fine arts and philosophy, social science, science and mathematics). The obvious effect of this curricular revision was to place new emphasis on academic specialization. For some time, individual departments had been mandating more courses for their majors; indeed, major-field requirements were beginning to assume the complexity of the group-elective curricula of the prewar era. Less explicit was the shift in educational philosophy that the 1969 reform suggested. No single discipline or even broad field of learning was any longer considered essential for a liberal arts education. The aim of the new curriculum was not exposure to a definite body of learning, nor even the acquisition of a set of intellectual skills, but rather a common procedure for students to randomly sample a burgeoning array of disciplines. The curricular reform of 1969, therefore, repudiated the traditional preeminence accorded substantive learning. Instead of an introduction to a common culture, the College of Arts and Sciences substituted a common rite of passage.

This shift in thinking about curriculum in the college was in some measure dictated by the extraordinary growth of the University over the course of the twentieth century, particularly after World War II. Expansion took place through yearly accretions, so that its long-range effect on the curriculum was not immediately perceived. To take its measure, one must make quantum leaps in the comparisons. What at the turn of the century had been a small university devoted primarily to the instruction of undergraduates had by the late 1960s become a comparatively large one with a variety of educational responsibilities.[5] The College of Arts and Sciences may still have enrolled a majority of the undergraduate students (54% in 1969), but it was no longer the academic center around which the professional colleges revolved.[6] Rather, it was only one in a number of growing constituencies, all of which had practical pedagogical objectives and most of which had ambitious research plans.

Not only did the four colleges (Arts and Sciences, Medicine, Engineering, and Agriculture) into which the University had been organized at the outset of the twentieth century grow and diversify. From midcentury, each spawned satellite schools that quickly acquired autonomous identities. The College of Arts and Sciences served as the matrix for the School of Education and Nursing (1946); the College of Medicine, for the School of Allied Health Sciences (1968); the College of Agriculture, for the School of Natural Resources (1973) and the School of Home Economics (1973); and the College of Engineering, for the School of Business Administration (1981). The problem of curriculum at UVM since midcentury has thus been intertwined with that of the organization of the University. In this respect, two eras of organizational reform are worth noting: the years immediately following World War II, when veterans eager for an education were returning to school in great numbers; and the late 1960s, a time of cultural ferment and pedagogical re-evaluation.

The organizational reforms of the late 1940s were tied to the dramatic expansion of the University in the postwar era. The creation of a School of Education and Nursing in 1946 paved the way. It consolidated instruction in a variety of curricula in teacher training that had taken shape haphazardly within the College of Arts and Sciences since the 1920s. There were by then five curricula (elementary education, junior high school education, secondary education, industrial arts education, and music education). Within this new structure, the Department of Nursing, inaugurated within the College of Arts and Sciences in 1944, found a temporary niche while awaiting a more logical home. Physical education (the department that has taught the only courses required of all undergraduates throughout the twentieth century) received departmental standing within the College of Education and Nursing in 1959.[7]

The College of Engineering was reconstituted as the College of Technology in the same year. Since the late nineteenth century it had offered highly prescribed courses of study in mechanical, civil and electrical engineering. All students enrolled in basic science and mathematics courses during their first two years and then proceeded to their field of specialization. To these long-standing programs, the college added a new curriculum in management engineering, offering a broader professional education for those with business ambitions. This program served as a point of connection with the Department of Commerce and Economics, simultaneously transferred from the College of Arts and Sciences. In its new setting, Commerce and Economics revised and expanded its offerings to include a theoretical program of core courses for the first two years and an array of more practical options for upper-level concentration.[8] The Departments of Chemistry and

Mathematics were also assigned here, although, like Commerce and Economics, they continued to offer programs for the B.A. within the College of Arts and Sciences.[9] Thus, the College of Arts and Sciences was divested not only of its professional programs but also of some of its traditional departments.

The expansion of the professional schools was in part dictated by the growing demand for and academic respectability of vocational education. Given its tradition as a comprehensive university, UVM was prepared to respond to this national trend. But the reasons for the organizational changes at UVM after the war were as much expedient as they were philosophical. They were designed to come to terms with the provision of the Wilbur Trust stating that funds would be forthcoming only as long as enrollment in the University did not exceed one thousand students. By that date the student population had already surpassed that limit, and university officials were working to modify its provisions. In 1932 university counsel Warren Austin successfully argued in chancery court that Wilbur certainly meant the College of Arts and Sciences in setting the figure that appeared in his will.[10] Although the college was obliged to keep the size of its student body within these limits, other academic units were permitted to grow freely. With the growth of the student body following World War II, however, even this reading of the provisions of the trust became a perplexing barrier to educational needs. University officials had no choice but to resort to organizational gerrymandering. In 1946, the Departments of Botany, Chemistry, Mathematics, and Commerce and Economics were parceled out among other colleges.

Such expedients notwithstanding, the professionalization of the curriculum was a long-range trend whose effects would have been visible anyway by midcentury. In this respect, the establishment of the Graduate College in 1952 was a sign of the times. Graduate degrees had been awarded as early as 1807, and graduate students were present in sufficient numbers by 1942 (twenty-five were enrolled in 1940; fifty-six advanced degrees were awarded in 1942) to prompt the creation of a graduate council to supervise their work.[11] The increase in their numbers was thenceforth steady, and the formation of the Graduate College heralded a future in which advanced professional education and postdoctoral research would occupy a more prominent place in the University.[12] In 1958 the first Ph.D. program was authorized (in biochemistry), and by 1971 fifteen more had been added.[13] The organizational reforms of the postwar years therefore signaled the official acknowledgment of the enhanced stature that programs in professional education had acquired and the role that research projects would thenceforth play in shaping the intellectual life of the University.

Equally significant were the organizational reforms of the late 1960s, which mainly concerned the biological sciences. These too represented the crystallization of long-range trends. As in the late 1940s, new academic units were created, and older ones were revamped. On an intellectual plane, they institutionalized the new technologies developed in medicine and biology. On a practical plane, they met the pressing need to group fields related to medicine that had been scattered about the University (dental hygiene, autonomous since 1949; medical technology, originally a hospital-based program, housed in the College of Arts and Sciences from 1946, transferred to the College of Technology in 1951) or were new to it (radiologic technology, physical therapy). A School of Allied Health Sciences, founded in 1968, brought them all together. At the same time, the programs in nursing were detached from the College of Education and given official standing within an autonomous school.[14]

The College of Medicine remained a preserve apart, but it too inaugurated significant curricular reforms in the late 1960s to take cognizance of the realities of practicing medicine in the late twentieth century. Medical students at UVM were still being trained in the image of the country doctor. As generalists, they pursued a common curriculum that provided for three years of classroom instruction followed by one year of clinical work. There were periodic curricular reforms, notably in 1928, 1937, and 1940, that introduced new fields of study and provided for more clinical training. But the college continued to prescribe a single academic program for all students, whose skills, independent of their interests, were regarded as interchangeable. By the 1960s, however, the image of the physician as general practitioner was a sentimental ideal, given the explosion of knowledge in the biological sciences and the refinement of medical technologies during and after World War II. Advances in surgical procedures, pharmacology, instrumentation, and diagnostic skills were such that no amount of classroom instruction could any longer survey their dimensions. The challenge facing college leaders, therefore, was to adapt the curriculum to the needs of the time without lengthening what was already a protracted course of postbaccalaureate study.[15]

Preliminary discussion of such a task had begun in the 1950s under the leadership of Dean George Wolf, and it was brought to fruition in the mid-1960s by Dean Edward Andrews and Associate Dean William Luginbuhl. This comprehensive reform (1967) balanced classroom study with a greater measure of clinical training begun earlier in the student's program, and it created major-field concentrations analogous to those of an undergraduate curriculum. Under the new program, students spent only their first 1½ years in the classroom; they then passed through a clinical rotation of major specialties during the following year. For the remaining 1½ years, each student chose an area of concentration in which there were both core subjects and elective offerings. Although abandoning a common course of study, the new program addressed the needs of medical education in an age in which nearly all physicians, even those engaged in family practice, were obliged to acquire some degree of specialization.[16]

The efforts of the College of Agriculture and Home Economics to respond to the intellectual changes in its fields led to a more troubling reassessment of its educational objectives. The formation of the college in 1911 still owed much to Vermont senator Justin Morrill's populist vision of the land grant college. Having headed off the challenge of a faction that wished to implement a narrow vocational curriculum, college leaders aspired to offer a scientific course of study that might serve as an alternative to the literary studies so prominent in the curriculum of the College of Arts and Sciences.[17] Deans Joseph Hills and Joseph Carrigan guided the college through a half-century of growth and rising academic respectability that might be characterized as its golden age.[18] By 1961, the College offered nine majors in agriculture, five in home economics, and one in forestry. But the economy and culture of a once rural state were changing, and agriculture and home economics were slated for a more modest role. In 1972 a task force appointed by President Andrews recommended that the college be reduced to the status of a department; meanwhile the college was trying to give its curriculum a more alluring scientific turn.[19] Taking advantage of the intellectual revolution in cell biology during the 1960s, the college instituted a core program in the biological sciences (1968) and expanded the options for majors.

This innovation helped forestall dissolution of the college, but it also reinforced the trend toward specialization. Many faculty members in home economics, who saw themselves as generalists bringing together diverse skills, greeted the changes with mixed feelings. The alliance between the fields, forged in 1916, had always been an uneasy one in which mostly female members of the home economics faculty felt that their interests were being sacrificed to those of the larger and mostly male agriculture departments.[20] Resentment was rising among the foresters as well. Founded in the early 1950s, their program had functioned for years as a two-year course in "pre-forestry," which obliged its students to transfer to other institutions to earn a bachelor's degree. A four-year program was finally begun in 1966 but remained a small-scale operation. The burgeoning interest in environmental studies in the late 1960s presented forestry with opportunities to diversify its curricular offerings. Both units, therefore, chose to separate from the College of Agriculture in 1973: home economics as an autonomous school, forestry as the nucleus of a School of Natural Resources.

Seeking to modernize its identity, the School of Home Economics stressed subjects of particular contemporary concern: clothing, nutrition, human development, and social welfare. Ironically, the broad-based curriculum in domestic skills being discarded as overly traditional had been conceived by the program's founder, Bertha Terrill, as an innovative way to promote women's independence. But Terrill's vision of what studies in home economics were supposed to do dissolved in this more professional curriculum; and amid declining enrollments, faculty quarrels, and the criticisms of a review committee, the school was dismantled in 1980. An interdisciplinary program in home economics was retained, but its constituent fields were either abandoned (housing), reabsorbed into the College of Agriculture (nutrition, textiles, home economics education), or put into the College of Education (human development).[21] The program in forestry, in contrast, was able to take advantage of a new-found identity as a School of Natural Resources. The school developed programs in wildlife ecology, recreational management, resource economics, and environmental studies, all subjects of topical interest in the public arena. Closely related to it was the highly innovative interdisciplinary program in environmental studies, designed to draw students from throughout the University by offering curricula in four colleges.[22]

Considered in their ensemble, the organizational reforms of the late 1940s and the late 1960s had a threefold effect on thinking about the curriculum. The first was to decentralize the process of decision making about curricular offerings. Technically, the president of the University retained responsibility for the curriculum until 1946, and officially the University Senate does so to this day. But as a practical matter, the individual colleges made their own decisions after 1946, and this accentuated differences in the ways in which the same courses were perceived by students from the various constituencies of the University. The common intellectual ground on which old and new colleges had been founded was increasingly viewed from divergent perspectives.

Consider, for example, the relationship between the College of Education and the College of Arts and Sciences. The former had emerged from the latter and under Dean Thomas King shared many of its educational goals. When education was still a department within Arts and Sciences in the years before World War II, the majority of its students were enrolled in the secondary education program. Although they received a B.S. in education, they satisfied many of the requirements expected of students in the Ph.B. programs. During the 1920s and 1930s, smaller programs in elementary and vocational education were added to the department, but they were taught apart according to standards set by the state Board of Education.[23] The proliferation of these programs led logically to a drive for autonomy, realized after the war with the formation of an autonomous School of Education. Therein the secondary education curriculum, formerly the more popular program, was rivaled by that in primary education, for which there was much demand in the years after the war.[24] In 1951 the school became a college, and all of its curricula thenceforth fell under the standards of a national board of teacher accreditation. Over the following decades the college placed an increasing emphasis on the professional formation of all prospective teachers, though majors in secondary education continued to meet high expectations in their subject matter areas through courses taught by the College of Arts and Sciences, and some work in subject areas was required for all other programs. But the trend was away from substantive learning toward professional preparation. The erosion of standards of general education culminated in a curricular reform of 1969 establishing a common distribution requirement of sixty credit hours in five broad areas of learning, but mandating just one course in each of these areas.

Correspondingly, the required hours in courses in professional education were periodically augmented, so by the late 1960s it was difficult for students in the College of Arts and Sciences to meet teacher certification standards (as many had before) without careful planning. Secondary education, the keystone of the education department of the 1930s, was relegated to a lesser place in the curriculum, especially after 1973 when the renamed College of Education and Social Services redefined its mission to emphasize educational administration and social work. The teacher education departments were consolidated, and departments in education administration, counseling, and special education were added,[25] while the curriculum committee of the college searched for a conception of general education based on "cognitive development" instead of substantive knowledge.[26] Thus, the organizational separation of education as a discipline from its roots in the College of Arts and Sciences fostered opposing conceptions of the curriculum and eventually obliged students thinking about a career in teaching to make a choice between their vocational and their intellectual goals.

Second, the trend toward curricular professionalization posed a dilemma for other expanding disciplines about their intellectual, as opposed to their vocational, identity. Commerce is a case in point. From 1899 until World War II the Department of Commerce and Economics was a large and popular field within the College of Arts and Sciences, offering a variety of practical and theoretical courses of study. The decision in 1946 to move the department to the newly formed College of Technology placed the accent on its professional rather than its theoretical side. Though the department was returned to the College of Arts and Sciences in 1963, its academic wing (economics) and its professional wing (renamed business administration in 1967) diverged. In 1973 the program in business administration opted for a place within the newly formed College of Engineering, Mathematics, and Business Administration (EMBA), while economics remained as a department within the College of Arts and Sciences. The schism followed national trends and may have made sense in terms of the way in which the discipline was being diversified and redefined. But it also obliged students doing work in this field to choose between an intellectual and a professional formation.

A third effect of organizational reform was to encourage the search for structuralist solutions to problems at all levels of the curriculum. Concomitant with the efforts of various colleges to revise their academic programs internally, university leaders devised a plan to organize the burgeoning array of disciplines relating to health care into a larger organizational structure. The Division of Health Sciences, grouping medicine, allied health, and nursing, was officially constituted in 1968. The reform was designed to coordinate the efforts of these academic units in their search for research funds and to plan the allocation of resources among them. It may also have been a mechanism for mitigating rivalries; the category of division permitted confederation where integration may not have been wanted. But it also provided a model for the reorganization of the University into academic superstructures, one that was gradually implemented across much of the campus. In 1981, a Division of Engineering, Mathematics, and Business Administration came into being, with business administration reorganized therein as an autonomous school. The prospect of creating a similar division to coordinate the programs of the College of Agriculture and Life Sciences with those of the School of Natural Resources was for a long time forestalled by the rivalries among its potential constituencies, but by the late 1980s it too had become a topic for long-range planning.[27] No proposal has yet been made to group Arts and Sciences with Education.

The concept of the division, invented to create administrative efficiency, had nothing directly to do with curricular issues. It revealed the pervasiveness of structuralist thinking within the University, with the search for abstract models of organizational and curricular coherence that had little to do with UVM's intellectual traditions. If courses could be clustered as subsets of a discipline and arranged hierarchically according to degree of difficulty, such thinking presupposed, a more nearly uniform course of study for all students might be achieved. More appealing still, such a schema created a unity of procedure where a unity of knowledge was no longer a realistic goal. It is worth noting that in the same year (1968) that university administrators unveiled the concept of a divisional superstructure to schematize the organization of the health sciences, they also set criteria for the numbering of courses in a five-tiered hierarchy of presumed difficulty.[28] Despite the semblance of overarching academic coherence, such superstructures helped obscure what remained of a common intellectual core. Unwittingly, this abstract schematization of the curriculum reinforced the notion that the foundation of the educational experience lies in the organization of the curriculum rather than in the substance of the individual courses.

As a practical matter, a greater measure of departmental autonomy in curricular issues had become necessary. Until World War I most departments offered fewer than ten courses, and they were typically identified in the bulletin through a system of single-digit numbering. By the 1930s some of the larger departments had begun to make distinctions between two and even three levels of intellectual sophistication. But as the number of departments burgeoned after World War II, so did the number of courses that each one offered, reinforcing the trend toward upper-level concentration as the place for intellectual formation. By the 1950s all departments were arranging their courses according to their perceived intellectual difficulty. Programs of study, hitherto conceived as a problem of curricula at the college level, were increasingly defined after the 1969 reforms along departmental lines, as each department specified more required courses for their majors, as well as the sequence in which such courses were to be taken.

The larger trend toward specialization was in some measure a function of the expansion of the University; it was also a response to the diversification of learning within higher education across the country. By the midtwentieth century, however, the trend itself had engendered a nostalgia for what was believed to be a lost curricular unity. In fact, as our history of the curriculum has underscored, such a unity never existed at UVM. The professional colleges stuck closely to their vocational missions from the time they were formed, and the various liberal arts curricula of the College of Arts and Sciences before 1942 were self-contained.

But where no tradition of university-wide education existed, one was about to be invented. In the early 1960s, precisely the time when everyone at UVM was beginning to sense how rapidly the curriculum was being professionalized, university leaders embarked on a quest for a program in the liberal arts that would serve as the foundation for all colleges in the University. This venture coincided with President John Fey's successful effort to annul the provisions of the Wilbur trust limiting enrollment. Departments from the College of Arts and Sciences assigned elsewhere in 1946 might now be returned, and university officials could now reassess the mix of professional and intellectual objectives in the curriculum. Fey came down emphatically on the intellectual side. In his report to the Board of Trustees in 1960 he pointed out the threats of too much professionalization and called for a reaffirmation of the University's commitment to its intellectual heritage:

If in the constantly changing environment of modern civilization a university finds itself in the role of a service agency, ready to meet every demand that society may make upon it, then there is a real danger that the vital purposes and goals of higher education may be lost. . . . What then, is the basic purpose of the University of Vermont—what is its philosophy of education? Basically, I should say that this is an institution which is dedicated to pure learning in the humanities, the physical sciences, and the social sciences.[29]

For several years the essentials of Fey's statement of principle were reprinted as an introduction to the university catalog but were dropped, significantly, after the 1969 curricular reforms.

Fey's viewpoint was buttressed by a faculty "self-study" committee, chaired by Professor Samuel Bogorad, which in 1962 recommended a "common freshman year" throughout the University.[30] Neither this nor the more far-reaching objective of the committee to strengthen the standing of the humanities and sciences within the University's curriculum was achieved. The Fey proposal was an abortive attempt to stay the trend toward the professionalization of the curriculum. By the 1960s it was too late to do so, even if Fey's policy initiative did inspire some measure of compliance by individual colleges. For the moment, the College of Arts and Sciences reaffirmed its commitment to the requirements established in 1942. The professional colleges mandated some electives in the humanities and the sciences, although no common principles or any requirements for proficiency beyond the introductory level were ever adopted.

Fey had raised an important philosophical issue that was bound to provoke further debate even within the College of Arts and Sciences. For the college, too, was being professionalized. Younger members of the faculty, hired in great numbers during the 1960s, brought with them a professional bias in favor of their newly acquired academic specializations and their expertise in research. From among their ranks, the devil's advocates to Fey's vision of a university were, by the end of the decade, beginning to be heard. The critics questioned whether there was any subject essential for a liberal arts education, and they charged that core requirements were arbitrary. Defenders of core requirements conceded that point while framing it in a different way. No single course might be considered indispensable in an abstract sense. But courses are taught not in abstract settings but rather within intellectual traditions. Because they are elaborated historically, traditions are unique and hence inherently arbitrary. But that, they concluded, is no reason to view them pejoratively, for they provide the only frameworks in which intellectual maturity may be achieved.[31] Given the intellectual iconoclasm of the late 1960s, it was not a propitious moment to raise this argument. The College of Arts and Sciences abandoned the remnants of its core requirements in 1969.[32]

The elusive quest for a core curriculum was nonetheless renewed in the late 1970s by the Inaugural Committee on Undergraduate Education appointed by President Lattie Coor. This time the agenda was even more ambitious. Not only would academic units be asked to provide some studies in the liberal arts, as they had been in 1962; now they would be asked to consider a program in "general education" in which all students in the University would be enrolled.[33] The renewed search for the University's common intellectual ground was motivated as it had been before by a concern about academic overspecialization.[34] But it was now accentuated by the unforeseen consequences of the abandonment of core requirements by the College of Arts and Sciences in 1969. The new curriculum shifted the responsibility for building the students' individual courses of study from guidelines devised by the faculty to free choices given to the students, and this created anxiety among those students who did not have clearly defined educational goals. What had been devised as a solution to arbitrariness in the curriculum in the late 1960s unintentionally gave rise to an "advising" problem by the mid-1970s, about which students and faculty alike complained.[35] Imbalances in the courses of study chosen by students also began to appear. Unacknowledged but significant was the shift of student interest toward the social and behavioral sciences (economics, sociology, political science, and psychology), whose enrollments grew dramatically during the 1970s while those in the traditional core disciplines (foreign languages, history, and mathematics) remained static or declined.[36]

In 1978 President Coor convened a Committee on Baccalaureate Education (COBE) under the leadership of political science professor Alan Wertheimer, with a mandate to study the implementation of common requirements across the curriculum.[37] After some study the committee rejected the notion of core requirements as impractical for UVM in the late twentieth century. Instead, it proposed a requirement for courses in three basic skills (expository writing, quantitative methods, and symbolic communication). It also proposed an ambitious distribution requirement covering seven broad areas of learning (literature, foreign language, history, cross-cultural studies, social institutions and analysis, artistic appreciation, and science). Within each area, specific courses were to be designated for fulfilling the requirement, and instructors were to be encouraged to create courses for the new curriculum. Follow-up courses in some of these areas would be required so that from fifty-four to seventy-two credit hours, or between 45 percent and 60 percent of a student's undergraduate course work, were to be given to general education.[38] Despite its ingenuity and boldness, the COBE proposal echoed the structuralist thinking that had shaped the discourse about curriculum since the late 1960s. The essential mechanism of the program was a common procedure for sampling broadly defined intellectual fields in which entire disciplines were interchangeable.

But as the University entered the 1980s, a set of fixed requirements that permitted even this degree of flexibility was certain to encounter resistance. Although comment on the COBE report was generally favorable, criticisms were wide-ranging. The definition of the rubrics was attacked as arbitrary, and the charge leveled against core requirements at the college level a decade before was now raised against distribution requirements at the university level: from a structuralist viewpoint, there were no sound intellectual grounds for preferring one field of learning over another.[39] With so much of the undergraduate education to be devoted to general studies, most of which fell within the province of the College of Arts and Sciences, faculty members in other colleges understandably worried about the fate of their professional programs. Some asked why general education should not draw more comprehensively on all of the offerings of the University.[40] The COBE was thus confronted with the ironical proposition that a program designed to counter the trend toward the professionalization of undergraduate education ought to accommodate the interests of the professional colleges in its requirements. In the face of such absurdities, the COBE proposal was quietly relegated to limbo.

Although this ambitious proposal proved as abortive as the Fey reform twenty years earlier, it did have a positive effect on individual colleges. Under the leadership of Dean John Jewett, the College of Arts and Sciences revised its curriculum to deal with the deficiencies of the one in place since 1969, and the plan that was implemented in 1986 was not that far removed from the one proposed by COBE. Requirements for the study of a foreign language, mathematics, and non-European culture were mandated, although another proposed in English composition (camouflaged as "expository writing") was tabled.[41] The distribution requirement was made more elaborate— students would choose eight courses from five areas, and within each of these specific course options were designated.[42] Provisions for a minor field, similar in intent to the "group elective" of the pre-1942 curricula, were also established to require some advanced work in a field other than the major. The 1986 reform represented a compromise, but the college had gone a long way toward reestablishing contact with its intellectual traditions severed in the 1969 curricular revision.

If the notion of general education through the establishment of university-wide requirements has proved to be an impossible dream, modest efforts to establish cooperation across disciplinary lines have emerged as a countervailing trend to specialization over the past three decades. Although departmental loyalties have become deeply entrenched at UVM, imaginative efforts have been made to create interdisciplinary programs on a more limited scale. Launching such initiatives was the creation in 1962 of the Program in Area and International Studies within the College of Arts and Sciences. Seeking to integrate the study of foreign languages with related work in literature, politics, and culture, the program originally established majors in Russian and Eastern European studies and in Latin American studies. Over the following decade similar courses of study were established in the Canadian (1964), Asian (1965), and Western European (1974) areas.[43]

Among the most innovative curricular reforms was the creation in 1968 of an Experimental Program (EP) within the College of Arts and Sciences. Instituted under the leadership of Professor Robert Daniels, the EP was a freshman–sophomore program in which students were randomly invited and faculty were volunteers. The students lived and studied together in small, informal classes, were free (subject to advising) to choose any of the courses the program offered, and received only pass/fail grades. Encouraged by the open intellectual climate of the late 1960s, the EP exuberantly challenged conventional thinking about curriculum, methods of learning, and scholastic evaluation. The venture survived for five years but could not prevail against the dominant curricular trend of specialized course sequences and the expectation of letter grades for admission to graduate schools. Faculty were tethered to departmental obligations and professional demands and so could rarely make a sustained commitment to teach in the program. Nor were its founders altogether happy about the direction the EP had taken, not toward a core curriculum of the sort that had existed in earlier days in the college but toward the opposite extreme. Course offerings changed from year to year, and faculty methods and expectations varied radically from course to course. The program revealed in an exaggerated way the consumerist mentality that an unstructured curriculum tends to breed.[44]

But other innovative programs that have bent the rules in less obtrusive ways have survived and flourished. Foreign study programs, beginning with the creation of the Vermont Overseas Study Program (VOSP) at the University of Nice in 1969, have expanded over the years, as have options for internships in public agencies in Washington, Montpelier, and elsewhere.[45] An honors and individual studies program has since the 1970s permitted highly motivated students to pursue advanced research and writing projects outside the conventional course system. To encourage students to explore unfamiliar avenues of learning, a pass/fail option for elective courses was instituted concurrently.

Just before the EP's demise, the Living/Learning Center was opened (1973). This was a poststructuralist solution to experimental education, that is, a space waiting to be filled with interchangeable contents. The center provided a setting for academic programs devised by faculty and nonacademic ones proposed by students from any quarter of the University. As a place for educational innovation or informal learning rather than a program itself, it permitted everything from language-study suites to adult and teacher education programs, pottery making, fitness, and public advocacy projects. Students who enrolled in these programs typically lived together in the residential suites the center provided, and some of the faculty members teaching in these programs lived with their families in the center's apartments. Juxtaposing such diverse interests, the center worried about its identity, but it enjoyed enough support to continue offering new approaches to learning to this day.[46]

Within the Living/Learning Center, the search for a core curriculum was realized in miniature in the Integrated Humanities Program (IHP), a small-scale venture teaching the literature, philosophy, and history of Western civilization, on parallel tracks, to some thirty freshmen annually. Similar in concept to the Great Books programs long central to the curriculum at St. John's, Columbia, and Stanford, it was planned and initiated in the mid-1970s by Professor Daniels, together with Professors Robert and Mary Hall, in an effort to create the rigorous intellectual program never realized in the EP. Under the direction of Professor Thomas Simone, the IHP continues to serve students who still wish to pursue the traditional education long since abandoned by the University at large.[47]

Discussions about curriculum typically center on administrative and faculty decisions, but whatever rules the faculty legislates at its meetings, individual teachers or, ideally, teachers and students in dialogue still decide what ideas are to be discussed in the classroom. An unwritten tradition about learning has been handed down from generation to generation among the UVM faculty as living legend. At the centennial celebration in 1904 of UVM's first graduating class, Professor James Wheeler characterized this tradition as a commitment to try to instill in students habits of mind that would lead them to intellectual maturity.[48] Many faculty members still hold as an article of faith that at UVM teaching comes first. As the University enters its third century, this belief should be counted among its greatest curricular assets.

Black Image in White Vermont: The Origin, Meaning, and Abolition of Kake Walk

JAMES W. LOEWEN

THE crowd quiets, until an electric stillness fills the darkened auditorium. A pencil-thin spotlight illuminates a black-gloved hand holding a white handkerchief at shoulder height. The hand opens. The handkerchief drops. A band begins a catchy ragtime tune. A larger spotlight picks up two dancers, both men, who kick their feet high into the air, toes pointed, arms around each other's back, moving as one being, in perfect time. The pace is rapid, the gestures staccato. The men move apart, still dancing. Then they slow, but their routine looks even more difficult. They seem to hang in the air between steps. The dancers face each other, link two feet, lean back at an impossible angle, leap high, and push their white-gloved hands skyward. This performance is at once difficult and athletic, graceful and aesthetic. The band, an integral part of the production, shows an uncanny ability to anticipate each tempo change. Even the crowd gets into the act, clapping and chanting rhythmically. It is like ice dancing in its rapid changes of tempo and mood. It is like free-form gymnastics, with certain steps that must be included in an overall routine. It is like ballet. It is like no other. It is UVM Kake Walk, an eighty-year tradition, the crowning event of the school calendar.

In a packed gymnasium, five thousand white people and perhaps two or three people of color watch intently as two white college students put on a caricature of African Americans. Their hands and feet are white, exaggerating the fact that, to some whites, blacks have large hands and feet, whose palms and soles are not the same color as the rest of them. The students' faces are colored black but not a human color. Rather, like the "pickaninny" dolls of the nineteenth century, this black is unnatural. Large white eye and mouth sockets exaggerate the perception whites have that the eyes and lips of African Americans are too big, stand out too vividly against their skin color. Outlandish kinky-haired wigs complete the effect, not so much comic as mildly repulsive, although the audience seems to view it with affection.

The students now begin to strut and kick up their legs in a ritual called "a-walkin' fo' de kake." When they have finished, they bow humbly to a white couple with crowns on, seated in a place of honor. They shuffle off like Stepin Fetchit in the old Hollywood movies. The crowd shows its appreciation with wild applause. This too is UVM Kake Walk, an eighty-year fascination with a stereotype of blacks in the whitest state in the Union.

Where did it come from? Why did it end? Was it just students having fun? Or was Kake Walk racist—and what does that question mean? Shall we now remember it fondly? Gloss over it? Or can we glean from this tradition some insights about our culture and our future?

Surely it is intriguing that an overwhelmingly white university, removed from slavery by several decades and hundreds of miles, should nonetheless fasten on a black image, or rather a white image of black slavery, as the theme for the most important event of its social calendar. Surely it is important that white students far from the nearest African American population center should maintain the theme for eight decades and then find it impossible to develop any other motif to hold their Winter Carnival together.

An educational institution celebrates itself best by inquiring into its past so that from the celebration, learning takes place. In that spirit this essay will journey to the roots of Kake Walk in Southern slavery and its founding at the University of Vermont in 1893. Always I will relate Kake Walk to the spirit of its time because UVM developed the tradition as part of our larger national culture. The essay will probe the growth of Kake Walk—the skits, ice statues, and other competitions. In the fifteenth year of the civil rights movement and growing controversy on campus, students put Kake Walk to rest in the fall of 1969. The essay will examine how the term "racist" might or might not apply to Kake Walk. Finally, it will explore reactions to the tradition by current students, to see what meanings Kake Walk and its demise still impart. Perhaps the journey will provide insights into American race relations that are consequential beyond one terminated tradition at one institution.

Happy Days on the Plantation

Everyone at UVM *thought* that Kake Walk started on the plantation, and in a way it did. However, the northern minstrel show plantation was not the reality of the southern slave plantation. Unlike the "Magnolia Myth" portrayed by Margaret Mitchell, historians since 1960 have painted a much bleaker portrait of slavery on the relatively few large plantations, a portrait that makes understandable such spirituals as "Nobody Knows the Trouble I've Seen."[1]

Defenders of slavery claimed that it was necessary because (according to the Magnolia Myth) blacks were inferior and actually *liked* slavery since their wants were looked after, they didn't have to work hard, and they were a care-free people anyway.[2] Cakewalk expressed that point. In the evening planters sometimes called on their slaves to perform for the amusement of visitors. Slaves hardly had time or freedom to work up an act, so one might play the banjo while the rest danced or strutted around in a circle, each trying to outdo the others in inventiveness and outrageousness. Slaves could make the show their own in style if not occurrence. It was an easier hour than their usual work. The slave who was most comical won the prize, often a lump of sugar or a cake, from which we get the expression "*That* takes the cake!"[3] Slavery was "a system of absolutism," as UVM historian Jeremy Felt would point out a century later. Cakewalk reminded slaves that planters controlled their lives, their leisure, and even their bodily motions. It told whites that they were powerful and important—the same conceit behind hiring only black waiters in fancy clubs today. It was safer for the black man to act happy and stupid "because he discovered that this conduct pleased the white man."[4] Guests fell for the suggestion: "I think them the most good-natured, careless, light-hearted, and happily-constructed human beings I have ever seen," said plantation visitor John Pendleton Kennedy in 1832.[5] As poet Paul Lawrence Dunbar wrote, in the year Kake Walk began at UVM, "We wear the mask that grins and lies."

The Rise of Minstrel Shows

Minstrel shows grew out of this plantation entertainment, gradually de-veloping a specific form, with an "interlocutor," or master of ceremonies, who introduced the various singers, dancers, and comedians. Sometimes he engaged in conversation with them, in which they told outrageous stories of their exploits, complete with humorous dialect or wrong choice of words. The cakewalk provided the climax. The performers walked about in a circle, each in his or her own style, and then each took a turn in the center while the rest formed a semicircle, open to the audience. Cakewalks could build for twenty minutes and typically formed the finale to the first half of the show.[6]

Blackface minstrel shows appeared in America by 1830, with mainly white performers. Always, they exaggerated their subjects. As Robert Toll, our foremost historian of the form, put it, "Although most Northerners did not know what slaves were like, they believed or wanted to believe that black slaves differed greatly from free white Americans. Thus, minstrels emphasized Negro 'peculiarities.'"[7] In the beginning, some skits showed the cruelty of slavery, but most minstrel shows emphasized happy singing "darkies" whose music and dance implied contentment.

During the Civil War and Reconstruction, when African Americans gained their freedom and considerable political rights, entertainment im-plying that they enjoyed bondage simply did not fit, and minstrel shows went into eclipse. Then came the "Nadir of Race Relations in America," from 1877 to 1901, when the white planter class in the South took back the rights guaranteed to African Americans by the Reconstruction Amendments, with Northern acquiescence. As Toll put it, minstrelsy then "provided a nonthreatening way for white Americans to cope with questions about the nature and proper place of black people in America." In the heyday of minstrel shows, from 1875 to 1900, songs like "Carry Me Back to Old Virginny" portrayed African Americans as nostalgic for the antebellum plantation. Always, Toll pointed out, "Heavily caricatured images of Blacks happy on the plantation and lost and incompetent off it"—obviously second-class citizen material—"remained the central message of minstrelsy."[8]

In our electronic age it is hard to imagine how prevalent minstrel shows were. According to Edith Isaacs, "For almost fifty years minstrels were the most popular form of American entertainment." Stephen Foster's and James Bland's famous songs from the nineteenth century—"Old Black Joe," "My Old Kentucky Home," "In the Evening by the Moonlight," and many more—were written for minstrel groups. Minstrel shows were the rage of London. When the Japanese entertained Commodore Perry and his sailors with sumo wrestling, the Americans responded by introducing cakewalk to Japan, where it became part of Japanese culture and was used in toothpaste advertisements and the like for over a century.[9]

Vermont did not escape. From New York City and Boston, minstrel shows toured the state like modern-day rock groups, traveling by steamboat and rail. In 1877 one troupe went "with a caravan of horses and wagons to all the small towns of New England not easily accessible by railroad," according to Carl Wittke's pioneering account of minstrelsy.[10] Publishers rushed booklets into print, supplying standard minstrel jokes and instructing how to apply the makeup and talk in dialect. "By the turn of the century," wrote historian Joseph Boskin, "practically every city, town, and rural community had amateur minstrel groups."[11] Minstrel shows "fixed the tradition of the Negro as only an irresponsible, happy-go-lucky, wide-grinning, loud-laughing, shuffling, banjo-playing, singing, dancing sort of being," according to James Weldon Johnson.[12] In Vermont, where few blacks existed to correct this impression, the stereotype provided the bulk of white "knowledge" about African Americans.

Kake Walk's Beginnings at UVM

Thus, for UVM students to turn to the blackface tradition to amuse themselves was not surprising. As one of its founders put it, the first UVM Kake Walk "was conducted along the usual lines of such functions."[13] African Americans were hardly salient in Vermont, but minstrelsy was a product of white culture and did not require that the object of its derision be present or even exist.

When Kake Walk began is a matter of interpretation. It goes back to the late 1880s, when UVM students occasionally put on "nigger shows," variety shows with a minstrel theme. By tradition its origin is December 19, 1893, when undergraduate Frederick Sharp invited male student friends to a masquerade ball, "Kake Walk," held in the old drill hall in Old Mill. According to one of the three or four student musicians who played for the dancing, "The 'Kake Walk' itself was the concluding event. . . . A procession of couples marched around the hall several times, and then each couple separately, doing their grotesque best." One member of each couple dressed in exaggerated woman's attire. Both wore blackface.[14]

Students repeated the event the next December. According to H. C. Shurtleff ('95), "At the minstrel show given by the students the following February in the old Howard Opera House some of the stunts of this latter cake walk were repeated, possibly introducing the affair to the public for the first time."[15] Some *Cynic* writers claim that UVM stopped Kake Walk for the next two years, but an undergraduate who later taught at UVM stated that he walked in 1895 and 1896. All sources agree that Kake Walk returned in 1897 much enlarged, now called "Kulled Koon's Kake Walk," a title used off and on for several decades. Skits became at least as important as the walking, and in 1908 the Briggs Cup was first awarded for best skit.[16]

The period of Kake Walk's founding, 1888–1893, saw more blacks lynched in the United States than at any other time in our history. During the 1890s whites took away black suffrage in the southern and border states. The image of African Americans in U.S. popular culture deteriorated still further. Major league baseball, which had included African-American players in the 1880s, expelled the last one in 1889. For several years the Bronx Zoo displayed an African in a cage, like a wild animal. Elsewhere in this volume, Kevin Dann shows how George Henry Perkins taught white supremacy as part of his popular anthropology classes at UVM. "The Clansman," by Thomas Dixon, enjoyed a Broadway triumph. "Coon songs," made popular on the minstrel stage, swept the nation in the 1890s. The coon, also called Jim Crow, Tambo, or Sambo, later immortalized on screen by Stepin Fetchit, "has always been used to indicate the black man's satisfaction with the system and his place in it," according to cultural historian Donald Bogle.[17] This image helped to legitimate a string of segregationist Supreme Court decisions from 1896 (*Plessy v. Ferguson,* legalizing "separate but equal") through 1927 (*Rice v. Gong Lum,* barring Chinese from white schools). Reflecting this white supremacist mentality, UVM students routinely built their skits around racial themes, including cannibals, lynchings, American Indians, "Orientals," Jews, and the Ku Klux Klan. It was no accident that Kulled

Koon's Kake Walk contained three K's. Later, "Kake Walk" was sometimes set in type that emphasized its three K's.

The Development of Kake Walk in the Twentieth Century

In 1903 students moved the event from the fall semester to the weekend nearest to Washington's Birthday, where it became the central event of the school year. Coon songs evolved into rags, and one such tune, "Cotton Babes," composed by Percy Weinrich about 1910, became the theme of the competition in 1912 or 1913.[18] In 1929 a fire destroyed UVM's copies, so Joseph Lechnyr, band director, rewrote them from memory. This incident became a part of Kake Walk lore, repeated in *Cynics* and programs ever after.

In 1917 Kake Walk "went to war": its directors donated their profits to the Red Cross. The national scene was still overtly racist; indeed, Woodrow Wilson's administration made segregation official national policy. *Birth of a Nation*, based on *The Clansman*, was our most popular movie. KKK membership soared; a rally near Montpelier in 1925 drew nearly ten thousand people.[19] UVM provided the institutional home for the Vermont Eugenics Survey.

In 1920 Kake Walk expanded to two nights, each including skits and walking. A typical program of the decade, 1922, called for the following:

The Grand Peerade, in which all the walking pairs, and sometimes other costumed, blackfaced students, made their grand entrance.

Stunts (often stunts did not have racial themes; they were judged on "originality, smoothness, and general excellence").

"A-Walkin'-Fo-De-Kake."

"Koon Kut-Ups" (these were done in blackface, had racial themes, and were judged on "originality of stunt and adherence to general lines of minstrelsy").

During the 1930s enthusiasm waned, so the event contracted to a single night for a time. King and queen were added in 1934, snow sculptures in 1940. World War II caused the 1944 Kake Walk to become a "condensed and rationed event," with an all-girl skit as well as two (male) stunts. Only three couples walked, all men, and five of the six walkers were first-year students, because sophomore males were being drafted.[20] But after the war, Kake Walk returned with a bang.

In the 1940s and early 1950s, magazines, movie cartoons, and other components of popular culture in the United States still demeaned African Americans. Stereotypical nonwhites peopled the series many children read— *Little House on the Prairie*, Bobbsey Twins, Dr. Doolittle, and Hardy Boys.[21] UVM Kake Walk itself was featured in *Life* magazine in 1952. At Kake Walk performances, "pickaninny ushers," also called "nigger babies"—coeds in blackface and raggedy dresses—still ushered audience members to their seats.

The peerade also lasted past World War II. So did the tradition of female attire for one member of each pair, at least for some couples. Later both walkers dressed alike, as males, in bright colors, often distinctive to each fraternity. The walking itself became ritualized and stylized; judges awarded points for "position of head and shoulders," "knee action," "position of toes," teamwork, costumes, and so on.

Kake Walk at Its Zenith

Today it is hard to realize how Kake Walk weekend, also called Winter Carnival, dominated the school calendar. By the 1960s four major competitions had evolved: king and queen, snow sculpture, skit, and "walkin'." Other honors included being a Kake Walk director, becoming Kake Walk secretary, and winning the poster competition. Exhorting students to show more spirit for athletic contests, *Cynic* sports editor Mike Rosenberg complained in 1969, "This campus is lethargic. It lives for Kake Walk."

Early each fall fraternities held their own competitions to choose their walking pair. Sometimes an independent group was also allowed to field a team. These men then attended workshops led by veteran walkers and judges and practiced all fall. The king and queen competition became so fierce that fraternity members spent four days and nights, in shifts, next to strategic trees on the UVM green, to reserve them for their candidates' posters. "Pops night," composed of skits that introduced the king and queen candidates, kicked off the voting on the weekend before Kake Walk. UVM declared Kake Walk Friday a holiday, so the weekend began with the ball on Thursday night. But as one student put it, "I don't know how you could go to school that week, if you were in a fraternity."

The Kake Walk issue of the *Cynic* marked the end of the editor's reign and of the volume number. Wrapped in a shiny front page with color illustrations, it was the most elegantly produced issue of the year. An editorial, written in 1948 and reprinted periodically later, sums up the importance of Kake Walk to participants: "When we think of college days, we will always remember Kake Walk. Winter Weekend is more than a tradition; it is a symbol of college life. The whole school becomes unified in one great surge of spirit—a spirit which is marked by the stimulating syncopations of 'Cotton Babes.'"

Kake Walk was also important to Burlington. Boy Scouts attended free and swept the floor between the skits and the walking. Walkers gave a special performance for children at the Baird Children's Center. Downtown merchants had special sales, and motel and restaurant owners braced for their biggest single weekend of the year. From time to time Kake Walk garnered national media attention. In the 1950s it grew so popular that directors considered adding a third night. Moving from Municipal Auditorium to Patrick

Gymnasium eased the crush, but by 1969 seats were again difficult to get except for favored groups.

Kake Walk almost always made a large profit. Each year the directors or a special committee disbursed part of those profits for campus projects, such as the chapel carillon. Profits in 1969 also purchased watches and pen sets for directors and apparently bailed the Interfraternity Council out of a $3,000 debt. After the last Kake Walk, in 1969, balances totaled $11,400.[22]

Women and Kake Walk

Before the Civil War, minstrelsy ridiculed not only blacks but also the woman suffrage movement, bloomers, pants, and other issues of importance to women. Indeed, according to Toll, "Throughout the nineteenth century, minstrels never varied from their complete condemnation of women's rights."[23] UVM Kake Walk skits sometimes parodied women. In 1904, for example, "Varsity vs. Coeds" won the cake for best skit. It depicted a mock football game "between the men and girls [sic] of the college," according to Gladys Neiburg, writing in the Cynic forty-four years later. "Time was called at short intervals to allow the 'girls' an opportunity to powder their noses with whisk brooms dipped into a conveniently placed bucket of corn starch." The skit might have been intended as an innocent spoof, but "it aroused the ire of the university women attending to the extent that they all left the hall in a body, some weeping copiously."[24] This was perhaps the first time that the object of a Kake Walk stereotype took offense. It would not be the last.

From the first Kake Walk in 1893, UVM men usually limited women's role to onlooker or "pickaninny usher." Women did "walk fo' de kake," however. In 1918 the woman's role in one couple was played by a woman. In 1934, 1938, 1940, and 1945, women pairs walked, but "non-competitively" according to some sources. In most years Kake Walk exemplified traditional sexist athletic patterns: men did, symbolically seeking women's approval; women applauded, symbolically granting it. Even the band was ROTC and all-male before World War II, but women suggested a "co-ed band" in 1943, and it stayed that way after the war.[25]

For two decades around World War II, sororities held their own snow sculpture competitions. Women came closest to equal participation in the semiformal ball that began the weekend, but even here, interesting differences remained. A Cynic page listed out-of-town girls who were guests of fraternity boys but usually not out-of-town boys hosted by sorority girls. At first, Kake Walk queen was chosen very differently from king. At the dance half a dozen of the "most attractive co-eds" were lined up, each represented by a number. The king, who had been elected by ballot, then rolled an enormous die, and the winning number was queen for the weekend. Later, queens were elected like kings. Even more coveted than queen was the role of Kake Walk secretary, perhaps the most honored role for a woman student on campus. The *Cynic*, yearbook, and Kake Walk program always commemorated her selection.

At the 1969 Kake Walk students raised the issue of sexism. Two women had prepared for months, joined the Independent Union, and thought they had received permission at least to stage an exhibition walk during intermission. They presented the directors with a petition with more than 1,100 student signatures, but the directors cited a "71-year tradition" against the participation of women (which we have seen was not always observed) and excluded them.[26]

Protests Build

Students never lost sight of Kake Walk's minstrel origins. As late as 1967, for example, Acacia fraternity put on a minstrel skit, complete with interlocutor. The blackface and dialect just wouldn't go away. But "the times, they were a-changin'," to paraphrase Bob Dylan, himself one of the catalysts of change. Several antiracist factors reverberated through American culture. World War II came to be fought partly against Nazi racism. The ideological impact of that struggle transformed our social science, which had supported white supremacy, into an opponent of ethnocentrism and racism. People of color in India, Southeast Asia, and Africa were mounting serious challenges to white colonialism. And within the United States, African Americans had been moving northward, making them a political force for the first time since the 1890s.[27]

By the 1950s American popular culture began to reflect these changes. Sambo was no longer welcome on the media. "Amos 'n' Andy," America's first and most famous national radio show, later on television, a show with direct minstrel antecedents, was canceled in the mid-1950s because of protests from black organizations.[28]

As early as 1950, a Swanton alum sent what she called "an open letter to the directors of Kake Walk," asking them to "convert the so-called Kake-Walk into a different type of vehicle, conveying . . . the great principles of democracy." She continued, "You must realize criticism is being directed at the university for presenting each year an entertainment whose basic theme tends to caricature the Negro race." In the same year, Constance Baker Motley of the national NAACP protested the blackface in a letter to the president of the University which was only made public in 1954.[29]

The first hint that students saw a problem with Kake Walk came in 1954. That year the Supreme Court was about to declare school segregation illegal in *Brown v. Board of Education,* thereby supplying a trigger of hope to the civil rights movement. In its Kake Walk issue the *Cynic* editorial read:

Please Look at the Front Page Again
Look at the "Blackface"
This Is the Tradition We Want to See Ended

The *Cynic* was "berated at every turn," according to an editor. Instead of getting rid of the blackface, some students tried to get rid of the *Cynic*! A rival paper, *The Vermont Skeptic,* published two issues that supported Kake Walk in blackface. However, Phi Sigma Delta walked in purple face, their house color, explaining that they "wouldn't perform in a disguise which stereotyped, unfavorably or falsely, a minority group."

The next year *Cynic* editors again called for removal of blackface and kinky wigs. They asked UVM's six African-American students their opinion of blackface. "Four objected vehemently while two reported it made them 'uncomfortable.'" Phi Sigma Delta again walked in purple face. The tiny local chapter of the NAACP again voiced its displeasure with the stereotype. Ironically, that year Kake Walk had its first black queen candidate. New editors took over the *Cynic,* and the issue seemed to disappear, but UVM was sitting on a time bomb, and its administrators knew it. Late in 1955 promotional copy that UVM supplied to the Burlington Chamber of Commerce noted that the University "does not encourage national publicity for its Kake Walk event," lest it be "misinterpreted." White professors knew it was problematic to African Americans and urged new black faculty members to be patient and not to leave because of Kake Walk.[30]

Meanwhile, the civil rights movement began to change America. After the first hesitant step of the Montgomery bus boycott in 1955, protests by African Americans shook every state in the South. Black college students sat in at lunch counters in Woolworth's in 1960, demanding service and enduring beatings. The following year integrated teams of Freedom Riders rode interstate buses and refused to separate when the buses crossed the Mason-Dixon Line. Black teenagers suffered fire hoses and police dogs in Birmingham in 1964. Whites murdered three civil rights workers in Mississippi that summer. Because the evening news televised these events, they provided images of African Americans—thoughtful, moral, outraged—that flatly opposed the old Sambo cartoon.[31]

UVM seemed isolated from the civil rights movement. There were no local chapters of such national organizations as Students for a Democratic Society (SDS) or Congress of Racial Equality (CORE). No part of the United States lay beyond the reach of these new images, however. Jules Older has described how UVM students demonstrated at the Woolworth's in downtown Burlington in support of the southern sit-ins. UVM professor

Alfred Haynes of the Burlington NAACP and a few students and other faculty continued to question Kake Walk, though they limited their criticism to the blackface and kinky wigs. At first they made converts. "In the situation which finds the Negro striving to find the place he deserves, it is really necessary to destroy the happy-go-lucky, carelessly-carefree image," said Bob Collier, president of the Interfraternity Council (IFC) in 1963. "If the Negro is being bombed in Alabama, then blackface in Vermont is no longer a joke." IFC decided to have the 1964 walkers wear a light green makeup, but retained the designation of the event in dialect, "walkin' fo' de kake," by a vote of 18 to 8.[32]

Professor Haynes was enthusiastic about the elimination of blackface: "The coming performance of Kake Walk should separate those who are interested in the skill and the beauty of the dance from those who are merely interested in blackface."[33] But many students and townspeople denounced the change from blackface. A *Vermont Sunday News* editorial complained, "The crowd could tell who the performers were and the whole program lost its usual color." Delma Crosier wrote to the *Free Press*, "The Negro people should feel real sad about the pale green face taking their place." Probably Mrs. Jeffrey Harvey said it best: "The moment that 'greenface' was applied on Friday night, all that ever went with the joy, excitement, and thrill of the minstrel show vanished."[34]

Nonetheless, the IFC voted against the return of blackface for 1965. For weeks the campus was in suspense as to what the walkers would look like. In the end the IFC and Kake Walk directors settled on dark green makeup and straight-haired black wigs. The change was not even cosmetic: from the stands, the new color was "almost indistinguishable from black," according to a Kake Walk supporter.[35]

Students End Kake Walk

Kake Walk seemed to have weathered the storm without real change, but the rush of events in the last half of the 1960s made Kake Walk an anachronism. When the United States continued to escalate the war in Vietnam, Kake Walk replied in 1966 with a new trophy honoring a Kake Walk alumnus, Thomas Eldridge ('62), killed in Vietnam. It was to be awarded to walkers "displaying the most spirit!" The war was tearing families and campuses apart; to respond with an honor for Kake Walk spirit was merely grotesque.

It is difficult for those who did not live through the period to appreciate the drumbeat of events of the late 1960s. Campus protests, ghetto riots, the Tet Offensive in Vietnam, the murders of Martin Luther King, Jr., and Bobby Kennedy, the counterculture, the beginnings of the women's movement—all clamored for attention on the evening news. UVM was caught up in the cadence. In the following listing of stories from just six weeks of the *Cynic*, the Kake Walk story stands out as an anomaly.

March 1, 1968: Dean concerned; U.S. will draft over half of all UVM graduate students for Vietnam

March 5, 1968: Naval aviation recruits in Billings Hall

March 8, 1968: 5,300 students at UVM, almost double 1958 numbers

March 12, 1968: Undercover drug investigations at UVM

March 19, 1968: Editorial favors affirmative action for racial minorities in UVM faculty recruitment

April 6, 1968: "New Dorms Go Co-Ed"

April 9, 1968: "Trustees Propose Memorial Scholarship in Honor of Dr. Martin Luther King" (Dr. King had been assassinated five days earlier.)

April 12, 1968: Editorial, "No Discrimination . . . But," favors recruiting more black students to UVM

April 16, 1968: Editorial, "The New England Ghetto," seeks exchange programs with black colleges

April 19, 1968: "Kake Walk Secretary Named"

Kake Walk was the property of the fraternities and, to a degree, the sororities. By the late 1960s, however, the entire Greek system had become an anachronism to some students and professors. Its emphasis on good times conflicted with students' serious concerns about the bad times of drug use and Vietnam. Some students were also upset that most houses discriminated against Jewish students, who then sought solace in four overwhelmingly Jewish chapters. Some national charters overtly limited membership to "Aryans," despite the notorious Nazi connotation of that term. In 1968 a Student Association (SA) report found some sororities and fraternities still guilty of anti-Semitism. Fraternity membership declined 15 percent in a single year. Since fraternities and sororities provided the core of Kake Walk supporters, this decline was like dry rot. Kake Walk still looked healthy, but its support was largely a matter of tradition and inertia.

As the walking wound down on the second night of the carnival in 1969, on the surface Kake Walk seemed unchanged. President Rowell had continued the custom of inviting the presidents of other Vermont colleges to the festivities. Snow sculptures still used so-called Negro dialect; the band still played "Cotton Babes." But cracks were appearing. Two white psychology graduate students picketed the walking, stating, "Kake Walk is offensive to humanity in general and to Black Americans in particular." One team, Phi Gamma Delta, refused the makeup and wigs "out of respect to the black community." Immediately after the event the IFC recommended that the directors drop darkface makeup and kinky wigs. A medical student wrote the *Cynic*, "I attended Kake Walk last weekend. I am ashamed for having been there." Kenneth Wibecan, a black Vermonter, wrote an op-ed piece, "Old Green Joe," in the Brattleboro *Reformer*. He noted Kake Walk's minstrel show origin and called for Vermonters to make known their opposition to the ritual.[36]

In March, Harold Collins, director of admissions, wrote to the Kake Walk directors that he was trying to recruit black students to UVM, and Kake Walk made that task difficult. In April the *Cynic* reprinted "Old Green Joe." Then "The Black Students" at UVM wrote to the *Cynic*: "We realize that in the past this act could have been performed with complete ignorance of its effects. However, now that it has been brought out in the open, it can no longer be done out of ignorance." This was a telling point. "Vermont at that time was extremely isolated from minorities," noted the 1969 Kake Walk finance director years later. "I'd never been around black people." With exposure to black displeasure, many minds were changing. "Most of us have come a long way in less than a year in our thoughts about black people," wrote UVM's director of admissions.[37]

Some minds had not changed. We'll recruit "negros," wrote President Rowell to several alumni, but "I am being careful to state in advance that we . . . do not intend to remake the University for their particular benefit." He denied that Kake Walk had any minstrel show origins and did "not feel that we have any reason for abandoning Kake Walk."[38]

The drumbeat of issues continued to stir the campus in the fall of 1969. Students wanted their school to be relevant to national issues. The president and first vice-president of SA had run and won as members of a new organization, Apple party, which favored student rights, student and faculty membership on the Board of Trustees, and the abolition of academic credit for ROTC. Kake Walk would not survive the year.

In its first issue of the semester, the *Cynic* called on UVM to "Abolish ROTC Now!" Freshman ROTC enrollment plummeted by 50 percent. On September 17 the Arts and Sciences faculty voted to abolish credit for ROTC. The English department introduced a course on American Negro literature. Professor Jeremy Felt offered a course titled Black History. Distribution requirements were loosened. A major curricular innovation, the Experimental Program in the College of Arts and Sciences, started with 120 students. Almost by definition, these students were in touch with calls for new programs and protests on other campuses. On September 23 the *Cynic* printed an editorial for women's equality at UVM. Fraternities and sororities hastened to pledge Jewish students; one fraternity that remained all-Gentile complained that they had rushed a Jewish student but he had turned them down. On October 1, about a thousand students met with trustee John Beckley to demand his resignation. (He had suggested earlier that students who do not approve of university policies "may go elsewhere" and faculty who do not approve "may teach elsewhere.") On October 4, SA president Brooks McCabe spoke to the trustees about scholarship aid for black students at UVM. He noted that UVM was spending much more on air conditioning. On October 15 UVM observed the national moratorium against the Vietnam War.

Early in the semester, Greek Week featured Father James Groppi, a white Catholic priest famed for his work in Milwaukee on behalf of African Americans. He was asked his opinion of Kake Walk, and when the tradition was explained to him, he suggested disruption if necessary to end it. Historian Felt declared in the *Cynic*, "Kake Walk is offensive to me *as a white person*." [39] A student–faculty committee under Roland Patzer, dean of students, recommended abolition. Professor Lawrence McCrorey told a gathering of students that Kake Walk celebrates a mythical "happy-go-lucky national banjo player." This argument convinced the president and vice-president of SA, Brooks McCabe and Louis Tesconi, that the ritual was irretrievably racist. In October they led the executive committee of SA to a unanimous decision against Kake Walk. Even if the IFC failed to act, said the executive committee, they would boycott the activity and ask others to do so. [40]

On October 21, 1969, the IFC urged the Kake Walk directors to keep the walking but abandon darkface, change the name, and give up "Cotton Babes" and the cakes. IFC was trying to rescue a doomed institution by reforms that were perceived as too little and too late. Its own constituents were not united behind its stand: ten houses voted for and four against the competition, with one abstention.

On October 23, at a two-hour university forum, "Students and faculty members present were almost unanimous in their belief that Kake Walk, as it now exists, should be discontinued," according to the *Free Press*. Black student Linda Patterson received "sustained applause" for her suggestion that "all students, white and black, celebrate the anniversary of Martin Luther King's birthday together," instead. [41] SA conducted a campus-wide opinion poll on October 27. Forty percent of the students took part. Two thirds of the respondents disagreed that "Kake Walk as it now exists (without kinky wigs, black make-up, and the expression 'walkin' fo' de' kake') is a racist activity." The same two thirds disagreed that "the 'walking' should be eliminated from the weekend." But students split evenly on specific changes in Kake Walk, such as eliminating "Cotton Babes," so the poll was not viewed as a ringing endorsement of the weekend. [42]

McCabe continued his campaign to stop Kake Walk. He claimed the poll showed that many students had an inadequate understanding of racism. Each day brought new support for abolition. Despite the poll the student senate voted 60–40 to end it. Governor Deane Davis and former governor Philip Hoff spoke against Kake Walk. On October 30, Phi Gamma Delta announced in the *Free Press*: "It will enter no walkers in the annual Kake Walking competition. . . . The Brotherhood empathizes with the feelings of the black community . . . [that Kake Walk] is a degrading activity not fit for any winter weekend or celebration, particularly at this period in our nation's history."

The next day the Kake Walk directors voted to end Kake Walk completely. "As of this date, the theme of Kake Walk and all of its inferences and manifestations are eliminated from the University of Vermont winter weekend," they declared. "In these sensitive times it is possible to interpret this tradition, as being racist in nature, and humiliating to the Black people of this nation. We feel that no amount of tradition and longevity can be used as a defense for the continuation of Kake Walk."

An interesting dispute arose regarding the directors' motivation. Rumors have persisted that Kake Walk was not ended by students but by administrators, frightened because any future performance would be disrupted by black militants. Angry Kake Walk supporters accused the administration of kowtowing to minority threats. Ironically, some opponents of Kake Walk made the same claim: that threats of disruption by "Black Panthers from Harlem" caused the administration to cave in.[43] This rumor made print: in a book about white stereotyping of blacks, *Sambo*, Joseph Boskin erroneously wrote that UVM canceled Kake Walk for fear of picketing by the NAACP.[44]

Undoubtedly, fear of disruption played a role: students had picketed Kake Walk the previous year, and much more opposition had now surfaced. When this concern was brought up at the October 23 university forum, Alfred Rollins, Jr., dean of the College of Arts and Sciences, countered, "We ought to act because we believe, not because we're scared." Similar false rumors had swept the campus in 1963 when blackface was eliminated, later to be replaced by dark green. One Burlingtonian wrote, "All of the credit for the change belongs solely to the students themselves."[45]

Another far-fetched rumor credited the UVM administration with ending Kake Walk under the threat of Nixon administration civil rights watchdogs. In reality, neither the college administration nor the federal government played much of a role. While the Kake Walk directors and SA wrestled with the issue, President Rowell said, "I feel that it is better that I wait and not attempt to influence discussion." Personally, Rowell liked Kake Walk. On the other side, Dean Rollins found Kake Walk "demeaning," "undignified," and "a bore." But students made the decision.[46] Probably their greatest motivator was fear of offending Black students. Moreover, if Kake Walk had ever been a unifying collegiate activity, it could unify no longer. Whatever the motivation, administrators did not end Kake Walk. Opposition from the SA leadership, most SA senators, and a few fraternities struck the mortal blow.

Protests and Revival Efforts

To replace Kake Walk in the Winter Carnival, the directors proposed a "Music and Film Festival" for 1970. Despite scant preparation time, the festival attracted eight film entries and nineteen slide shows, more entries than had ever participated in the old skits and walking. However, off-campus support plummeted: alumni bought eight hundred tickets to the 1969 Kake Walk and tried to buy more, but they purchased only sixty to the Film Festival. Technical problems also plagued the festival. The audience, already relegated to a more passive role than the clapping, chanting Kake Walk crowd, grew restless as long delays intervened between numbers. For 1971 a new "Festival 71 Committee" proposed an "ice follies competition" but attracted only two entrants, so they canceled the event. The film and slide shows continued another year, then faded away.

The *Free Press* called the decision to discontinue Kake Walk "in a word, shameful."[47] But alumni protested the demise of Kake Walk the loudest. Donations dropped sharply. One couple explained, "If our University agrees to be eroded by militant minority groups, we can no longer feel an allegiance or financial responsibility to further its causes."[48] Not all alumni agreed: Howard Delano of Williston enclosed a contribution in support of the university and noted, "Where human rights and human dignity are concerned there can be no compromise."[49]

Initial reaction on campus was mild. One student, Theodore Riehle III, planned to rent Memorial Auditorium in March to continue Kake Walk off campus. Riehle recruited eight walking teams, but without business support his revival fell through for lack of funding.[50]

Nonetheless, on February 15, 1970, "a group of UVM fraternity brothers staged a quickly organized Kake Walk Sunday night," according to the *Free Press*: "Close to 500 students crowded in the Simpson Hall cafeteria on the Redstone Campus to watch the spontaneous walking as rapidly organized teams of clean-faced fraternity men took the floor to compete for the cake."[51] However, "there was nothing spontaneous about it," as the *Vermont Freeman* pointed out. "Teams of walkers were ready to perform after months of rehearsal; cakes were on hand for prizes; a crowd was watching; the word was sufficiently broadcast in advance to attract students from St. Michael's in Winooski."[52]

Among the St. Michael's students who attended were eight to ten black students and an equal number of whites, who strode onto the floor after the fifth team. One student challenged spectators, "If there's going to be any walking done here tonight, it'll be over my dead body." Twenty years later, a participant remembered the tense standoff as "the closest Vermont ever came to a race riot." The crowd broke into two factions, some chanting "No trouble, no trouble!" and others "We want Kake Walk." After "mild harassing" of the blacks outside and the intervention of campus security forces, everyone dispersed.[53]

Each year between 1970 and 1978 some fraternity members tried to revive Kake Walk. Each year they practiced. Administrators waffled. When the students ended Kake Walk, President Rowell consoled distraught alumni: "I have no doubt that at sometime in the future this whole area may be re-examined and Kake Walk could very possibly be re-instituted." President Edward Andrews suggested in the spring of 1974 that students would have to hold the event off campus, without UVM's support. If the weekend was successful and did not meet with opposition, in a few years the University might help. As late as 1978, Arthur (Rusty) Brink, director of alumni affairs, complained of "a continuing feeling among students and alumni that a possibility exists for the return of Kake Walk." Brink went on to blame the administration: "I believe the University has helped perpetuate these feelings and surrounding myths by not forcefully stating its position opposing Kake Walk's return."[54]

Efforts to Revive Kake Walk Fail

In fact, the fraternities never mounted a major campaign to revive Kake Walk. A leader of the revival effort explained that "fear of the opposition, not the opposition itself," deterred them.[55] Their fear was well founded. Although the Vietnam War had wound down by 1975 and with it much student activism, UVM had changed irrevocably. Gone was the sense of isolation from national issues. In 1971 students, faculty, and President Andrews took the lead in protesting and changing the names of Niggerhead Mountain and Niggerhead Pond in Marshfield, Vermont. Sixty students staged a four-day peaceful sit-in in the ROTC building in 1972; others worked for George McGovern for president.[56] Eighteen-year-old voting helped connect students to political issues. By the mid-1970s, as Jules Older relates, the handful of black students who attended UVM during Kake Walk's last years had grown to about seventy. They would never permit Kake Walk's revival. Neither would many whites.

An example from 1976–1977 will show what happened to revival efforts. Jim Rock of Kappa Sigma led meetings at other fraternities to revive Kake Walk. "The final outcome of this was a meeting of all of the fraternity and sorority presidents," according to a graduate assistant to the director of student activities. Thirteen of fourteen chapters voted no; Kappa Sigma abstained. Fraternity and sorority leaders followed up to write a united open letter to President Lattie Coor stating that they were "overwhelmingly opposed to any revival of this type activity at any time. We feel that this decision supports the development of a multicultural environment for all at UVM." Coor had taken a forthright stand against Kake Walk after his inauguration in 1976.[57]

Moreover, the country had changed. In 1969, the year that Kake Walk ended, federal courts ordered massive school desegregation in the South. White attitudes about black people changed abruptly in the following years.

"Black" replaced "Negro" in the media. Many historically white universities found their curricula challenged as "racist" and "irrelevant" by minority students calling for Black and Third World studies. Minstrel shows lingered in Morrisville and Tunbridge, Vermont, and in a few small towns in other states, but as historian Boskin put it, "minstrelsy as a force, as an aspect of white perceptions, swiftly receded in the national consciousness."[58]

In today's climate of rhetoric, talk of reviving Kake Walk is reserved for those private gatherings where ethnic jokes can still be told. In confidential interviews some alumni and others privately support Kake Walk but will not say so on the record. Their reticence shows they know that something was wrong with Kake Walk. They don't want to let others know they support it because it might not be proper, might even be racist. They still remember it fondly, however, and alumni groups around New England still show the old Kake Walk movie from time to time as the program for their meetings.[59]

Was Kake Walk Racist?

Certainly no participant thought Kake Walk was racist. Neither did most townspeople, alumni, or students. In a sense, they were right: Kake Walk played many functions that were not racist. The ritual gave positive sanction to deviance, in the same way deviance is sanctioned in Mardi Gras and other festivals, some of which also formerly relied on blackface. Males could dance together without stigma. Skits satirizing UVM administrators or traditions could be hard-hitting, without fear of offense. Kake Walk also exemplified values of school spirit, competition, and athleticism.

Defenders of Kake Walk argued that since the walkers didn't *intend* to be racist, they were not and could not be racist. In a letter to the *Free Press*, Clara Kellogg put it this way: "I doubt if anyone participating in or watching the "walkin' fo' de Kake" ever had any thoughts of racial discrimination."[60] Therefore, the problem lay in the minds of those who perceived it to be racist. A 1963 lead editorial in the Vermont *Sunday News*, owned by William Loeb, a supporter of Kake Walk, quoted a black IBM employee: "There wasn't any racial slur or degradation. I think the ones who protested the blackface have tainted minds." Progressive acts in Vermont's past were invoked to show that Vermonters were not racist; hence, Kake Walk could not be racist. If Kake Walk offended African Americans, that was their problem, according to its defenders.[61] "I think that the black people in America should view this performance as a tribute to them and be glad," wrote Lawrence Kimball (UVM '51). Pushing this line of thinking one step closer to blatant racism, another Vermonter said, "I think it's an honor to the Negro. . . . There is a limit to what the whites have to endure because God made the Negroes." In a classic example of what sociologists call "blaming the victim," William Snyder of Underhill, Vermont, wrote that Kake Walk should not be blamed for the "unfavorable image of the Negro" in the United States. "If this image does exist," he continued, "it is not one which has been created by the textbooks and minstrel shows. It has been created by the conduct of the contemporary Negro himself."[62]

To understand these reactions, we must clarify "racism." Defined most simply, racism means to treat members of a racial group worse because of their membership in the group. Sociologists typically divide racism into three types: individual, institutional, and cultural. Individual racism requires that the perpetrator be conscious of what she or he is doing; hence, it requires some kind of animus. Those who claimed that racial antagonism did not motivate Kake Walkers were perfectly correct. To this day, undergraduates whose parents participated in Kake Walk are deeply relieved when the distinction between individual and cultural racism is drawn and their relatives are absolved of the former. Their reaction exemplifies whites' fear of being considered racist, hence whites' tendency to define the term to include only cross-burning KKK members.

But if individual racism did not motivate walkers, nonetheless Kake Walk was culturally racist to its core. From "flesh-colored" Band-Aids to "little white lies," our language suggests that white is right, nonwhite is otherwise. Forty years ago sociologist E. Franklin Frazier wrote of cultural racism, "The entire culture of the American people has until World War II and the years following stamped the Negro as an inferior human being unfit for assimilation into American life." Kake Walk was just the kind of cultural element he meant.[63] Indeed, part of white cultural racism is the tendency for whites to define the images of "others." Kake Walk dialect, because it rendered black speech differently from white, with absurd spellings and mislocutions, was a textbook example of racism: "treating members of a racial group worse because of their membership in the group." The racism of Kake Walk was largely unthinking, unconscious. As Clara Kellogg said, defending Kake Walk, "It was pure entertainment and that was all there was to it."[64] However, the entertainment value of Kake Walk decreased without the blackface. South Burlington High School senior Sarah Dopp pointed this out: "If you do away with the black faces and kinky hair why not do away with Kake Walk entirely. Kake Walk is not Kake Walk without them."[65]

Moderate opponents of blackface didn't understand how intrinsic the coon stereotype was, even to the evolved dance competition of the modern period. Alfred Haynes said, "I fail to see how blackface is any more essential to the beauty of the dance than blonde hair and blue eyes to the beautiful performance of a waltz." He was wrong: blackface *was* fundamental to Kake Walk. Marie Lawlor of Burlington said it best: "To eliminate the black faces and substitute white ones would make the performance a farce and absurdity."[66] Thus, the *meaning* of Kake Walk was intrinsically culturally racist; the coon was a cultural icon. That's why giving up the blackface and the dialect proved so difficult. The NAACP pointed out, reacting to the attempted Kake Walk revival of February 1970, "Kakewalk has been a vehicle for perpetuation of the Magnolia Myth—a subtly vicious stereotype which has done staggering harm to the interests of black people." Responding to that revival effort and a pro–Kake Walk editorial by WCAX-TV, Professor McCrorey demanded and received equal time to make the same point:

White Americans, in order to justify black slavery, invented the image of the *Negro*—the so-called Magnolia Myth which stereotyped the black man as an inferior being. . . . Black people are not condemned in America because they are poor, uneducated or even black, but rather because they are *Negroes*—that is, because of an idea, an image. . . . Kake Walk was conceived as an extension of this racist thinking.

"Imitation is the sincerest form of flattery," said several Kake Walk defenders. But this stereotyped compliment was dangerous because it credited African Americans only with physical rather than mental achievement. One Vermonter wrote, "I think the black people should be proud. Kake Walk has been accredited to them as something they can do"—implying that African Americans could not be accomplished brain surgeons, economists, or pilots.[67] During the Kake Walk abolition campaign in 1969, a black undergraduate told the SA senate, "One of the questions asked of her [by other students] was how well she could dance. The student's comment was, 'Damn it, I can think well and I am going to show you that first.' "[68]

We have seen that the stereotype of African Americans as inferior has been used to keep them out of schools, baseball, politics, and other areas of American life. Thus, cultural racism can promote institutional and individual racism. Moreover, when the cultural racism of Kake Walk was pointed out, some white reactions shaded into individual racism. Robert O'Brien was making this point when he criticized greenface as "even more distressing pseudo-blackface." Pseudo-blackface showed that whites knew better yet still would not change. On the other hand, when some students became convinced of Kake Walk's fatal flaw, they became antiracist individuals. Brooks McCabe began as a Kake Walk supporter; after his change he "single-handedly wrote a hundred or so radio spot histories and broadcast them during Negro History Week." Louis Tesconi spoke widely before alumni groups, helping them come to terms with Kake Walk's abolition. Rusty Brink had been king of Kake Walk as a student. The sincerity of his conversion was shown by his private letter to administrators, already cited, when he was director of alumni affairs.[69]

Thinking about Kake Walk Today

It is particularly sad that a university, part of whose basic mission is to prompt young adults to rethink unthinking stereotypes, should have perpetuated them instead. Thus, it is altogether fitting and proper that UVM should now lay Kake Walk thoroughly to rest. But we must exhume its image for a final postmortem examination.

At the back of the classroom, without much introduction, the professor starts a film. It is old and jumpy, in black and white, and the sound is bad. Students strain forward, for they have heard rumors about Kake Walk, but most don't know what it looked like. Some have brought friends, so the classroom is crowded. At the end of the half-hour documentary, students look at each other, some in disbelief. "I can't believe that happened at my school," says a sophomore. "It makes me want to transfer." "I wish they could bring it back," responds another. "There's nothing like that now, nowhere near that spirit."

The campus has no oral tradition of the role of students in ending Kake Walk. In a three-part series on Kake Walk and race relations in 1985, the *Cynic* editor implied Kake Walk had been ended by a few conspirators, without campus support. But in the first issue after Kake Walk's demise, the *Cynic* had editorialized, "We are now the possessor of America's youngest winter carnival, and we should be proud of this fact, proud of the motivation behind the change, proud of the manner in which the change occurred." [70] This pride has been mislaid.

Since then students have continued to play the leading role in helping UVM reduce the third kind of racism—institutional—and become a multicultural institution. In the early 1970s student initiative spurred the initial recruitment of significant numbers of black students at UVM. Students led a campaign, including a campus "shantytown" in the autumn of 1985 that caused UVM to be one of the first universities to sell its investments in firms operating in South Africa. In April 1988, as described in Jules Older's chapter, students occupied the president's offices, demanding more diversity among students, faculty, and courses, and won a written agreement promising change.

So Vermont's tradition of positive steps in race relations, dating back to its abolition of slavery, has some recent additions. In this series the abolition of Kake Walk can take its honored place. Until now the University has had a sort of amnesia about Kake Walk. Kake Walk has been painful to recall, difficult to think about, because of the issue of racism. It's embarrassing now that the rite lasted as long as it did. But Kake Walk *is* part of our history, whether we wish it or not. To end discrimination in America and at UVM we must understand our national and institutional past. Kake Walk forces us to remember that white culture could go on being racist for decades, in the absence of blacks and in the absence of controversy. Its abolition shows us that whites can become nonracist, even antiracist. As UVM relates to an ever-more-multiracial environment, recapturing the memory of Kake Walk and its abolition as part of our living tradition is vital to our continued institutional health.

The Faculty Role in University Governance

BEAL B. HYDE

"It must be leadership that will forcibly remind those within the academy that independence and self-governance can survive only if they are willing to shoulder the burden of making it not merely a matter of pious rhetoric, but a living working reality."[1]

THE faculty struggle to find an appropriate role in university governance continues without end. Successes, and there are a number, come fitfully, as in any democracy; and old battles must be fought again and again. Heroes, if any, are as rare as the villains.

What, then, is the conflict? The faculty in most institutions of higher education regards itself as the center and the continuity of the university. The faculty attends to the primary purposes of a university: investigation, scholarship, and teaching. Professors are highly trained for these functions and have direct and enduring stewardship over almost all academic activity. Presidents, deans, and students, on the other hand, come and go on much shorter cycles. Yet in the public eye it is the administration and the students that are most in evidence; the faculty remain relatively invisible. Moreover, as the university becomes more complex and consumer-oriented, the centrality of the faculty is threatened. Whereas at one time the president and faculty worked together to solve nearly all university problems, now there is a large staff of admissions officers, counselors, health providers, resident hall administrators, security officers, and so on, who serve student needs. The faculty is most sensitive, however, to the increasing size and all-pervasive presence of the higher administration (deans, provosts and presidents). The conflict comes as professors struggle to maintain their centrality and to re-establish control over the direction their professional lives are taking.

The Faculty Role in the Nineteenth Century

The earliest accounts of organized and regular faculty direction over the University of Vermont are recorded in the minutes of faculty meetings.[2] These begin in 1827 when the faculty, including President James Marsh, were five men. Much of the deliberation concerned whether or not to dismiss erring students who were, of course, well known to all faculty members: "Whereas C. L. Putnam having shown by his exhibitions at the annual examination now past, as well as by his previous conduct that he is incorrigibly neglectful of his duties as a student & also having on the night previous to commencement been engaged in intemperate & disorderly conduct *Resolved* that his guardian be directed to remove him from College." This decision (August 7, 1827) was reversed in September, and Mr. Putnam was placed on probation.

The faculty took responsibility for many details; grading, for example: "*Voted* [13 September 1827] that 10 shall be the standard number for a perfect recitation." And it set the daily lives of students: "Breakfast shall be at 7½ hours A.M. Evening prayers at five o'clock P.M."

They were actively concerned about maintenance of the physical plant. "Professor Benedict [July 27, 1843] made a verbal report on the college roof that it should be strongly urged upon the corporation to authorize the new roofing of the N[orth] and S[outh] buildings immediately, as the rooms leak so badly now during storms as scarcely to be habitable—subjecting the tenant to great inconvenience and exposing them to unhealthy influences." He estimated the cost to be about $1,000 if done with tin.

On September 20, 1827, it was "*Voted* that the students be prohibited from placing any wood in front of the Colleges, or so as to obstruct the way between the Colleges, or against the Colleges, or in the entrances. That the bell-man be required to provide candles when necessary for evening prayers in the chapel." In 1849 the faculty voted to build a woodhouse.

Evidence that the faculty had other than the good of the students on their minds comes from the minutes of the corporation (Board of Trustees) of August 4, 1831: "A verbal report from the faculty that the Corporation would take measures to have their salaries punctually paid was referred" to a committee of three trustees.

Throughout its history the university calendar has been determined by the faculty, and during the nineteenth century there are frequent references to the scheduling of examinations and holidays. Admissions policy was fully under faculty control until, after an indecisive faculty discussion of the matter, the Corporation decided in 1871 to admit women.

The library properly occupied faculty attention. On April 29, 1841, the faculty discussed scientific periodicals and voted "in favour of taking the Comptes Rendues Hebdomadaire of the French Academy of Sciences and the Berlin Jahr-bücher." They also ordered back volumes.

Faculty Committees around 1900

After the Civil War the University grew only slowly until close to the turn of the century. When faculty committees were first employed is not clear, but this mechanism became logical when the four earliest departments—agriculture, arts and sciences, engineering, and medicine—began to take on distinct missions and curricula, and all university business became more specialized. Standing committees of the faculty are listed for the first time during the presidency of Matthew Buckham, in the university catalog of 1892–1893. There were five: library, status of students, military, absence, and athletic. These committees covered most of the problems deliberated in the early years of the University by the entire faculty. They addressed mostly noncurricular matters because the curricula were already largely determined within the several departments. Note also that these committees did not concern themselves with university finances, administrative policy, or decisions concerning hiring and promotion of faculty. At this time the president presided over faculty meetings, which were held at irregular intervals but more than once a month on average during the academic year. Of the thirty to thirty-five faculty members, four or five might be absent.

During the rest of Buckham's presidency the number of standing faculty committees gradually increased to twelve. They included general, advanced degrees, athletics, gymnasium, military, library, scholarships, chapel services and attendance, catalog, student finances, summer school, and extension (not agricultural extension). The list reflects the growing responsibilities and commitments of the faculty not only to an expanding university but also, in the case of the catalog and extension committees, to the world beyond the university.

Establishment of the University Senate

The University Senate was established abruptly and by authoritarian fiat. In his first speech, to the "Educational Staff" of UVM in September 1911, the newly inaugurated president, Guy Benton, announced:

The united faculties of all the colleges, henceforward, by order of the Executive Committee [of the Board of Trustees], to be known as the University Senate, will recognize the President of the University as its official presiding officer. This is the only legislative body of the Academic community, and all recommendations as to rules, regulations, policies, standards, etc. must come from the several Faculties and Committees of the University Senate to the Senate for final action. It is expected that the University Senate will meet at least once each month and it is hoped that the deliberations of the body may prove of professional help as well as of legislative value to all who are connected therewith.[3]

There is no evidence that any faculty member was ever consulted prior to this decision, nor do other statements in President Benton's address suggest that he intended to give the faculty much authority. Moreover, faculty meetings up to this time included all of the faculty and were almost always chaired by the president. The form, then, remained unchanged.

President Benton's speech continued reassuringly: "The original University was a community of scholars brought together in voluntary association for study and service to the youth who might submit to their leadership. . . . If this sacred trust is to be administered with credit and efficiency, there should be frequent meetings of the teaching body." But Benton was skeptical of any right of the "community of scholars" to advise the president:

It is difficult to conceive of a more painful caricature on true manhood than that made up of a little professorial group gathered together in a darkened corridor or behind a building gesticulating wildly against the administration, unless it be the same small crowd in the study of one of the number, or in the same club-room, planning surreptitiously for the overthrow of their chief. . . . The vulgar swagger assumed by some university and college professors in the latter day would be pitiable if it were not positively mischievous.

Committees and Administrative Centralization, 1911–1941

Under Benton the number of committees increased abruptly. In the 1912–1913 catalog, twenty-two committees are designated for the first time as senate committees. The officers of the senate listed in 1914–1915 were President Benton and his personal secretary. Benton designated himself an ex officio member of all committees and used senate meetings to promulgate "Administrative Orders," mainly pronouncements on how faculty and staff were to do their jobs. These changes were all clear evidence that he had no intention of granting any real authority to the faculty or the University Senate. The faculty share in university governance was probably at its smallest during the six years of Benton's effective presidency.

As might be expected, President Benton's style did not sit well with everyone. Henry Holt, a distinguished New York City publisher and part-time Burlington resident, wrote to Professor Samuel Bassett, "I may as well tell you that the signs are as unmistakable as any signs of the future I ever saw, that Benton has to go. The Alumni are aroused against him."[4] In a more balanced account of the Benton presidency, Dean Joseph Hills wrote, "The U.V.M. trustee, and to some extent the [State Agricultural College] trustee, board was being made over as rapidly as might be, a slow process, into an anti-Benton body."[5]

The imperial President Benton and his board of trustees typified the "duumvirate" that controlled most of the great universities at the time. Nevertheless, events of surpassing importance to faculty governance were taking place elsewhere. The American Association of University Professors (AAUP) was established in 1915, and that same year prepared the "General Declaration of Principles," which stated the rationale for academic freedom and the need for trustees to protect that freedom, as well as faculty rights as citizens and fair procedures in hiring, firing, and grievances.[6] The AAUP grew in numbers and influence, profiting from increasing faculty impatience with the unresponsiveness of contemporary university administrations.

President Guy Bailey, trained in law, business, and public relations, naturally left many academic decisions to the faculty. Nevertheless, during his twenty-year term, five senate committees were composed only of administrators, that is, the president, deans, and directors of certain nonacademic university offices,[7] who also made up the University Council. Senate meetings became increasingly rare during the Bailey years and dealt with less and less important matters. The ten or twelve other senate committees evidently worked independently of the senate as a whole.

Senate Agenda between the Wars

The matters discussed in senate meetings during the early Bailey presidency deserve detailed attention as a baseline for the transition that lay ahead. During this period the senate agenda was not greatly different from that of the nineteenth century, but it contrasted sharply with what followed World War II. For instance, at Bailey's first senate meeting, on September 20, 1919, it was decided not to review the problem of chapel attendance, no longer compulsory. Student discipline continued to be a major topic. In November 1919 a set of "Rules for Regulating Dances given by College Organizations" worked out by a joint faculty–student committee was adopted. This kind of regulation occupied the entirety of several senate meetings in the early 1920s. At this same meeting the senate voted (and did so again exactly one year later) to place on probation those students absent the day before and after a recess. The fact that a second vote was required suggests that mechanisms for carrying out the substance of a faculty vote were not effective.

In October 1920 a report of a student dishonesty committee was adopted. The policy gave the faculty responsibility for determining the fact of dishonesty but left with the University Council responsibility for enforcing sanctions specified in the report.

In the spring of 1921 the senate voted sanctions for students on probation for violating university rules and regulations: "While on probation, the student shall be excluded from beneficiary aid for the current half year, from employment for remuneration by the University, and from membership in athletic teams, musical, dramatic and debating clubs and from analogous organizations."

Finally, the minutes of June 14, 1923, show that the senate adopted the report of the Committee on Degrees, which consisted entirely of a list of the graduates. From this time until June 1940, with only one or two exceptions, the senate met only once a year, in June. The minutes for most of the Bailey years are simply lists of graduating students. Nevertheless, faculty deliberation in committee did occur at the college and department level, and the faculty continued to control the traditional areas of academics. Minutes of the meetings of the College of Arts and Sciences begin in 1920. They record details of disciplinary decisions, curriculum revisions, and other academic affairs in that major undergraduate college.

Real faculty participation in university governance thus languished through the presidencies of both Benton and Bailey but for different reasons. Benton was high-handed and opinionated, almost inviting faculty insurrection. Bailey rose to the presidency from the position of comptroller and ran the university from his vest pocket. Reminiscences by Professor George Dykhuisen give some indication of faculty feelings about President Bailey:

He had never left Vermont and therefore had a narrow viewpoint, and an oldtime paternalistic attitude toward the University of Vermont. He sat like a king over in his office in the Medical College Building [now Dewey Hall] and nobody could get to see him. . . .

The reason why the University went into such financial difficulties was that Bailey had an old Vermont attitude about accepting no outside help.[8]

Emeritus dean George Kidder recalls that under Bailey most direction in the University "came from the top down. . . . Whatever the President said, went. Everything was left to him even by the trustees." But the faculty accepted this kind of presidency. Bailey was "trusted by the people in the state and could have been elected governor. . . . He bore the burden himself and protected the faculty."[9]

The UVM chapter of the AAUP, formed in 1930, held monthly luncheon meetings. Its membership, numbering sixty-five in 1938, was clearly not a group dissatisfied with Bailey's leadership. Major Elbridge Colby wrote, "For want of critical personal issues of the sort which the AAUP exists to affect . . . , the University of Vermont Chapter has devoted its attention primarily to keeping its membership intact and getting it together."[10]

During these years neither the senate nor the AAUP discussed salaries, promotion, tenure, or sabbaticals. The financial policies and fortunes of the University were fully in the hands of the president and Board of Trustees. Faculty influence on these matters was informal at best.

The Wartime Transition

To address the financial crisis revealed after President Bailey's death in November 1940, the Board of Trustees appointed a joint advisory committee consisting of Temporary President Paul Packer; Hardy A. Kemp, dean of medicine; Roy L. Patrick and Asa S. Bloomer, members of the Board of Trustees; J. Howard Moore, president, and Horace H. Powers, president-elect of the alumni council (but with no one other than Dean Kemp from the faculty).[11] Governor Wills also set up a general committee to make recommendations on how the state could help the University, consisting primarily of businessmen and farmers; the only academic representative was Dr. Caroline S. Woodruff of Castleton, past president of the National Education Association.[12]

The acting controller of the University, F. W. Kehoe, recommended, among other steps to deal with the crisis, "Salaries must be sharply reduced" by an average of 12½ percent.[13] Both the executive committee of the Board of Trustees and the full Board heard presentations by Deans Hills (agriculture), Swift (arts and sciences), and Eckhard (engineering) about the opinions of their respective faculties toward these cuts. This is the only evidence of any faculty input into the solution of the financial crisis. Perhaps upon a petition of the deans, in February 1941 the Trustees "*voted* faculty have one representative on Committee to choose a President. No action taken on faculty request that they have representative on Committee to revise budget."[14] Nevertheless, the Board excluded faculty from the special committee of four set up to complete the search for a permanent president.[15]

Meanwhile, Governor Wills recognized the centrality of the faculty when he asked them to make the necessary financial sacrifices: "The body of scholars making up the Faculty constitute the heart and soul of that organism. . . . The courage and strength and virility of the institution are not merely *dependent* upon the Faculty, since *they* are the courage, strength, and virility of the Faculty itself."[16] His talk was roundly applauded.

Temporary President Packer also pushed to establish a "complete retirement system as soon as university finances permit."[17] At this time there were a number of senior faculty members aged sixty-seven or older, some of whom had served for thirty to forty years. Such lifetime service may in part have been because of the lack of a suitable retirement system. At a board of trustees meeting in November 1941 it was recommended that seven of these senior faculty members be retired in the next two years. The allowance for fully retired faculty was set at one half maximum salary but not to exceed $2,000 annually.[18] The recommendations were put into effect as of September 1, 1942.

John Millis was formally appointed to the presidency by the Trustees on November 1, 1941. Under his leadership major changes were to alter the University in a remarkably short time. The faculty had been sensitized by the salary cuts and the retirement of senior faculty at the behest of the Board of Trustees at a time when retirement support was meager. Nationally, the AAUP was beginning strongly to influence faculty thinking about their status, while the Carnegie plan to provide retirement funds was soon to find itself in serious financial difficulties that forced it to discontinue. The Teachers Insurance and Annuity Association was not to be initiated until the late 1940s.

President Millis faced a difficult future and was all business. In the opinion of Dean George Kidder, he was "academically sound, personally aggressive . . . , uncouth in relationships with people . . . , and gave the appearance of not giving a damn about anybody," but he "improved the quality of the Board of Trustees and put them to work." In Kidder's view, the coming effort by the faculty to increase their participation in decision making was more in reaction to Millis's leadership style than to a recollection of the all-controlling approach of President Bailey.

A Major Change in Senate Committee Policy

The new president had mobilized the faculty in new ways during the earliest days of his presidency, and from this time on, senate meetings were held regularly. The minutes are more detailed and informative of business discussed and accomplished than they had been for a quarter century.

On February 16, 1942, in the early weeks of formal U.S. participation in World War II, Professor Paul Evans presented to the senate a report of an emergency committee on reorganizing senate committees, appointed by the president. This document, adopted at the March meeting, marks a real turning point in a number of ways. The discussion associated with its acceptance is predictive of many of the forces and opinions with which the senate has struggled ever since.

The most important recommendation was to form a Policy Committee. The five members of the committee were to be elected in their colleges: Arts and Sciences was given two members; Agriculture, Engineering, and Medicine, one each. "Members and chairmen of all other Senate committees shall be appointed annually by the president from lists of nominees submitted by the Policy Committee after consultation with the several faculties, or, at his discretion, from other members of the Senate."

Other functions of the Policy Committee were spelled out in October when all members of the new committees had been designated. At that time, "a consolidated statement of the functions of the several Senate committees as formulated by themselves and revised by the policy committee" was presented to the senate. The Policy Committee was to meet regularly with the president and to serve as an intermediary between the president and the faculty. It was also to represent the faculty to the Board of Trustees. The proposal added, "It is understood that, in order to perform these functions, the committee must be informed by the President of all important proposed changes in either policy or personnel, whether administrative or instructional, and must have access to the details of the budget at all times. Such information will necessarily be confidential to the members of the committee." Thus, for the first time the faculty decisively and formally injected itself into all the affairs of the university.

With the establishment of the Policy Committee, the senate assumed a major responsibility for both the composition and quality of university committees, resolving that "no members [of the Policy Committee] be retained except for those who can give their best services in their present positions; that chairmanships should not be reserved for [full] professors; that several places on most committees should be given to members of other ranks." The Policy Committee began to function immediately, with a recommendation to the Trustees on retirement and pensions, adopted by the Board in April 1943.[19] A reorganization of the standing committees of the senate reduced the previous twenty to twelve, only three of which—admissions, library, and publications—specifically included members of the staff or administration. This step clearly suggests that all committees are faculty committees and that membership from other components of the University is an exception.

The AAUP Plays a Role

The 1940 revised version of the AAUP Declaration of Principles stated concisely the meaning of academic freedom in research, in the classroom, and for teachers as citizens, and it very specifically spelled out the nature of a desired agreement between a university and its professors both during the probationary appointment and after the tenure award. Millis made quick use of this document, inviting a committee of the local AAUP to formulate a statement of policy concerning academic freedom and tenure. It quoted nearly all of the 1940 statement. Changes and deletions were made necessary by the fact that there was no preceding policy on such matters at UVM; tenure was being established for the first time. The senate passed the new policy unanimously and with uncommon alacrity on January 9, 1943.

In contrast, less than a decade later, in the divisive and inflammatory atmosphere of the McCarthy era—and on the UVM campus, of the Novikoff case especially—the AAUP principles underwent far more serious scrutiny. Following the first dismissal of Professor Novikoff, the senate and the AAUP drew up a statement on faculty loyalty, a set of procedures for termination of faculty on continuous appointment, and a reiteration of the AAUP Principles of Academic Freedom and Responsibility.

Several versions of the faculty loyalty policy, addressing loyalty in general rather than Communism in particular, were discussed by the senate, but none was formally voted. A procedure for termination for cause was adopted by the senate, after much revision, in March 1954 and was included in the first edition of the faculty handbook. The second edition (1956) included a revised statement on academic freedom and tenure, with a much stronger preamble, still in effect today. These faculty handbooks, or officer's handbooks, constitute the primary legal contract between the University and faculty members.

With the publication of the handbooks the AAUP principles had become an essential bulwark in the defense of faculty rights, in accord with the needs and purposes of the institution and fully accepted by all of its components.

The University had been transformed from the benign yet overly central-ized leadership of President Bailey to a much more organized interaction between the Board of Trustees, president, and faculty.

During the 1940s another organization of professors was formed to ad-vance their causes, particularly to improve their salaries. This was Local 703 of the American Federation of Teachers (AFT). Professor Benjamin Wain-wright kept the minutes for its entire history (1942–1954); his wry, even scathing, comments shed a great deal of light on the frustrations of this small faculty organization.[20] Probably at no time did it consist of more than ten to twelve members. On March 12, 1943, "Mr. DeForest [president of the local] reported on his visit to President Millis, who admitted that the faculty had taken a $120,000 loss [salary cut] in two years but told a sob story of his financial troubles." At the next meeting, in April, there was a "lively discus-sion of the need of an adequate salary scale at UVM and the importance of continued agitation for annuities and a tenure plan."

Local 703 of the AFT voted itself out of existence in early 1954, prob-ably because, with a more active AAUP and an increasingly well organized senate, it was unable ever to augment its membership.

The Struggle to Form a More Perfect Senate, 1963–1979

Efforts to enhance the role of the senate began by codifying the organiza-tion that had existed in name since the time of President Benton in 1911 and in form since the earliest days of the University. Up to the 1950s the senate had been a de facto organization, without bylaws, recognized officially in the catalog and in the early faculty handbooks only as a set of faculty commit-tees. In December 1963, President John Fey announced that "a Committee of the Senate has been appointed for the purpose of preparing a constitution and by-laws of this body."[21] Two years later, in February 1966, the bylaws prepared by this committee passed the senate "without dissent." They de-fined membership of the senate, excluding most people not holding academic rank; specified the committee structure; and established a town meeting for-mat for senate meetings. Thus was enshrined for the first time a de jure senate. It was to survive a bare three years.

By the 1960s many forces were changing the position of the faculty with respect to the administration, their disciplines and the political world outside the University. The number of students, staff, faculty, and administrators doubled or tripled during the thirty-year period from 1940 to 1970. UVM had metamorphosed from a seemingly private liberal arts college combined in an unusual way with a medical college and a land grant college, to become a developing multiversity with a state charter incorporating all parts into a quasi-public institution. Many of the responsibilities previously assumed by the faculty became the province of professional administrators, only a few of whom held or had held faculty status. The support staff grew and gradually organized itself as a separate voice within the burgeoning institution. The functions and outlooks of administrators, faculty, and staff became increasingly disparate. With increasing research funds, the faculty had new opportunities and were taking on new responsibilities in scholarship, investigation, and graduate instruction, on which their professional status (and salaries) depended more and more. As a consequence, purposeful participation in university governance appealed to a smaller and smaller proportion of the faculty. The easy collegiality between faculty and administration that had not reliably existed since the end of the nineteenth century could not be sustained at all, let alone enriched, by the older forms of organization. The faculty were in a dilemma, wishing to wield strong influence over administrative decisions but not inclined to perform many administrative functions.

Nevertheless, the faculty wanted to maintain a strong, independent, cohesive voice within the University. The next step was to remove the president from the chair at senate meetings. A brief amendment to the bylaws was passed unanimously on March 13, 1970: "The Senate shall elect from members of the Faculty a Chairman (Speaker), Vice Chairman, and Secretary."

Professor William White, the first professor elected to preside over the senate, ushered in, on September 11, 1970, a decade of senate reorganization. His own remarkably prescient words describe the situation well:

We are entering upon a new period in our Senate experience—the University president no longer serves as Senate Chairman. This small change considerably alters the posture of the Senate in university government. . . . [But] no single individual feels responsible to attend Senate meetings—he is only one vote in 800 or more likely, 180. Many other important and interesting affairs occupy the attention of our faculty. . . . Some state that the principal function of the Senate is to serve as a faculty forum. Obviously decisions rendered by this body cannot carry the weight that is due them if they are made by a small percentage of the membership. More frightening is the possibility that a special interest group could take over the Senate at some meetings. If [the Senate] is to have the greatest credibility it should adequately represent all interest groups on campus. Members must feel a distinct responsibility for carrying on the business of the University. Our town meeting style of university government does not seem to be meeting these requirements.

The senate wrangled over two major issues for almost a decade before its present structure was established. The first, the issue of a town meeting versus some sort of elected representative senate, occupied many hours of ad hoc committee anguish as well as full senate debate and maneuver, including several mail referenda of the entire faculty. So violent were the battles and so ponderously unsuccessful was the method finally decided on for electing the senate that many faculty members and several senate chairs have declined to participate in senate affairs ever since.[22] This election procedure, combined with faculty apathy, rendered the senate nearly impotent. By 1975 attendance at senate meetings by elected senators was so small that the body was in danger of losing its ability to speak with any authority for the faculty as a whole.

Finally, at a dispirited senate meeting in October 1975 (twenty-seven of forty-one senators present), Professor Donald Moser moved "That the Chairman of the Faculty Senate appoint a committee to investigate the reasons why the Faculty has not elected its full complement of senators this year and why attendance at Senate meetings has been so low recently, and to make recommendations to the Senate aimed at generating a greater spirit of cooperation among faculty and administration in the conduct of University affairs." The motion carried, and a senate review committee composed of seven members, chaired by Professor Roger Cooke, was formed. This committee met regularly until the end of the 1975–1976 academic year; its report set the stage for several improvements.

Discussion and maneuver over the next fifteen months eventually brought back the town meeting form, that is, every faculty member was entitled to vote again. In addition, however, the following statement came into force in September 1977: "Each department shall elect a representative from its faculty who will assume special obligation to attend all Senate meetings." This hybrid town meeting/departmental representative form continues today.

The second issue, that of enhancing faculty participation in university governance, has generally been addressed by modifying the senate's committee structure. In 1970 the Policy Committee was carved up, pursuant to a recommendation by a local AAUP committee, into three committees: academic policy, financial policy, and administrative policy. Each would meet regularly with appropriate members of the administration so as to participate in these three administrative areas. The full senate approved this idea in November 1970. In 1972, when the constitution and bylaws for the elected senate were finally voted, the Academic Policy Committee was renamed the Faculty Affairs Committee, with responsibility for reviewing all promotion and tenure decisions. A new committee, Academic Affairs, would supervise academic programs and all-university curricular requirements. On December 2, 1972, the Board of Trustees adopted the recommendation of its governance committee that the "Constitution and Bylaws of the University of Vermont Faculty be approved without, however, in any way relinquishing any responsibility or authority vested in the Board." The Administrative Policy Committee, resisted by administrators, functioned only until 1977. Reworking of the committee structure continued through the long-drawn-out campaign over the town meeting problem. The present committee structure was not codified until 1979 and continues occasionally to be modified.[23]

Can the Senate Solve Real Problems?

Despite the vicissitudes of its structure and the many external pressures on the University, the senate has accomplished a great deal for the faculty.

Three simultaneous developments threatened the faculty during the 1971–1972 academic year. First, the University was suffering financial stringency owing to an unexpected drop in enrollment; the possibility arose that certain units might be reduced and certain faculty dismissed. Second, the Board of Trustees refused to renew the appointment of Professor Michael Parenti, against nearly unanimous university support for him. And third, the Vermont Legislature was considering a bill to amalgamate the Vermont State Colleges with UVM. These issues, and concern over the rights of faculty to participate in their resolution, occupied part of each regular senate meeting and all of two special sessions in the fall term of 1971.

In response to the financial issue, the senate prepared strong new language to regulate dismissal of faculty under conditions of financial stringency. The administration maneuvered through this financially tight period without violating that language. The substance of the new language was incorporated into the revision of the officers' handbook in 1976–1977.

Both the financial threat and the Parenti case raised the possibility that faculty grievances might be brought against the administration in the future. The senate resolved (68–35) on December 2, 1971, "that the President of the Senate appoint a committee to consider establishing a full-time faculty ombudsman." This effort was not to mature for some years.

The third issue—union of UVM with the Vermont state college system—which to many professors threatened the academic quality of UVM at a time when it was struggling to keep up with rapid growth on inadequate funds, contributed to a feeling of helplessness. In the event, of course, the Legislature dropped the idea. Suggestions for faculty–trustee committees to provide more faculty input in such long-range decisions never bore fruit.

There were, however, nonvoting professors on six committees of the Board of Trustees as early as 1971. During the first year (1976–1977) of the incumbency of President Lattie Coor and Vice-President Robert Arns a major revision of the officers' handbook was undertaken. That revision specified members of the senate executive council to sit regularly with their counterpart committees of the Board of Trustees. Their influence under these circumstances continues to be circumscribed.

Another significant addition at this time was provision for a faculty ombudsman and a grievance procedure. As the University grew in size and administrative layers became increasingly ordered and separate, professors increasingly needed help when the normal appeal process up through the academic bureaucracy failed to bring a satisfactory resolution to their complaints. The idea for an ombudsman, as we have seen, had been in the minds of faculty for five or six years. Moreover, grievance hearing procedures were being used in other universities, and models were available. In this new system the part-time ombudsman's principal responsibilities are to help aggrieved faculty to negotiate the normal appeal sequence—from chair to dean to provost to president—and to serve as mediator during this process. The grievance committee's main function is to carry out hearings when the appeal process has been exhausted and to decide on the merits of the grievant's case. During the life of the grievance system there have been fewer than one hearing per year. The grievance procedure has thus encouraged both faculty and administration to resolve disputes through the due process of normal appeal. Decisions by the grievance committee have almost always been carried out by the provost. Nevertheless, some faculty members still wanted grievance committee decisions to be binding on the administration and grievants to be able to choose to be represented by an attorney. The State Labor Relations Act extended to UVM by the Vermont Legislature in 1988 provides binding arbitration of grievances by the Vermont Labor Relations Board after remedies within the University have been exhausted.

The present grievance system is an excellent example of a faculty initiative carefully thought out by an ad hoc committee, ironed out with the administration, and made legally binding in the officer's handbook. By rule the system is reviewed at least every five years, and it has been modified at each review.

Another area in which faculty participation has increased is the selection of officers of the academic administration—presidents, provosts, and deans. The Board of Trustees designated a committee to select a successor to President Millis that included eight trustees, one member of the Policy Committee, one dean, one member of the Alumni Council and, ex officio, President Millis. Two years later the committee to select a successor to President Carlson included seven trustees, five members of the Policy Committee, and one dean. The shift in the ratio of trustees to faculty may, in part, have resulted from discussion of the matter in the senate. Sixteen years later, in November 1968, owing to the quick appointment of Lyman Rowell to the presidency by the Trustees, the senate urged "continuation of sound academic tradition at the University of Vermont in the choice of a President. Such appointments should be made after full participation of representatives of the faculty throughout the process leading up to the final decision." Except on this occasion, faculty members have increasingly participated in the selection of the presidents since Millis. The requirements that professors be part of search committees for the president, provost, and deans and the procedure for selecting them are carefully spelled out in the contemporary officers' handbook.

From time to time since the Vietnam War was escalated in the 1960s the senate has considered resolutions dealing with issues beyond the borders of the University, often in response to student initiatives. In 1966 a student demonstration generated a senate debate over U.S. participation in the Vietnam conflict. Again in May 1972, a student petition prompted the motion, "The faculty of the University of Vermont calls for an immediate withdrawal of U.S. land, air and naval forces from Indo-China." Although dissent on such issues has often led to considerable disruption on the campus and opinions are strongly expressed, only a minority of the faculty have participated in these conflicts on the floor of the senate or elsewhere. The moral voice of the senate has often been effective only to the extent that it is in concert with other groups in the university community.

Conclusions

Where, then, does the UVM faculty stand when it comes to university governance? Can the assiduous faculty member influence the University to comply with his or her financial aspirations as well as professional and moral standards? An excellent article in the *Cynic*, by an undergraduate, Susan Khodorahmi,[24] presents a good amalgam of faculty opinion about senate power to influence administrative decisions: "Despite its authority 'to review and establish policy' regarding, among other matters, academic freedom, all matters relating to the curriculum, research and scholarship, general admission standards, regulations for attendance, examinations and degrees, teaching quality and the academic calendar, there are a variety of instances in which the administration has the final say." Khodorahmi also points out that many faculty members fail to attend meetings or otherwise participate in the senate because they consider it a "stagnant, faltering organization." On the other hand, many faculty members blame sporadic attendance and interest in the senate for its lack of effectiveness.

Service in governance has always appealed to a relatively minor fraction of the faculty, unless it directly affects an individual's future or finances. With the present hybrid town meeting/department representative form of the senate, no faculty members except the executive council take any responsibility for the quality or outcome of senate deliberations. Those who participate in the senate often meet with indifference and criticism on the part of their colleagues. When Professor David Holmes was chair of the Faculty Affairs Committee in 1981, he wrote: "The faculty as a body must be willing to delegate significant responsibility to colleagues who are elected to work on behalf of the faculty and the university. At the same time, the number of faculty experienced in the business of the university needs to be broadened in a systematic way." But, he adds, "it is not clear whether the faculty is willing or in a position to invest considerable time and effort in helping to govern the university."[25]

Thus, neither the long struggle to establish a faculty senate having substantial voice in university affairs nor its clear achievement in a number of cases, has won universal admiration or, more important, meaningful support among its constituents. Professor Holmes, reflecting on this low esteem, remarks, "The faculty governance system neither accepts, rejects, perfects nor selects an alternative to a tentative course of action.

In these circumstances some faculty members are attempting once again, through the National Education Association, to persuade their colleagues to form a bargaining unit. And the faculty as a whole may fail them too. Perhaps Professor Dolores Sandoval, who in 1982 resigned the senate chair in discouragement, has it right: "The Faculty Senate is only as vigorous as its members demand it to be. It is only as efficient as its members' expectations require it to be. It is only as useful a tool in the overall governance structure of the university as its members decide it shall be."[26]

Appendix A

Presidents of the University of Vermont, 1800–1990

(Full name; birth and death dates; college and class; previous position, if other than Congregational minister, and location; dates elected and retired from presidency.)

Daniel Clarke Sanders (1768–1850), Harvard '88; Vergennes; 1800–14
Samuel Austin (1760–1830), Yale '83; Worcester, Mass.; 1815–21
Daniel Haskel (1784?–1848), Yale '02; Burlington; 1821–24
Willard Preston (1785–1856), Brown '06; Burlington; 1825–26
James Marsh (1794–1842), Dartmouth '17; Classics, Hampden-Sydney College, Va.; 1826–33
John Wheeler (1798–1862), Dartmouth '16; Windsor, Vt.; 1833–49
Worthington Smith (1795–1856), Williams '16; St. Albans; 1849–55
Calvin Pease (1813–1863), UVM '38; Classics, UVM; 1855–61
Joseph Torrey (1797–1867), Dartmouth '16; Philosophy, UVM; 1862–66
James Burrill Angell (1829–1916), Brown '49; Editor, Providence, R.I., *Journal*; 1866–71
Matthew Henry Buckham (1833–1910), UVM '51; Greek and English literature, UVM; 1871–1910
Guy Potter Benton (1865–1927), Baker U., Baldwin, Kan., '93; President, Miami University of Ohio; 1911–19
Guy Winfred Bailey (1876–1940), UVM '00; Comptroller, UVM; 1919–1940
John Schoff Millis (1903–88), U. Chicago '24; Carnegie Foundation; 1941–49
William Samuel Carlson (1905–   ), U. Mich.'29; President, University of Delaware; 1950–52
Carl William Borgmann (1905–   ), U. Colorado '31; Dean of the Faculties, University of Nebraska; 1952–58
John Theodore Fey (1917–   ), Washington & Lee '37; Clerk, U.S. Supreme Court, Washington, D.C.; 1958–64
Shannon McCune (1914–   ), College of Wooster '35; Assistant to the President, University of Illinois, Champaign-Urbana; 1965–66
Lyman Smith Rowell (1904–84), UVM '25; Vice President for Administration, UVM; 1966–70
Edward Clinton Andrews (1925–   ), Middlebury '43; Dean, College of Medicine, UVM; 1970–75
Lattie Finch Coor (1936–   ), U. Northern Arizona '58; Vice Chancellor, Washington U., St. Louis; 1976–89
George H. Davis (1942–   ), College of Wooster '64; Interim Vice President for Business Affairs, U. Arizona; 1990–

Appendix B

UVM Professors, 1804–1869

(Name, college and year graduated, birth and death dates; subjects, and dates taught. Brown, BU (2); Columbia, CU (1); Dartmouth, DC (4); Hamilton (1); Harvard, HC (1); University of Vermont, UV (12); Williams, WC (3); Yale, YC (6); University of Zurich (1). Omits professors in the Medical Department after it was organized in 1822 and the 13 tutors who were not also professors.)

John Pomeroy,* 1764–1844; anatomy and surgery, 1804–1817

James Dean, DC '00, 1776–1849; math, physics, astronomy, 1809–1814, 1822–1824 (tutor, '07–'09)

Jason Chamberlain, BU '04, 1783–1821; Classics, 1811–1814

Jairus Kennan, UV '04, ?–1816; natural history, chemistry, 1813–1814**

Ebenezer Burgess, BU '09, 1790–1870; math, physics, 1815–1817

James Murdock, YC '97, 1776–1856; Classics, 1815–1819

Gamaliel S. Olds, WC '01, 1777–1848; math, physics, 1819–1821

Lucas Hubbell, UV '18, 1778–1847; Classics, 1819–1824 (tutor, '16–'19)

John J. Robertson, CU '16, 1796–1881; Classics, 1824–1825

George W. Benedict, WC '18, 1796–1871; math, 1825–1829; physics, 1825–1839; chemistry, 1829–1847; natural history, 1839–1847

William A. Porter, WC '18, 1798–1830; Classics, 1825–1827

Joseph Torrey, DC '16, 1797–1867; Classics, 1827–1842; philosophy, 1842–1866

Geo. R. Huntington, UV '26, 1800–1872; math, civil engineering, 1829–1832 (tutor, '28–'29)

Farrand N. Benedict, Hamilton '23, 1803–1880; math, civil engineering, 1833–1854 (tutor, '33)

James Marsh, DC '17, 1794–1842; philosophy, 1833–1842

Henry Chaney, UV '31, 1808–1885; physics, chemistry, 1837–1849

Calvin Pease, UV '38, 1813–1863; Classics, 1842–1855

Wm. G. T. Shedd, UV '39, 1820–1894; English literature, 1845–1852

Zadock Thompson, UV '23, 1796–1856; natural history, 1851–1856 (tutor, '25–'26)

Nathaniel G. Clark, UV '45, 1825–1896; English literature, 1852–1863; Latin, 1857–1863 (tutor, '49–'50)

Henri Erni, Ph.D. UZurich, 1822–1885; chemistry, pharmacy, 1853–1857

McKendree Petty, UV '49, 1827–1887; math, physics, 1854–1886 (tutor, '53–'54)

Leonard Marsh, DC '27, MD '32, 1800–1870; Classics, 1855–1857; "vegetable and animal physiology," 1857–1870

Matthew H. Buckham, UV '51, 1832–1910; English literature, 1856–1857; Greek, 1857–1871 (tutor, '53–'54)

Edward Hungerford, YC '51, 1829–1911; chemistry, geology, 1857–1862

Chas. W. Thompson, UV '54, 1832–1897; pro tem. Latin, 1863–1867 (tutor, '56–'57)

Eli Whitney Blake, YC '57, 1836–1895; pro tem. chemistry, physics, 1866–1867

Henry W. Haynes, HC '51, 1831–1912; Latin, 1867–1871; Greek, 1871–1873

Peter Collier, YC '61, 1835–1896; chemistry, minerals, 1866–1877

Henry A. P. Torrey, UV '58, 1837–1902; philosophy, 1868–1902

George H. Perkins, YC '67, 1844–1933; zoology, 1869–1902; botany, 1869–1892; geology, 1869–1933; anthropology, 1885–1933

Volney G. Barbour, YC '67, 1842–1901; civil engineering, 1889–1893; sanitary science, 1886–1888 (Med. Dept.); mechanics and bridge engineering, 1894–1901

*Only professor who was also a trustee (1807–1810, 1813–1822); taught at his Battery Street residence right through the War of 1812 with assistance from Jairus Kennan (above), his son John N. Pomeroy (1814), and John LeComte Cazier (1816–1817).

**Returned in October 1814 but was too sick to teach.

The median age at appointment as professor was just under thirty; their age when they stopped teaching was just over forty-two. Six were still teaching when they died (James Marsh, Zadock Thompson, Leonard Marsh, H. A. P. Torrey, George H. Perkins, Volney G. Barbour); three taught until their final illness of a year or two (Jairus Kennan, Joseph Torrey, McKendree Petty).

Royall Tyler held a professorship from 1811 to 1814, but it is not clear whether he actually lectured.

Appendix C

Roster of Professors, by Years, to 1870

1801–1809
Sanders

1809–1811
Sanders
Chamberlain
Dean

1811–1812
Sanders
Dean
Chamberlain

1812–Mar 1814
Sanders
Dean
Chamberlain
Kennan

1815–1816
Austin
Kennan
Burgess
Murdock

1816–1817
Austin
Burgess
Murdock

1817–1819
Austin
Murdock

1819–1821
Austin
Hubbell
Olds

1821–1822
Haskell
Hubbell

1822–May 1824
Haskell
Hubbell
Dean

1824–1825
Dean
Robertson

1825–1826
Preston
Benedict
Porter

1826–1827
Marsh
Benedict
Porter

1827–1829
Marsh
Benedict
Torrey

1829–1832
Marsh
Benedict
Torrey
Huntington

1832–1833
Marsh
Benedict
Torrey

1833–1837
Wheeler
Marsh
G. Benedict
Torrey
F. Benedict

1837–1842
Wheeler
Marsh
G. Benedict
Torrey
F. Benedict
Chaney

1842–1847
Wheeler
G. Benedict
Torrey
F. Benedict
Chaney
Pease
Shedd (1845–)

1847–1849
Wheeler
Torrey
F. Benedict
Chaney
Pease
Shedd

1849–1851
Smith
Torrey
F. Benedict
Chaney
Pease
Shedd

1851–1853
Smith
Torrey
F. Benedict
Chaney
Pease
Thompson
Shedd (to 1852)
Clark (1852–1853)

1853–1854
Smith
Torrey
F. Benedict
Pease
Thompson
Clark
Erni

1854–1855
Smith
Torrey
Pease
Thompson
Clark
Erni
Petty

1855–1856
Pease
Torrey
Thompson
Clark
Erni
Petty
L. Marsh

1856–1857
Pease
Torrey
Clark
Erni
Petty
L. Marsh
Buckham

1857–1862
Pease
Torrey
Clark
Petty
L. Marsh
Buckham
Hungerford

1862–1863
Torrey
Clark
Petty
L. Marsh
Buckham

1863–1866
Torrey
Petty
L. Marsh
Buckham
C. Thompson

1866–1867
Angell
Petty
L. Marsh
Buckham
Blake
Collier
C. Thompson

1867–1868
Angell
Petty
Marsh
Buckham
Collier
Haynes

1868–1869
Angell
Petty
Marsh
Buckham
Collier
Haynes
H. Torrey

1869–1870
Angell
Petty
Marsh
Buckham
Collier
Haynes
H. Torrey
Perkins
Barbour

Notes

Part One. Origins of UVM, Overview (pp. 9–17)

1. John A. Williams, ed., *Laws of Vermont*, vol. 15 of *State Papers of Vermont*, (Montpelier: Secretary of State, 1967), p. 33. The official date of the charter was November 2, 1791.

2. John S. Whitehead, *The Separation of College and State: Columbia, Dartmouth, Harvard, and Yale, 1776–1876* (New Haven: Yale University Press, 1973), p. 3 and passim.

3. Julian I. Lindsay, *Tradition Looks Forward, The University of Vermont: A History, 1791–1904* (Burlington: University of Vermont, 1954), pp. 49–50.

4. Sidney Willard, *Memories of Youth and Manhood* (Cambridge, Mass.: 1855), p. 230.

5. Trustees' statement to the Legislature, 20 October 1810, in Sanders's handwriting, in Vermont State Papers, Vermont State Archives, vol. 67, p. 19.

6. James Dean, *An Oration on Curiosity, Pronounced in the University of Vermont, 24th April, 1810, on Induction into Office* (Burlington, Vt.: Samuel Mills, 1810); Jason Chamberlain, *An Inaugural Oration, Delivered at Burlington, August 1, 1811* (Burlington, Vt.: Samuel Mills, 1811).

7. Trustees' statement to the Legislature, 20 October 1810, in President Sanders's handwriting, in Vermont State Papers, vol. 67, p. 10. Accessible copies of the original 1791 charter and the charter as amended in 1810 are in *Organization of the University of Vermont and State Agricultural College* (Burlington, Vt.: Free Press Publishing, 1917), pp. 18–27.

8. Report of Governor Martin Chittenden and trustee Heman Allen to the Legislature, 22 October 1814, Vermont State Papers.

9. Ibid.

10. MS, "Autobiography of Daniel Clarke Saunders," in the possession of Nancy Wolcott of Scituate, Mass.; photocopy and typescript copies in the UVM archives.

11. Unsigned biographical sketches of Presidents Austin and Haskell appear in Abby M. Hemenway, ed., *Vermont Historical Gazeteer*, 5 vols. (Burlington: A. M. Hemenway, 1867–1892), vol. 1, pp. 525–7.

12. Daniel Haskell and J. Calvin Smith, *A Complete Descriptive and Statistical Gazetteer of the United States of America* (New York: Sherman and Smith, 1843, 1844).

13. *Records of the Governor and Council of the State of Vermont*, ed. E. P. Walton, 8 vols. (Montpelier: J. & J. M. Poland, 1873–1880), vol. 7, p. 342.

14. *Acts Passed by The Legislature of the State of Vermont at their October Session, 1825* (Windsor, Vt.: Simeon Ide, 1825), p. 116, and *1826* (Bennington, Vt.: William Haswell, 1826), p. 89; Kevin T. Dann, "The College of Natural History at the University of Vermont, 1826–1850," *Vermont History* 53 (Spring 1985): 77–94.

15. Alonzo B. Rich to Royal D. King, 5 May 1842, MSS 22, #13, Vermont Historical Society.

Chapter 1. A Hard Founding Father to Love (pp. 18–33)

1. University of Vermont trustee minutes, 23–24 March 1814, UVM Archives, vol. 2, pp. 47–57.

2. The only biography of Ira Allen is James B. Wilbur's uncritical *Ira Allen: Founder of Vermont 1751–1814*, 2 vols. (Boston: Houghton Mifflin, 1928). The best collections of Ira Allen manuscripts are the Allen Family Papers, University of Vermont Library (hereafter AP, UVM); the Allen sections of the Stevens Collection, Vermont State Archives; and the holdings of the Vermont Historical Society, Montpelier, Vermont.

3. See Allen's unfinished autobiography, published in Wilbur, *Ira Allen*, vol. 1, pp. 1–59.

4. Onion River Land Company advertisement, *Connecticut Courant*, 29 May 1773.

5. Ira Allen autobiography, in Wilbur, *Ira Allen*, vol. 1, p. 53.

6. Ibid., chap. 1.

7. Matt B. Jones, *Vermont in the Making* (1939; reprint, New York: AMS Books, 1968), chaps. 13–14; *Records of the Governor and Council of the State of Vermont*, ed. E. P. Walton (Montpelier, Vt.: J. & J. M. Poland, 1873–1880), vol. 1; *Records of Conventions in the New Hampshire Grants for the Independence of Vermont 1776–1777*, ed. Redfield Proctor (Washington, D.C.: n.p., 1904).

8. Sarah V. Kalinoski, "Sequestration, Confiscation, and the 'Tory' in the Vermont Revolution," *Vermont History*, 45 (Fall 1977): 236–46.

9. See Ira Allen, *The Natural and Political History of the State of Vermont* (1798; reprint ed., Rutland, Vt.: Charles E. Tuttle Co., 1969), pp. 106–108.

10. Wilbur, *Ira Allen*, chaps. 12–16.

11. AP, UVM, boxes 6–10; Chilton Williamson, *Vermont in Quandary: 1763–1825* (Montpelier: Vermont Historical Society, 1949), chaps. 9–11; H. N. Muller III, "The Commercial History of the Lake Champlain–Richelieu River Route 1760–1815" (Ph.D. diss., University of Rochester, 1968).

12. Wilbur, *Ira Allen*, chaps. 13–16; Benny F. Cockerham, "Levi Allen (1746–1801): Opportunism and the Problem of Allegiance" (M.A. thesis, University of Vermont, 1965).

13. *The Constitution of the State of Vermont* (Hartford: Watson and Goodwin [1778]), p. 22.

14. Julian I. Lindsay, *Tradition Looks Forward, The University of Vermont: A History 1791–1904* (Burlington: University of Vermont, 1954), pp. 6–12.

15. Ibid., pp. 18–20.

16. Vermont Historical Society, MSS 7 789372.

17. Windsor *Vermont Journal*, 23 September 1789; typescript in Samuel Williams Papers, UVM Library, box 2, folder 29.

18. MSS of pledge lists, 1 September 1790, in AP, UVM, box 11, folder 109, and box 12, folder 59A.

19. Text in Lindsay, *Tradition*, pp. 23–28.

20. Samuel Williams to Allen, 13 May 1791, MS in Allen Papers, Stevens Collection, Vermont State Archives.

21. Lindsay, *Tradition*, pp. 28–29; John A. Williams, ed., *Laws of Vermont*, vol. 15 of *State Papers of Vermont* (hereafter *SPOV*; Montpelier: Secretary of State, 1967), pp. 32–35.

22. Allen to State of New York, 27 January 1792, MS in AP, UVM, box 13, folder 31.

23. Allen's promise to honor original pledge to UVM, 16 June 1792, MS in AP, UVM, box 11, folder 111.

24. Allen's agreement with UVM Board of Trustees, 13 October 1793, photocopy in AP, UVM, box 14, folder 70.

25. Allen's memorial to Vermont Legislature, 23 October 1793, photocopy in AP, UVM, box 14, folder 69.

26. Allen's draft of memorandum on objectives in founding UVM, [1793?], MS in AP, UVM, box 14, folder 81-A.

27. The committee's report is in John A. Williams, ed., *Journals and Proceedings of the General Assembly of the State of Vermont 1795–1796*, vol. 3, part 7 of *SPOV* (Montpelier: State of Vermont, 1973), pp. 145–9; quotation appears on p. 147.

28. Allen's bond to UVM, October 1795, photocopy in AP, UVM, box 16, folder 17; AP, UVM, box 16, contains photocopies of several Allen leases for his mills and other properties, November 1795.

29. Wilbur, *Ira Allen*, vol. 2, pp. 79–82; Thomas Chittenden, appointment of Allen as agent to solicit gifts for UVM, 27 October 1795, MS in UVM Archives.

30. Allen's journal, 11 December 1795–19 August 1796, includes copies of letters to the Duke of Portland, MS in AP, UVM, box 16, folder 28.

31. Wilbur, *Ira Allen*, chaps. 24–29; Jeanne A. Ojala, "Ira Allen and the French Directory, 1796: Plans for the Creation of the Republic of United Columbia," *William and Mary Quarterly*, 36 (July 1979): 436–8. Allen's *Olive Branch* manuscripts are in AP, UVM, box 30.

32. Wilbur, *Ira Allen*, chaps. 26–28. Photocopies of Allen's manuscripts of 1797–1800 are in AP, UVM, boxes 18–21.

33. Thomas S. Webster, "Ira Allen in Paris, 1800, Planning a Canadian Revolution," Canadian Historical Association *Annual Meeting Report* (1963), pp. 74–80. Copies of Allen's 1800 United Columbia manuscripts are in AP, UVM, box 30.

34. Report of Nathaniel Chipman, Daniel Chipman, and Noah Chittenden in Onion River Land Company lawsuit, 11 December 1802, photocopy in AP, UVM, box 23, folder 67; Ira Allen, *State of Vermont. To the Honorable the Court of Chancery to be Holden at Middlebury . . . the 29th Day of June, . . . 1802* (Middlebury?: Huntington & Fitch?, 1803?).

35. See Lindsay, *Tradition*, pp. 39–44, for the texts of Allen's 1796 correspondence with European associates concerning UVM.

36. Ibid., chap. 4; David M. Stameshkin, *The Town's College: Middlebury College, 1800–1915* (Middlebury, Vt.: Middlebury College Press, 1985).

37. MS of 28 July 1800, Chittenden County Court order for attachment of Plainfield as payment of Allen's 1793 pledge to UVM, in AP, UVM, box 21, folder 77.

38. Allen advertisement in Burlington *Northern Centinel*, 4 June 1801; photocopy of 18 May 1801, MS in AP, UVM, box 22, folder 53; published in Wilbur, *Ira Allen*, vol. 2, p. 316.

39. Allen to David Russell, 15 July 1801, photocopy in AP, UVM, box 22, folder 59; published in Wilbur, *Ira Allen*, vol. 2, pp. 333–4.

40. Benjamin Boardman et al., advertisement for sale of Allen's Colchester properties, in Burlington *Vermont Centinel*, 5 August 1802.

41. Allen bankruptcy documents, September 1803, MSS at Vermont Historical Society, * X MS B AL535 and MSS 26 #16.

42. Ira Allen, Gen. Allen's Statement, Respecting a Large Cargo of Cannon and Arms Purchased in France, for the Use of the Militia in Vermont ([Philadelphia?: 1804?]).

43. Vermont House of Representatives resolution, 7 November 1804, Journals of the General Assembly of the State of Vermont . . . October 11, 1804 (Bennington, Vt.: Haswell & Smead, 1805), p. 335.

44. Allen published nine Olive Branch books and pamphlets between 1804 and 1809. The longest, 551 pages, is Particulars of the Capture of the Ship Olive Branch (Philadelphia: Author, 1805).

45. Allen, Copies of Letters to the Governor of Vermont (Philadelphia: Author, January 1810), pp. 21–27.

46. MSS and photocopies of Allen's letters to his family, 1805–1813, in AP, UVM, box 24, and at Vermont Historical Society.

47. In 1810–1811 Allen published three slightly different editions of his pamphlet Copies of Letters to the Governor of Vermont.

48. Wilbur, Ira Allen, chap. 41; photocopies of Allen letters concerning the Texas expedition, AP, UVM, box 24; Harris G. Warren, The Sword Was Their Passport: A History of American Filibustering in the Mexican Revolution (Baton Rouge: Louisiana State University Press, 1943).

49. Burlington Northern Sentinel, 11 February 1814.

50. Ira Hayden Allen to Elijah Paine, 12 June 1838, MS in AP, UVM, box 25, folder 20.

51. John Wheeler, A Historical Discourse (Burlington, Vt.: Free Press Print, 1854), pp. 10–11.

52. John E. Goodrich, The Founder of the University of Vermont ([Burlington: n.p., 1892]), p. 44.

53. Wilbur, Ira Allen, vol. 1, p. vi.

54. Copies of the Wilbur–Bailey correspondence are in the James B. Wilbur Papers, UVM Library, and the UVM Archives.

Chapter 2. Years of Trial (pp. 34–47)

1. David Stameshkin, The Town's College: Middlebury College, 1800–1915 (Middlebury, Vt.: Middlebury College Press, 1985), p. 27.

2. E. P. Walton, Records of the Governor and Council of the State of Vermont, 8 vols. (Montpelier: J. & J. M. Poland, 1837–1880), vol. 4, p. 279; Laws and Acts of the State of Vermont, 1800, pp. 34–40.

3. Perry Miller, The Life of the Mind in America (New York: Harcourt, Brace & World, 1967), pp. 4–5.

4. Timothy Dwight, The Nature and Danger of Infidel Philosophy Exhibited in Two Discourses (New Haven, Conn.: 1798), p. 89.

5. Nathan Perkins, Narrative of Tour through the State of Vermont (Woodstock, Vt.: Elm Tree Press, 1930), p. 22.

6. Ibid., p. 26; Timothy Dwight, Travels through the U.S. and Canada (New Haven, Conn.: T. Dwight, 1821), vol. 2, p. 402; Paul Jeffrey Potash, "Welfare of the Regions Beyond," Vermont History 46 (1978): 109–28.

7. University of Vermont charter, in John A. Williams, ed., Laws of Vermont, 1791–1795, vol. 15 of State Papers of Vermont (Montpelier: Secretary of State, 1970), p. 33.

8. Dwight, Travels, vol. 2, pp. 415–16; Stameshkin, Town's College, pp. 26–27, 69.

9. UVM Trustees Minutes, 11 September 1807, University of Vermont Archives (hereafter UVA); Sanders Notebook, UVA; *President Sanders' Discourse on the Death of Mrs. Martha Russell* (Bennington, Vt.: Haswell & Smead, 1805), pp. 20–22.

10. Miller, *Life of the Mind*, pp. 103–104, 108.

11. Daniel Sanders to William C. Harrington, 6 October 1806, UVA.

12. Quoted in H. N. Muller III, "Smuggling into Canada: How the Champlain Valley Defied Jefferson's Embargo," *Vermont History*, 38 (1970): 5–21.

13. *The Hundredth Anniversary of the First Church in Burlington, February 23, 1905* (Burlington: The First Church, 1905), pp. 15–17.

14. Daniel Sanders to Royall Tyler, 5 December 1810, UVA.

15. Asa Burton, *The Life of Asa Burton Written by Himself*, ed. Charles Latham, Jr. (Thetford, Vt.: First Congregational Church, 1973), pp. 34–36.

16. John Wheeler, *Historical Discourse on the Semi-centennial of the University of Vermont, 1854* (Burlington: Free Press, 1854), pp. 18–19.

17. UVM Trustees Minutes, 1 August 1811, UVA. See also Daniel Sanders to Royall Tyler, 5 December 1810, UVA.

18. Daniel Sanders to President John T. Kirkland, 3 September 1811, UVA.

19. Daniel Sanders, *A History of the Indian Wars with the First Settlers of the United States, Particularly of New England* (Montpelier, Vt.: Wright & Sibley, 1812), p. 307.

20. John Hough, "Review of *A History of the Indian Wars with the First Settlers of the United States, Particularly of New England*," *The Literary and Philosophical Repertory* ([Middlebury, Vt.], 1813): 349–75.

21. Joshua Bates, "Revivals of Religion at Middlebury College," *American Quarterly*, February 1840, pp. 307–11.

22. Richard D. Birdsall, "The Second Great Awakening and the New England Social Order," *Church History*, 39 (1976): 345–64.

23. Daniel Sanders, "Autobiography," UVA.

24. Samuel Austin, *Inaugural Address Presented at the University of Vermont, July 26, 1815* (Burlington: Francis G. Fish, 1815).

25. Wheeler, *Historical Discourse*, p. 23.

26. Stameshkin, *Town's College*, pp. 52–53.

27. University students to University of Vermont Board of Trustees, 21 March 1821, UVM Trustees Minutes, UVA; also Wheeler, *Historical Discourse*, p. 23.

28. Zadock Thompson, *History of Vermont, Natural, Civil and Statistical* (Burlington, Vt.: C. Goodrich, 1842), p. 145.

29. Wheeler, *Historical Discourse*, p. 24.

30. James Marsh, *The Remains of the Rev. James Marsh* (Boston: Crocker & Brewster, 1843), p. 27.

31. Ibid., pp. 9–12.

32. James Marsh, *Inaugural Address Delivered at the University of Vermont, November 28, 1826* (Burlington, 1826), p. 8.

33. Bates, "Revivals," pp. 311–17.

34. Joshua Bates, *The Scriptures Our Only Guide* (Middlebury, Vt.: Copeland & Allen, 1820); Joshua Bates, *An Inaugural Oration Pronounced March 18, 1818* (Middlebury, Vt.: Copeland, 1818), pp. 4, 20.

35. Marsh, *Remains*, p. 109.

36. Wheeler, *Historical Discourse*, p. 31.

37. Ibid., p. 32.

38. Figures from Congregational Church of Vermont, *Annual Minutes of the General Convention*, 1831, p. 7.

39. *Vermont Chronicle*, 18 March, 3 and 24 June 1831.

40. Thomas Merrill, "Complete List of the Congregational Ministers in Addison County," *Quarterly Register*, August 1839, pp. 9–12; Bates, "Revivals," pp. 318–19.

41. Bates, "Revivals," p. 320; Charles G. Eastman, ed., *Sermons, Addresses & Exhortations by Rev. Jedidiah Burchard* (Burlington, Vt.: C. Goodrich, 1836), pp. 89–90.

42. John Henry Hopkins, *The Primitive Church* (Burlington, Vt.: Smith & Harrington, 1835), pp. 126–54.

43. Marsh, *Remains*, pp. 126–30.

44. Eastman, *Sermons*, p. 90.

45. Benjamin Labaree, *A Baccalaureate Discourse Delivered at Middlebury, Vermont, August 6, 1865, in the Twenty-Fifth Anniversary of His Presidency* (Boston: T. R. Marvin & Son, 1865), p. 11.

46. Stameshkin, *Town's College*, pp. 141–43.

47. Report of the Committee on the Project of a Charter Uniting the University of Vermont and Middlebury College, 12 October 1847, UVM Trustees Minutes, UVA.

Chapter 3. Student Debates . . . and Thaddeus Stevens (pp. 48–62)

1. "Semi-Centennial Anniversary of the University of Vermont, A.D. 1854," in *A Historical Discourse of Reverend John Wheeler, D.D.* (Burlington: Free Press, 1854), p. 119, remarks by Charles Adams, Esq., of Burlington.

2. UVM Archives. Judiciary Records (1791–1814). Sanders Papers. Record Group One.

3. Dean Joseph Hills, "History of the University of Vermont" (unpublished manuscript), UVM Archives.

4. Zadock Thompson, *History of Vermont, Natural, Civil, and Statistical* (Burlington: C. Goodrich, 1842), pt. 2, "Civil History of Vermont," p. 94.

5. Ibid.

6. Ralph R. Gurley, *Life of Jehudi Ashmun, Late Colonial Agent in Liberia*, 2nd ed. (New York: Robinson & Franklin, 1839).

7. Altha L. B. Bass, *Cherokee Messenger* (Norman: University of Oklahoma Press, 1936).

8. David P. Thompson, *History of the Town of Montpelier* (Montpelier, Vt.: E. P. Walton, 1860), pp. 249–62; Louise E. Koier, "The Story of a Sword and a Pistol," *News and Notes* (Vermont Historical Society) 5 (February 1954): 41–42.

9. Andrew Robertson, "An Analysis of Thaddeus Stevens' Support in Lancaster County 1843–1866," *Journal of the Lancaster County Historical Society*, 84 (1980): 51.

10. Hills, "History."

11. Fawn M. Brodie, *Thaddeus Stevens, Scourge of the South* (New York: Norton, 1959), pp. 27–28.

12. Samuel A. McCall, *Thaddeus Stevens* (Boston: Houghton Mifflin, 1899), p. 12; Elsie Singmaster, *I Speak for Thaddeus Stevens* (Boston: Houghton Mifflin, 1947), p. 53.

13. Singmaster, *I Speak for Thaddeus Stevens*, p. 53.

14. Ibid.

15. Caledonia County Grammar School, Peacham, Vt., *Hundredth Anniversary of the Caledonia County Grammar School, Peacham, Vt. Report of the Commemorative Exercises, August 11–12, 1897* (Peacham, Vt.: The Alumni Association, 1900), pp. 36ff.

16. David McClure and Elijah Parish, *Memoirs of the Reverend Eleazer Wheelock, D.D.* (Newburyport, Mass.: E. Little & Co., 1811), p. 153.

17. Julian I. Lindsay, *Tradition Looks Forward, The University of Vermont: A History, 1791–1904* (Burlington: University of Vermont, 1954), pp. 93–104.

18. For a more detailed reconstruction of the play's contents, see Betty Bandel, "Thaddeus Stevens, Playwright," *Vermont History*, 40 (1972): 138–59.

19. For the life of La Harpe, see Jean C. F. Hoefer, *Nouvelle biographie générale depuis les temps les plus reculés jusqu'a nos jours* (Paris: Firmin Didot, 1861).

20. Ernest Ludlow Bogart, *Peacham: The Story of a Vermont Hill Town* (Montpelier: Vermont Historical Society, 1948), p. 128, n. 38.

21. Joseph Planta, *The History of the Helvetic Confederacy* (London: J. Stockdale, 1807), vol. 1, p. 294, note.

22. Dorothy Canfield Fisher, *Vermont Tradition* (Boston: Little, Brown, 1953), p. 153.

23. Frédéric César de La Harpe, *Aux Habitants du pays de Vaud: Esclaves des oligarques de Fribourg et de Berne* (Paris, 1797).

24. Wilhelm Oechsli, *History of Switzerland, 1599–1914*, trans. Eden and Cedar Paul (Cambridge: The University Press, 1922), p. 318.

25. Brodie, *Thaddeus Stevens*, p. 366.

26. Ibid., pp. 266ff.

27. Ibid., pp. 207, 165–67.

28. Ibid., pp. 29–30.

29. Ibid., p. 339.

30. Alphonse B. Miller, *Thaddeus Stevens* (New York: Harper, 1939), p. 410.

31. Hoefer, *Nouvelle biographie*, vol. 28, p. 886.

Chapter 4. James Marsh (pp. 63–77)

1. UVM Trustees Minutes, 17 October 1826, University of Vermont Archives.

2. Quoted in David Lowenthal, *George Perkins Marsh: Versatile Vermonter* (New York: Columbia University Press, 1958), p. 76.

3. Joseph Torrey, ed., *The Remains of the Rev. James Marsh, D. D., Late President, and Professor of Moral and Intellectual Philosophy, in the University of Vermont; with a Memoir of His Life* (Boston: Crocker and Brewster, 1843).

4. On these years at Dartmouth, see Frederick Chase, *History of Dartmouth College* (Cambridge, Mass., 1897).

5. Torrey, *Remains*, pp. 18–20.

6. George Ticknor to James Marsh, 16 April 1822, in John Duffy, ed., *Coleridge's American Disciples: Selected Correspondence of James Marsh* (Amherst: University of Massachusetts Press, 1973); hereafter cited as *CAD*.

7. Rufus Choate to James Marsh, 1821, Baker Library, Dartmouth College.

8. James Marsh to Lucia Wheelock, 1823, in Torrey, *Remains*, pp. 58–59.

9. James Marsh to Lucia Wheelock, 1 July 1821, in Torrey, *Remains*, pp. 45–46.

10. Torrey, *Remains*, p. 34.

11. Quoted in Torrey, *Remains*, pp. 37–38. (James Marsh's journal has been lost.)

12. James Marsh to Leonard Marsh, 27 April 1822, James Marsh Collection, Bailey Howe Library, University of Vermont.

13. James Marsh, Inaugural Address, in Torrey, *Remains*, pp. 582–83.

14. John Wheeler, *A Historical Discourse at the Celebration on the Occasion of the Semi-Centennial Anniversary of the University of Vermont* (Burlington, Vt.: Free Press 1854), pp. 117ff.

15. James Marsh, Report to the Corporation of the University of Vermont, Burlington, Vermont, 25 March 1827, UVM Trustees Minutes, UVM Archives.

16. James Marsh, "Tract on Eloquence," in Torrey, *Remains*, p. 613.

17. [James Marsh], "Ancient and Modern Poetry," *The North American Review*, 22 (July 1822): 123–24.

18. Ibid.

19. *An Exposition of the System of Instruction and Discipline Pursued in the University of Vermont* (Burlington: Chauncey Goodrich, 1827; revised 1831).

20. Wheeler, *Historical Discourse*, pp. 37–40.

21. For Coleridge on the distinction between Reason and Understanding, see, e.g., his *Statesman's Manual* (Burlington, Vt.: C. Goodrich, 1832).

22. Wheeler, *Historical Discourse*, p. 39 (emphasis added).

23. See Marsh's letters to Archibald Alexander and others in *CAD*, pp. 75ff.

24. Torrey, *Remains*, p. 65.

25. Samuel Taylor Coleridge, *Aids to Reflection, in the formation of a Manly Character, on the Several Grounds of Prudence, Morality, and Religion; illustrated by select passages from our elder divines, especially Archbishop Leighton. 1st American edition, from 1st London edition. With an appendix and illustrations from other works of the same author, together with a preliminary essay and additional notes from James Marsh* (Burlington, Vt.: Chauncey Goodrich, 1829).

26. *CAD*, p. 31, n. 3.

27. Ralph Waldo Emerson, *The Journals and Miscellaneous Notebooks of Ralph Waldo Emerson* (Cambridge, Mass.: Belknap Press of Harvard University Press, 1964), vol. 1, pp. 412–13, vol. 4, pp. 1636–39; *The Letters of Ralph Waldo Emerson* (New York: Columbia University Press, 1939), pp. 244–45.

28. *CAD*, p. 321, n. 3.

29. James Marsh to Joseph Torrey, 14 February 1829, in *CAD*, pp. 68–73.

30. "Popular Education," under the pen name "Philopolis," *The Vermont Chronicle*, vol. 4, nos. 3, 4, 6, 8, 9, 11, 12, 14, 16 (January 16–April 17, 1829).

31. James Marsh to Samuel Taylor Coleridge, March 1829, in *CAD*, pp. 79–84.

32. James Marsh to Joseph Torrey, 16 July 1829, in *CAD*, pp. 89–93.

33. James Marsh to Samuel Taylor Coleridge, 24 February 1830, in *CAD*, pp. 108–11.

34. Emerson, *Journals*, vol. 1, p. 413.

35. W. G. T. Shedd, ed., *The Complete Works of Samuel Taylor Coleridge*, 7 vols. (New York: Harper & Brothers, 1853).

36. Quoted in Wheeler, *Historical Discourse*, p. 117.

37. John Wheeler to Joseph Henry Green, in Julian I. Lindsay, *Tradition Looks Forward, The University of Vermont: A History, 1791–1904* (Burlington: University of Vermont, 1954), pp. 145–47.

38. Henry Raymond, obituary of James Marsh, *The New World*, 16 July 1842.

39. Bissell's recollections of Marsh are reprinted in Lindsay, *Tradition*, pp. 163–64.

40. Torrey, *Remains*, p. 589.

41. Corliss Lamont, ed., *Dialogue on John Dewey* (New York: Horizon, 1959), pp. 15–16.

42. Lindsay, *Tradition*, p. 168.

43. John Dewey, *Problems of Men* (New York: Philosophical Library, 1946).

Part Two. The Classical College, Overview (pp. 79–88)

1. George Gary Bush, *History of Education in Vermont* (Washington, D.C.: Government Printing Office, 1900), p. 156.

2. John Wheeler, *A Historical Discourse . . . on the Occasion of the Semi-Centennial Anniversary of the University of Vermont* (Burlington, Vt.: Free Press, 1854), p. 34.

3. Cushing Strout, "Faith and History: The Mind of William T. Shedd," *Journal of the History of Ideas*, 15 (January 1954): 153–62.

4. M. H. Buckham, "President Pease," in Abby M. Hemenway, ed., *Vermont Historical Gazetteer*, 5 vols. (Burlington: A. M. Hemenway, 1867–1892), vol. 1, pp. 652–54.

5. Joseph Torrey, *A Theory of Fine Art* (New York: Scribner, Armstrong, 1874).

6. The UVM Archives has various copies of James Marsh's lectures. The entry of 20 October 1848 in the diary of Roswell Farnham ('49), UVM Archives, refers to this medieval practice.

7. John Wheeler to John Henry Green, Kings College, London, 16 February 1843, text in Julian I. Lindsay, *Tradition Looks Forward, The University of Vermont: A History, 1791–1904* (Burlington: University of Vermont, 1954), pp. 145–47.

8. Lindsay, *Tradition*, p. 221.

9. See T. D. S. Bassett, "Student 'Violence' at UVM in 1843," Burlington *Free Press*, 5 June 1977.

10. Lindsay, *Tradition*, pp. 163–65.

11. *Catalogue of the Sigma Phi E.P.V.* (n.p.: The Society, 1949), p. 241.

12. *Delta Psi Fraternity, University of Vermont, 1850–1950; Ninth General Catalogue, Centennial Edition* (Burlington, Vt.: The Fraternity; Champlain Printers), pp. 2–3.

13. Leonard Marsh, "The Practical Determination of Species" (manuscript, n.d.), p. 9, UVM Archives.

14. Leonard Marsh's publications are listed in Marcus D. Gilman, *Bibliography of Vermont* (Burlington, Vt.: Free Press Association, 1897), p. 161.

15. *College Maul*, 16 May 1861, p. 1.

16. Leonard Marsh to George Perkins Marsh, 22 April 1862, Marsh Papers, Bailey/Howe Library, University of Vermont.

17. *The University of Vermont . . . Centennial . . . of the Graduation of the First Class . . . 1904* (Burlington, Vt.: The University, 1905), pp. 274–75.

18. See Thomas Le Duc, "State Disposal of Agricultural College Land Scrip," *Agricultural History*, 28 (July 1954): 100. UVM saw none of the income before 1867.

19. Jessie Elvira Wright ('84; Mrs. G. H. Whitcomb) wrote her first novel reflecting UVM student life in the early 1880s (under the pseudonym Elvirton Wright), *Freshman and Senior* (Boston: Congregational Sunday School Publishing, 1889).

20. *University Cynic*, 25 April 1883.

21. Samuel F. Emerson, "The Mediate University," *Ariel*, 1918, pp. 331–38; two Philosophy 2 lecture notebooks of May Olive Boynton ('94) are in the UVM Archives.

22. Thomas Reed Powell, "Our Academic Heritage," *Vermont Alumnus*, 21 (May 1942): 178.

23. Ibid., pp. 169–70.

Chapter 5. The Curriculum—I (pp. 89–106)

1. Erastus Root, Journal, Special Collections, Bailey-Howe Library, UVM.

2. Jason Chamberlain, *Inaugural Address*, 1 August 1811 (Burlington: University of Vermont, 1811).

3. Chamberlain names Homer, Hesiod, Socrates, Plato, and Aristotle among the "grave" scholars; Xenophon, Thucydides, Demosthenes, the Plinies, Livy, Cicero, Terence, and Virgil among the "accomplished"; Anacreon, Pindar, Lucretius, Tibullus, Juvenal, Ovid, Catullus, and Horace among the "gay gentlemen of antiquity." Quintilian, Isocrates, and Longinus were noted for eloquence; Pythagoras, for astronomy; Archimedes, Apollonius, and Euclid, for mathematics; Herodotus, Plutarch, Pausanias, Sallust, Tacitus, and Julius Caesar, for history.

4. Julian I. Lindsay, *Tradition Looks Forward, The University of Vermont: A History, 1791–1904* (Burlington: University of Vermont, 1954), p. 109.

5. Samuel Eliot Morison, *Harvard College in the Seventeenth Century* (Cambridge, Mass.: Harvard University Press, 1936), vol. 1, p. 188.

6. The main evidence for this evolution is the *Catalogue*, which sets forth in tabular form all required subjects and their meeting times. Documentation is more difficult before 1822, the year of the first *Catalogue*. Lindsay, *Tradition*, provides some of the relevant information.

7. Ira Allen to L'Abbé Vaire, quoted in Lindsay, *Tradition*, pp. 39–42.

8. Ira Allen to Fulwar Skipwith, quoted in Lindsay, *Tradition*, p. 45.

9. Lindsay, *Tradition*, p. 81.

10. On the Laws, see Lindsay, *Tradition*, pp. 84ff.

11. Ibid., p. 81.

12. Ibid., p. 87.

13. John Wheeler, *A Historical Discourse at the Celebration on the Occasion of the Semi-Centennial Anniversary of the University of Vermont* (Burlington, Vt.: Free Press, 1854), p. 29.

14. Ibid., p. 13, citing a pamphlet published in 1829 and enlarged in 1832.

15. George Benedict to Abner Benedict, 17 January 1826, Benedict Family Papers, UVM Special Collections, carton 1.

16. George Benedict to Abner Benedict, 14 April 1826, Benedict Papers.

17. George Benedict to Abner Benedict, 28 January 1827, Benedict Papers.

18. Lindsay, *Tradition*, p. 193.

19. See *Catalogue of the Books Belonging to the Library of the University of Vermont* (Burlington, Vt.: Vernon Harrington, 1836), p. 49. In the 1840s Calvin Pease's diary (UVM Archives) often notes his use of Müller's work to prepare his classes. For Torrey's buying trip, see Anne Torrey Frueh, "Josephy Torrey and the Early Development of the University of Vermont Library" (master's thesis, McGill University Graduate School of Library Science, 1970).

20. Calvin Pease, *Inaugural Address* (Burlington, Vt.: Free Press, 1856), esp. pp. 12, 28.

21. Calvin Pease, Diary, 11 October 1860, UVM Archives.

22. W. H. Crockett in *Vermont Alumni Weekly*, vol. 3, no. 16.

23. Calvin Pease, Diary, 17 and 24 September 1860, UVM Archives.

24. James B. Angell, Inaugural Address, 1 August 1866, quoted in Lindsay, *Tradition*, p. 225.

25. Quoted in Lindsay, *Tradition*, p. 233.

26. A note attached to a sketch in the Benedict Family Papers indicates that the window was probably designed by Benedict himself.

27. Quoted in Lindsay, *Tradition*, pp. 240–41.

28. Farnham Papers, UVM Special Collections.

29. Both Root and Farnham found their teaching duties onerous but occasionally noted moments of delight. In his student journal Farnham writes: "My family [i.e., his pupils in the school] has increased to eighty, and one of them is *black*—an African—a Negroe [sic]—perhaps . . . the descendant of a long line of princes. Who knows but his grandfather was king of some mighty tribe of Ethiopia?" (p. 28).

30. Farnham Papers, UVM Special Collections.

Chapter 6. President Matthew Buckham and the University (pp. 107–20)

1. Matthew Henry (1662–1714) of Chester, author of *Exposition of the Old and New Testament*. The picture of Buckham arriving in England is imaginary.

2. T. D. S. Bassett, "Father of a College President: James Buckham, 1795–1886," Chittenden County Historical Society *Bulletin*, 24 (Summer 1989): 4–6: William Parmelee Marsh, "Rev. James Buckham and President Matthew Henry Buckham, Their Families, and Descendants to 1941," typescript in Special Collections, Bailey/ Howe Library, University of Vermont, p. 20.

3. Thomas Reed Powell comments on the mature Buckham's aloof exterior and warm heart in "Our Academic Heritage," *Vermont Alumnus*, 21 (May 1942): 174.

4. M. H. Buckham to James Buckham, 16 December 1854, Buckham Papers, UVM Archives.

5. Trustee Henry Loomis to Freeman Nye, Champlain, N.Y., 21 March 1862, in McLellan Collection, Special Collections, Feinberg Library, SUNY–Plattsburgh, Plattsburgh, N.Y., brought to my attention by Professor Allan S. Everest of SUNY–Plattsburgh.

6. On the death certificate Dr. Leroy M. Bingham stated the cause of death as "Insanity," lasting two years, but her son spoke of it as "a long illness."

7. John W. Buckham's reminiscences in Marsh, "Rev. James Buckham and President Matthew Henry Buckham," pp. 20–21.

8. *Sigma Phi Magazine*, tearsheet without volume number or date, filed with Buckham obituaries, therefore 1910–11, pp. 99–100.

9. *Inauguration of Prof. M. H. Buckham as President of the University of Vermont and State Agricultural College, August 2, 1871* (Burlington: Free Press Association, 1871), p. 4.

10. Buckham to Angell, 29 September 1869, in the James B. Angell Papers, box 1, folder 1, Michigan Historical Collections, Bentley Historical Library, University of Michigan.

11. Buckham to Angell, 21 September, 12 November 1871, 5 September 1872, box 1, folders 11, 12, 14, and box 2, folder 50, Michigan Historical Collections.

12. Buckham to Angell, 21 September 1871, ibid., box 1, Folder 11.

13. President's Report to the Trustees (1872), UVM Archives.

14. Buckham to Angell, 5 September 1872, Angell Papers, box 1, folder 14, Michigan Historical Collections.

15. President's Report to the Trustees (1875), p. [16], UVM Archives.

16. Burlington *Daily News*, 6 December 1910.

17. Matthew H. Buckham, *The University of Vermont: Its History, Rank, Relation to the State: Its Degrees and Honors, Alumni and Student Body. The Opening Address, September 22, 1910* (Burlington, Vt.: Free Press, 1910), pp. 4–5.

18. *General Catalogue of the University of Vermont and State Agricultural College, Burlington, Vermont, 1791–1900* (Burlington: Free Press, 1901), pp. 18–20.

19. Buckham to J. W. Stewart, 17 April 1874, Buckham Letter Book, pp. 3,2, UVM Archives.

20. Joseph L. Hills, connected with the College of Agriculture for sixty years, has written extensively on this and the subsequent separation fight. See also Edwin C. Rozwenc, *Agricultural Policies in Vermont, 1860–1945* (Montpelier: Vermont Historical Society, 1981).

21. Nancy Price Graff, "The Gallery: In the 1870s Trenor Park of Bennington Brought Culture to the Green Mountains," Burlington *Free Press Vermonter*, 18 June 1978, pp. 6–8; Jacob G. Ullery, comp., *Men of Vermont* (Brattleboro, Vt.: Transcript Publishing, 1894), pp. 296–98.

22. Bryant F. Tolles, Jr., "The 'Old Mill' (1825–29) at the University of Vermont," *Vermont History* 57 (Winter 1989): 22–34.

23. Unsigned editorial, presumably provided by Buckham, in *The University Cynic*, 6 (8 November 1888): 61–62.

24. Thomas Reed Powell, "Our Academic Heritage," *Vermont Alumnus*, 21 (May

1942): 176, 178. T. D. S. Bassett, "The College Street Congregational Church, Burlington, and Its First Pastor, 1860–82," *Vermont History*, 57 (Spring 1989): 116–17.

25. Powell, "Our Academic Heritage," p. 174.

26. "The Greek Play at Cambridge," signed M.H.B., Burlington *Free Press* (undated clipping, April 1879).

27. "Hospitality," *U.V.M. Notes*, 6(1):5, quoted in Blair Williams, *A Backward Look—Ahead: Home Economics at The University of Vermont* (Burlington, Vt.: Home Economics Program, 1987), p. 1.

28. *Annual Address of the President of the Association of American Agricultural Colleges and Experiment Stations* (Washington, D.C.: Government Printing Office, 1907), reprinted from the Association's *Proceedings* at its 20th Annual Convention, pp. 40–46.

29. Papers in the Probate Court office, Burlington, Vt., for Matthew Henry Buckham, intestate.

30. UVM Trustees Minutes, vol. 5, p. 47 (June 26, 1911), UVM Archives.

31. *The Very Elect: Baccalaureate Sermons and Occasional Addresses of Matthew Henry Buckham. D. D. LL. D. President of the University of Vermont, 1871–1910. With Biographical Notes and Studies in Appreciation*, comp. John W. Buckham and J. E. Goodrich. (Boston: Pilgrim Press, 1912).

Buckham's widow and sister-in-law occupied a duplex at 41 South Prospect Street until the 1930s and probably passed on their mementoes to other family members. Goodrich turned over a few choice manuscripts to the Billings Library. According to hearsay, a truckload of Professor Goodrich's papers, presumably including some of Buckham's, went to the dump after Goodrich died in 1915. John Wright Buckham's house in Berkeley, California, burned in the 1920s. A few scraps were rescued and eventually donated to UVM in 1958 by Margaret Buckham, granddaughter of the president. His daughter Laura gave a few more pieces, and the papers of his son James, including a diary kept while he was living with his father, were given to UVM by James's son, Waldo Brigham Buckham. With less than two linear feet of President Buckham's papers in the UVM Archives, it is no wonder he is remembered largely for his publications and his buildings.

Chapter 7. John Dewey's Vermont Inheritance (pp. 121–37)

1. Alfred North Whitehead, "John Dewey and His Influence," in Paul Arthur Schlipp, ed., *The Philosophy of John Dewey* (Evanston and Chicago: Northwestern University, 1939), p. 478.

2. John Dewey, "James Marsh and American Philosophy," *Journal of the History of Ideas* 2 (April 1941): 147.

3. Corliss Lamont, ed., *Dialogue on Dewey* (New York: Horizon Press, 1959), p. 15.

4. John Dewey, "From Absolutism to Experimentalism," in George P. Adams and William Pepperill Montague, eds., *Contemporary American Philosophy*, vol. 2 (New York: Macmillian, 1930), p. 13.

5. Ibid., pp. 14–15.

6. Ibid., p. 14.

7. Ibid., p. 19.

8. John Dewey, *The Quest For Certainty* (New York: Paragon Books, 1929), p. 308.

9. John Dewey, *A Common Faith* (New Haven, Conn.: Yale, 1934), p. 28.

10. George Dykhuizen, *The Life and Mind of John Dewey* (Carbondale: Southern Illinois University Press, 1973), p. 3.

11. Ibid., p. 9.

12. Ibid., pp. 30–31.

13. Lamont, *Dialogue*, p. 89.

14. For an account of the hoopla surrounding Dewey's visit, see *The Vermont Cynic*, 2 November 1949, p. 2.

15. Jane Dewey "Biography of John Dewey," in Schlipp, *Philosophy of John Dewey*, pp. 43, 3.

16. Sidney Hook, *John Dewey: An Intellectual Portrait* (New York: John Day, 1939), p. 5.

17. Neil Coughlan, *Young John Dewey* (Chicago: University of Chicago Press, 1973), p. 112.

18. Ibid., pp. 90–91; Lewis S. Feuer, "John Dewey and the Back to the People Movement in American Thought," *Journal of the History of Ideas* 20 (1958): 545–68.

19. Ibid., p. 565.

20. "Burlington, Vermont 1865–1965" (Burlington, Vt.: League of Women Voters, n.d.), p. 7.

21. See Coughlan, *Young John Dewey*, pp. 90–91.

22. Max Eastman, "John Dewey," *Atlantic* 168 (1941): 672.

23. Dewey to George Dykhuizen, 15 October 1949, University of Vermont Archives, Dykhuizen File #16.

24. Dykhuizen, *Life and Mind*, p. 12.

25. The records of Dewey's library transactions were discovered and published by Lewis Feuer, "John Dewey's Reading at College," *Journal of the History of Ideas* 19 (1958): 415–21.

26. R. J. Hinton, *English Radical Leaders* (New York: G.P. Putnam's Sons, 1875), p. 76.

27. Julian Ira Lindsay, *Tradition Looks Forward, The University of Vermont: A History, 1791–1904* (Burlington: University of Vermont, 1954), p. 234.

28. Ibid., p. 252.

29. There is no reference in Feuer's list to Dewey having checked out writings by Comte from the library, but Dewey mentions having read Comte in the library. See Dewey, "From Absolutism to Experimentalism," p. 20.

30. Ibid.

31. Jane Dewey, "Biography of John Dewey," p. 11.

32. Lewis S. Feuer, "H.A.P. Torrey and John Dewey: Teacher and Pupil," *American Quarterly* 10 (1958): 53.

33. H.A.P. Torrey, "In Memoriam—Abraham Lincoln," MS, UVM Archives.

34. Ibid., p. 18. (Page numbers refer to typewritten transcription of the document made by Lewis Feuer, located with the original.)

35. The phrase comes from Dewey's book, *The Quest for Certainty*.

36. Torrey, "In Memoriam," p. 13.

37. Ibid., p. 9.

38. Sidney Hook, *Pragmatism and the Tragic Sense of Life* (New York: Basic Books, 1974), p. 101.

39. H.A.P. Torrey, "The 'Theodicy of Leibnitz,'" *Andover Review* 4 (October–December 1885): 497.

40. Ibid., p. 511.

41. Ibid., p. 509.

42. Levi P. Smith, introductory essay, "A Masterpiece in Living," in Matthew Buckham, *The Very Elect* (Boston: Pilgrim Press, 1912), p. 5.

43. Buckham, *The Very Elect*, p. 48.

44. See, e.g., Sidney Ratner, *The Philosopher of the Common Man* (New York: G. P. Putnam's Sons, 1940).

45. See Buckham, *The Very Elect*, p. 34.

46. Ibid., p. 80.

47. Ibid., p. 329.

48. Ibid., p. 201.

49. Ibid., p. 200.

50. Minutes of the first meeting of Young People's Society of Christian Endeavor of First Congregational Church of Burlington, Vt., 21 November 1881; Special Collections, Bailey Howe Library, UVM, First Congregational Church documents, vol. 15.

51. Lewis O. Brastow, "Religion and Government," *Burlington Free Press*, 6 April 1876, p. 4.

52. *Minutes of the Eighty-Fourth Annual Meeting of the General Convention of Congregational Ministers and Churches of Vermont Held at Burlington, June 1879* (Montpelier: Vermont Chronicle, 1879), pp. 19–20.

53. Frank C. Porter, "Lewis Orsmond Brastow, D.D.," *Yale Divinity Quarterly*, January 1913, p. 6.

54. Quoted, ibid., p. 10.

55. Brastow remarked, for example, that it was the "extreme development of the theories of individualism which have resulted in a loose public sentiment." "Comments about a Divorce Reform Bill," *Burlington Free Press*, 16 February 1884, p. 1. Although Brastow made this comment well after Dewey had left Burlington in 1882, it is the type of opinion Dewey was likely to have heard from him.

56. Lewis O. Brastow, "The True Estimate of Life." *Burlington Free Press*, 17 February 1879, p. 2.

57. James Marsh, introduction to Samuel Taylor Coleridge, *Aids to Reflection* (Burlington, Vt.: Chauncey Goodrich, 1829), p. xlv.

58. Ibid., p. xiv.

59. Ibid., p. xx.

60. Joseph Torrey, *The Remains of The Rev. James Marsh, With a Memoir of His Life* (Boston: Crocker and Brewster, 1843), p. 42.

61. Ibid., p. 115.

62. Ibid., pp. 114–15.

63. Ibid., p. 490.

64. Dewey, "James Marsh and American Philosophy," p. 142.

65. Ibid., p. 145, quoted from Torrey, *Remains*, pp. 607–608.

66. John Dewey, *The Public and Its Problems* (Athens, Ohio: Swallow Press, 1927), p. 96.

67. John Dewey, *Liberalism and Social Action* (New York: G. P. Putnam's Sons, 1935), p. 28.

68. Ibid., see especially chapter 1.

69. In Dewey's own time, perhaps the best expression of this perspective is found in Walter Lippmann's *Public Opinion* (New York: Harcourt, Brace, 1922).

70. Dewey, *The Public and Its Problems*, p. 207.

71. John Dewey, *Reconstruction in Philosophy* (Boston: Beacon Press, 1957), p. 177.

72. Ibid., p. 186.

73. Dewey, *The Public and Its Problems*, p. 148.

74. John Dewey, *Experience and Nature* (LaSalle, Ill.: Open Court, 1925), p. 138.

75. Dewey, *The Public and Its Problems*, p. 33.

76. John Dewey, "Democracy Is Radical," *Common Sense*, 6 (January 1937): 11.

77. See, for example, Dewey's attack on Kantianism and his understanding of its political implications in John Dewey, *German Philosophy and Politics*, vol. 8 of *John Dewey: The Middle Works*, ed. Jo Ann Boydston (Carbondale: Southern Illinois University Press, 1979), pp. 135–204.

78. Paul Conklin, *Puritans and Pragmatists* (New York: Dodd, Mead, 1968), p. 346.

79. Ibid., p. 402.

80. See Dewey, *German Philosophy and Politics.*

81. Cushing Strout, *Intellectual History In America*, vol. 2 (Ithaca, N.Y.: Cornell University Press, 1968), p. 77.

82. John Wright Buckham, "God and the Ideal: Professor Dewey Reinterprets Religion," *The Journal of Religion* 15 (January 1935): 1–9, 309–15.

Chapter 8. The Natural Sciences and George Henry Perkins (pp. 138–59)

1. See Kevin T. Dann, "The College of Natural History at the University of Vermont, 1826–1850," *Vermont History* 53 (1985): 77–94.

2. Charles Rosenberg, "On Writing the History of American Science," in Herbert J. Bass, ed., *The State of American History* (Chicago: University of Chicago Press, 1975), p. 185; Thomas Bender, "Science and the Culture of American Communities: The Nineteenth Century," *History of Education Quarterly* 16 (1976): 72.

3. George H. Perkins, "The Molluscan Fauna of New Haven," *Proceedings of the Boston Society of Natural History*, vol. 13, October 6–November 3, 1869.

4. *Catalogue of UVM and State Agricultural College, 1869–1870.*

5. Joseph Torrey, quoted in "Recollections of the Botanical Work of Joseph Torrey," *Vermont Botanical Club Bulletin* 1 (1906): 7–9.

6. Lucius Bigelow to Lewis Ralph Jones, 13 November 1907. Jones Papers, UVM Archives.

7. Charles A. Converse's lecture notes from Leonard Marsh's geology class, UVM Archives.

8. See Kevin T. Dann, "John Bulkley Perry and the Taconic Question," *Earth Sciences History* 3(2): 153–9.

9. "Lectures on Geology," John Bulkley Perry Papers, Special Collections, Bailey-Howe Library, University of Vermont.

10. Thomas F. Glick, ed., *The Comparative Reception of Darwinism* (Austin: University of Texas Press, 1974); B. J. Louewenberg, "The Controversy over Evolution in New England, 1859–1873," *New England Quarterly* 8 (1935): 232–57.

11. Frederick Trenck Perkins to George Henry Perkins, 13 November 1864, Perkins Papers, UVM Archives.

12. G. H. Perkins, "The Antiquity of Man," in *Winnowings from the Mill* (n.p., 1876).

13. *University Cynic*, vol. 1 (1883), no. 7, pp. 80–81; vol 2 (1884), no. 5, p. 57, no. 10, pp. 113–14.

14. "Lecture before Unity," *Burlington Free Press*, 14 December 1895, p. 6.

15. *Burlington Free Press*, 10 February 1871.

16. Henry Drummond, *The Lowell Lectures on the Ascent of Man* (London: Hodder and Stoughton, 1894); Joseph LeConte, *Religion and Science: A Series of Sunday Lectures on the Relation of Natural and Revealed Religion or the Truths Revealed in Nature and Scripture* (New York: D. Appleton, 1873); G. Frederick Wright, *Studies in Science and Religion* (Andover, Mass.: M. F. Draper, 1882).

17. Faculty Circulation Records, 1889–1906, UVM Archives.

18. George Henry Perkins, "The Early History of Natural Science at UVM," *Vermont Alumni Weekly*, vol. 13 (1933), no. 7, p. 6; *Cynic*, vol. 1 (1884), no. 8, p. 145; Record of the Proceedings of the Executive Committee of the Corporation of the UVM and SAC, UVM Archives; UVM and SAC Financial Statements, UVM Archives.

19. *Cynic*, vol. 1 (1883), no. 2, p. 17.

20. Ibid., no. 1, pp. 4–5, no. 2, pp. 16–17; vol. 2 (1884), no. 1, pp. 4–5, no. 9, p. 102.

21. Lewis S. Feuer, "John Dewey's Reading at College," *Journal of the History of Ideas* 19 (1958): 415–21.

22. George Dykhuizen, "An Early Chapter in the Life of John Dewey," *Journal of the History of Ideas* 13 (1952): 563–72.

23. George H. Perkins, "Exchange of Extras" list in undated museum catalog, Perkins Geology Museum, UVM; G. H. Perkins, "Notice of a Recent Landslide on Mount Passaconway, *American Journal of Sciences* 49 (1870): 158–61; Library Record, Faculty and Others, 1844–1873, UVM Archives; Faculty Circulation Records, 1889–1906, UVM Archives; scrapbook of G. H. Perkins's publications, Perkins Papers, UVM Archives.

24. T. D. S. Bassett, "George Henry Perkins and UVM Public Relations, 1869–1898," *Burlington Free Press*, 31 October 1976; T. D. S. Bassett, *A History of Vermont State Geological Surveys and State Geologists* (Burlington: Vermont Geological Survey, 1976), pp. 16, 19–24.

25. Ezra Brainerd to Cyrus Pringle, 4 December 1882, Pringle Herbarium Papers, University Archives, UVM.

26. Brainerd to Pringle, February 13, 1888, Pringle Herbarium Papers, UVM Archives.

27. R. H. Howe, review of G. H. Perkins, "A Preliminary List of the Birds Found in Vermont," *Contributions to North American Ornithology*, vol. 2 (1902), no. 5, p. 23.

28. Frances Horton to G. H. Perkins, 30 December 1901, Perkins Papers, UVM Archives.

29. Board of Control, Minutes, 1887–1916, p. 138, UVM Archives.

30. UVM Catalog, 1878.

31. *Cynic*, vol. 1, no. 57 (September 1883), p. 26.

32. Mary Perkins to Henry F. Perkins, 5 August 1899, Perkins Papers, UVM Archives.

33. Mary Perkins to her sister, no date, Perkins Papers, UVM Archives.

34. Richard H. Eyde and E. S. Barghoorn, "Morphological and Botanical Studies of the Nyssaceae: 2. The Fossil Record," *Journal of the Arnold Arboretum* 44:343.

35. G. H. Perkins to family, 25 July 1907, Perkins Papers, UVM Archives.

36. Evan Thomas, "Random Recollections and Reflection," *Vermont Alumnus*, January 1939.

37. UVM Trustees Minutes, 30 June 1880, UVM Archives; Lyman S. Rowell, "The Early History of Natural Science at UVM," *Vermont Alumni Weekly*, 15 November 1933, p. 76.

38. *Vermont Alumni Weekly*, 25 March 1931.

39. A. P. Atwood, "The Glacial Geology of Quincy, Massachusetts," Master's thesis, UVM, 1914.

40. President's Annual Report to the Trustees, 1886, UVM Archives.

41. List of apparatus with a total value of $30,000, Williams Science Hall Contracts, UVM Archives.

42. UVM Trustees Minutes, 16 June 1933, UVM Archives.

43. G. H. Perkins to F. W. Putnam, 26 June 1887, Peabody Museum Director Files, Harvard University Archives.

44. See Kevin Dann, "The Prince of Plant Collectors Finds a Home at UVM," *Vermont*, Winter 1986, pp. 7–10.

45. Anthropology notebook of Harry Way, fall 1895, UVM Archives; William

Haviland and Louise Basa, "Anthropology and the Academy: George H. Perkins and the Nineteenth Century," *Man in the Northeast* 8 (1974): 120–5; William Haviland, personal communication, 26 January 1989; University Catalogue, 1886; G. H. Perkins to Irving C. Tomlinson, 17 August 1886, Peabody Museum Director Files, Harvard University Archives.

46. See for example, G. H. Perkins to F. W. Putnam, 28 June 1887, 23 October 1897, Peabody Museum Director Files, Harvard University Archives; Haviland and Basa, "Anthropology and the Academy," p. 121; anthropology notebook of Harry Way, fall 1895, UVM Archives.

47. Anthropology lecture notes of May Boynton, 1893, UVM Archives.

48. Henry F. Perkins, "Development of *Gontonemus Murbachii*," *Proceedings of the Philadelphia Academy of Sciences* (n.p., 1902).

49. Henry F. Perkins, "Double Reproduction in the Medusa *Hyboodon prolifter*," *American Naturalist*, vol. 38 (1904), n.p.; Henry F. Perkins, "Notes on the Medusae of the Western Atlantic," *Carnegie Institution of Washington Publication #102* (1905), pp. 133–56.

50. Henry F. Perkins, "Mollusks of Lake Champlain," *Science* (1913), n.p.

51. H. F. Perkins to G. W. Bailey, 14 May 1920, 9 April 1924, President's Papers, UVM Archives.

52. H. F. Perkins to W. J. Fox, 10 October 1902, 14 August 1902, 12 March 1903, Faculty File, UVM Archives; Biographical materials, Faculty File, UVM Archives.

53. C. B. Davenport to H. F. Perkins, 13 February 1922, Zoology Papers, UVM Archives; Jones Papers, UVM Archives.

54. Guy Bailey to Mrs. E. P. Eggleston, 6 February 1926, Bailey Papers, UVM Archives.

55. Perkins's reading included some of Francis Galton's original papers on the subject. Faculty Circulation Records, 1889–1906, UVM Archives; Henry F. Perkins, 1930, "Heredity Factors in Rural Communities," *Eugenics* 3:288.

56. Moody had joined the UVM faculty in 1927; he was a national leader in serology research, demonstrating evolutionary relationships among mammals by comparing their blood proteins. His two textbooks—*Genetics of Man* (1967) and *Introduction to Evolution* (1972)—were grounded in his pre–World War II research and in the training he had received under H. F. Perkins. (*Introduction to Evolution*, used by over 70 colleges and universities in the United States, was dedicated to Perkins). The Moody Papers in the UVM Special Collections, as yet uncataloged, record the legacy of eugenics at UVM.

57. Brigham, a disciple of ardent eugenicist Madison Grant, was a firm believer in Nordic superiority. Along with popularizing intelligence tests, he advocated the view that there were definite correlations between race and intelligence. Metcalf continued to administer the intelligence tests until his retirement in 1945, after which they were conducted by UVM's Office of Student Personnel.

58. H. F. Perkins to J. S. Millis, 2 January 1942, 1 October 1942; see, for example, the description of the discarding of the mammal collection, *Vermont Alumnus*, May 1938, p. 234.

59. J. S. Millis's memorandum of conversation with G. P. Burns regarding E. J. Dole, 12 February 1945, Faculty Vertical File of E. J. Dole, UVM Archives.

60. E. C. Jacobs Faculty Vertical File, UVM Archives.

61. Roger L. Geiger, *To Advance Knowledge: The Growth of the American Research Universities: 1900–1940* (New York: Oxford University Press, 1986), p. 19; *Vermont Alumnus*, 22(3):1, 58.

Chapter 9. Medicine at UVM (pp. 160–76)

In preparing this chapter I have referred extensively to Martin Kaufman, *The University of Vermont College of Medicine* (Hanover, NH: University Press of New England, 1979).

1. Lyman Allen, "A Sketch of Vermont's Early History," *New England Journal of Medicine* 209 (19 October 1933): 16.

2. "Petition to the Vermont General Assembly, 1834" from a group of inhabitants of Bennington, Vermont State Papers, MS vol. 62, p. 102, Vermont State Archives, Montpelier. Vermont State Papers hereafter cited as VSP.

3. Benjamin Lincoln, *Hints on the Present State of Medical Education and the Influence of Medical Schools in New England* (Burlington: Author, 1833), p. 15.

4. See, for example, VSP, MS vol. 3, p. 80. See also "Minutes for Third Medical Society in Vermont 1803," MS, Special Collections, Bailey Library, University of Vermont. Special Collections hereafter cited as SC.

5. John W. King, "Dr. John Pomeroy and the College of Medicine of the University of Vermont," *Journal of the History of Medicine* 4 (Autumn 1949): 393–406. See also Lester Wallman, "Pomeroy, John" in *Dictionary of American Medical Biography* (Westport, Conn.: Greenwood Press, 1984), p. 600.

6. Emily A. Smith, *The Life and Letters of Nathan Smith, M.B. M.D.* (New Haven, Conn.: Yale University Press, 1914), p. 5.

7. Gerald N. Grob, *Edward Jarvis and the Medical World of Nineteenth-Century America* (Knoxville: University of Tennessee Press, 1978), pp. 21–25.

8. *General Catalogue of the University of Vermont and State Agricultural College, 1791–1900* (Burlington, Vt.: Free Press, 1901).

9. Charles Caldwell, *Thoughts on the Impolicy of Multiplying Schools of Medicine* (Lexington, Ky.: Clarke, 1834), pp. 32–34, quoted in James M. Cassedy, *Medicine without Doctors* (New York: Science History Publications, 1977), p. 38.

10. Benjamin Lincoln, *An Exposition of Certain Abuses Practiced by Some of the Medical Schools in New England* (Burlington: Author, 1833), pp. 71–76.

11. Lester J. Wallman, "Benjamin Lincoln, M.D., Vermont Medical Educator," *Vermont History*, October 1961, p. 29.

12. Abby Maria Hemenway, *Vermont Historical Gazetteer*, vol. 2 (Burlington: A. M. Hemenway, 1868–91), p. 309.

13. Ibid., p. 598.

14. See account books of Rufus Chaffee, Joel Fairchild, Overseer of the Poor of Panton, Vt., and Joel Holton, SC.

15. Barnes Riznik, "The Professional Lives of 19th Century New England Doctors," *Journal of the History of Medicine* 19 (January 1964): 8.

16. UVM Trustee Minutes, 29 March 1853, UVM Archives.

17. See Kenneth M. Ludmerer, *Learning to Heal* (New York: Basic Books, 1985), chap. 2.

18. An Act to Prevent the Spreading of Contagious Diseases and to Establish a State Board of Health, Public Act #93, State of Vermont, Montpelier, 1886.

19. Lester Wallman, "Vermont State Board of Health, 100 Years," unpublished manuscript, State Health Department, Burlington, 1986.

20. Dean's Book, Medical Department, UVM, 1854–1884; MS, 2 vols., Registrar's Office, UVM.

21. *General Catalogue, UVM, 1791–1890*, p. 154.

22. Deed, John P. Howard to UVM, UVM Land Records Office (microfilm #028855).

23. Catalogs of the UVM Medical Department from 1855, Dana Medical Library, UVM (hereafter cited as DL).

24. *Transactions of the Vermont State Medical Society*, Burlington, 18 and 19 October 1965, p. 5.

25. Faculty Information File, Henri Erni, UVM Archives.

26. Ibid.

27. *Burlington Daily Free Press and Times*, 23 January 1879.

28. *University of Vermont Medical Department, General Catalogue, 1823–36 and 1854–1903* (Burlington: Free Press, 1904).

29. *Minutes of the Chittenden County Medical Society*, MS, 3 vols.: 1864–73, 1873–77, 1893–1919, DL.

30. Kaufman, *College of Medicine*, p. 78.

31. *Bulletin, Medical Department, Washington University, 1904*, quoted in Ludmerer, *Learning to Heal*, p. 81.

32. Henry Crain Tinkham in Minutes of the UVM Medical Faculty, 12 June 1906, UVM Archives.

33. Abraham Flexner, *Medical Education in the United States and Canada* (New York: Carnegie Foundation, 1910).

34. Ibid., p. 262.

35. A. Bradley Soule, oral history interview, July 1972, UVM Collection of Folklore and Oral History (SC).

36. George Wolf, oral history interview, 7 October 1969, UVM Collection of Folklore and Oral History (SC).

37. "William E. Brown, Dean of UVM's Medical College, 1945–52, an Oral History Interview," interview by Paul K. French, *Vermont History* 41 (Summer, 1973): 158–72.

Chapter 10. Agricultural Education and Extension (pp. 177–96)

1. Alfred Charles True, *A History of Agricultural Education in the United States, 1785–1925*. U.S.D.A. Miscellaneous Publication No. 36 (Washington, D.C.: Government Printing Office, 1925), pp. 2–7, 31.

2. Ibid., pp. 31, 34.

3. Ibid., pp. 41–42, 83.

4. "A Chronological History of the University of Vermont and State Agricultural College, 1777–1922," Mimeographed, Special Collections, Bailey-Howe Library, University of Vermont, pp. 84–87.

5. Memorial Address by Senator George Hoar of Massachusetts, delivered in the Senate of the United States, 55th Congress (Washington: Government Printing Office, 1899), p. 27.

6. *Chronological History*, p. 6.

7. Quoted in True, *Agricultural Education*, p. 108.

8. Ibid., p. 180.

9. "Legislative History of the University of Vermont and State Agricultural College," unpublished manuscript, 1955, UVM Archives.

10. Edwin C. Rozwenc, *Agricultural Politics in Vermont, 1860–1945* (Montpelier: Vermont Historical Society, 1981).

11. Quoted in Julian I. Lindsay, *Tradition Looks Forward, The University of Vermont: A History, 1791–1904* (Burlington: University of Vermont and State Agricultural College, 1954), p. 225.

12. *The First Annual Report of the University of Vermont and State Agricultural College* (Burlington: University of Vermont, 1866), p. 6.

13. *Second Annual Report of the University of Vermont and State Agricultural College* (Burlington: University of Vermont, 1867), pp. 6, 7.

14. *Third Annual Report of the Trustees of the University of Vermont and State Agricultural College* (Burlington: University of Vermont, 1868), p. 5.

15. Lindsay, *Tradition*, p. 234.

16. *Biennial Report of the Trustees of the University of Vermont and State Agricultural College* (Burlington: University of Vermont, 1873–74), p. 10, 11. Italics added.

17. Rozwenc, *Agricultural Politics*, p. 60.

18. Ibid., p. 60.

19. Ibid., p. 66.

20. Ibid., p. 60.

21. *Biennial Report of the Trustees of the University of Vermont and State Agricultural College* (Burlington: University of Vermont, 1887–88), p. 9.

22. *Biennial Report of the Trustees of the University of Vermont and State Agricultural College* (Burlington: University of Vermont, 1879–80), pp. 8, 9.

23. Rozwenc, *Agricultural Politics*, p. 60.

24. *Biennial Report of the Trustees of the University of Vermont and State Agricultural College* (Burlington: University of Vermont, 1885–86), p. 8.

25. Ibid.

26. Joseph L. Hills, *The Semi-Sesquicentennial of the State Agricultural College* (Burlington: University of Vermont, 1941), p. 5.

27. Howard Allen Kerr, *The Legacy: A Centennial History of the State Agricultural Experiment Stations, 1887–1987* (Columbia: Missouri Agricultural Experiment Station, 1987), p. 2.

28. Rozwenc, *Agricultural Politics*, pp. 64–65.

29. Ibid., p. 67.

30. Ibid., p. 66.

31. Hills, *The Semi-Sesquicentennial of the State Agricultural College*, p. 8.

32. Joseph L. Hills, *The Attempted Disruption of the University of Vermont and State Agricultural College*, unpublished manuscript, much still in longhand, UVM Archives.

33. Ibid.

34. Joseph L. Hills, *Memoirs*, unpublished manuscript, UVM Archives.

35. Guy P. Benton, Inaugural address, *The Vermonter*, vol. 16, no. 11, November 1911.

36. Carnegie Foundation for the Advancement of Teaching, *A Study of Education in Vermont*, Bulletin No. 7, parts 1 and 2 (New York: The Foundation, 1914).

37. Ibid., p. 167.

38. Rozwenc, *Agricultural Politics*, pp. 80–81.

39. Charles R. Cummings, "The Better Farming Special," *The Vermonter*, vol. 16, nos. 6–7, June–July 1911.

40. Joseph L. Hills, unpublished manuscript on early days of Extension, UVM Archives.

41. Deacy Leonard, *The Vermont Farm Bureau Story, 1915–1985* (Montpelier: Vermont Farm Bureau, 1985).

42. Robert P. Davison et al., *Highlights of the Vermont Extension Service: From the Beginning* (Burlington: Vermont Extension Service, University of Vermont, 1982).

43. *Bulletin of the University of Vermont* (Burlington: University of Vermont, 1941).

44. Reprinted in *Vermont Alumni Weekly*, vol. 27, no. 22 (1942).

45. *Report of the Task Force on Collegiate Reorganization*, printed as a special supple-

ment in *This Week* (Burlington: University of Vermont), 1 December 1972.

46. Burlington *Free Press* and Rutland *Daily Herald*, 4 December 1972.

Part Three. A Small University with Ivy Aspirations, Overview (pp. 197–205)

1. *Ariel*, 1918, pp. 334–38.

2. UVM Trustees Minutes, vol. 5, pp. 41, 77, UVM Archives; James Dewey Benedict file, Benton Papers, UVM Archives.

3. *Organization of the University of Vermont and State Agricultural College, Including the By-Laws of the Board of Trustees* (Burlington, Vt.: Free Press, 1917); "Record of a Meeting of Full Professors of the University of Vermont and State Agricultural College, April 6, 1916," galleys of proposed bylaws and organization distributed for discussion, with professors' comments, Benton Papers, UVM Archives.

4. UVM Trustees Minutes, 19 January 1914, vol. 5, pp. 81–82, UVM Archives.

5. Matthew Buckham to Levi P. Smith, 14 November 1907, in the possession of Levi P. Smith, Jr., who called it to my attention.

6. Vermont Medical Society *Transactions*, 1913, p. 93.

7. Joseph L. Hills, "History of the University of Vermont," MS, UVM Archives, J, p. 5. I have also heard the story of Tupper's calling Benton's fatuous bluff from my father, Samuel E. Bassett, and Julian Lindsay, who were on the faculty under Benton.

8. Henry B. Shaw's "The Benton Bible Class" papers, UVM Archives.

9. UVM Trustees Minutes, 14 October 1918, vol. 5, p. 188, UVM Archives. Mrs. G. Grenville (Katharine) Benedict to her son George W. Benedict, 16 October 1918, Benedict Family Papers, Special Collections, Bailey/Howe Library, UVM.

10. J. L. Hills, "History," UVM Archives, sec. J, p. 14.

11. Lawrence J. Doolin, Floyd H. James, and John L. Beckley, eds., *Thank You, Guy Bailey* (North Caldwell, N.J.: John L. Beckley, 1976). See also Chester B. Eaton, interview by the author, 26 January 1990, transcript in the Oral History Archives, UVM Special Collections.

12. See Martin Kaufman, *The University of Vermont College of Medicine* (Hanover, N.H.: University Press of New England, 1979), chaps. 11, 12.

13. Stephen C. Terry ('64), *The Sunday Herald-Times-Argus*, 5 June 1977, sec. 3, p. 3.

14. George W. Alger Memorandum, "What Is the Matter with the University of Vermont?" 25 February 1941 (initialed GWA:ERP), typescript in Rehabilitation folder, Reference files, UVM Archives.

Chapter 11. Guy Bailey and the University (pp. 206–18)

1. See the Burlington *Free Press* obituary, 23 October 1940, and the trustee resolution of 9 November, Trustee Minutes, vol. 6, p. 169, UVM Archives.

2. Essex Town Land Records, vol. 20, p. 137 (lease of 2 April 1888, from M. L. and Jane H. Snyder, partners with Mrs. Bailey in the stonecutting company); 28:152 (John W. Bailey's deed for the Railroad Avenue lot, for $1,300, 7 March 1907). See also Frank Bent, *History of the Town of Essex* (Essex Junction, Vt.: Essex Publishing, 1963), p. 99; obituary of John W. Bailey in Burlington *Free Press*, [8?] July 1922 (undated clipping) in Guy W. Bailey Reference File, UVM Archives.

3. Loyal Legion Circular No. 5 (15 November 1940); unpublished Bailey genealogy supplied to the author by Anne K. Batten of East Hardwick.

4. Allen Martin, "Memorial to Guy Winfred Bailey," Vermont Bar Association *Proceedings* 35 (1941): 39.

5. *Portfolio of the Class of 1900 of the University of Vermont* (Boston: Heliotrope, 1900), unnumbered.

6. Allen Martin, "Memorial," p. 38; Thomas Reed Powell, "Our Academic Heritage," *Vermont Alumnus* 21 (May 1942): 176.

7. Birth and death certificates by Dr. A. T. Arkley in Essex Town Office.

8. Editorial, 23 October 1940.

9. Montpelier *Journal*, 1 July 1908, pp. 1, 4.

10. Harry Holden, Burlington *Daily News*, 26 October 1940.

11. Guy W. Bailey, *Report on Uniform Town Accounting* (Montpelier, Vt.: Secretary of State, 1915).

12. Interview of Samuel Saiger by Samuel B. Hand, at Ohavi Zedek Synagogue.

13. Barre *Times*, 25 June 1917.

14. UVM Trustee Minutes, 13 April 1917, vol. 5, pp. 153–4, UVM Archives.

15. Cornelius Howard Patton and Walter Taylor Field, *Eight O'clock Chapel* (Boston: Houghton-Mifflin, 1927), p. 304.

16. *The University: Its Duty and Its Relation to the State. Address by Acting President Guy W. Bailey at the Opening Exercises of the University of Vermont, September 24, 1919* (Burlington: University of Vermont, 1919).

17. Carnegie Foundation for the Advancement of Teaching, *A Study of Education in Vermont* (Montpelier, Vt.: 1914), pp. 123, 129.

18. Viola L. Lugenbuhl, "The Richardsonian Influence at Redstone," paper for American architecture course, University of Vermont, typescript with plans, copy in Special Collections, Bailey-Howe Library, University of Vermont.

19. Irene E. Allen, ed., *Project "Laundry Case", 1921–1975, for the 50th Reunion of the Class of 1925* (Burlington, University of Vermont Alumni Office, 1975), p. 4.

20. *Project "Laundry Case"* is full of such stories, e.g., pp. 22, 24, 87–88, 104–5. See also unpublished parts of Irene Allen's 6 January 1976 statement in "The Bailey Project," UVM Archives; conversation with Mrs. Lyman Rowell, 19 May 1990.

21. See *Thank you, Guy Bailey*, ed. John L. Beckley, Lawrence J. Doolin, and Floyd M. James (North Caldwell, N.J.: John L. Beckley, 1976), pp. 81–82.

22. The Burlington *Free Press*, 24 October 1924; William M. Hall, "Radio Broadcasting Comes to Vermont," *Vermont History* 49 (Spring 1981): 92–96.

23. "Self Study Report," 14 November 1961, p. 2, UVM Archives.

24. *Who Was Who*, vol. 1 (1897–1942), outlines Wilbur's career.

25. *Ira Allen, Founder of Vermont, 1751–1814,* 2 vols. (Boston: Houghton Mifflin, 1928).

26. Herbert W. Congdon, *Old Vermont Houses: The Architecture of a Resourceful People* (Brattleboro, Vt.: Stephen Daye, 1940).

27. George W. Alger, "Memorandum: What Is the Matter with the University of Vermont?" 25 February 1941, UVM Archives, Alumni Files, Alger, G. W.

28. *A Graduation Address from Upstate Vermont*, LP record (Foster, R.I.: Droll Yankees, 1962).

29. Alger memorandum of 25 February 1941.

30. Trustees Minutes, 18 June 1934, vol. 6, p. 74, UVM Archives.

31. Interview of Chester B. Eaton by T. D. Seymour Bassett, 26 January 1990, pp. 19–21, Oral History Collection, Special Collections, Bailey/Howe Library, University of Vermont.

32. *Thank You, Guy Bailey*, p. 6; summary of Haskins and Sells report in special *Vermont Alumni Weekly*, August 1941.

33. *Thank You, Guy Bailey*, pp. 108, 111.
34. Trustees' Minutes, vol. 6, pp. 122, 135, 137, 138, 164, UVM Archives.
35. Estate of Guy W. Bailey, No. 14151, Chittenden County Probate Court files.
36. "Memorial to Guy Winfred Bailey," Vermont Bar Association *Proceedings* (1941), p. 41.
37. *Thank You, Guy Bailey*, p. 39.
38. "The Bailey Project," 6 January 1976, UVM Archives.

Chapter 12. Women at UVM (pp. 219–33)

1. Mary Woodruff, "In Search of Usefulness: The University of Vermont's First Women Graduates" (M.A. thesis, University of Vermont, 1985), pp. 14–17, 30–34; Julian Ira Lindsay, *Tradition Looks Forward, The University of Vermont: A History, 1791–1904* (Burlington: University of Vermont and State Agricultural College, 1954), pp. 229, 234, 237–39; *Inauguration of Professor M. H. Buckham, as President of the University of Vermont and State Agricultural Colleges, August 2, 1871* (Burlington: Free Press, 1871); "Biennial Report of the Trustees of the University of Vermont and State Agricultural College for 1871–72" in *Vermont Legislative Documents and Official Reports Made to the General Assembly, Biennial Session, 1872,* (Montpelier, Vt.: n.p., 1872), vol. 1, pp. 6–9; UVM Faculty Meetings, 1871–1885, Faculty Records, 1853–1894, and Trustee Minutes, 1865–1906, UVM Archives; and U.S. Congress, Senate, Senator Justin S. Morrill speaking for National Colleges, S. 693, 42nd Congress, 3rd session, 5 December 1872, *Congressional Globe*, pt. 1: 36.
2. Wilfred B. Shaw, ed., *The University of Michigan: An Encyclopedic Survey* (Ann Arbor: University of Michigan Press, 1942), vol. 1, pp. 63–65, vol. 4, pp. 1783–85, and *From Vermont to Michigan: Correspondence of James B. Angell, 1869–1871* (Ann Arbor: University of Michigan Press, 1936), pp. 138, 196, 202–203, 205, 217, 226; Burke A. Hinsdale, *History of the University of Michigan* (Ann Arbor: Published by the University, 1906), pp. 130, 133–8; Shirley W. Smith, *James Burrill Angell: An American Influence* (Ann Arbor: University of Michigan Press, 1954), pp. 75–83, 95; Elizabeth M. Farrand, *History of the University of Michigan* (Ann Arbor: Register Publishing House, 1885), pp. 273–76; Dorothy Gies McGuigan, *A Dangerous Experiment: 100 Years of Women at the University of Michigan* (Ann Arbor: Center for the Continuing Education of Women, 1970), pp. 39–42; T. D. S. Bassett, *Burlington Free Press*, 19 June 1977.
3. UVM catalogs, 1850–1872; "Fifth Annual Report of the Trustees of the University of Vermont and State Agricultural College for 1870" in *Vermont Legislative Documents*, 1870–1871, pp. 7–9; *James Burrill Angell: Addresses at the Dinner Given in His Honor by Professional and Business Men of Detroit on May Fifth, Nineteen Hundred and Ten* (Detroit: Pohl Printing Company, 1910), pp. 42–43.
4. Shaw, *From Vermont to Michigan*, pp. 66, 147–8, 187; *James Burrill Angell: Addresses*, pp. 42–43; Smith, *James Burrill Angell*, pp. 75–80.
5. David M. Stameshkin, *The Town's College: Middlebury College, 1800–1915* (Middlebury, Vt.: Middlebury College Press, 1985), chap. 8; UVM Faculty Meetings, 30 May [misdated; should read April], 14 May, and 4 September 1871, and Trustee Minutes, 1 August 1871, UVM Archives.
6. Trustee Minutes, 1 August 1871, UVM Archives; C. Carroll Parker to George G. Benedict, Women file, UVM Archives; Lindsay, *Tradition*, pp. 234, 227; Shaw, *University of Michigan*, vol. 4, p. 1783; McGuigan, *A Dangerous Experiment*, chaps. 3–4.
7. *Inauguration of M. H. Buckham*, p. 17; "Annual Report of the Trustees of the University of Vermont and State Agricultural College for 1872" in *Vermont Legislative Documents* 1872, p. 8.

8. *General Catalogue of the University of Vermont and State Agricultural College, 1791–1901* (Burlington, Vt.: Free Press, 1901).

9. Trustee Minutes, 31 October 1871, UVM Archives; Faculty Records, 20 September 1871, 4 February 1888, 1 October 1887, 22 October 1894, 9 November 1894, 17 November 1894, and 1 January 1902, UVM Archives; "Thirty Years of Athletics for the Women at the University of Vermont," *Vermont Alumni Weekly*, 15 April 1931, p. 357; "To The Ladies," *Vermont Alumni Weekly*, 18 April 1928, p. 356.

10. UVM catalogs, 1871–1900; *General Catalogue*.

11. *Cynic*, 2 October 1895; UVM Faculty Minutes, 4 December 1872 and 5 November 1873 and Faculty Records, 10 March 1875, 21 February 1877, 17 September 1886, and 1 June 1887, UVM Archives.

12. Trustee Minutes, 25 June 1895, UVM Archives; *Cynic*, 2 November 1895; UVM catalogs, 1871–1900.

13. *Cynic*, 12 November 1885, 20 May 1909; Richard J. Storr, "Marion Talbot" and Janet Wilson James, "Ellen Richards" in Edward T. James, ed., *Notable American Women, 1607–1950: A Biographical Dictionary* (Cambridge: Harvard University Press, 1971), pp. 423–24, 143–6; Blair Williams, *A Backward Look Forward: Home Economics at the University of Vermont* (n.p., n.d.).

14. Williams, *A Backward Look Forward*; "Bertha Mary Terrill," prepared by the Vermont Home Economics Association in April, 1950, UVM Archives; Dorothy Mayo Harvey's *Teachers of Stature* (n.p., n.d.); *Burlington Free Press*, 2 December 1965, 24 December 1968; *Panorama* (22 March 1947), pp. 4–5; T. D. S. Bassett, folder of clippings on Mary Jean Simpson, UVM Archives.

15. Trustee Minutes, 8 May 1911, 24 June 1914, UVM Archives; "A Brief Description of the Development of Teacher Preparation at the University of Vermont," *Vermont Alumni Weekly*, 30 November 1932, pp. 99–100; "Professor Terrill to Retire," *Vermont Alumnus*, June 1940, 195.

16. Trustee Minutes, 4 December 1908, 25 June 1920, UVM Archives; Faculty Records, 21 November 1919, 16 June 1927, UVM Archives; "A Brief Description of the Development of Teacher Education."

17. UVM Senate Minutes, 19 January, 12 February 1943, UVM Archives; *Cynic*, 1 May 1955.

18. "Medical College Graduates First Woman This Year: Every College Now Has Woman Graduate," *Vermont Alumni Weekly*, 2 July 1924, p. 539; Trustee Minutes, 25 June 1920, UVM Archives; L. W. Dean, "Three Women Graduates of the College of Agriculture," *Vermont Alumni Weekly*, 28 October 1925, pp. 52, 58; Alumni Files of Alma Carpenter, Marie McMahon, and Dorothy Mary Lang; catalogs, 1909–1930.

19. Williams, *A Backward Look Forward*, pp. 5–6; Trustee Minutes, 28 June 1905, 27 June 1906, UVM Archives; *Cynic*, 20 May 1909; "A Brief Description of the Development of Teacher Education."

20. Trustee Minutes, 22 October 1894, 9 November 1894, 17 November 1894, 16 April 1916, 28 April 1916, 4 August 1917, 14 May 1918, UVM Archives; Trustee Executive Committee Minutes, 2 February 1918, 28 March 1918, UVM Archives.

21. *Cynic*, 25 March 1936, 24 April 1936.

22. *Cynic*, 22 April 1922, 12 May 1936; *Handbook of the Women's Athletic Association* (n.p., 1927), UVM Archives.

23. WSGA records; 1960 typescript history of WSGA by Margaret W. Wing, UVM Archives.

24. Ruellen Ottery, "UVM Faculty Women, 1910–1930" (typescript in author's possession).

25. "Ladies of the Faculty" records, UVM Archives; "37-Year-Old Club Admits Women," *The Vermont Alumnus*, April 1942, p. 161.

26. Ottery, "UVM Faculty Women."

27. Guy Potter Benton to Pearl Randall Wasson, 7 June 1919, Benton MSS, UVM Archives; "Dean Wasson Memorial;" Bassett folder on Pearl Randall Wasson (especially letter from Charlotte B. Murray to Lattie Coor, 7 July 1982); *Cynic*, 5 June 1926; Marian Patterson, "Lilac Day at the University," *Vermont Alumni Weekly*, 6 November 1932, p. 71.

28. Bassett File, Marian Patterson (especially letter from Mary V. Holman to T. D. Seymour Bassett, 23 December 1972); Marian Patterson, "Time to Live: Avocations Instead of Jobs," *Vermont Alumni Weekly*, 26 April 1933, p. 279; "An Invitation to Alumni," *Vermont Alumni Weekly*, 8 November 1933, pp. 63, 66.

29. Mary Jean Simpson to her mother, 4, 6, 10, 13, 16, 20, 22, 24 June 1937, and memo from Mary Jean Simpson to Mr. Abbott, 2 November 1937, Mary Jean Simpson MSS, UVM Wilbur Collection; Betsy Farrell, "Mary Jean Simpson: A Paradox in American Feminism," typescript, Wilbur Collection.

30. Patterson, "Time to Live" and "An Invitation to Alumni"; *Cynic*, 23 October 1936, 1 November 1935, 4 February 1936.

31. *Cynic*, 14 January 1936; "Year's Only Co-ed M.D. States Views," *Vermont Alumni Weekly*, 15 July 1936, p. 374.

32. UVM Senate Minutes, 13 October 1944, UVM Archives; *Cynic*, 15 December 1943, 1 March and 14 April 1944; "Today's Challenge to Organized Women" (21 January 1942) and "Woman Power Mobilized," Simpson MSS.

33. UVM Senate Minutes, 1 February 1944, 12 February 1943, UVM Archives; *Cynic*, 15 December 1943.

34. UVM Senate Minutes, 1 November 1946, UVM Archives; *Cynic*, 1 March 1944, 14 April 1944, 7 October 1954, 18 November 1954.

35. *Cynic*, 21 October 1954, 10 March 1967, 10 November 1955.

36. *Cynic*, 23 September 1954.

37. Burlington *Free Press*, 18 May 1968; *Cynic*, 17 March 1967, 3 November 1967, 8 December 1967.

38. Memo from Mary Jean Simpson, 1953, WSGA MSS; *Cynic*, 11 March 1969, 3 October 1969, 27 February 1970.

39. *Cynic*, 19 November 1971.

40. Ibid.

41. UVM catalogs, 1955–1988; 1979 Report on Salaries, American Association of University Women MSS, Wilbur Collection.

42. Trustee Minutes, 16 June 1922, UVM Archives.

Chapter 13. UVM Goes Modern (pp. 234–55)

A large part of this chapter is based on taped interviews by the author with UVM alumni, as indicated in the text.

1. UVM *Catalogue*, 1900–1901.

2. Quoted in Julian I. Lindsay, *Tradition Looks Forward, The University of Vermont: A History, 1791–1904* (Burlington: University of Vermont, 1954), p. 266.

3. Ibid., pp. 263–64.

4. *Cynic*, 27 November 1915.

5. UVM Archives, Hendrick folder.

6. M. J. Simpson, DOC Box 203, Simpson Letters, Vermont Historical Society.

7. Bassett interviews, Oral History Collection, Wilbur Collection, Bailey-Howe Library, UVM.

8. Telephone interview of Margaret P. Gilbert by the author, May 1989.

9. "The University of Vermont in the Great War," report of the War Service Committee of the University of Vermont, 1924, UVM Archives.

10. *Cynic*, 28 June 1919.

11. *Vermont Alumni Weekly*, 24 January 1926.

12. *Cynic*, 31 May 1919.

13. Joseph C. Carter and Stanley K. Carter, "Four Semesters at Our Dear UVM," ed. Joseph Cleveland Carter, 1980, manuscript, Vermont Historical Society, XB C 245.

14. Bassett interviews.

15. *Vermont Alumni Weekly*, 16 March 1932.

16. *Ariel*, 1947.

17. *Cynic*, 4 March 1938.

18. Ibid., 23 September 1941.

19. Ibid., 27 February 1943.

20. Ibid., 7 March 1945.

21. Ibid., 15 September 1951.

22. UVM Office of Admissions, Director's Report, 1950.

Chapter 14. The Arts at UVM (pp. 256–69)

The author would like to thank several colleagues for their generous contributions of time and information to her research. Among others are Merlin Acomb, Glenn Markoe, and Milly Meeks of the Fleming Museum staff, art historian William Lipke, and theatre department faculty members George Bryan and Edward Feidner.

1. *Grandmother Tyler's Book*, The Recollections of Mary Palmer Tyler (Mrs. Royall Tyler), 1775–1866, ed. Frederick Tupper and Helen Tyler Brown (New York and London: G. P. Putnam's Sons, 1925).

2. Julian Ira Lindsay, *Tradition Looks Forward, The University of Vermont: A History, 1791–1904* (Burlington: University of Vermont, 1954), p. 103.

3. Julie Becker, "The Fleming at 50," *Vermont*, Spring 1982, pp. 13–14.

4. George Poole, "History of the Museum," *The Vermont Alumnus*, November 1928, p. 136.

5. Glenn E. Markoe, "Fleming Museum History," manuscript at the Fleming Museum, University of Vermont, n. 42.

6. The Park Gallery of Art: Announcement (Burlington: University of Vermont and State Agricultural College, 1873). For more information on Park and his life-style, see Anne Knapp, *The Park-McCullough House: A Small History of the Place and the People* (North Bennington, Vt.: Park-McCullough House Association, 1979).

7. Markoe, "Fleming Museum History," p. 8.

8. Special Collections, Bailey/Howe Library. The Wilbur Collection was housed at the Fleming Museum in the Wilbur Room until it was transferred to the new Bailey Library in 1961.

9. "If You Haven't Seen the Fleming . . . ," *Vermont Alumnus*, October 1955, p. 7.

10. Ibid.

11. Robert Hull Fleming Museum, Director's Report (Henry F. Perkins), Wilbur Collection.

12. Herbert Wheaton Congdon, *Old Vermont Houses: The Architecture of a Resourceful People* (Brattleboro, Vt.: Stephen Day Press, 1940).

13. Glen E. Markoe, Raymond J. DeMallie, and Royal B. Hassrick, eds., *Vestiges of a Proud Nation: The Ogden B. Read Northern Plains Indian Collection* (Burlington: Robert Hull Fleming Museum, 1986).

14. Tom Slayton, introduction to *Francis Colburn: This I Remember*, exhibition at the Robert Hull Fleming Museum of the University of Vermont, 26 March–18 July 1984; catalog edited by Ildiko Heffernan (Burlington: Robert Hull Fleming Museum, 1984).

15. For more information on the Lane Series, see "Report of Team C," oral history project by Ilicia J. Sprey and Patrick Reirden under the supervision of Alfred Andrea; typescript in the Lane Series office. See also John Alexander, "Dr. Jack Trevithick and the Lane Series: 1955–1976," UVM honors paper, 1985, typescript in Wilbur Collection.

16. Bulletins of the music department, 1925–1926, 1926–1927, 1927–1928.

17. George B. Bryan in the dedication program for the Royall Tyler Theatre, March 14, 1974.

18. Account books for the "Histrionic Develings," UVM Archives; Lindsay, *Tradition Looks Forward*, p. 267.

19. Tyler dedication program.

20. A pair of female busts by Gould were the first original sculptures acquired by the Park Gallery in 1881. Markoe, "Fleming Museum History," p. 11.

Part Four. The Many-Sided University, Overview (pp. 271–81)

1. *Vermont Alumni Special*, August 1941, contains summaries of the auditors' report, the Governor's Advisory Committee report, Paul Packer's report, and the Alumni Committee's recommendations, with a chronology of events since President Bailey's death. Governor William Wills chaired his advisory committee, consisting of Representative Asa Bloomer; Elbert S. Brigham, president of the National Life Insurance Co.; the future U.S. Senator Ralph E. Flanders, president of the Jones & Lamson machine tool company; L. Douglas Meredith, Brigham's treasurer and assistant; Arthur H. Packard, president of the Vermont Farm Bureau; Henry A. Stoddard, master of the Vermont State Grange; and Caroline Woodruff, recently retired head of Castleton Normal School.

2. *Vermont Alumnus*, October 1941, p. 3.

3. John S. Millis, interview, ca. 1958, Oral History Collection, Special Collections, Bailey/Howe Library, UVM.

4. Lyman S. Rowell, "Five Decades of Change," *Ariel*, 1970, p. 10; UVM Trustees Minutes, 30 April, 19 June 1943, vol. 6, pp. 364–69, UVM Archives.

5. "War Service of the University of Vermont during World War II" [1948], Millis Reference File, UVM Archives.

6. Donald F. Wetzell ('49) to the author, 16 April 1990.

7. UVM Trustees Minutes, 20 December 1947, vol. 6, pp. 563, vol. 7, p. 6, UVM Archives.

8. UVM Trustees Minutes, vol. 7, p. 18; Lyman-Carlson correspondence, Carlson Papers, UVM Archives.

9. "Presidential Hunt 1952" folder, Senate Policy Committee box, RG 5, UVM Archives.

10. UVM Trustees Minutes, 16 October 1948, vol. 7, p. 2, UVM Archives.

11. Chester B. Eaton, interview, 26 January 1990, Oral History Collection, UVM Special Collections.

12. Ibid., and Elmer L. Nicholson, interview, 22 April 1971, Oral History Collection, UVM Special Collections.

13. *Memorandum of the University of Vermont on S 1321, February 19, 1960,* a 9-page, mimeographed argument, presumably by President Fey; UVM Trustees Minutes, vol. 6, pp. 240, 249, 253, 369, UVM Archives. See also the "Wilbur Fund" folders in the UVM Archives Reference File and the Wilbur Collection Curator's file.

14. UVM Trustees Minutes, 6 August 1966, vol. 9, pp. 163–82, UVM Archives. Together with Professor Samuel B. Hand (history) I interviewed the principals in the McCune matter; some of the transcripts, tapes, and files are not yet open for research. See UVM Trustees Minutes, 6 August 1966, vol. 9, pp. 163–82, UVM Archives.

15. James R. Overfield, chair of history, "Faculty Evaluation Guidelines," to Howard Ball, dean, College of Arts and Sciences, 18 March 1990.

16. Peter Collier, *Opening Address Delivered Before the Medical Class of the University of Vermont, Thursday, March 9, 1876* (Burlington, Vt.: R. S. Styles, 1876).

17. Richard Moll, *The Public Ivies: a Guide to America's Best Public Undergraduate Colleges and Universities* (New York: Viking, 1985), pp. 141–60, described UVM along with the California system (especially Berkeley), the Universities of Colorado, Illinois, Miami of Ohio, Michigan, North Carolina, Pittsburgh, Texas, Virginia, Washington, Wisconsin; also Georgia Institute of Technology, New College (Florida), Pennsylvania State University, SUNY–Binghamton, and College of William and Mary, on an impressionistic basis. He concluded that UVM was low in resources, high in resourcefulness; high in academic and social vitality; high in selectivity, particularity among out-of-staters; "politically conservative, personally liberal" (p. 147), with 55% of its students on campus.

Chapter 15. UVM, Carl Borgmann, and the State (pp. 282–97)

1. Carl W. Borgmann, interview by the author, 10 June 1989. All comments directly attributed to Dr. Borgmann and not taken from news accounts of the day or his writings are from interviews by the author, 18 March, 10 June, and 14 June 1989.

2. Texts of the original charter and subsequent charters and changes are in *The Organization of the University of Vermont and State Agricultural College, 1791–1959* (Burlington: University of Vermont, 1959).

3. Carl W. Borgmann, interview by T. D. Seymour Bassett, 1972, tape in Special Collections, Bailey-Howe Library, University of Vermont.

4. Chester R. Eaton, interview by the author, 11 July 1990.

5. *The Vermont Cynic,* editorial, 8 November 1888.

6. Eaton interview.

7. Richard Hopwood, interview by the author, July 1989.

8. Betty Bandel, interview by the author, May 1989.

9. Handwritten chart, ca. 1954, Borgmann papers, UVM Archives.

10. Hopwood interview.

11. Carl W. Borgmann, speech manuscript, ca. 1954, Borgmann Papers, UVM Archives.

12. Carl W. Borgmann, memorandum, ca. 1954.

13. Frederick P. Smith, quoted in the Rutland *Daily Herald,* 24 February 1955.

14. Burlington *Free Press,* editorial, 10 December 1954.

15. Members of the board of directors of Research and TV Education, Inc., in addition to Ellis and Barber, were Foster Gibbie of Greensboro (president of the Orleans County Farm Bureau); attorney Clarke A. Gravel of Burlington, a former probate judge; and Howard C. Rice, then publisher of the Brattleboro *Reformer.* The *Reformer* published several editorials in 1954 and 1955 that opposed the legislative action to make UVM more clearly public.

16. Record of Hearing, 27 January 1955, Joint House–Senate Education Committee, Vermont State Archives.

17. Carl W. Borgmann, quoted in the Rutland *Daily Herald*, 28 January 1955.

18. Bennington *Banner*, editorial, 10 February 1955.

19. The bill was officially Act 66 of the 1955 Legislature, and was subsequently referenced in Title 16, *Vermont Statutes Annotated*, though because of its special one-time purpose it was not actually included in the published statutes.

20. The total appropriation would be higher under either proposal because some state funds already went to help support the medical college, agriculture, and other purposes. The amounts cited are those earmarked solely for tuition reduction for Vermont students.

21. Carl W. Borgmann, speech to a legislative forum, 22 January 1955, text in Borgmann papers, UVM Archives.

22. Fred Reed, Opinion no. 311, 1959, Attorney General's Office, State of Vermont.

23. Philip H. Hoff, interview by the author, 25 January 1990.

24. Robert V. Daniels, interview by the author, 21 May 1990.

25. George A. Wolf, interview by the author, May 1990.

26. Franklin S. Billings, in *Sprague v. The University of Vermont*, 9 June 1987.

27. National Labor Relations Board, in *University of Vermont and State Agricultural College v. The State of Vermont*, 9 May 1990.

28. Willard M. Miller, quoted in the Burlington *Free Press*, 15 May 1990.

29. Comment by a UVM administrator, not for attribution, ca. 1989.

30. Rutland *Daily Herald*, editorial, 4 January 1989.

31. Hoff interview.

32. Michael J. Obuchowski to John C. Candon, 31 August 1989, appendix A, in *UVM Record*, 22 September 1989.

33. John C. Candon to Michael J. Obuchowski, 25 September 1989, in *UVM Record*, 6 October 1989.

34. Garrison Nelson, signed column, Burlington *Free Press*, 7 October 1989.

35. Figures cited are from *State of Vermont General Fund Appropriations* (Burlington: University of Vermont, 1990).

36. "Analysis of State Funds for Higher Education," *Chronicle of Higher Education*, 24 October 1990.

Chapter 16. Academic Freedom and the Novikoff Affair (pp. 298–312)

1. Dorothy Canfield Fisher, *Vermont Tradition* (Boston: Little, Brown, 1953), p. 395.

2. Walter Metzger, *Academic Freedom in the Age of the University* (New York: Columbia University Press, 1955), pp. 194–221.

3. See Betty Bandel to Edward Andrews, 9 December 1971 (copy in papers of Dr. Ethan A. H. Sims), for background on this affair.

4. See Michael Parenti, "Struggles in the Temple of Knowledge," in Phillip Meranto, Oneida Meranto, and Matthew Lippman, eds., *Guarding the Ivory Tower* (Denver: Lucha Publications, 1985), pp. 55–72.

5. The Burlington *Free Press*, 12 November 1970, 6, 7, 8, 9 December 1971.

6. More detailed descriptions of the episodes discussed in this chapter appear in David Holmes, *Stalking the Academic Communist: Intellectual Freedom and the Firing of Alex Novikoff* (Hanover, N.H.: University Press of New England, 1989).

7. Arnold Schein to David R. Holmes, 12 April 1987.

8. Testimony by Dean William Brown, *In Re: Dr. Alex Novikoff*, Stenographic Record of Final Hearing, 29 August 1953, UVM Archives, indicated that Novikoff's controversial political past did not come up for discussion during the interviews in Vermont.

9. Holmes, *Stalking the Academic Communist*, pp. 62–79.

10. Novikoff stated on a passport application in 1958 that he had left the party in "approximately 1945" (Novikoff private papers). Interviews by the author with Novikoff (12 March and 18 May 1984) elicited a similar recollection.

11. Brown testimony.

12. After his testimony Albaum told a mutual friend that he "had to name Novikoff." See author's interview with Novikoff, 18 May 1984. Also, an FBI report (SAC, New York, to Director, FBI, 24 April 1953, FBI file 100-94031) indicated that Albaum had furnished the names of Brooklyn College Communists.

13. Holmes, *Stalking the Academic Communist*, pp. 127–8.

14. Minutes of the University Senate, 26 March 1953, pp. 2–3, UVM Archives.

15. Novikoff told Borgmann that he "might be willing not to use the privilege of the Fifth Amendment for the time that I had been associated with the university." See hearing transcript, testimony of Alex Novikoff, Committee on the Judiciary, U. S. Senate, *Subversive Influence in the Educational Process*, pt. 2, 23 April 1953, pp. 800–801.

16. Ibid., pp. 796–816.

17. Burlington *Daily News*, 23 April 1953.

18. See Burlington *Free Press*, 1 and 27 March 1948; *The Caledonian Record*, 27 March 1948.

19. Burlington *Free Press*, 16 August 1950.

20. Ibid., 31 March 1953.

21. Emerson papers, Vermont State Archives.

22. See Martin Trow, "Right-Wing Radicalism and Political Intolerance: A Study of Support for McCarthy in a New England Town," Ph.D. diss., Columbia University, 1957. Trow's study is summarized and analyzed in Holmes, *Stalking the Academic Communist*, pp. 120–2.

23. Zechariah Chaffee and Arthur Sunderland, letter to the editor, *Harvard Crimson*, 8 January 1953.

24. Lewis Webster Jones, *Academic Freedom and Civic Responsibility*, Board of Trustees of Rutgers University, 24 January 1953.

25. Lee Emerson to Carl Borgmann, 28 April 1953, Novikoff file, UVM Archives.

26. Hearing transcript of Trustee–Faculty Committee to Investigate Alex Novikoff, 30 April 1953, Novikoff file, UVM Archives.

27. Report of the Findings of the Trustee–Faculty Committee to Investigate Alex Novikoff, 12 June 1953, Novikoff file, UVM Archives.

28. These events are recapitulated in Novikoff's "Outline of Events at the University of Vermont," prepared 28 July 1953, Novikoff file, UVM Archives.

29. UVM Trustees Minutes, 20 June 1953, UVM Archives.

30. Burlington *Daily News*, 21 June 1953.

31. Burlington *Free Press*, 23 June 1953.

32. Ibid., 24 June 1953.

33. Burlington *Daily News*, 23 June 1953.

34. Holmes, *Stalking the Academic Communist*, pp. 156–7.

35. Swanton *Courier*, 14 May 1953.

36. Essex Junction *Suburban List*, 21 May 1953.

37. The text of the letter was printed in the Burlington *Daily News*, 9 July 1953.

38. Holmes, *Stalking the Academic Communist*, pp. 161–3, 167–8.

39. See Loya Metzger, "Professors in Trouble: A Quantitative Analysis of Academic and Tenure Cases," Ph.D. diss., Columbia University, pp. 76–81.

40. Holmes, *Stalking the Academic Communist*, pp. 166–7.

41. Minutes of the University Senate, 30 June 1953, UVM Archives.

42. Borgmann took the blame for the errors of procedure in a letter to Governor Emerson (with copies to the other board members). Copy in the Novikoff file, UVM Archives.

43. Holmes, *Stalking the Academic Communist*, pp. 182–9.

44. Francis Peisch, Memorandum of 22 August 1953, Novikoff papers, UVM Archives.

45. Louis Lisman, interview by the author, 7 February 1986.

46. Stenographic record of hearing, *In Re: Dr. Alex Novikoff before Board of Review*, pp. 12–18, UVM Archives.

47. Ibid., pp. 22–23, 29–30.

48. Robert Joyce, interview by the author, 29 June 1984.

49. Holmes, *Stalking the Academic Communist*, pp. 208–209, 212–14.

50. UVM Trustees Minutes, 5 September 1953.

51. Ellen Schrecker, *No Ivory Tower* (New York: Oxford University Press, 1986).

52. Burlington *Free Press*, 22 May 1983.

Chapter 17. Jews, Blacks, and Catholics (pp. 313–32)

1. Raul Hilberg to Lyman S. Rowell, 3 June 1959.

2. Ibid.

3. Lewis S. Feuer, "The Stages in the Social History of Jewish Professors in American Colleges and Universities," *American Jewish History* 76 (June 1982): 432–61.

4. Quoted, ibid., p. 455.

5. Leonard Dinnerstein, "Anti-Semitism Exposed and Attacked, 1945–50," *American Jewish History* 76 (September 1986): 136.

6. Quoted, ibid.

7. Julian I. Lindsay, *Tradition Looks Forward, The University of Vermont: A History, 1791–1904* (Burlington: University of Vermont, 1954).

8. Samuel Williams, *The Natural and Civil History of Vermont*, 2nd ed. (Burlington, Vt.: Samuel Mills, 1809), vol. 2, pp. 382–83.

9. Lindsay, *Tradition*, p. 14.

10. UVM Trustees Minutes, 6 December 1969, UVM Archives.

11. Lattie F. Coor, Memorandum, 25 April 1988, p. 1.

12. Robert V. Daniels, "Affirmative Action Has Its Obstacles," Burlington *Free Press*, 11 May 1988, p. 16a.

13. "Student Takeover of Waterman Bldg.," SP. 88. (SPARC video tape), UVM Media Library.

14. Lattie F. Coor, Memorandum to the UVM Campus Community, 25 April 1988.

15. "The Fight Against Apartheid," *Ariel*, 1986, pp. 74–77.

16. Crystal M. Brown, personal communication, 22 September 1989.

17. "Committee Adopts Plan of Action to Promote Tolerance," *Vermont Cynic*, 20 November 1945, p. 1.

18. "The Time Is Now," *Vermont Cynic*, 20 November 1945, p. 2.

19. "Sororities to End Discrimination as Rushing Commences," *Vermont Cynic*, 15 January 1946, p. 1.

20. "Sorority Fight: Vermont Chapter Stirs Nationwide Controversy by Admitting a Negro," *Life*, 20 May 1946, p. 31.

21. Ibid.

22. "Pledging of Crystal Malone Causes Furor," *Vermont Cynic*, 26 April 1946, p. 1.

23. Peter Mallett, letter to the editor, *Vermont Cynic*, 7 May 1946, p. 2.

24. "Sorority Pledging Negro Is Inactive," New York *World-Telegram*, 31 January 1947.

25. "Segregation in Vermont," *Vermont Cynic*, 28 February 1957, p. 4.

26. Letter to the editor, *Vermont Cynic*, 28 February 1957, p. 4.

27. Judy Gerber, "Community Acts on Segregation Incident," *Vermont Cynic*, 7 March 1957, p. 1.

28. "Anti-Segregation Unit Sees Need for Legislation," *Vermont Cynic*, 14 March 1957, p. 3.

29. "Bill Made on Segregation," *Vermont Cynic*, 11 April 1957, p. 1.

30. "Pickens Elected SA President," *Vermont Cynic*, 11 April 1957, p. 1.

31. Jules Older, "UVM Students Picket to Protest Segregation," *Vermont Cynic*, 31 March 1960, p. 1.

32. "SA Opposes Discrimination," *Vermont Cynic*, 31 March 1960, p. 1.

33. Roger Zimmerman, "The Melting Pot," *Vermont Cynic*, 31 March 1960, p. 5.

34. "Students Protest," *Vermont Cynic*, 31 March 1960, p. 4.

35. Sheila Whitney, "Opposes Pickets," *Vermont Cynic*, 31 March 1960, p. 9.

36. Gordon Sprigg, "Official SA Stand on Resolution," *Vermont Cynic*, 5 May 1960, p. 5.

37. "CYNIC Opposes SA Resolution," *Vermont Cynic*, 5 May 1960, pp. 1, 4.

38. "SA Revises Resolution," *Vermont Cynic*, 12 May 1960, p. 4.

39. "Victory in Nashville," *Vermont Cynic*, 19 May 1960, p. 4.

40. See Maudean Neill, *Fiery Crosses in the Green Mountains* (Randolph Center, Vt.: Greenhills Books, 1989).

41. Rowland E. Robinson, *Vermont: A Study of Independence* (Boston: Houghton-Mifflin, 1892; reprinted, Rutland: Charles E. Tuttle, 1975), pp. 330–31.

42. Elin L. Anderson, *We Americans: A Study of Cleavage in an American City* (Cambridge, Mass.: Harvard University Press, 1937, pp. 14–15; reprinted, New York: Russell & Russell, 1967).

43. Philip H. Hoff, Introductory letter, in *Franco-Americans in Vermont: A Civil Rights Perspective* (Washington, D.C.: U.S. Commission on Civil Rights, 1983).

44. Ibid., p. 38.

45. Martin Kaufman, *The University of Vermont College of Medicine* (Hanover, N.H.: University Press of New England, 1979), p. 115.

46. Ibid., p. 211.

47. James L. Kingsland to Lawrence McCrorey, 29 August 1987.

48. Ibid.

49. C. H. Beecher to Scott Nearing, 25 July 1944, UVM Archives.

50. Kaufman, *College of Medicine*, p. 215.

51. Ibid.

52. Ibid.

53. James N. Jenne to Morris S. Lazaron, 10 July 1934, American Jewish Archives, Cincinnati.

54. Edward C. Halperin, "Frank Porter Graham, Isaac Hall Manning, and the

Jewish Quota at the University of North Carolina Medical School," unpublished manuscript; Dinnerstein, "Anti-Semitism."

55. Fred Zapffe interview, 22 November 1937, Medical College Reorganization Box, UVM Archives.

56. Kaufman, *College of Medicine*, p. 168.

57. Anderson, *We Americans*, pp. 90–91.

58. Kaufman, *College of Medicine*, pp. 180–1.

59. Ibid., pp. 183–4.

60. Ibid., p. 196.

Chapter 18. The Curriculum—II (pp. 333–48)

1. John Converse, *The Twentieth-Century University* (Philadelphia: Lippincott, 1898), pp. 3–21.

2. In 1889 Departments of Arts, Applied Science, Medicine, and Agriculture; in 1911, Colleges of Arts and Sciences, Engineering, Medicine, and Agriculture. *Catalogue of the University of Vermont and State Agricultural College*, 1889–90, p. 13; 1911–12, p. 155. (Hereafter cited as *UVM Cat.*)

3. *UVM Cat.*, 1934–1935, pp. 226–229.

4. *UVM Cat.*, 1946–47, p. 75.

5. University of Vermont, Office of Institutional Studies (hereafter cited as OIS), "UVM Undergraduate Headcount Enrollment, 1900–1989," 8 May 1990. By decade the undergraduate population increased as follows: 1900, 278; 1910, 302; 1920, 936; 1930, 1,161; 1940, 1,314; 1950, 2,695; 1960, 2,992; 1970, 5,861. All OIS statistics appearing in this essay were compiled by Keith Coutu, to whom the author expresses gratitude.

6. In 1969, 2,933 students were enrolled in the College of Arts and Sciences out of a total undergraduate enrollment of 5,466 (54%). In 1979 the figures were 3,347 out of 7,896 (42%); in 1989, 3,642 of 8,029 (45%). OIS, "UVM Headcount Undergraduate Enrollment by College/School," 8 May 1990.

7. Archives of the College of Education (hereafter Arch. Coll. Ed.), dossier "Education and Nursing: Constitution of the College," self-study memoirs "The School of Education and Nursing," 1950 and 1956. The basic two-year course in ROTC was compulsory for all male undergraduates from 1918 to 1964.

8. *UVM Cat.* (1946–47), pp. 53, 109–15.

9. Ibid., p. 108.

10. "Wilbur Fund History" file, UVM Archives.

11. Donald B. Johnstone, ed., *A History of Graduate Study at the University of Vermont in Commemoration of the Silver Jubilee of the Graduate College, 1952–1977* (Burlington: University of Vermont: 1977), pp. 5–7.

12. Graduate enrollment increased as follows: 1950, 111; 1955, 56; 1960, 154; 1965, 307; 1970, 646; 1975, 797; 1980, 901; 1985, 1,014. OIS report "UVM Headcount Graduate Enrollment," 9 May 1990.

13. Johnstone, *History of Graduate Study*, p. 37, lists Ph.D. programs with their year of inauguration. The first Ph.D. was awarded in 1962.

14. "A Report about the University of Vermont," conducted by the New England Association of Colleges & Secondary Schools, March 1972, pp. 14–15 (Wilbur Collection, UVM Library).

15. Martin Kaufman, *The University of Vermont College of Medicine* (Hanover, N.H.: University Press of New England, 1979), pp. 135, 143, 151–67, 224, 227.

16. William H. Luginbuhl and Edward C. Andrews, Jr., "A New Curriculum: Its

Evolution, Design, and Implementation," *Journal of Medical Education* 42 (1967): 826–32.

17. Joseph L. Hills, "The Attempted Disruption of the University of Vermont and State Agricultural College in 1890," MS, UVM Archives, pp. 12–312.

18. Agriculture enrollment increased as follows: 1911, 76; 1920, 137; 1930, 112; 1940, 243; 1950, 472; 1955, 417. OIS, "UVM College of Agriculture Headcount Enrollment, 1910–1985," 9 May 1990.

19. The percentage of majors in traditional agricultural disciplines in the College decreased from 48% in 1962 to about 15% by 1972. "Addendum to the Task Force Report on University Reorganization," *This Week*, supplement, 23 January 1973.

20. Blair Williams, *A Backward Look—Ahead: Home Economics at the University of Vermont* (Burlington: University of Vermont, 1987), pp. 14, 43.

21. Ibid., pp. 59–65; *The University of Vermont and State Agricultural College Self-Study Report, 1988* (September 1988), p. 82.

22. David Holmes, *Reform from Within; Case Studies of Faculty-Initiated Educational Change at the University of Vermont* (Burlington: University of Vermont, 1979), pp. 14–20.

23. Two-year and four-year programs in elementary and junior high school teaching were introduced in 1921 and 1922 respectively; programs in business education (1932), music education (1935), and industrial education (1939) followed. Arch. Coll. Ed.: Memo, "An Incomplete Chronology of the College of Education and Social Services at the University of Vermont," 23 August 1989.

24. Arch. Coll. Ed.: dossier "Education and Nursing: Constitution of the College," report "The School of Education and Nursing," 1950. See also Marguerite Dow McNeil, "A Study of the Professional Sequence for Elementary-School Teachers at the University of Vermont," (Ph.D. diss., Columbia University, 1963).

25. "Addendum to the Task Force Report on University Reorganization."

26. Arch. Coll. Ed.: dossier "Curriculum Committee, 1970s–1980s," reports of the Curriculum Committee, 21 December 1973, 12 February 1974, 30 April 1975.

27. College of Agriculture and Life Sciences, "New Directions, Reorganization: A Discussion Document," report May 1989; The *UVM Self-Study Report, 1988*, p. 82.

28. *UVM Cat.* (1969–70), p. 138.

29. *UVM Bulletin: Report of the President*, no. 58 (31 December 1960), p. 3.

30. Samuel N. Bogorad, *The University of Vermont Self-Study: Report of the Final Evaluation Committee, 1962* (Burlington: University of Vermont, 1962), pp. 26, 33–34.

31. *Minutes of the Meeting of the Faculty of the College of Arts and Sciences*, 11 and 17 March, 1 April 1969.

32. The reform passed 139 to 30. An amendment to retain an English requirement was defeated 89–81. *Ibid.*, 14 April 1969.

33. *Report of the Inaugural Committee on Undergraduate Education*, June 1977, p. 2.

34. Robert G. Arns, "General Education in the Baccalaureate: Is There a Need for Renewal?" essay prepared for the UVM Academic Council, 16 March 1978.

35. *Minutes, College of Arts and Sciences*, 9 October 1979.

36. Majors in the social and behavioral sciences increased from 629 in 1974 to 1,039 in 1981 (+65%). By contrast, those in history declined from 114 to 102, in foreign languages from 96 to 92, in mathematics from 87 to 69. OIS, "College of Arts and Sciences, Headcount Enrollment of Selected Disciplines, 1974–89," 8 May 1990.

37. Although appointed as a presidential committee, the COBE was reconstituted as a subcommittee of the Senate Academic Affairs Committee in September 1979 so that its recommendations might be acted on by the faculty. Alan P. Wertheimer,

"General Education at the University of Vermont: An Interim Report," presented to the Faculty Senate, 26 February 1980.

38. Alan P. Wertheimer, *General Education at the University of Vermont: A Working Paper* (Burlington: University of Vermont, 1979), pp. 69–90.

39. See the *Minutes of the College of Arts and Sciences*, 12 March 1980, for the spirited debate on the proposal. See also Wertheimer, "Interim Report."

40. Ibid., pp. 5, 9–10.

41. It should be noted that the English department's faculty workshops on writing across the curriculum, inspired by Professor Toby Fulwiler, have had a far-reaching impact on the teaching of writing skills at UVM since the mid-1980s.

42. The areas are fine arts, literature, humanities, social sciences, natural sciences. Curriculum Committee of the College of Arts and Sciences, "Proposal for a New Curriculum," 24 April 1985, appendix to the *Minutes of the College of Arts and Sciences*, 2 May 1985. For the prior debate on the curricular proposal, see *Minutes of the College of Arts and Sciences*, 20 October, 6 and 20 November 1984.

43. Thomas H. Geno, "Area & International Studies at the University of Vermont: Programs, Perceptions, Presumptions, Problems, and Possibilities," report of the director, Spring 1981.

44. Robert V. Daniels, "Personal Observations on the Experience of the Experimental Program to Date," report to the faculty of the College of Arts and Sciences, 10 November 1970. Daniels and Dean Alfred Rollins had originally envisaged the EP as the first of a cluster of subcolleges around which Arts and Sciences might be remodeled, but this concept failed to materialize.

45. Patrick H. Hutton, "An Evaluation of the Vermont Overseas Study Program," Report of the Director to the Dean of the College of Arts and Sciences, August 1978, College of Arts and Sciences archives, University of Vermont.

46. Paul J. Magnarella, "The University of Vermont's Living–Learning Center: A First Year Appraisal," mimeographed, Living/Learning Center, 1974. Also *Self-Study, The University of Vermont and State Agricultural College*, presented to the Commission on Institutions of Higher Education, New England Association of Schools and Colleges (Burlington: University of Vermont, 1978), Appendix L (Living/Learning Center).

47. See Report of the Curriculum Committee of the College of Arts and Sciences, 9 December 1986.

48. James R. Wheeler, "The Nature of Liberal Education," in *The University of Vermont: The Centennial Anniversary of the Graduation of the First Class, July 3–7, 1904* (Burlington: University of Vermont, 1905), pp. 114–123.

Chapter 19. Black Image in White Vermont (pp. 349–69)

1. James Loewen and Charles Sallis, eds., *Mississippi: Conflict and Change* (New York: Pantheon, 1974), p. 94; Kenneth M. Stampp, *The Peculiar Institution* (New York: Random House Vintage, 1956), p. 30.

2. Ibid., p. 28.

3. Edith Isaacs, *The Negro in the American Theatre* (College Park, Md.: McGrath, 1947, 1968), pp. 21–23; James Weldon Johnson, *Black Manhattan* (New York: Knopf, 1930), p. 87; Joseph Boskin, *Sambo* (New York: Oxford University Press, 1986), p. 50; William and Mary Morris, *Morris Dictionary of Word and Phrase Origins* (New York: Harper and Row, 1988), p. 562.

4. Jeremy P. Felt, "Kake Walk—A White Man's View," *Vermont Cynic*, 17 October 1969.

5. John Pendleton Kennedy, *Swallow Barn, or a Sojourn in the Old Dominion* (1832), quoted in Boskin, *Sambo*, p. 95.

6. Isaacs, *The Negro in the American Theatre*, pp. 23, 44.

7. Robert C. Toll, *Blacking Up: The Minstrel Show in Nineteenth-Century America* (New York: Oxford University Press, 1974), p. 34.

8. Ibid., p. 57; Boskin, *Sambo*, p. 129; Gunnar Myrdal, *An American Dilemma* (New York: Harper and Row, 1944, 1962), p. 989; Robert C. Toll, introduction to Ike Simond, *Old Slack's Reminiscence and Pocket History of the Colored Profession* (Bowling Green, Ohio: Popular Press, 1974), p. xxv.

9. Isaacs, *The Negro in the American Theatre*, pp. 23–25; Boskin, *Sambo*, p. 76.

10. Carl Wittke, *Tambo and Bones* (Westport, Conn.: Greenwood, 1930, 1968), p. 93.

11. Boskin, *Sambo*, p. 85.

12. Johnson, *Black Manhattan*, p. 93.

13. Edward Randall ('95), letter to the editor, *Cynic*, 16 March 1907.

14. The two best sources on early Kake Walks are Randall (n. 13) and H. C. Shurtleff ('95), "Prehistoric Kake Walks," *Vermont Alumni Weekly*, 29 February 1923. Other useful information was found in UVM Archives files on Kake Walk, fraternity papers, and presidential papers.

15. Shurtleff, "Prehistoric Kake Walks."

16. Cf. "The Great Tradition—Ghosts of Kake Walk Past," *Cynic*, 25 February 1966; The Burlington *Free Press*, 21 February 1952; Julian I. Lindsay, *Tradition Looks Forward, The University of Vermont: A History, 1791–1904* (Burlington: University of Vermont, 1954), p. 267.

17. E. Franklin Frazier, *The Negro in the United States* (New York: Macmillan, 1949, 1957), p. 160; Rayford Logan, *The Negro in American Life and Thought: The Nadir, 1877–1901*, republished as *The Betrayal of the Negro* (New York: Macmillan Collier, 1954, 1965); Donald Bogle, *Toms, Coons, Mulattoes, Mammies, and Bucks* (New York: Bantam, 1974), p. 9.

18. Myrdal, *An American Dilemma*, p. 990; Kake Walk files, UVM Archives, including John Mullins, "Published Arrangement of 'Cotton Babes' Loaned to UVM in Time for Kake Walk," *Free Press* clipping, not dated.

19. John Turner, *The Ku Klux Klan: A History of Racism and Violence* (Montgomery, Ala.: Southern Poverty Law Center, 1981); Sue Burton, lecture at UVM, February 1990; *Free Press*, 1 June 1925.

20. *Cynic*, 17 March 1944.

21. Boskin, *Sambo*, pp. 108–112.

22. Kake Walk files, UVM Archives.

23. Toll, *Blacking Up*, pp. 162–64.

24. Gladys Neiburg, "Fleeting Glimpses of Fifty-One Gala Years in UVM Kake Walk History," *Cynic*, 20 February 1948.

25. "'Joe' Lechnyr, 'Cotton Babes' Arranger, Hails 28th Kake Walk," *Cynic*, 20 February 1948; *Free Press*, 14 February 1969; UVM Archives.

26. *Free Press*, 29 January, 8 and 14 February 1969.

27. Boskin, *Sambo*, p. 199. Cf. Myrdal, *An American Dilemma*.

28. Boskin, *Sambo*, pp. 167, 201–202.

29. Florence Beebe to Kake Walk directors, 24 January 1950; Bob Bernard, "Reflections of an Ex-Editor," *Cynic*, 21 February 1964; E. K. Breger, "Kake Walk Committee Ends Blackface," *Cynic*, 25 February 1969.

30. *Free Press*, 14 January 1955; David Spector ('56), Letter to the editor, *Cynic*,

23 January 1970; Kake Walk files, UVM Archives; William Bright, interview by the author.

31. Boskin, *Sambo*, p. 204.

32. "IFC Votes to End Blackface," University of Vermont *Bulletin*, Winter 1963–1964; "Kake Walk Is Bleached," Montpelier *Argus*, 9 October 1964.

33. Albert Haynes, Letter to the editor, *Free Press*, 24 October 1963.

34. Kake Walk files, UVM Archives; *Free Press*, 2 and 24 February, 6 March 1964.

35. Kake Walk files, UVM Archives.

36. *Cynic*, various numbers, February–April 1969; Kake Walk files, UVM Archives.

37. Eric Lipton, "Kake Walk: When Ritual Became Racism," *Cynic*, 25 September 1986; *Cynic*, various numbers, February–April 1969; Kake Walk files, UVM Archives.

38. Lyman Rowell to John Lord, 18 March 1969, President Rowell Papers, UVM Archives.

39. *Cynic*, 17 October 1969 (italics in the original).

40. *Cynic*, various numbers, 1969; Lawrence McCrorey, interview by the author.

41. "UVM Administration Hedges on Kake Walk," *Free Press*, 24 October 1969.

42. *Cynic*, 30 October 1969; *Free Press*, 12 October 1969.

43. Various letters to Lyman Rowell, President Rowell Papers, UVM Archives; interviews by the author (not for attribution).

44. Boskin, *Sambo*, pp. 223–24.

45. Pierson Ostrow, Letter to the editor, *Free Press*, 22 October 1963.

46. "Student Referendum Planned as Groups Ask Kake Walk's End," *Commentary* (Bulletin of the University of Vermont), vol. 67, no. 6 (1 October 1969), p. 2; "UVM Administration Hedges on Kake Walk," *Free Press*, 24 October 1969.

47. *Free Press*, Editorial, 1 November 1969.

48. Peter Lakis and Inese Ringmanis to Alumni Director, 16 November 1969, UVM Archives.

49. Howard Delano to Lyman Rowell, 3 November 1969, UVM Archives.

50. Moses Anderson to Dean Roland Patzer, 11 December 1969, and enclosed correspondence.

51. *Free Press*, 16 and 17 February 1970.

52. *Vermont Freeman*, undated clipping, Kake Walk files, UVM Archives.

53. *Free Press*, 16 and 17 February 1970; James Barrett, interview by the author.

54. H. D. Thibault, Jr., graduate assistant to director of student activities, memo to Kake Walk file, January 1976; David Platka, "The Demise of Kakewalk," typescript, 1975; Lyman Rowell to Donald Fuller, 17 November 1969; conversation between Platka and Edward Andrews, reported by Platka in "The Demise of Kakewalk"; Arthur Brink to Barbara Snelling, undated memo, ca. 1978; all in Kake Walk file, UVM Archives.

55. Platka, "The Demise of Kakewalk."

56. *Free Press*, 19 and 25 March 1971, 15 May, and 9 June 1972.

57. Thibault, memo to Kake Walk file, 22 February 1975; Brian Pluff (president, Greek Coordinating Council) and Marjory Read (president, Panhellenic Council) to Lattie F. Coor, 24 February 1977; both in UVM Archives.

58. Boskin, *Sambo*, p. 93.

59. Martha Day (UVM Media Services), interview by the author.

60. Clara Kellogg, Letter to the editor, *Free Press*, 14 October 1963.

61. *Vermont Sunday News*, Editorial, 20 October 1963.

62. *Vermont Catholic Tribune*, 8 October 1969; *Free Press*, 4 October 1963; Kake Walk files, UVM Archives.

63. Frazier, *The Negro in the United States*, p. 669.

64. Clara Kellogg to the *Free Press*, 14 October 1963.

65. *Free Press*, 11 October 1963.

66. *Free Press*, 23 and 24 October 1969. Cf. Boskin, *Sambo*, pp. 93, 120.

67. Connie Marshall, Letter to the editor, *Vermont Sunday News*, November 9 1969.

68. Dan Beegan, "Senate Slates Seminars on Merits of Weekend," *Cynic*, 10 October 1969.

69. Robert O'Brien, Letter to the editor, *Free Press*, 10 October 1963; Lawrence McCrorey, interview by the author, May 1988; Arthur Brink, interview by the author, October 1976.

70. *Cynic*, Editorial, 4 November 1969.

Chapter 20. The Faculty Role in University Governance (pp. 370–85)

1. *The Control of the Campus: A Report on the Governance of Higher Education* (Washington, D.C.: Carnegie Foundation for the Advancement of Teaching, 1982).

2. Much of the information recorded in this report comes from the minutes of faculty meetings, 1827–1919, UVM Archives. In sharp contrast to earlier and more informal handwritten minutes, those for the Benton years are notable for careful typing, systematic reporting of committee recommendations and their adoption, but they record almost no faculty discussion or dissent. Minutes of senate meetings from 1919 to the present are stored in the Faculty Senate Office. Since about 1950 debate has been recorded much more completely.

3. Guy Benton, Address to the Senate of the University of Vermont and State Agricultural College, 22 September 1911, Benton Papers, UVM Archives.

4. Henry Holt to Samuel Bassett, Professor Samuel Bassett Papers, UVM Archives.

5. Joseph L. Hills, "Guy Potter Benton 1911–1919" (unfinished history of Benton's presidency), Benton information file, UVM Archives.

6. "The 1915 Declaration of Principles: Academic Freedom and Tenure," *Bulletin of the AAUP*, vol. 40 (1954–55), pp. 93–112; W. P. Metzger, "Origins of the Association," *Bulletin of the AAUP*, pp. 229–37.

7. The committees were Admissions and Advanced Standing, Buildings and Grounds, Military Science, Regulations and Discipline, and Scholarships.

8. George Dykhuisen, interview by David Blow, UVM Archives.

9. George V. Kidder, personal communication.

10. Major Elbridge Colby, *The Vermont Alumnus* 17 (March 1938): p. 161.

11. F. W. Shepardson and C. N. Bailey, "Rehabilitation of the University of Vermont and State Agricultural College," 1943 pp. 170–1, 201–202, UVM Archives.

12. Ibid., pp. 30–31.

13. Ibid., pp. 3–8.

14. Ibid., p. 165.

15. Ibid., p. 231.

16. William H. Wills, Address to a Special Meeting of the UVM Faculty, May 1941, pp. 41–47, UVM Archives.

17. Ibid., p. 220.

18. Ibid., p. 238.

19. UVM Trustees Minutes, 30 April 1943, UVM Archives.

20. American Federation of Teachers, Local 703, Minutes, 18 December 1943–12 May 1952, UVM Archives.

21. The members were Professor Jay Gould, chair, Dean Clinton Cook, Dean Lyman Rowell, Professors William Adams, Raymond Donaghy, Donald Gregg, Merton Lambden, and Alexander Rippa.

22. Candidates would be elected if they received ten votes from the faculty at large, each member casting only one vote. Thus the maximum size of the senate could be one tenth of the faculty if all members of the faculty voted. The new senate had 61 elected members of a possible 78. Thus, additional members could be added to the senate if they obtained ten votes not previously registered. Since the term of the senators was two years, a second election was held in the fall of 1974. This time only 44 faculty members ran; only about half the eligible faculty bothered to vote, and only 39 were elected. Large segments of the University were not represented.

23. See Constitution and Bylaws of the University of Vermont Faculty Senate, Officer's Handbook. In 1979 there were seven standing committees: Academic Affairs, Faculty Affairs, Financial Policy, Admissions, Student Affairs, Physical Planning, and Nominating. There is also an important executive committee. Faculty representatives are designated to the several committees of the Board of Trustees.

24. Sue Khodorahmi, "Professors Disagree on Effectiveness and Power of the Faculty Senate," *Cynic*, vol. 106 (26 February 1987), p. 1.

25. David Holmes, "University Governance and the Role of Faculty," *This Week*, 13 October–5 November 1981.

26. Dolores Sandoval, "Senate Wants Faculty Pay Evaluations in Writing," *This Week*, 26 March–8 April 1982.

Index

UNIVERSITY PRESS OF NEW ENGLAND publishes books under its own imprint and is the publisher for Brandeis University Press, Brown University Press, Clark University Press, University of Connecticut, Dartmouth College, Middlebury College Press, University of New Hampshire, University of Rhode Island, Tufts University, University of Vermont, and Wesleyan University Press.

Library of Congress Cataloging-in-Publication Data

The University of Vermont : the first two hundred years / Robert V. Daniels, senior editor.
      p.   cm.
Includes index.
ISBN 0–87451–549–1
      1. University of Vermont—History.   I. Daniels, Robert Vincent.
LD5633.U55   1991   90–50919
378.743′17—dc20